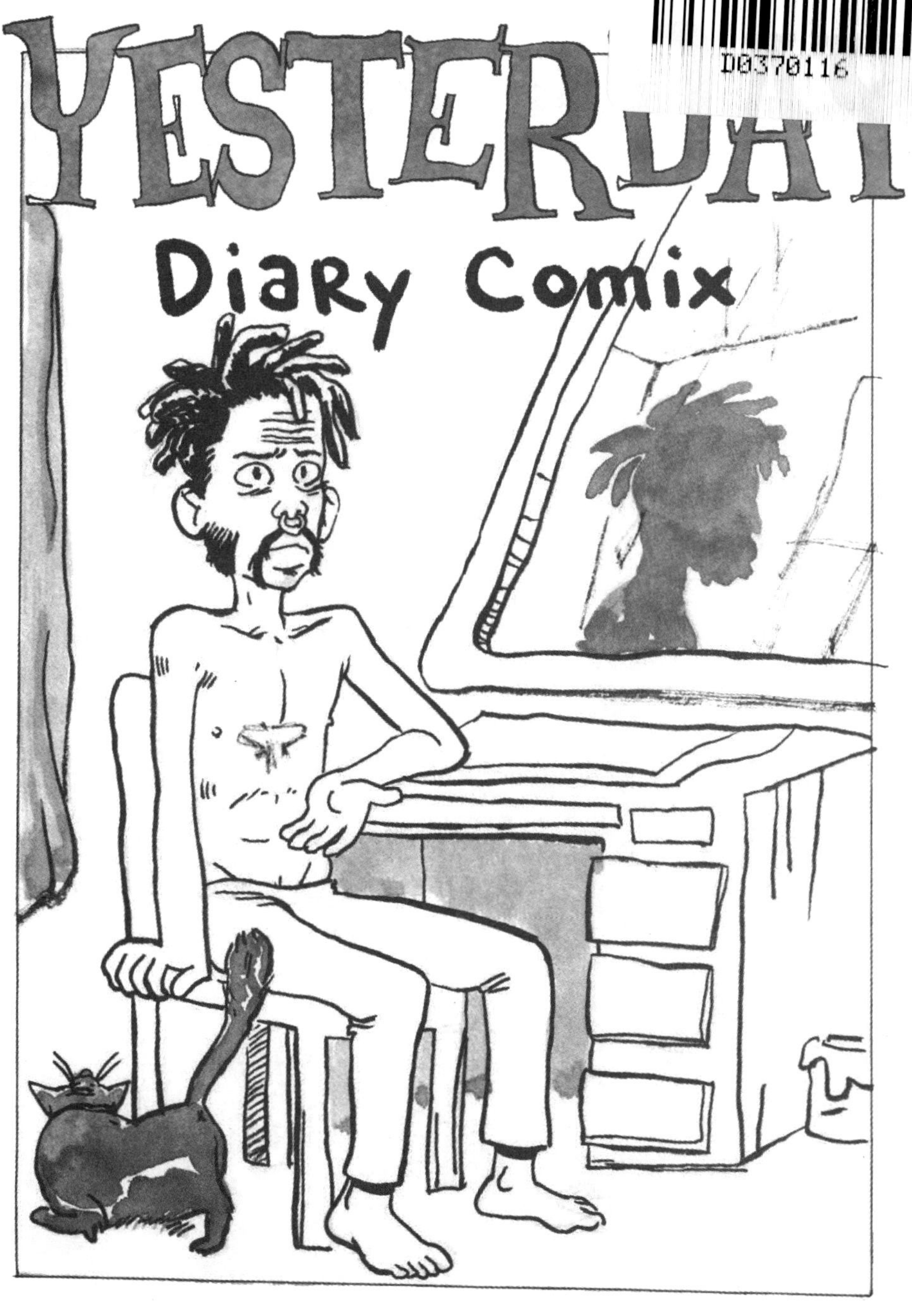
YESTERDAY
Diary Comix

Yesterday: Diary Comix
by Brother Malcolm

Published by Birdcage Bottom Books
324-A West 71st St.
New York, NY 10023
United States of America

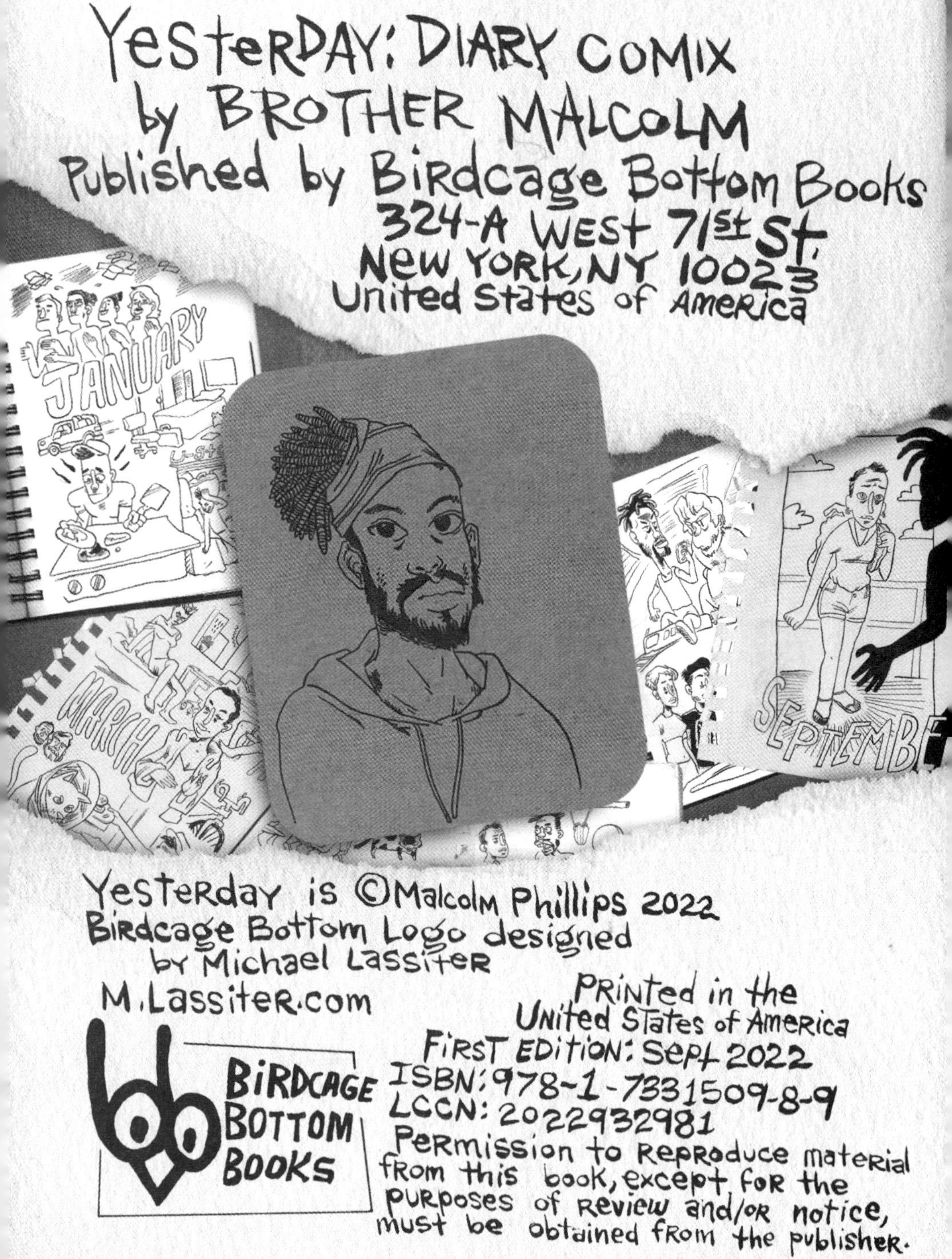
JANUARY
MARCH
SEPTEMBE

Birdcage Bottom Logo designed
by Michael Lassiter
M.Lassiter.com

BIRDCAGE
BOTTOM
BOOKS

Printed in the
United States of America
First Edition: Sept 2022
ISBN: 978-1-7331509-8-9
LCCN: 2022932981

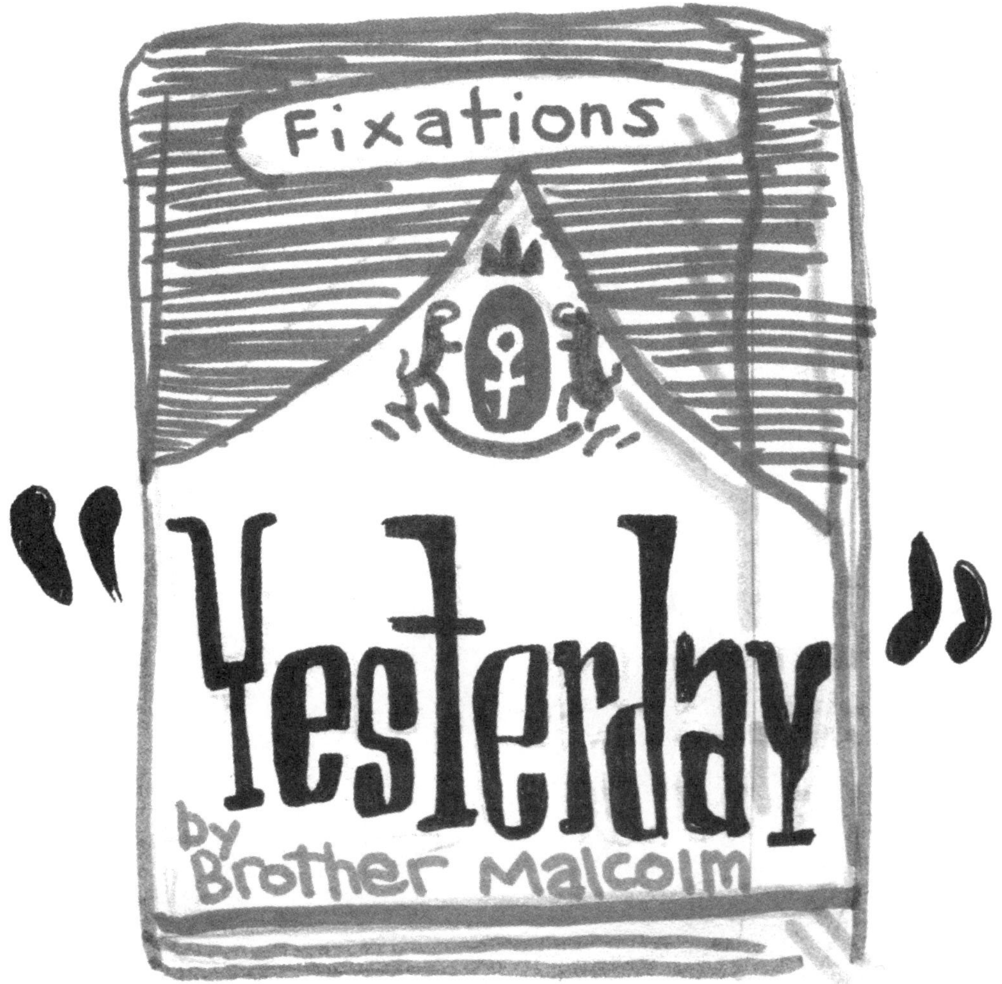
Fixations
"Yesterday"
by Brother Malcolm

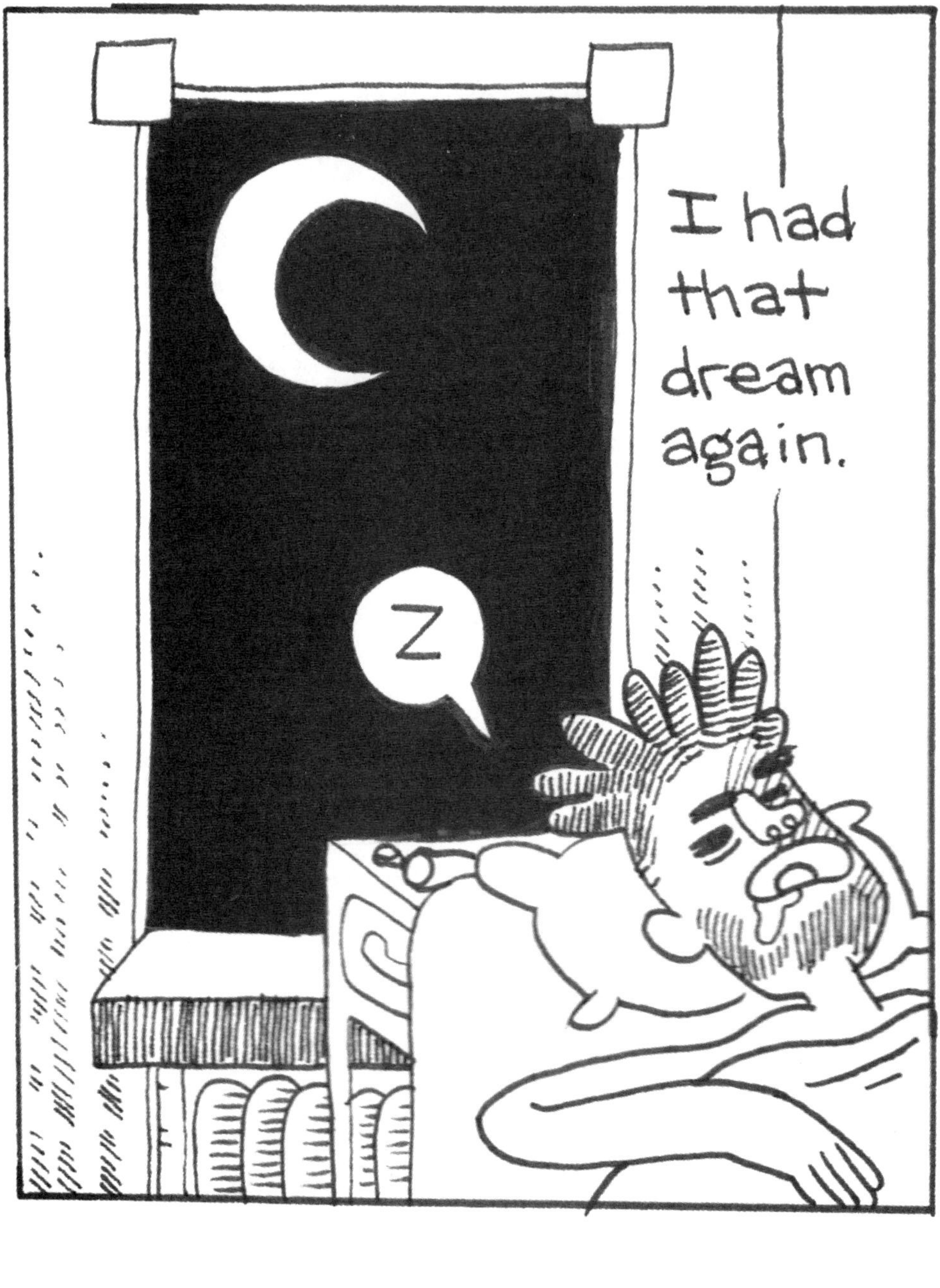

I had that dream again.
Z

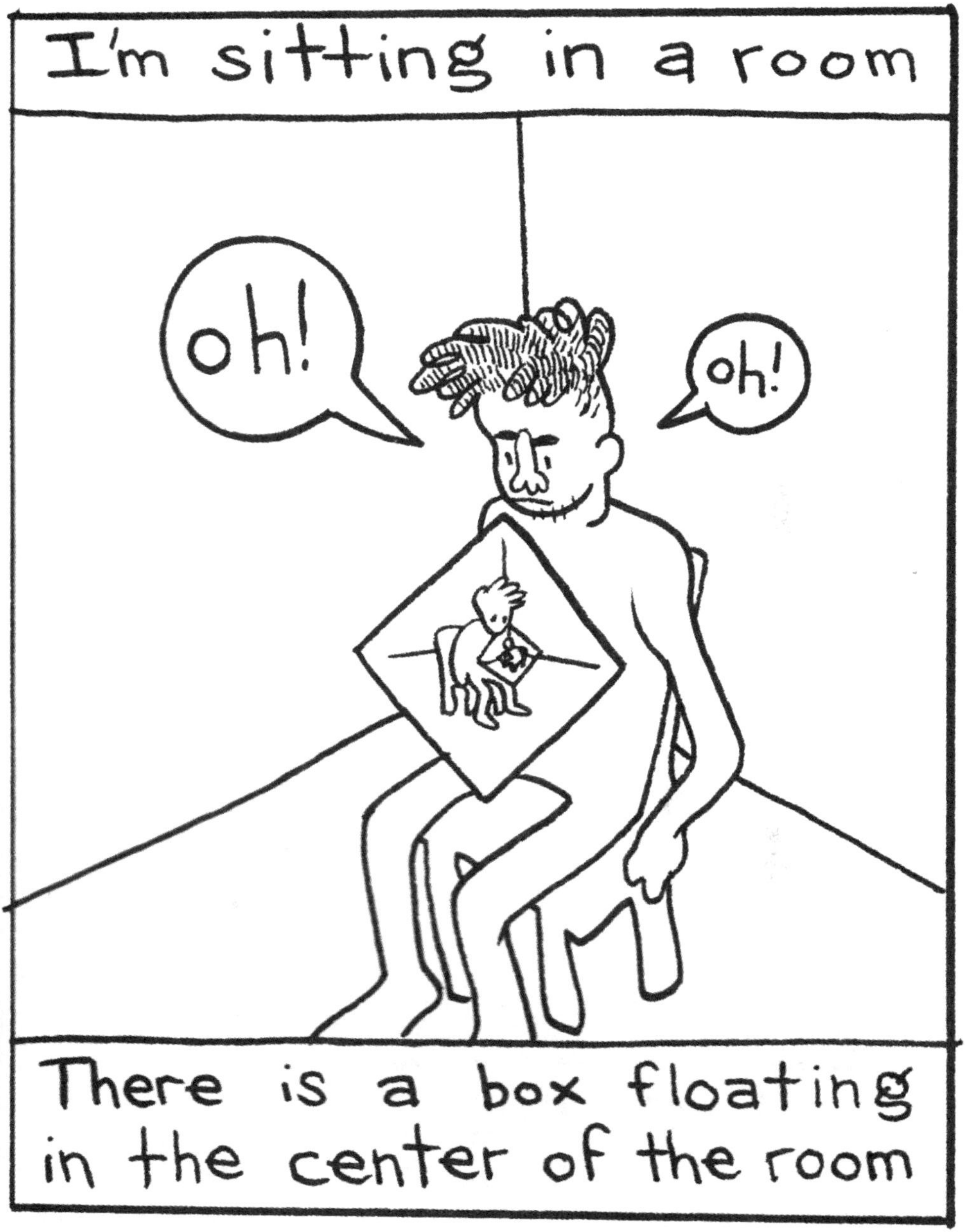
I'm sitting in a room
oh!
oh!
There is a box floating in the center of the room

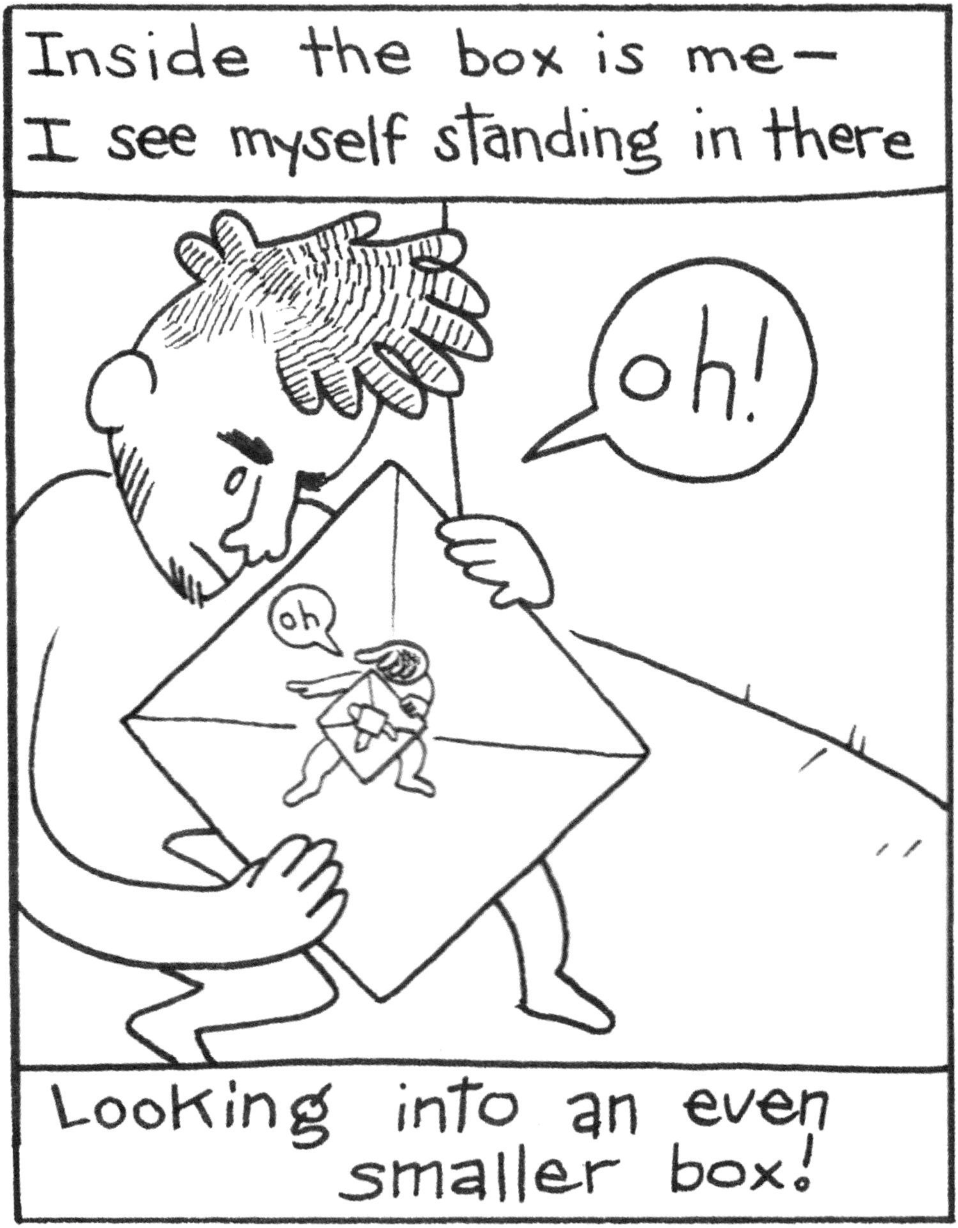
Inside the box is me—
I see myself standing in there
oh!
oh
Looking into an even
smaller box!

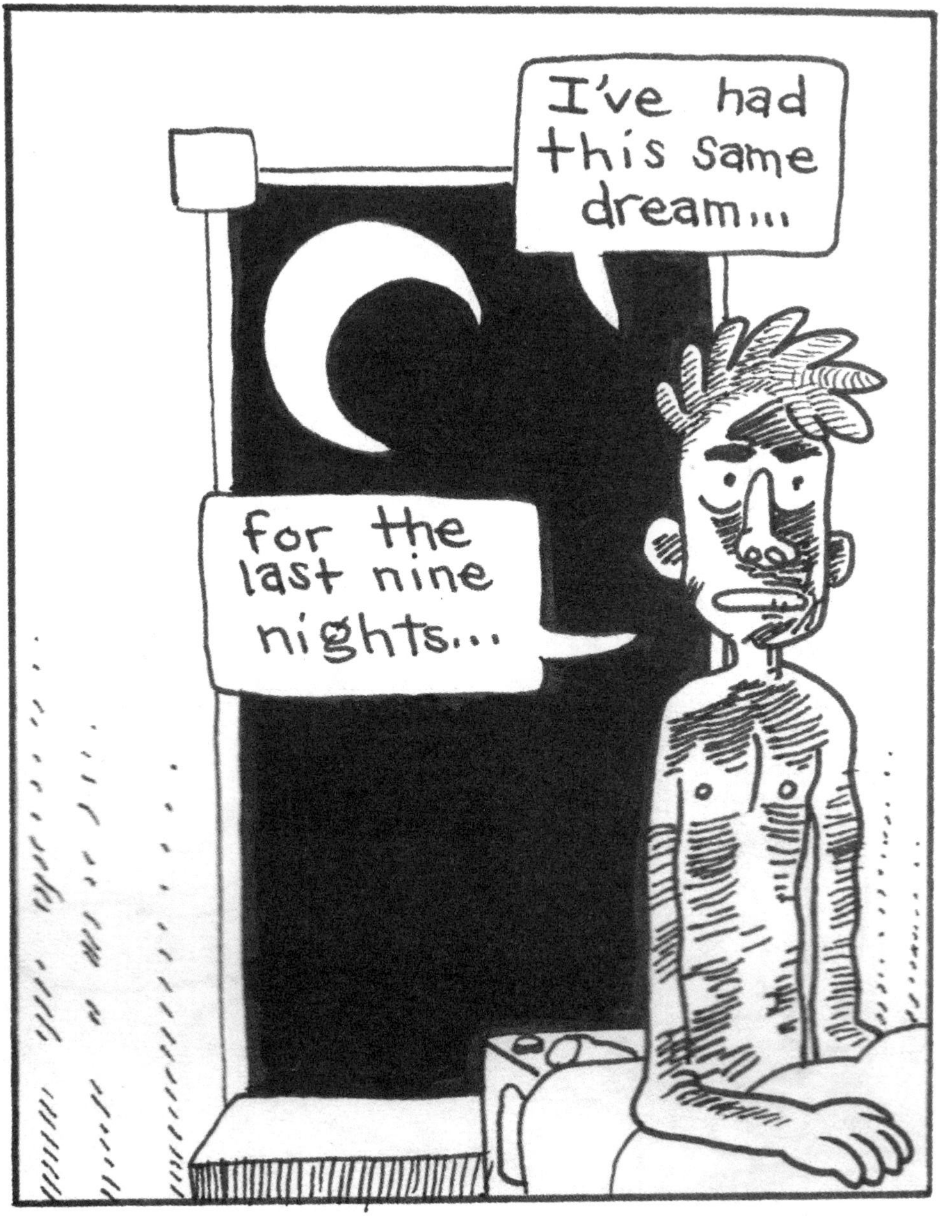
I've had this same dream...
for the last nine nights...

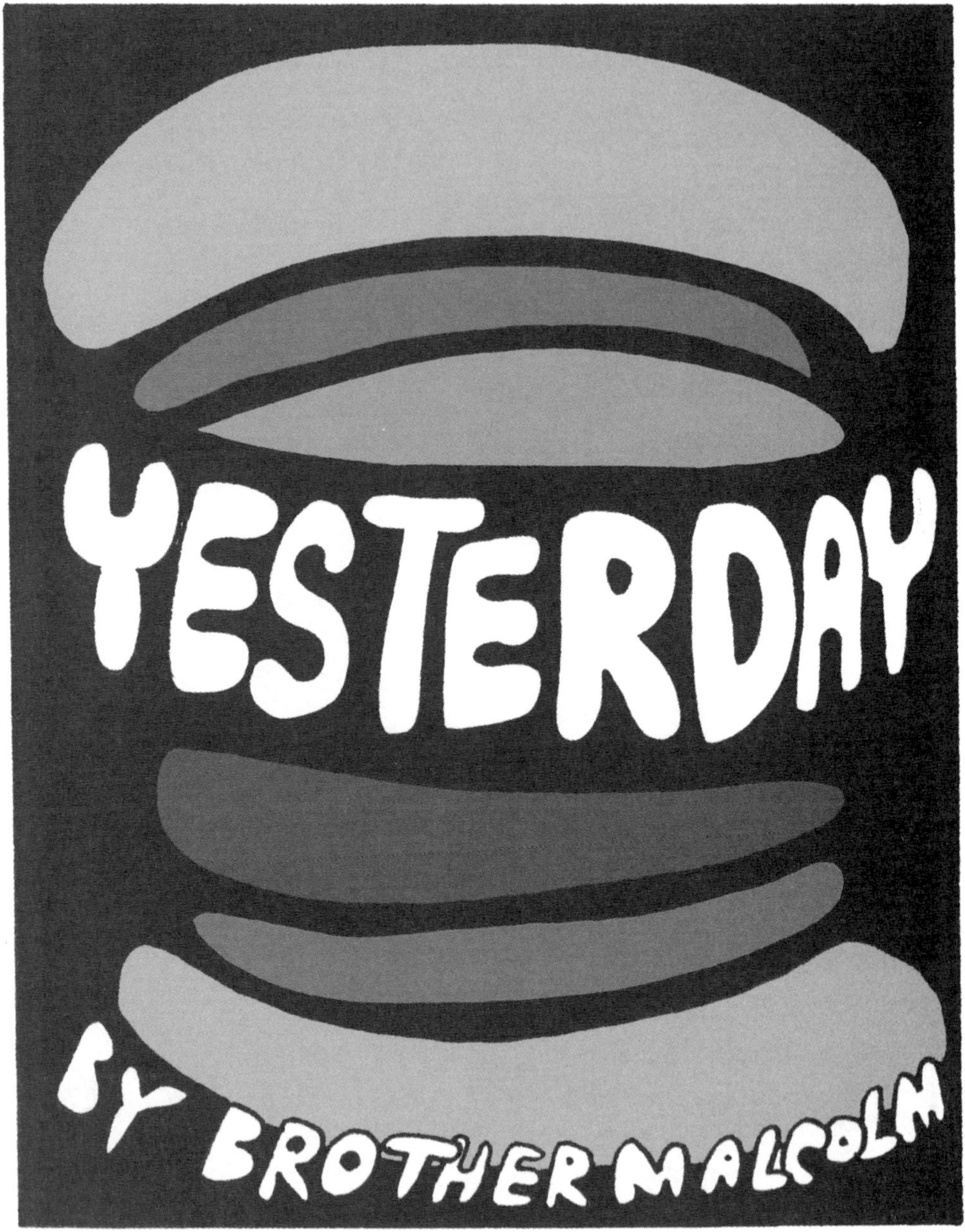
YESTERDAY
BY BROTHER MALCOLM

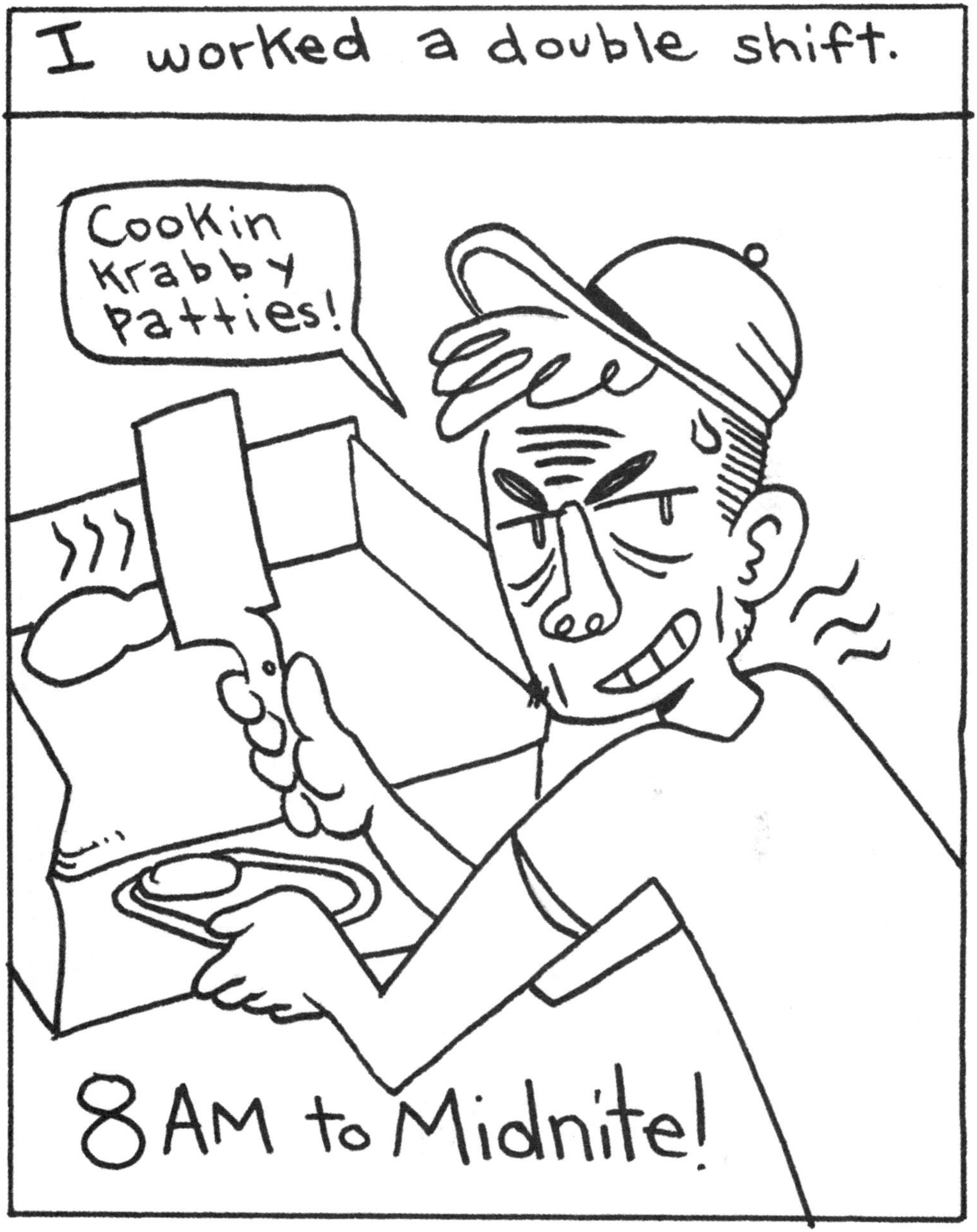
I worked a double shift.
Cookin Krabby Patties!
8 AM to Midnite!

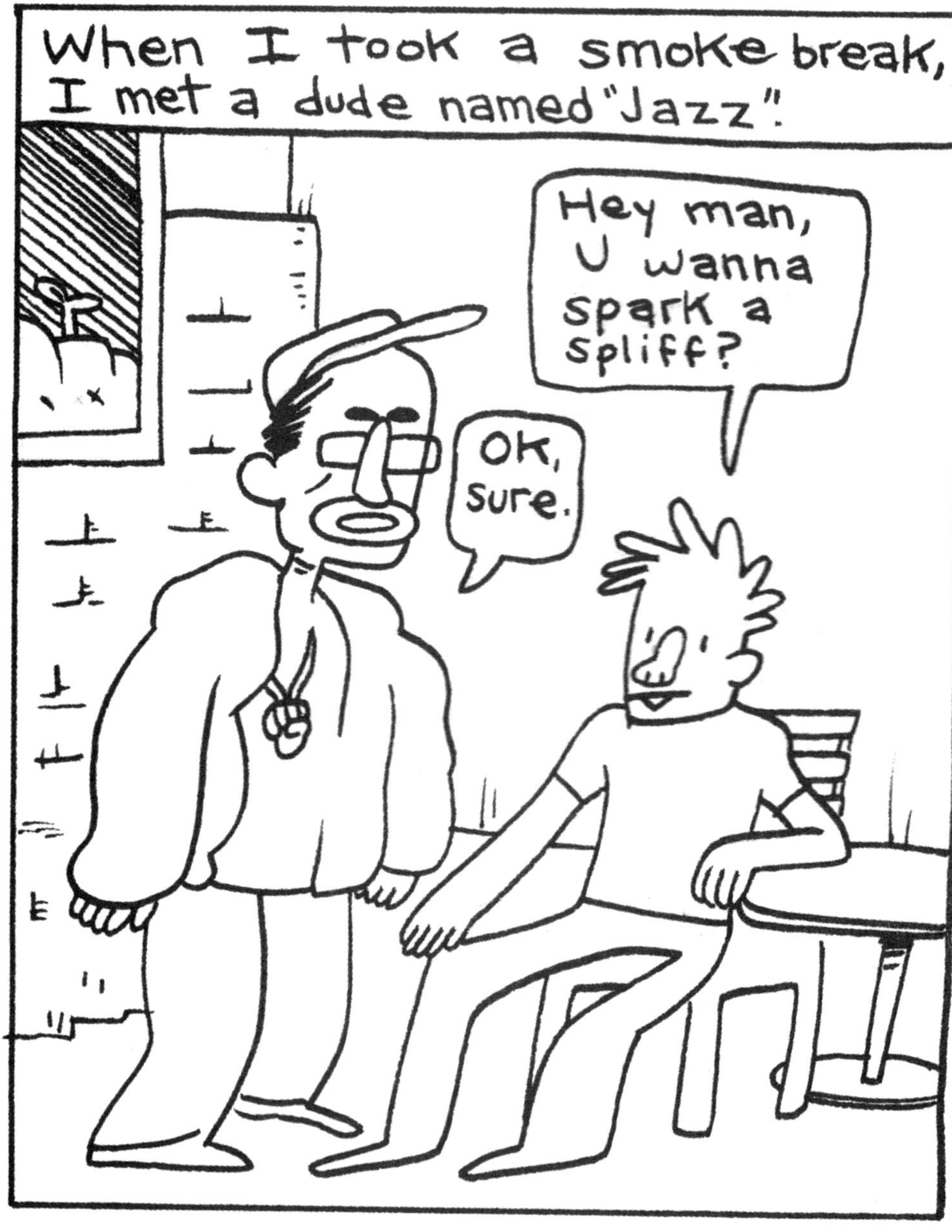
When I took a smoke break, I met a dude named "Jazz".
Hey man, U wanna spark a spliff?
Ok, sure.

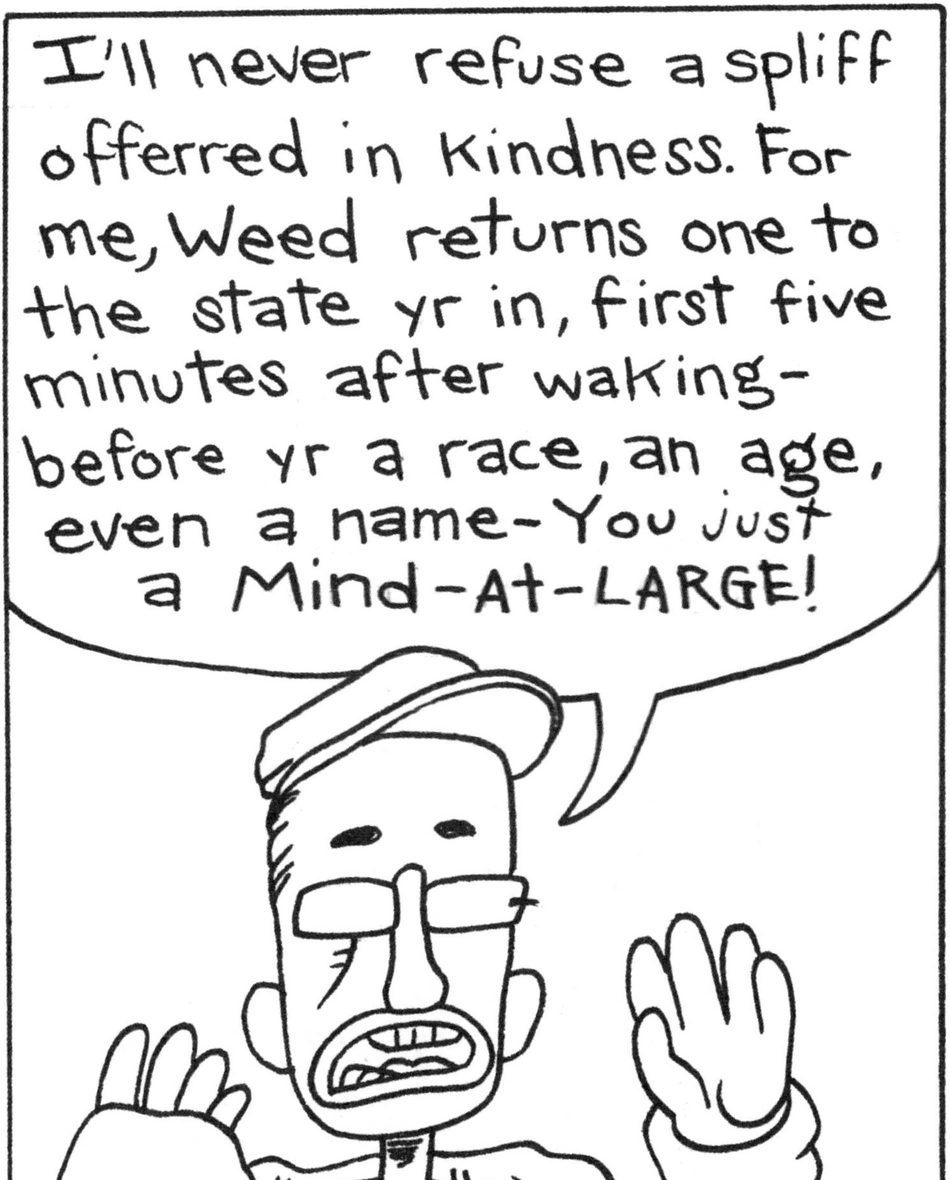
I'll never refuse a spliff offerred in Kindness. For me, Weed returns one to the state yr in, first five minutes after waking- before yr a race, an age, even a name- You just a Mind-At-LARGE!

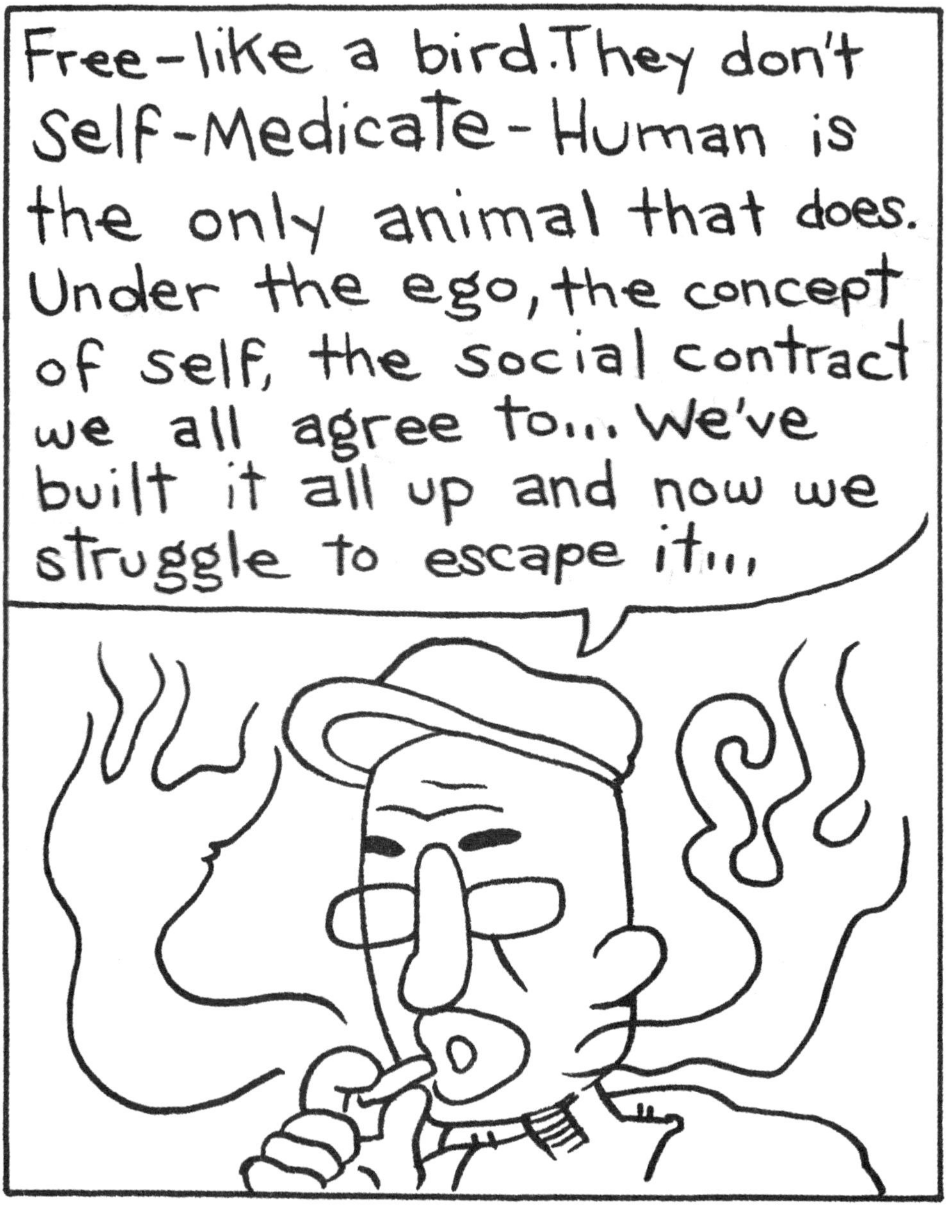
Free-like a bird. They don't Self-Medicate-Human is the only animal that does. Under the ego, the concept of self, the social contract we all agree to... We've built it all up and now we struggle to escape it...

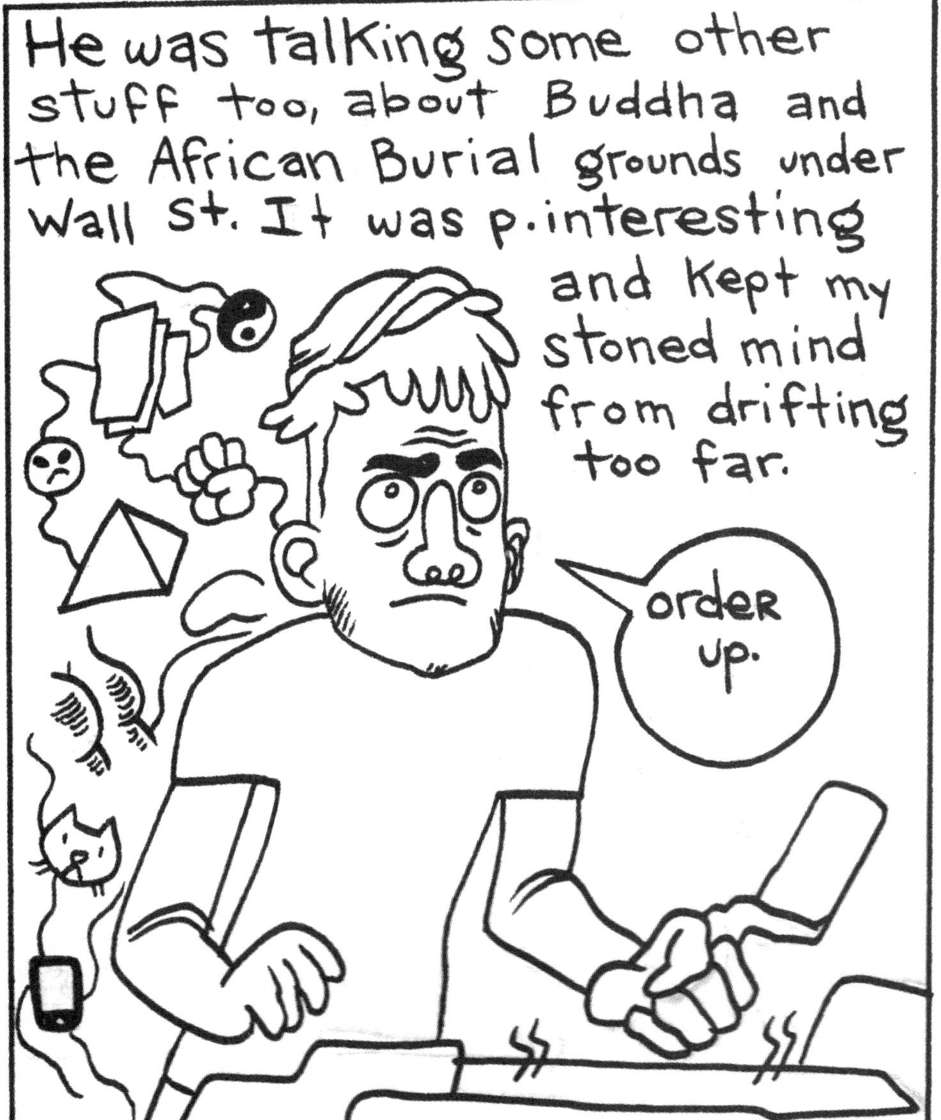
He was talking some other stuff too, about Buddha and the African Burial grounds under Wall St. It was p. interesting
and kept my stoned mind from drifting too far.
order up.

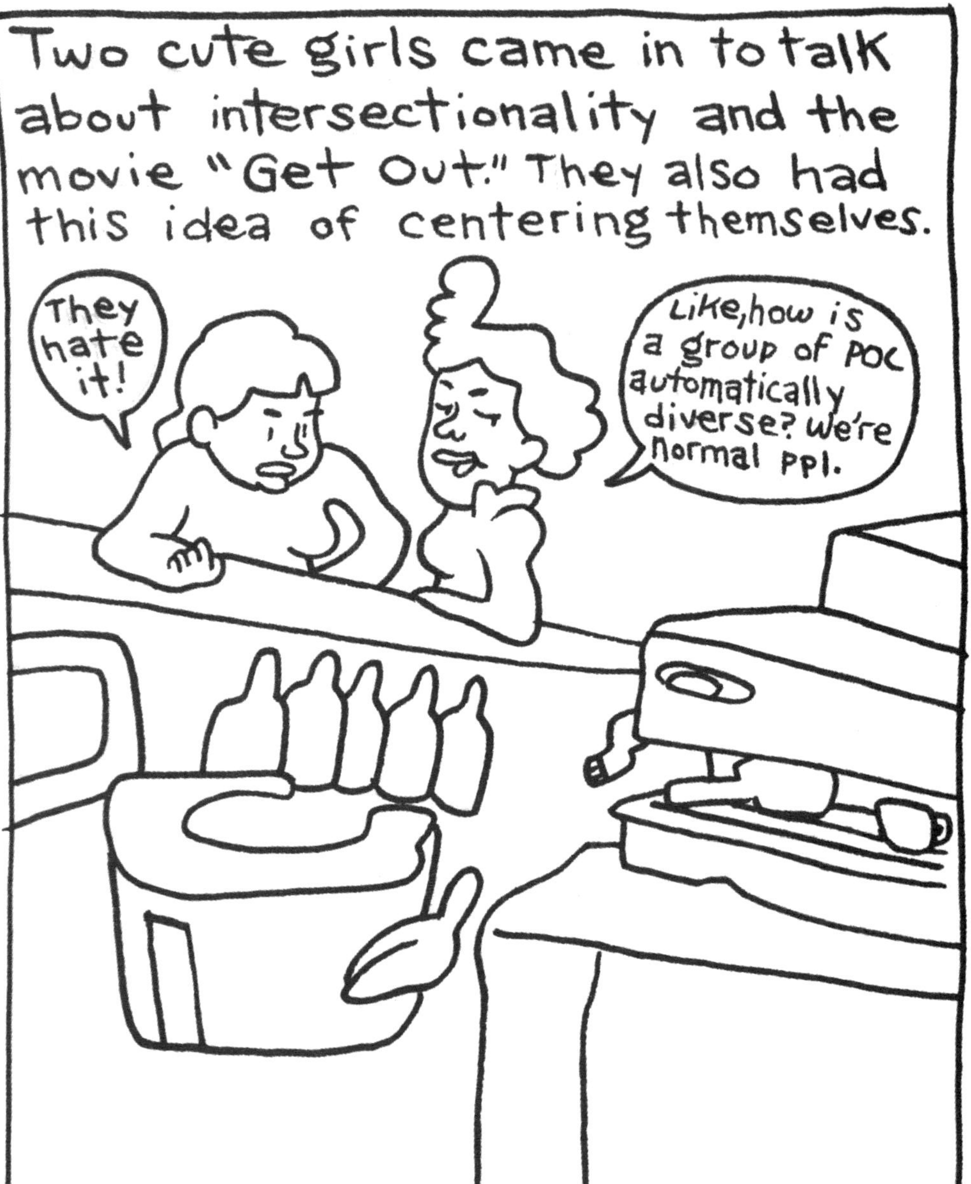
Two cute girls came in to talk about intersectionality and the movie "Get Out." They also had this idea of centering themselves.
They hate it!
Like, how is a group of POC automatically diverse? We're normal ppl.

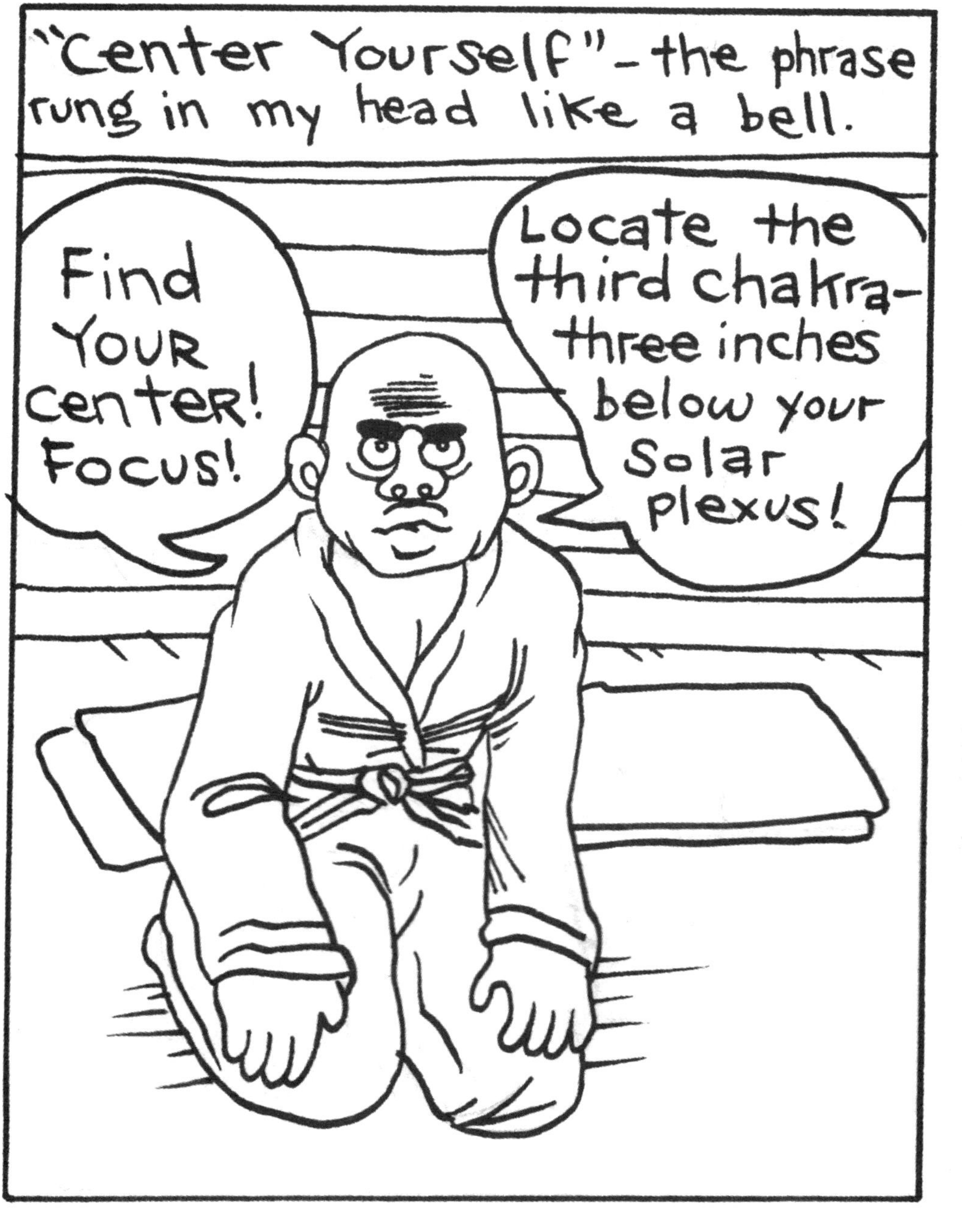
"Center Yourself" - the phrase rung in my head like a bell.
Find Your Center! Focus!
Locate the third chakra- three inches below your Solar plexus!

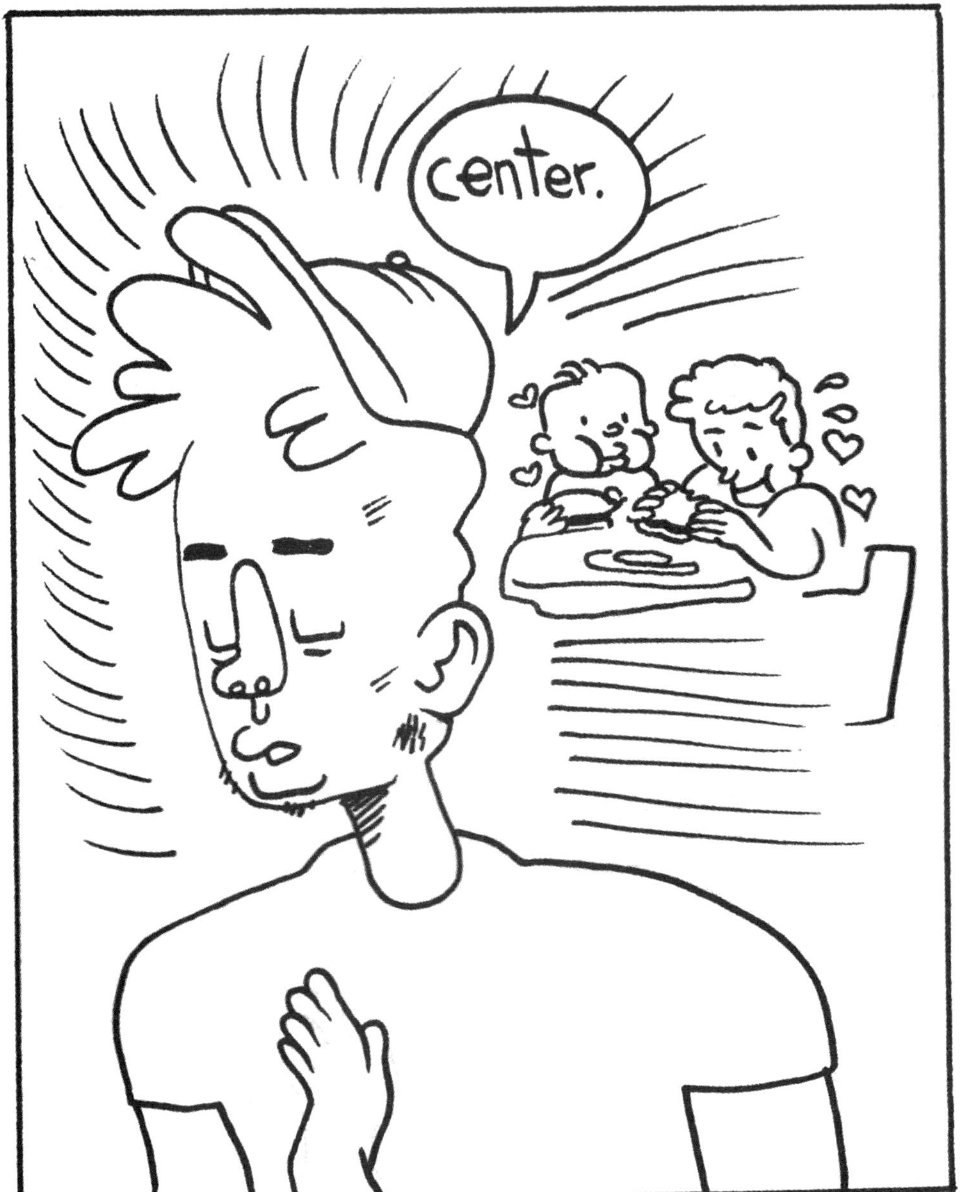
center.

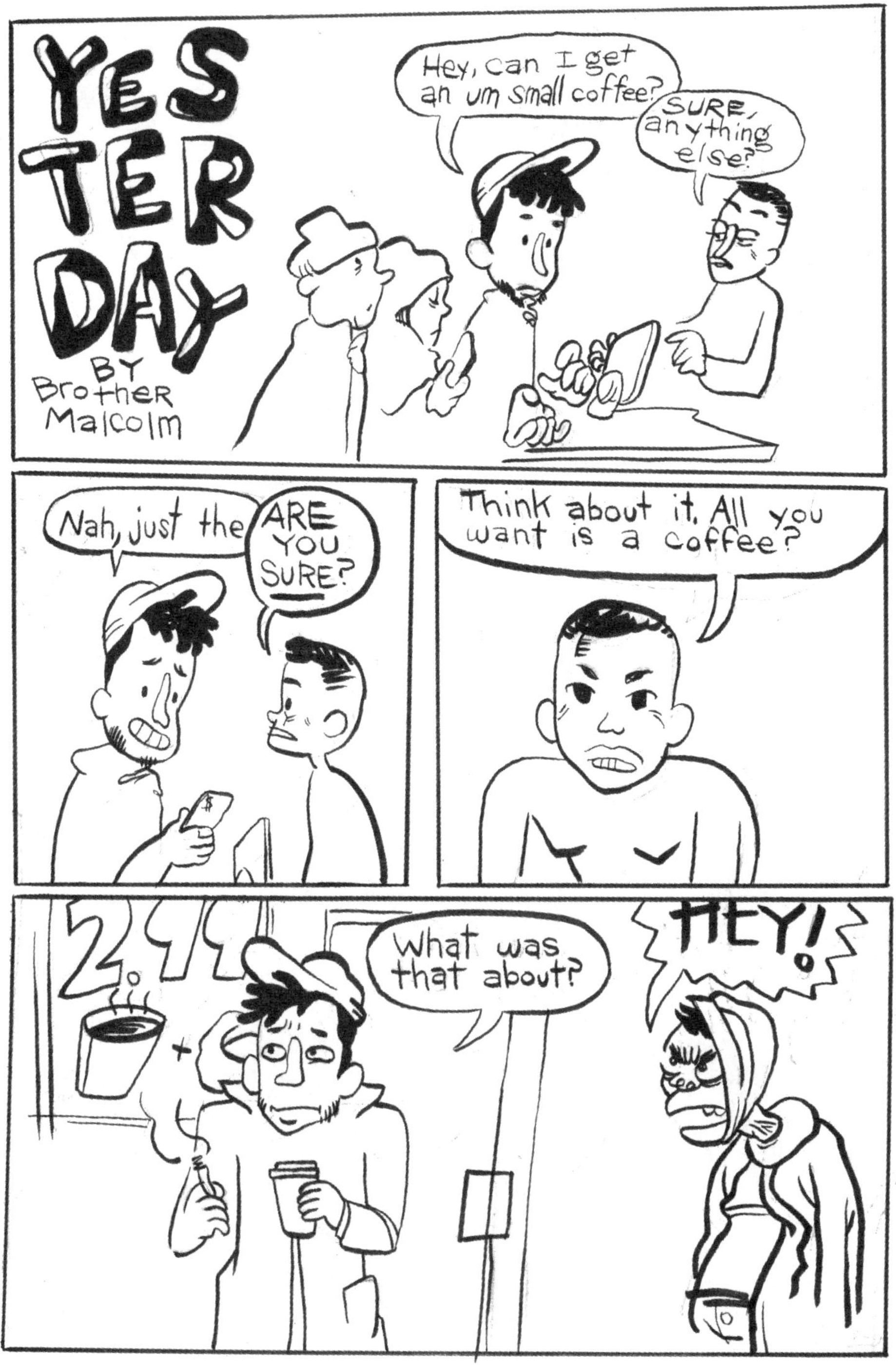
YES TER DAY
BY Brother Malcolm
Hey, can I get an um small coffee?
SURE, anything else?
Nah, just the
ARE YOU SURE?
Think about it. All you want is a coffee?
2.99
What was that about?
HEY!

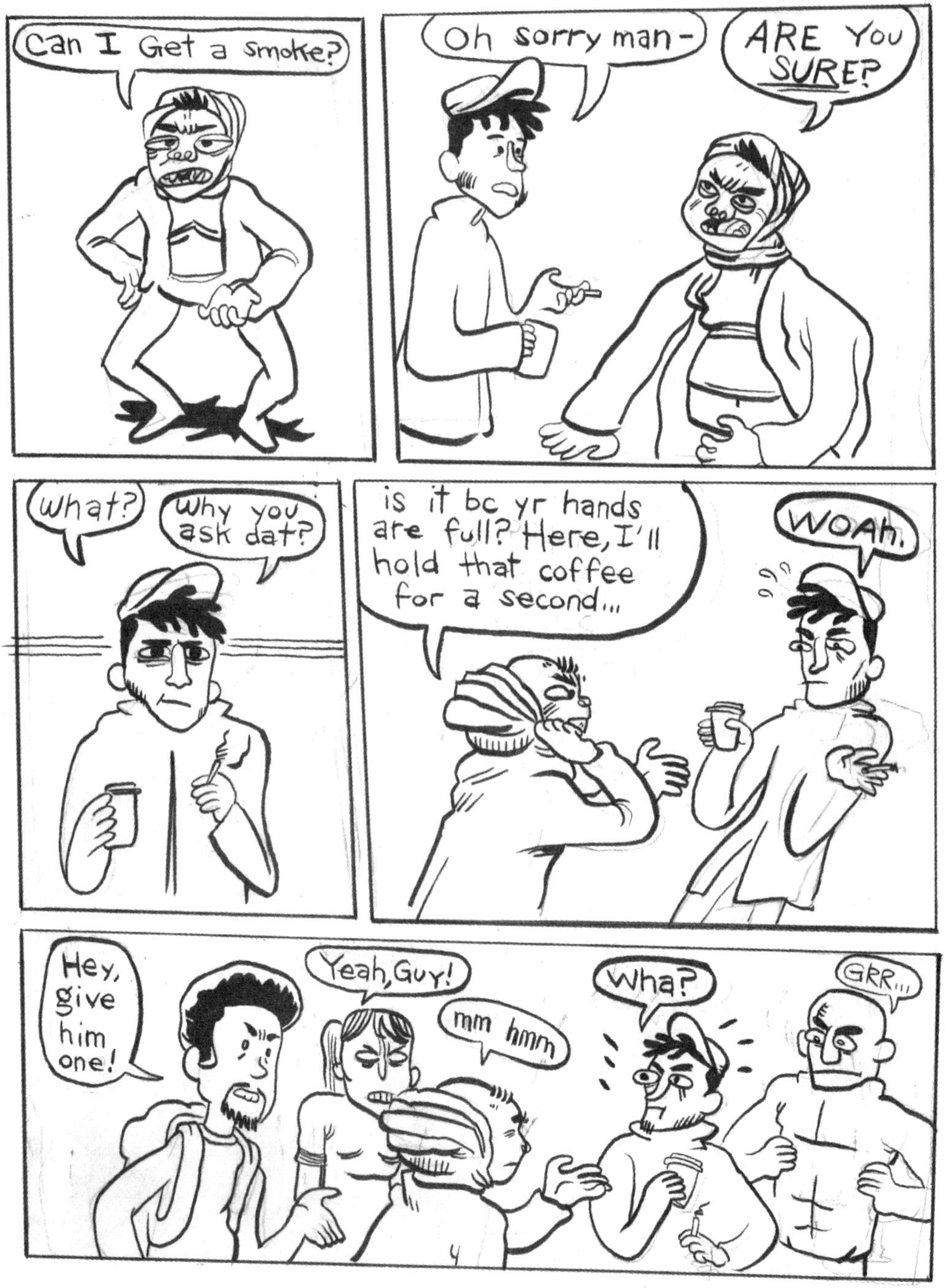
Can I Get a smoke?
Oh sorry man-
ARE You SURE?
what?
why you ask dat?
is it bc yr hands are full? Here, I'll hold that coffee for a second...
WOAh.
Hey, give him one!
Yeah, Guy!
mm hmm
Wha?
GRR...
4

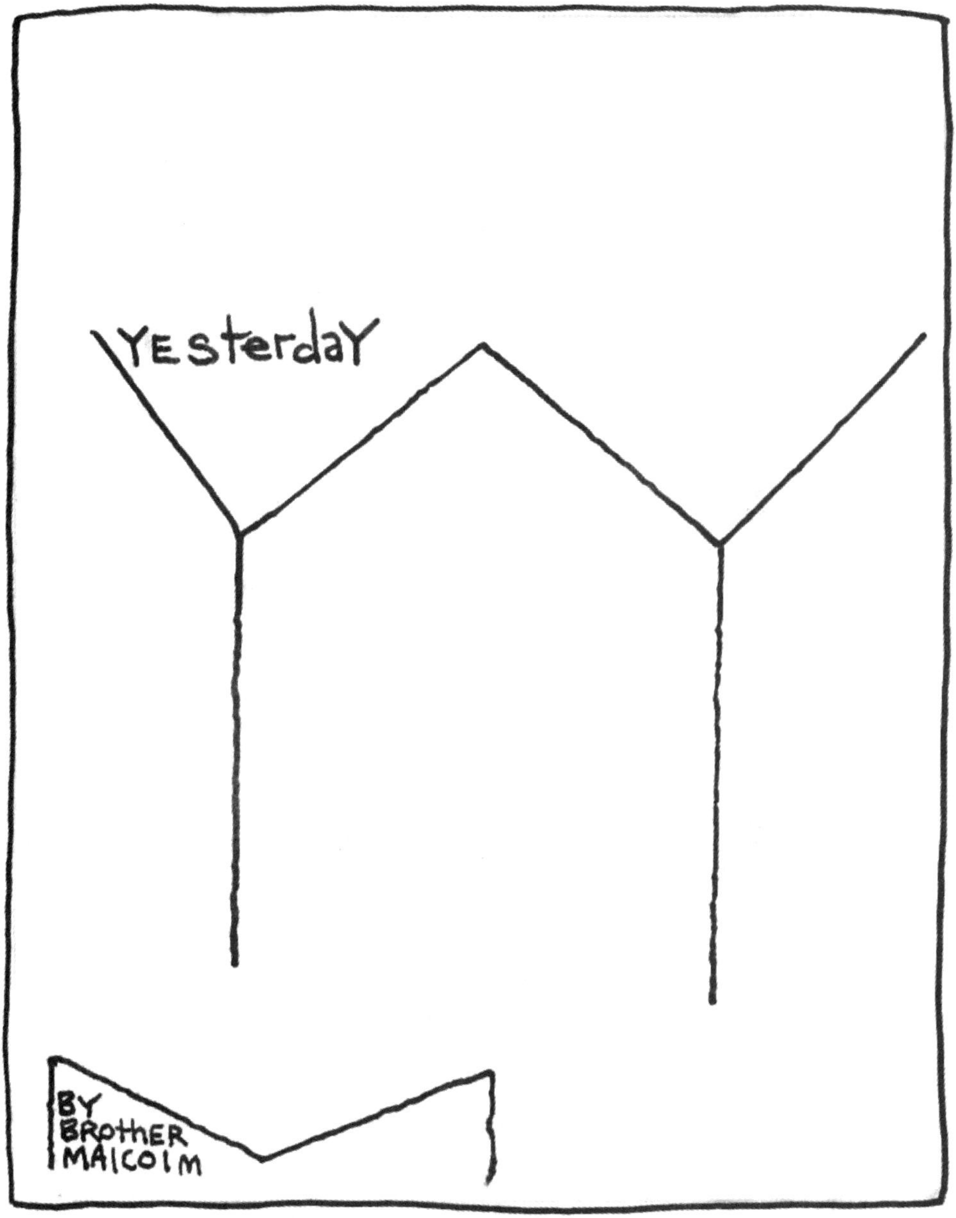
YESterdaY
BY
BROtHER
MAlCOlM

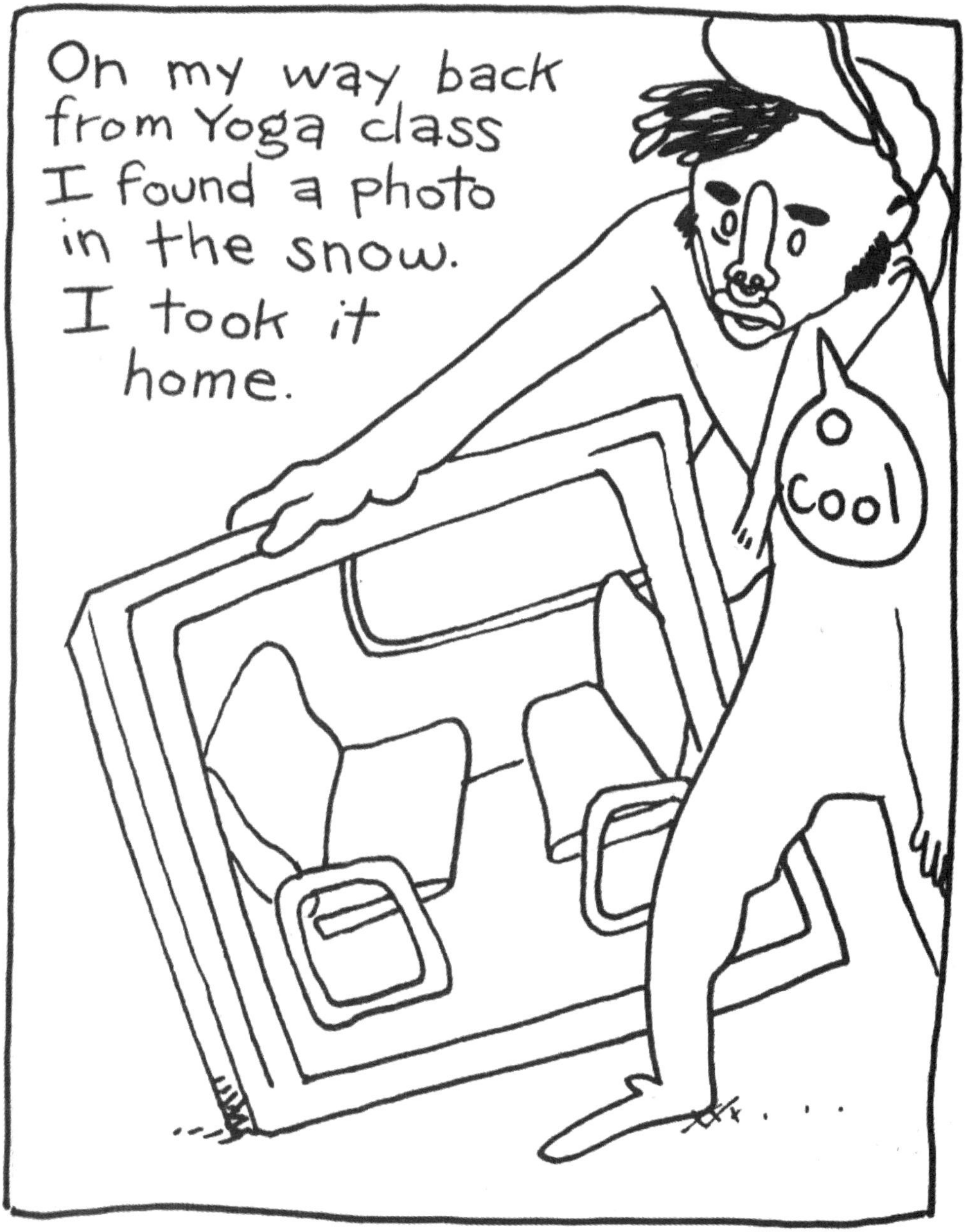
On my way back from Yoga class I found a photo in the snow. I took it home.
O Cool

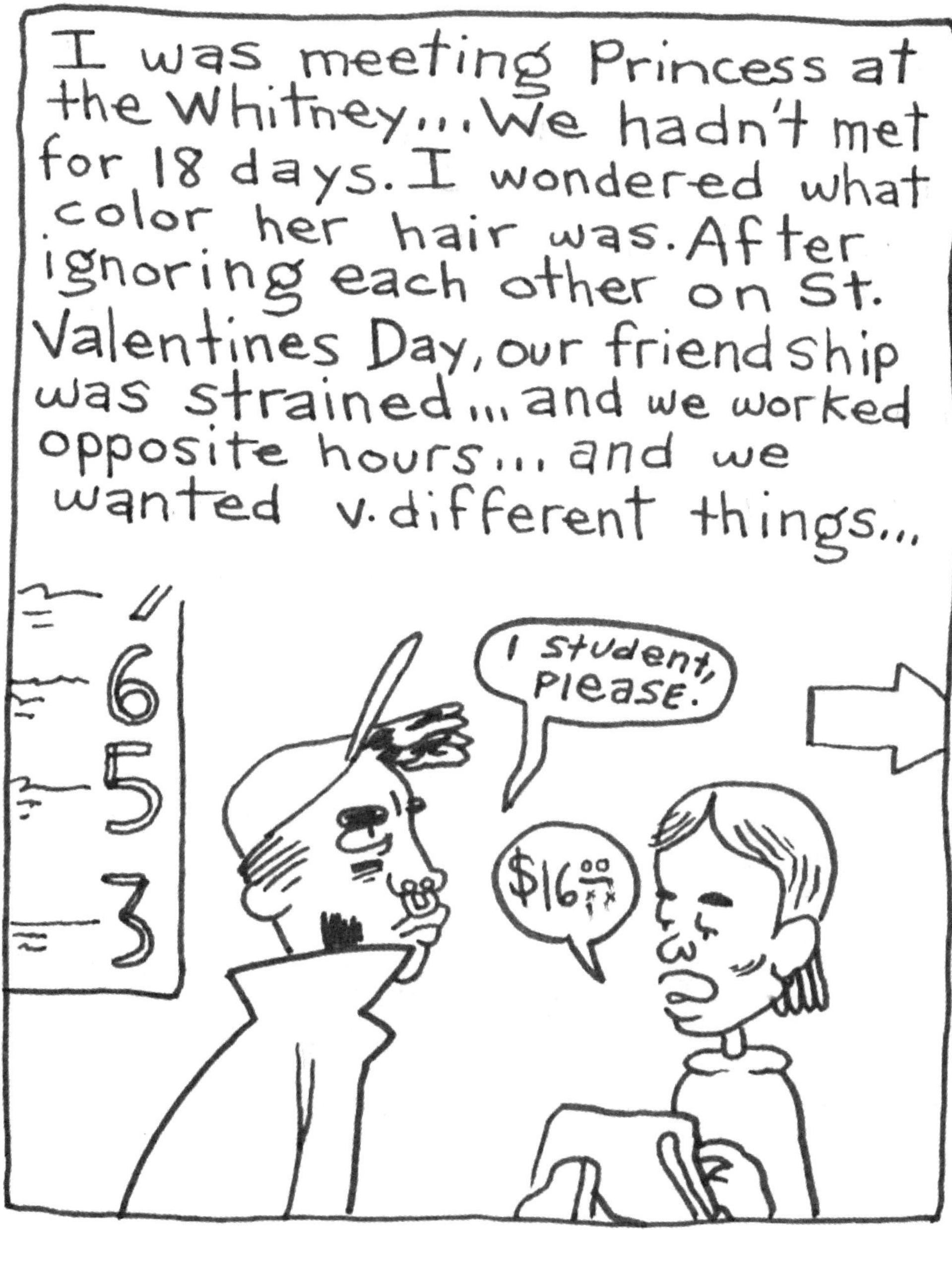
I was meeting Princess at the Whitney... We hadn't met for 18 days. I wondered what color her hair was. After ignoring each other on St. Valentines Day, our friendship was strained... and we worked opposite hours... and we wanted v. different things...
6 5 3
1 student, please.
$16 00

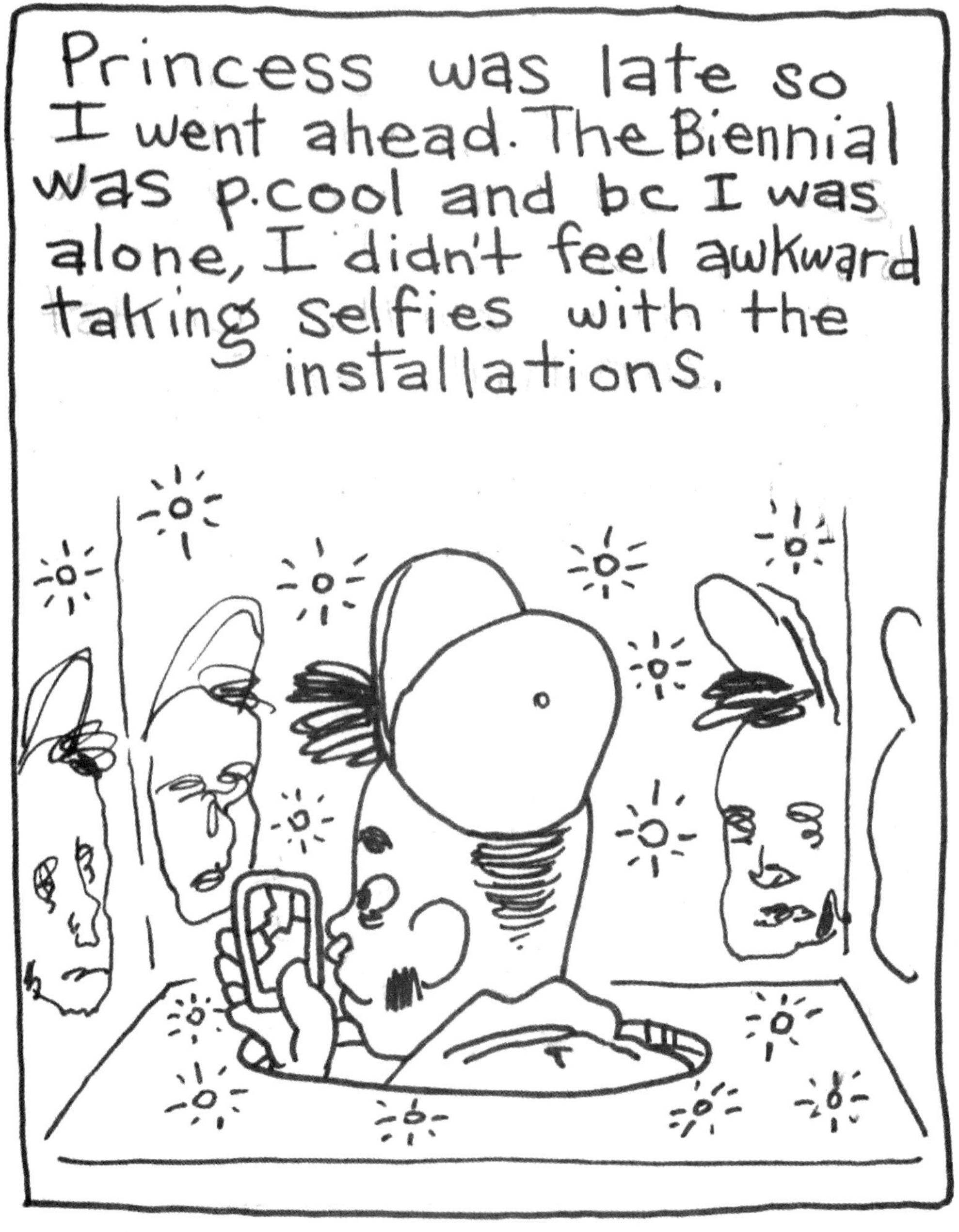

Princess was late so I went ahead. The Biennial was p.cool and bc I was alone, I didn't feel awkward taking selfies with the installations.

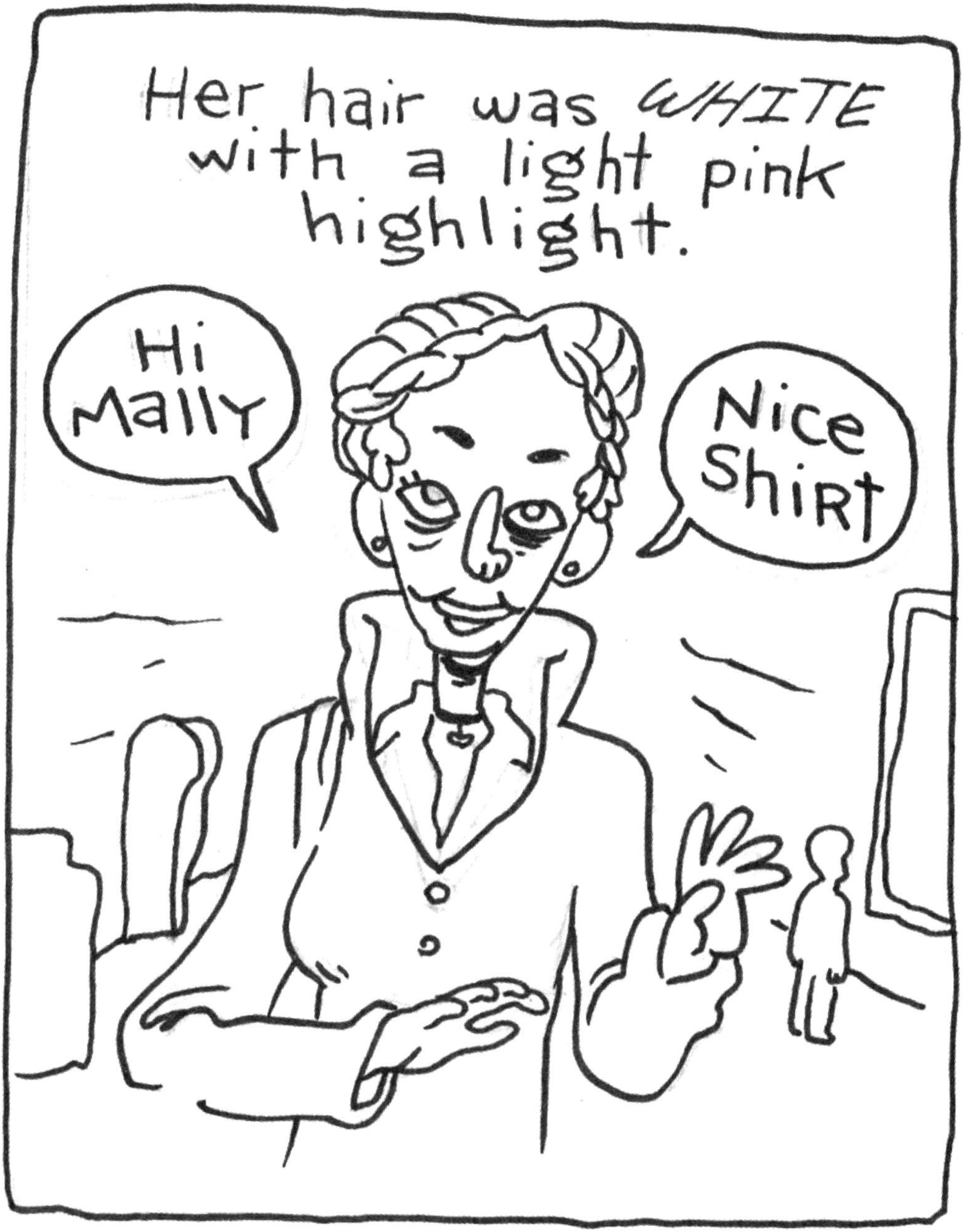
Her hair was WHITE with a light pink highlight.
Hi Mally
Nice Shirt

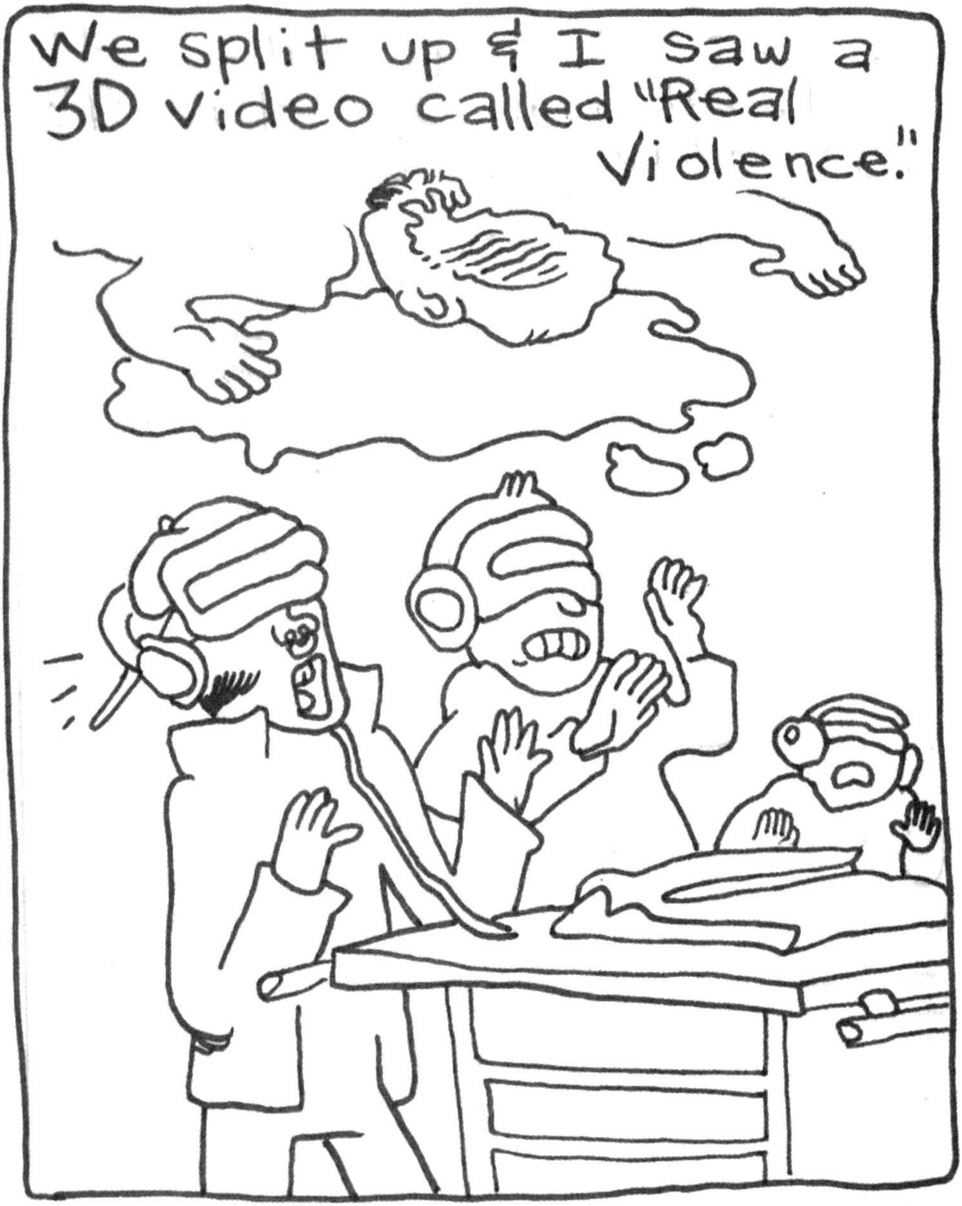
We split up & I saw a 3D video called "Real Violence."

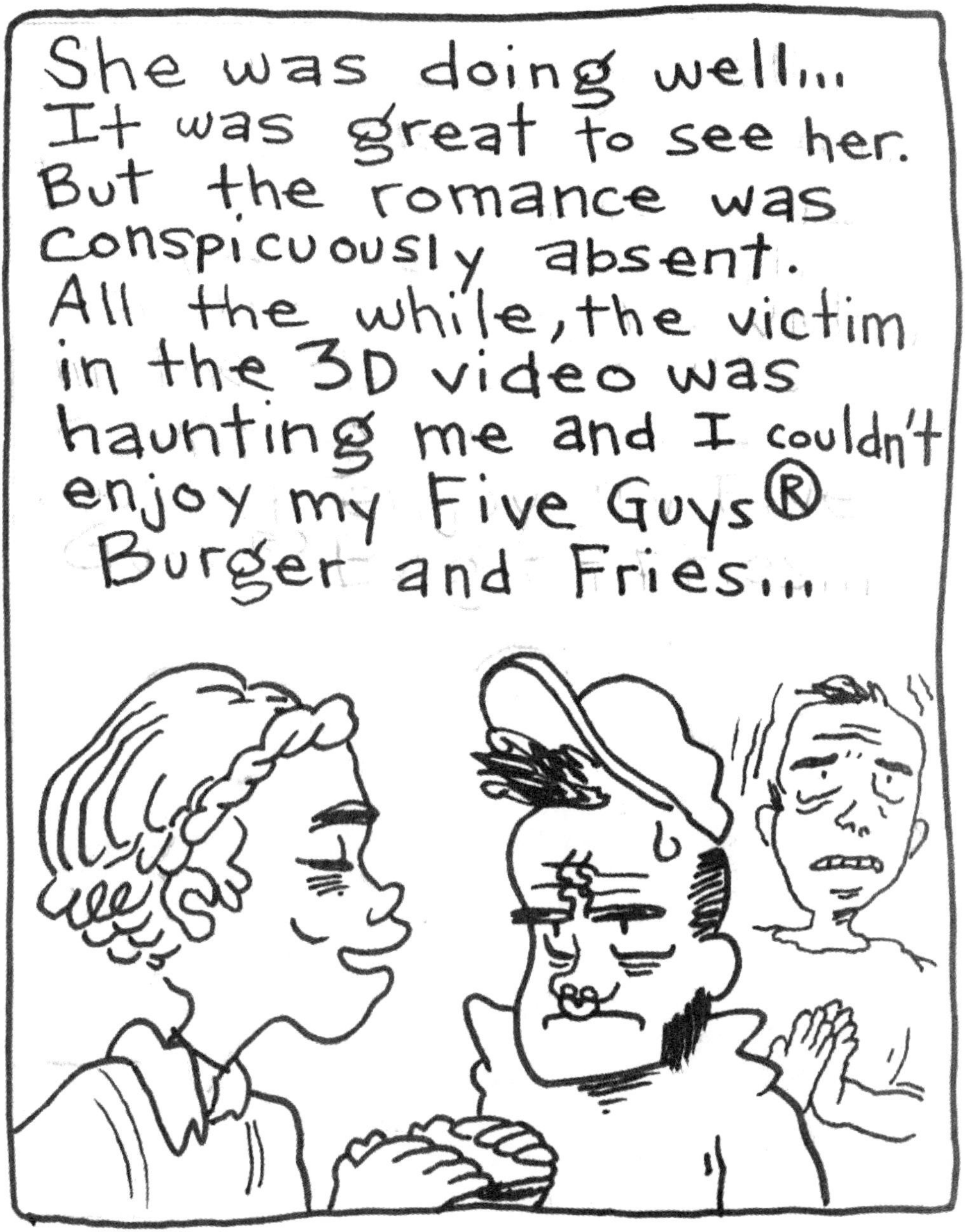
She was doing well...
It was great to see her.
But the romance was conspicuously absent.
All the while, the victim in the 3D video was haunting me and I couldn't enjoy my Five Guys® Burger and Fries...

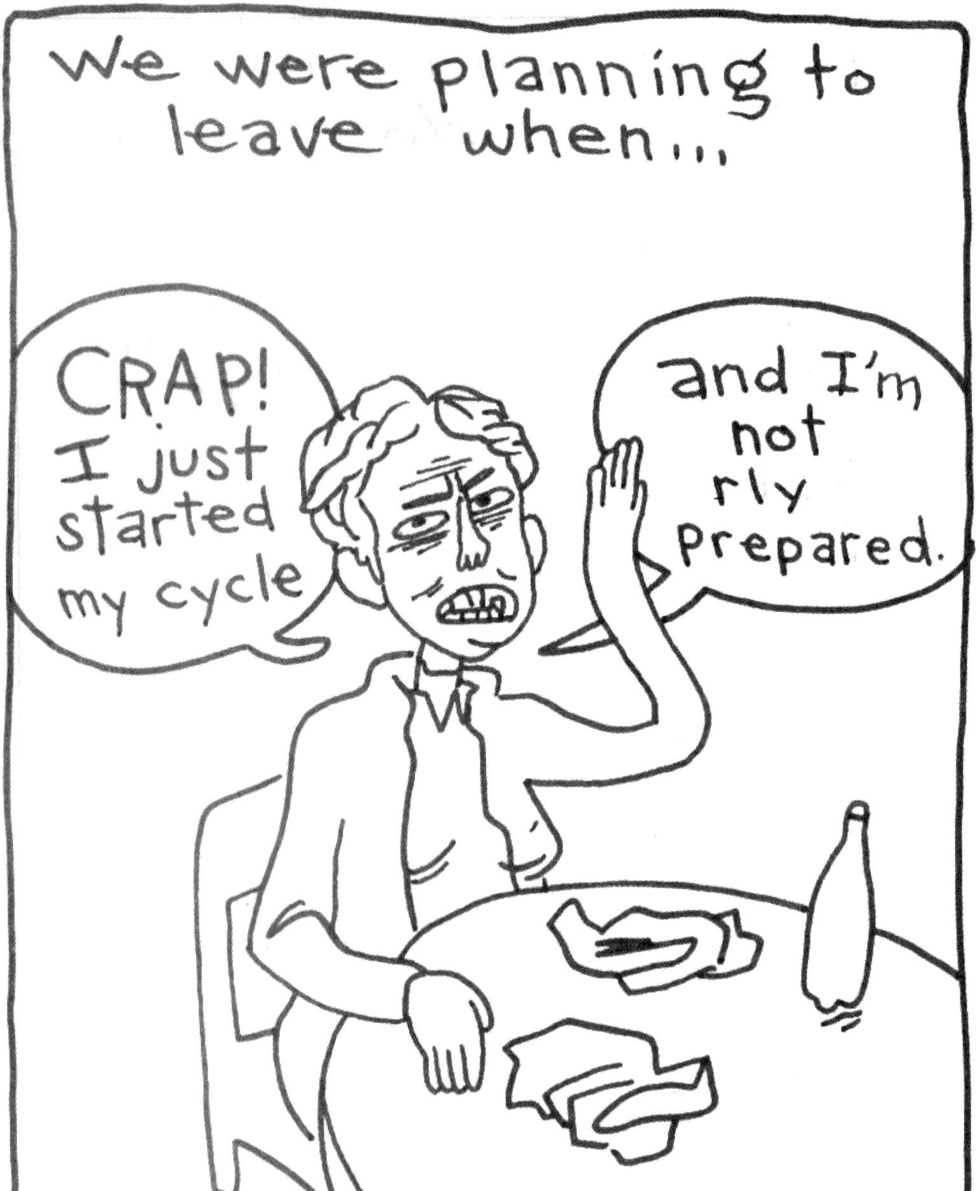
We were planning to leave when...
CRAP! I just started my cycle
and I'm not rly prepared.

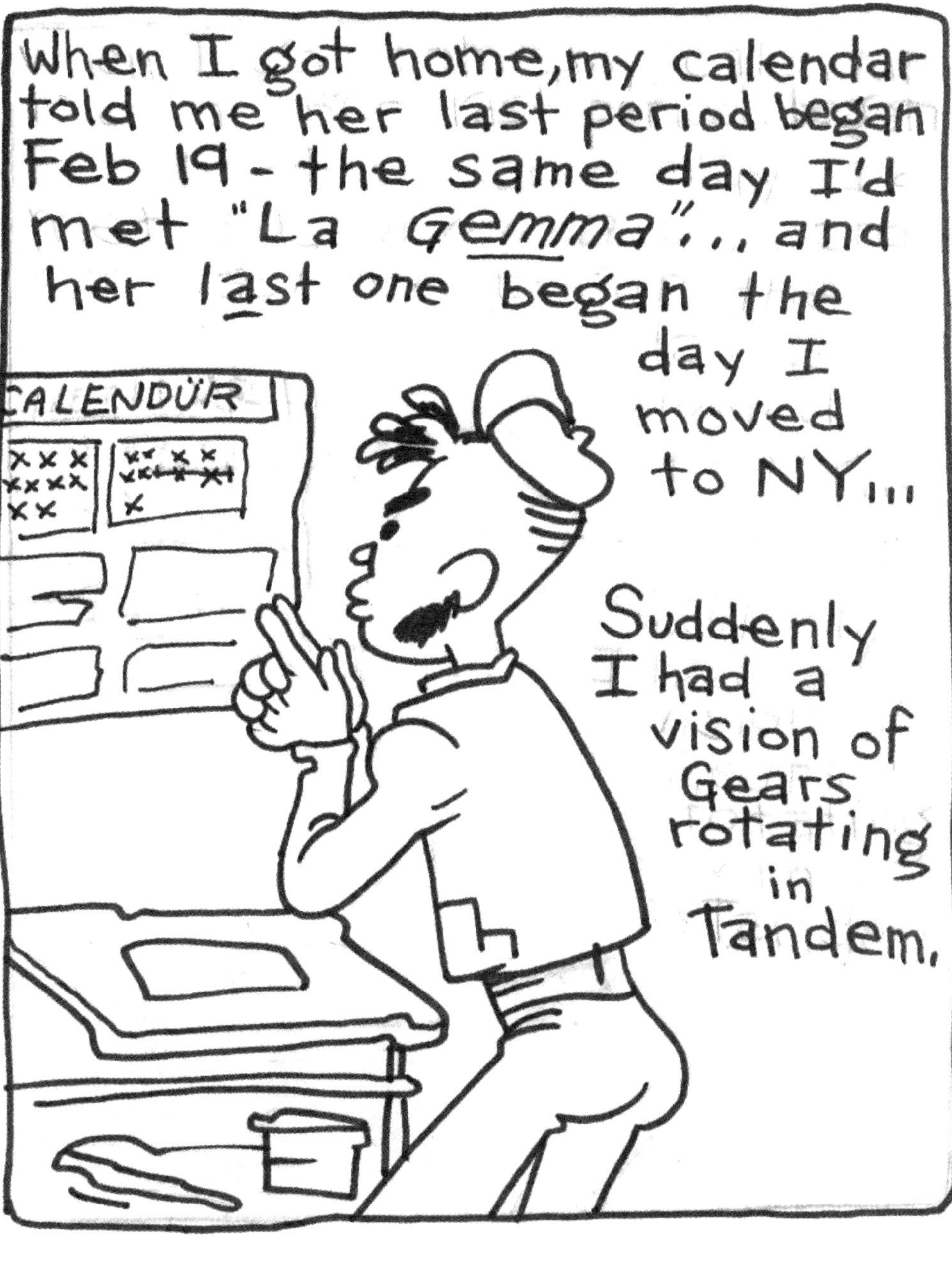
When I got home, my calendar told me her last period began Feb 19 - the same day I'd met "La Gemma"... and her last one began the day I moved to NY...
CALENDÜR
Suddenly I had a vision of Gears rotating in Tandem.

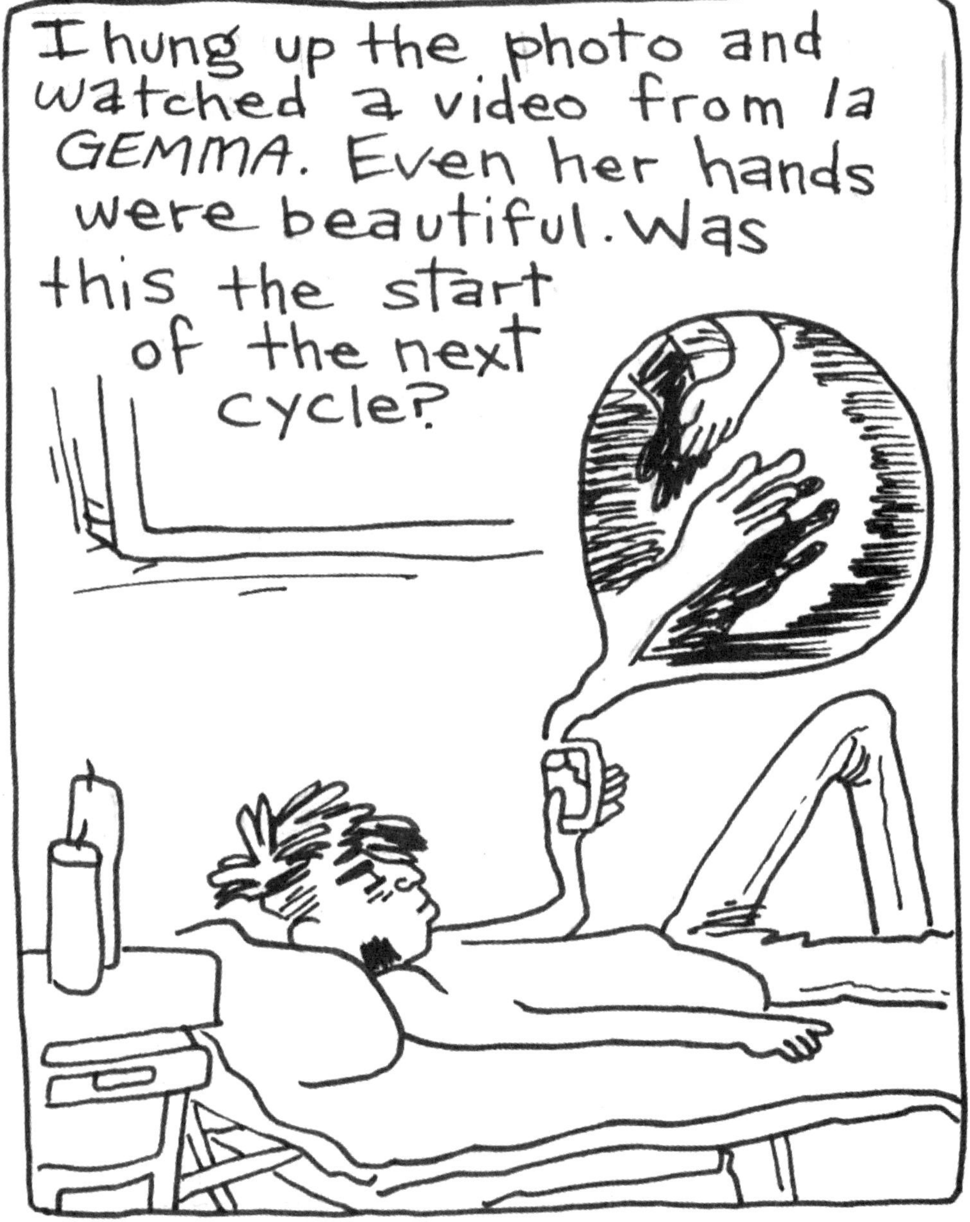
I hung up the photo and watched a video from *la GEMMA*. Even her hands were beautiful. Was this the start of the next cycle?

YESTERDAY

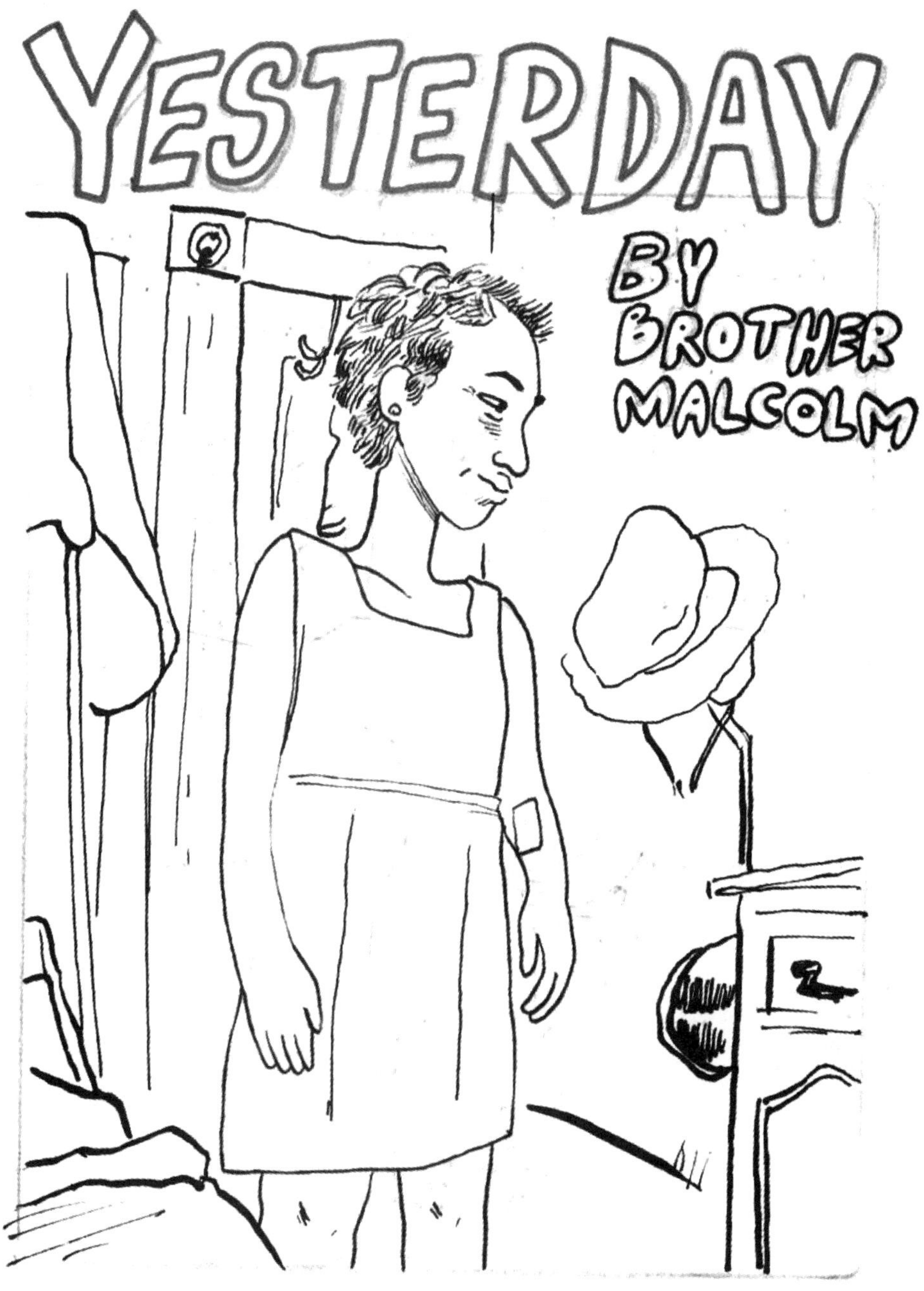
BY BROTHER MALCOLM

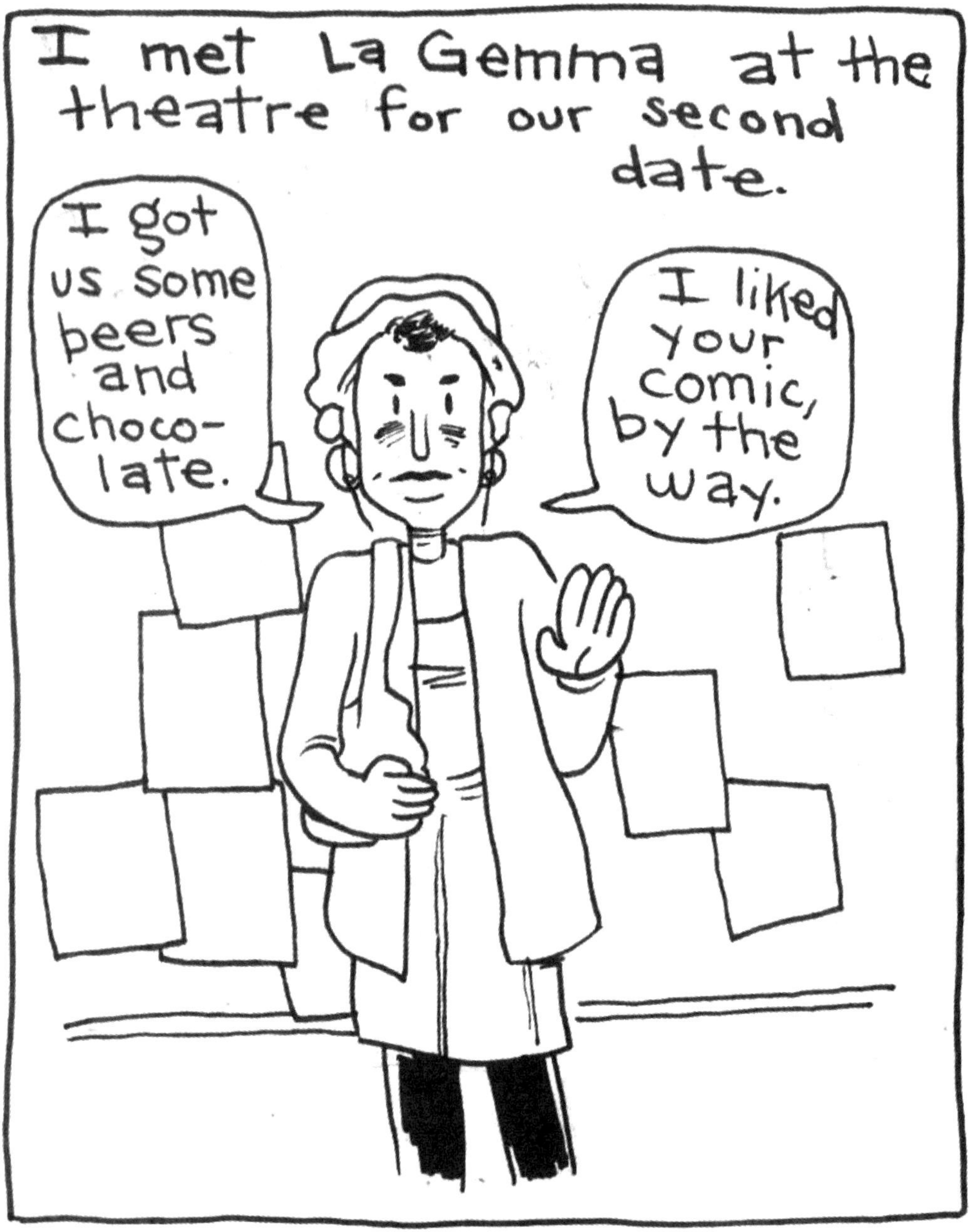
I met La Gemma at the theatre for our second date.
I got us some beers and choco-late.
I liked your comic, by the way.

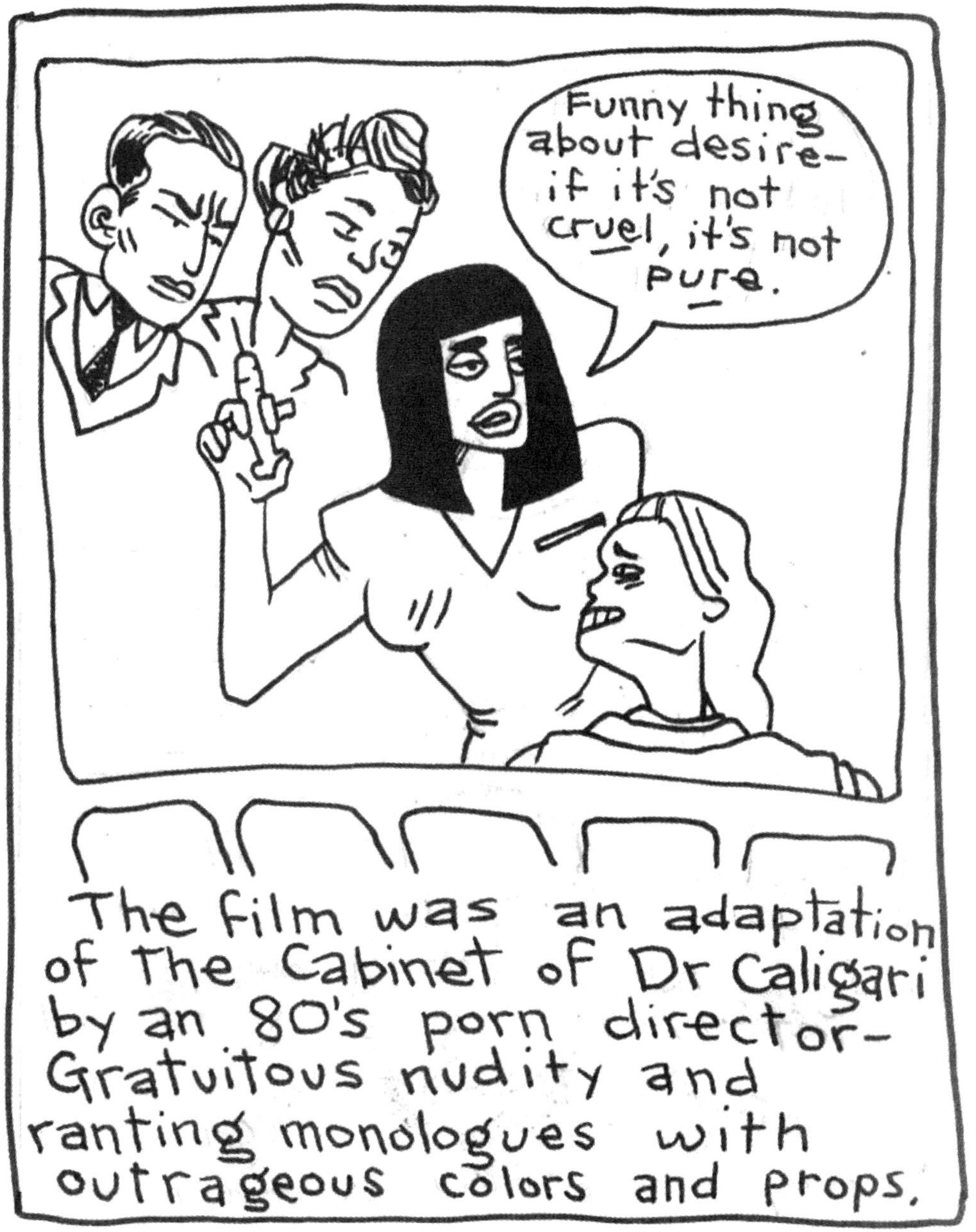
Funny thing about desire- if it's not cruel, it's not pure.
The film was an adaptation of The Cabinet of Dr Caligari by an 80's porn director- Gratuitous nudity and ranting monologues with outrageous colors and props.

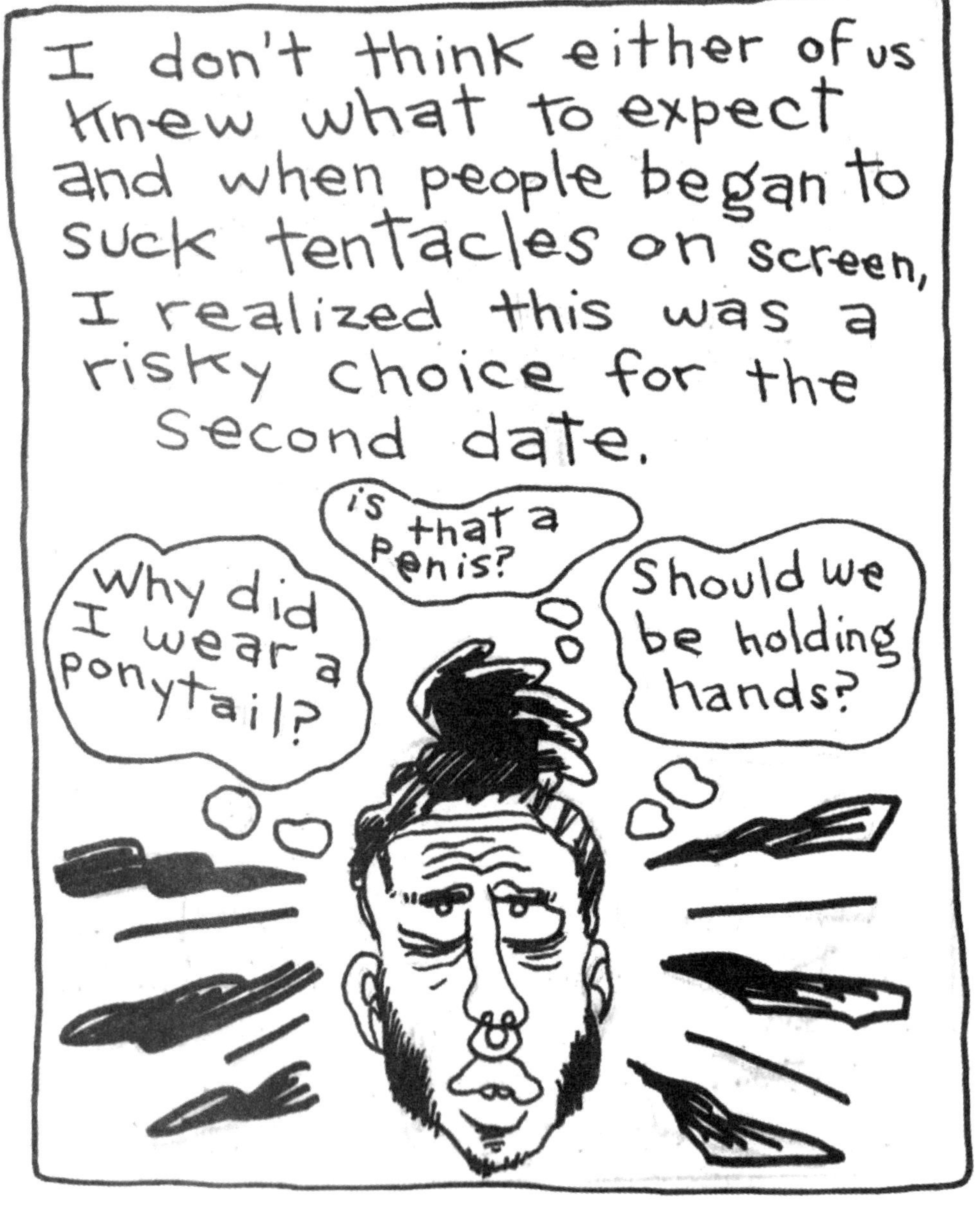
I don't think either of us knew what to expect and when people began to suck tentacles on screen, I realized this was a risky choice for the second date.
Why did I wear a ponytail?
is that a penis?
Should we be holding hands?

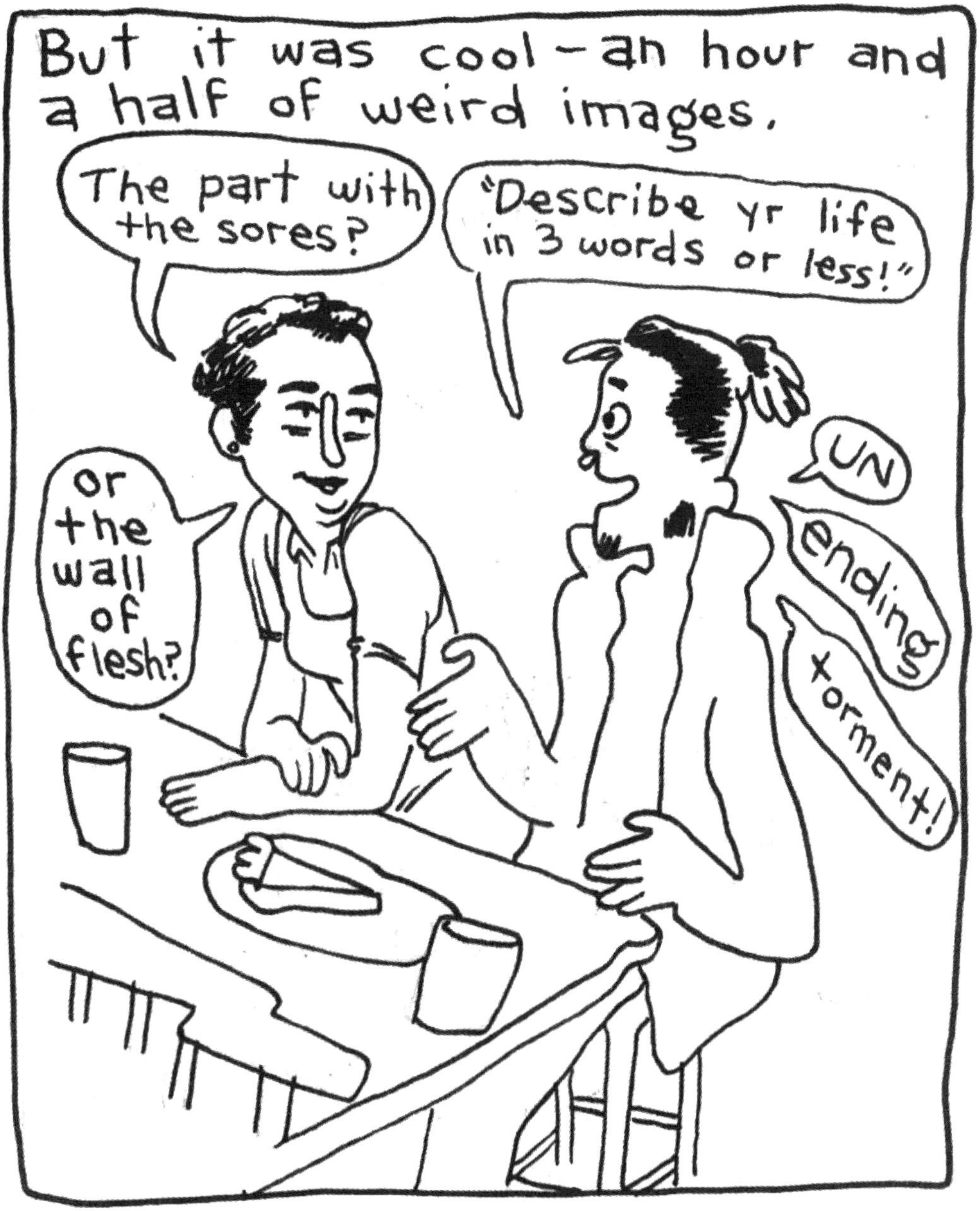

But it was cool - an hour and a half of weird images.
The part with the sores?
"Describe yr life in 3 words or less!"
or the wall of flesh?
UN
ending
torment!

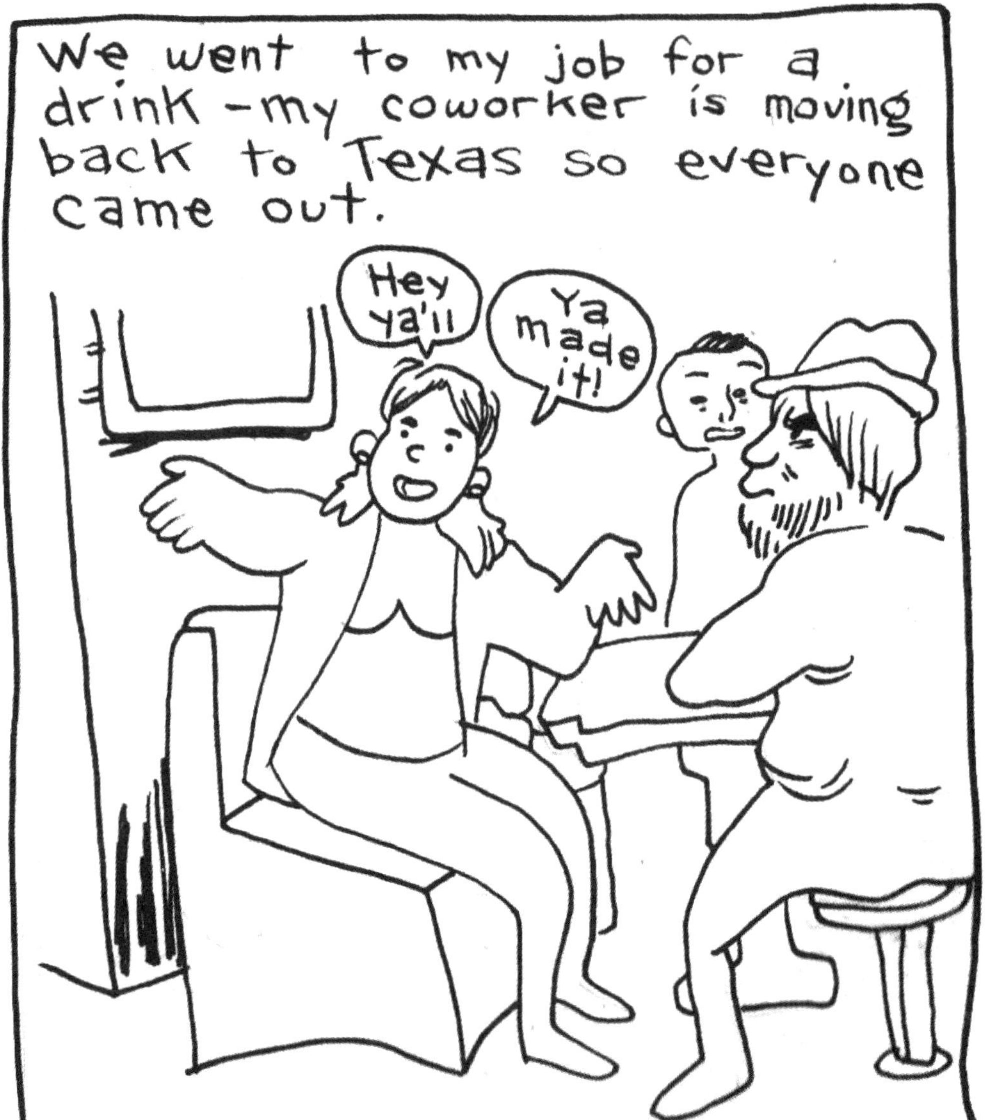
We went to my job for a drink - my coworker is moving back to Texas so everyone came out.
Hey ya'll
Ya made it!

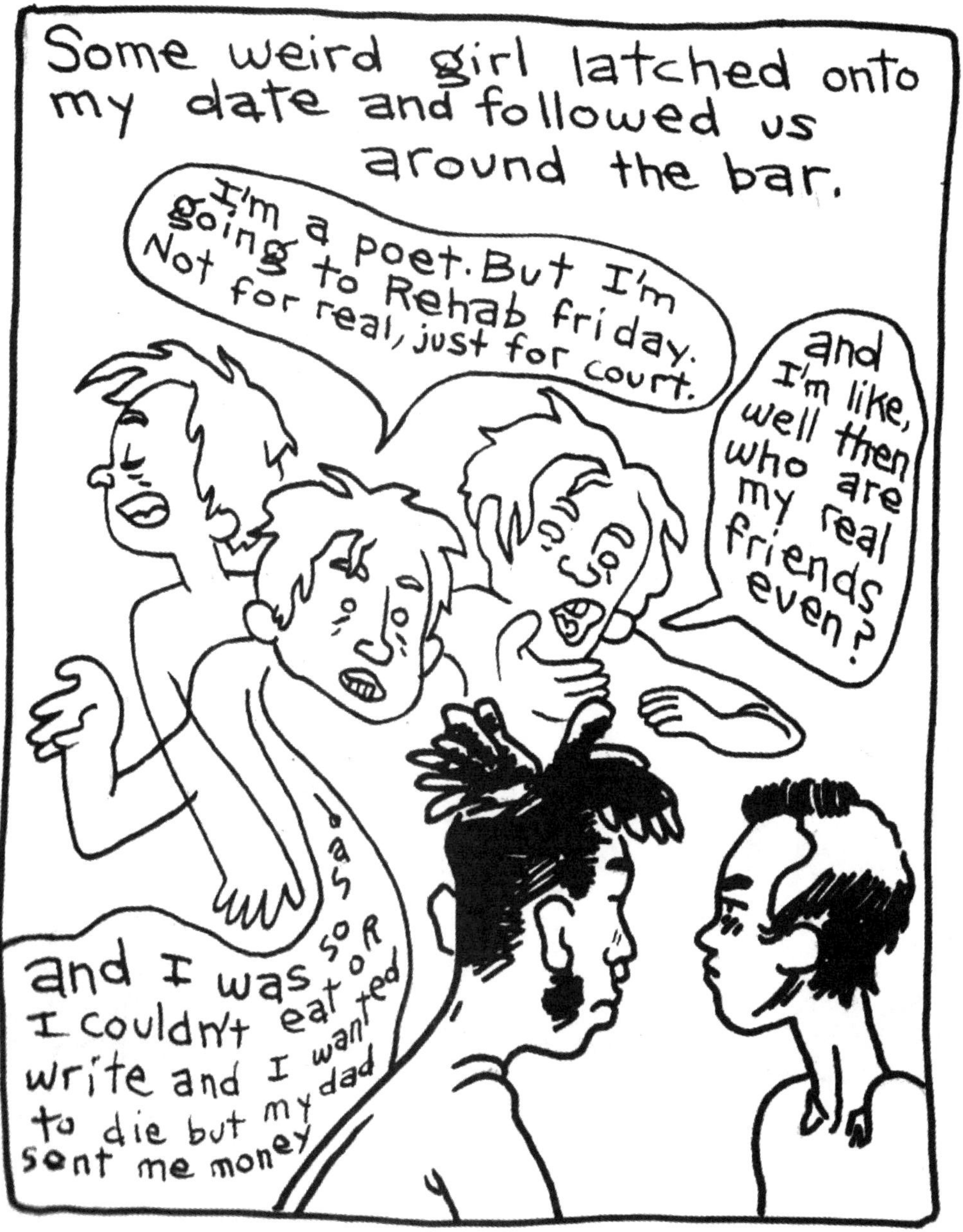
Some weird girl latched onto my date and followed us around the bar.
I'm a poet. But I'm going to Rehab friday. Not for real, just for court.
and I'm like, well then who are my real friends even?
and I was so sad
so poor
I couldn't eat
write and I wanted to die but my dad sent me money

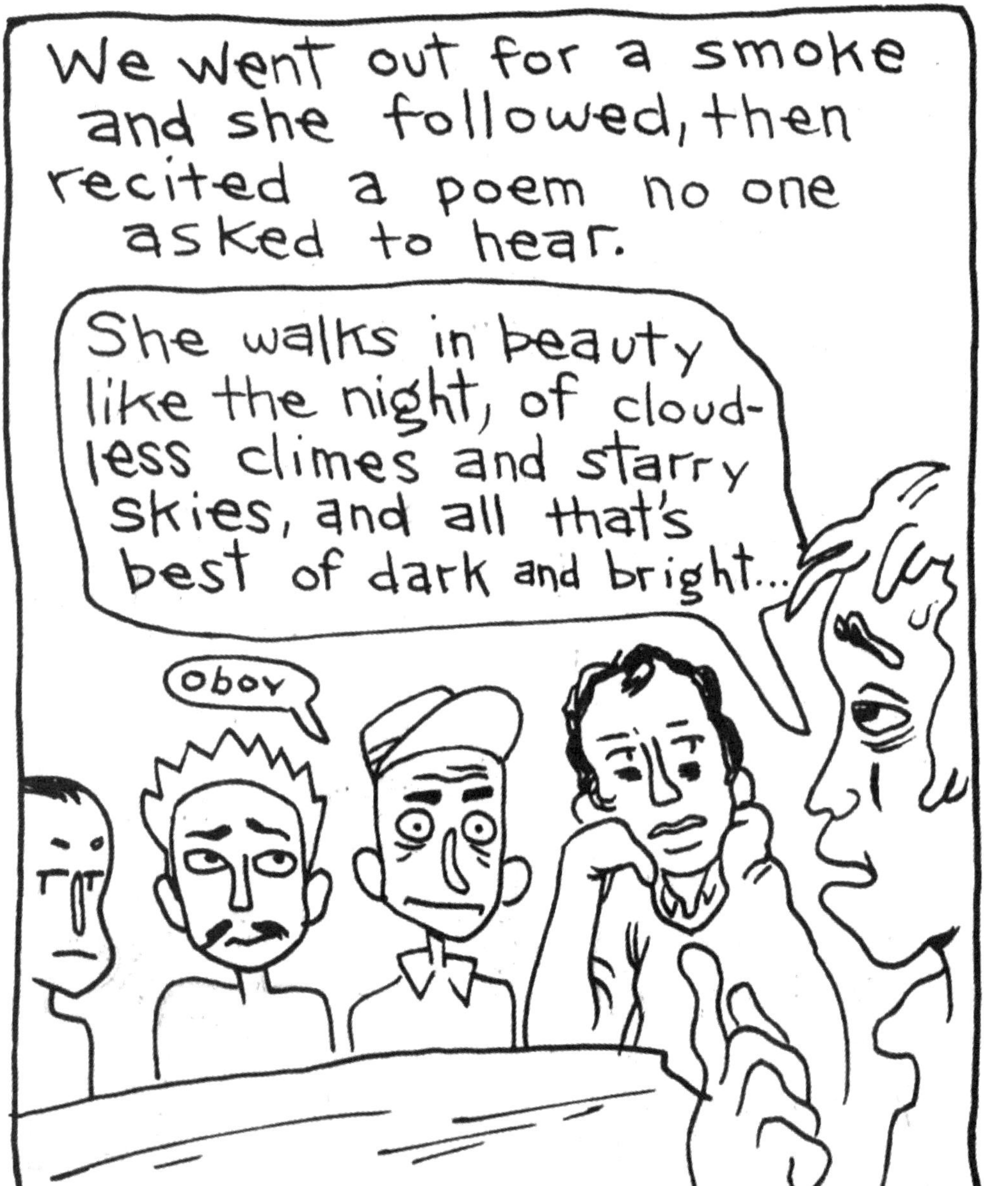
We went out for a smoke and she followed, then recited a poem no one asked to hear.
She walks in beauty like the night, of cloudless climes and starry skies, and all that's best of dark and bright...
oboy

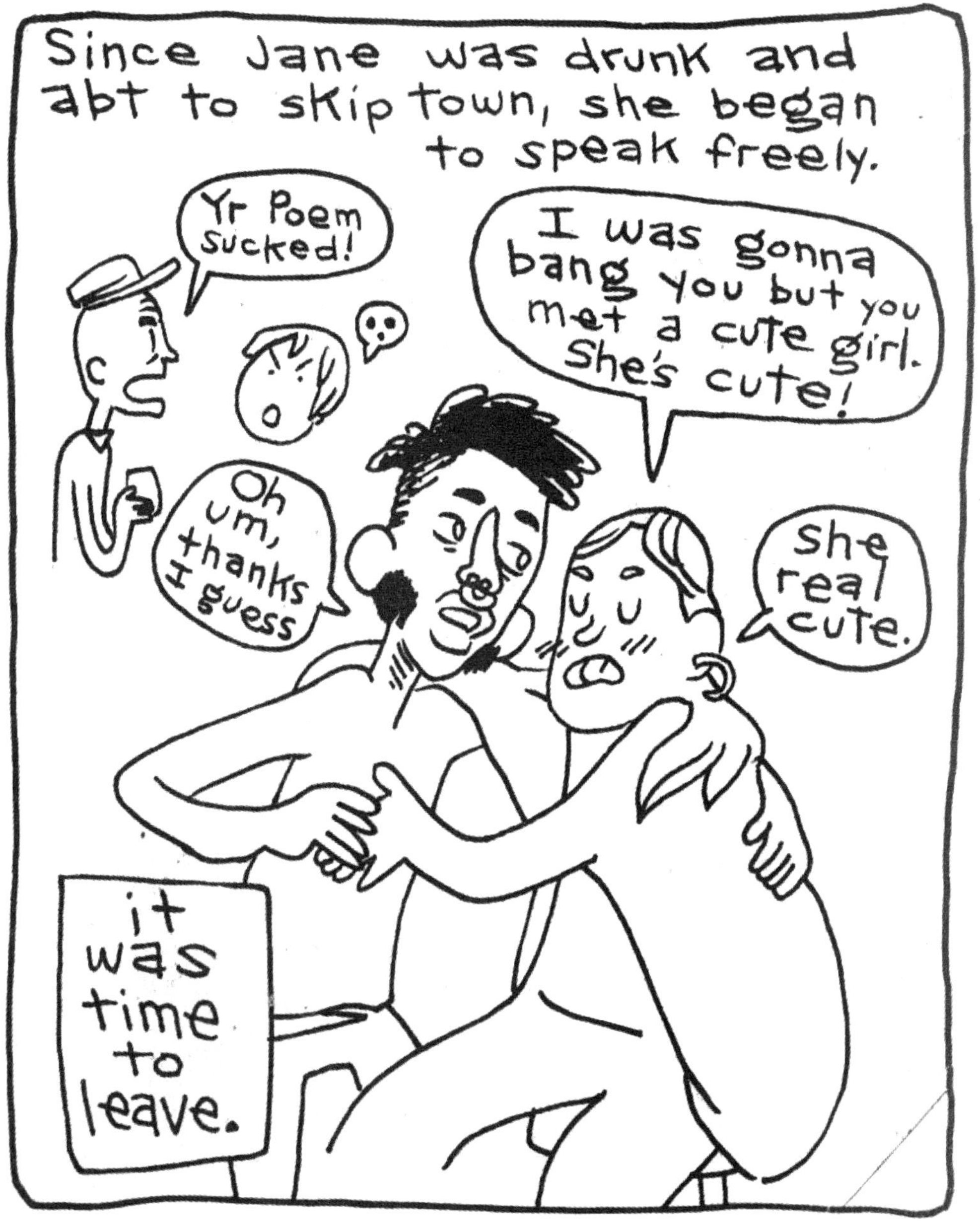

Since Jane was drunk and abt to skip town, she began to speak freely.
Yr Poem sucked!
I was gonna bang you but you met a cute girl. She's cute!
Oh um, thanks I guess
She real cute.
it was time to leave.

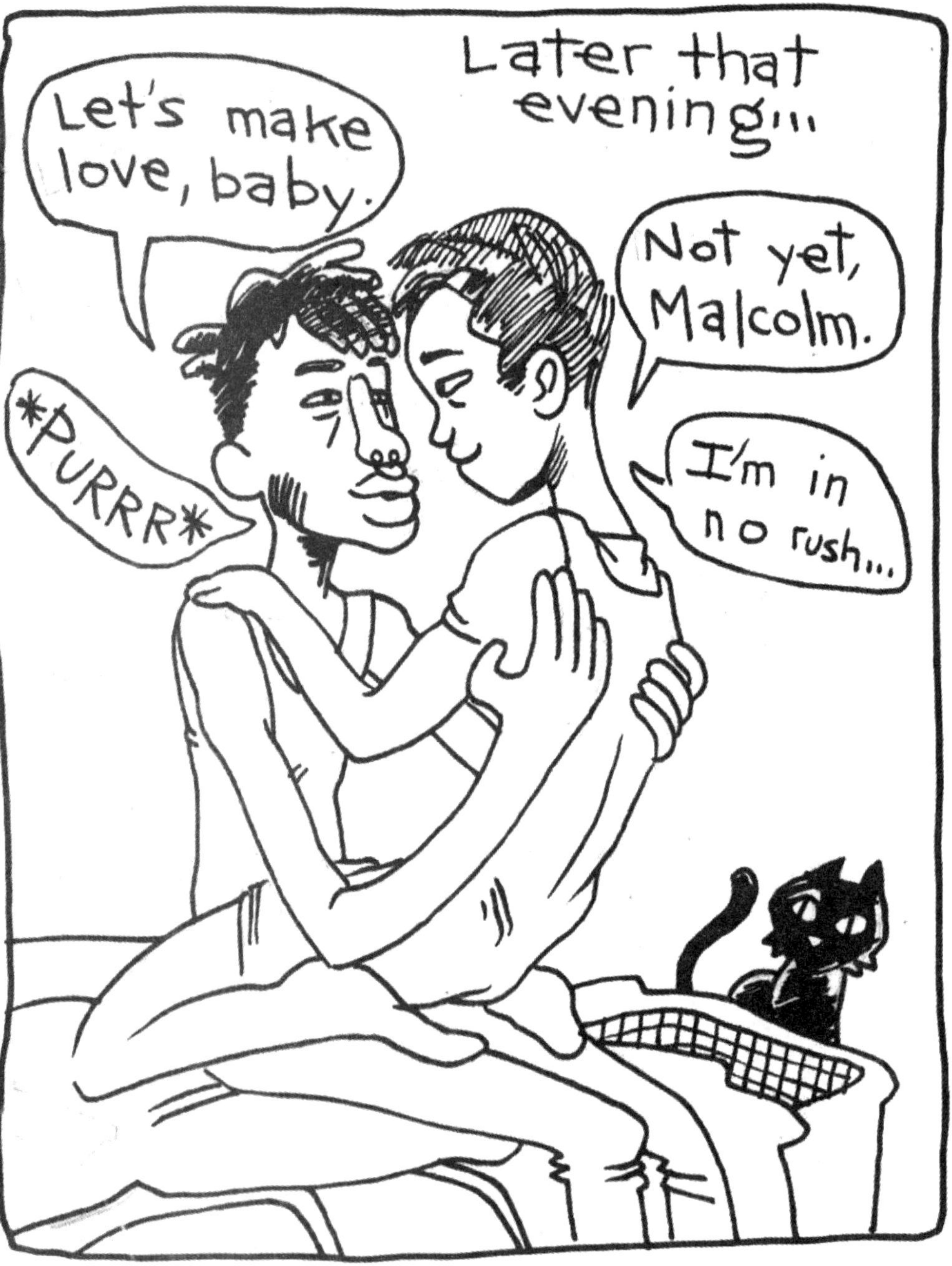
Later that evening...
Let's make love, baby.
Not yet, Malcolm.
PURRR
I'm in no rush...

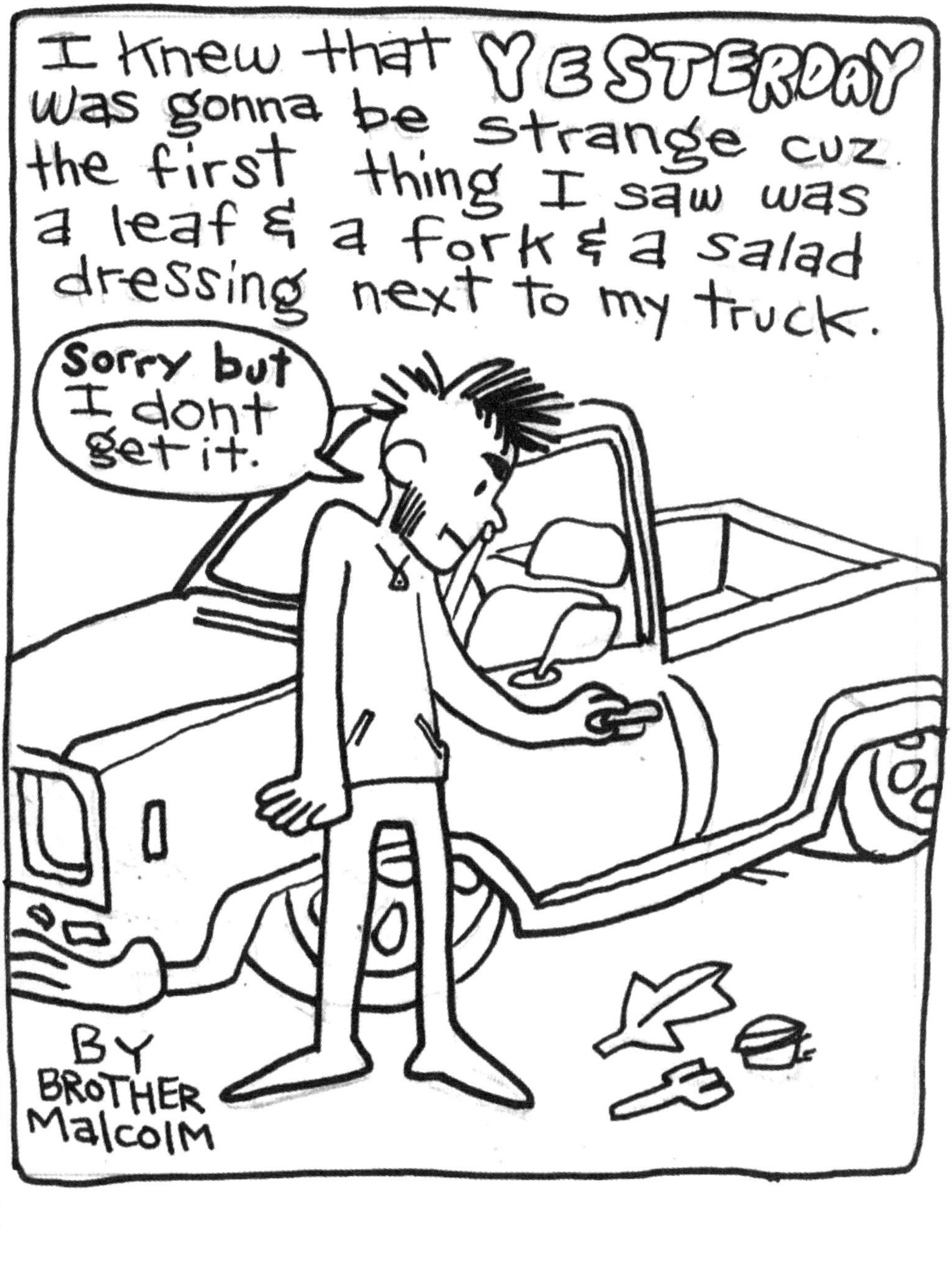
I knew that YESTERDAY was gonna be strange cuz the first thing I saw was a leaf & a fork & a salad dressing next to my truck.
Sorry but I dont get it.
BY BROTHER Malcolm

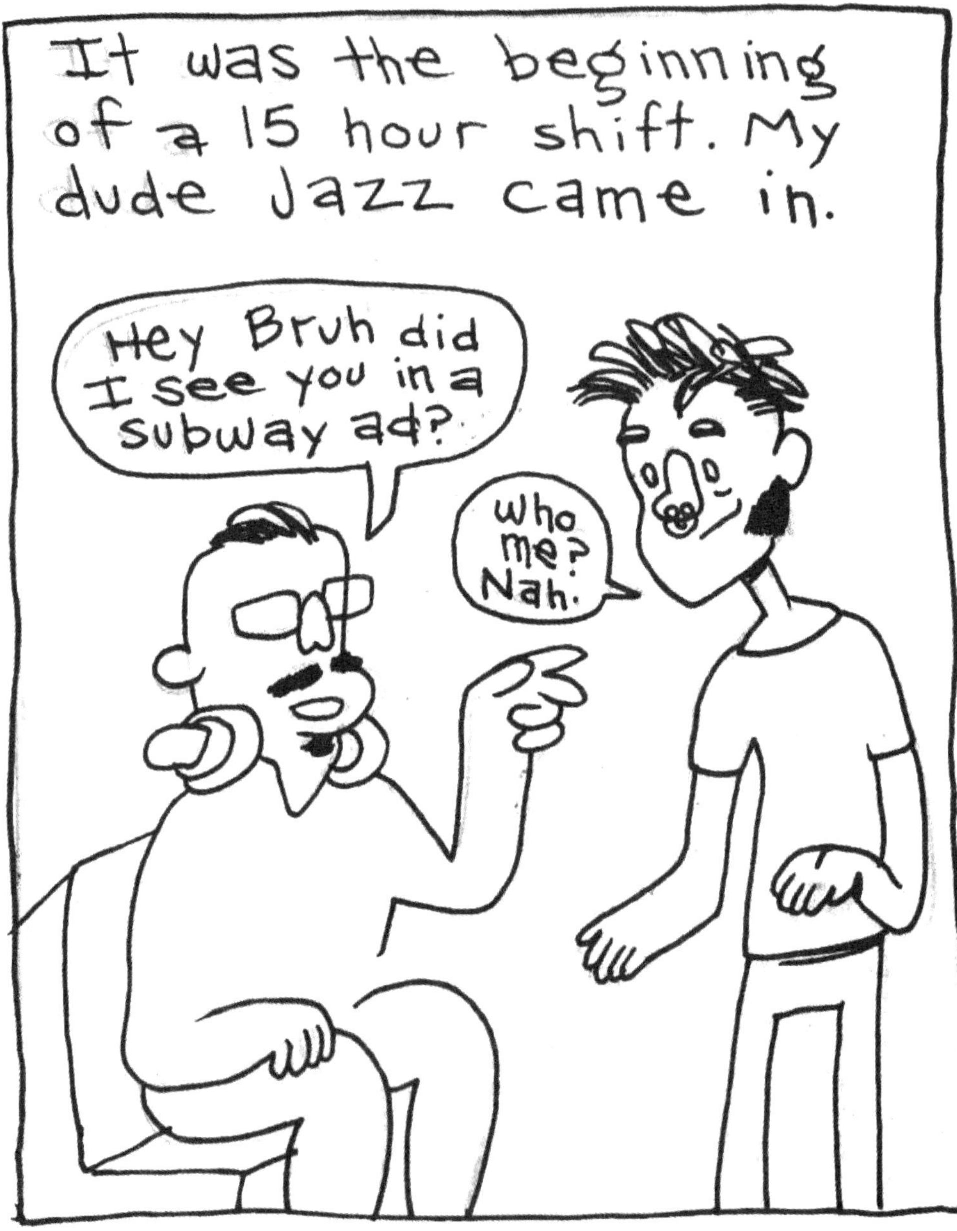
It was the beginning of a 15 hour shift. My dude Jazz came in.
Hey Bruh did I see you in a subway ad?
Who me? Nah.

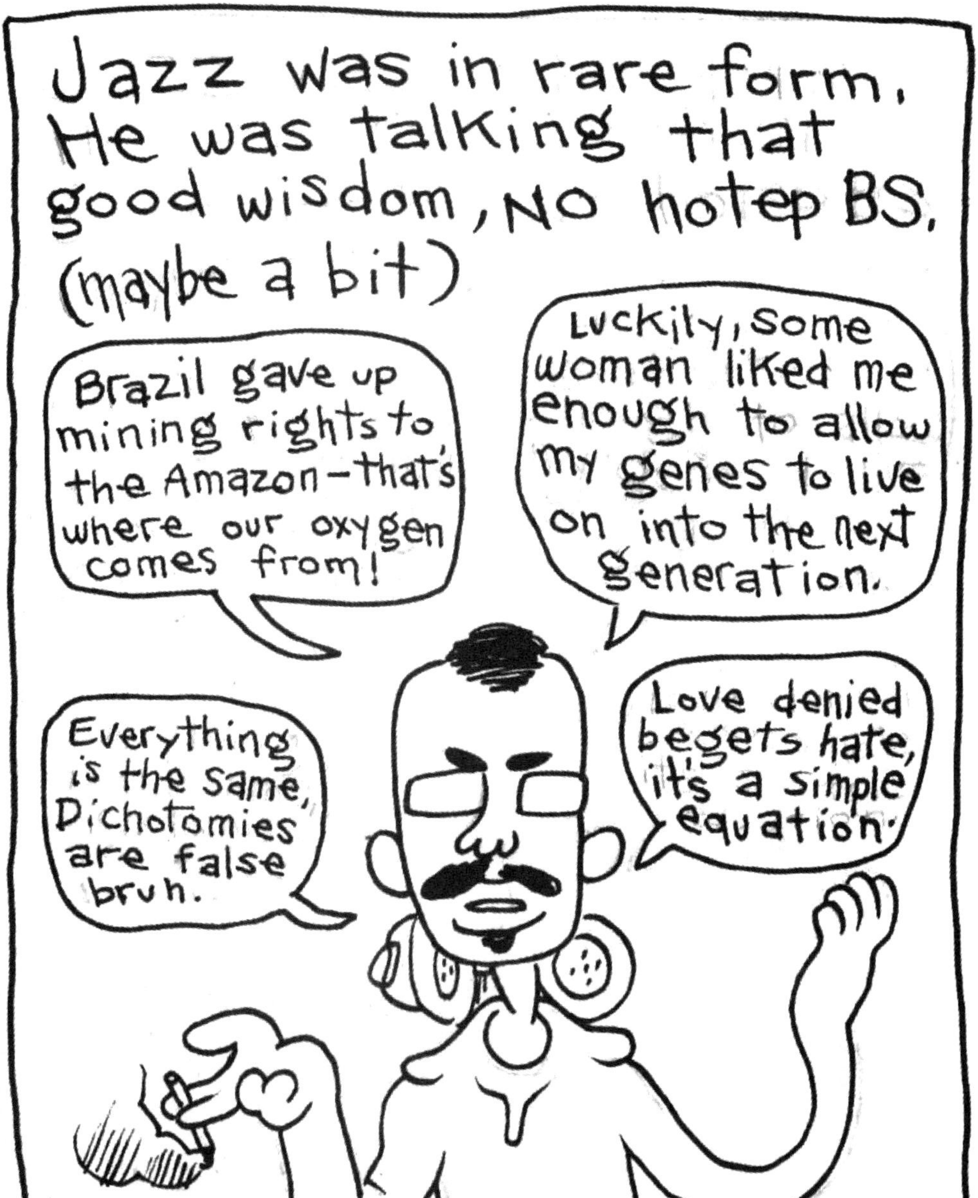
Jazz was in rare form. He was talking that good wisdom, NO hotep BS. (maybe a bit)
Brazil gave up mining rights to the Amazon—that's where our oxygen comes from!
Luckily, some woman liked me enough to allow my genes to live on into the next generation.
Everything is the same, Dichotomies are false bruh.
Love denied begets hate, it's a simple equation.

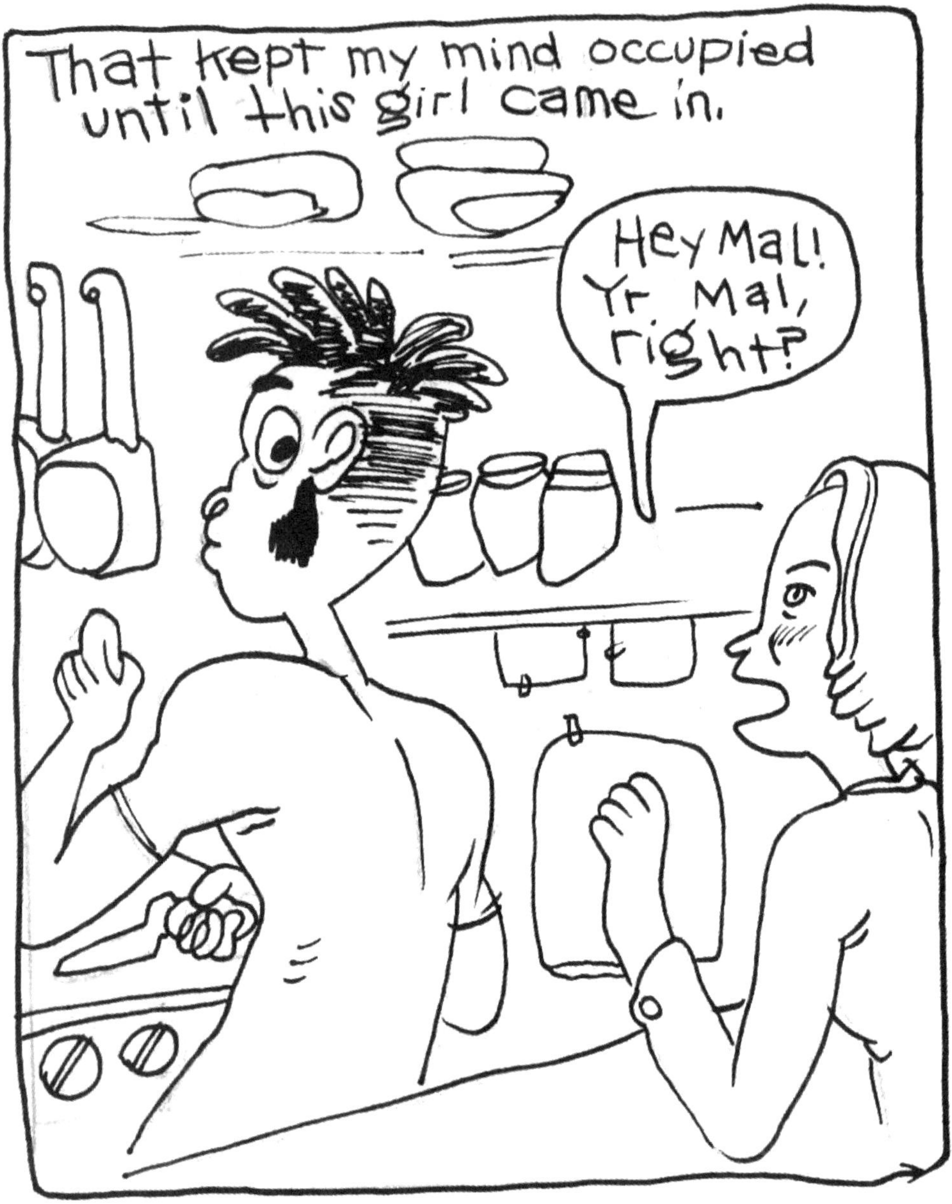
That kept my mind occupied until this girl came in.
Hey Mal! Yr Mal, right?

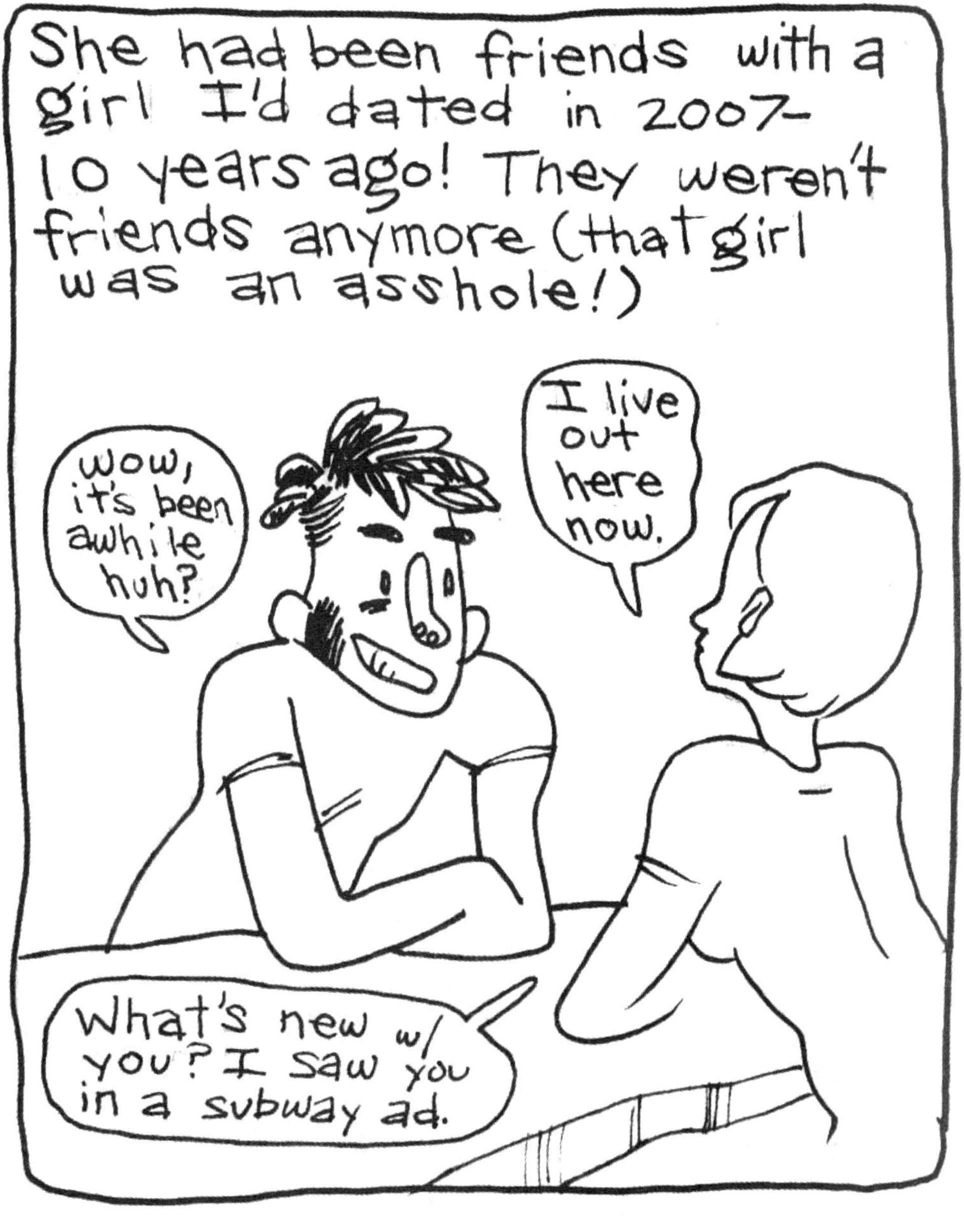
She had been friends with a girl I'd dated in 2007- 10 years ago! They weren't friends anymore (that girl was an asshole!)
wow, it's been awhile huh?
I live out here now.
What's new w/ you? I saw you in a subway ad.

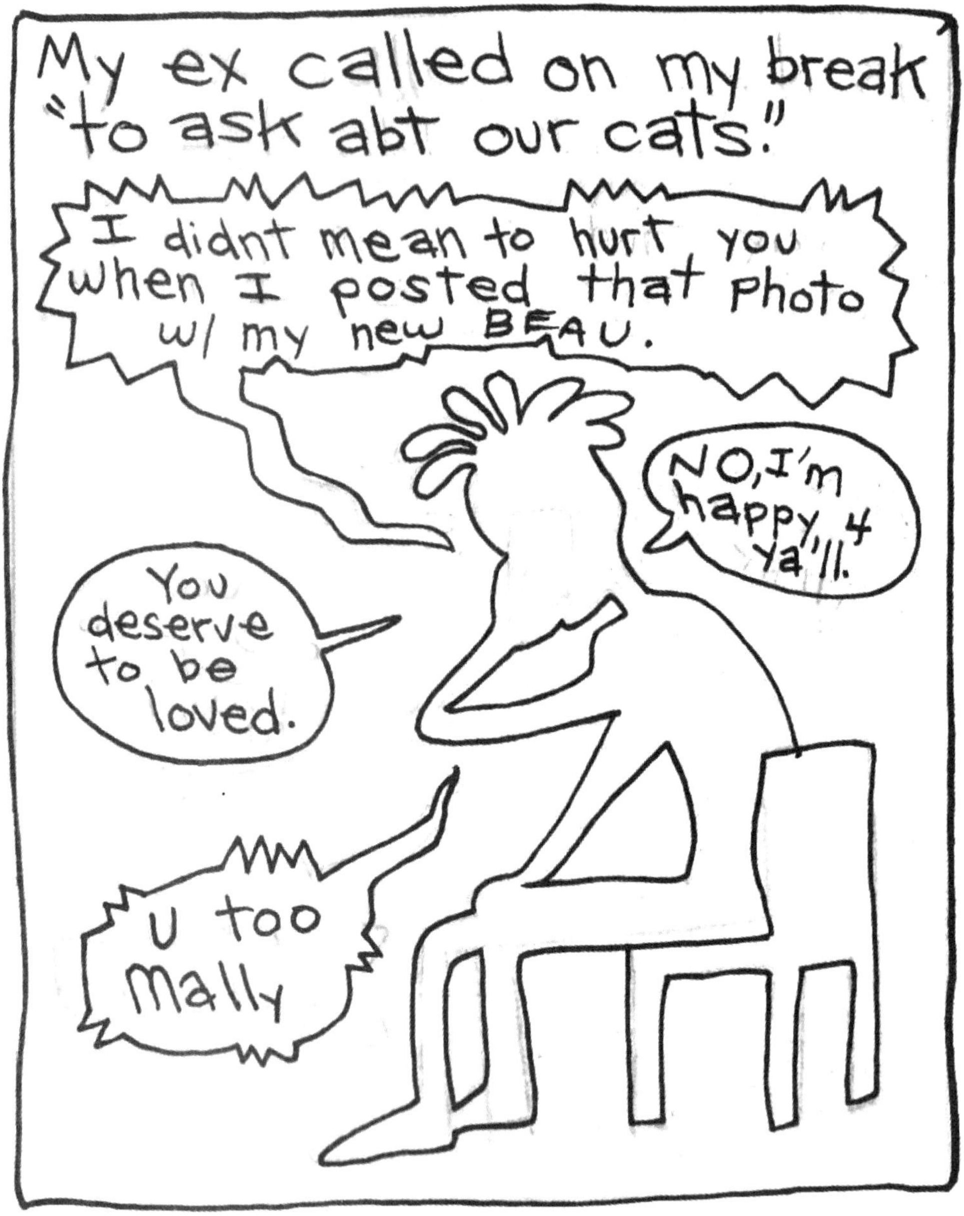
My ex called on my break "to ask abt our cats."
I didnt mean to hurt you when I posted that photo w/ my new BEAU.
NO, I'm happy 4 ya'll.
You deserve to be loved.
U too Mally

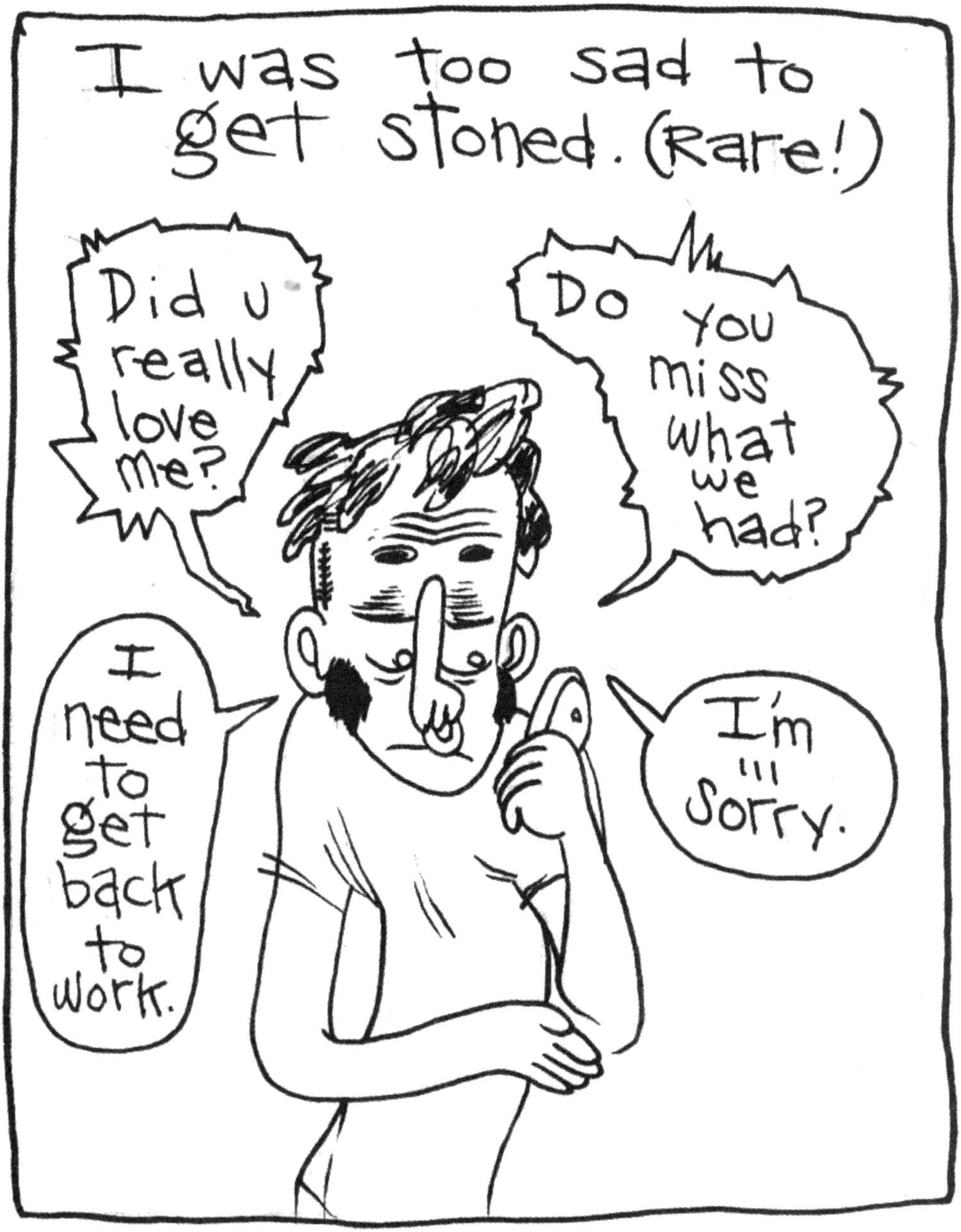
I was too sad to get stoned. (Rare!)
Did u really love me?
Do you miss what we had?
I need to get back to work.
I'm ... sorry.

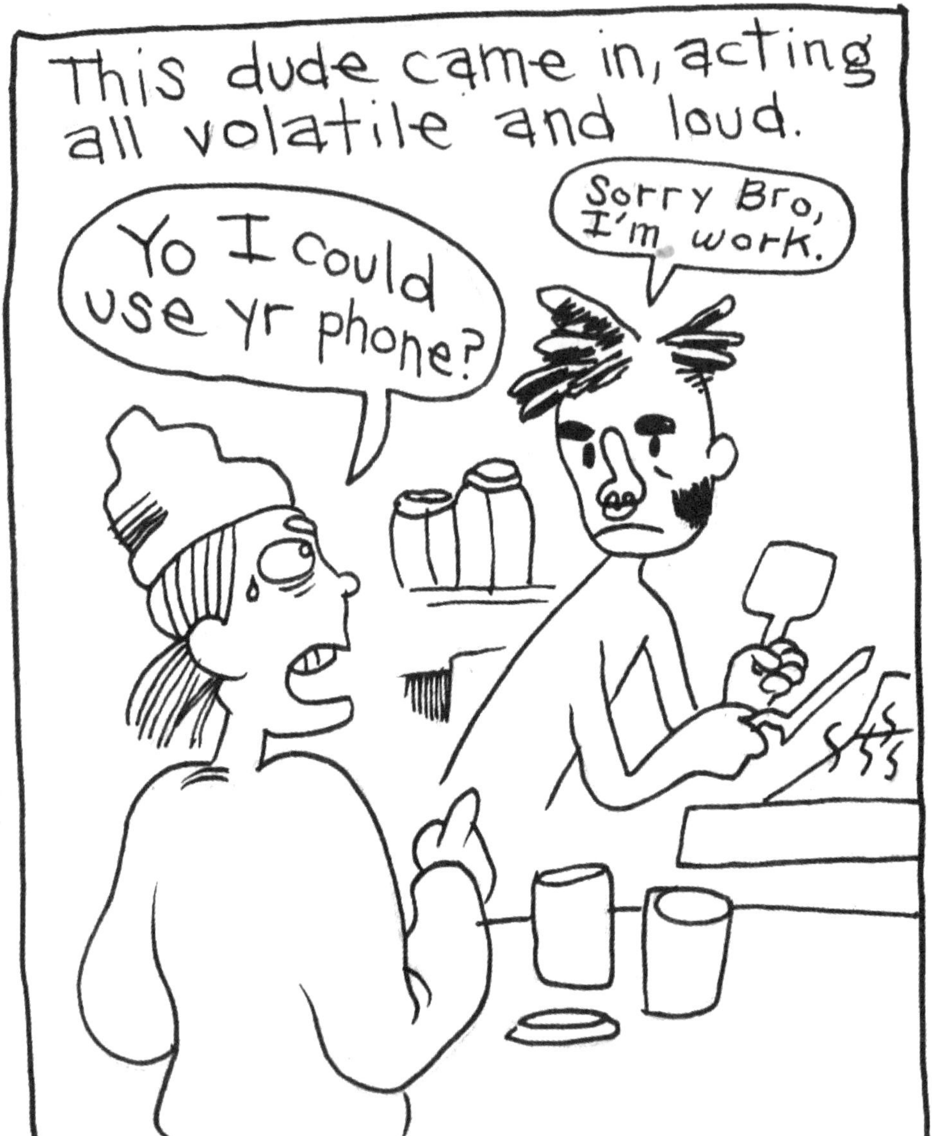
This dude came in, acting all volatile and loud.
Yo I could use yr phone?
Sorry Bro, I'm work.

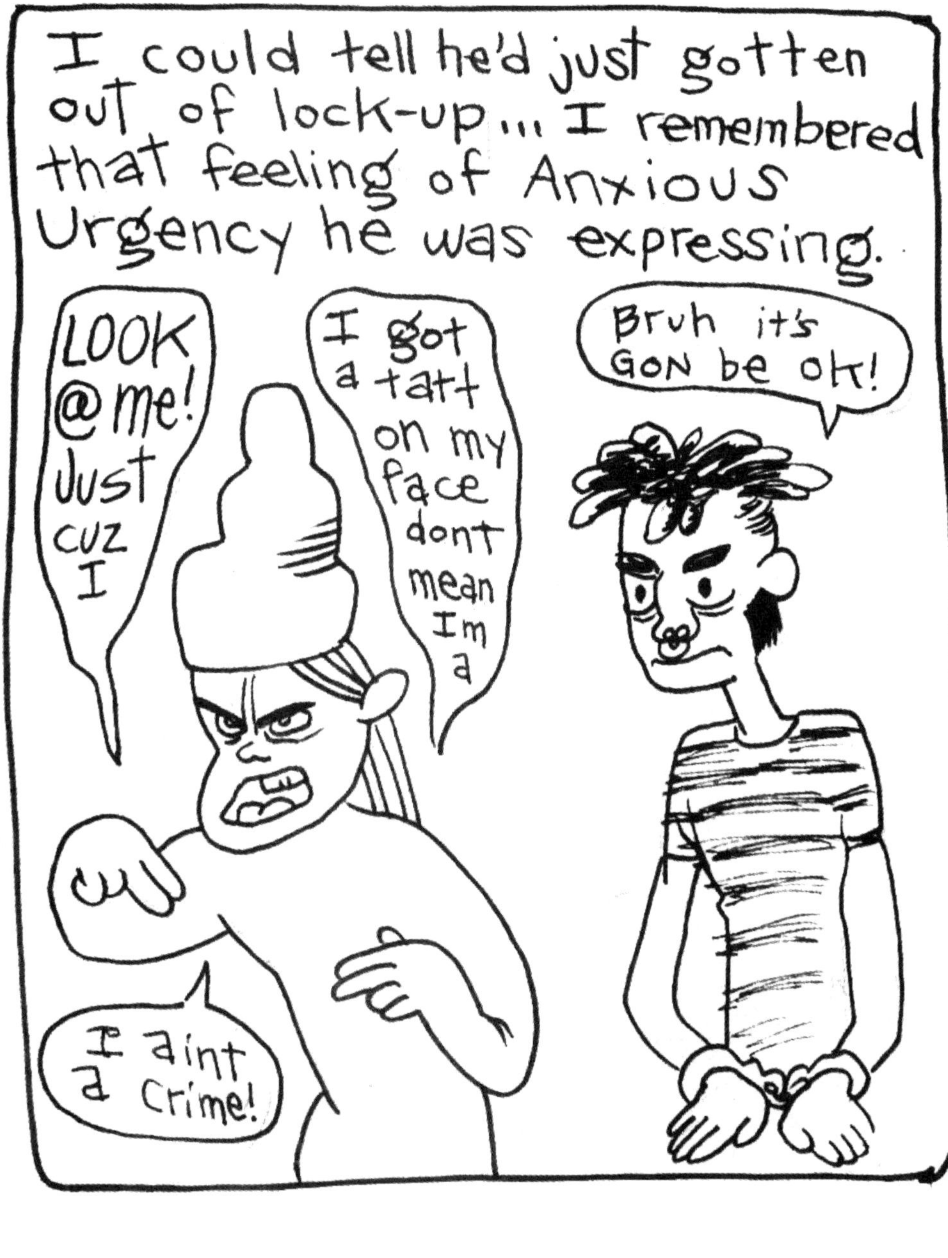
I could tell he'd just gotten out of lock-up... I remembered that feeling of Anxious Urgency he was expressing.
LOOK @ me! Just cuz I
I got a tatt on my face dont mean Im a
I aint a crime!
Bruh it's GON be ok!

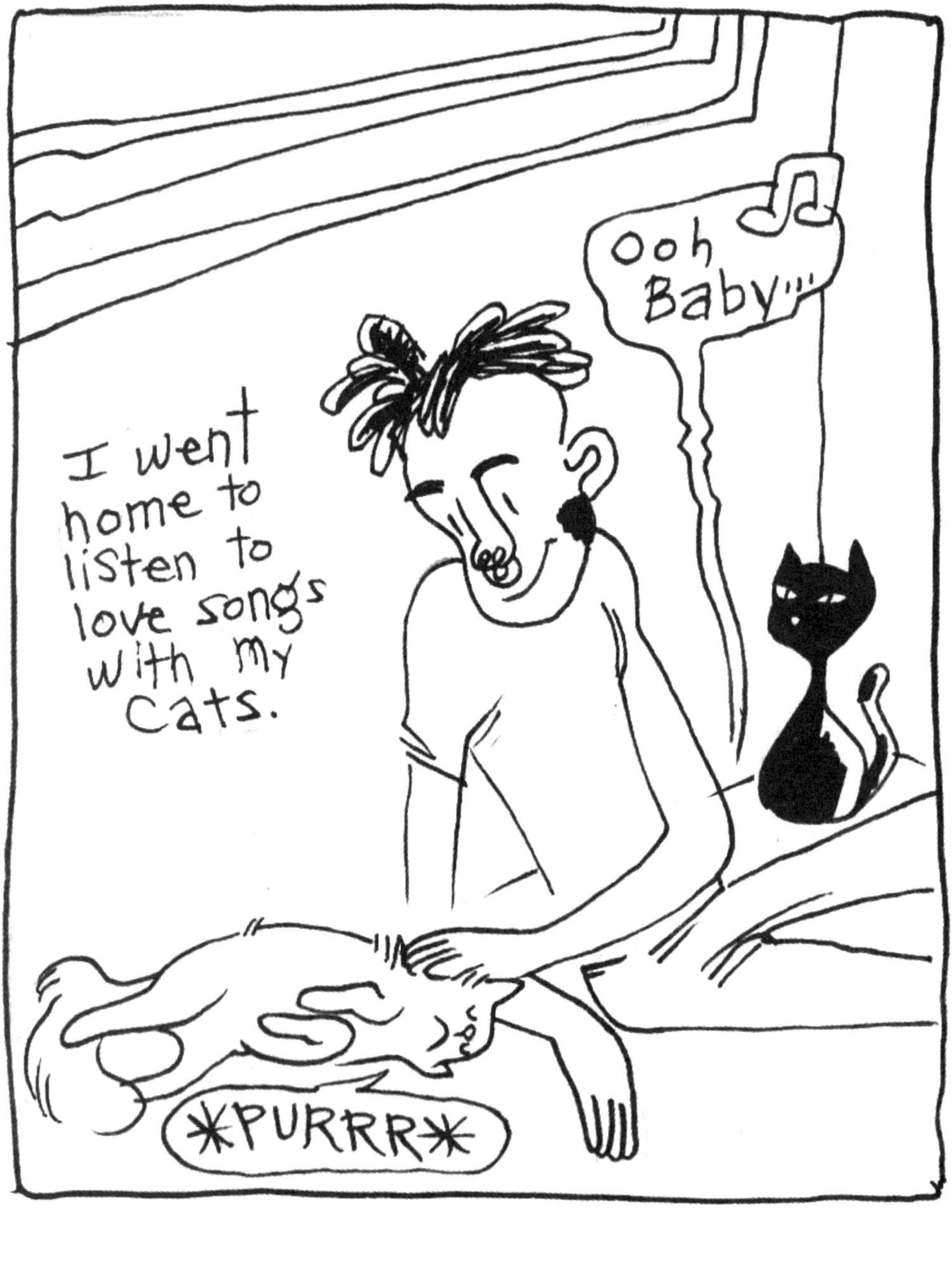

I went home to listen to love songs with my cats.
Ooh Baby...
PURRR

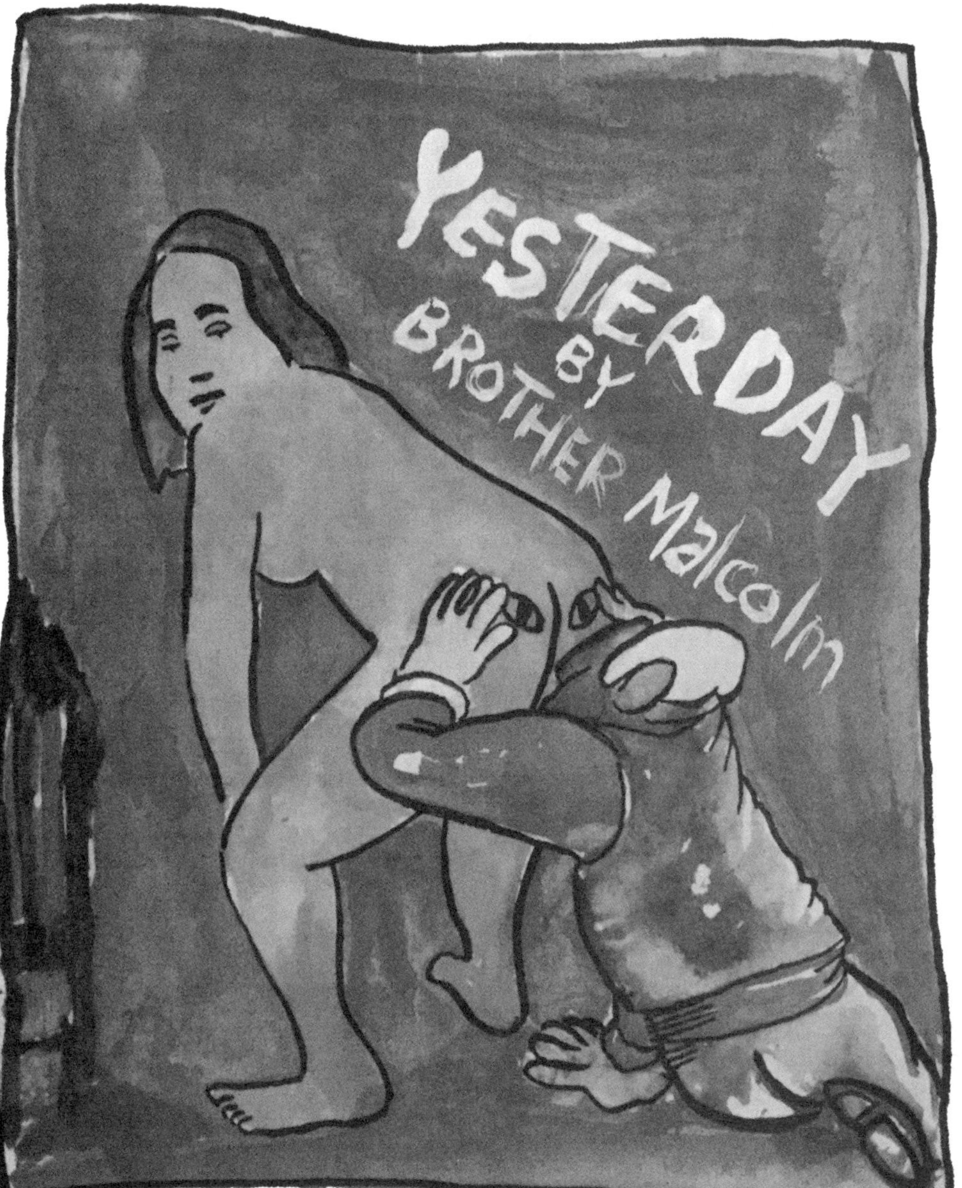
YESTERDAY
BY
BROTHER Malcolm

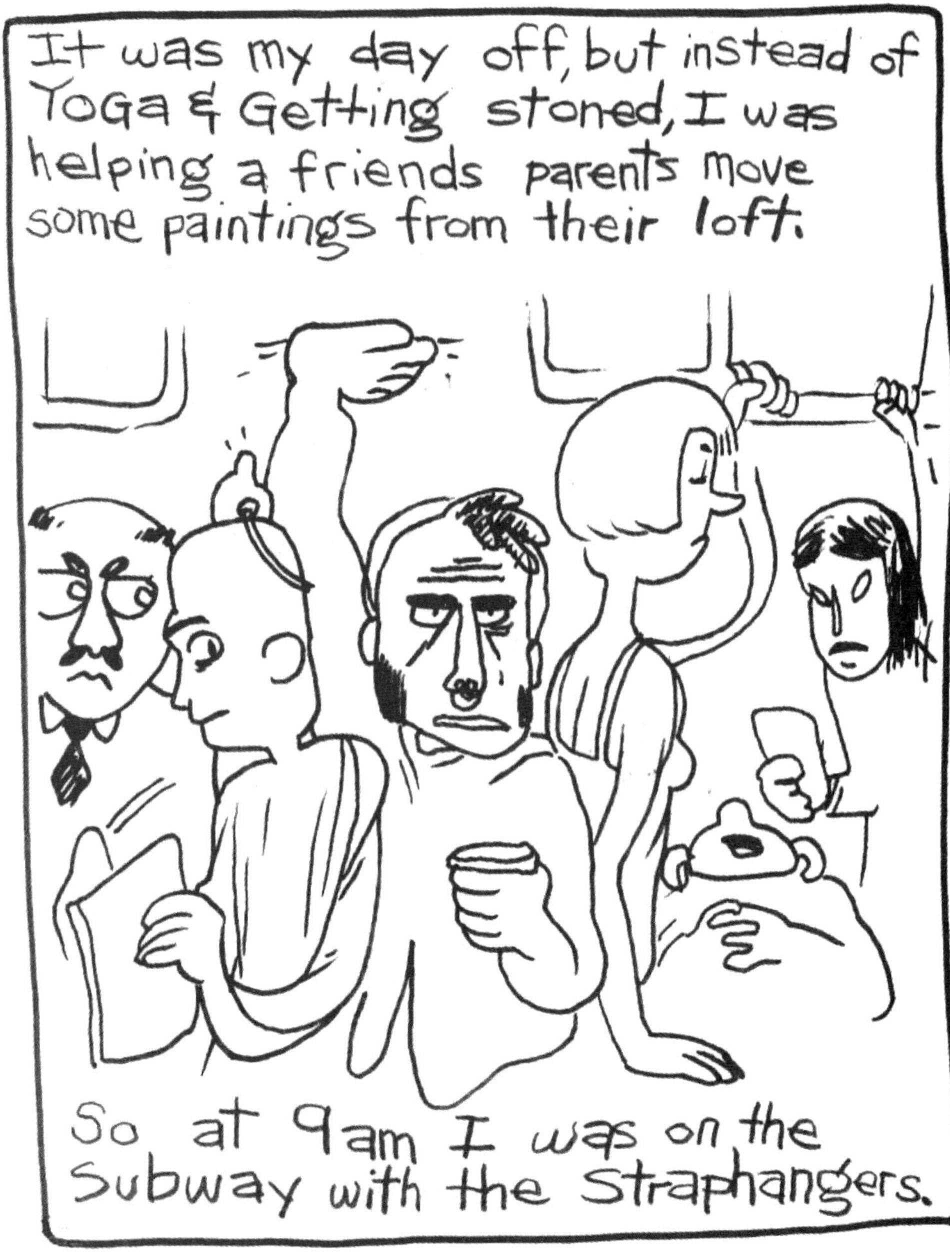
It was my day off, but instead of YOGA & Getting stoned, I was helping a friends parents move some paintings from their loft.
So at 9am I was on the Subway with the Straphangers.

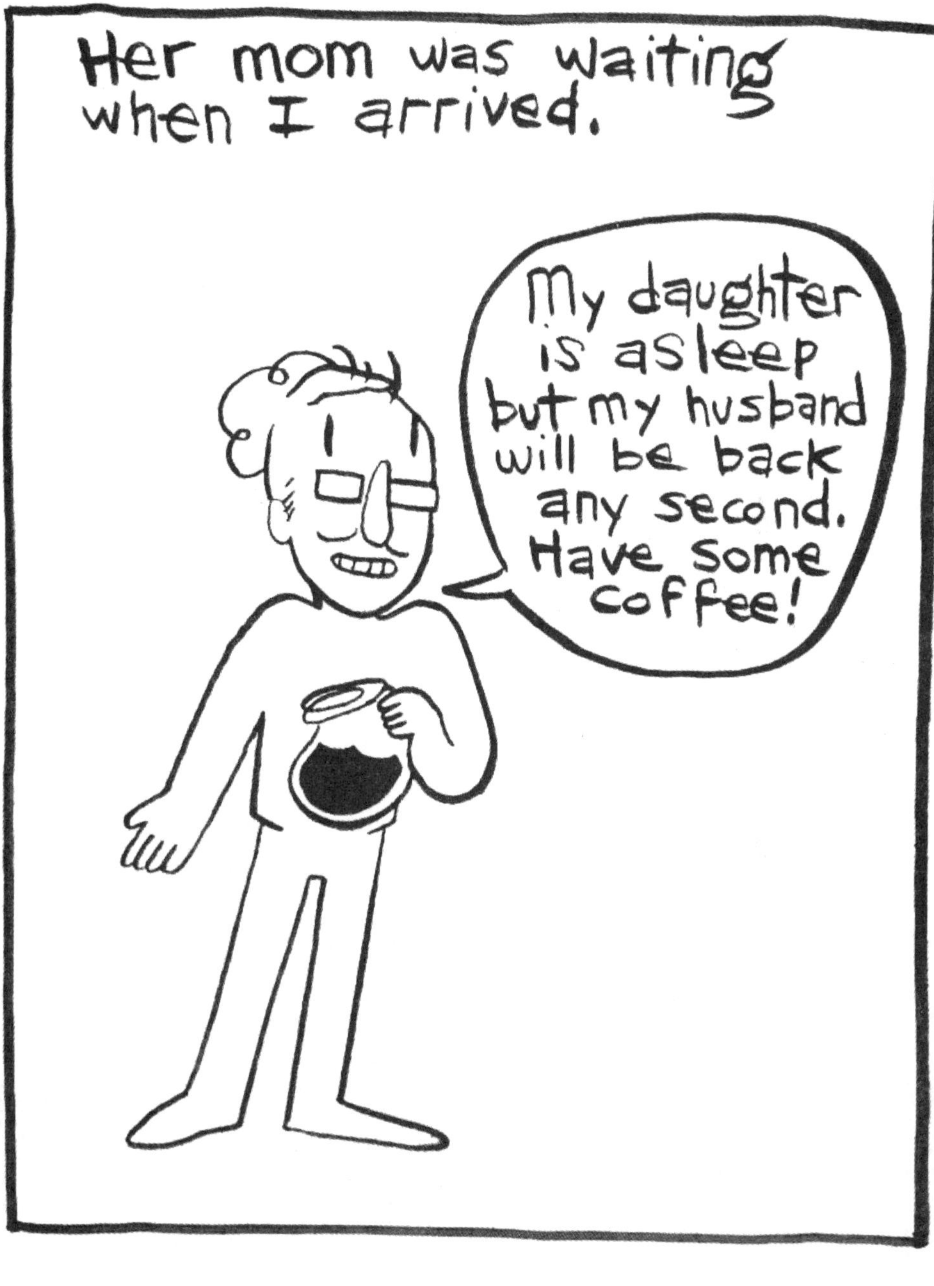
Her mom was waiting when I arrived.
My daughter is asleep but my husband will be back any second. Have some coffee!

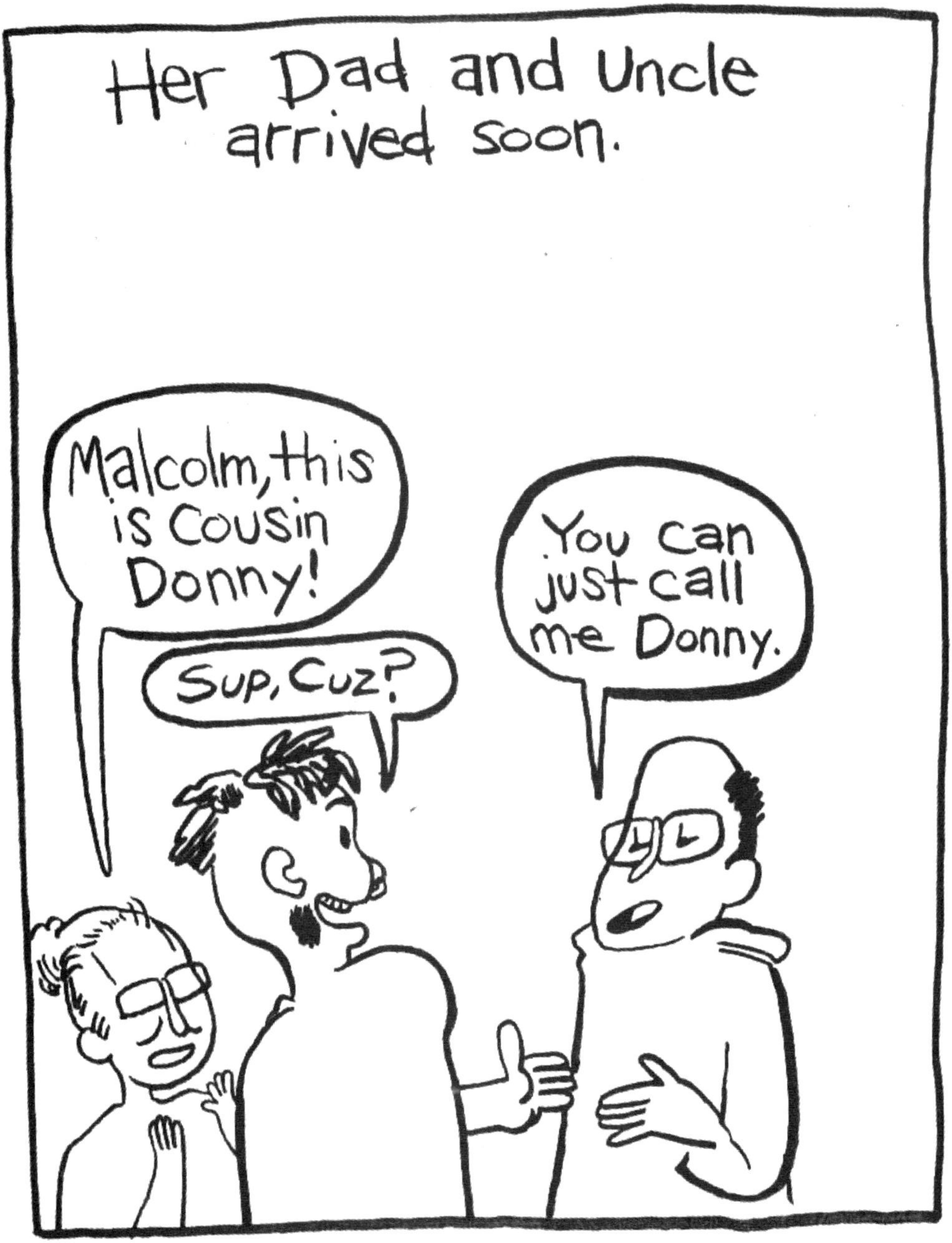
Her Dad and Uncle arrived soon.
Malcolm, this is Cousin Donny!
Sup, Cuz?
You can just call me Donny.

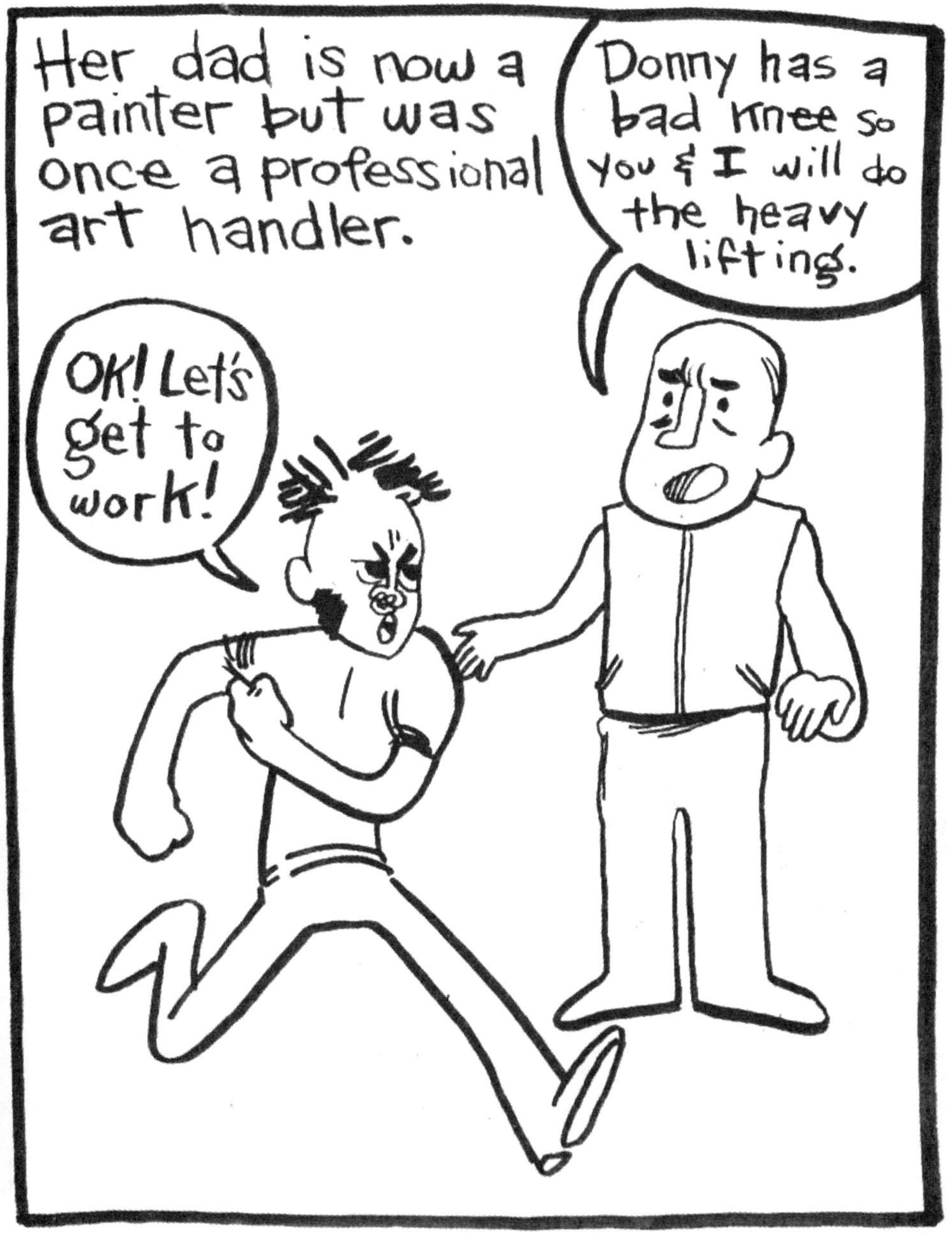
Her dad is now a painter but was once a professional art handler.
Donny has a bad knee so you & I will do the heavy liftings.
OK! Let's get to work!

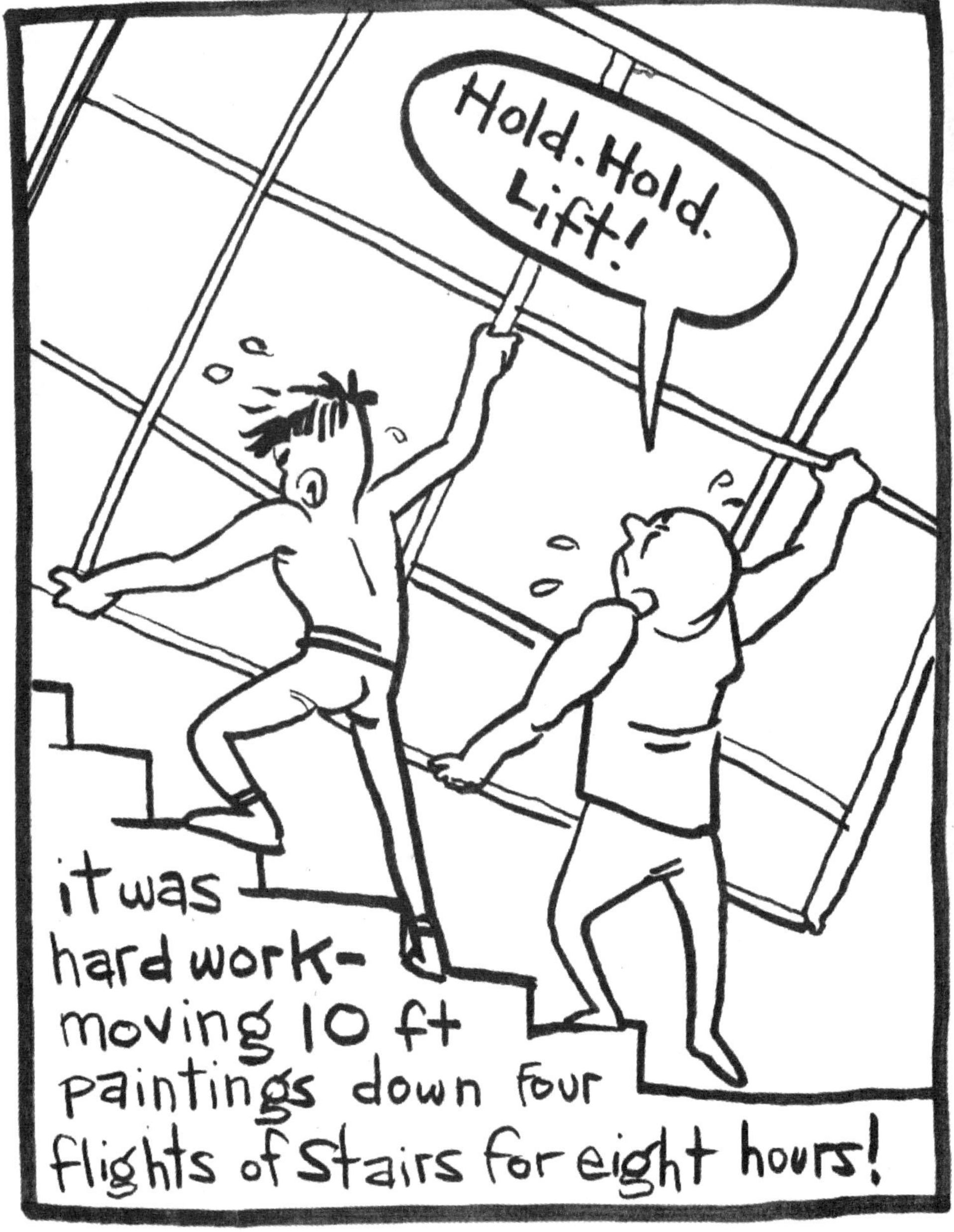
Hold. Hold. Lift!
it was hard work- moving 10 ft paintings down four flights of stairs for eight hours!

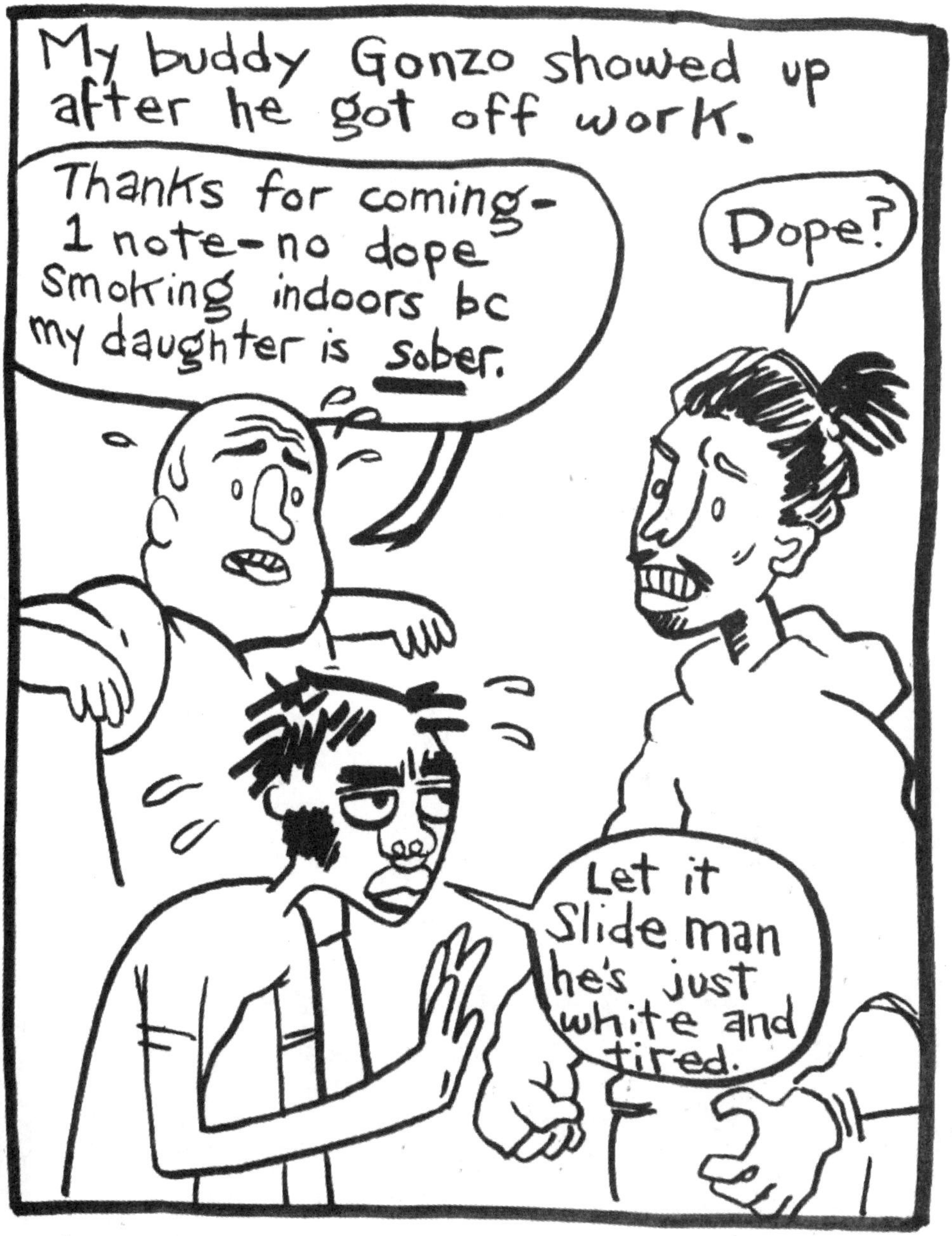
My buddy Gonzo showed up after he got off work.
Thanks for coming- 1 note-no dope smoking indoors bc my daughter is sober.
Dope?
Let it Slide man he's just white and tired.

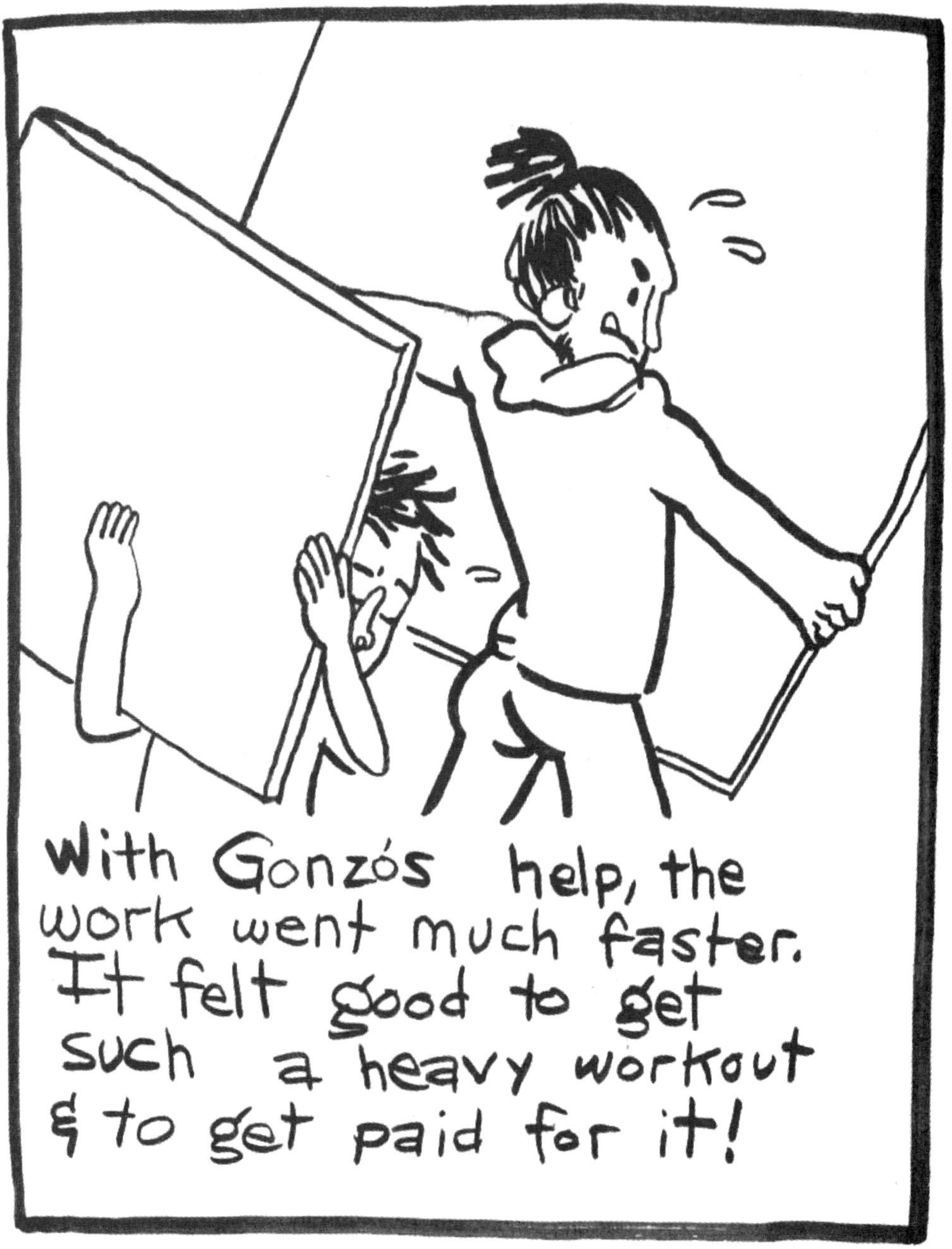
With Gonzós help, the work went much faster. It felt good to get such a heavy workout & to get paid for it!

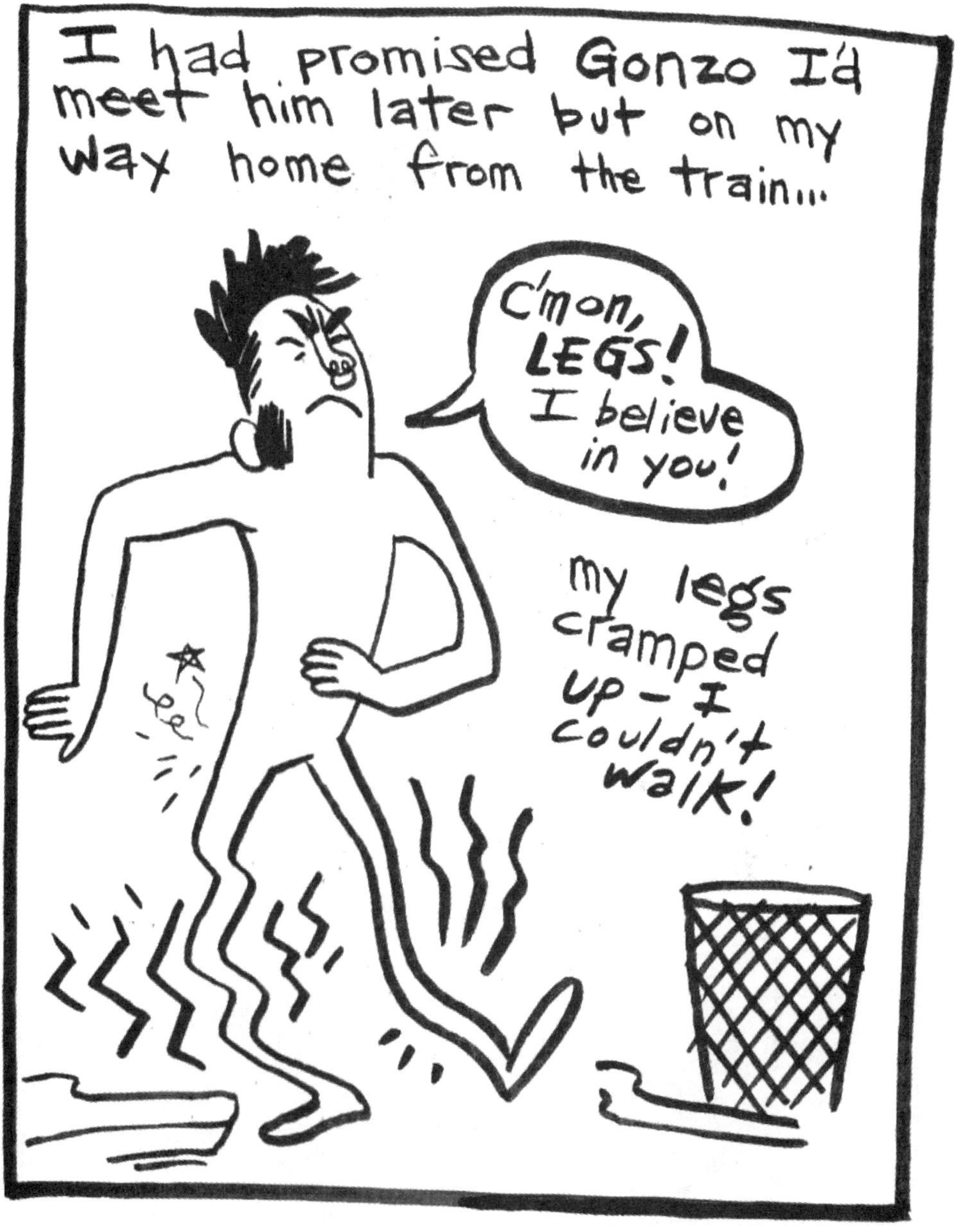
I had promised Gonzo I'd meet him later but on my way home from the train...
C'mon, LEGS! I believe in you!
my legs cramped up – I couldn't walk!

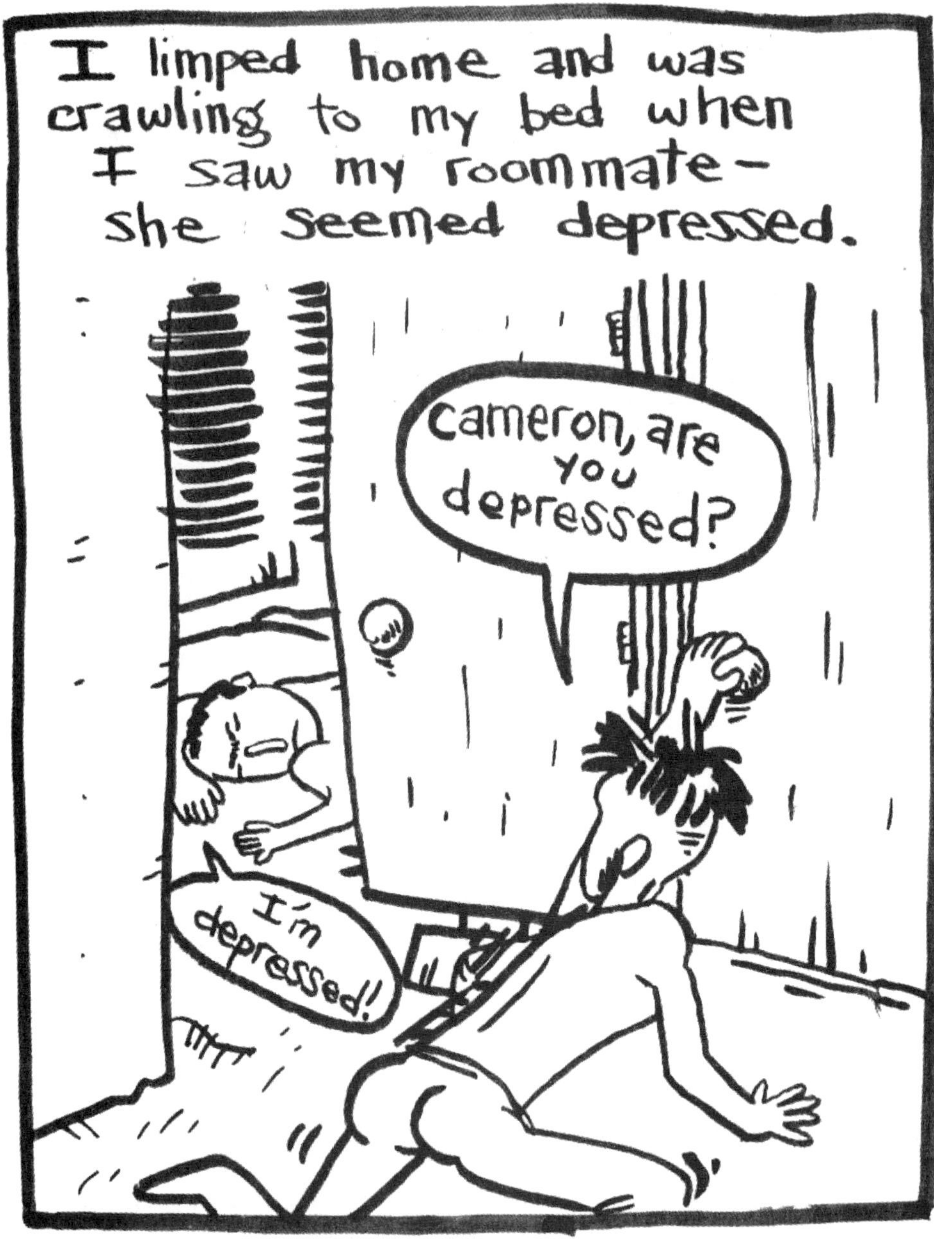
I limped home and was crawling to my bed when I saw my roommate- she seemed depressed.
Cameron, are you depressed?
I'm depressed!

Yesterday

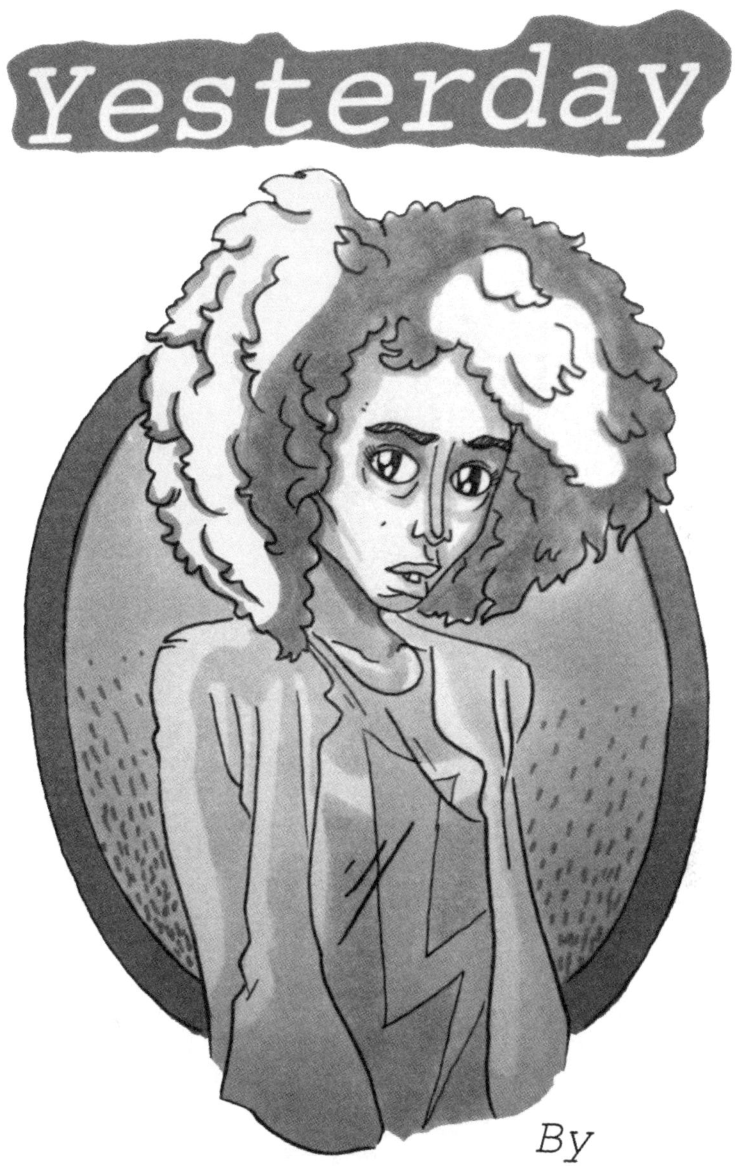

By
Brother Malcolm

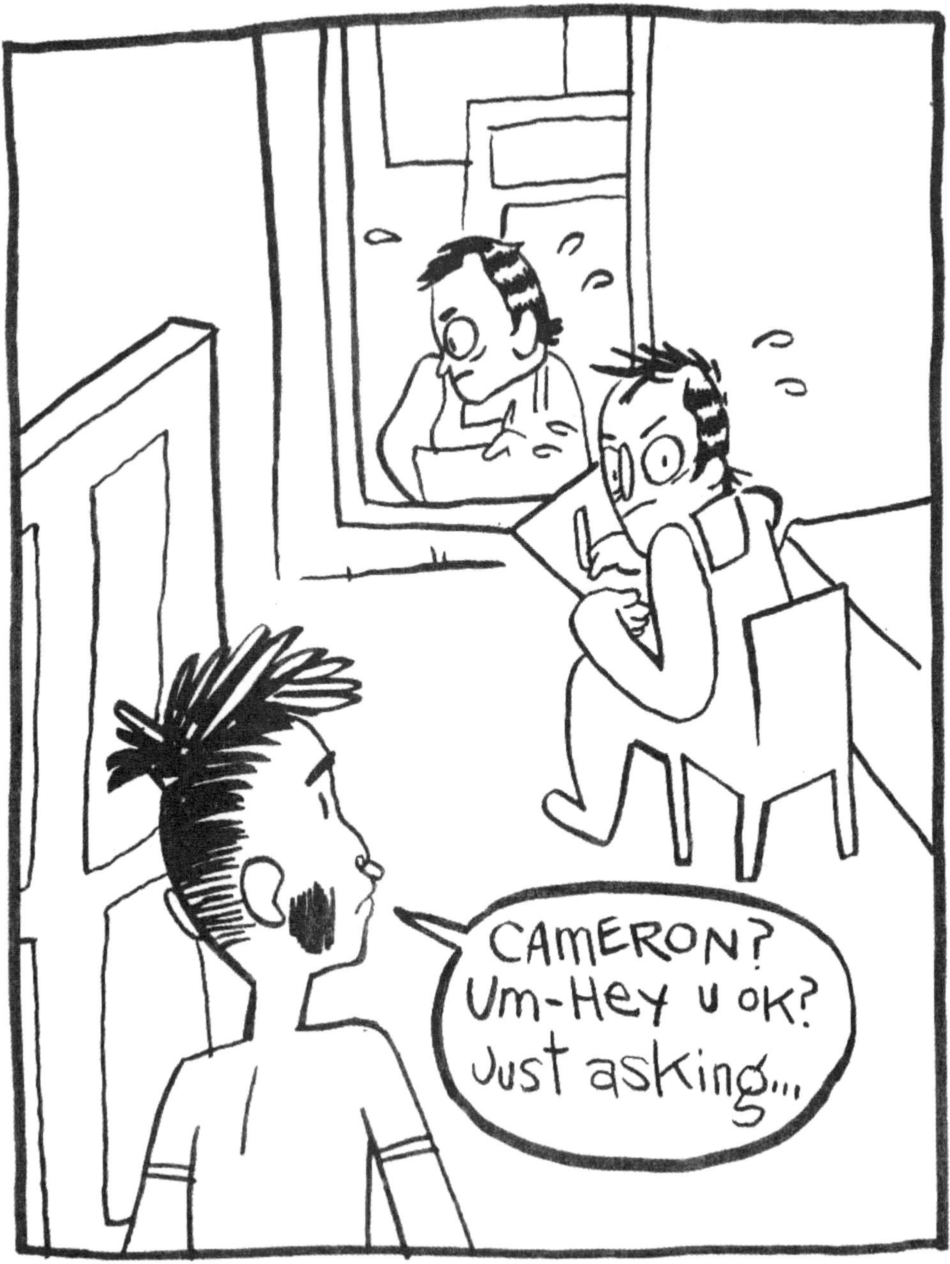
CAMERON? Um-Hey u ok? Just asking...

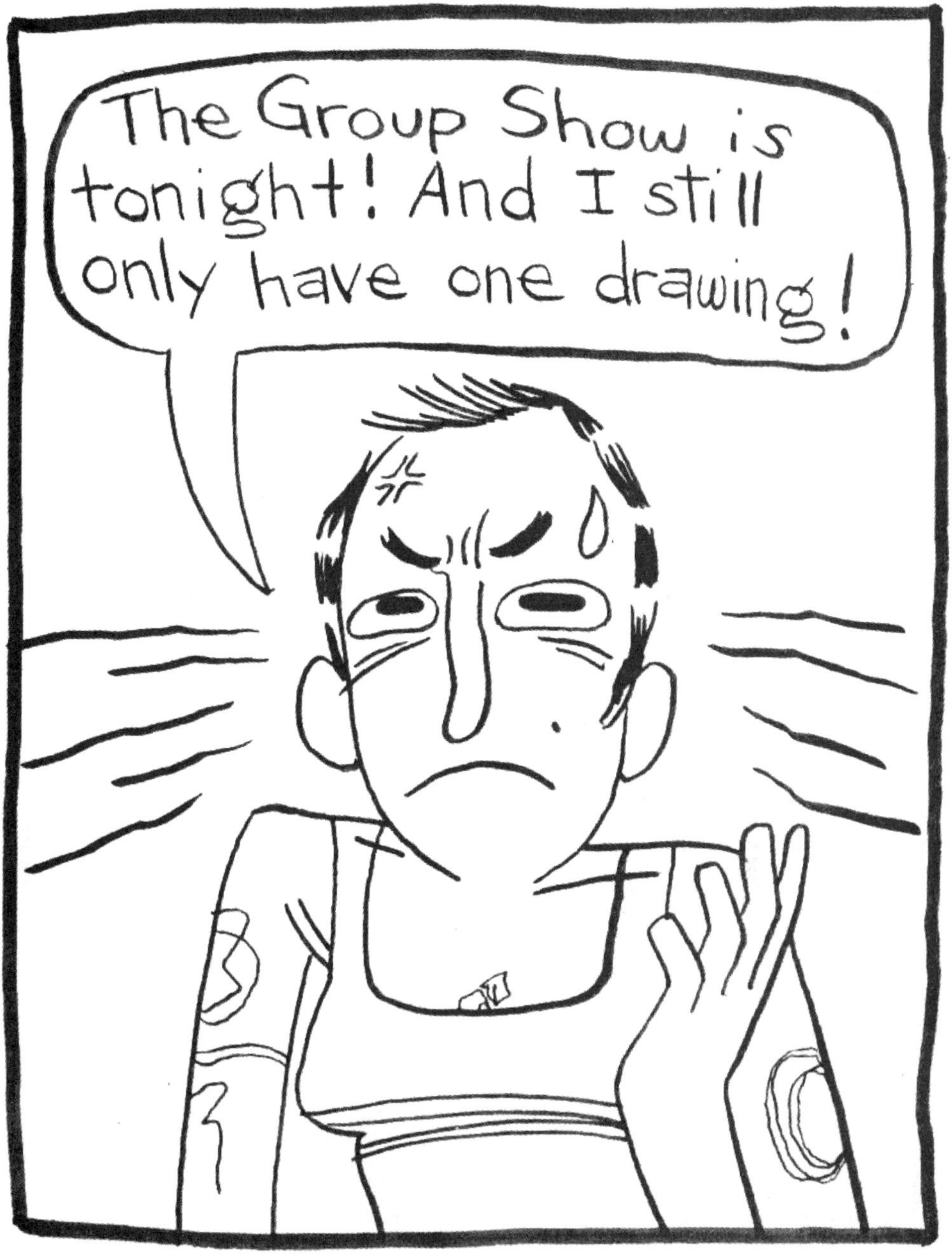
The Group Show is tonight! And I still only have one drawing!

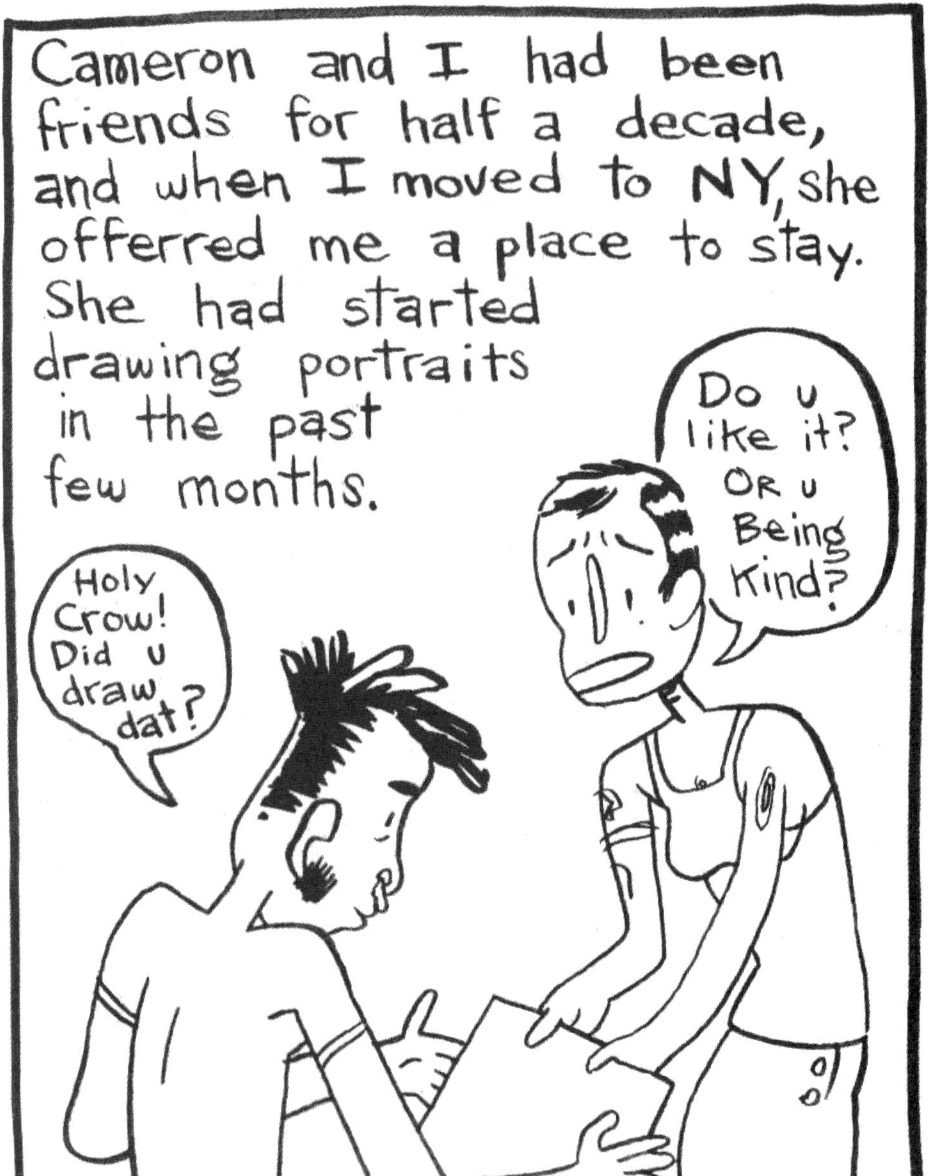
Cameron and I had been friends for half a decade, and when I moved to NY, she offerred me a place to stay. She had started drawing portraits in the past few months.
Holy Crow! Did u draw dat?
Do u like it? OR u Being Kind?

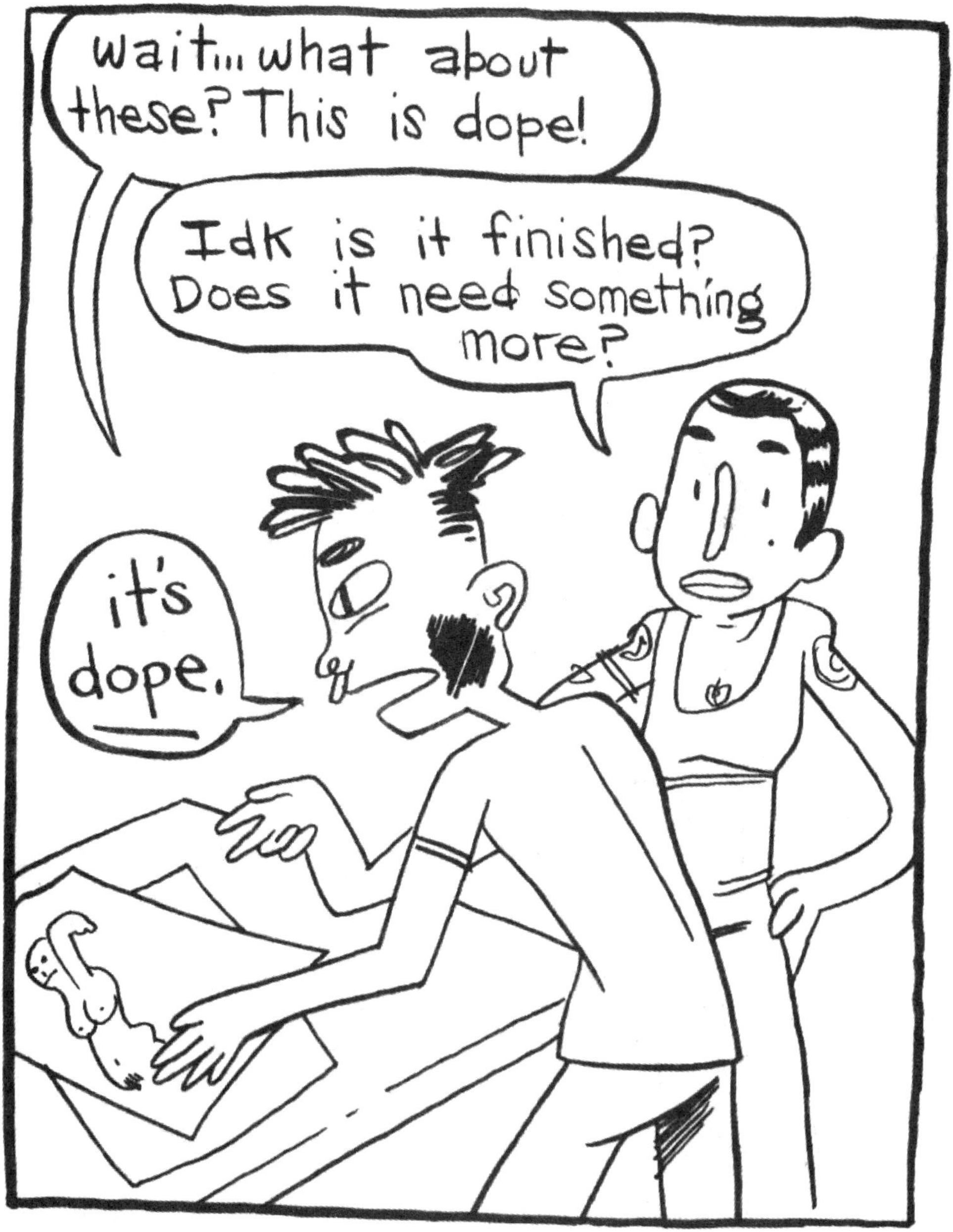
wait... what about these? This is dope!
Idk is it finished? Does it need something more?
it's dope.

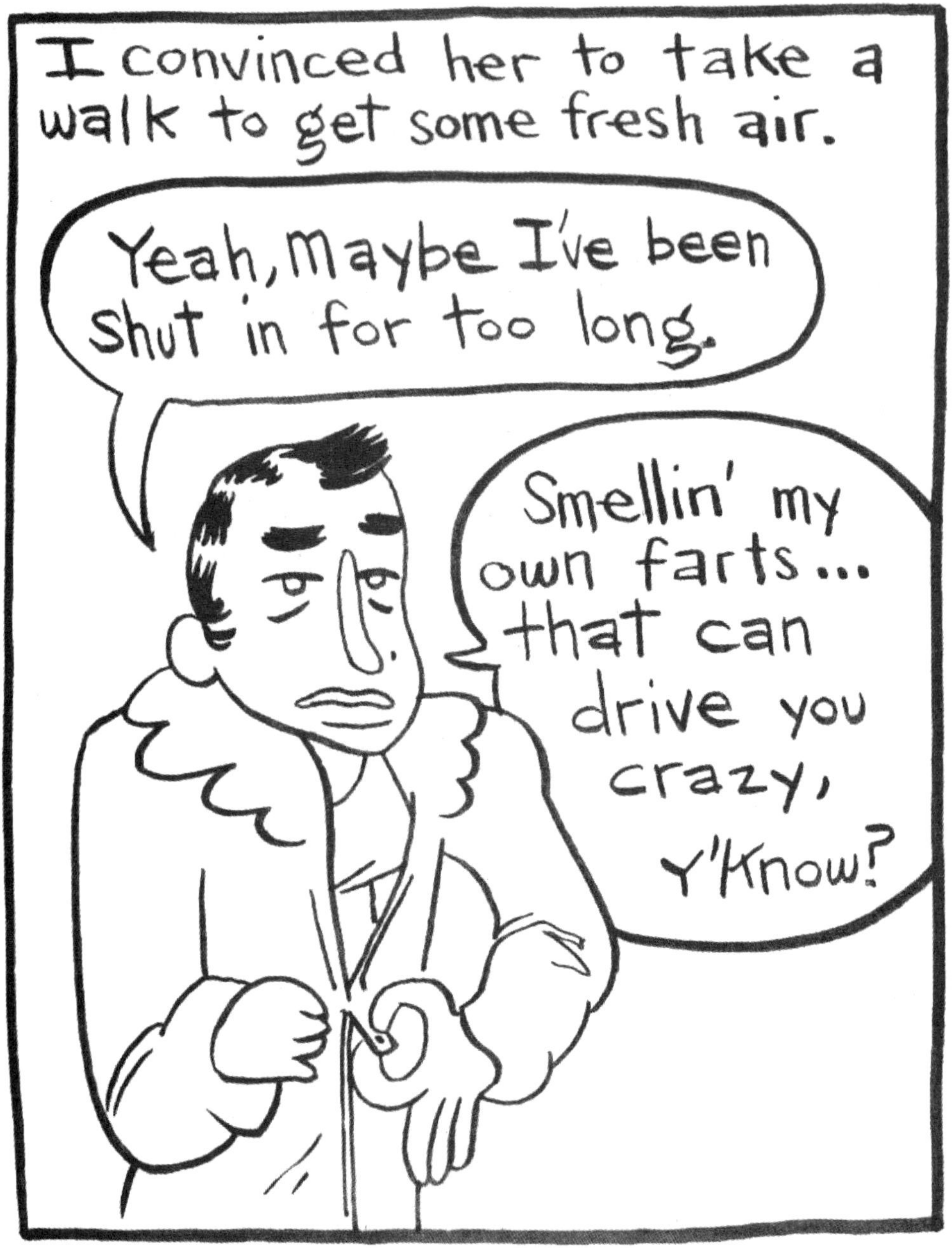
I convinced her to take a walk to get some fresh air.
Yeah, maybe I've been shut in for too long.
Smellin' my own farts... that can drive you crazy, y'know?

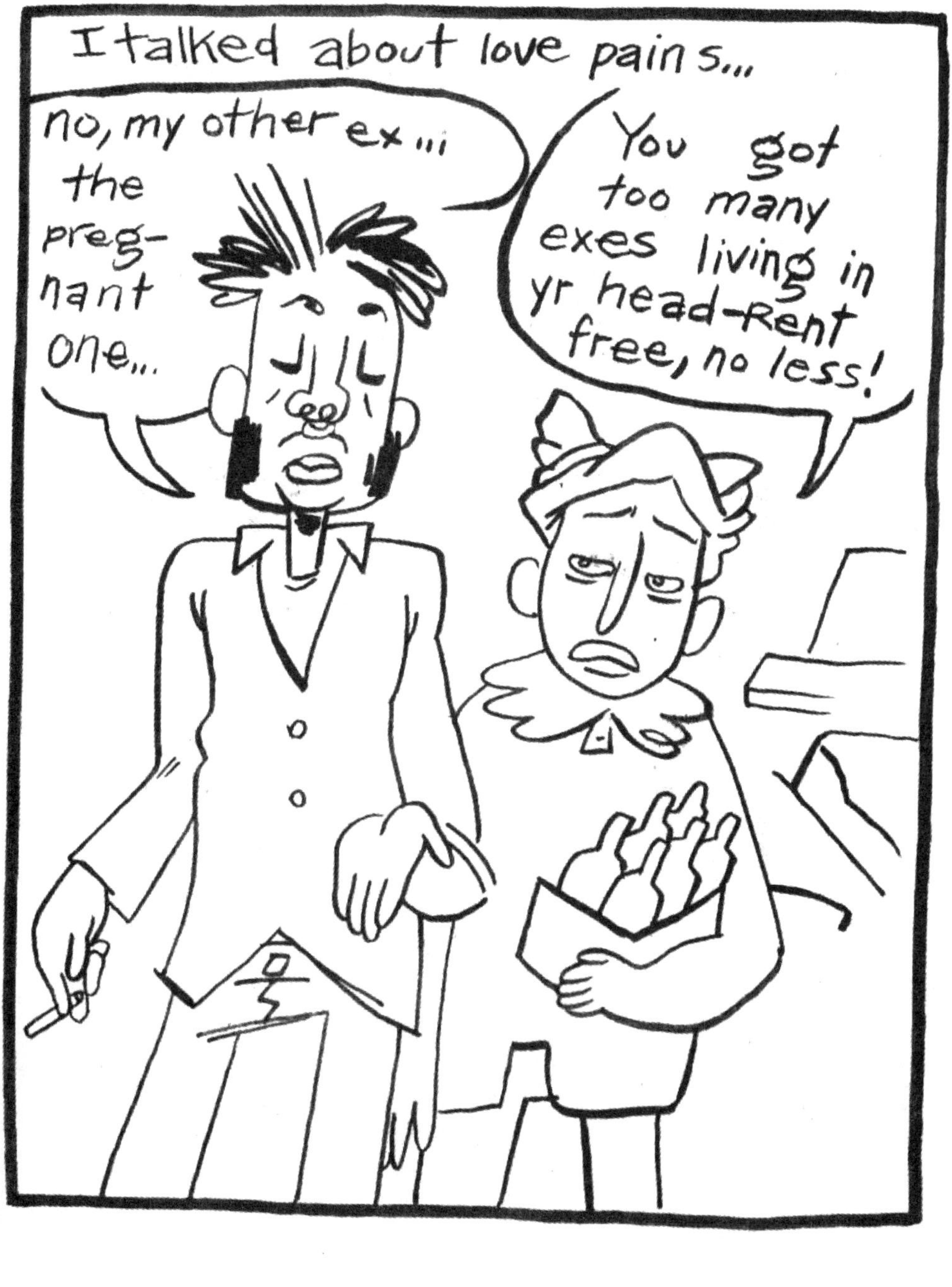
I talked about love pains...
no, my other ex... the pregnant one...
You got too many exes living in yr head-Rent free, no less!

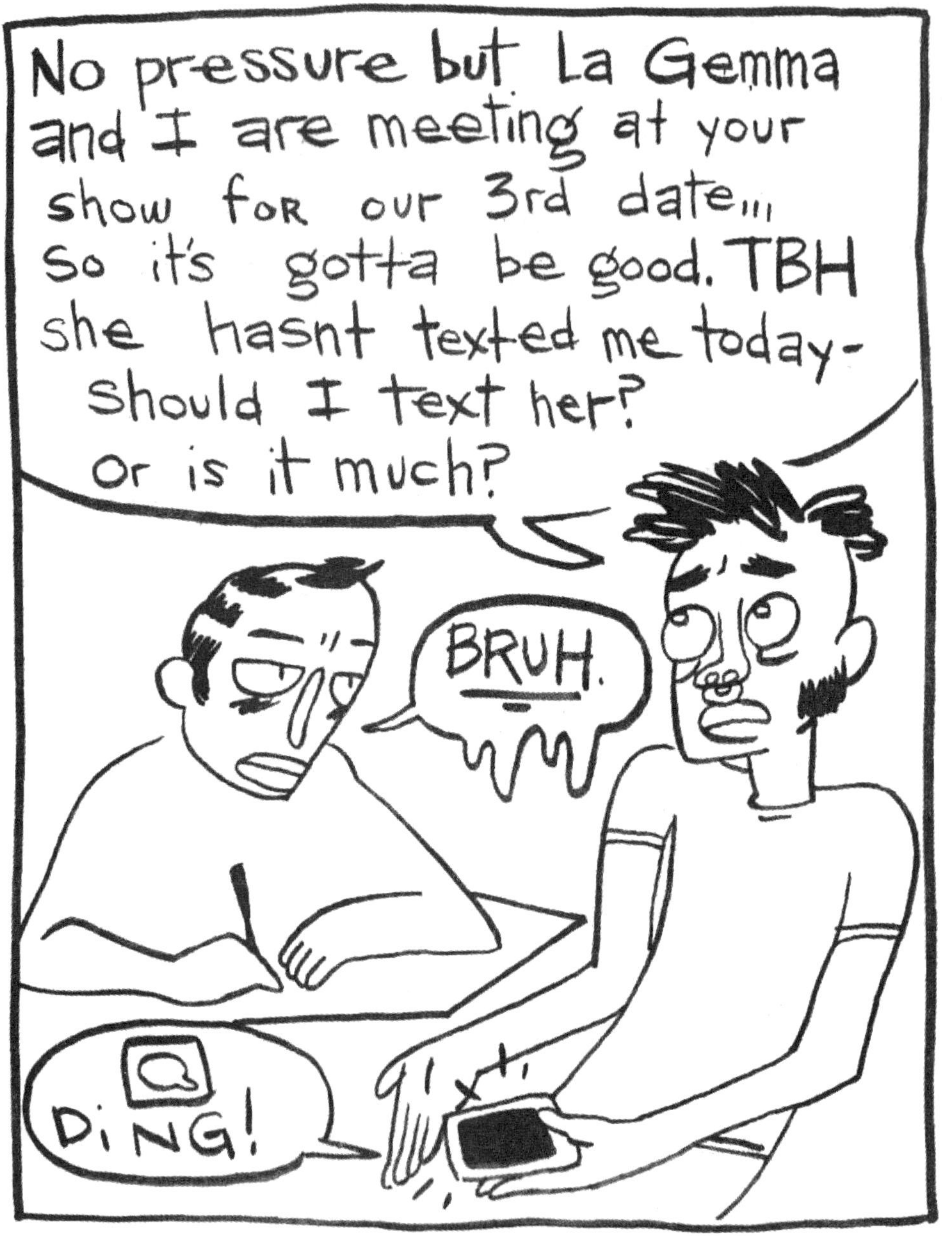
No pressure but La Gemma and I are meeting at your show for our 3rd date... So it's gotta be good. TBH she hasnt texted me today- Should I text her? Or is it much?
BRUH.
DiNG!

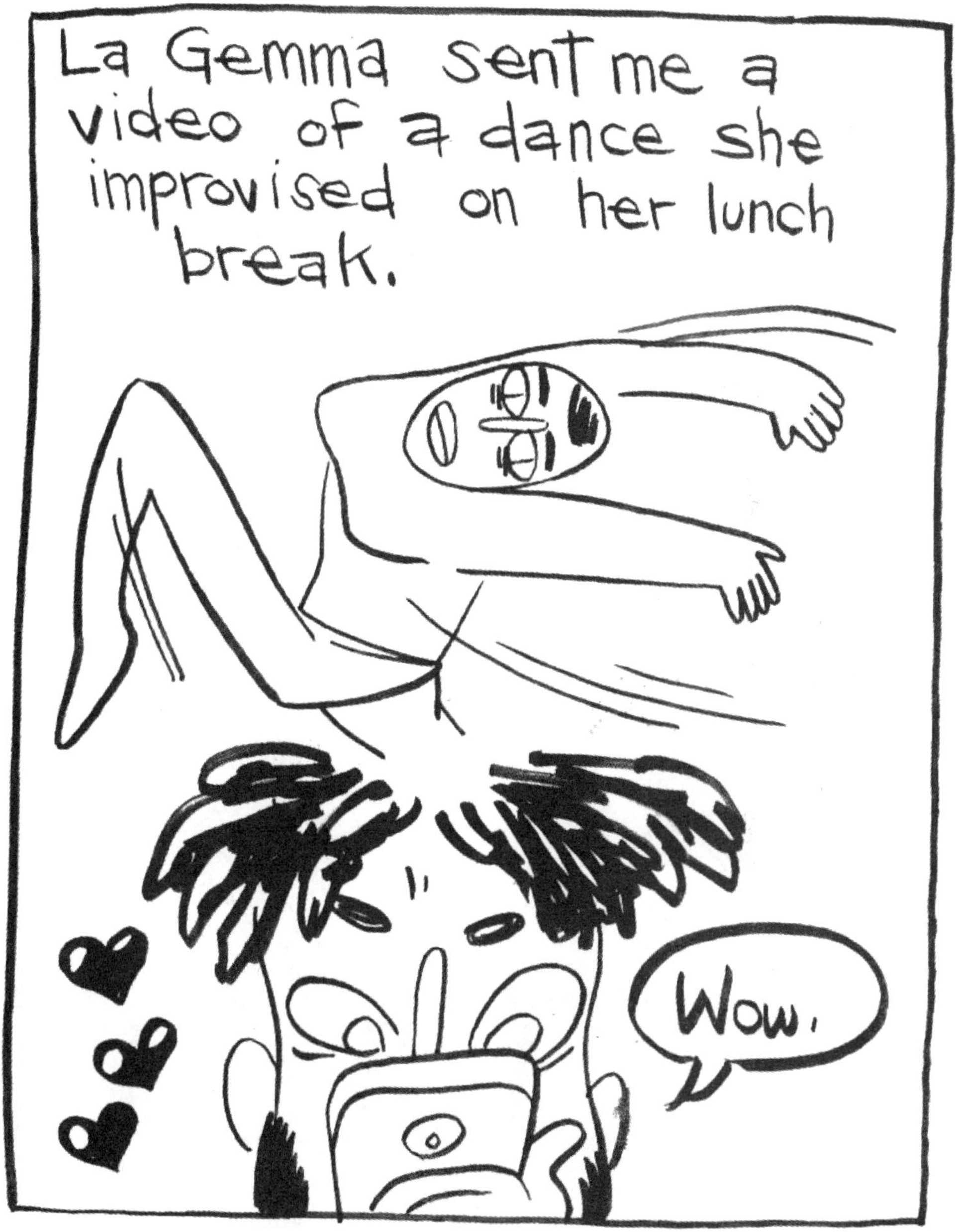
La Gemma sent me a video of a dance she improvised on her lunch break.
Wow.

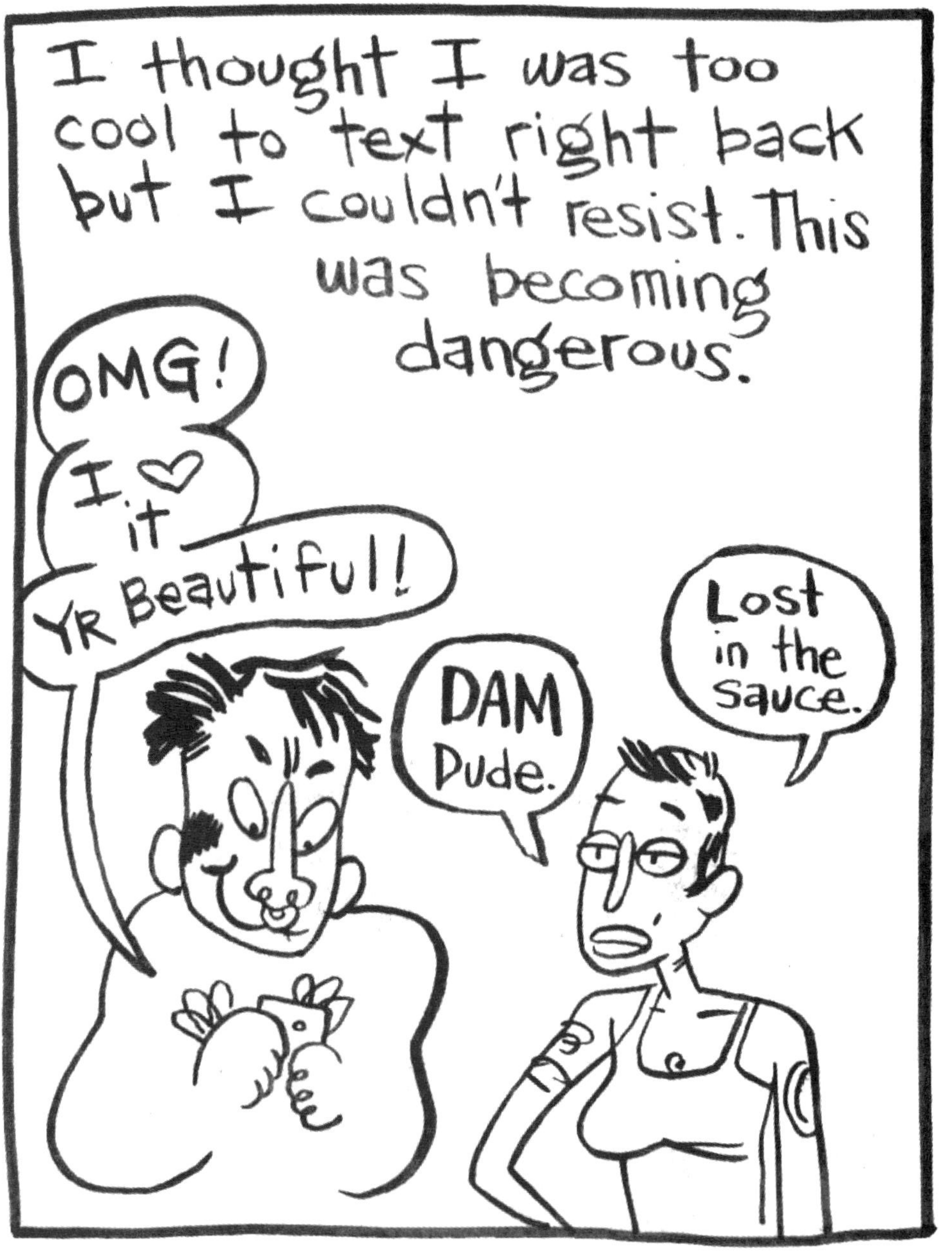
I thought I was too cool to text right back but I couldn't resist. This was becoming dangerous.
OMG!
I ♡ it
YR Beautiful!
DAM Dude.
Lost in the sauce.

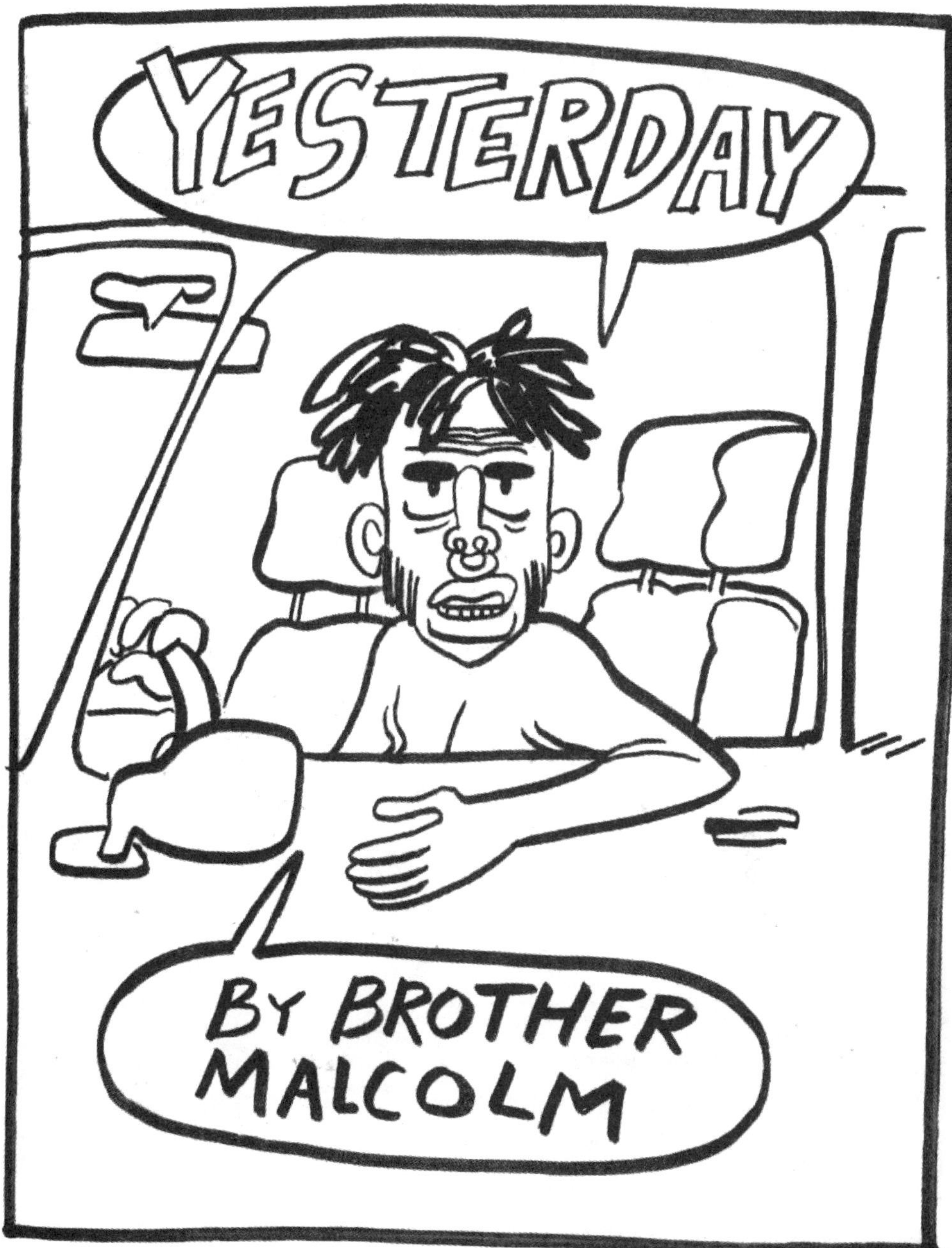
YESTERDAY
BY BROTHER MALCOLM

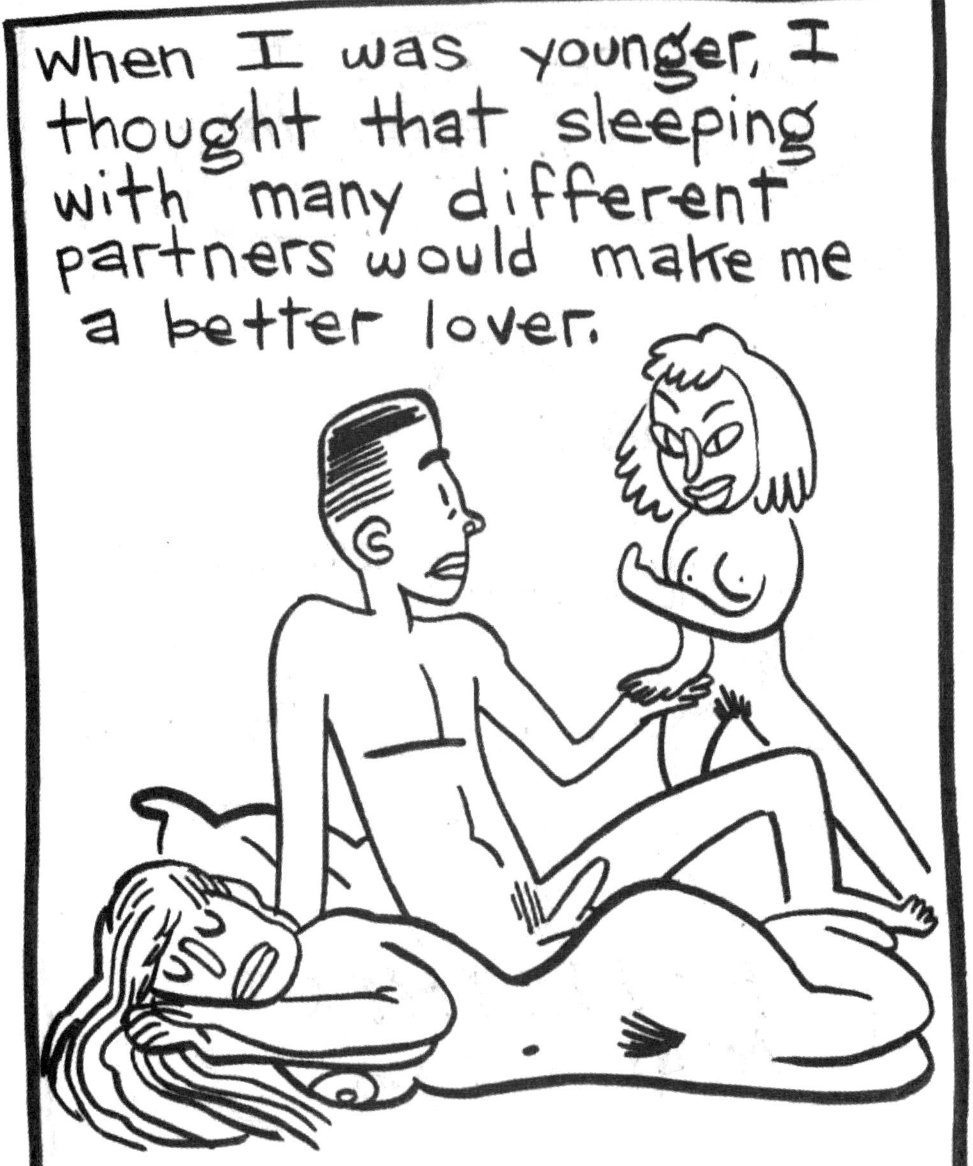
When I was younger, I thought that sleeping with many different partners would make me a better lover.

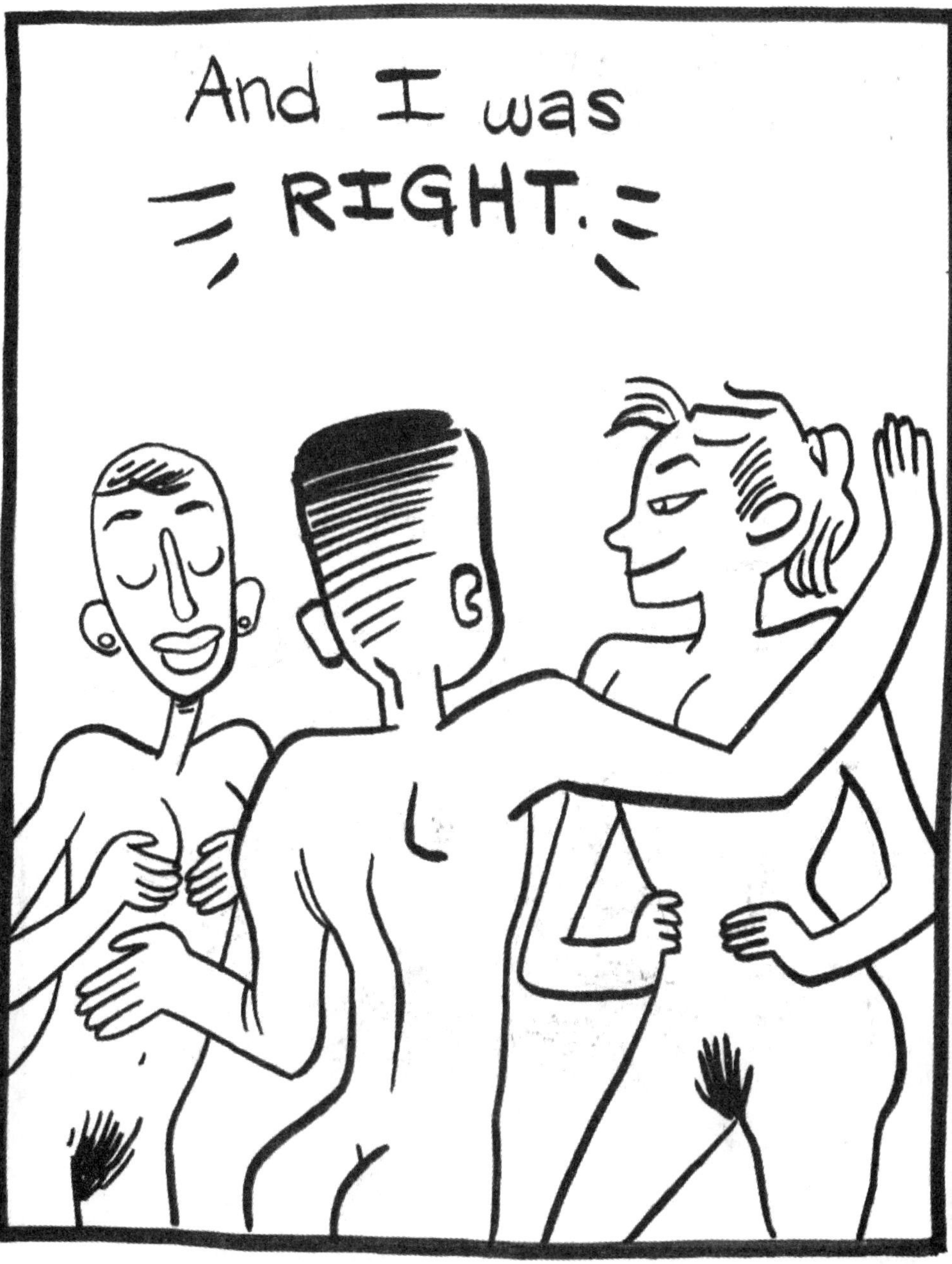
And I was
RIGHT.

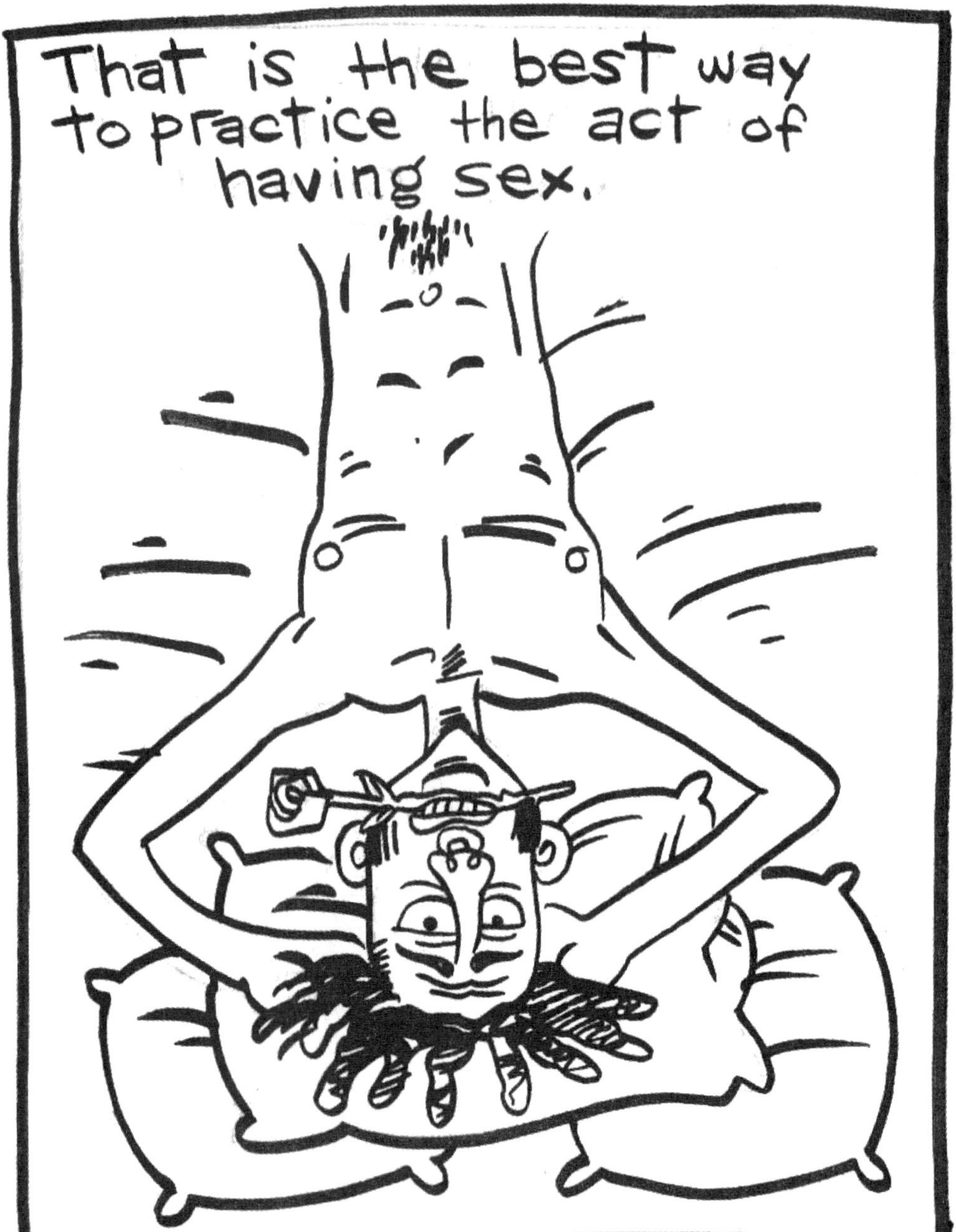
That is the best way to practice the act of having sex.

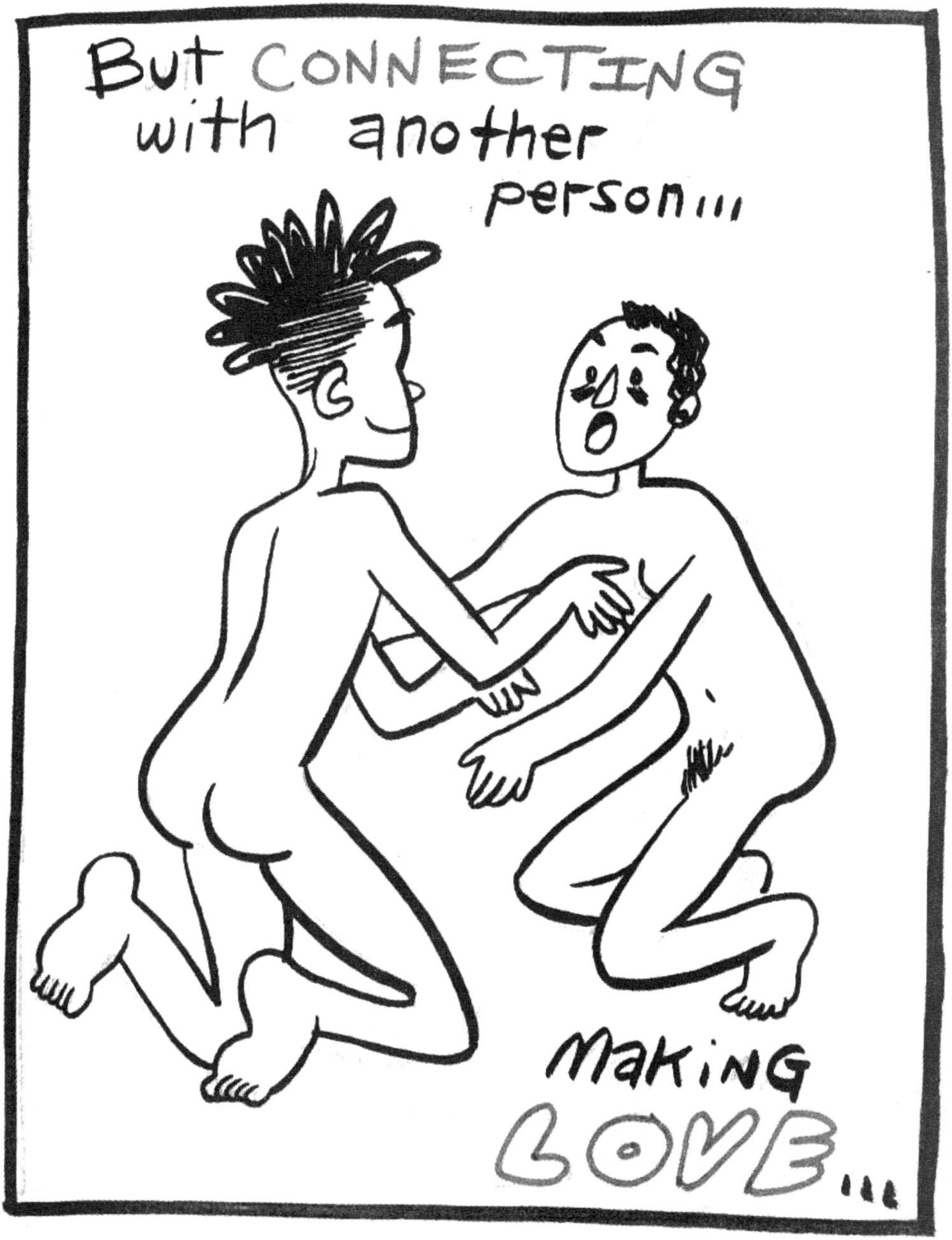
But CONNECTING with another person...
Making LOVE...

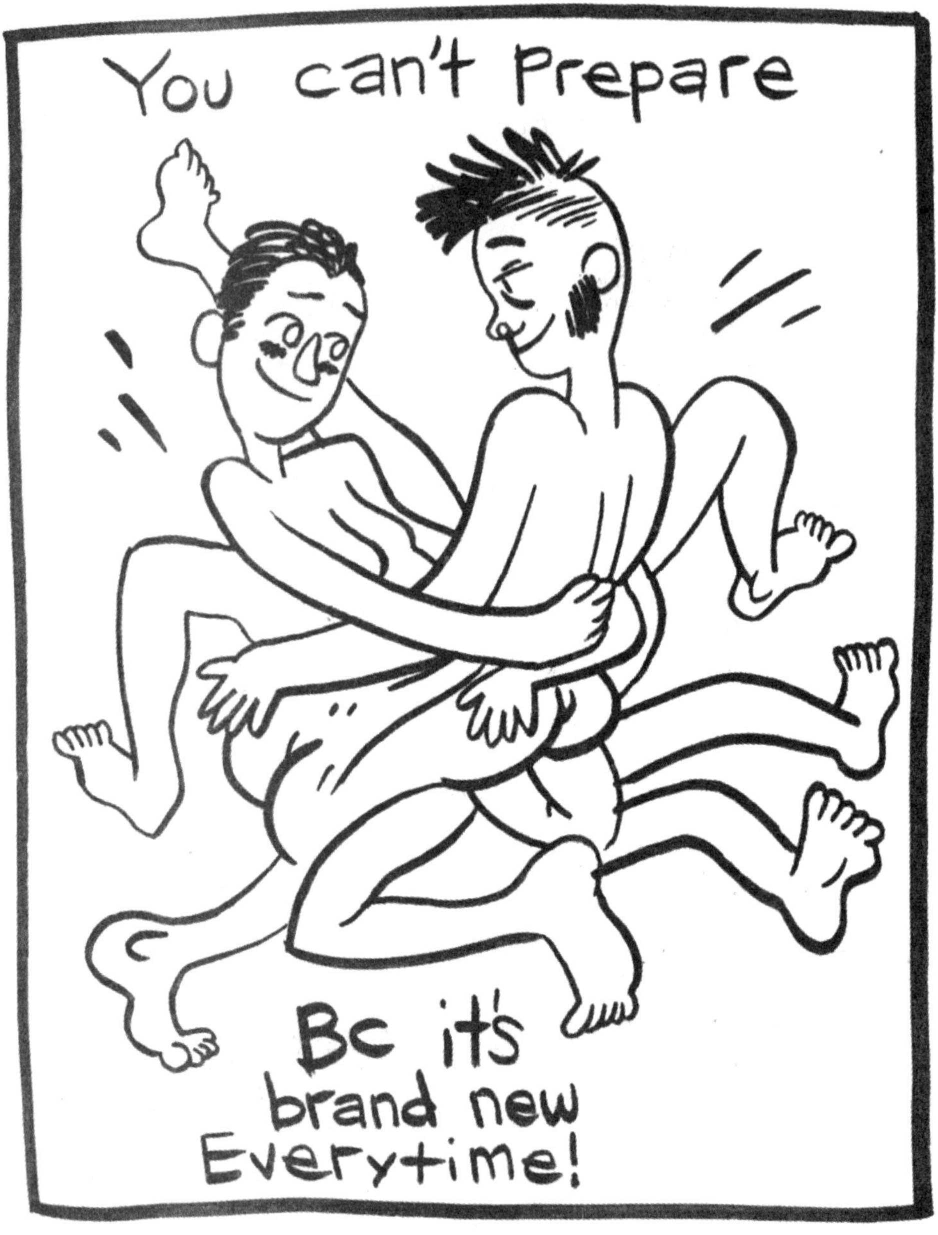
You can't prepare
Bc it's
brand new
Everytime!

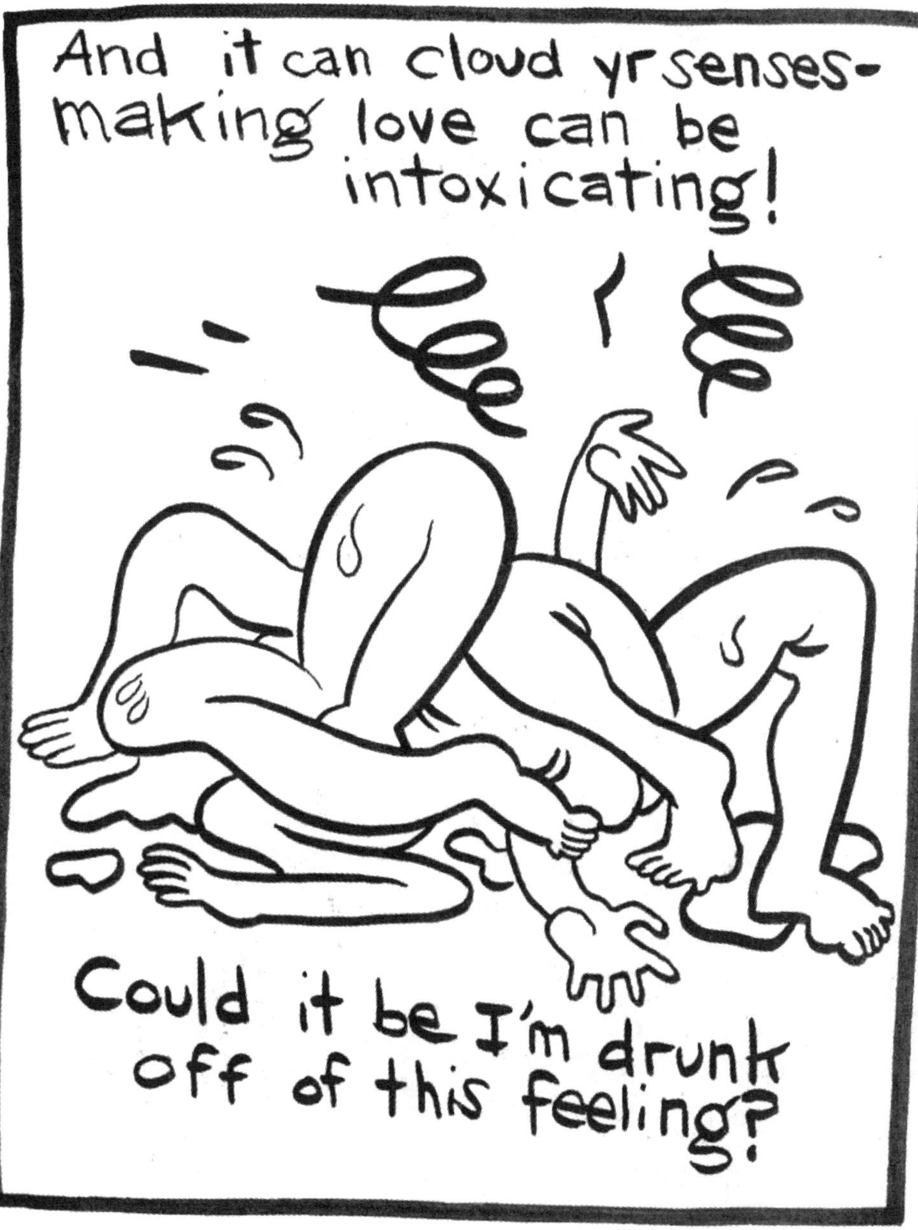
And it can cloud yr senses-
making love can be
intoxicating!
Could it be I'm drunk
off of this feeling?

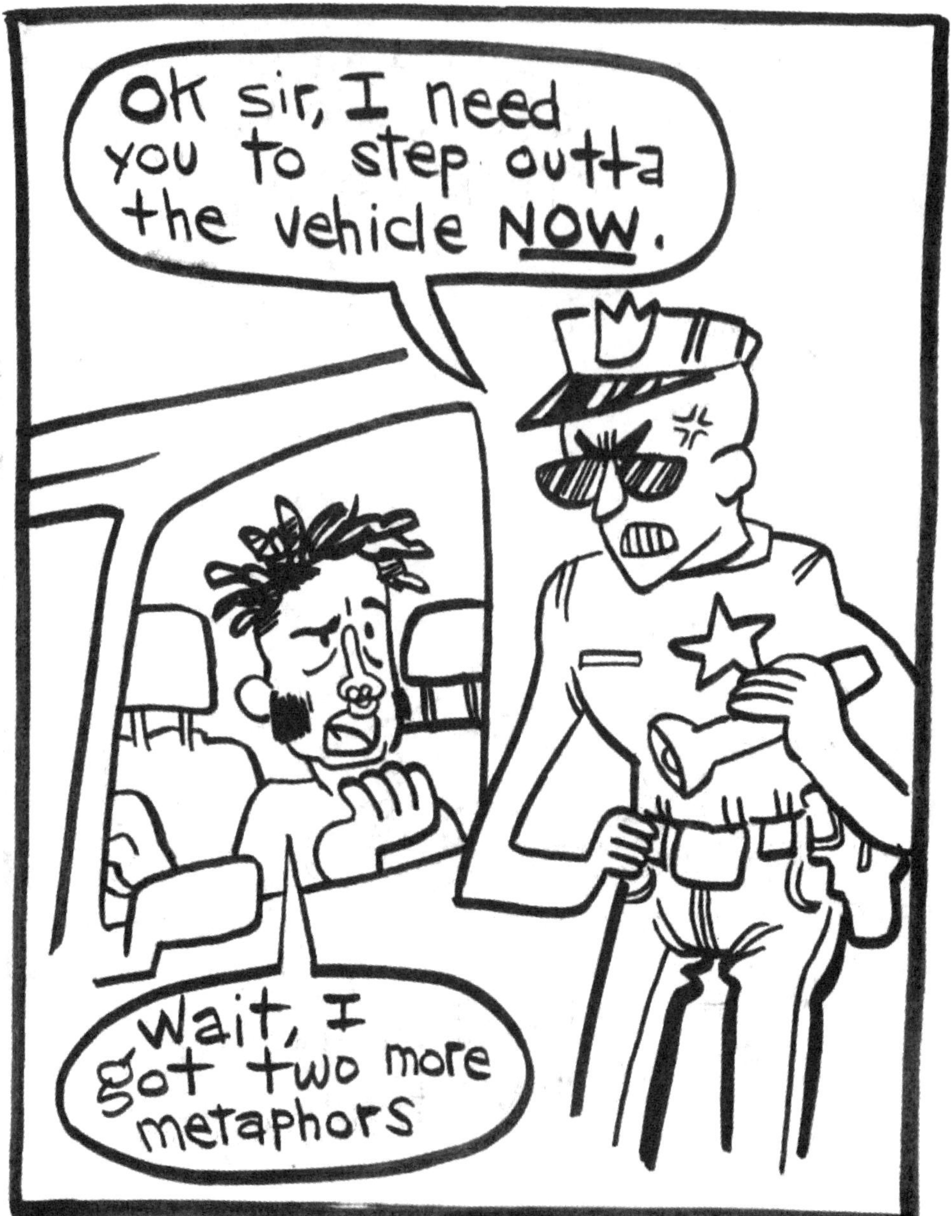
Ok sir, I need you to step outta the vehicle NOW.
Wait, I got two more metaphors

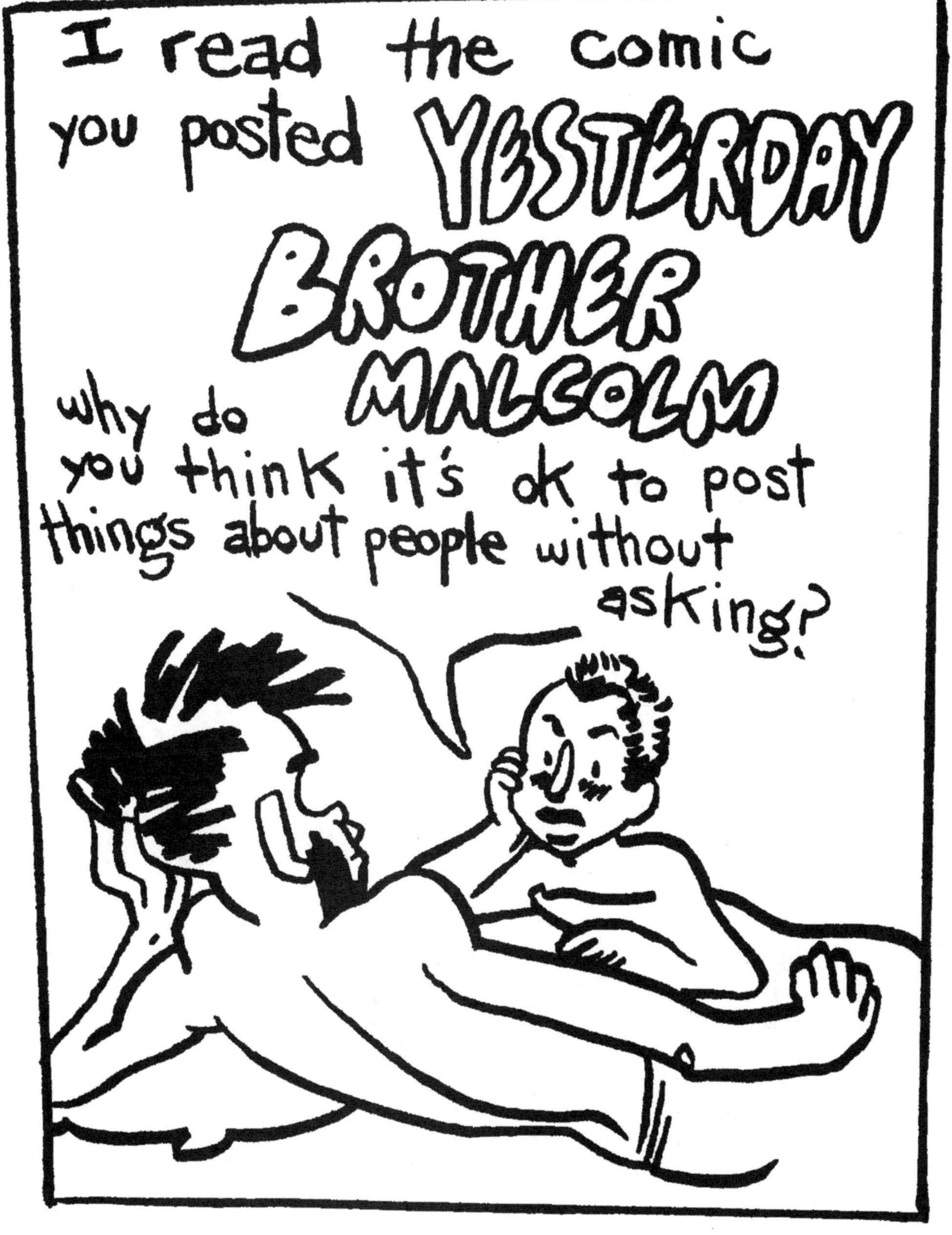
I read the comic you posted YESTERDAY BROTHER MALCOLM
why do you think it's ok to post things about people without asking?

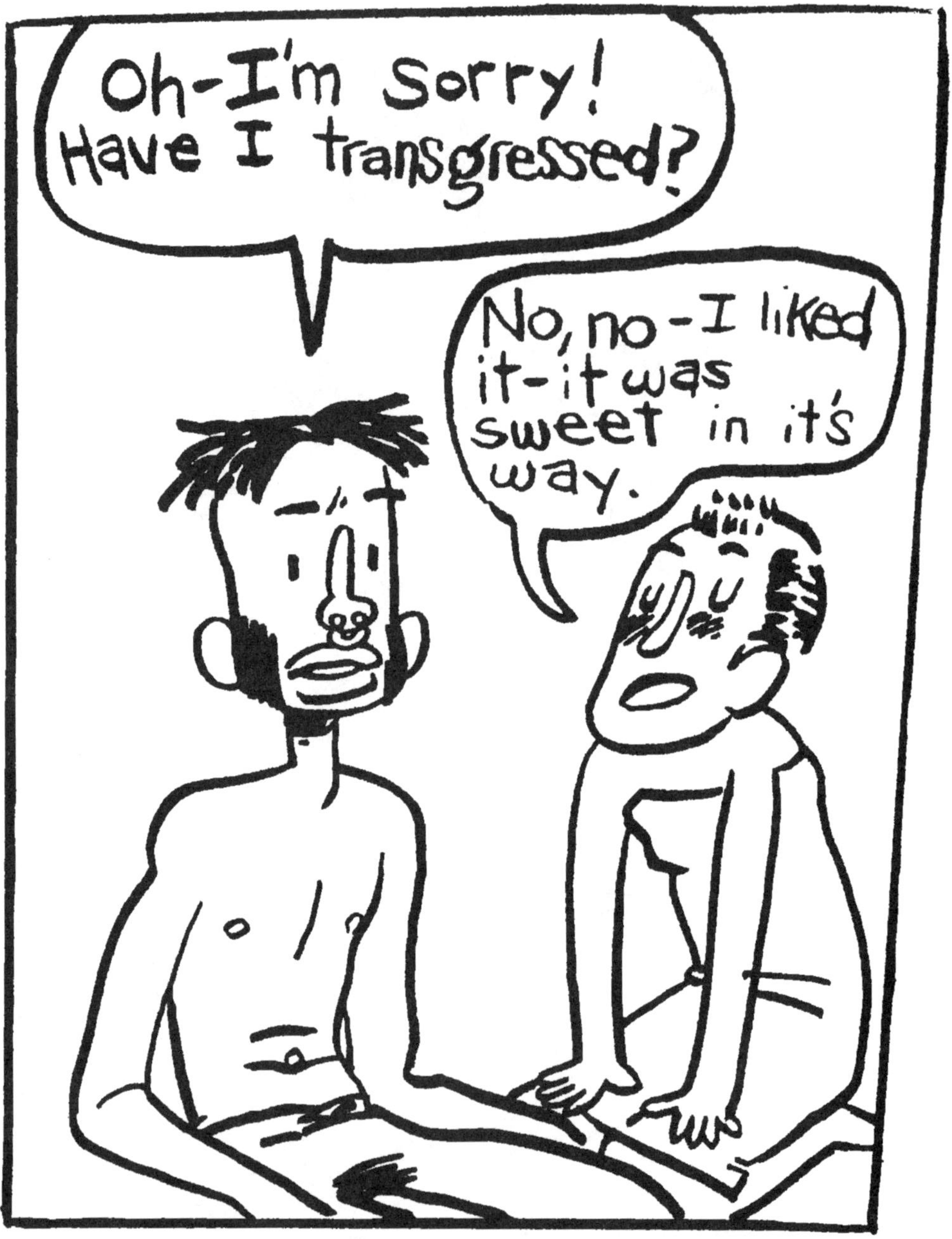
Oh-I'm Sorry! Have I transgressed?
No, no-I liked it-it was sweet in it's way.

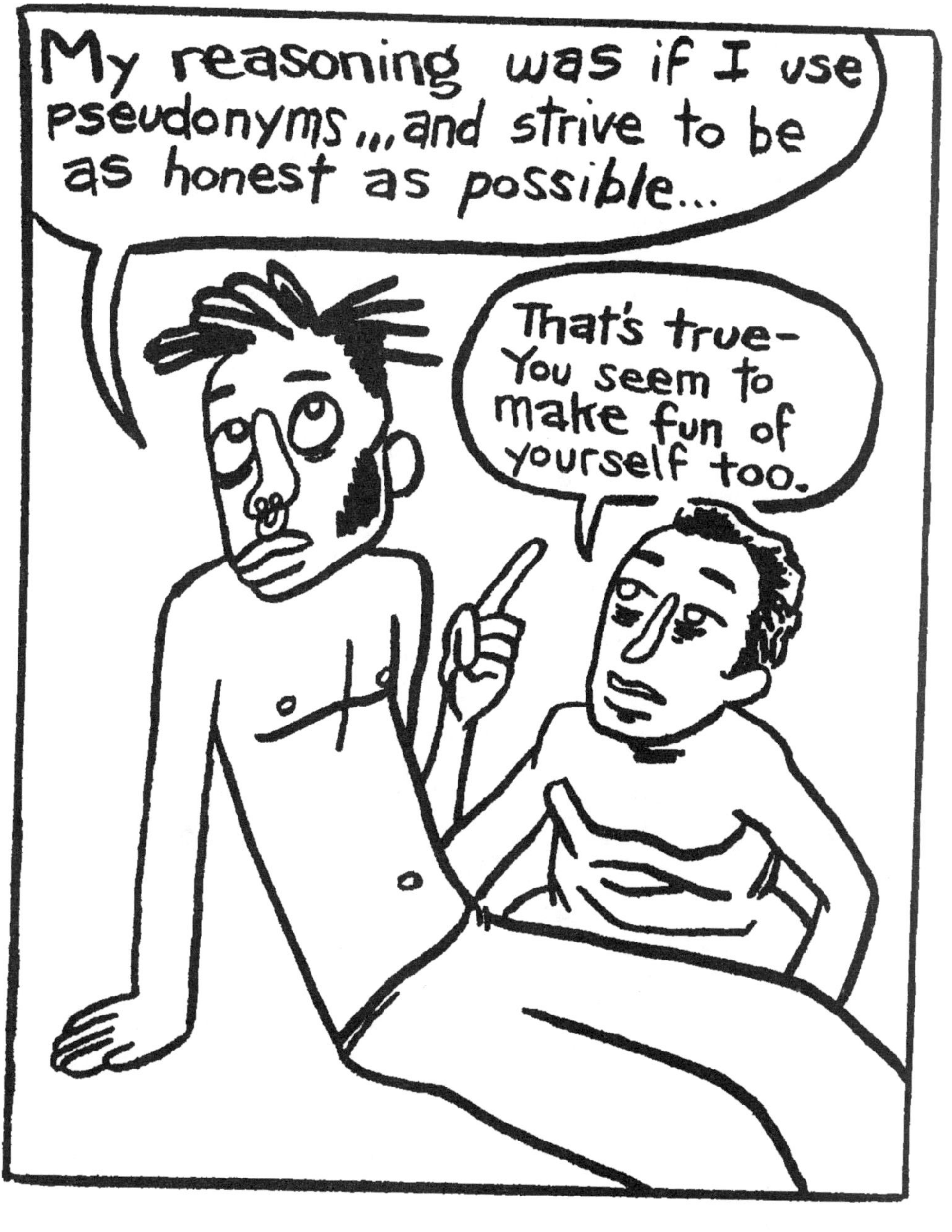
My reasoning was if I use pseudonyms,,, and strive to be as honest as possible...
That's true- You seem to make fun of yourself too.

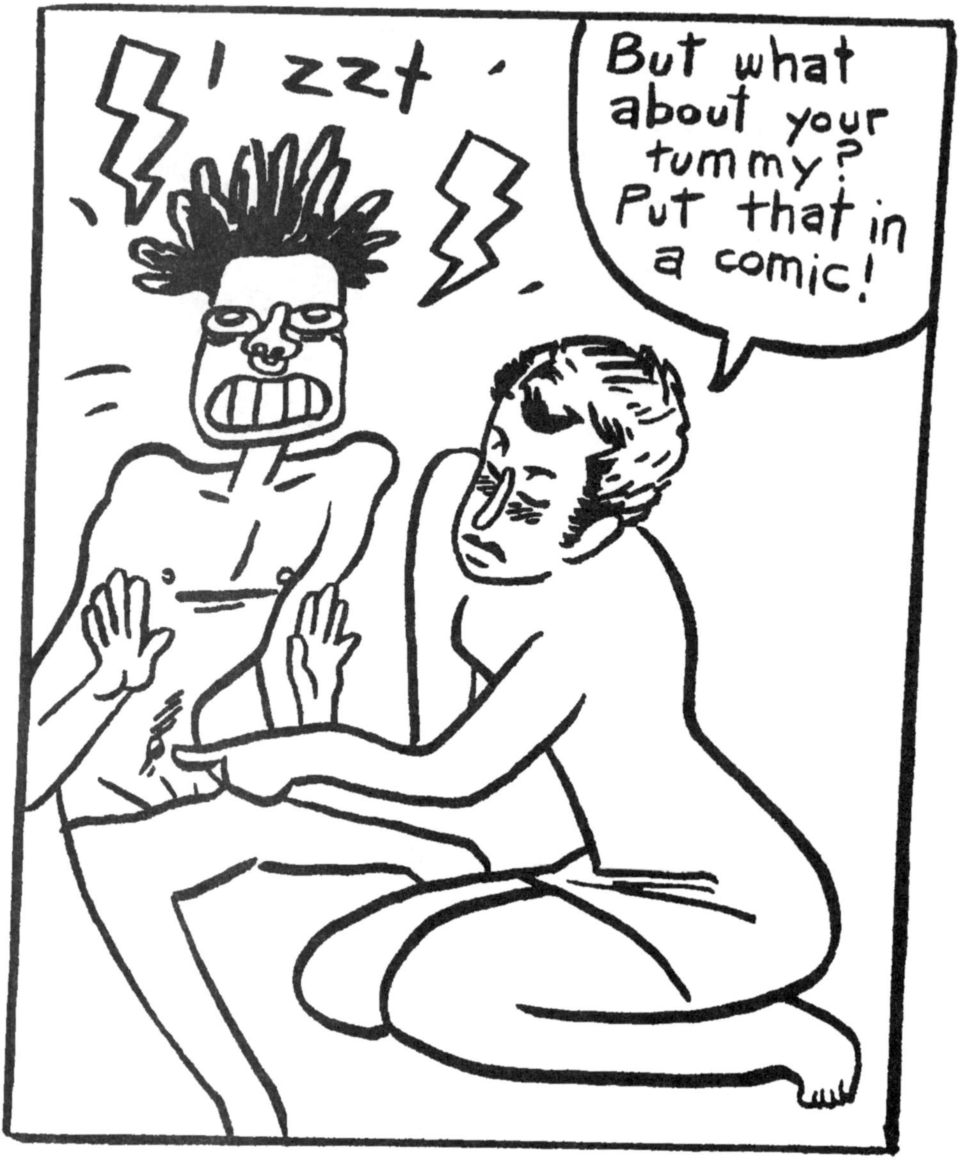
zzt
But what about your tummy? Put that in a comic!

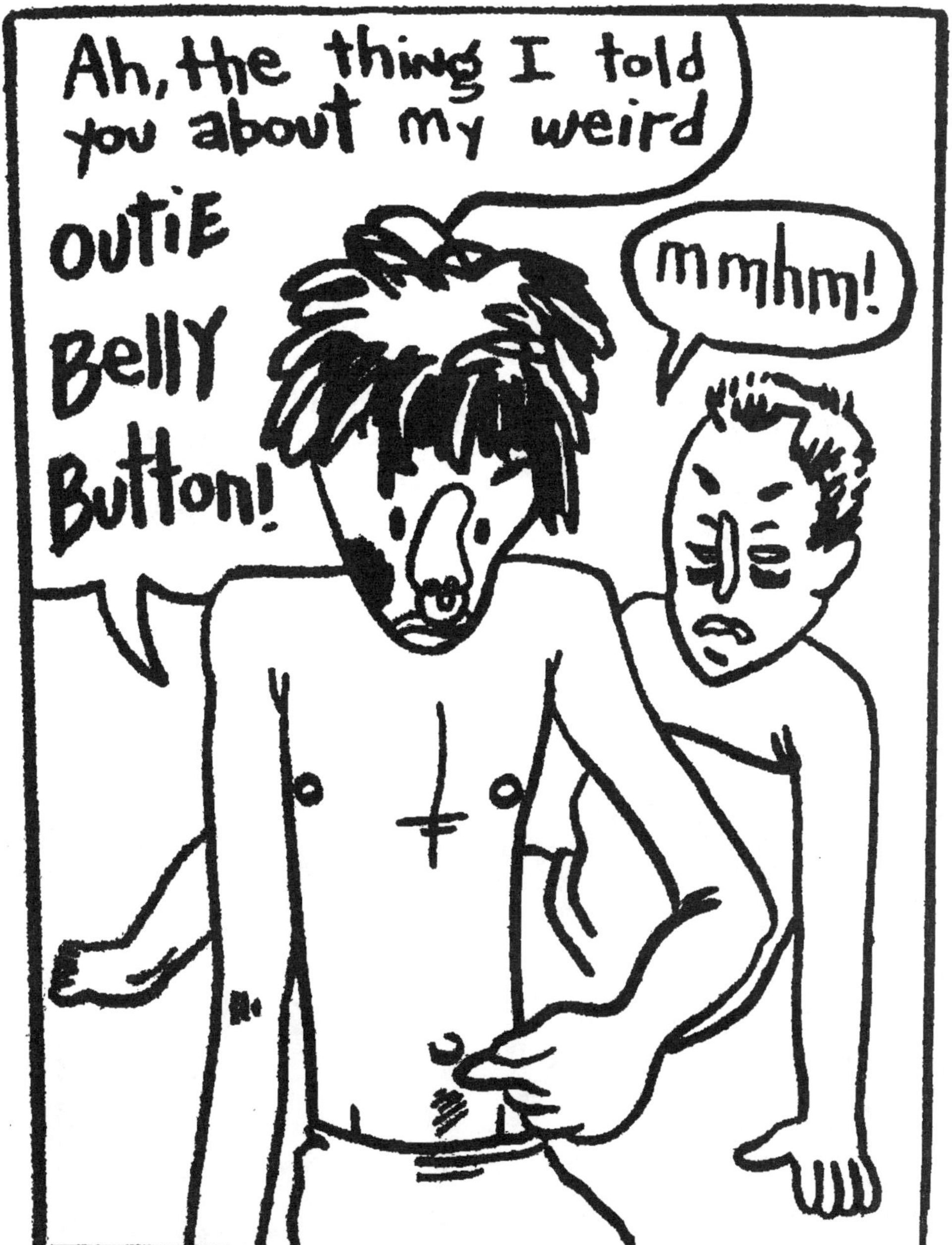
Ah, the thing I told you about my weird OUTIE BELLY Button!
mmhm!

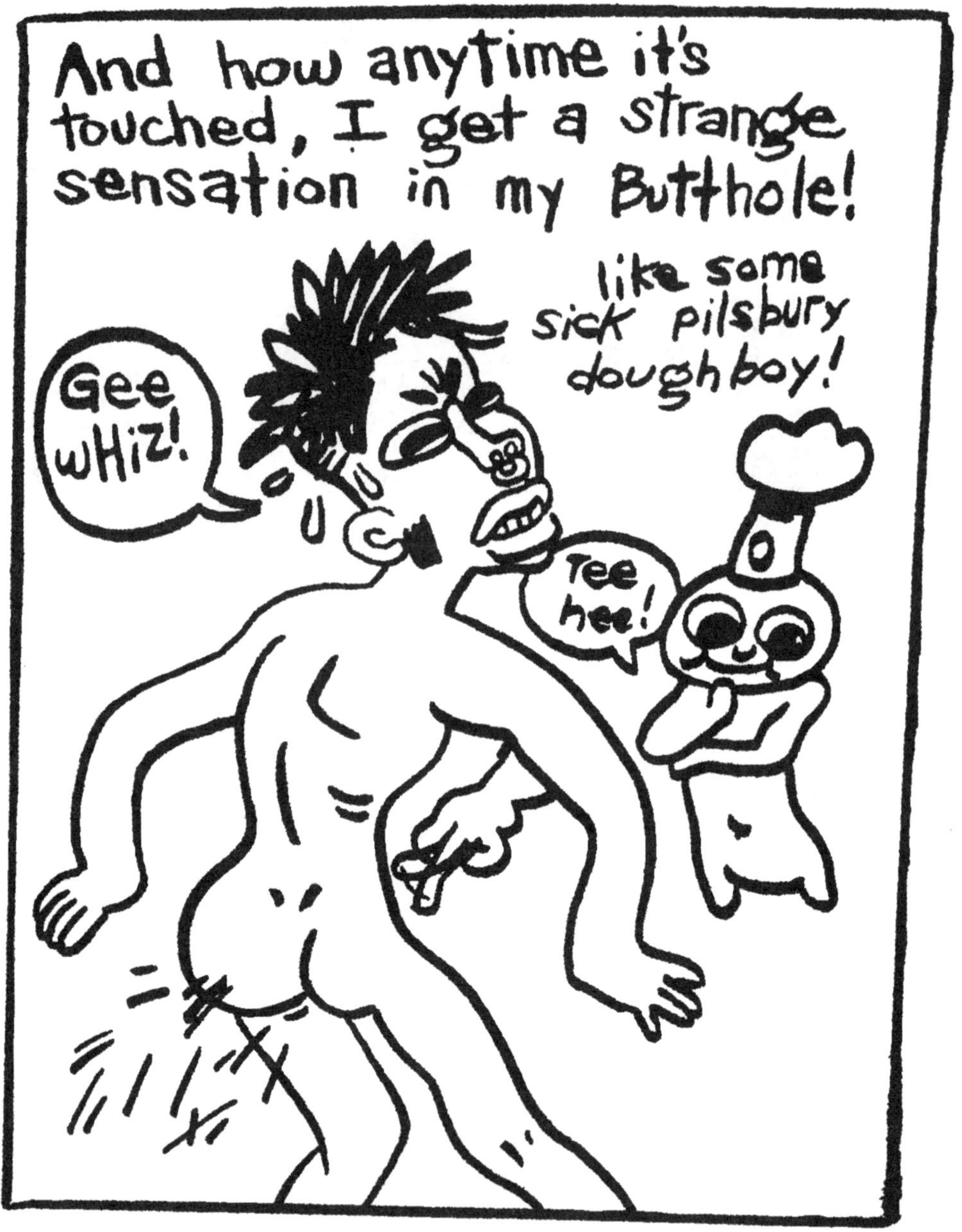
And how anytime it's touched, I get a strange sensation in my Butthole!
Gee wHiz!
like some sick pilsbury doughboy!
Tee hee!

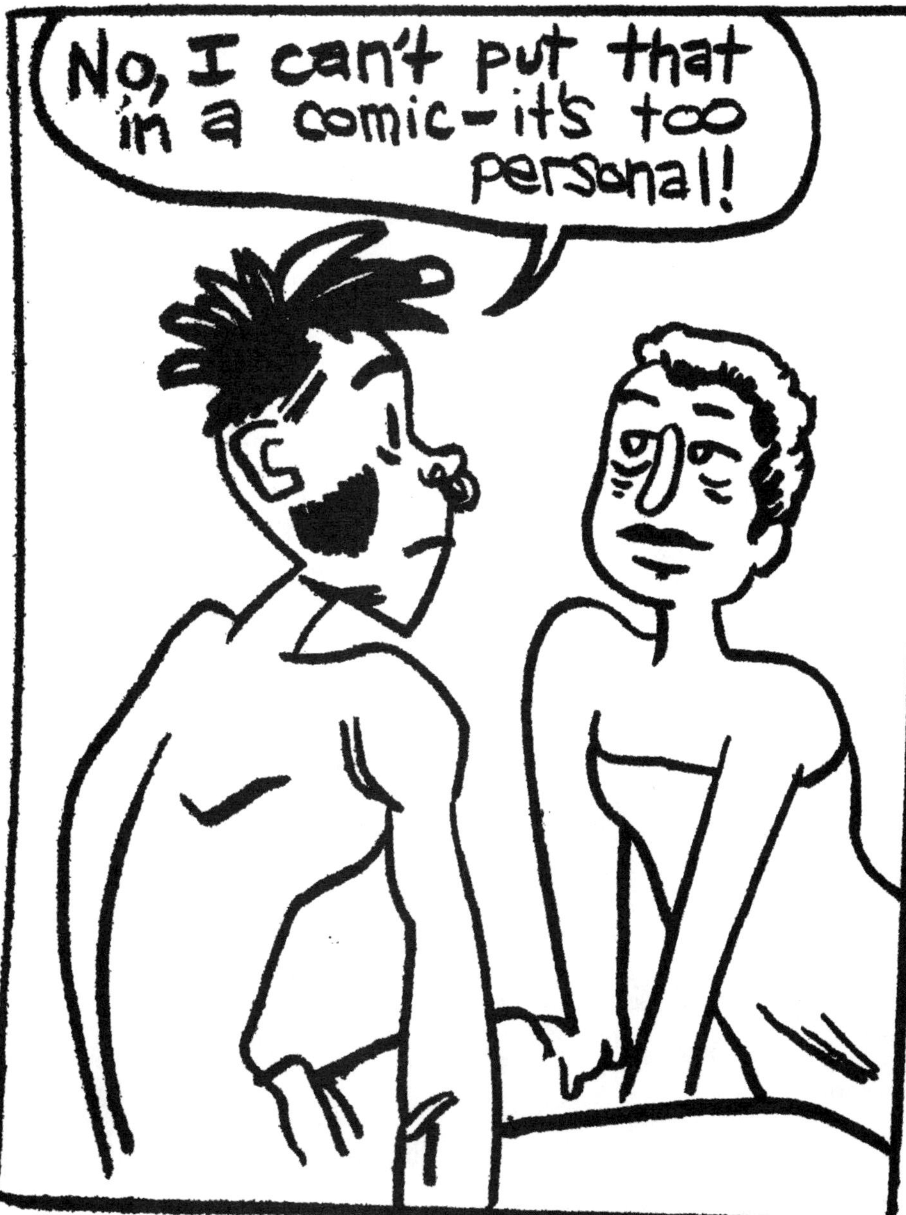
No, I can't put that in a comic-it's too personal!

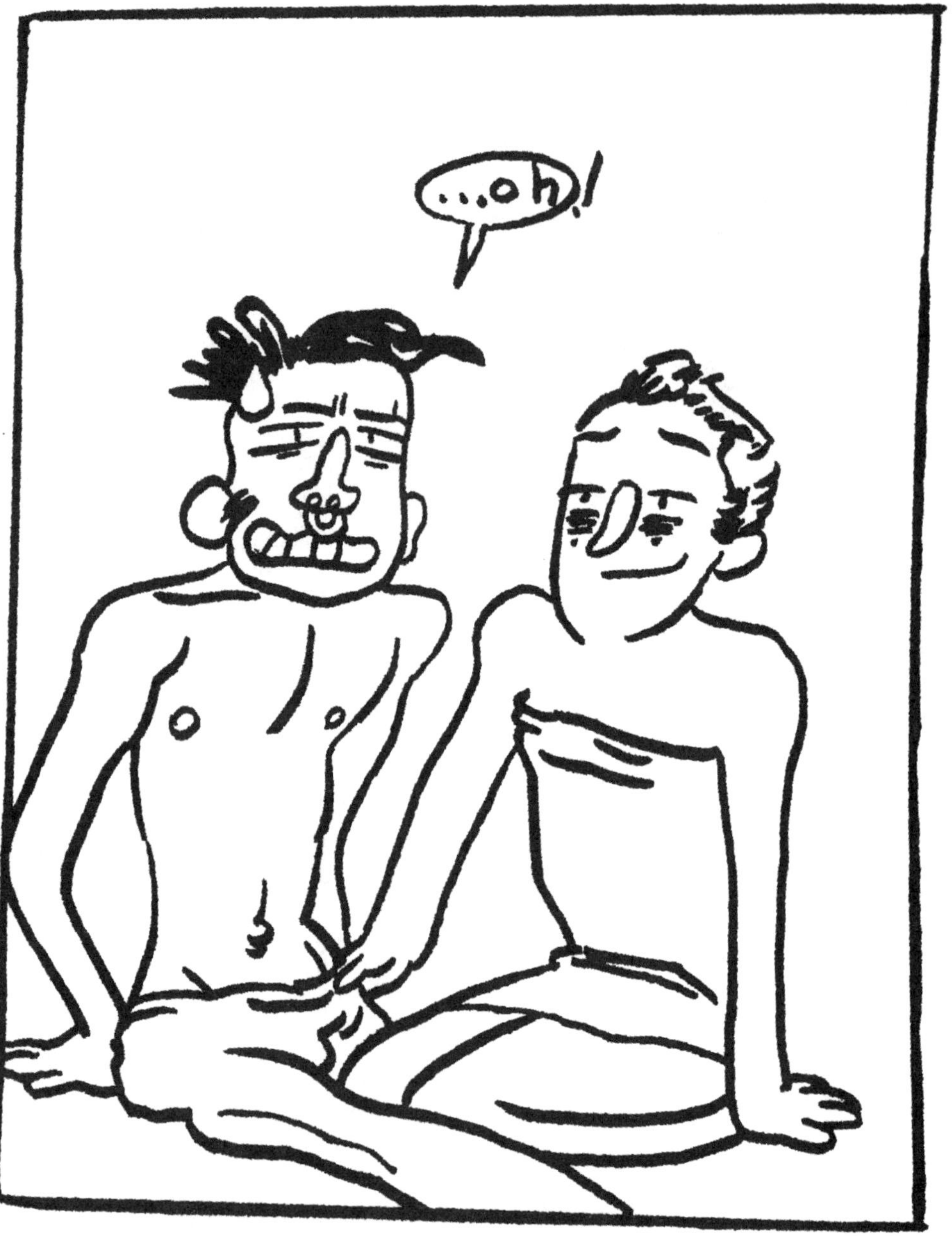
...oh!

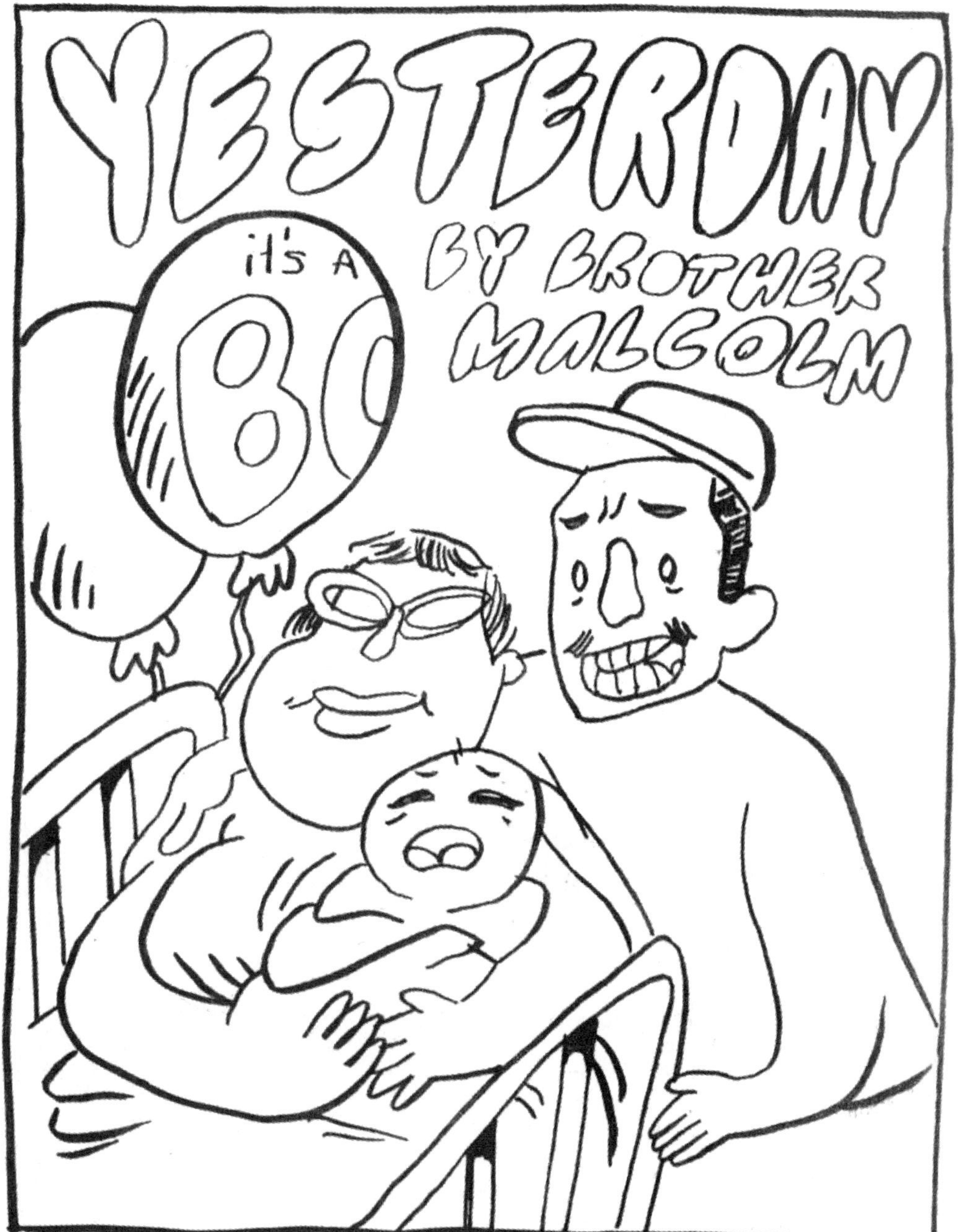
YESTERDAY
BY BROTHER MALCOLM
it's a
80

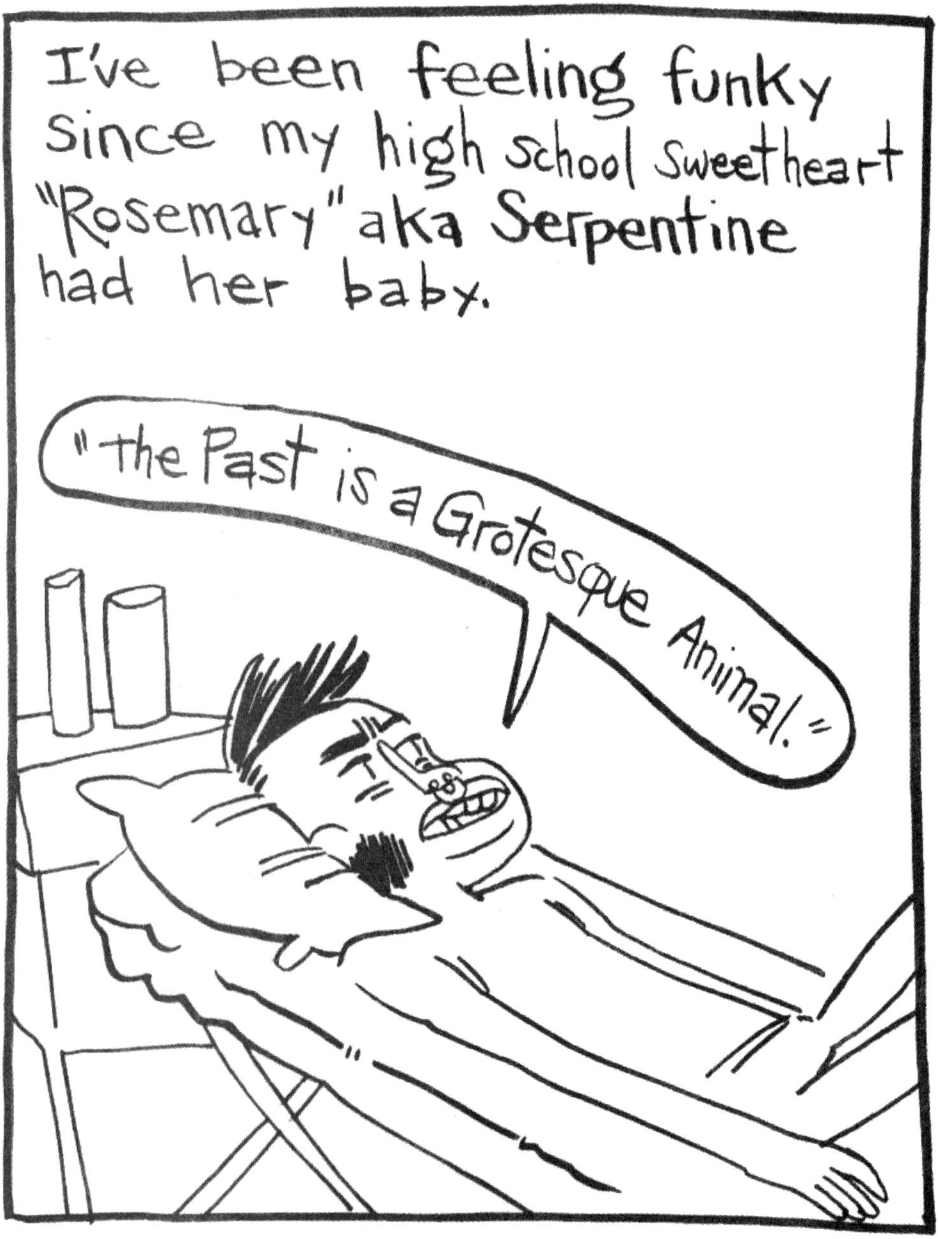
I've been feeling funky since my high school sweetheart "Rosemary" aka Serpentine had her baby.
"the Past is a Grotesque Animal."

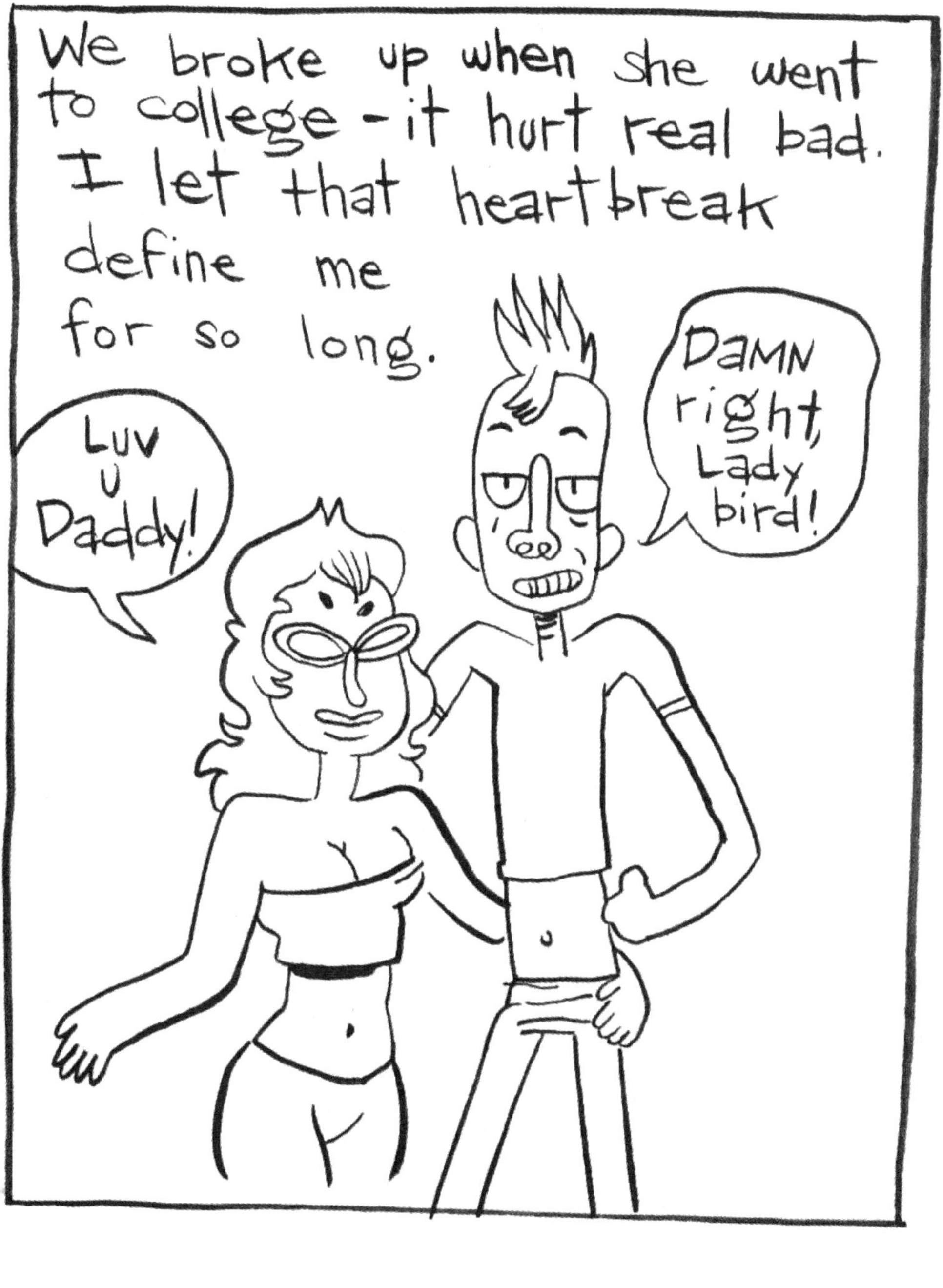
We broke up when she went to college - it hurt real bad. I let that heartbreak define me for so long.
Luv U Daddy!
DAMN right, Lady bird!

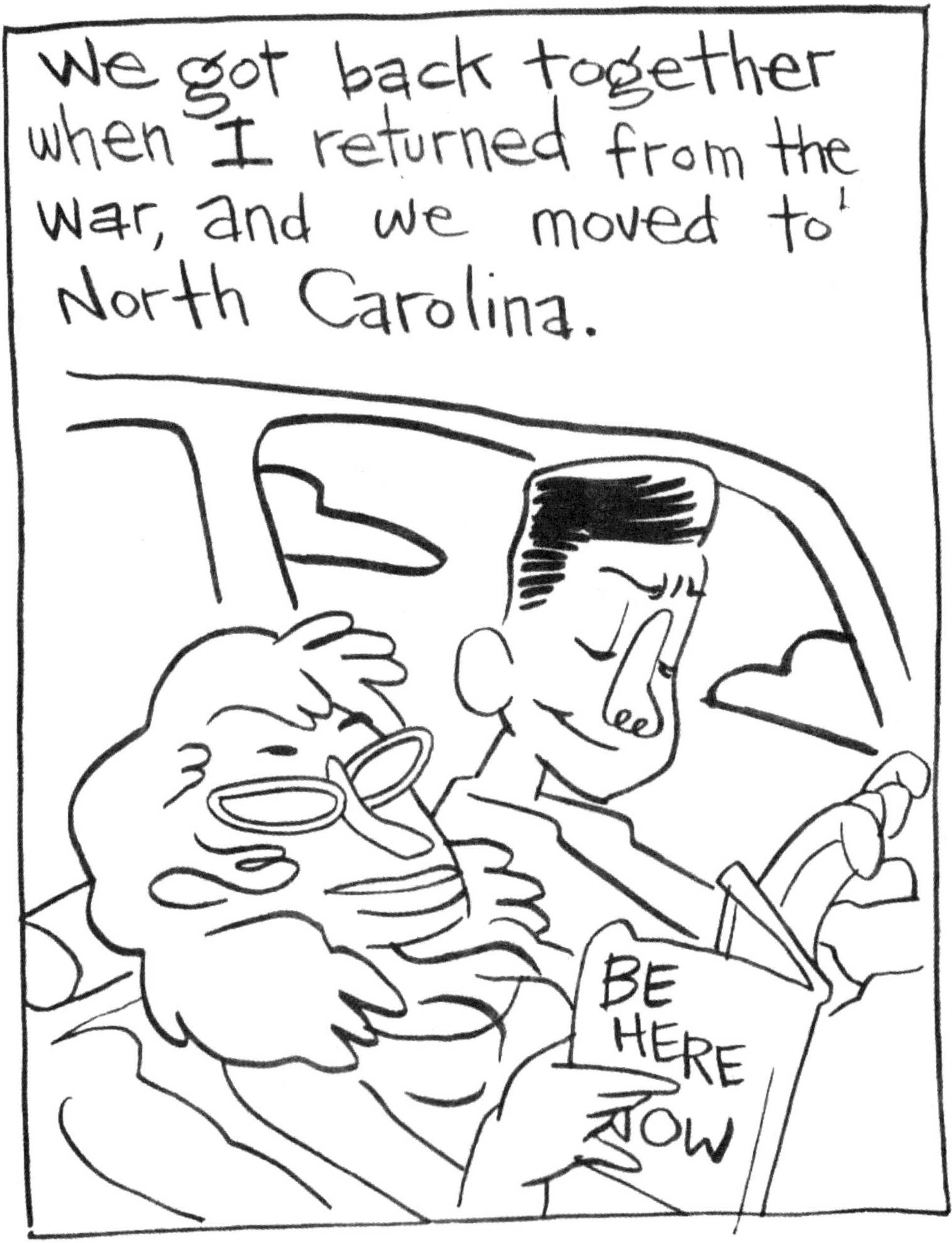
We got back together when I returned from the war, and we moved to North Carolina.
BE HERE NOW

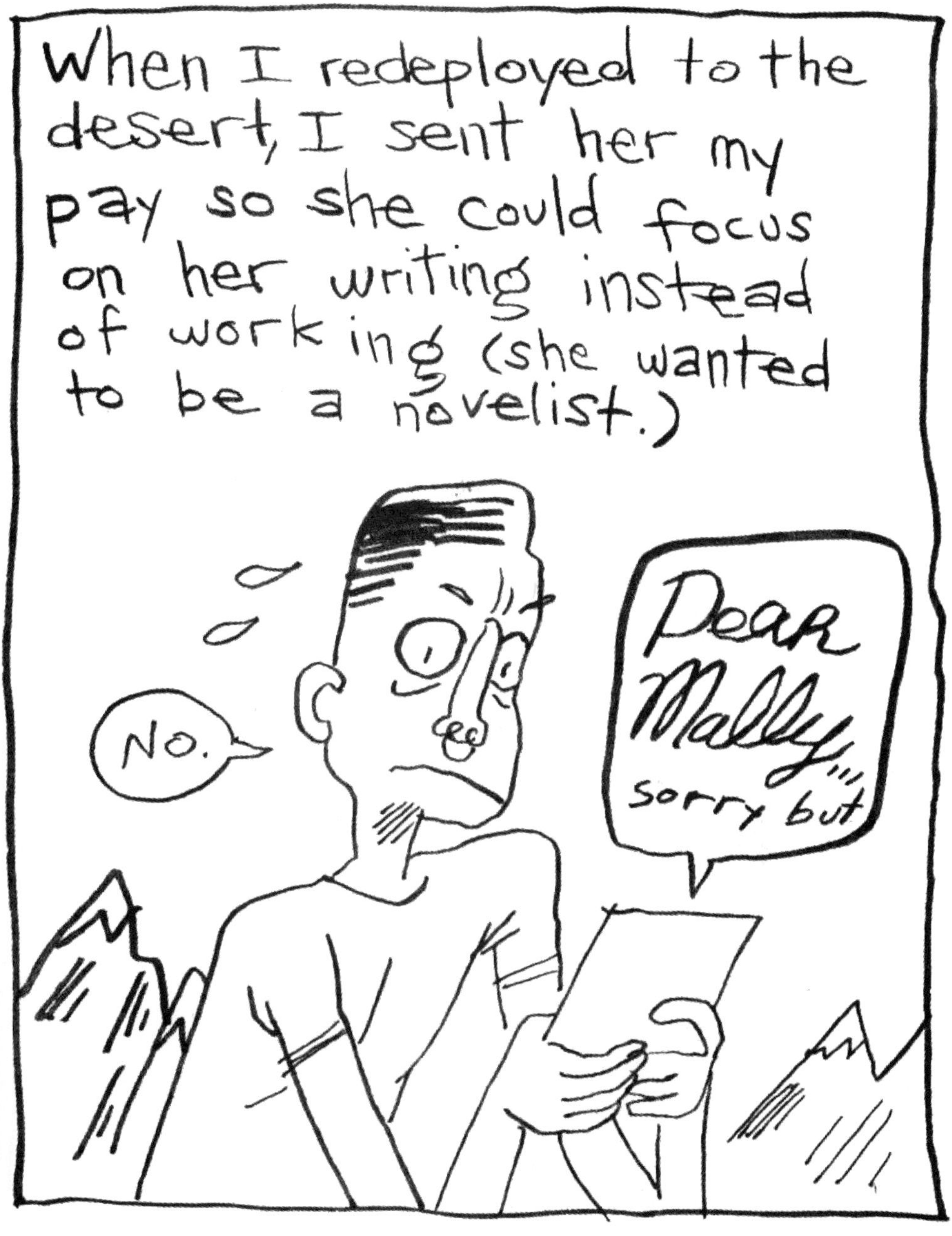
When I redeployed to the desert, I sent her my pay so she could focus on her writing instead of working (she wanted to be a novelist.)
No.
Dear Mally, sorry but

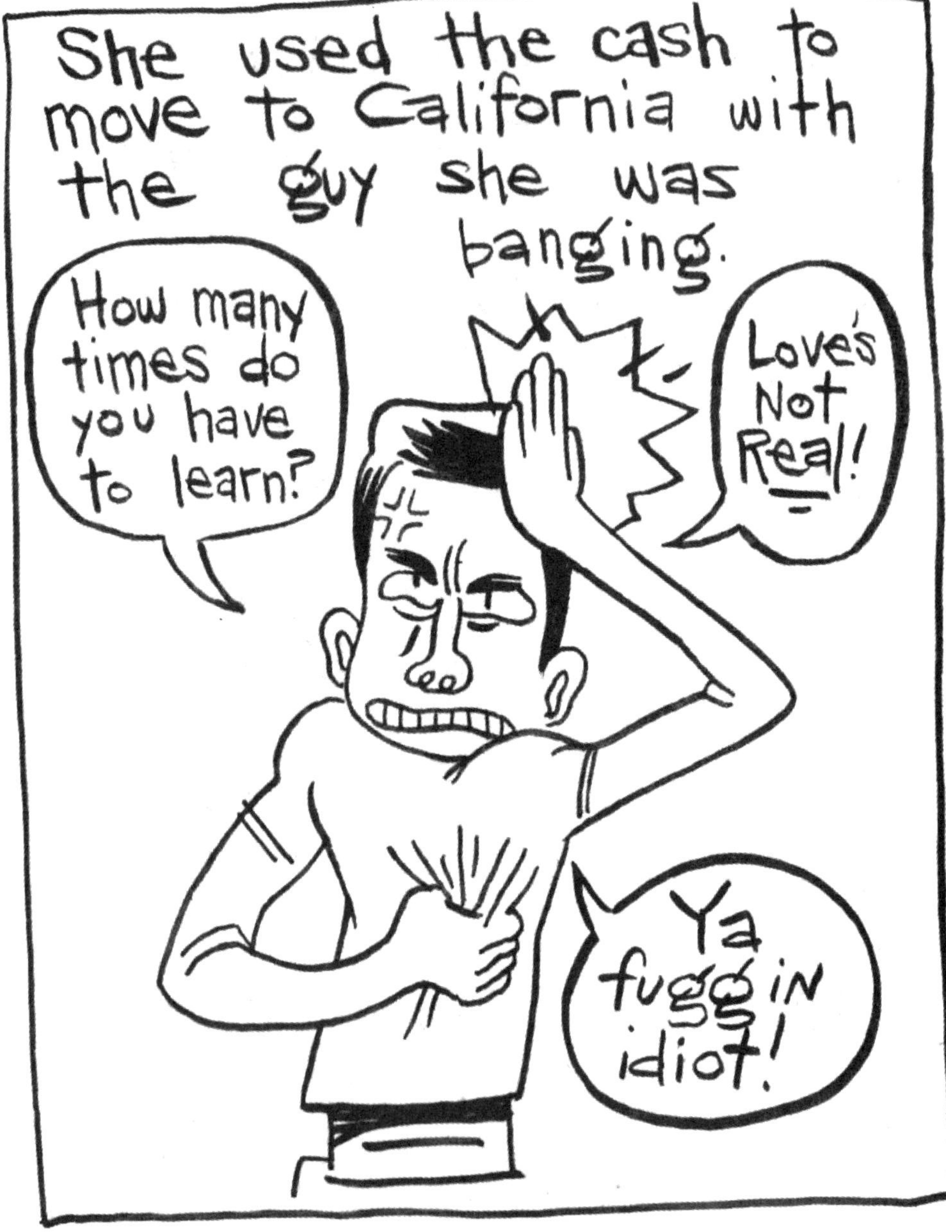
She used the cash to move to California with the guy she was banging.
How many times do you have to learn?
Love's Not Real!
Ya fuggin idiot!

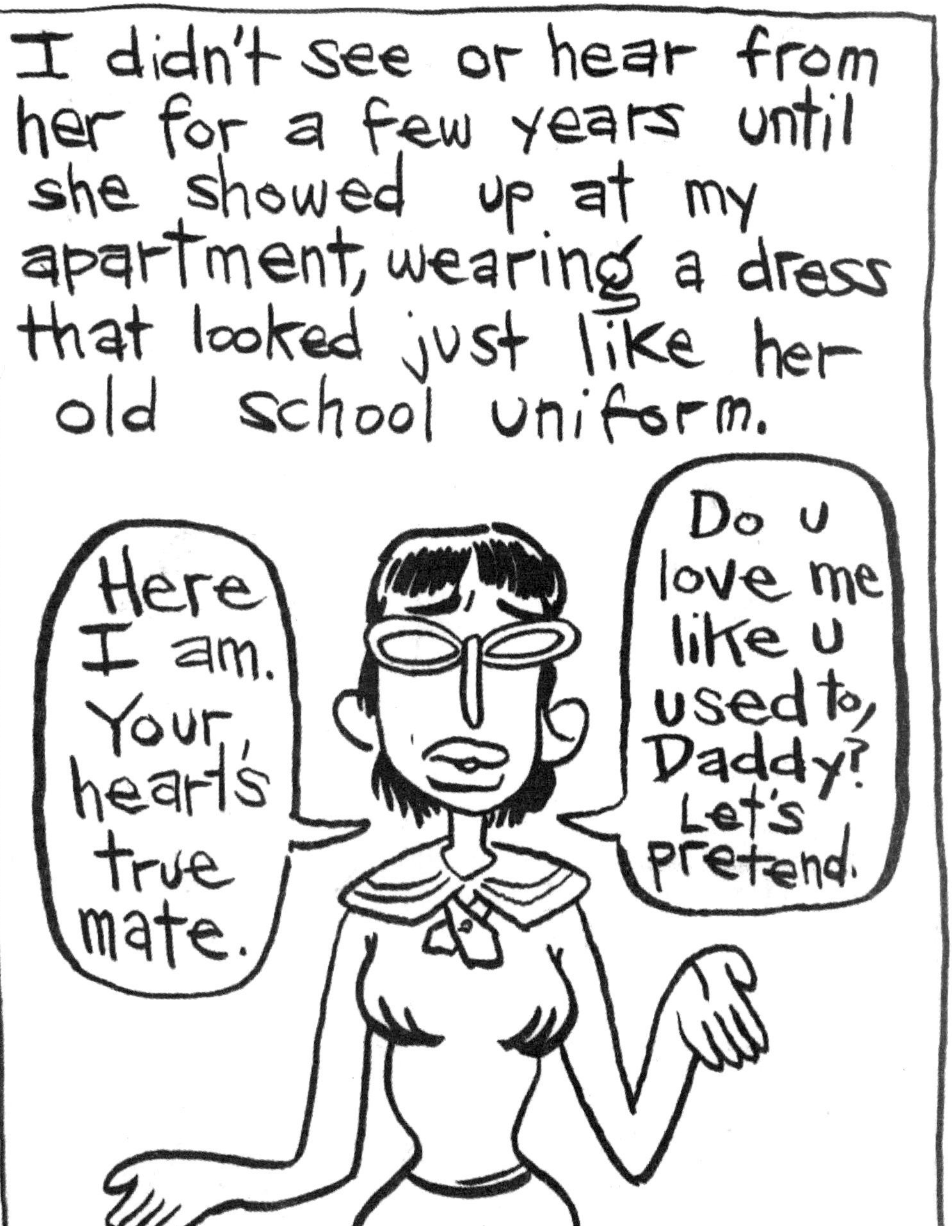
I didn't see or hear from her for a few years until she showed up at my apartment, wearing a dress that looked just like her old school uniform.
Here I am. Your heart's true mate.
Do u love me like u used to, Daddy? Let's pretend.

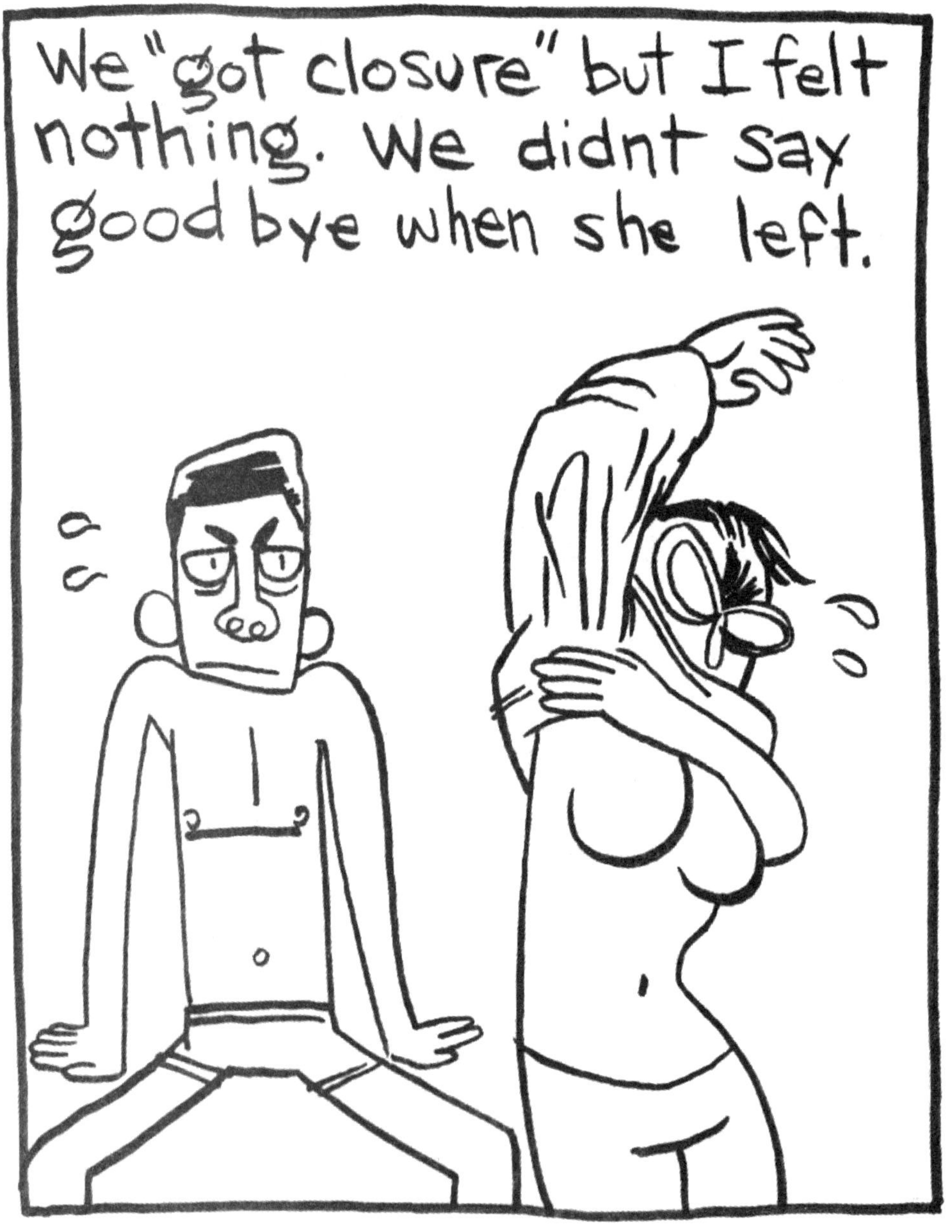
We "got closure" but I felt nothing. We didnt say good bye when she left.

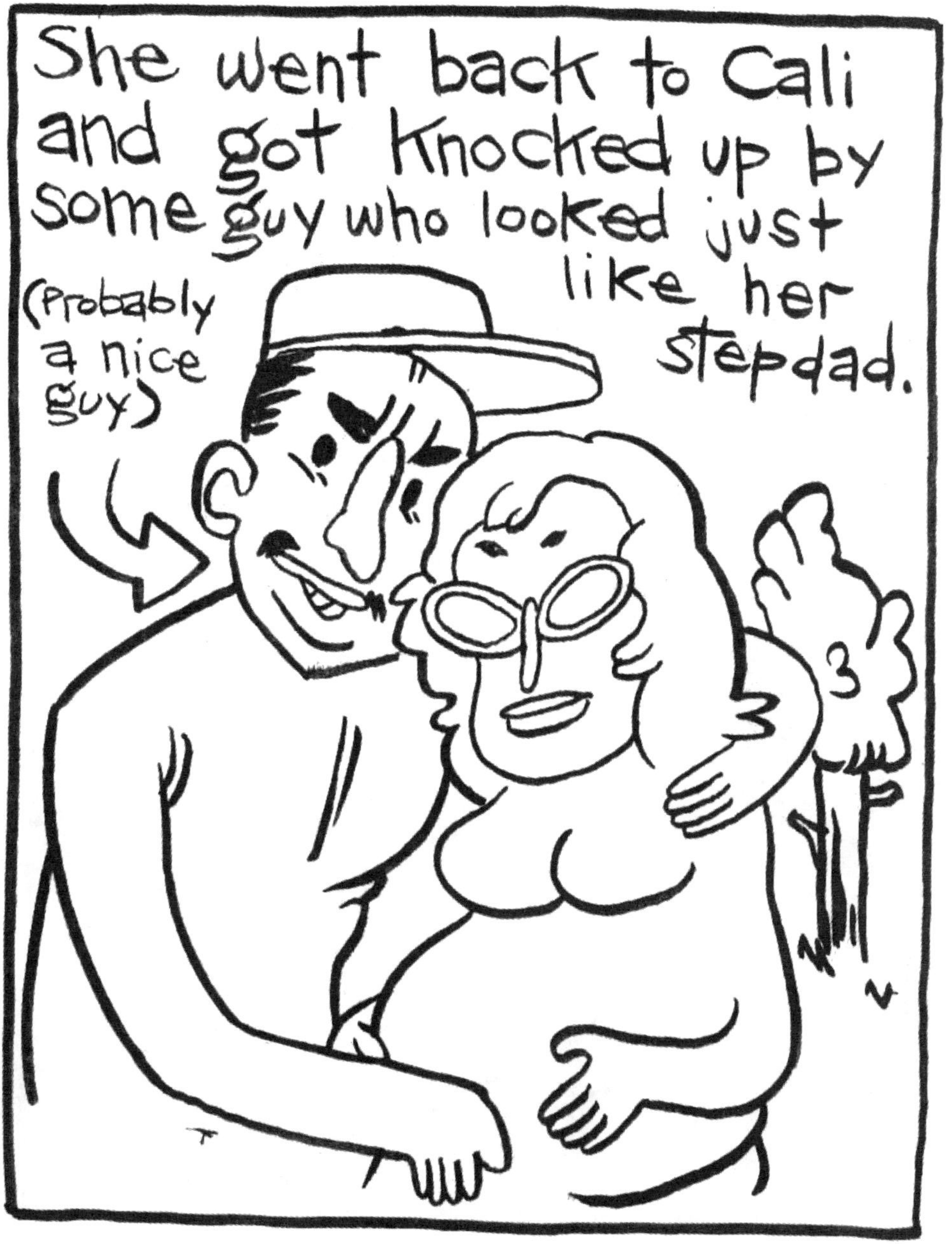
She went back to Cali and got knocked up by some guy who looked just like her stepdad.
(probably a nice guy)
3

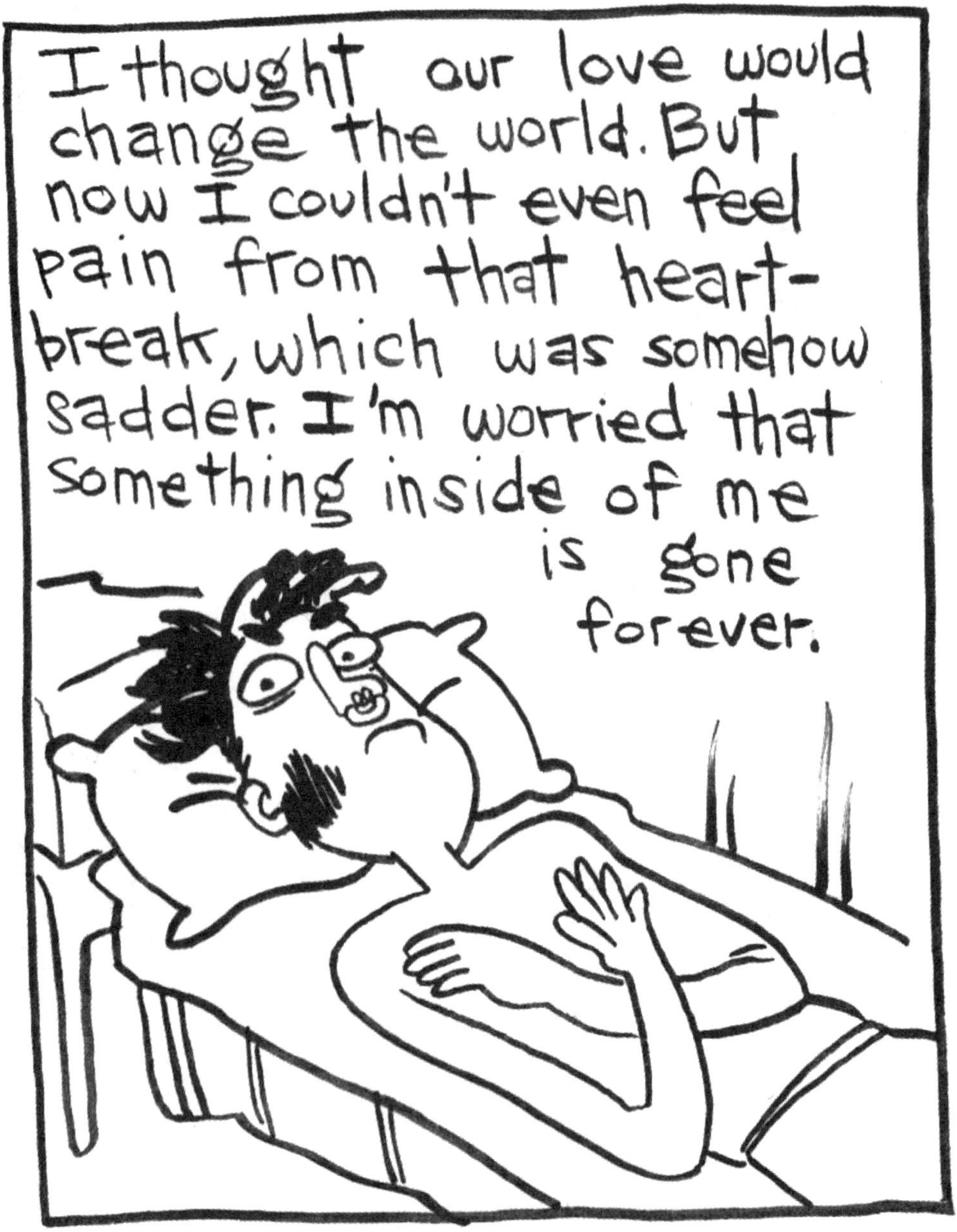
I thought our love would change the world. But now I couldn't even feel pain from that heart-break, which was somehow sadder. I'm worried that something inside of me is gone forever.

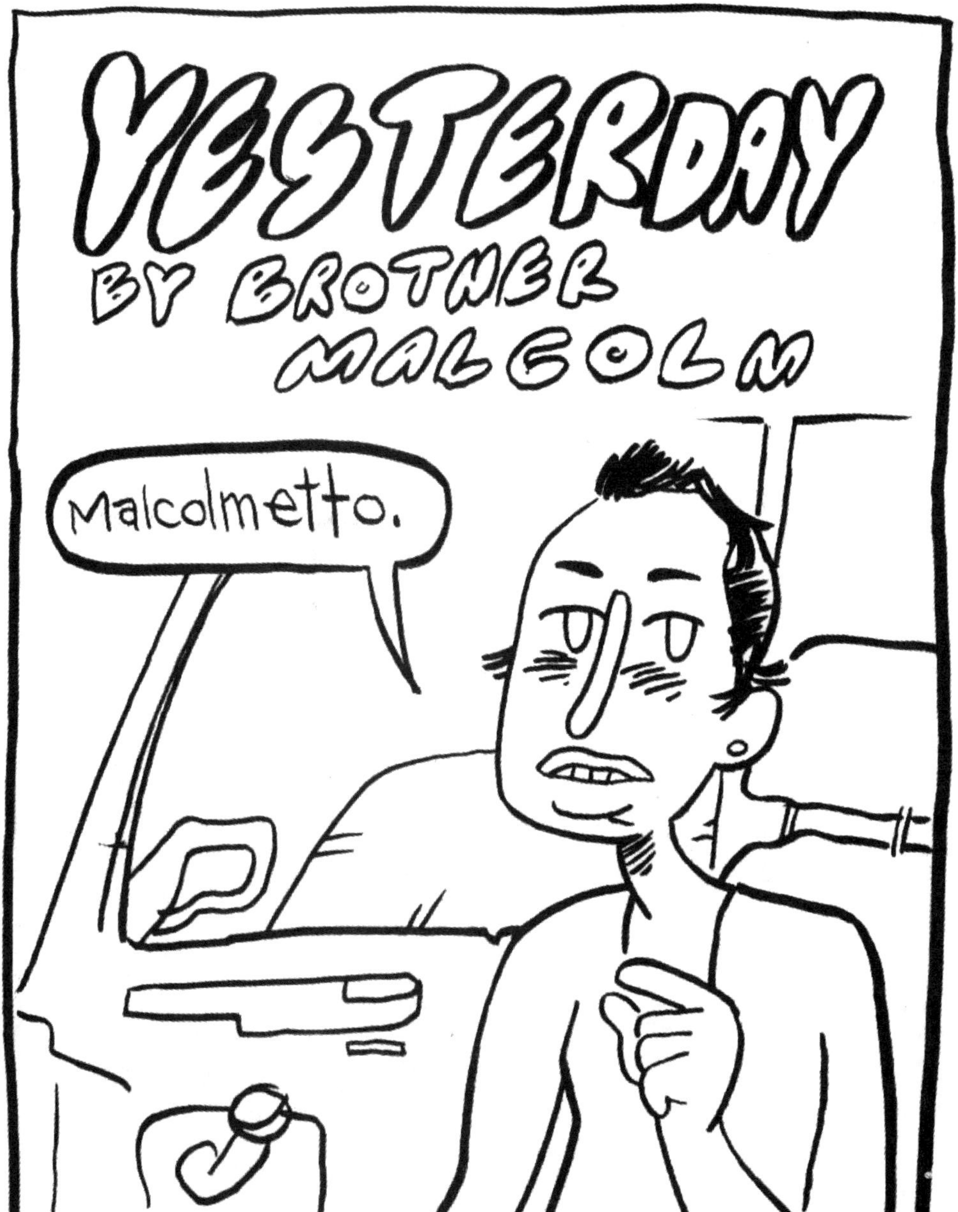
YESTERDAY
BY BROTHER MALCOLM
Malcolmetto.

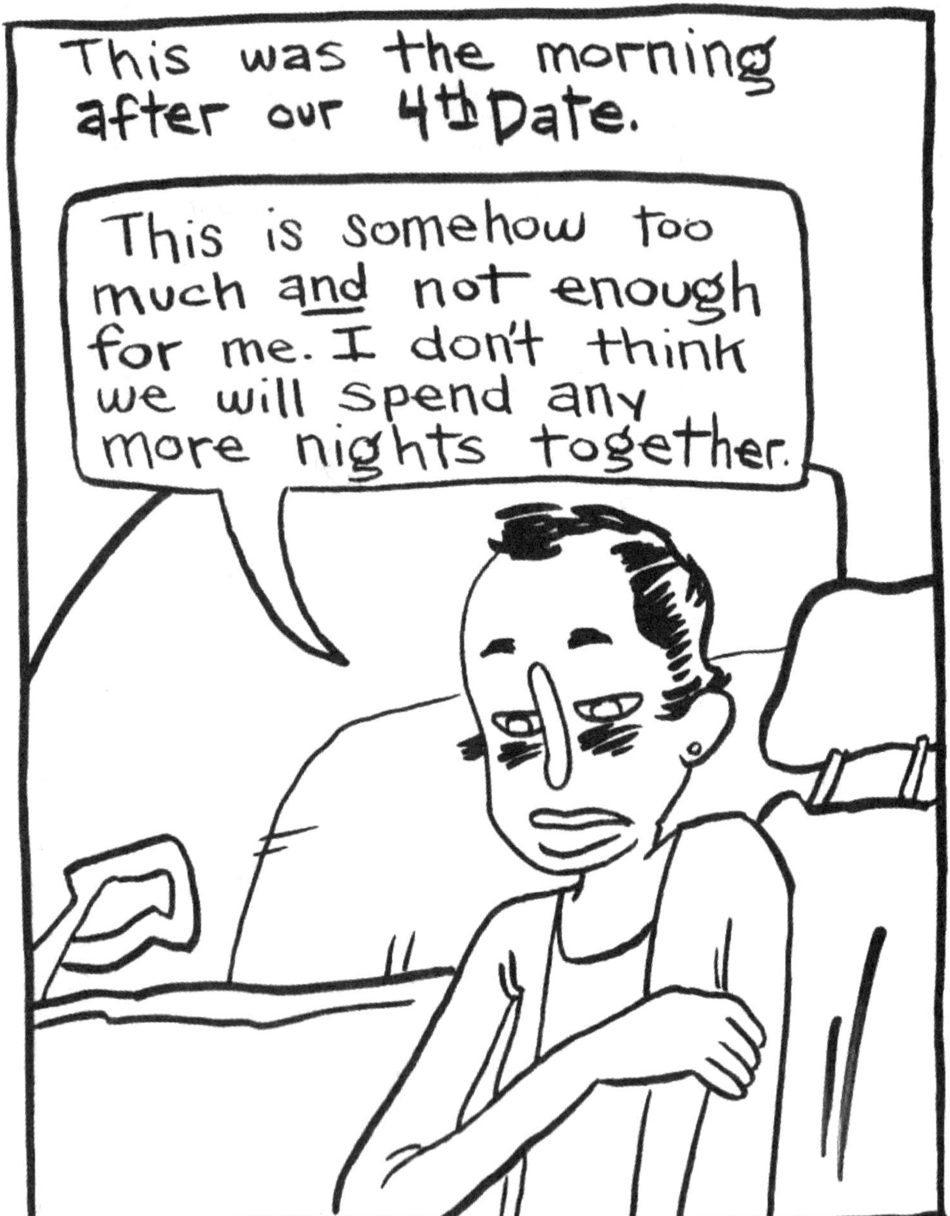
This was the morning after our 4th Date.
This is somehow too much and not enough for me. I don't think we will spend any more nights together.

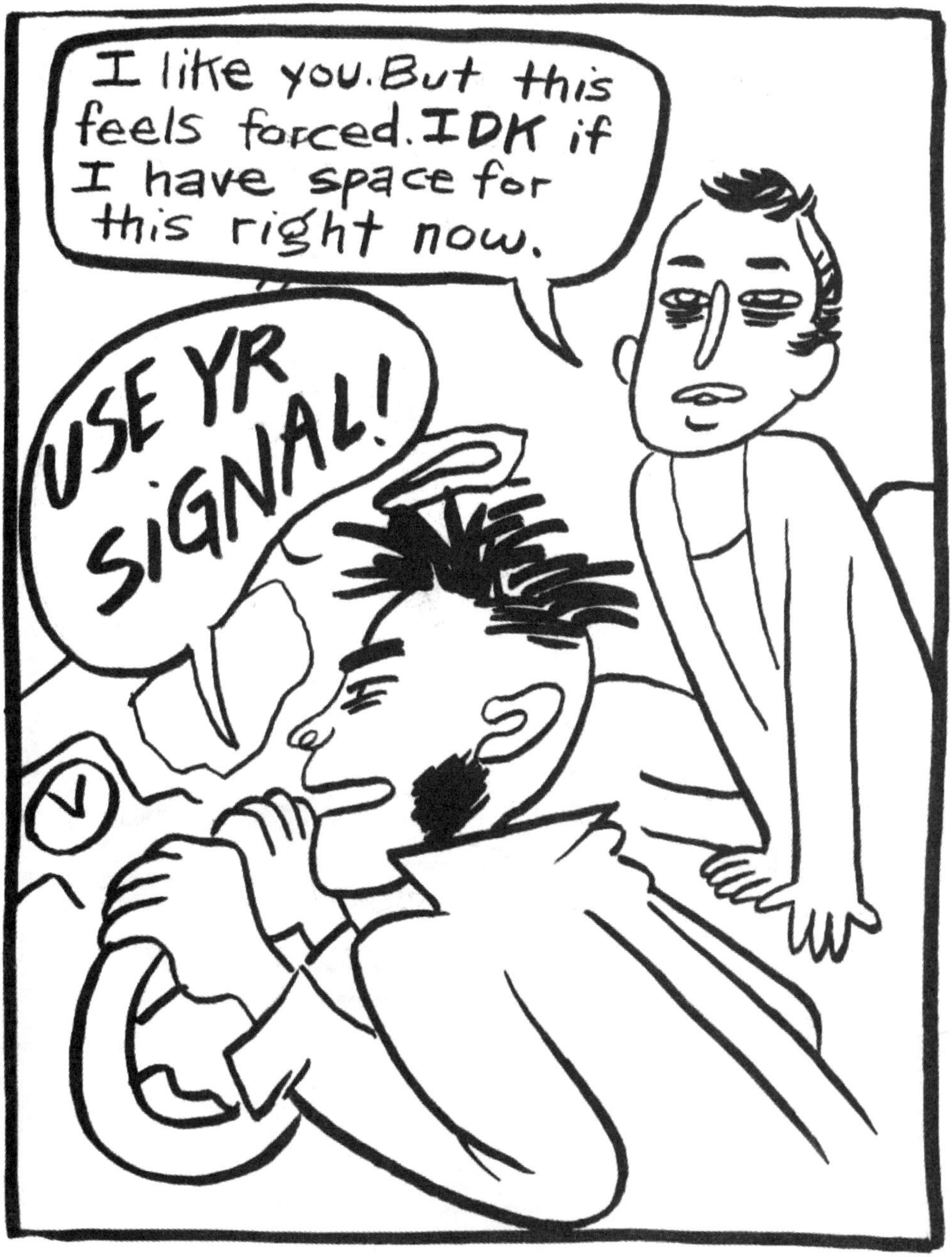
I like you. But this feels forced. IDK if I have space for this right now.
USE YR SIGNAL!

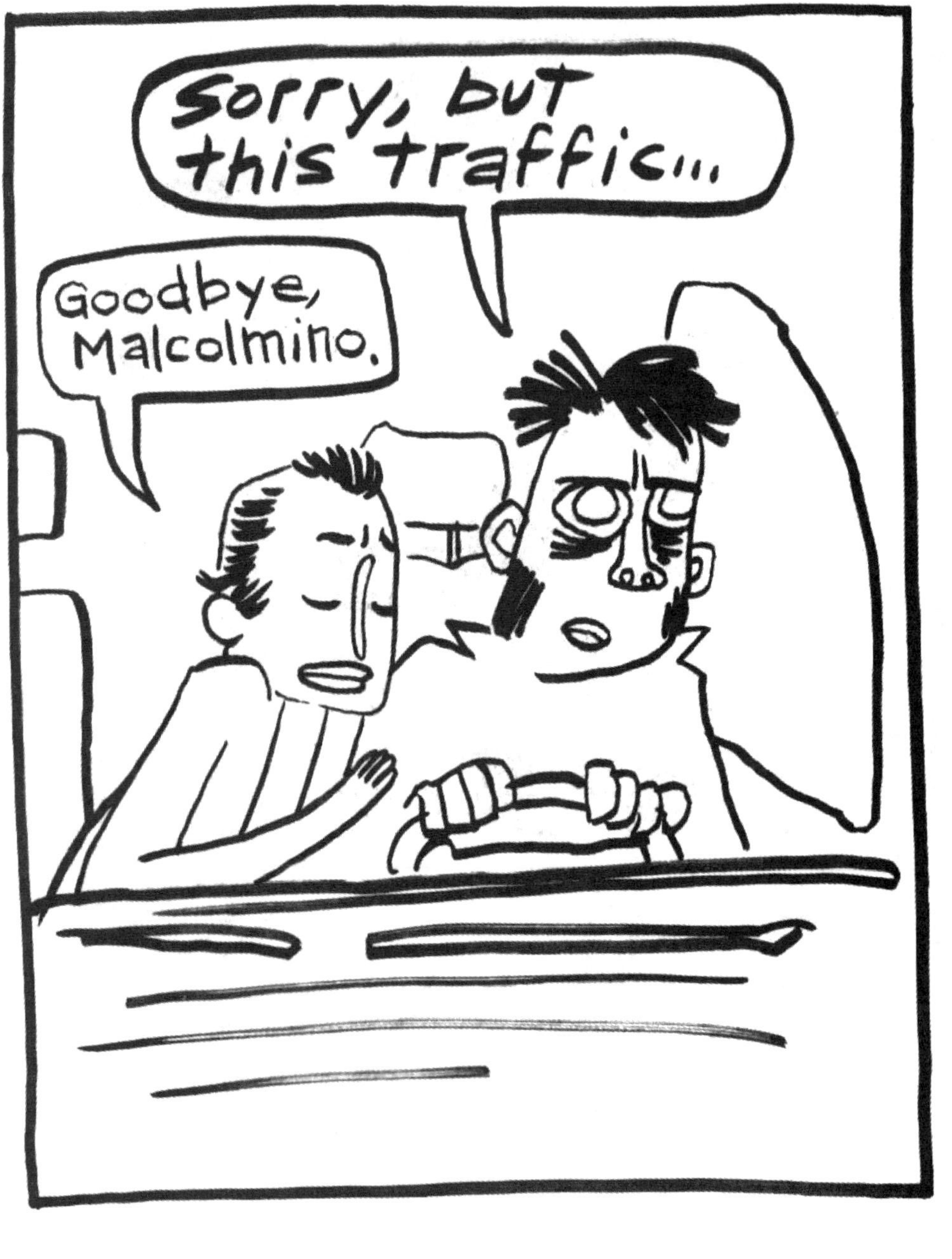
Goodbye, Malcolmino.
Sorry, but this traffic...

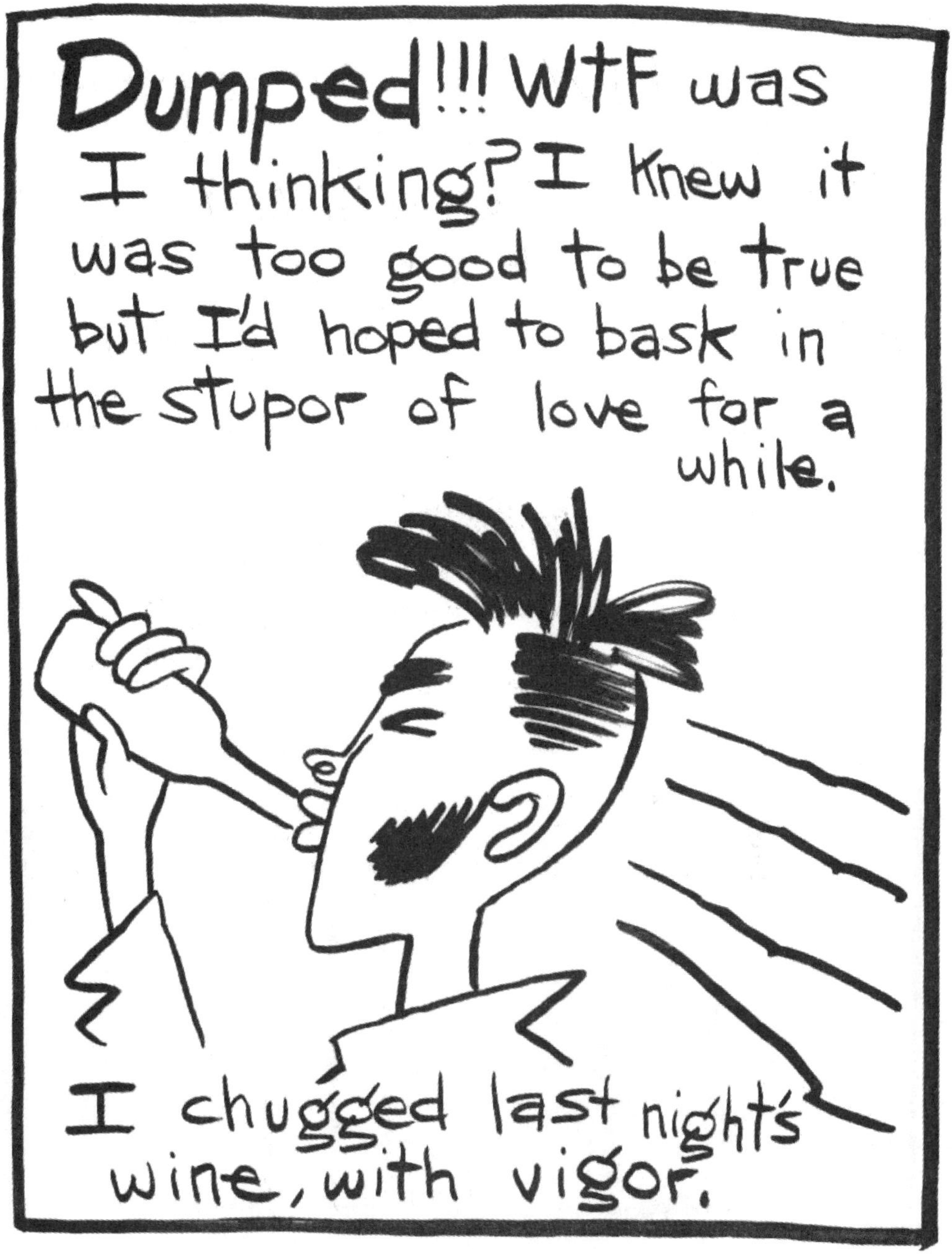
Dumped!!! WTF was I thinking? I knew it was too good to be true but I'd hoped to bask in the stupor of love for a while.
I chugged last night's wine, with vigor.

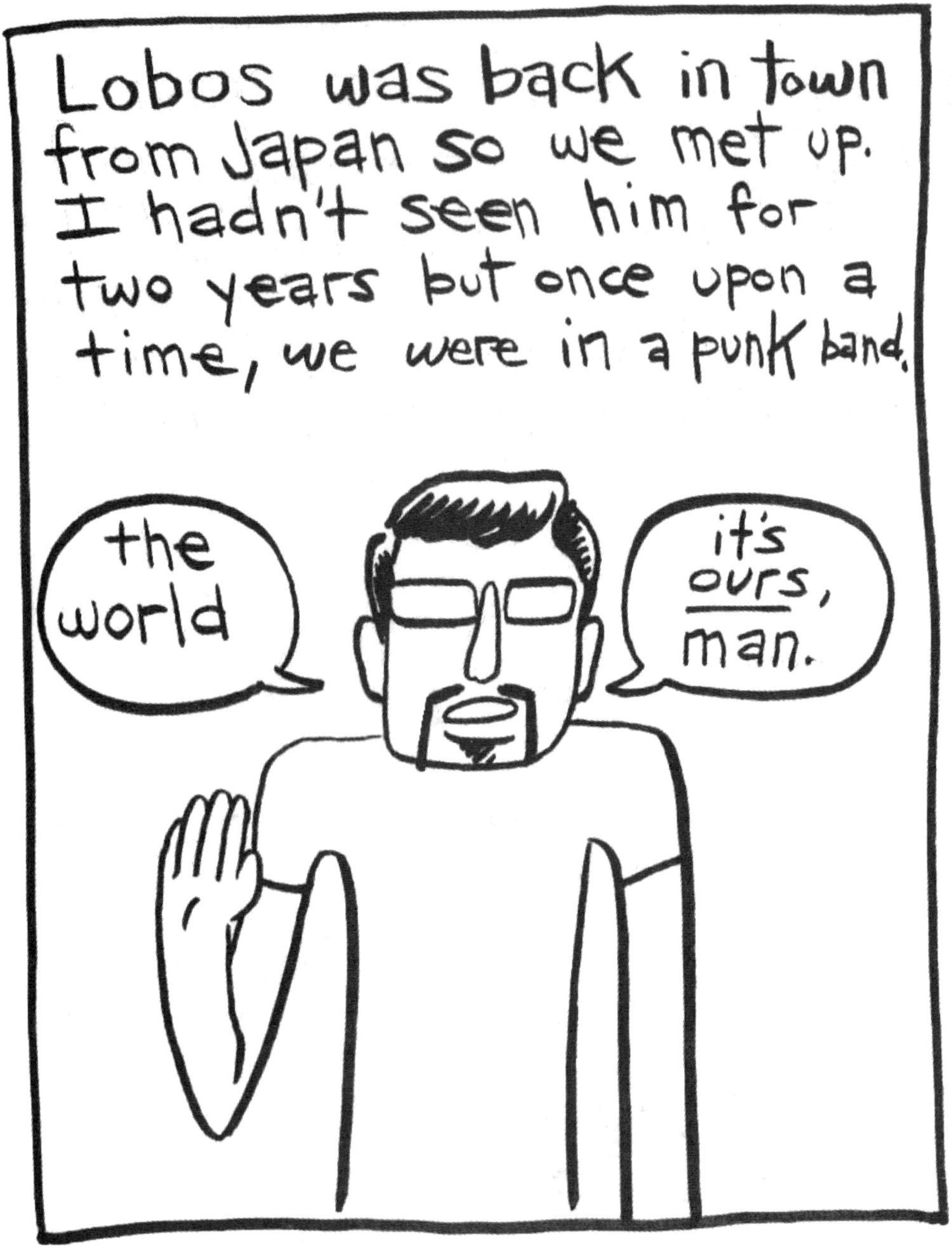
Lobos was back in town from Japan so we met up. I hadn't seen him for two years but once upon a time, we were in a punk band.
the world
it's ours, man.

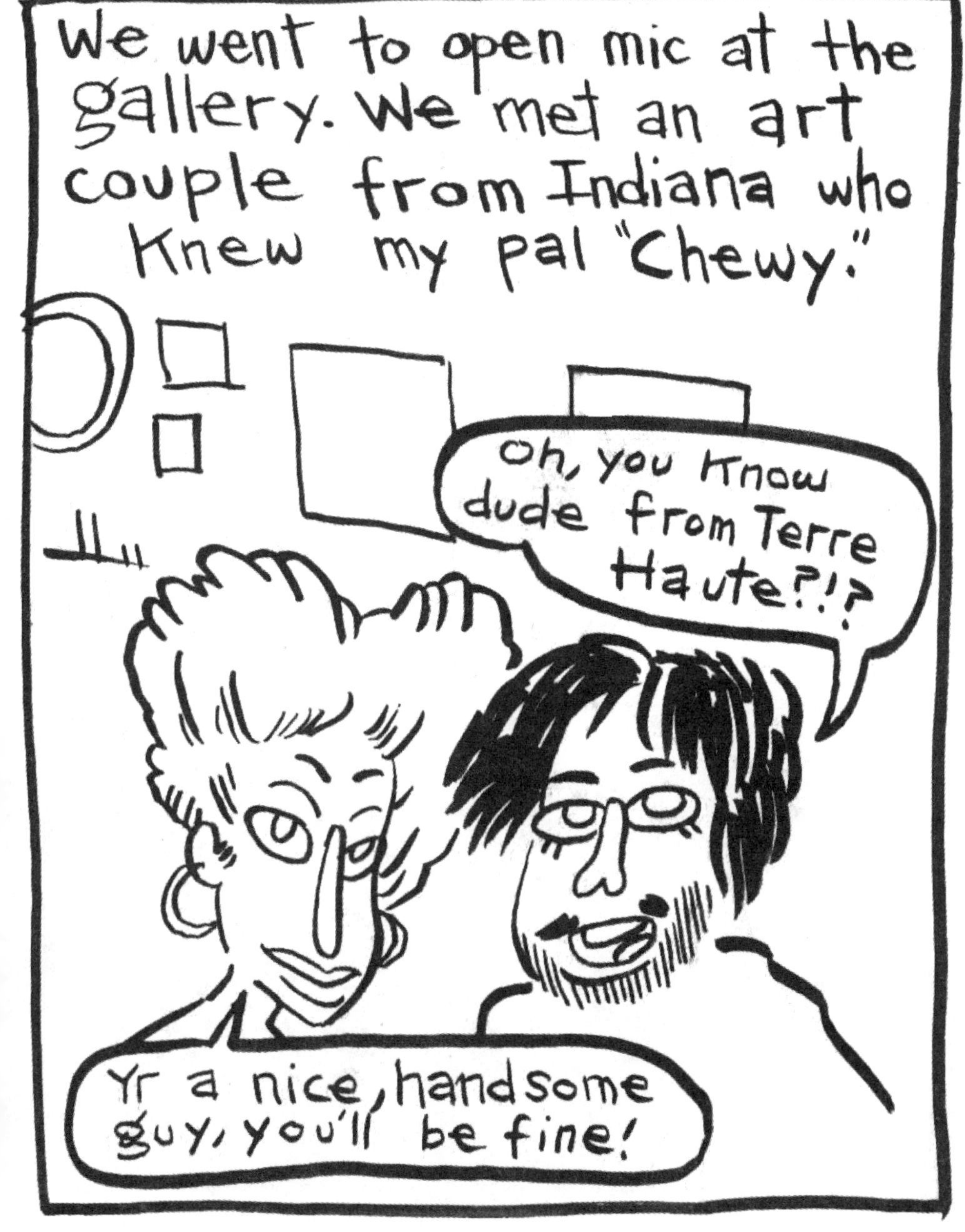
We went to open mic at the gallery. We met an art couple from Indiana who knew my pal "Chewy."
Oh, you know dude from Terre Haute?!?
Yr a nice, handsome guy, you'll be fine!

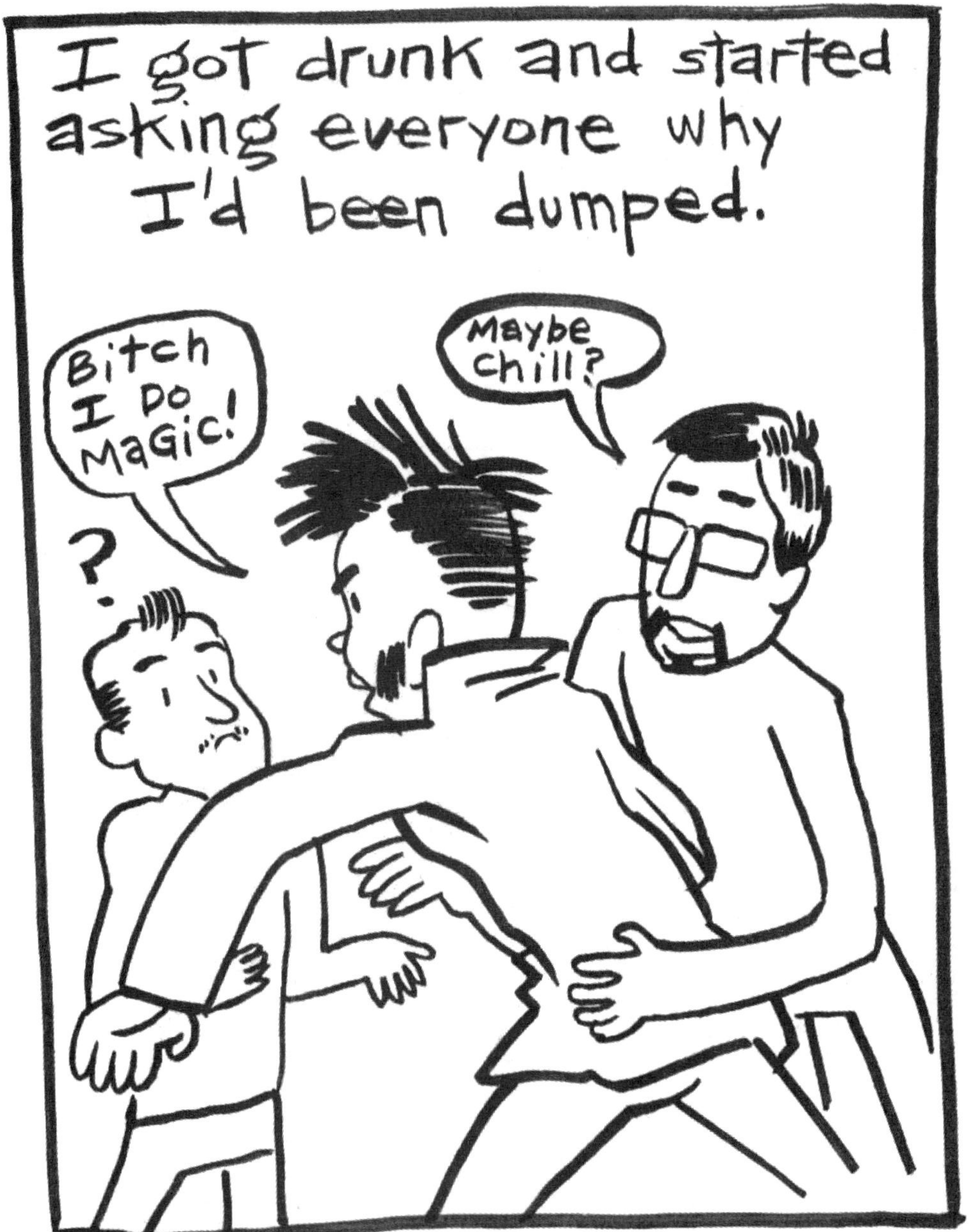
I got drunk and started asking everyone why I'd been dumped.
Bitch I Do MaGic!
?
Maybe chill?

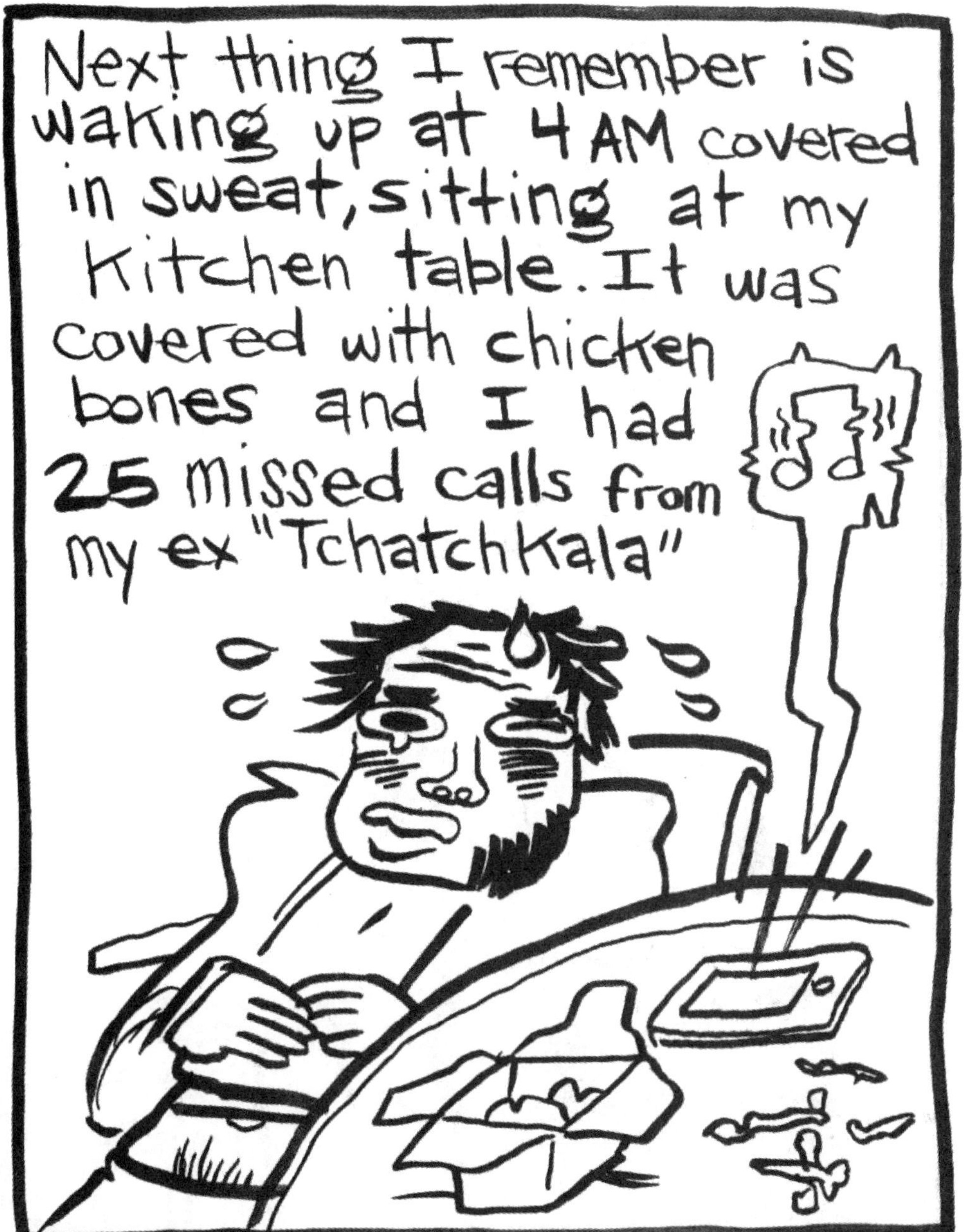
Next thing I remember is waking up at 4 AM covered in sweat, sitting at my kitchen table. It was covered with chicken bones and I had 25 missed calls from my ex "TchatchKala"

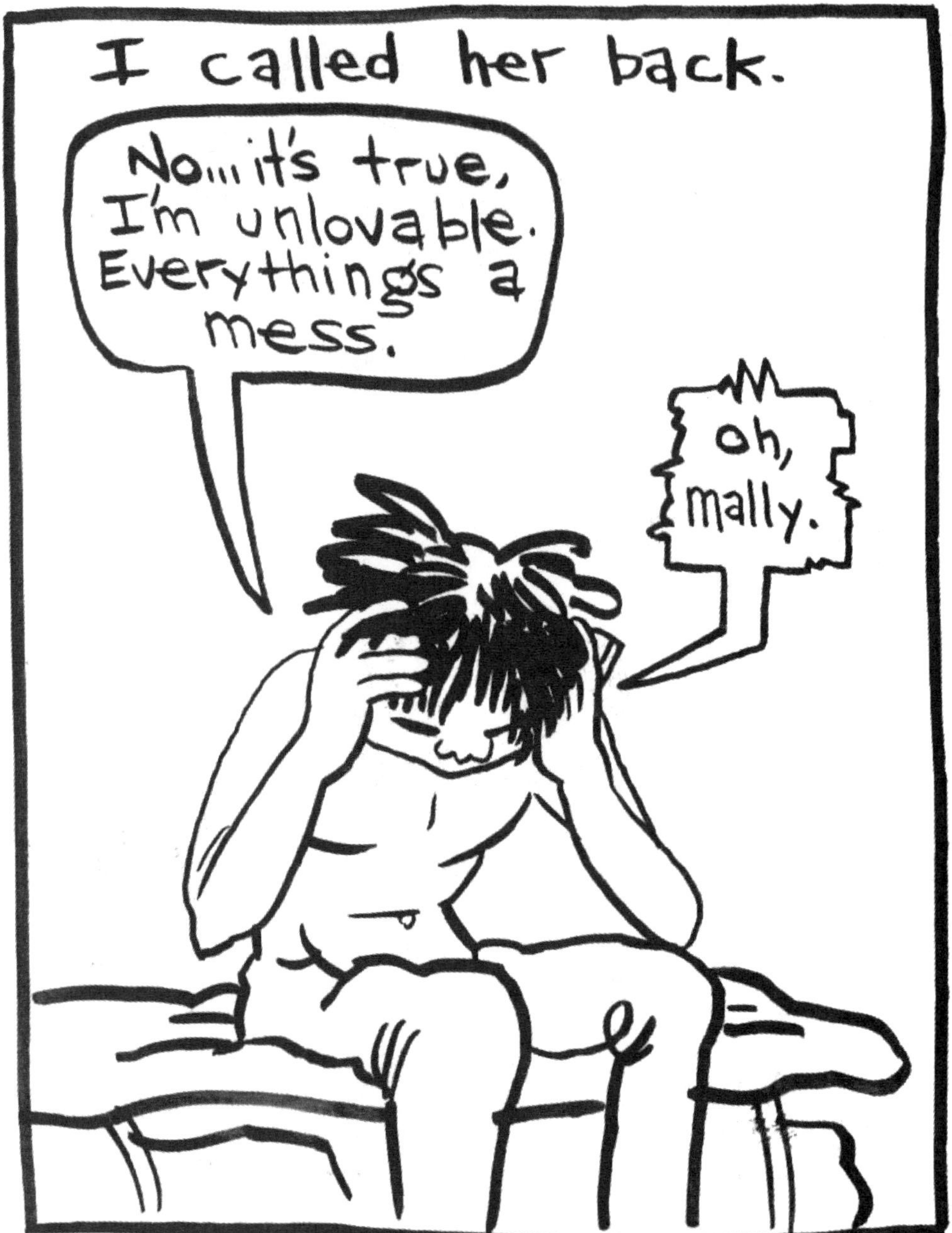
I called her back.
No... it's true, I'm unlovable. Everythings a mess.
oh, mally.

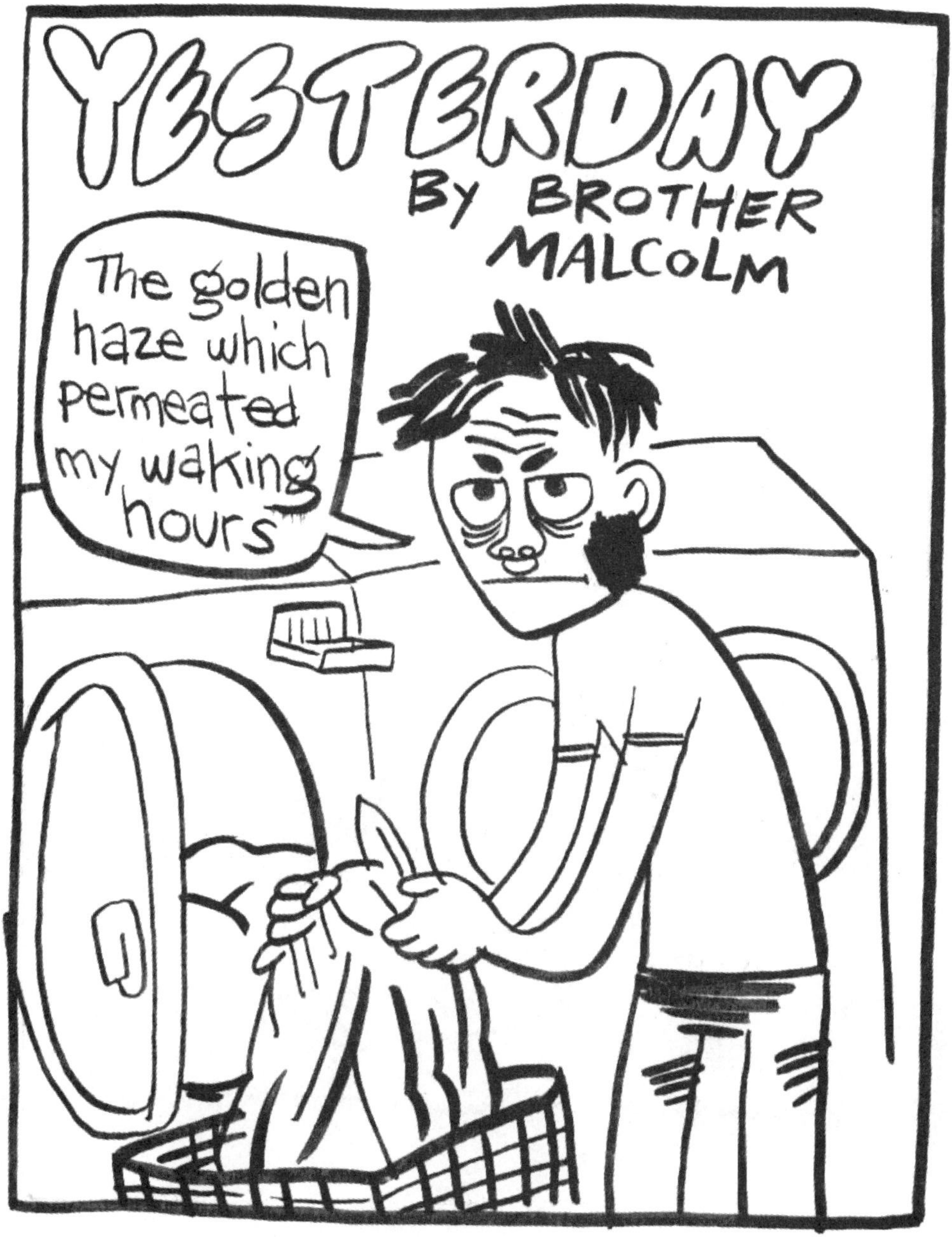
YESTERDAY
BY BROTHER MALCOLM
The golden haze which permeated my waking hours

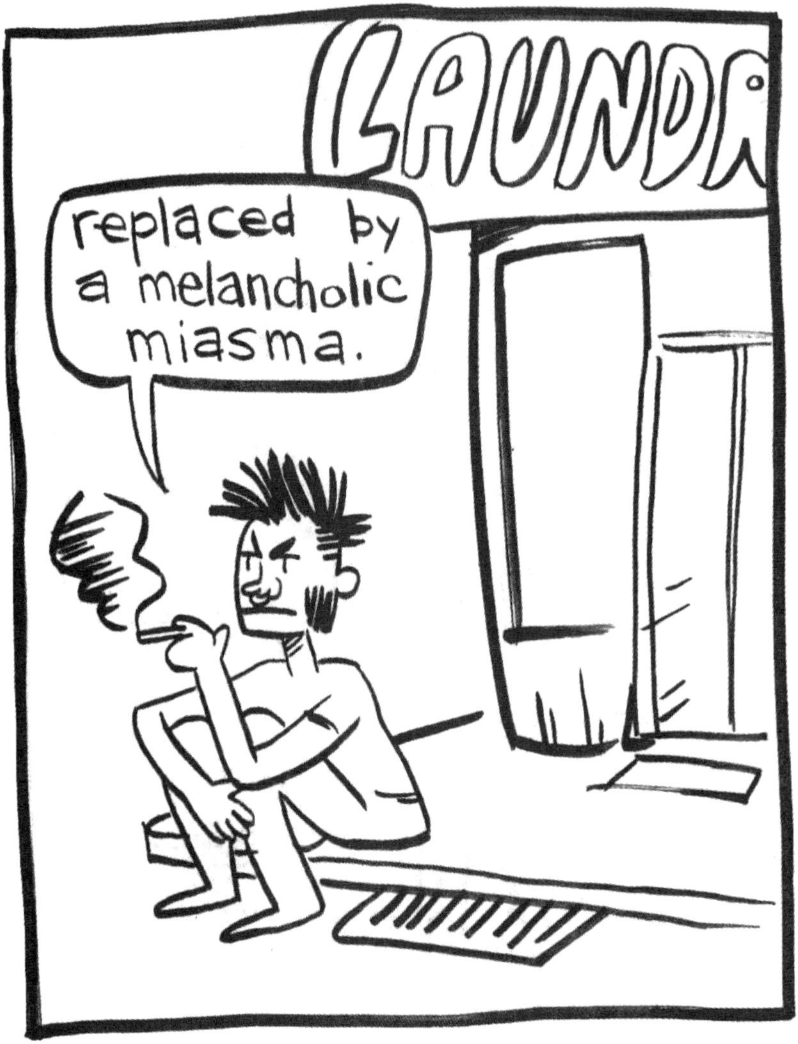
LAUNDR
replaced by a melancholic miasma.

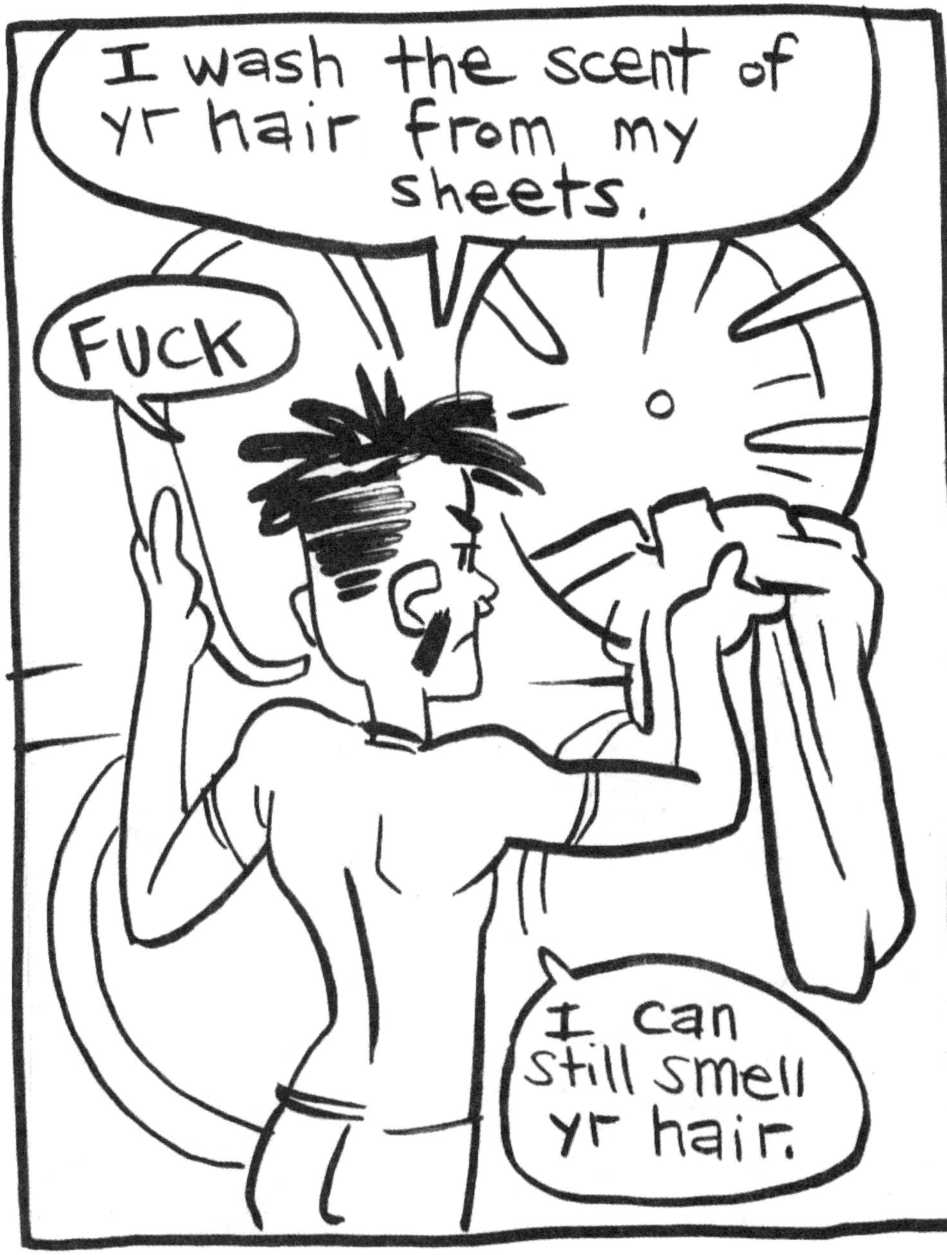
I wash the scent of yr hair from my sheets.
FUCK
I can still smell yr hair.

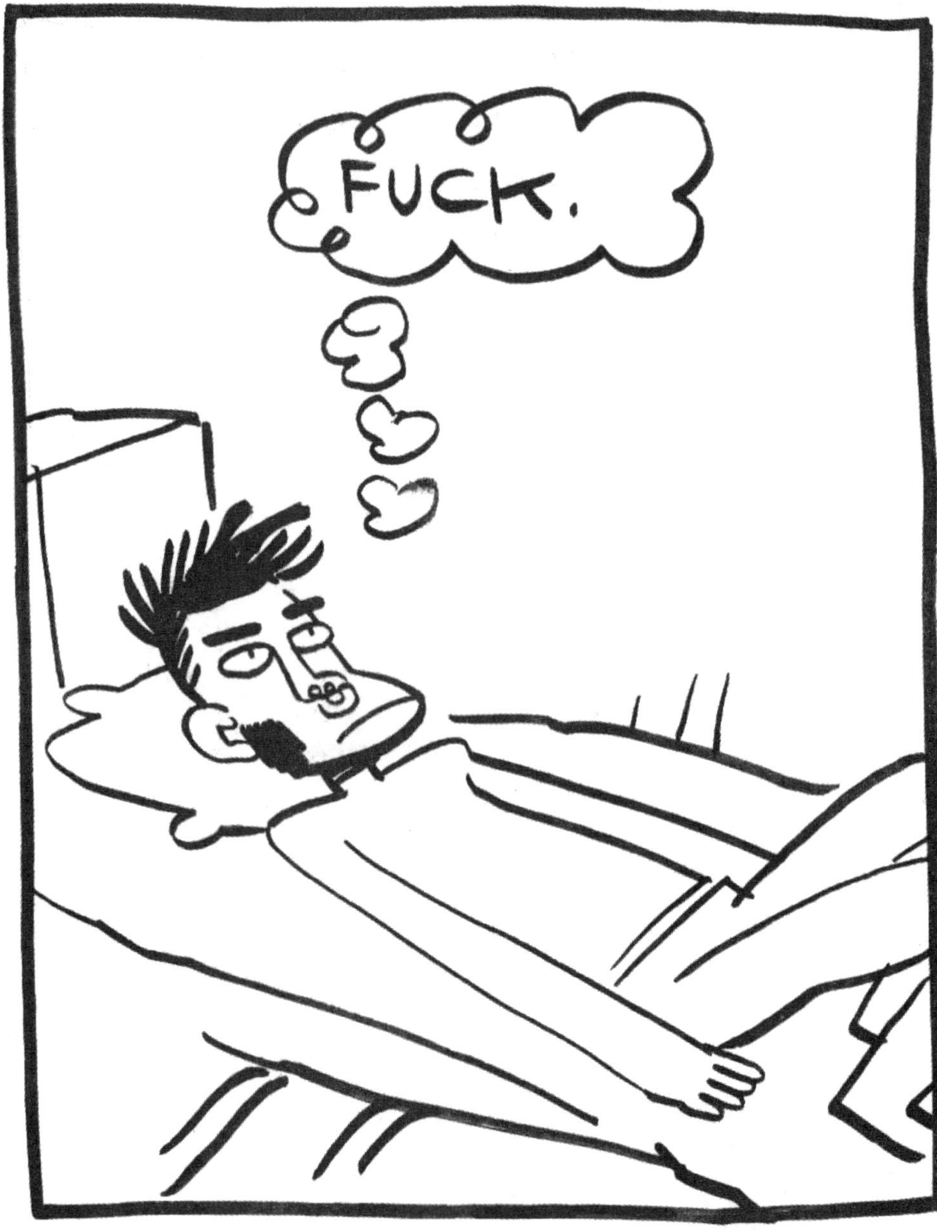
FUCK.

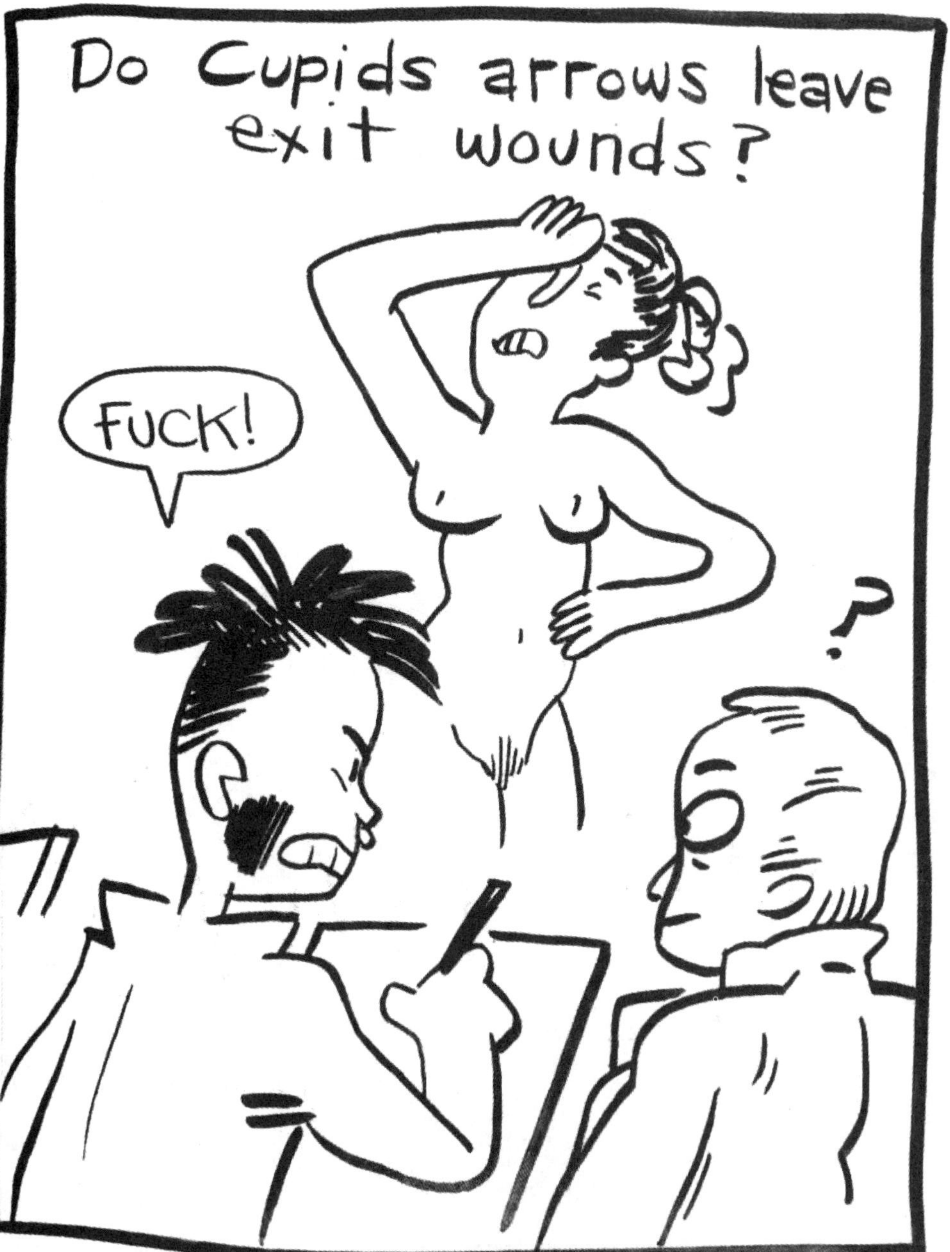
Do Cupids arrows leave exit wounds?
FUCK!
?

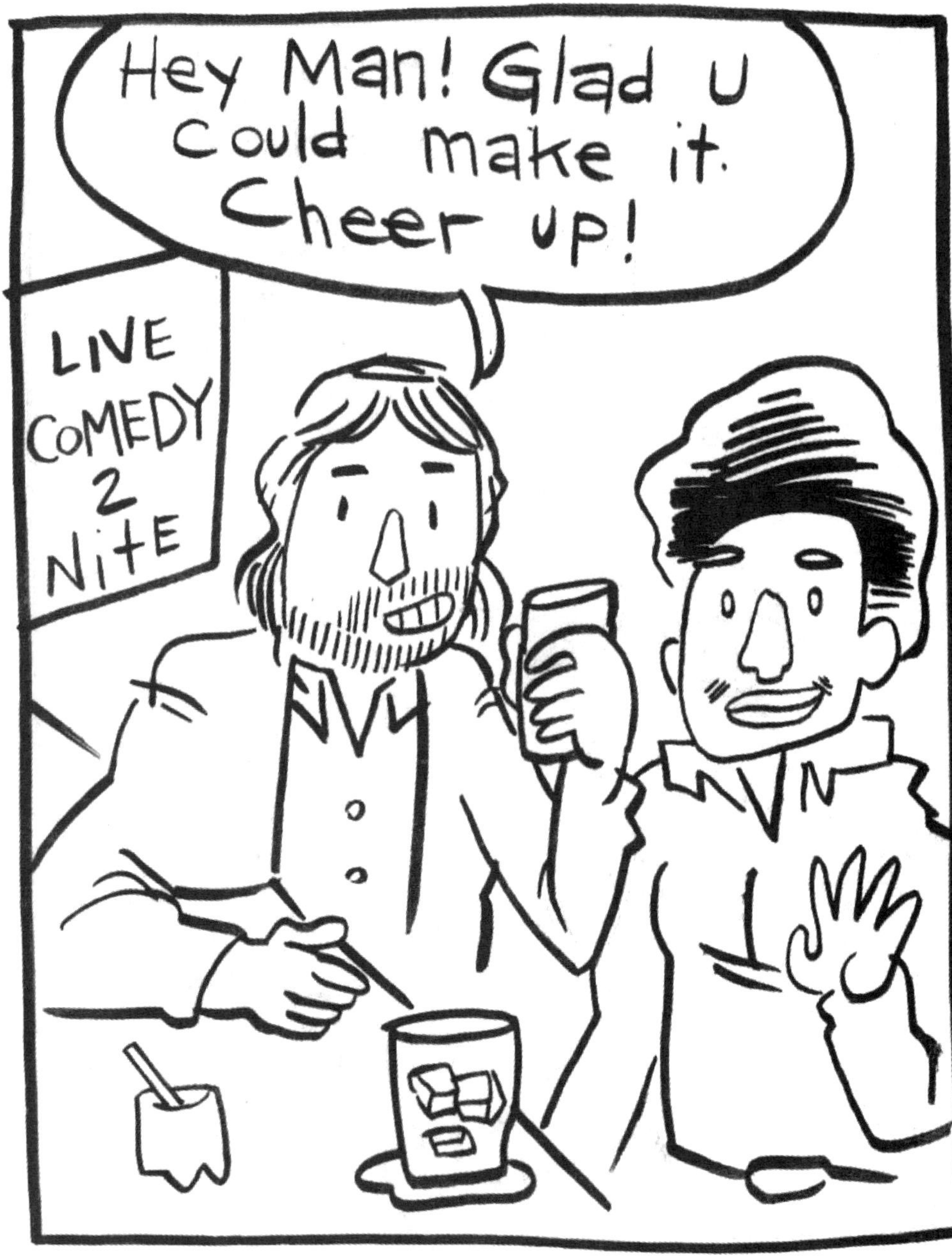
Hey Man! Glad U could make it. Cheer up!
LIVE COMEDY 2 NITE

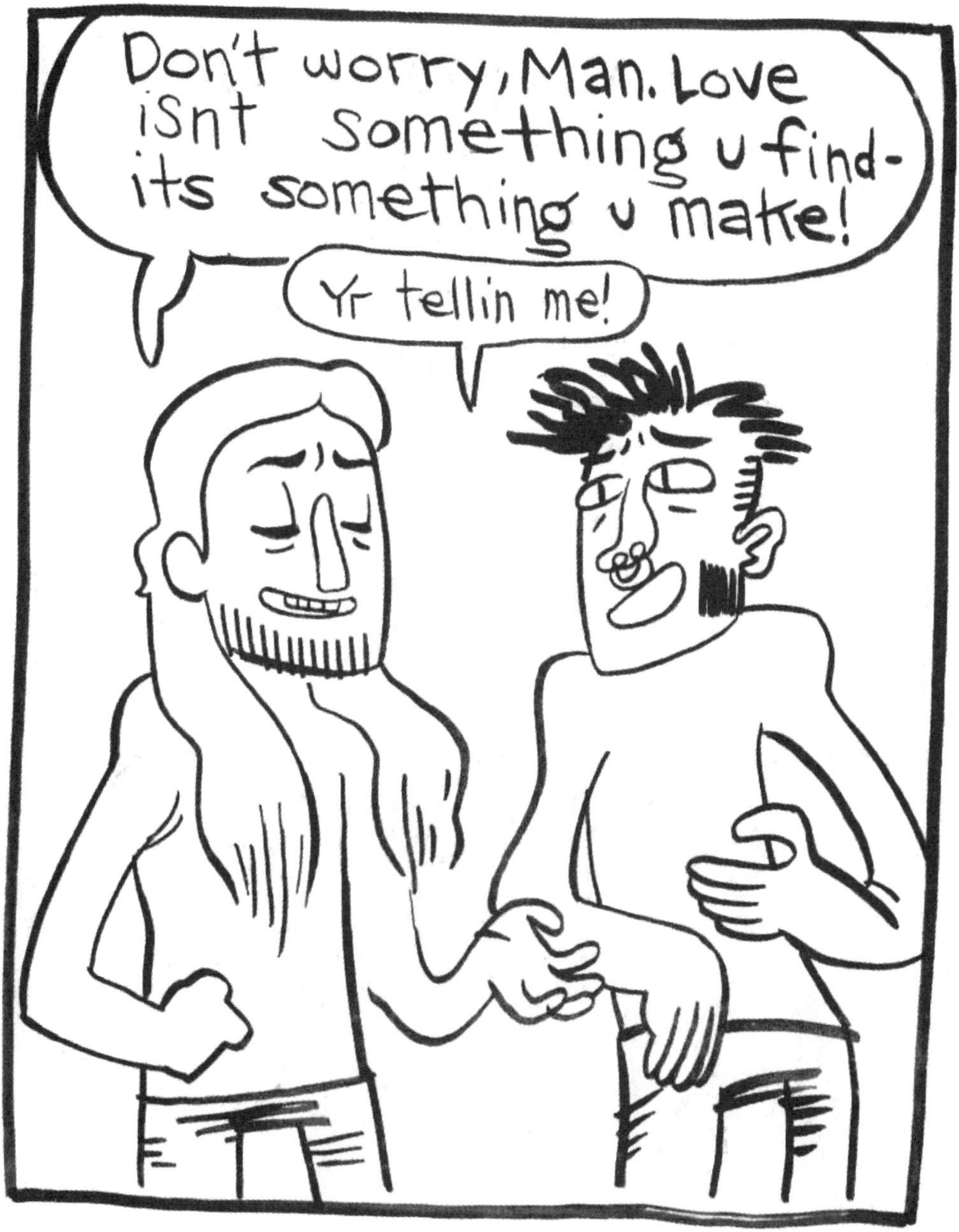
Don't worry, Man. Love isnt something u find- its something u make!
Yr tellin me!

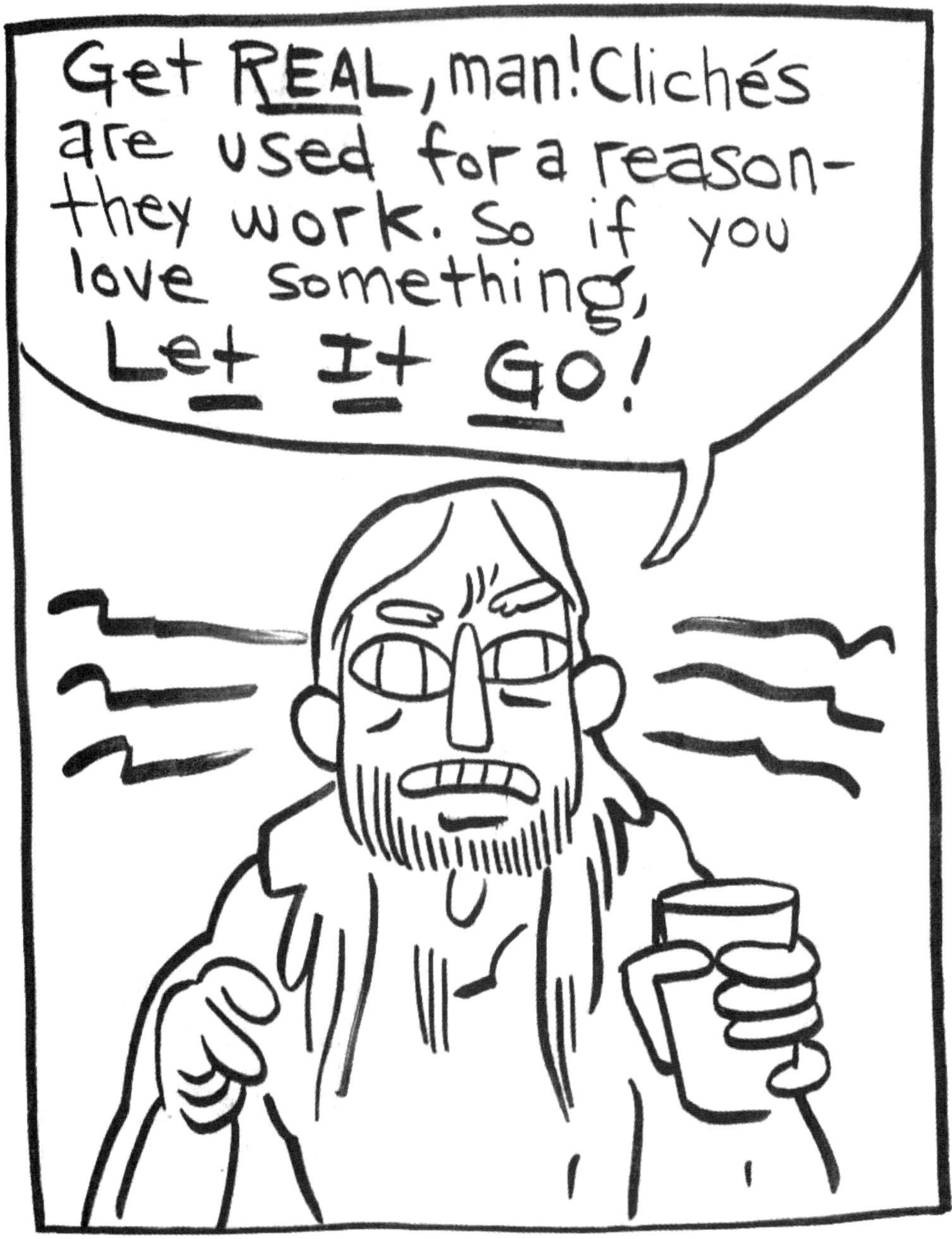
Get REAL, man! Clichés are used for a reason- they work. So if you love something, Let It GO!

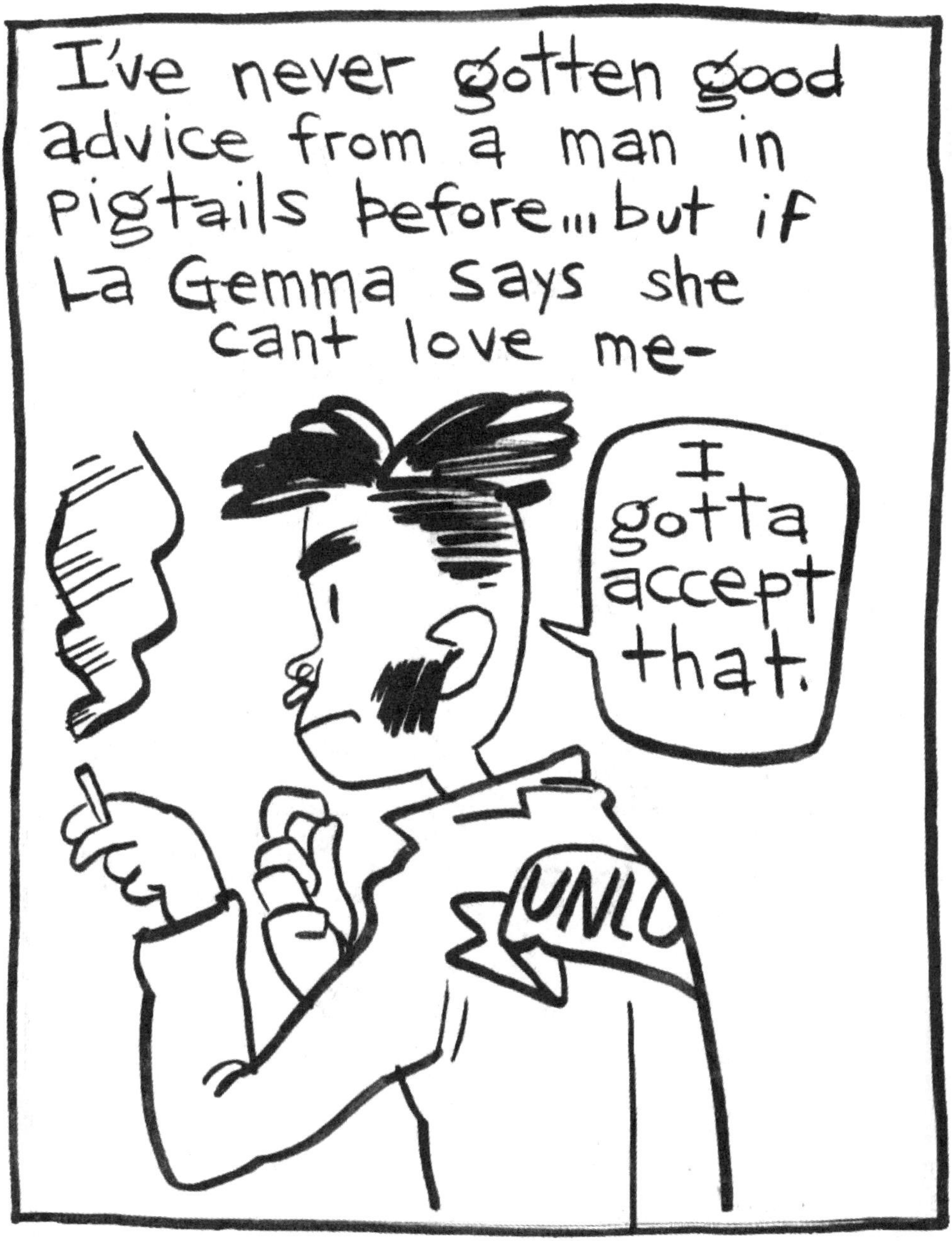
I've never gotten good advice from a man in pigtails before... but if La Gemma says she cant love me-
I gotta accept that.
UNLO

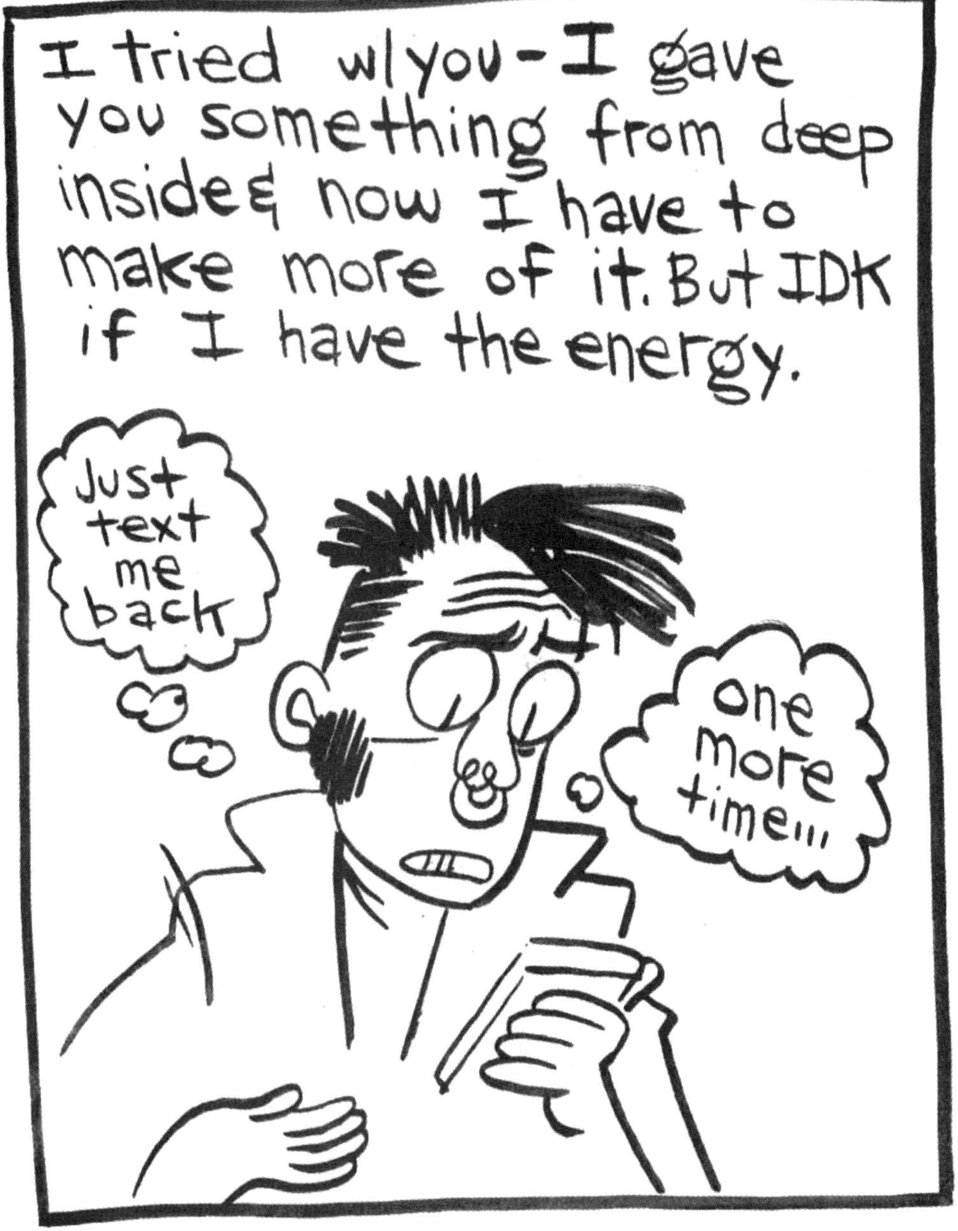
I tried w/you - I gave you something from deep inside & now I have to make more of it. But IDK if I have the energy.
Just text me back
one more time...

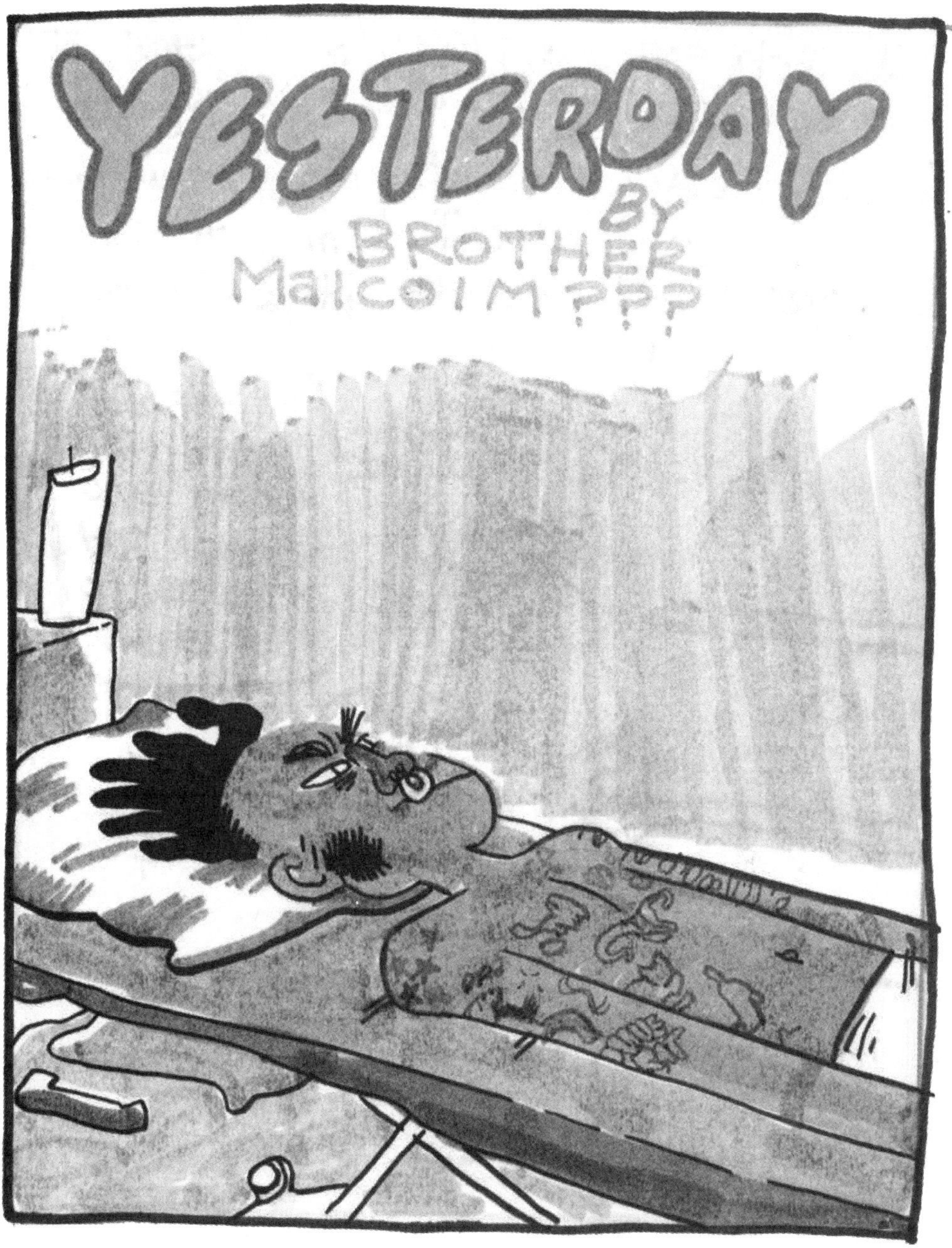
YESTERDAY
BY
BROTHER
Malcolm ???

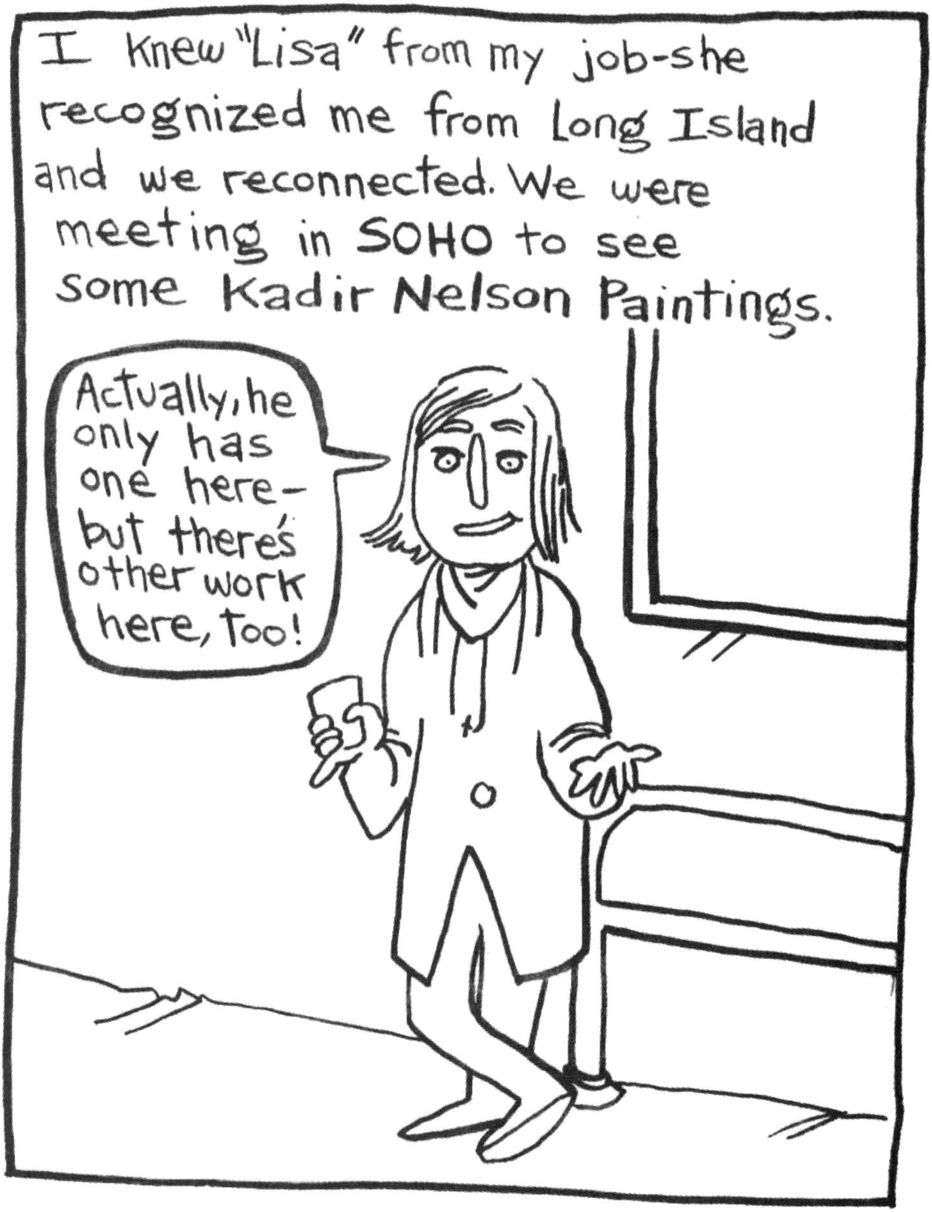
I knew "Lisa" from my job-she recognized me from Long Island and we reconnected. We were meeting in SOHO to see some Kadir Nelson Paintings.
Actually, he only has one here-but there's other work here, too!

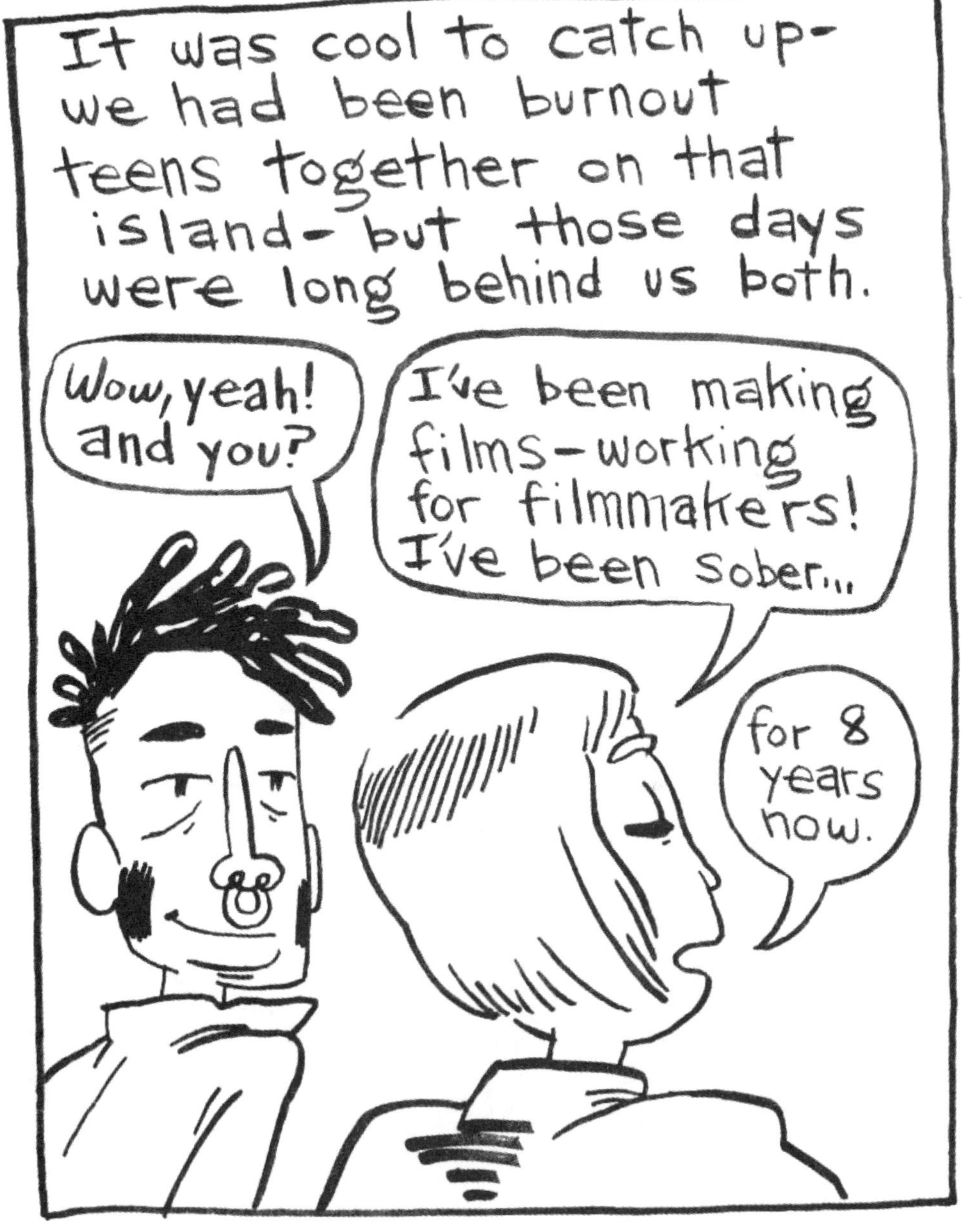
It was cool to catch up-we had been burnout teens together on that island- but those days were long behind us both.
Wow, yeah! and you?
I've been making films-working for filmmakers! I've been sober...
for 8 years now.

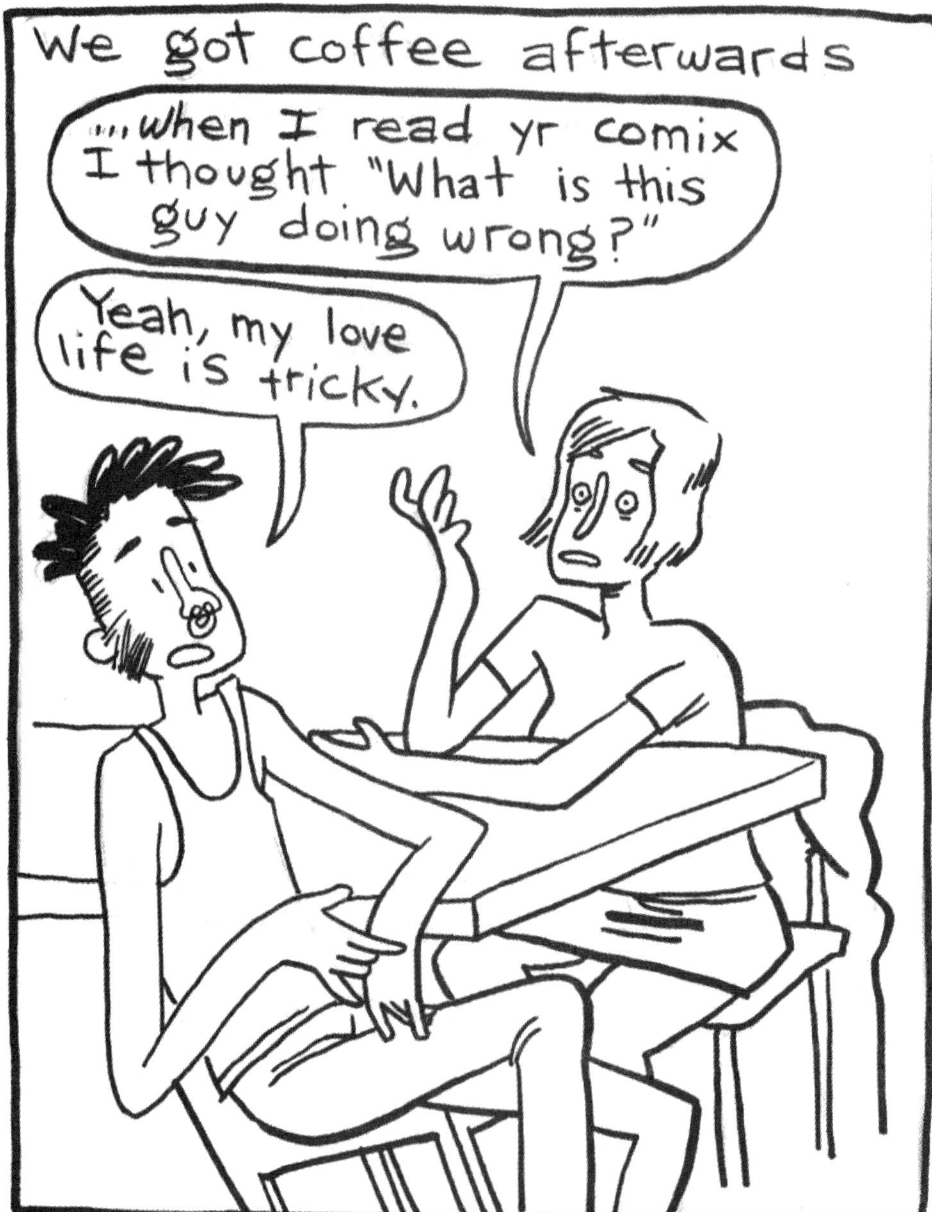
We got coffee afterwards
...when I read yr comix I thought "What is this guy doing wrong?"
Yeah, my love life is tricky.

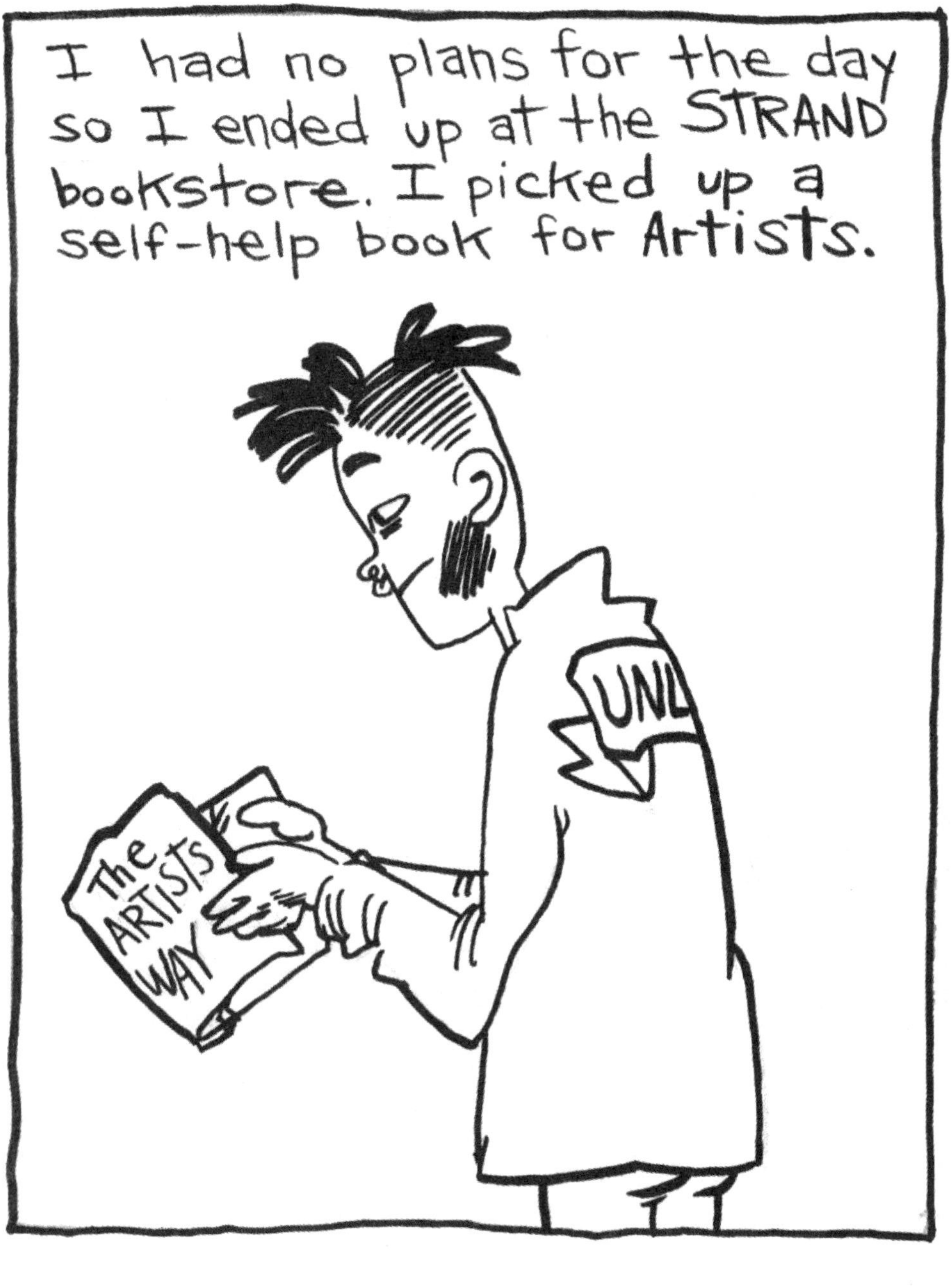
I had no plans for the day so I ended up at the STRAND bookstore. I picked up a self-help book for Artists.
UNL
The ARTISTS WAY

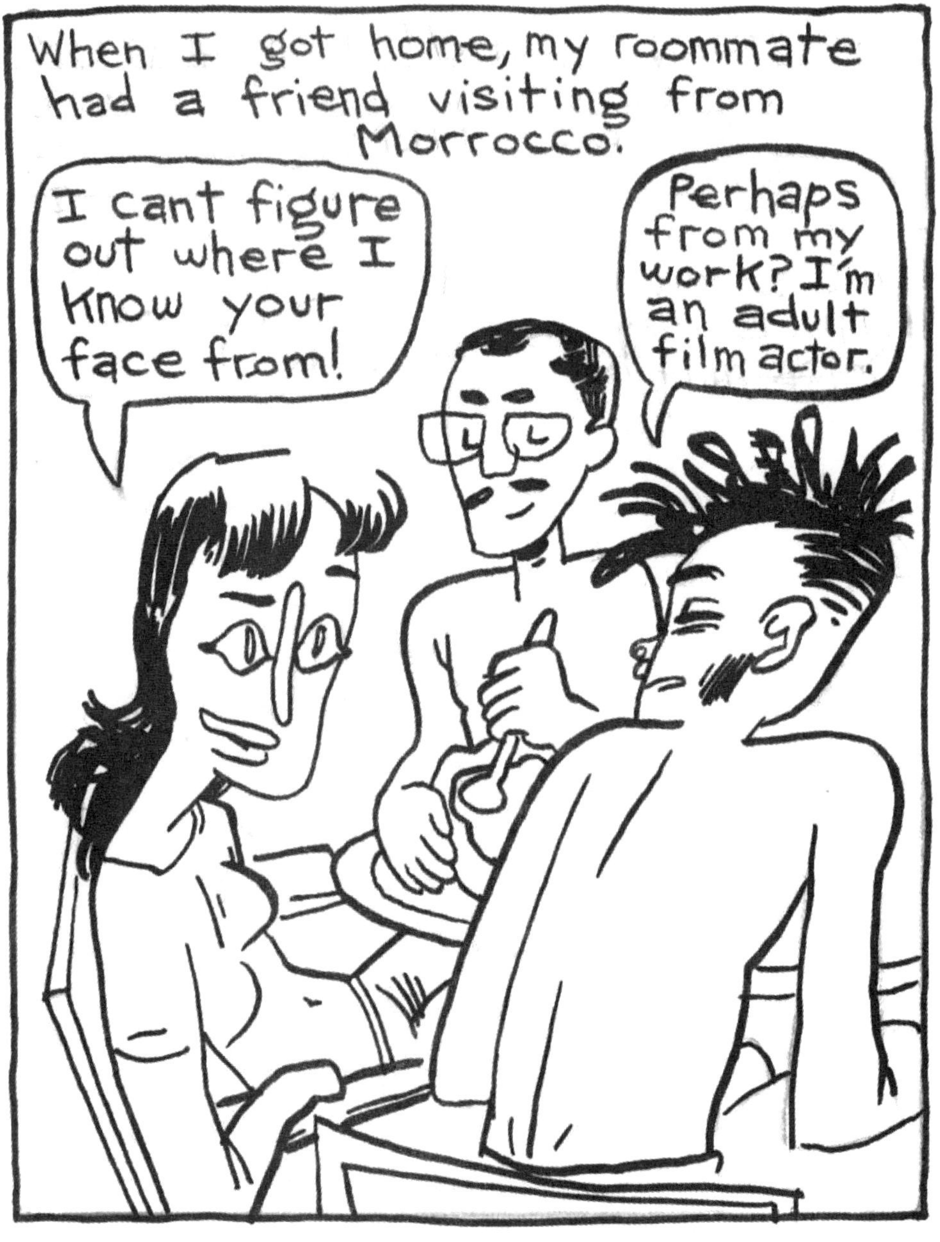
When I got home, my roommate had a friend visiting from Morrocco.
I cant figure out where I know your face from!
Perhaps from my work? I'm an adult film actor.

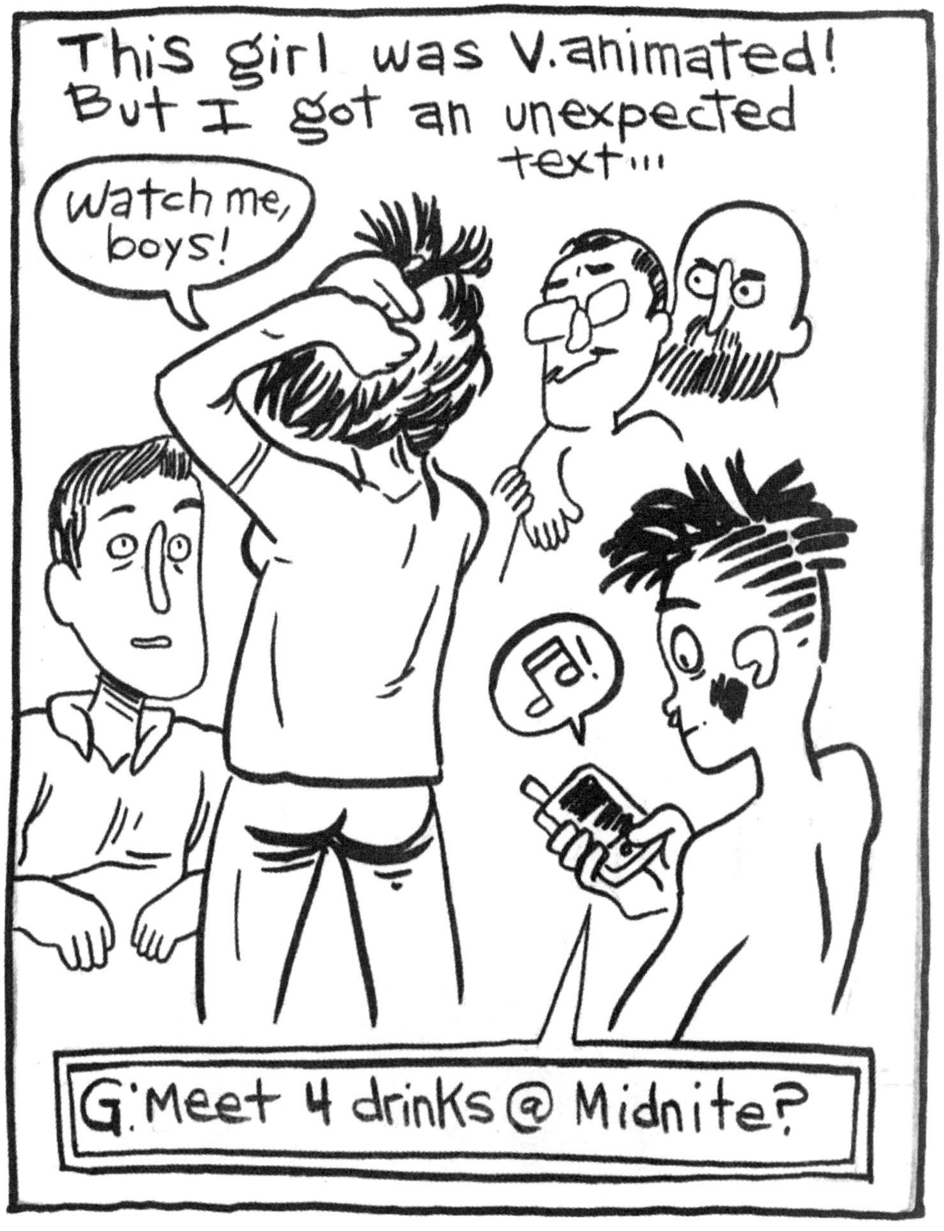
This girl was V. animated! But I got an unexpected text...
Watch me, boys!
♫!
G: Meet 4 drinks @ Midnite?

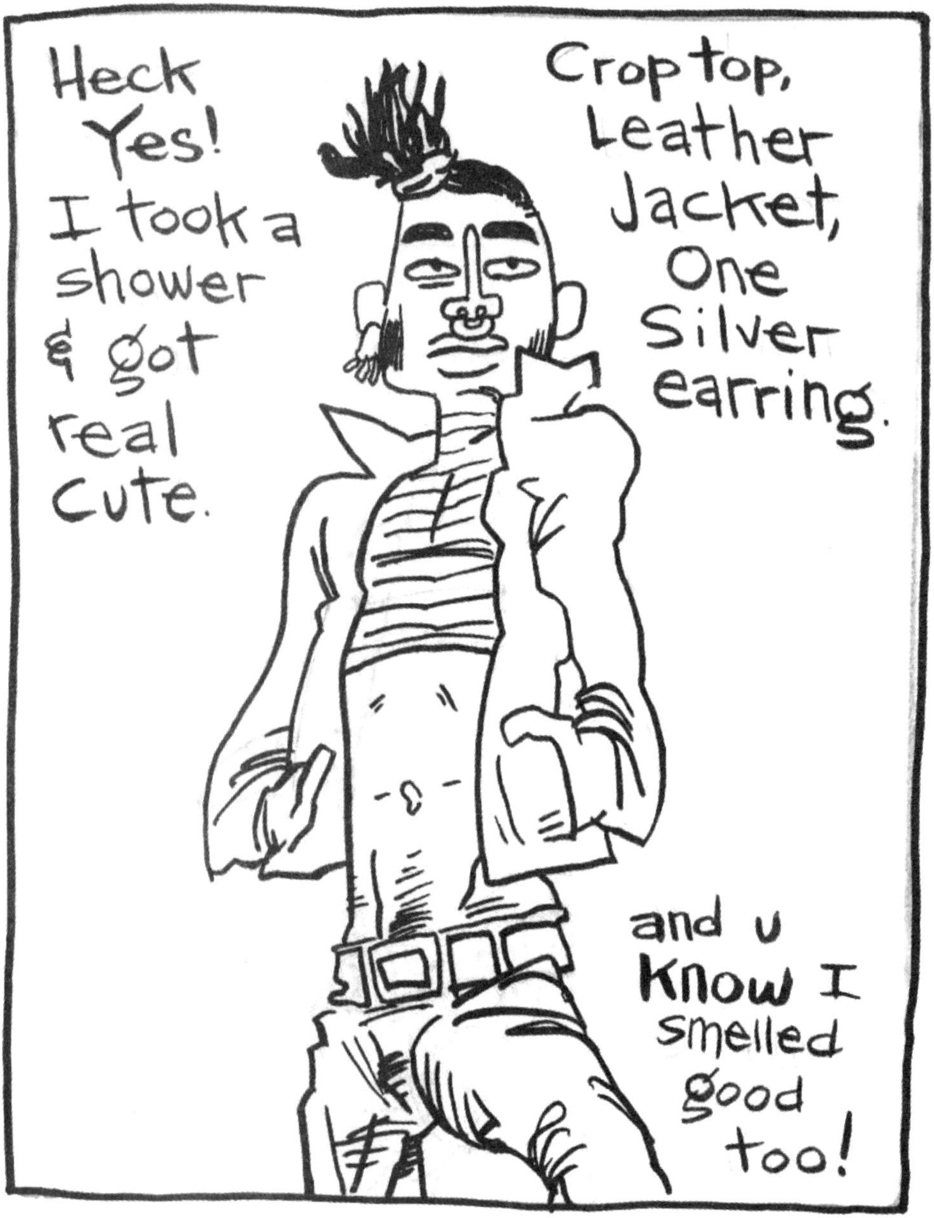
Heck Yes! I took a shower & got real cute.
Crop top, Leather Jacket, One Silver earring.
and u Know I smelled good too!

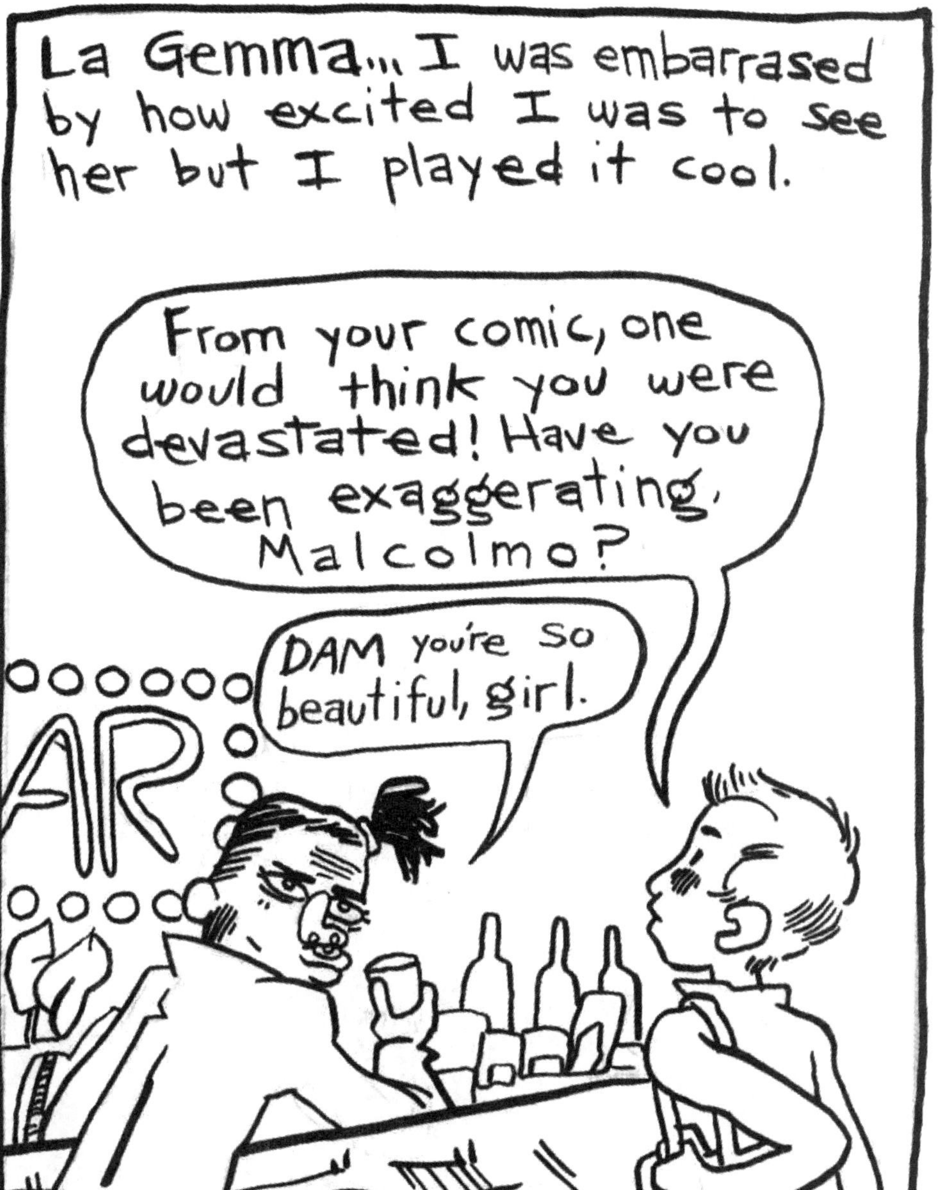
La Gemma... I was embarrased by how excited I was to see her but I played it cool.
From your comic, one would think you were devastated! Have you been exaggerating, Malcolmo?
DAM you're so beautiful, girl.

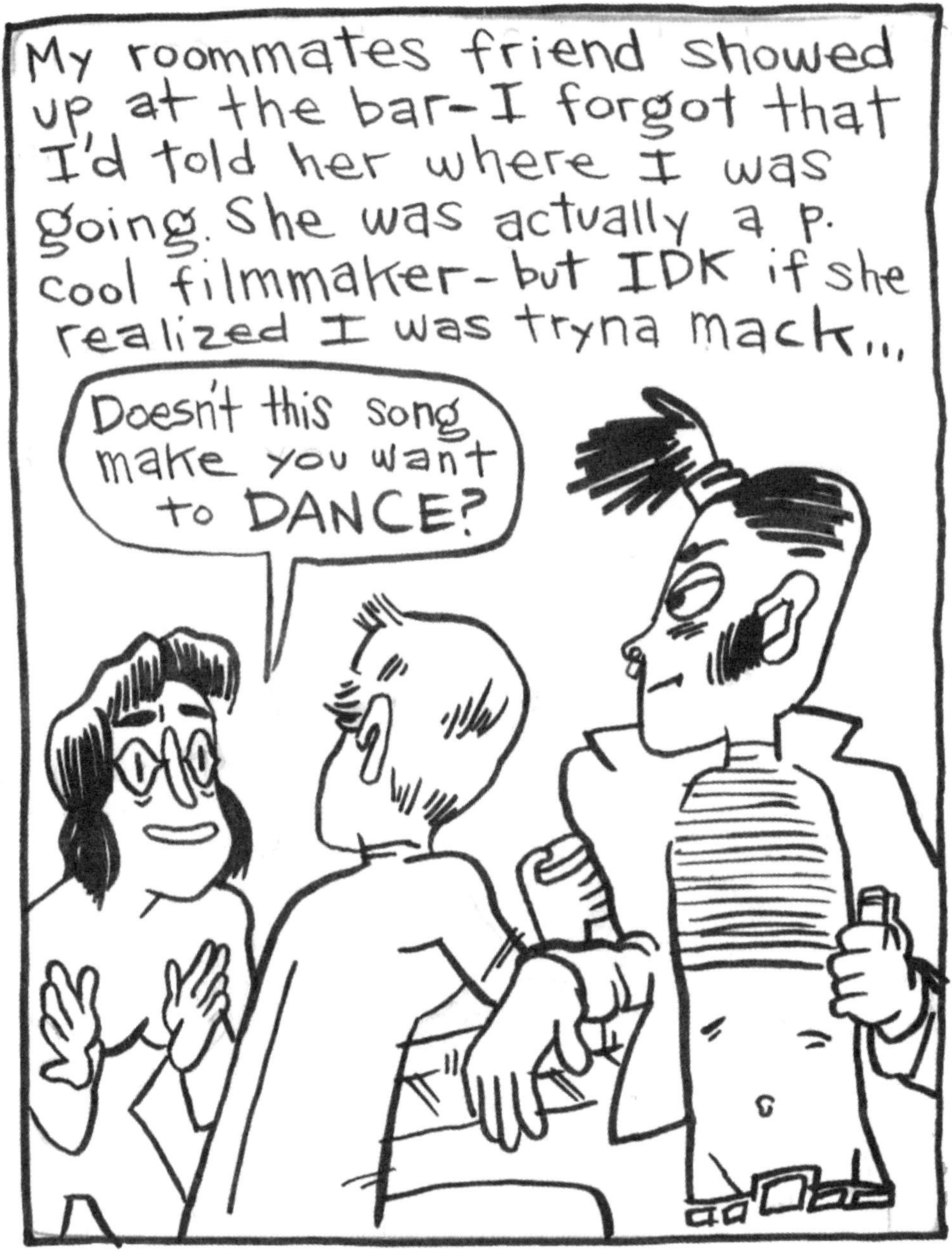
My roommates friend showed up at the bar- I forgot that I'd told her where I was going. She was actually a p. cool filmmaker- but IDK if she realized I was tryna mack...
Doesn't this song make you want to DANCE?

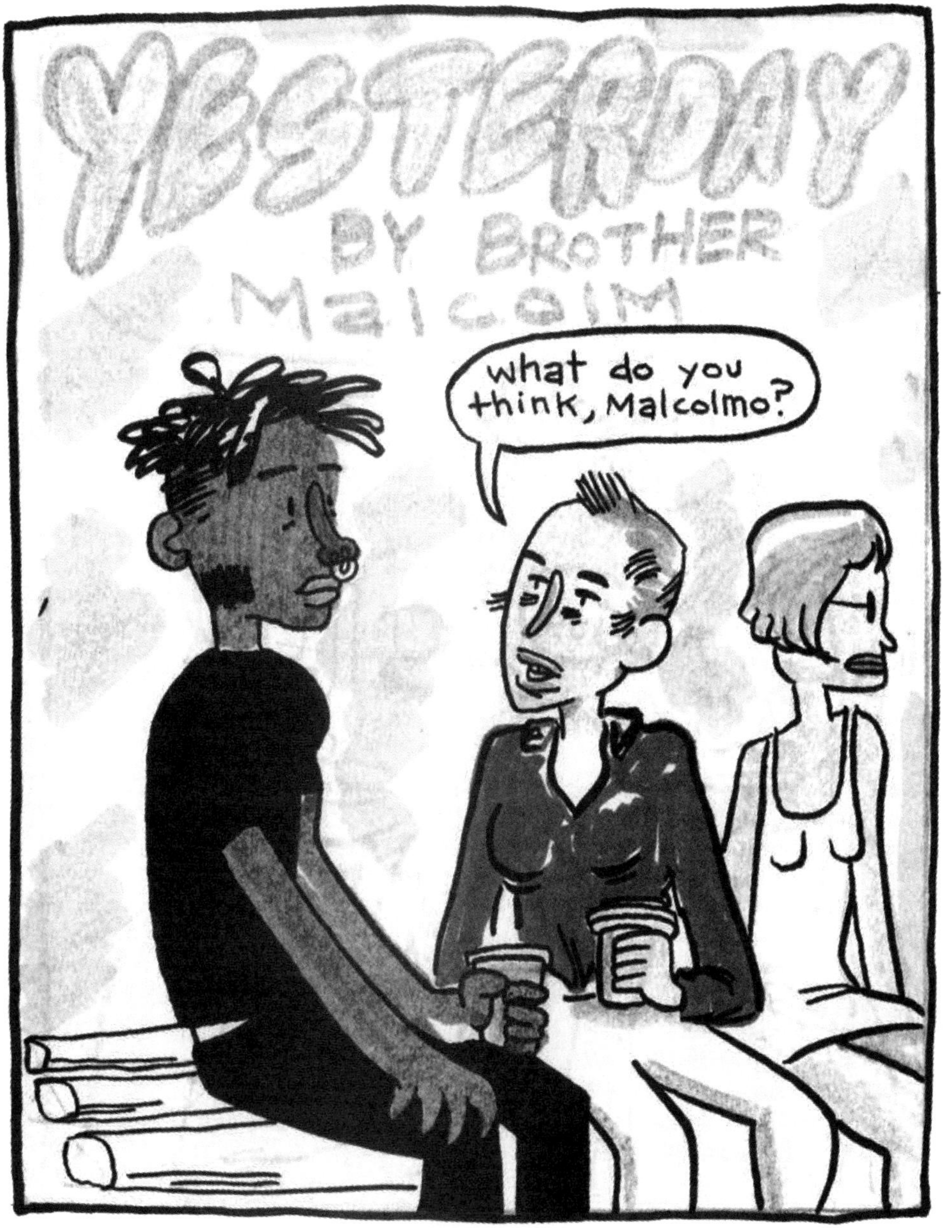
YESTERDAY
BY BROTHER
Malcolm
what do you think, Malcolmo?

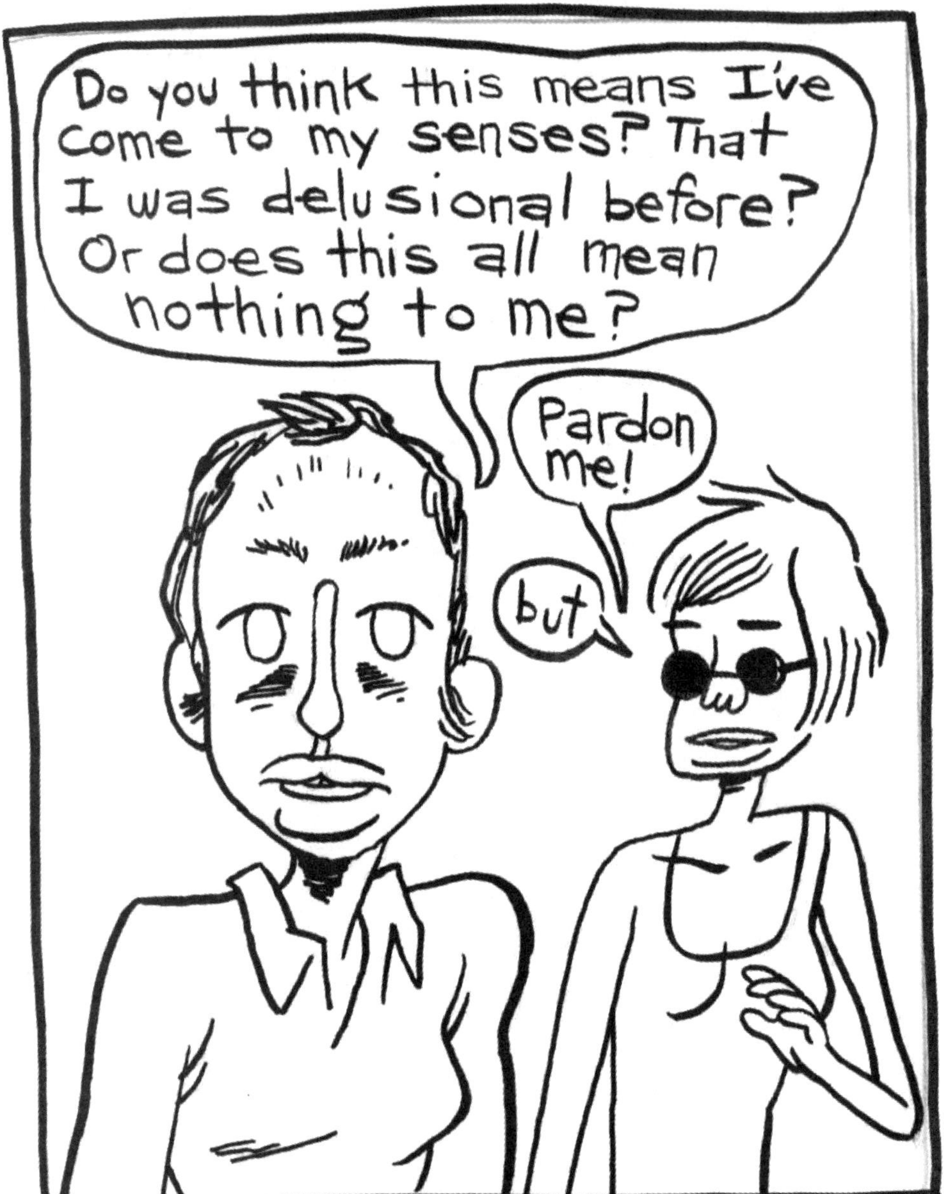
Do you think this means I've come to my senses? That I was delusional before? Or does this all mean nothing to me?
Pardon me!
but

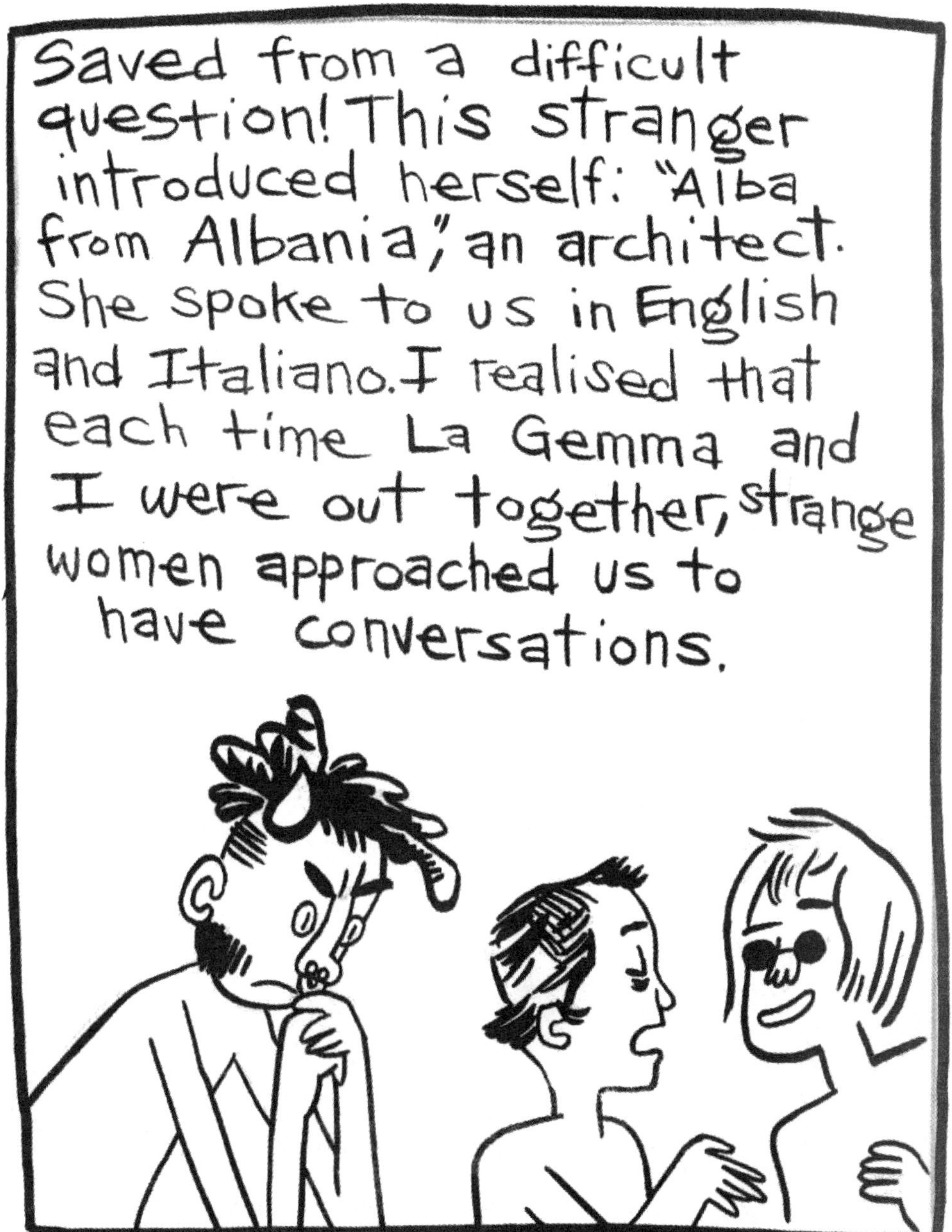
Saved from a difficult question! This stranger introduced herself: "Alba from Albania," an architect. She spoke to us in English and Italiano. I realised that each time La Gemma and I were out together, strange women approached us to have conversations.

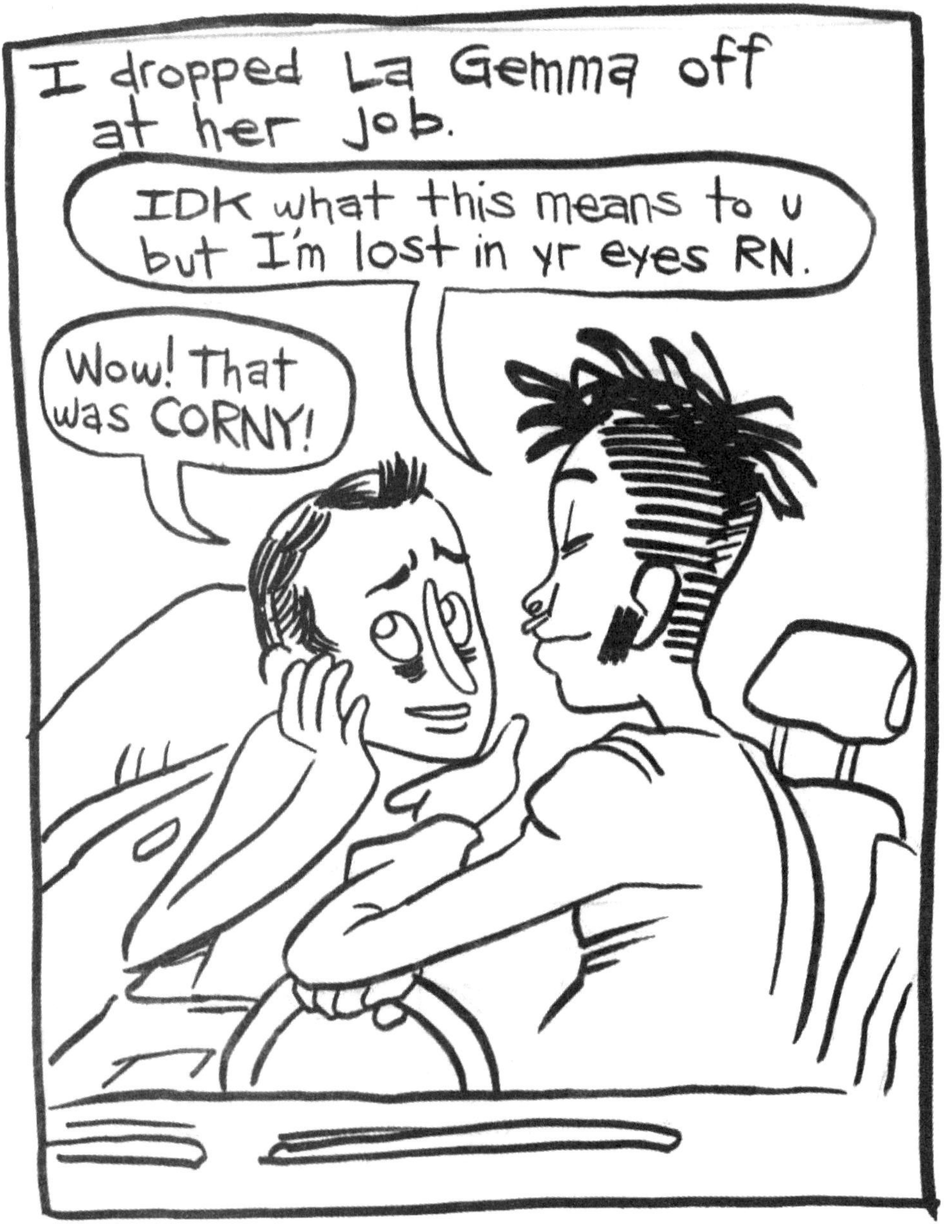
I dropped La Gemma off at her job.
IDK what this means to u but I'm lost in yr eyes RN.
Wow! That was CORNY!

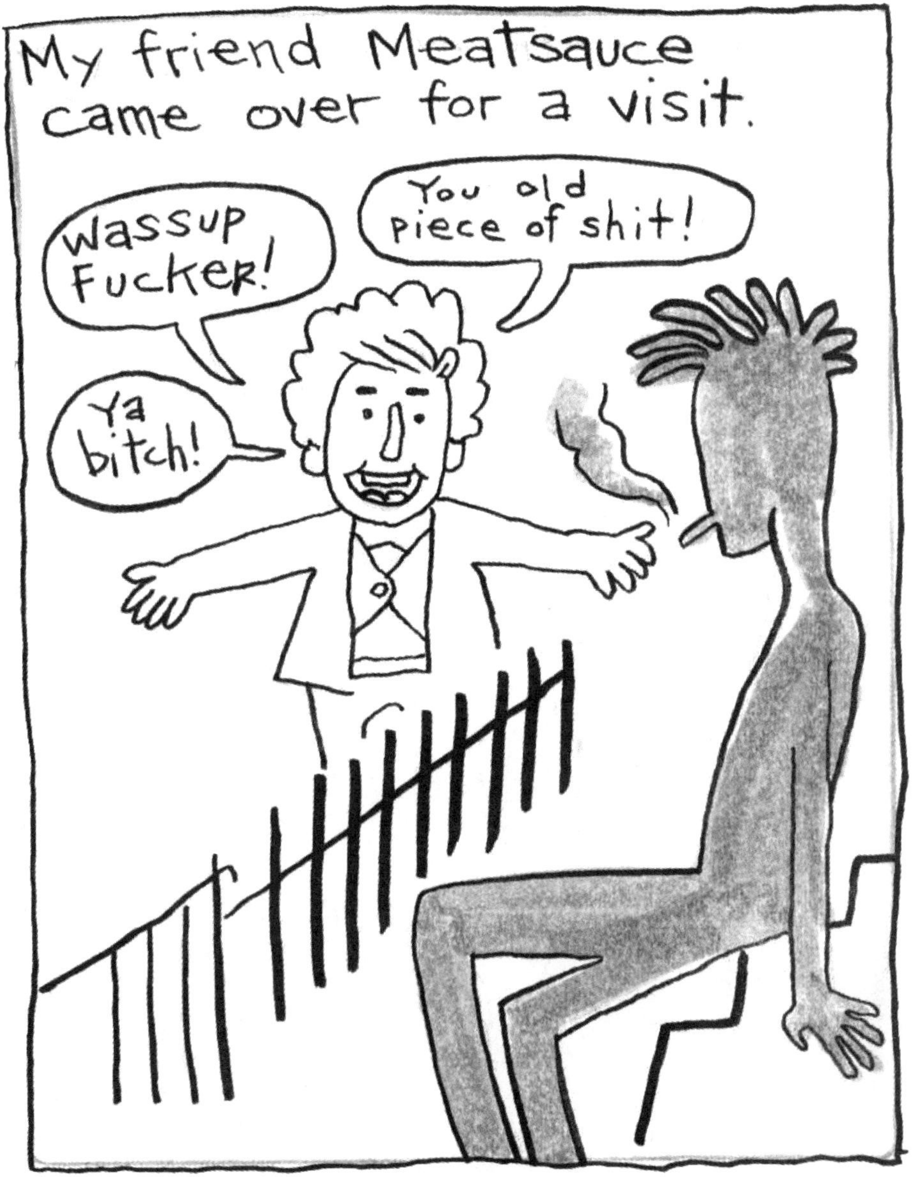
My friend Meatsauce came over for a visit.
Wassup Fucker!
You old piece of shit!
Ya bitch!

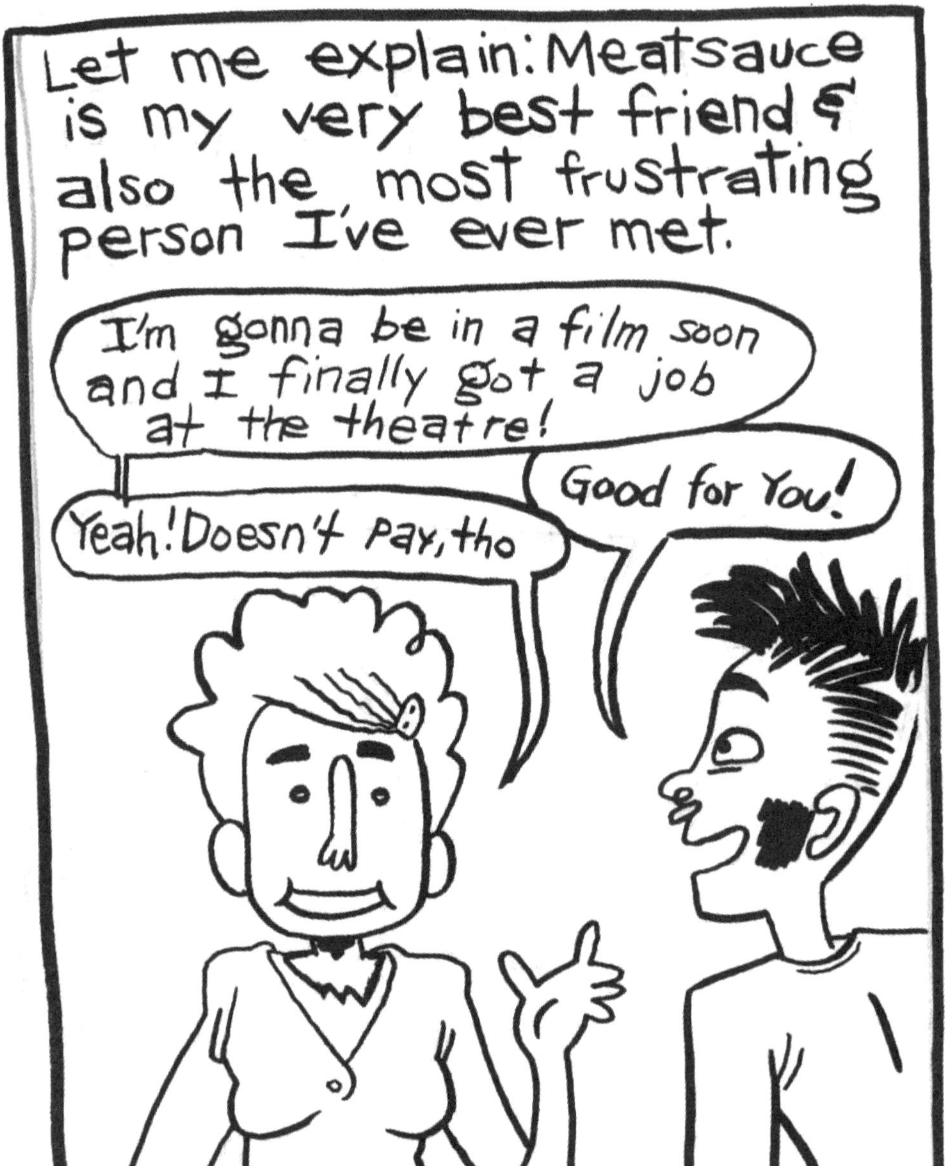
Let me explain: Meatsauce is my very best friend & also the most frustrating person I've ever met.
I'm gonna be in a film soon and I finally got a job at the theatre!
Yeah! Doesn't pay, tho
Good for You!

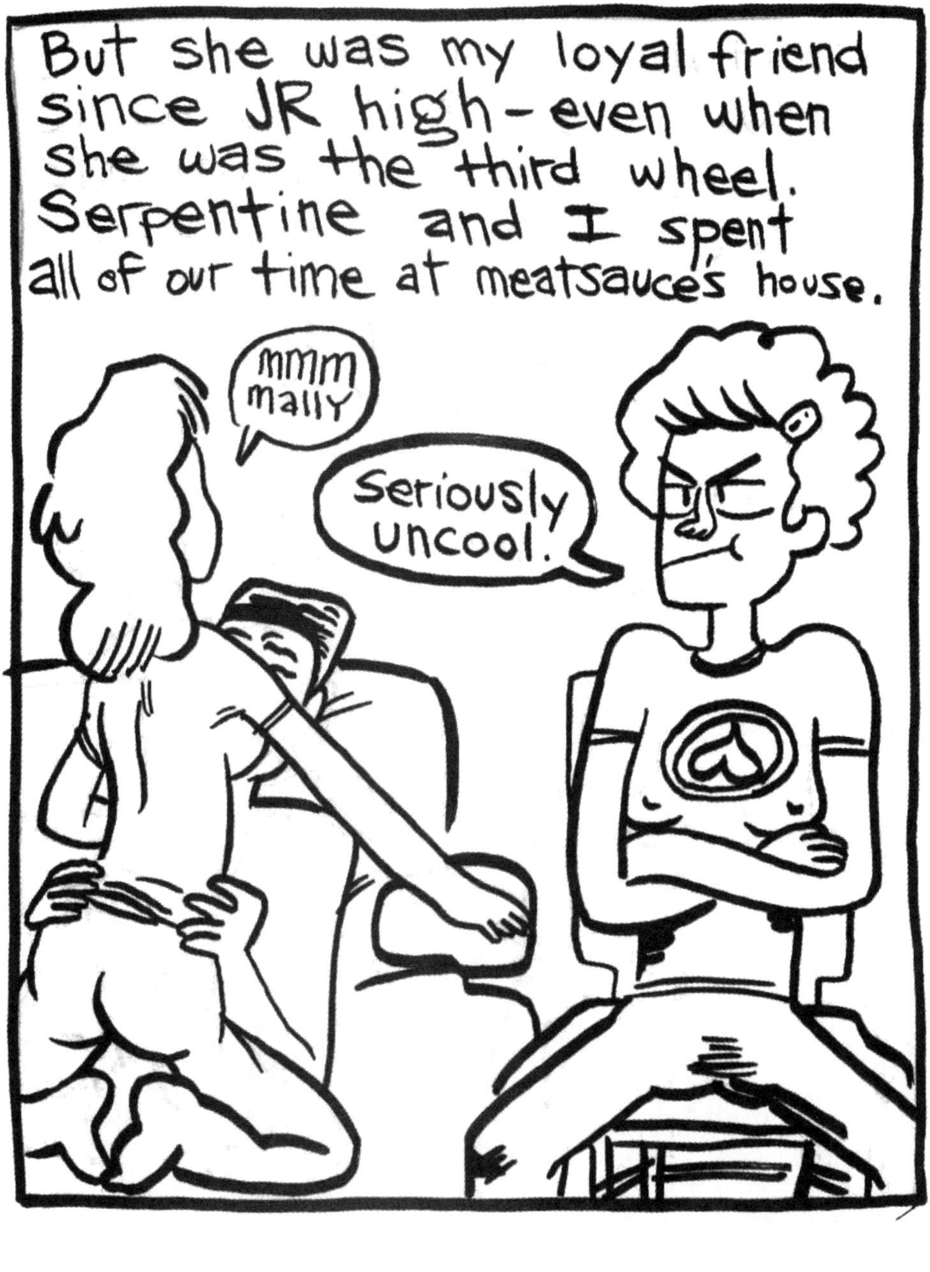
But she was my loyal friend since JR high - even when she was the third wheel. Serpentine and I spent all of our time at meatsauce's house.
mmm mally
Seriously uncool.

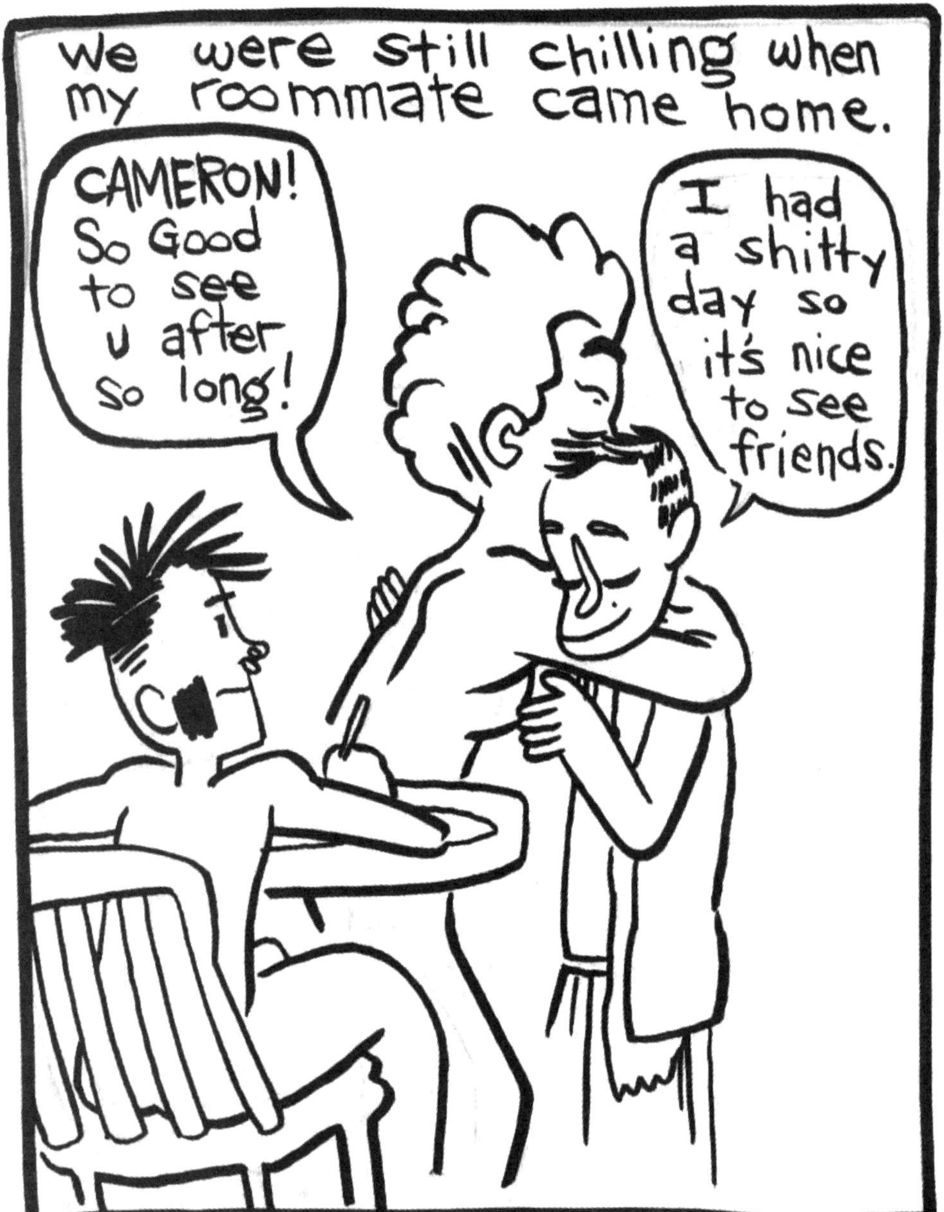
We were still chilling when my roommate came home.
CAMERON! So Good to see u after so long!
I had a shitty day so it's nice to see friends.

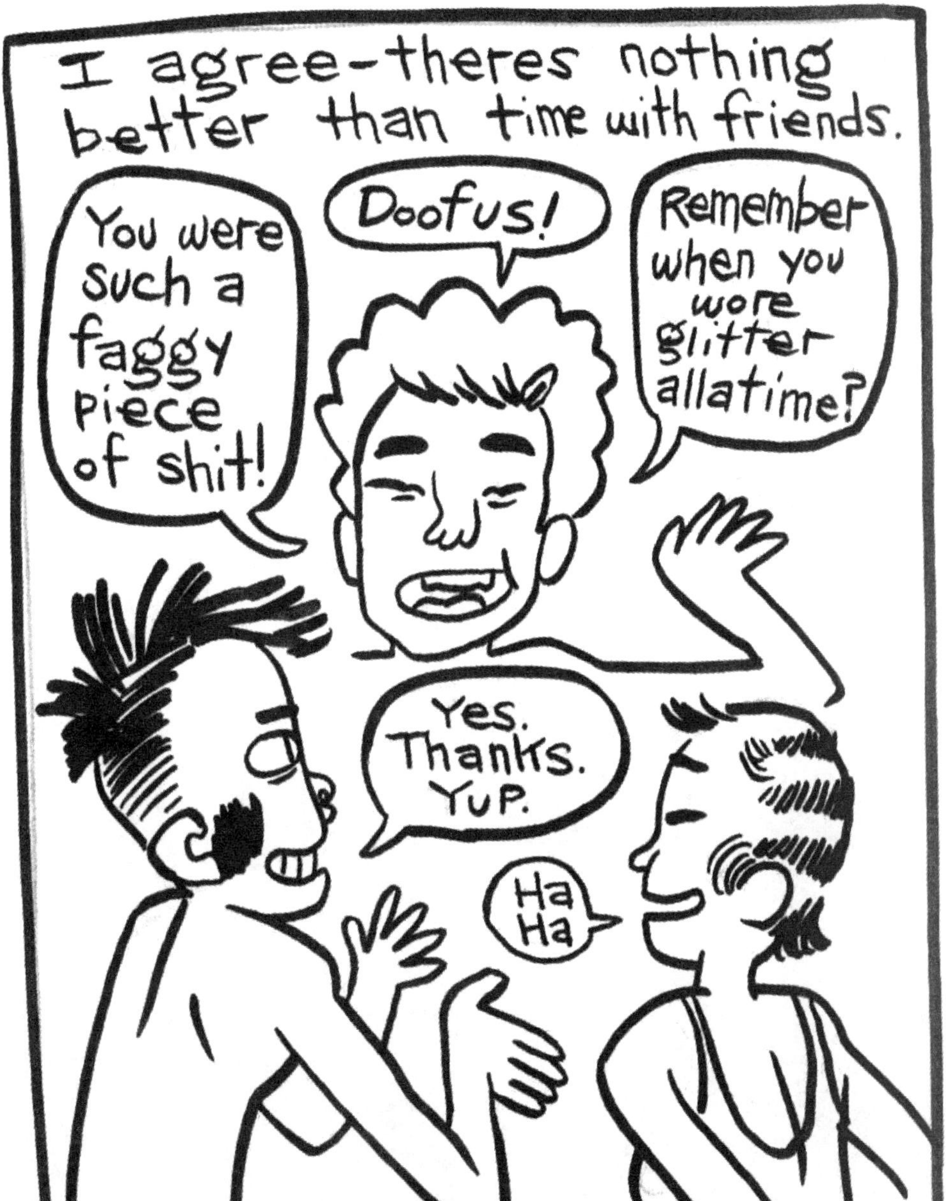
I agree-theres nothing better than time with friends.
You were such a faggy piece of shit!
Doofus!
Remember when you wore glitter allatime?
Yes. Thanks. Yup.
Ha Ha

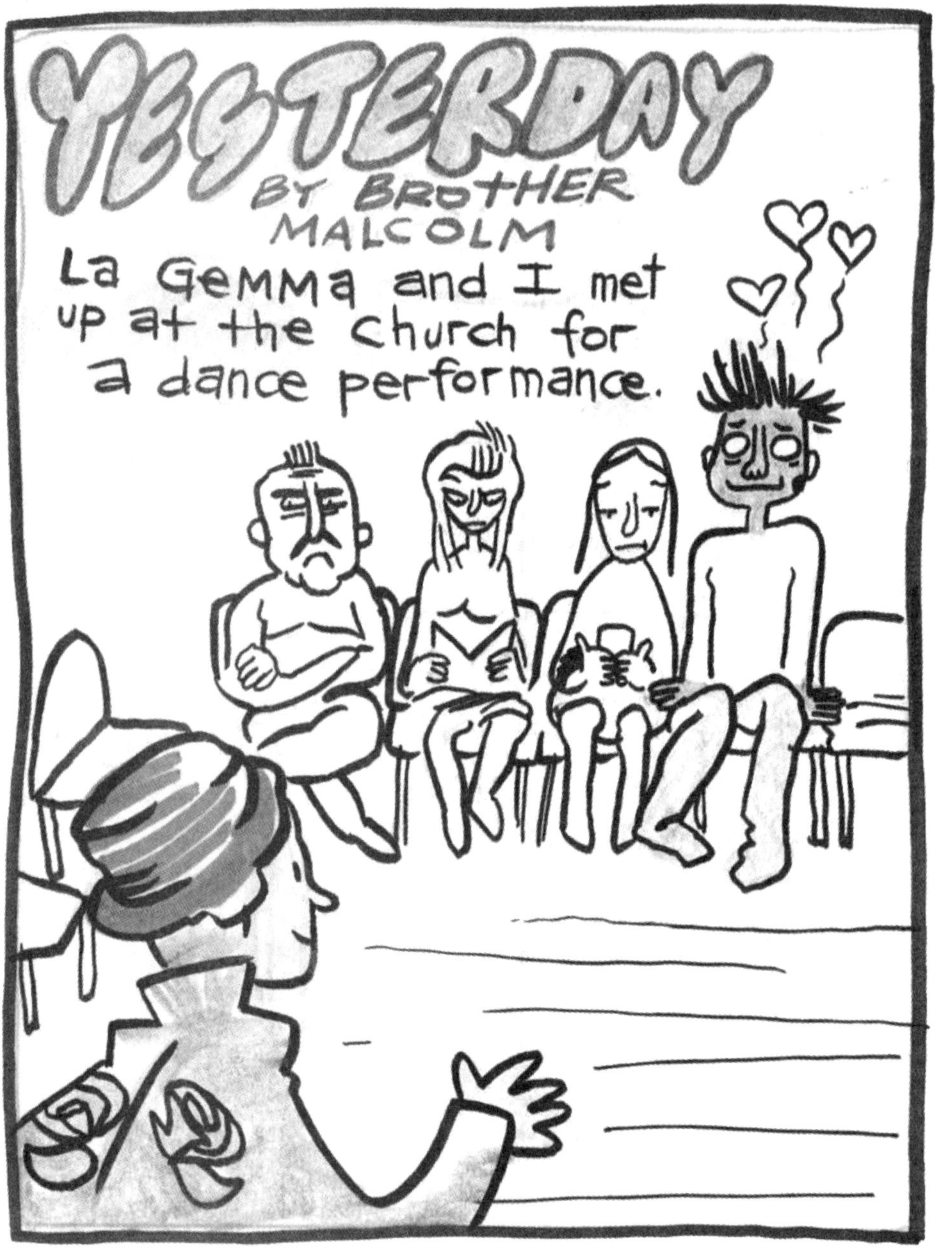
YESTERDAY
BY BROTHER MALCOLM
La Gemma and I met up at the church for a dance performance.

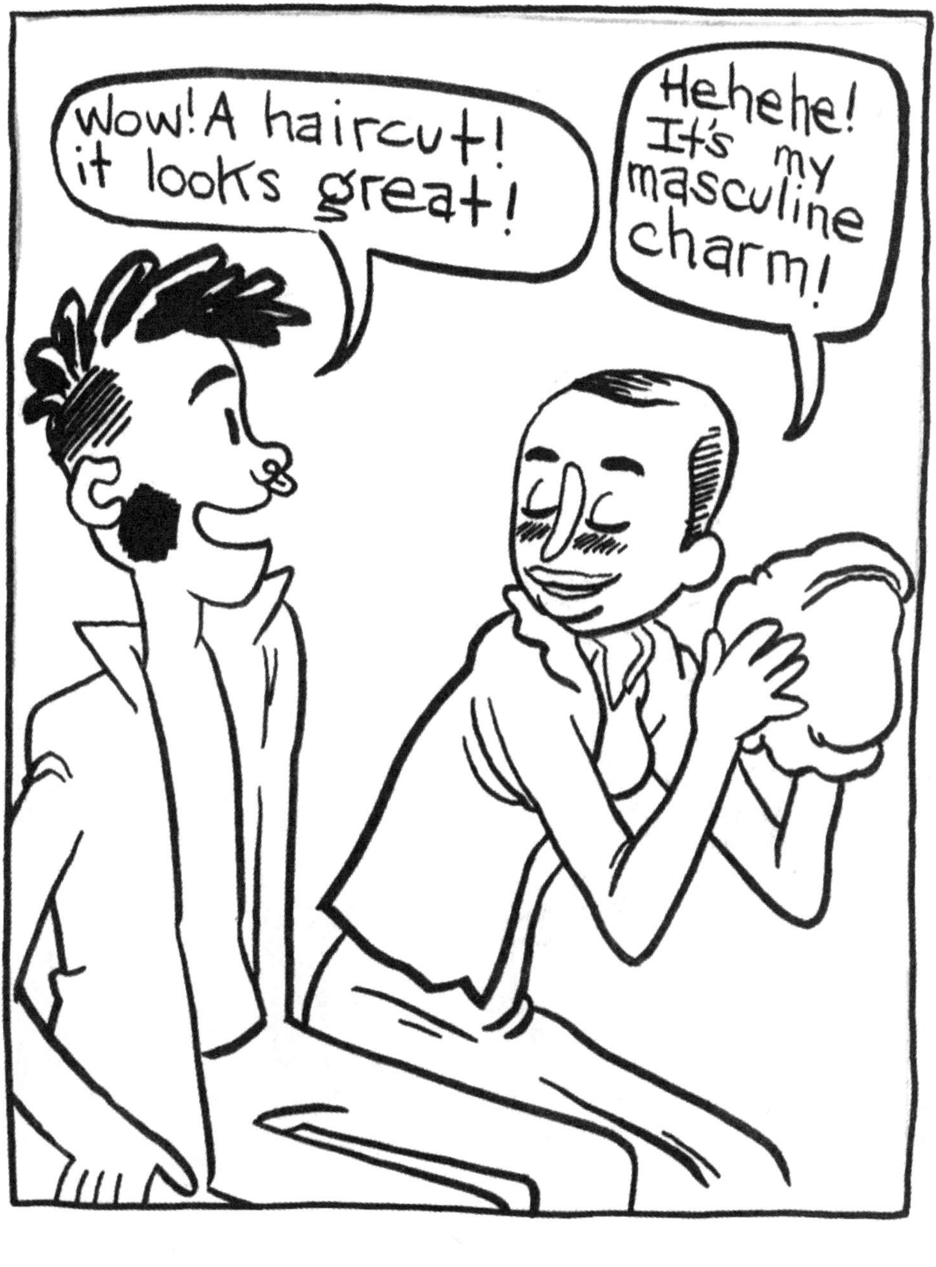
Wow! A haircut! it looks great!
Hehehe! It's my masculine charm!

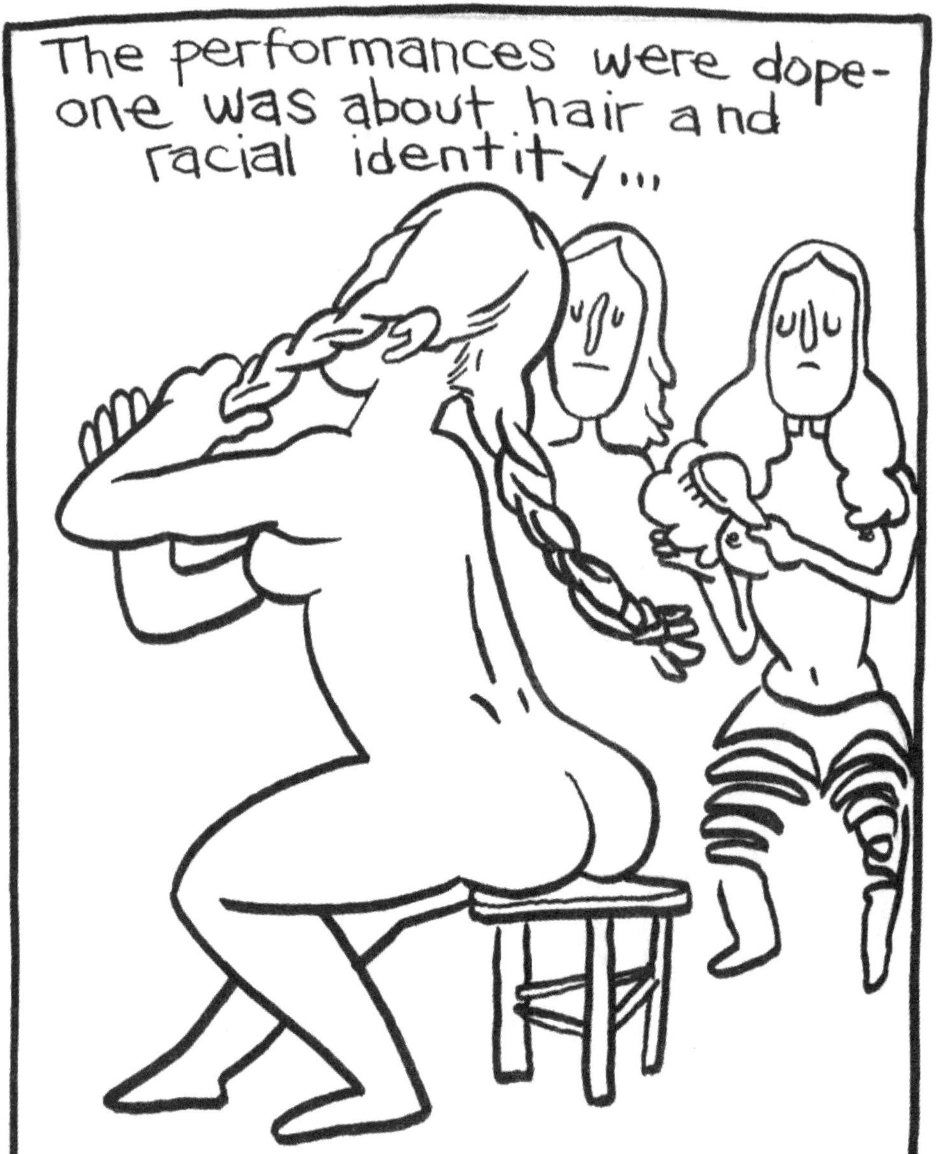
The performances were dope-
one was about hair and
racial identity...

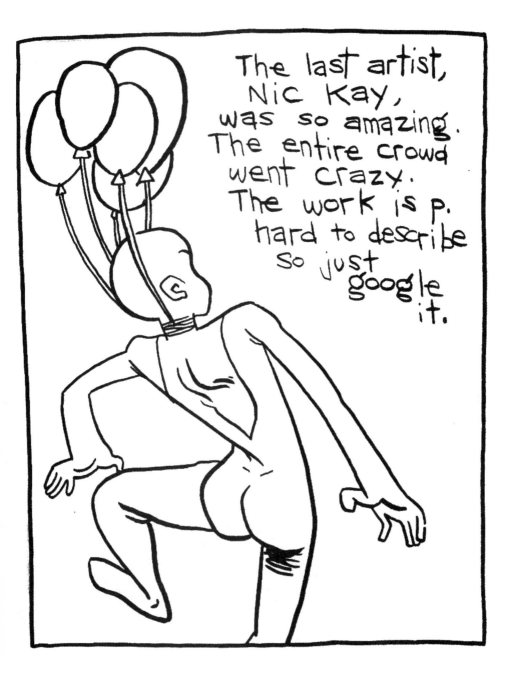

The last artist, Nic Kay, was so amazing. The entire crowd went crazy. The work is p. hard to describe so just google it.

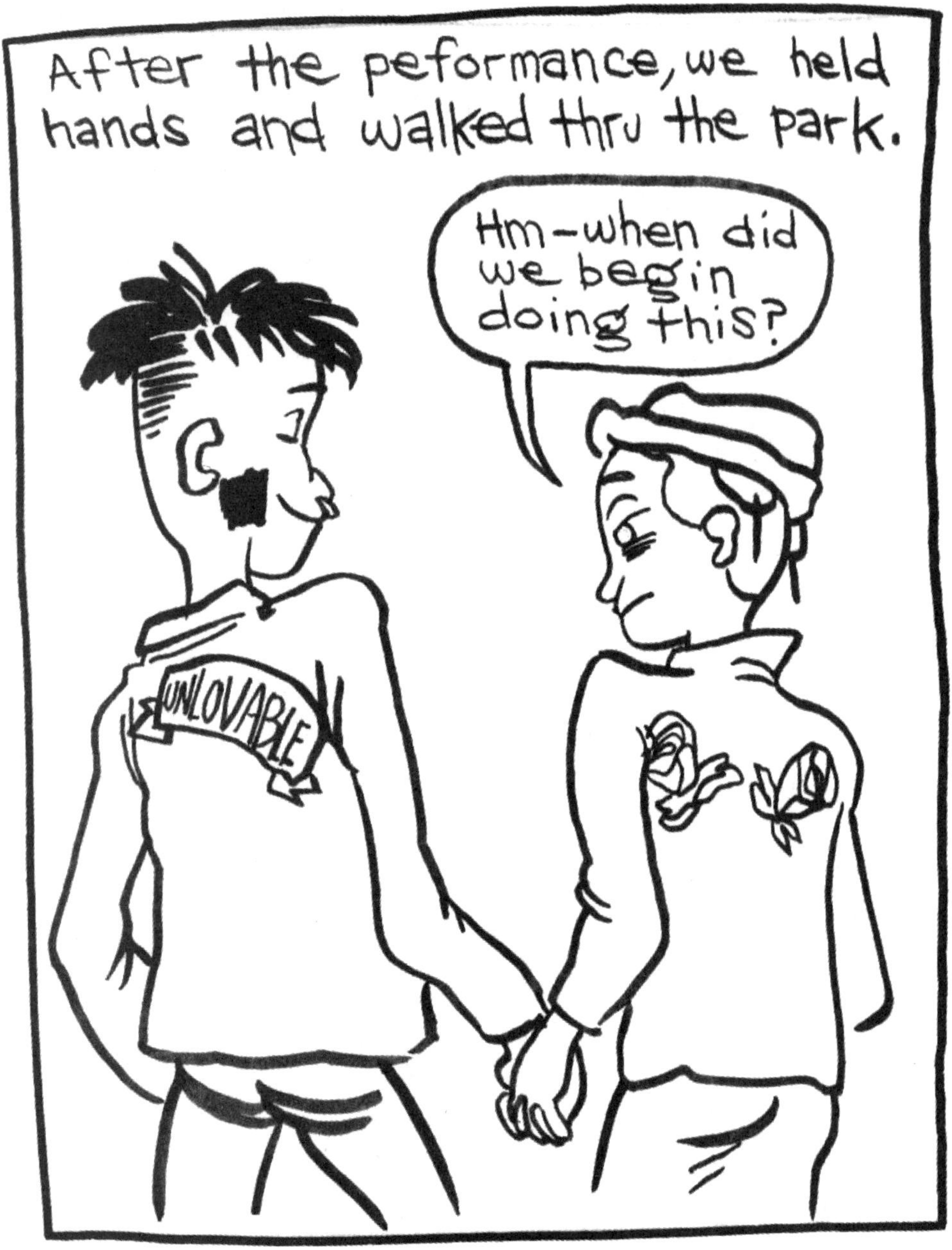
After the peformance, we held hands and walked thru the park.
Hm-when did we begin doing this?
UNLOVABLE

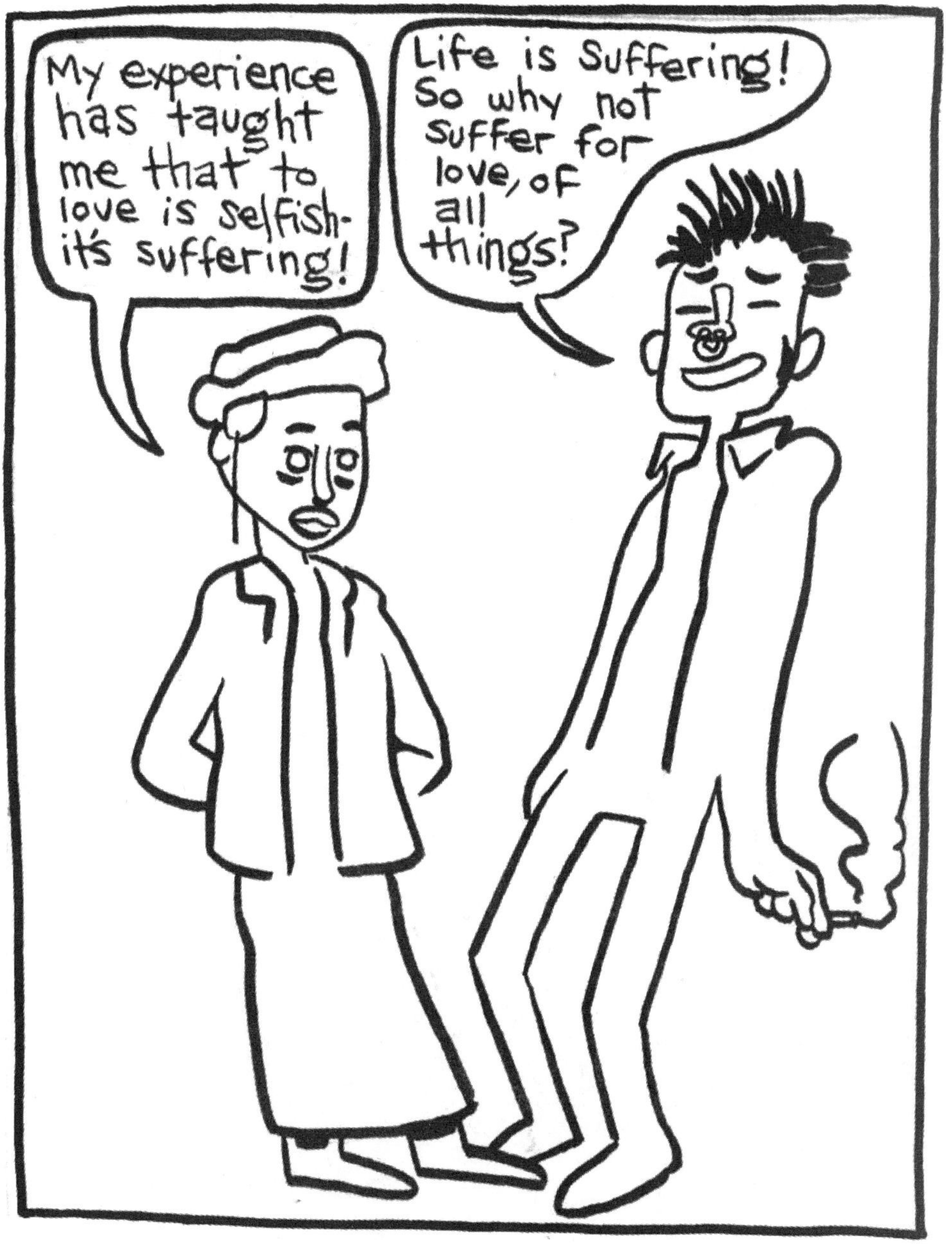
My experience has taught me that to love is selfish- it's suffering!
Life is suffering! So why not suffer for love, of all things?

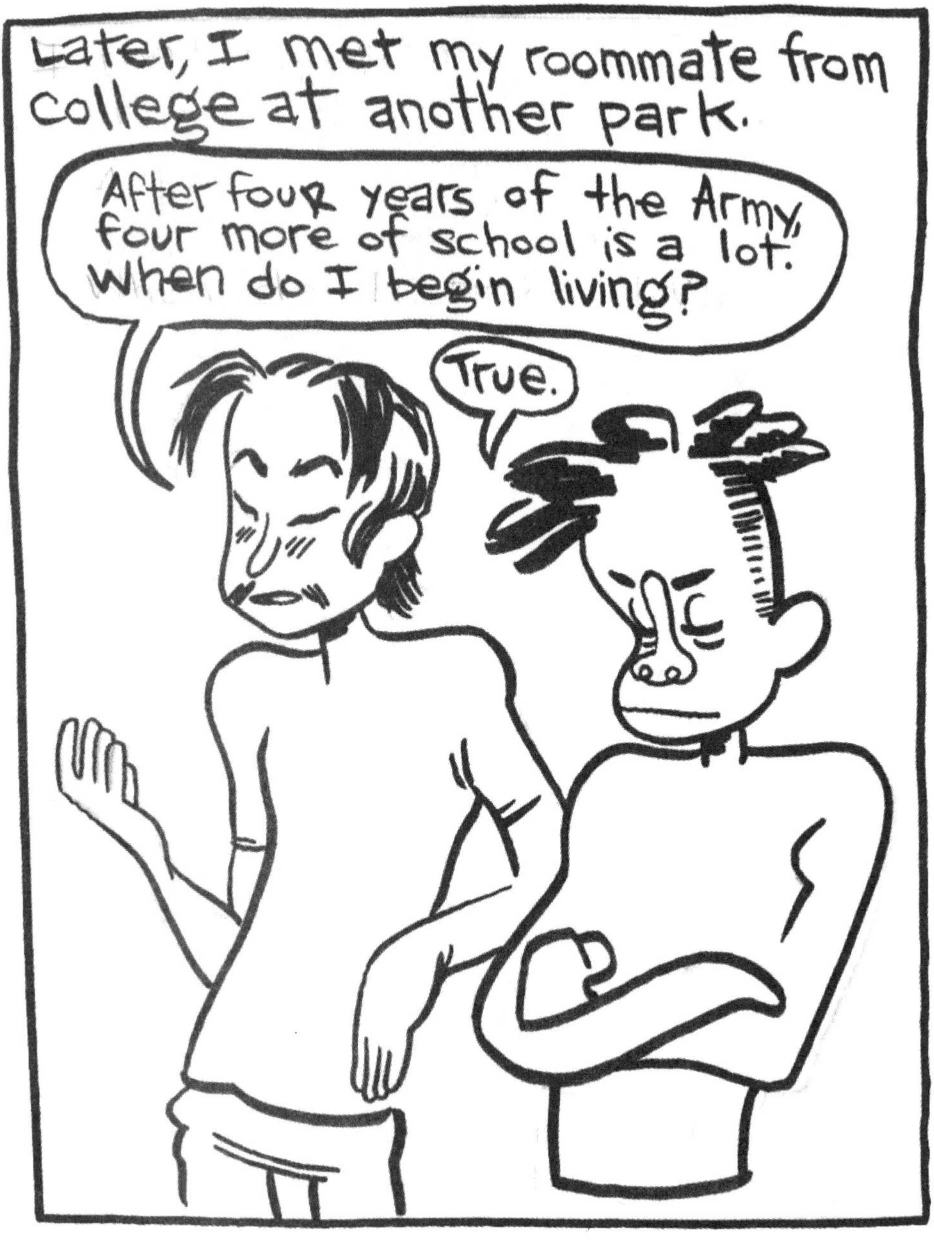
Later, I met my roommate from college at another park.
After four years of the Army, four more of school is a lot. When do I begin living?
True.

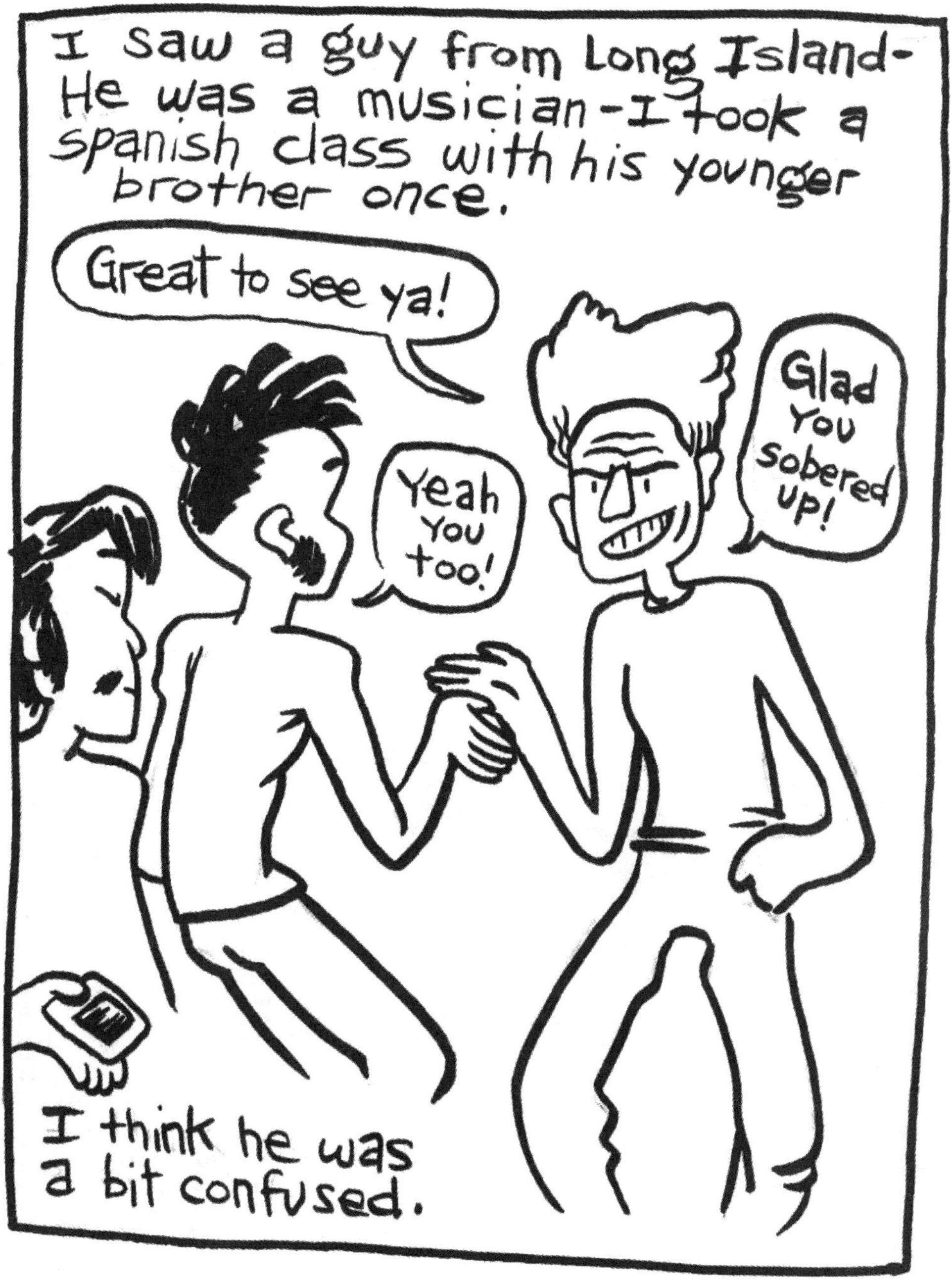
I saw a guy from Long Island-
He was a musician-I took a
spanish class with his younger
brother once.
Great to see ya!
Yeah You too!
Glad You sobered up!
I think he was
a bit confused.

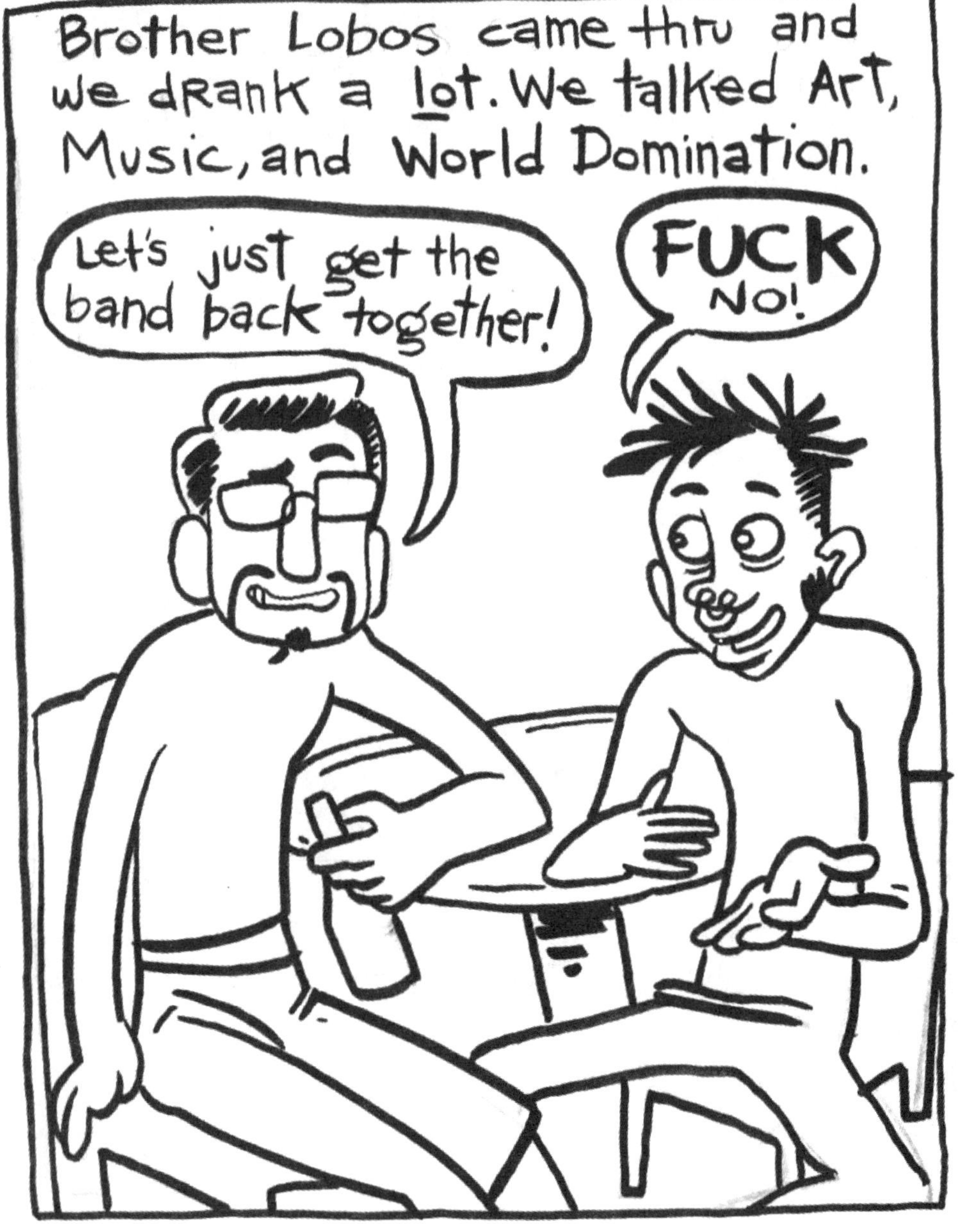
Brother Lobos came thru and we drank a lot. We talked Art, Music, and World Domination.
Let's just get the band back together!
FUCK NO!

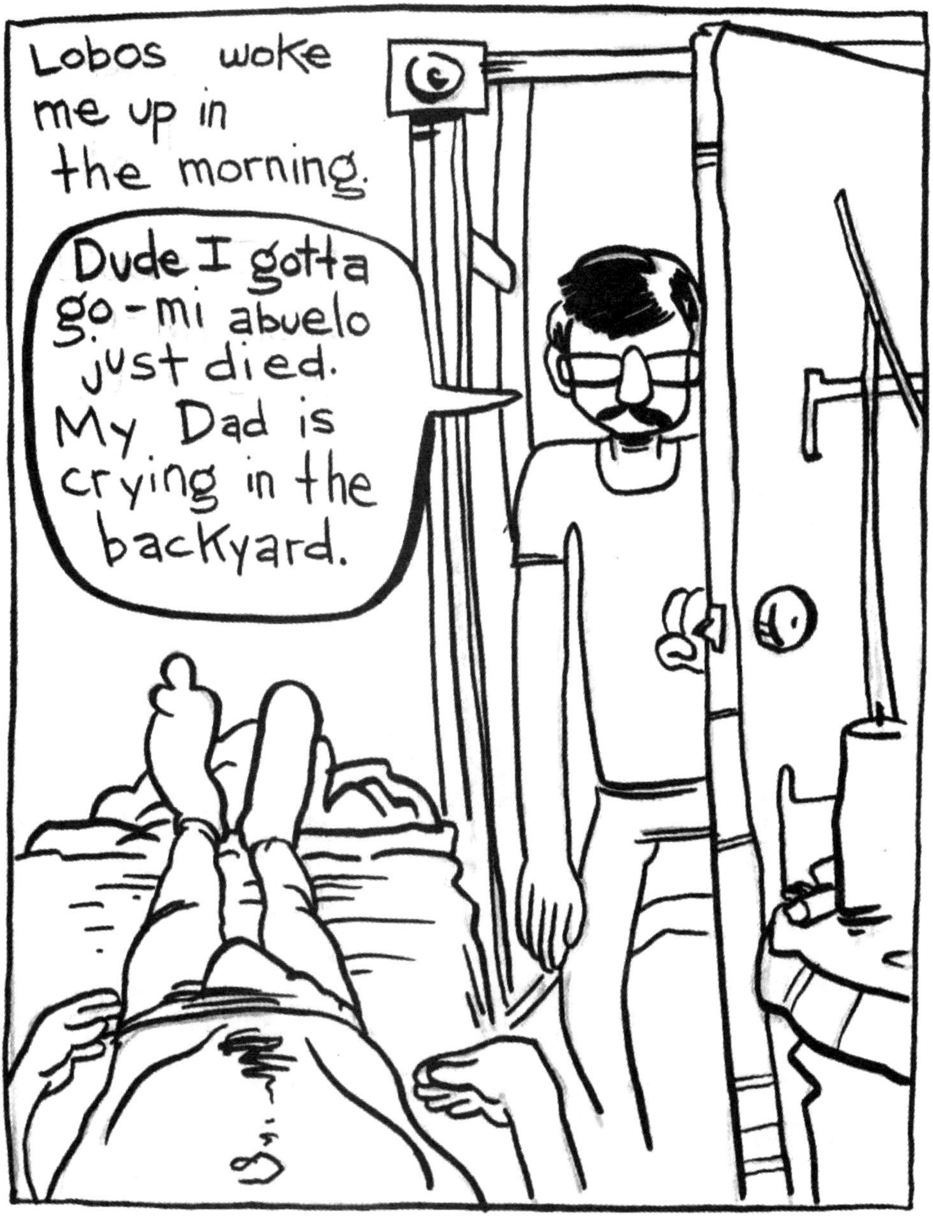
Lobos woke me up in the morning.
Dude I gotta go-mi abuelo just died. My Dad is crying in the backyard.

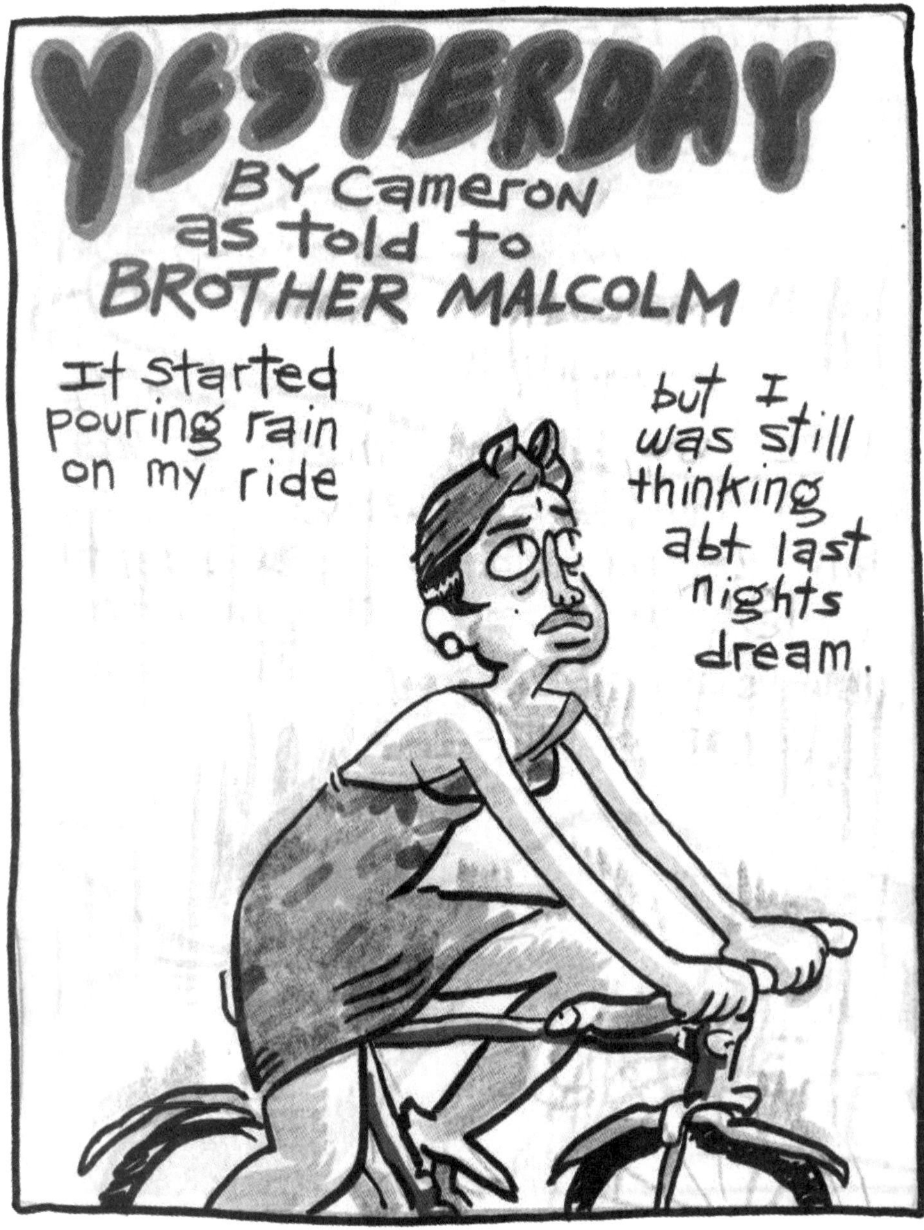
YESTERDAY
BY Cameron
as told to
BROTHER MALCOLM
It started
pouring rain
on my ride
but I
was still
thinking
abt last
nights
dream.

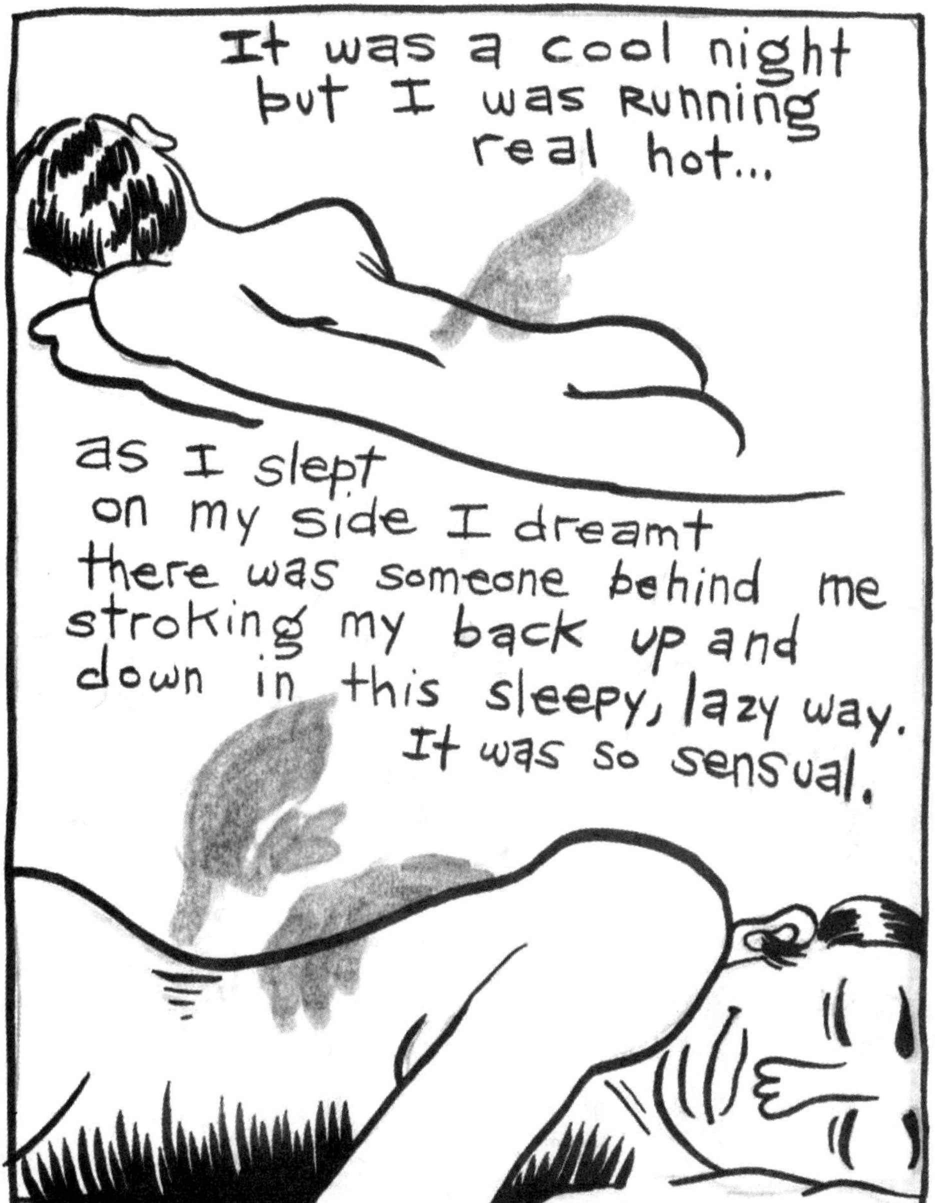
It was a cool night but I was running real hot...
as I slept on my side I dreamt there was someone behind me stroking my back up and down in this sleepy, lazy way. It was so sensual.

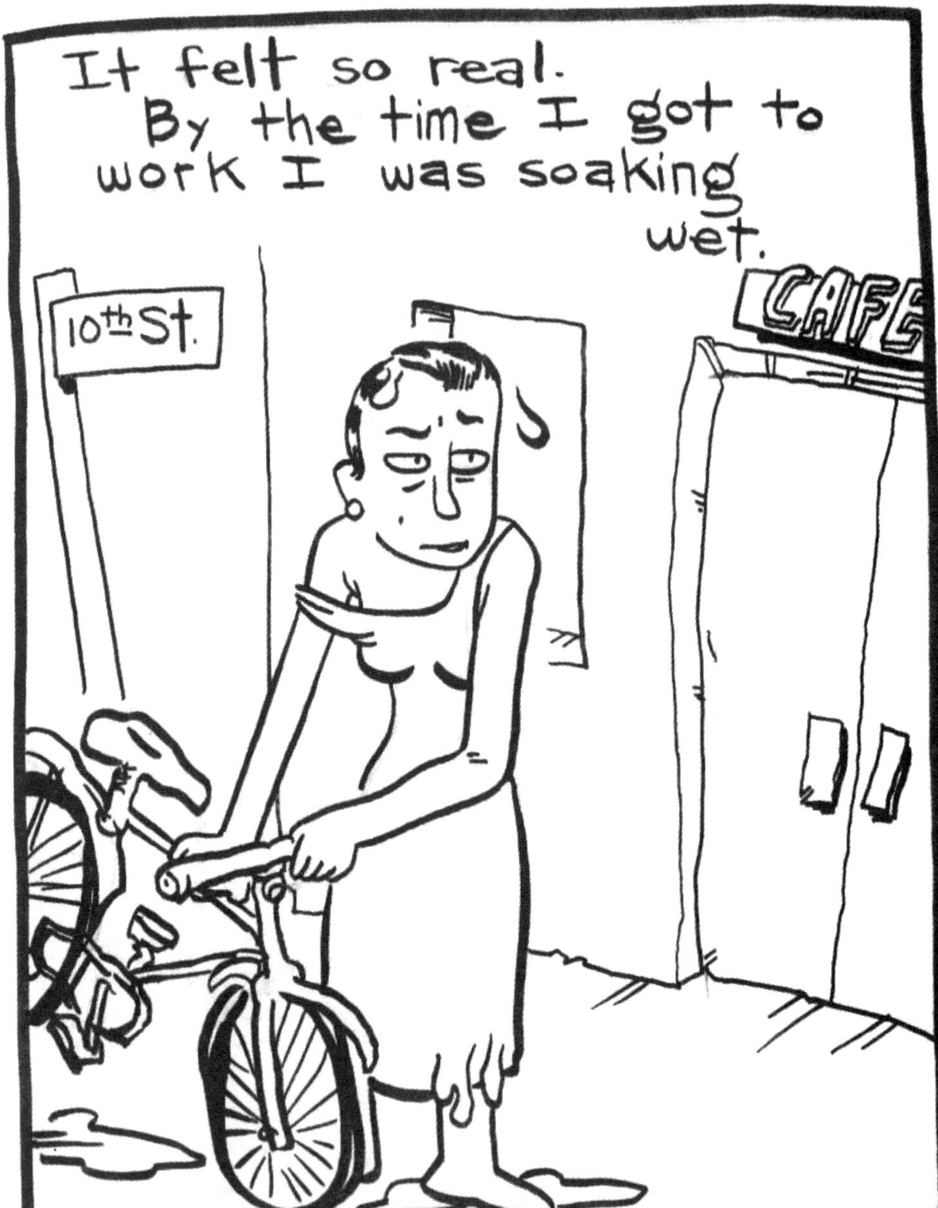
It felt so real.
By the time I got to work I was soaking wet.
10th St.
CAFE

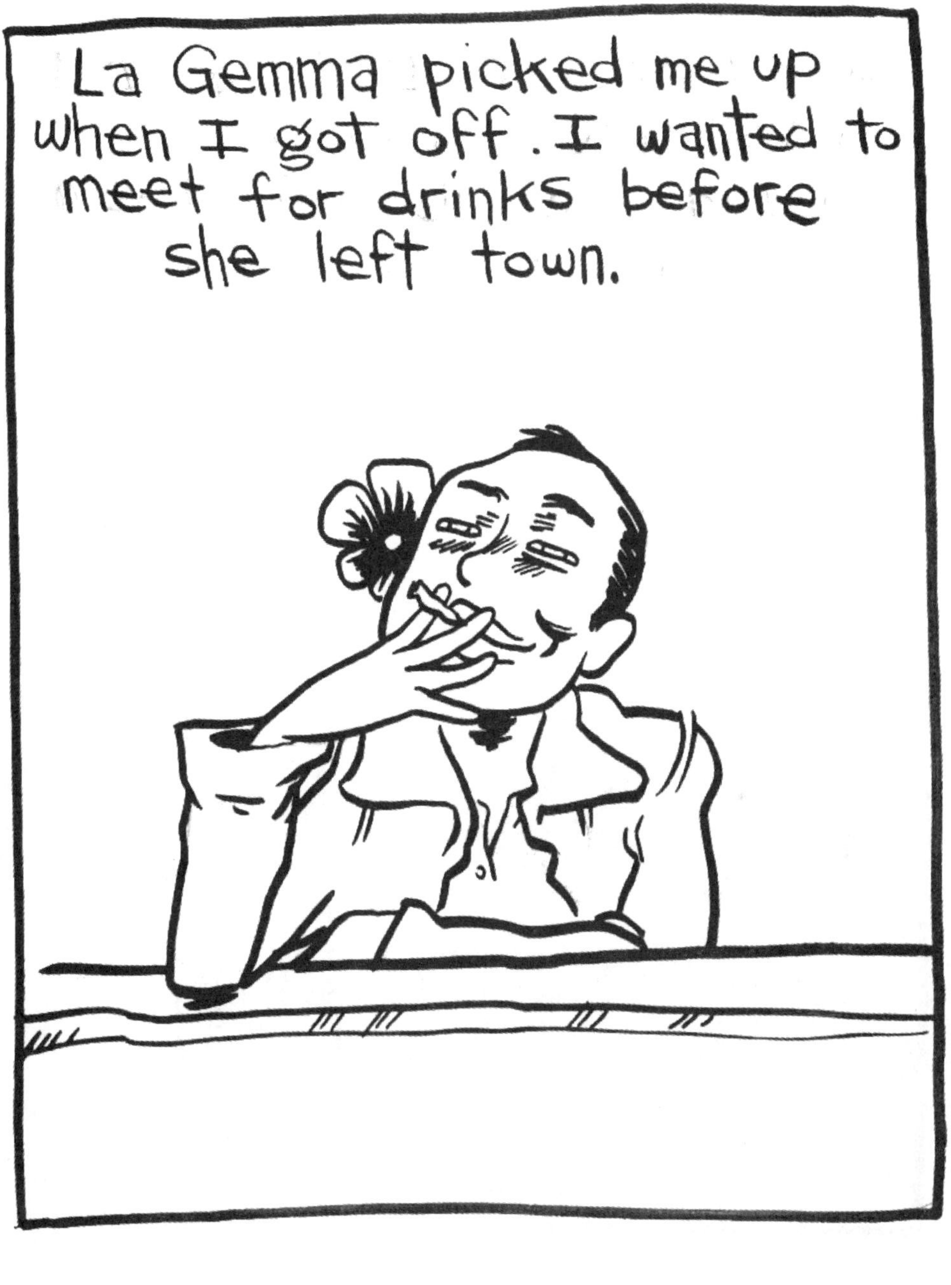
La Gemma picked me up when I got off. I wanted to meet for drinks before she left town.

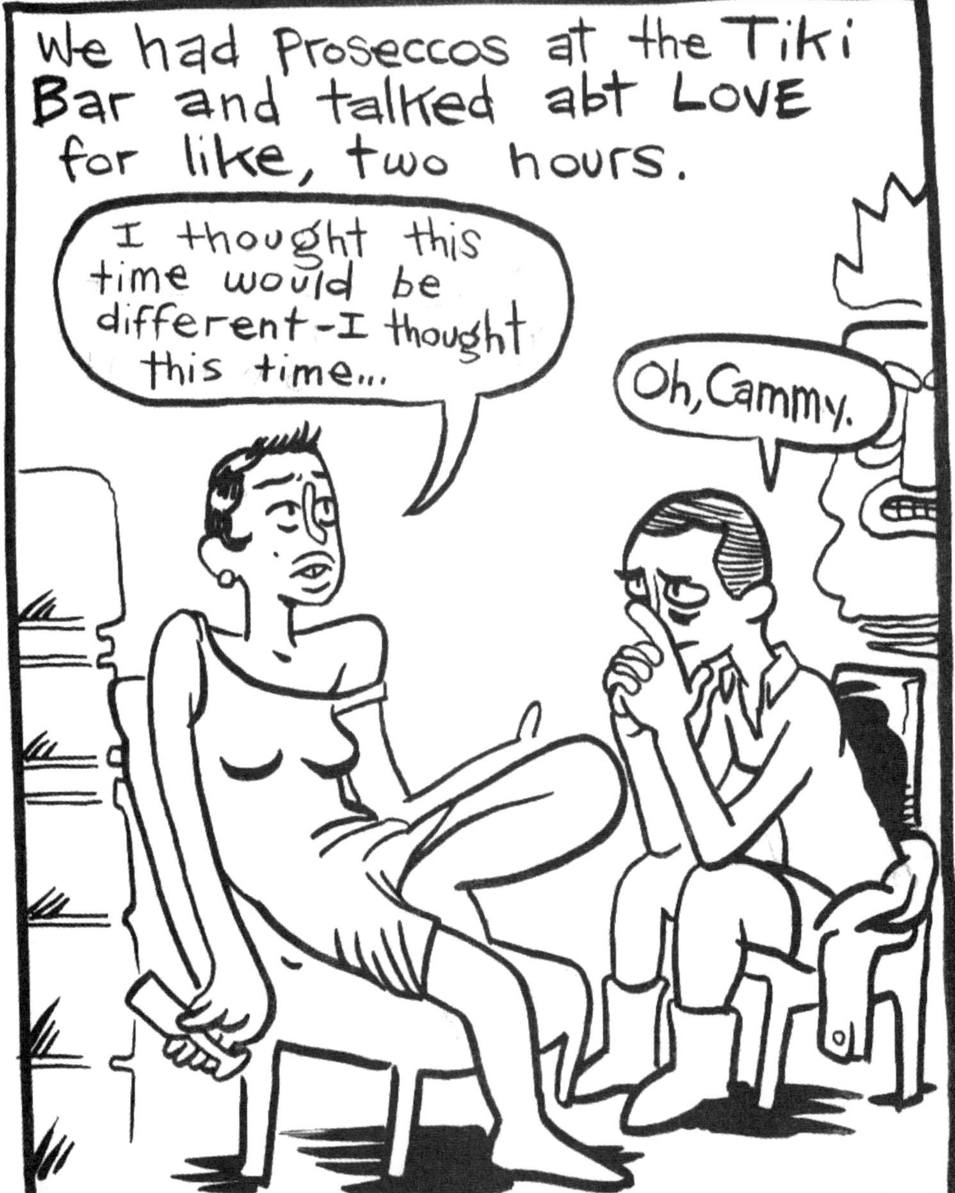
We had Proseccos at the Tiki Bar and talked abt LOVE for like, two hours.
I thought this time would be different-I thought this time...
Oh, Cammy.

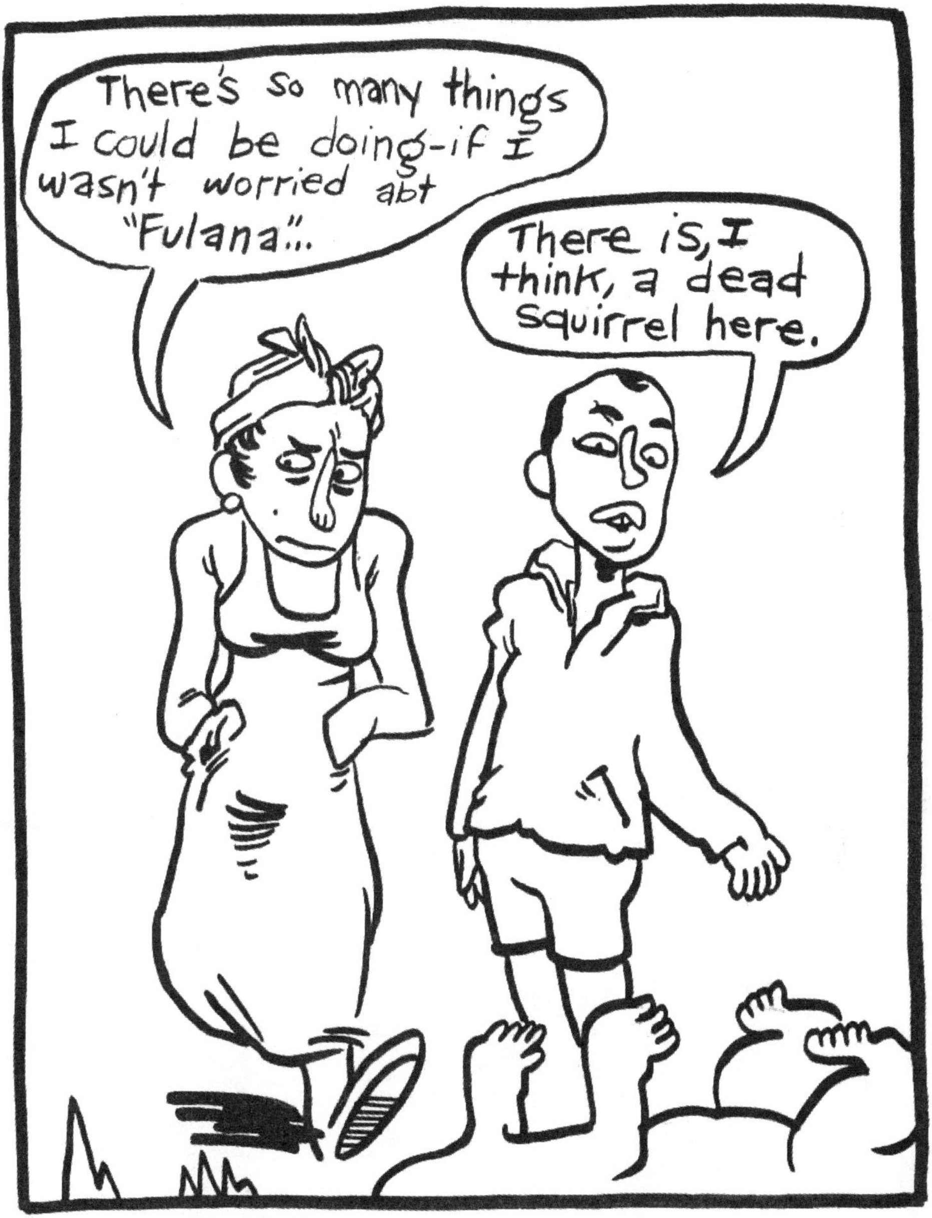
There's so many things I could be doing-if I wasn't worried abt "Fulana"...
There is, I think, a dead squirrel here.

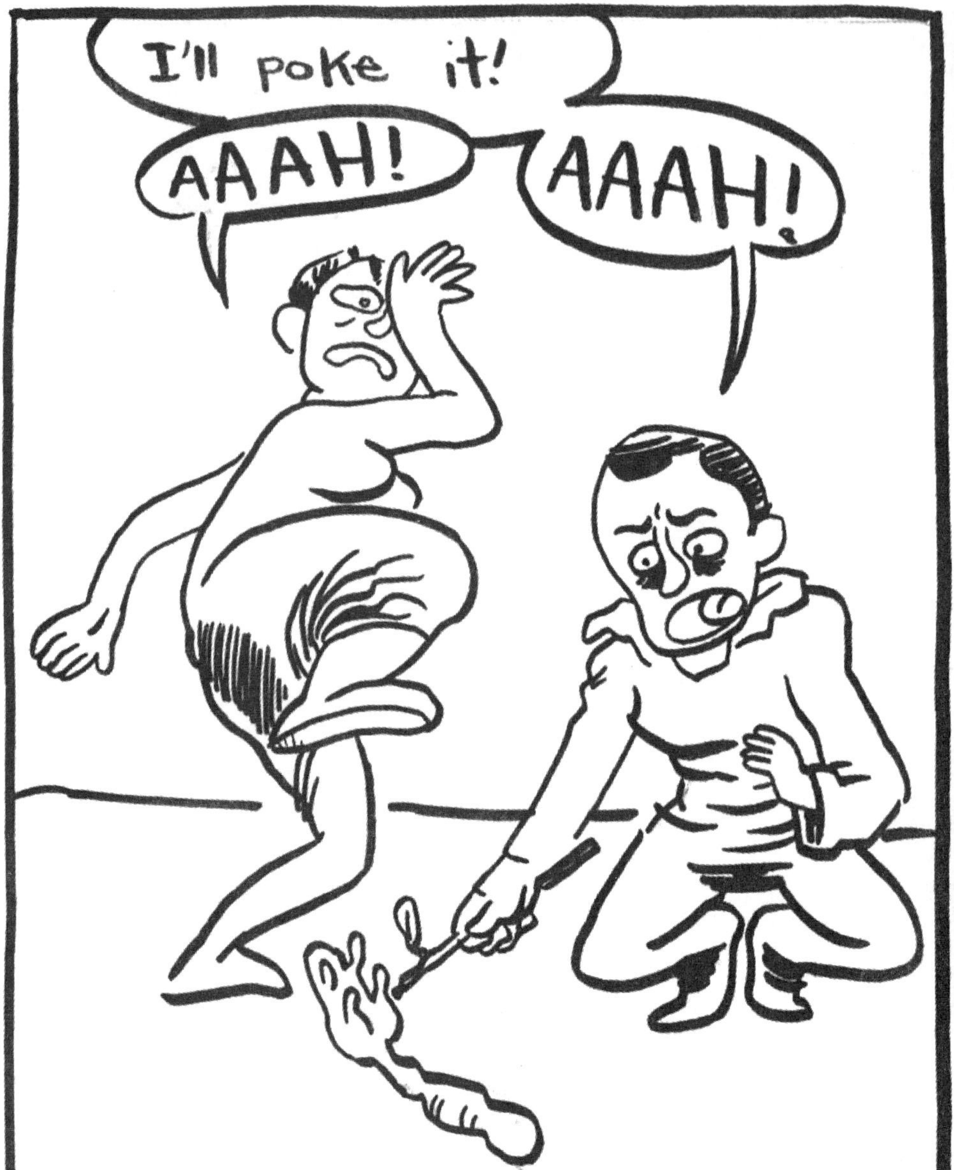
I'll poke it!
AAAH!
AAAH!

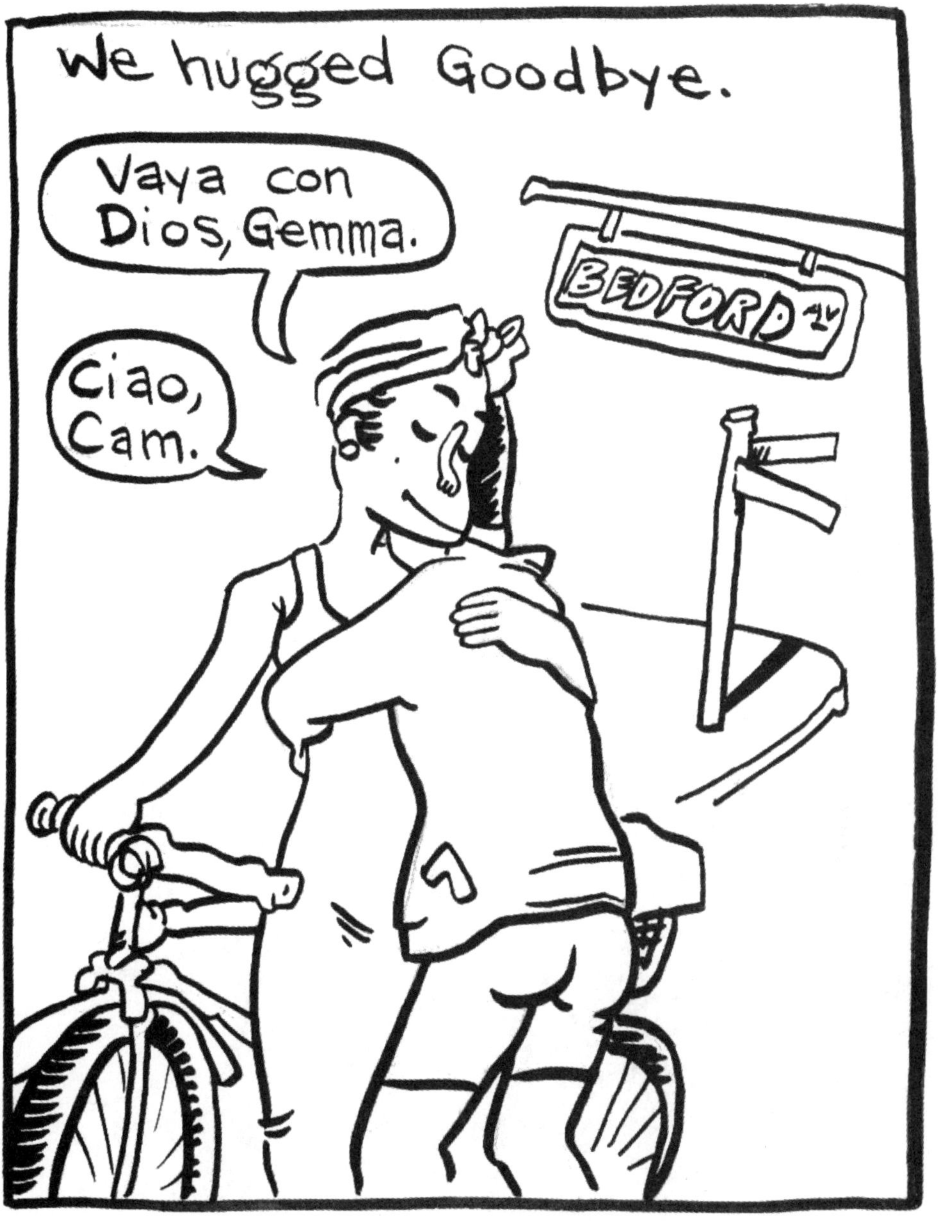
We hugged Goodbye.
Vaya con Dios, Gemma.
Ciao, Cam.
BEDFORD AV

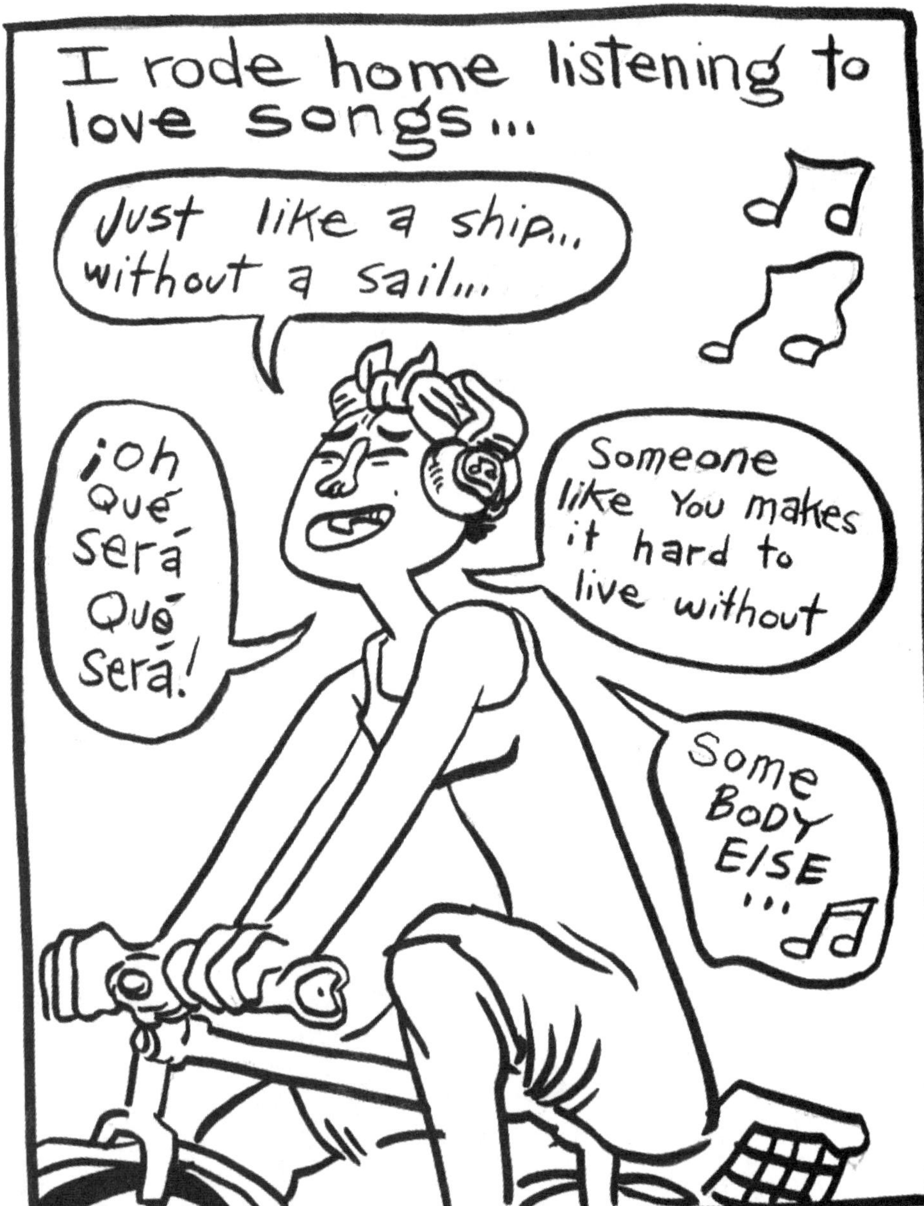
I rode home listening to love songs...
Just like a ship... without a sail...
¡Oh Qué será Qué será!
Someone like You makes it hard to live without
Some Body Else...

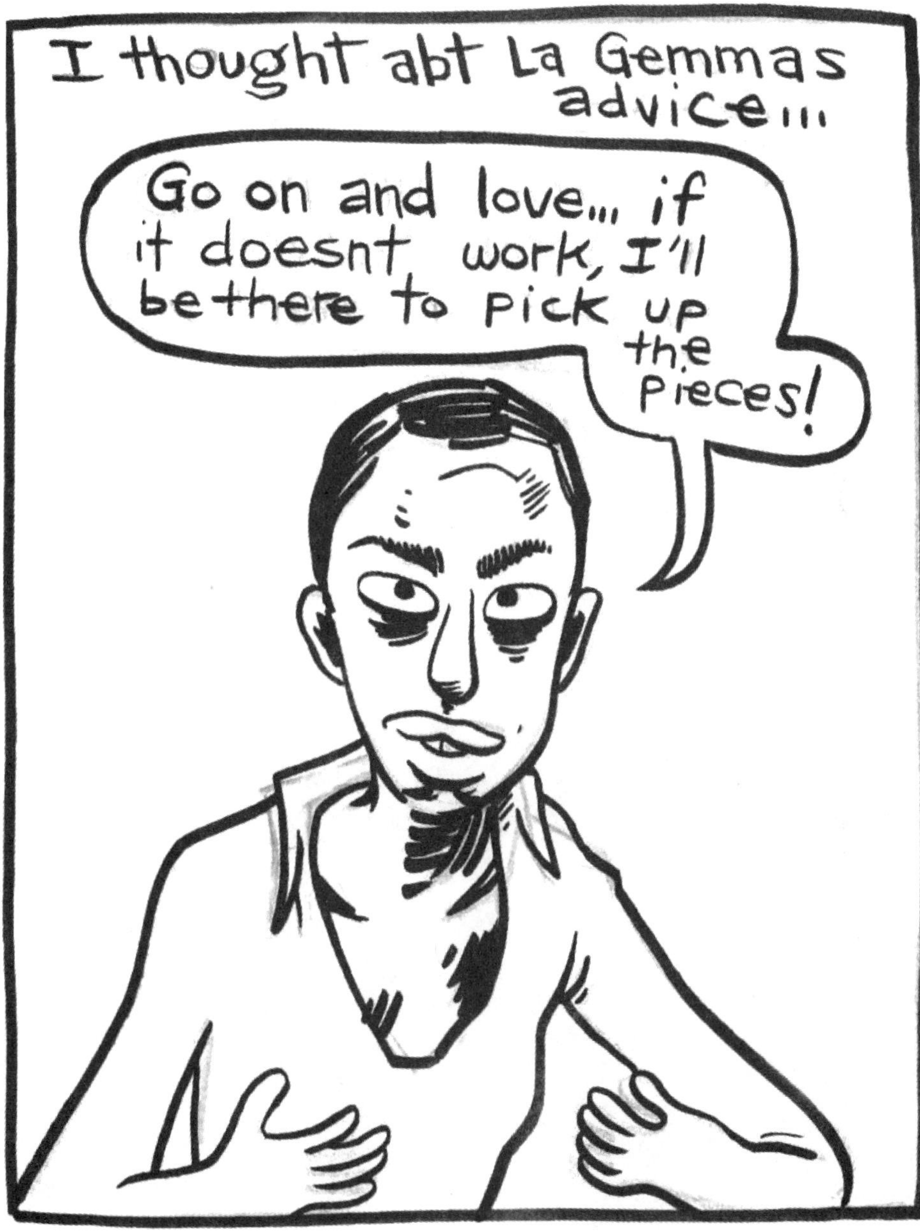
I thought abt La Gemmas advice...
Go on and love... if it doesnt work, I'll be there to pick up the pieces!

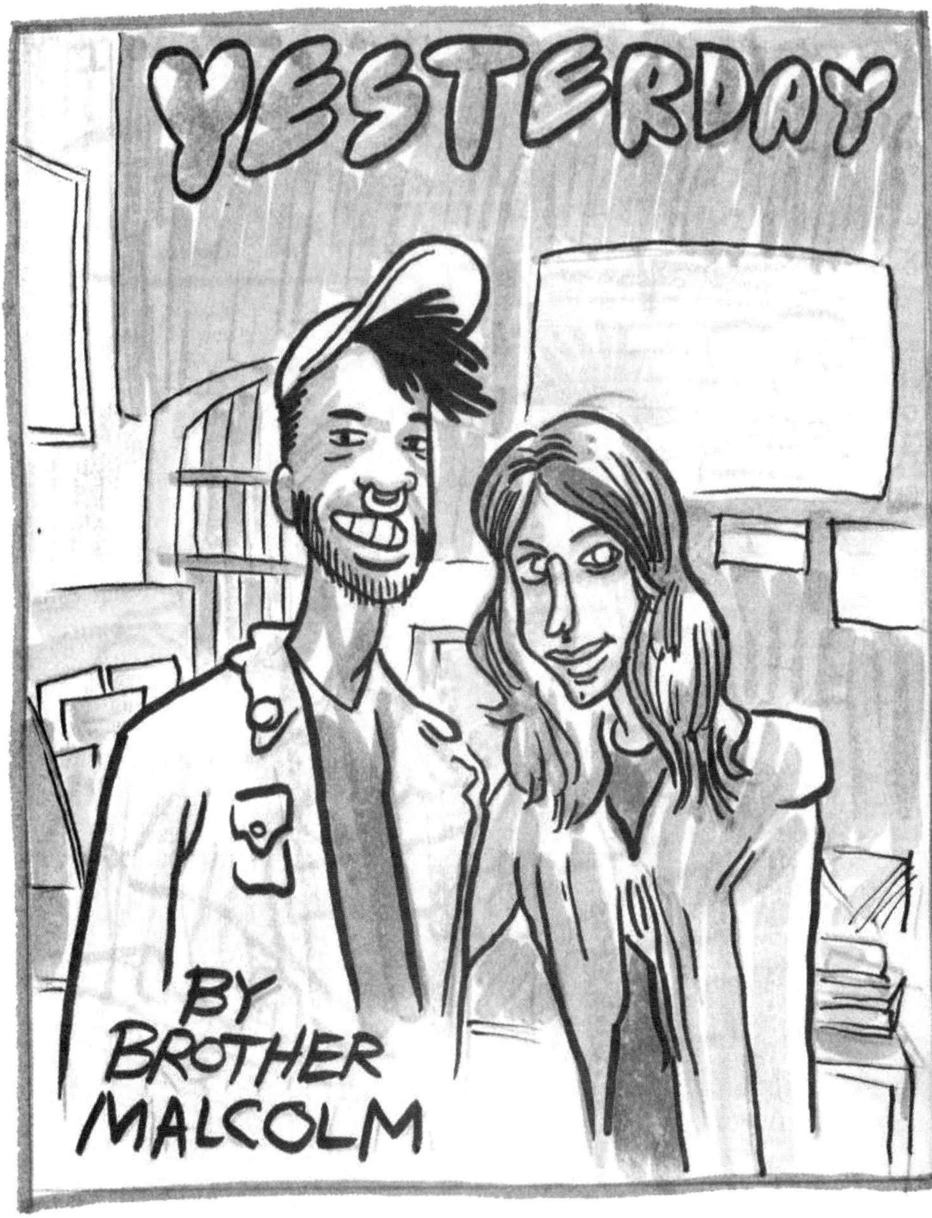
YESTERDAY
BY
BROTHER
MALCOLM

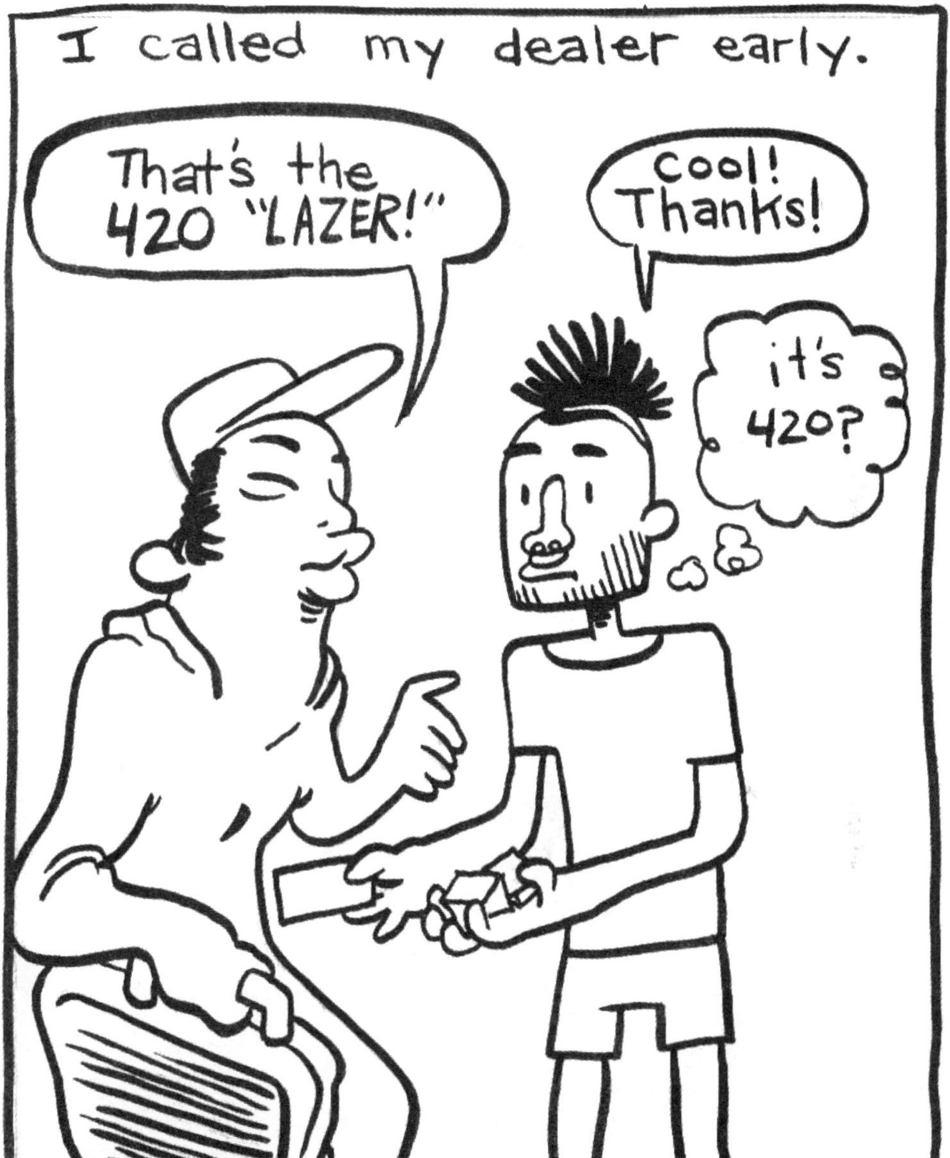
I called my dealer early.
That's the 420 "LAZER!"
Cool! Thanks!
it's 420?

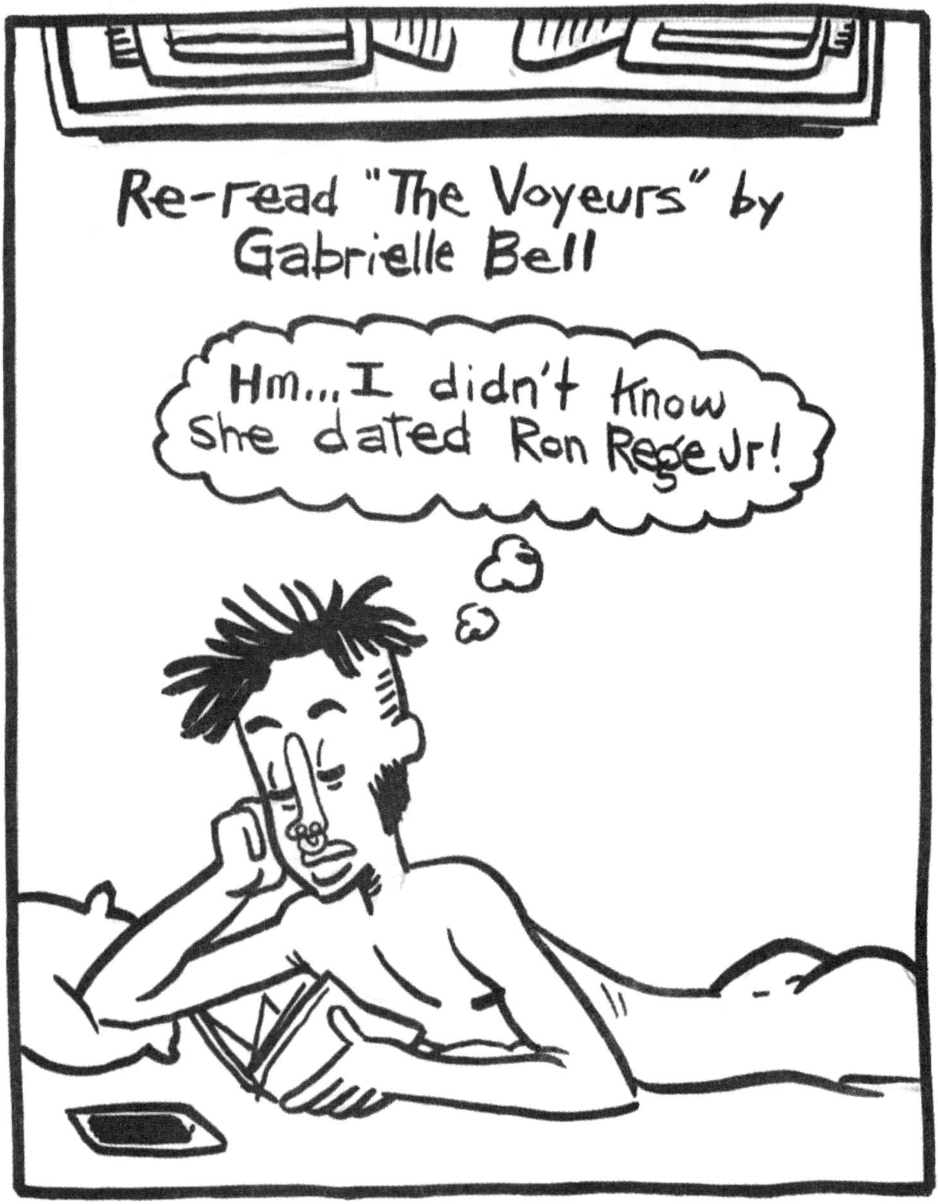
Re-read "The Voyeurs" by Gabrielle Bell
Hm... I didn't know she dated Ron Rege Jr!

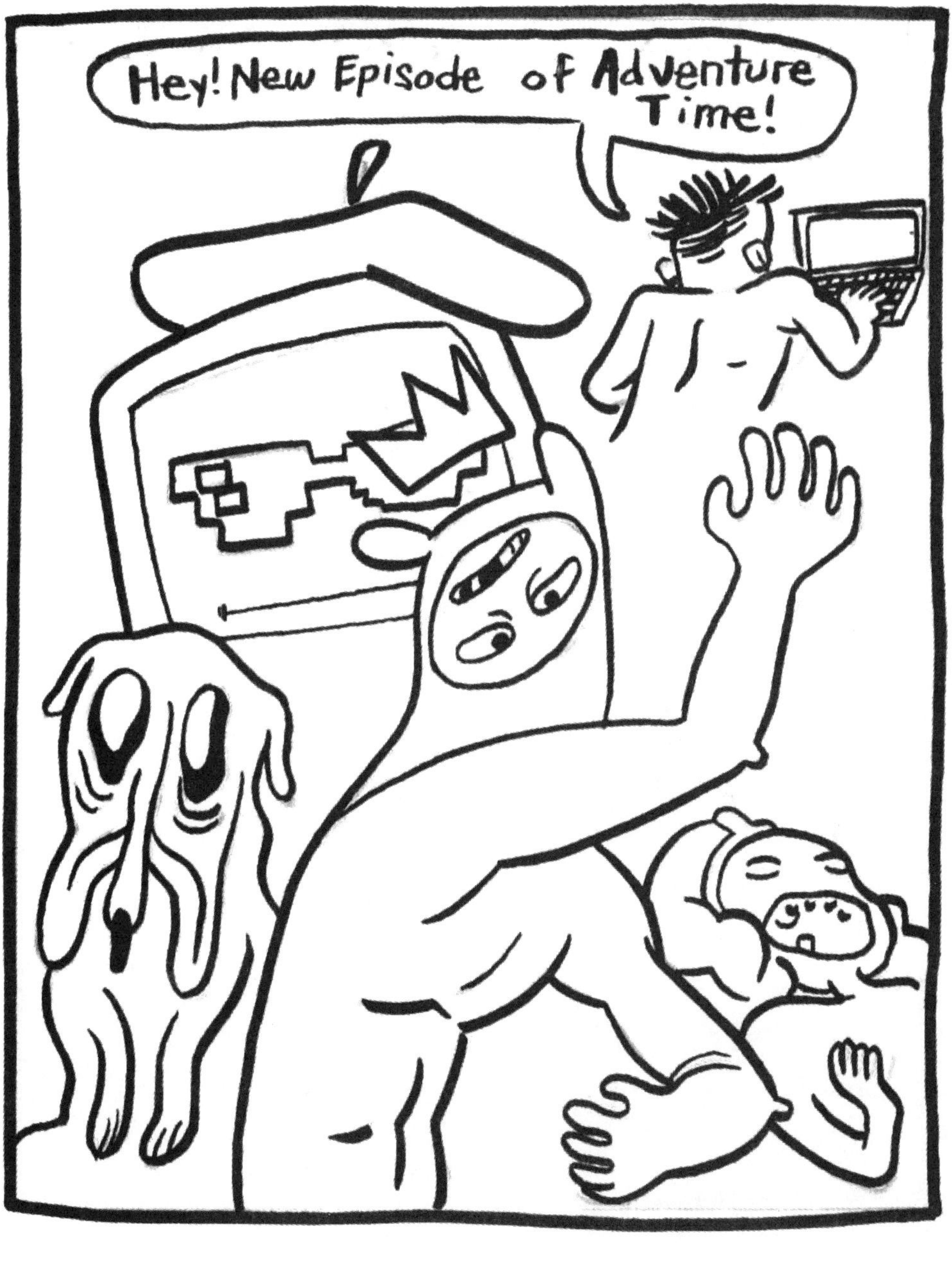
Hey! New Episode of Adventure Time!

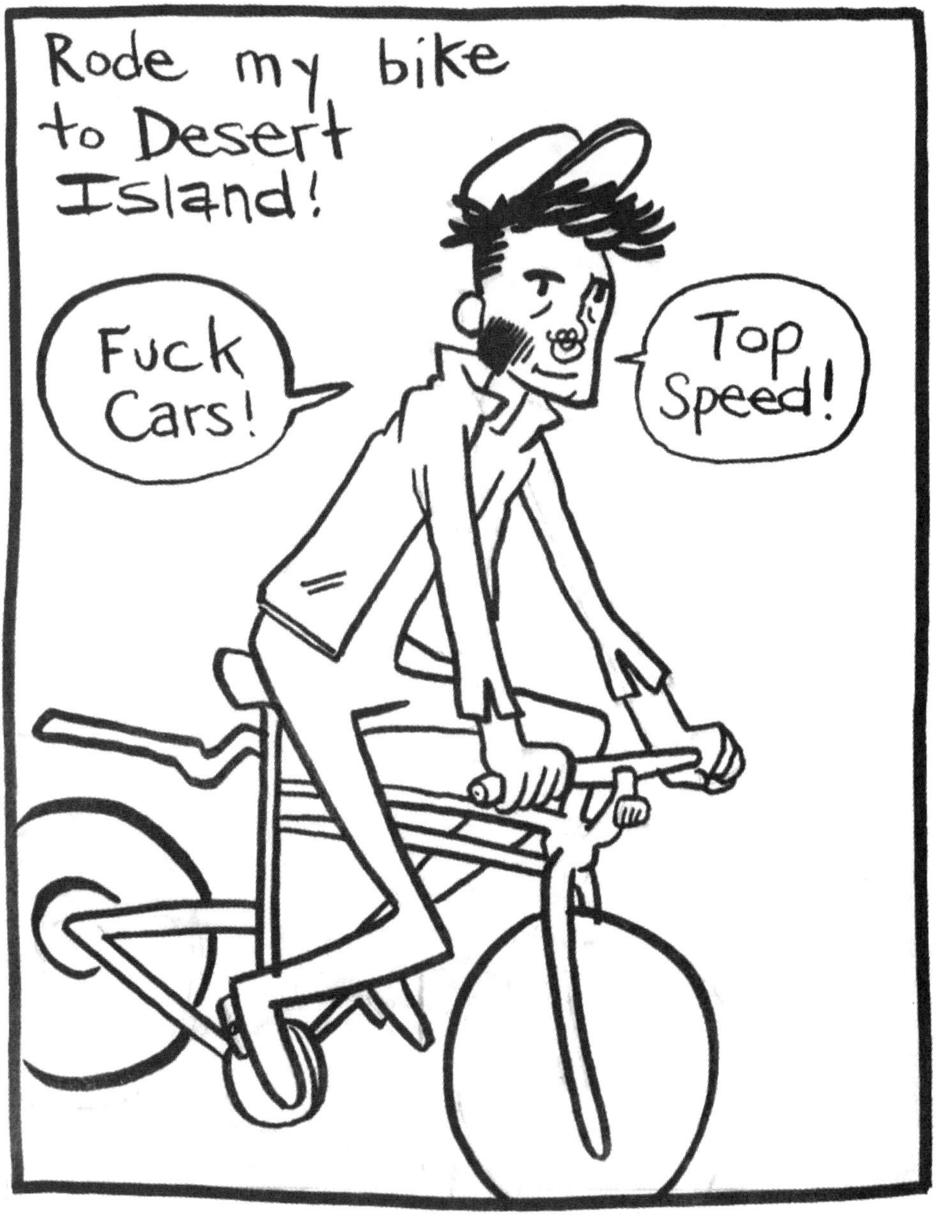
Rode my bike to Desert Island!
Fuck Cars!
Top Speed!

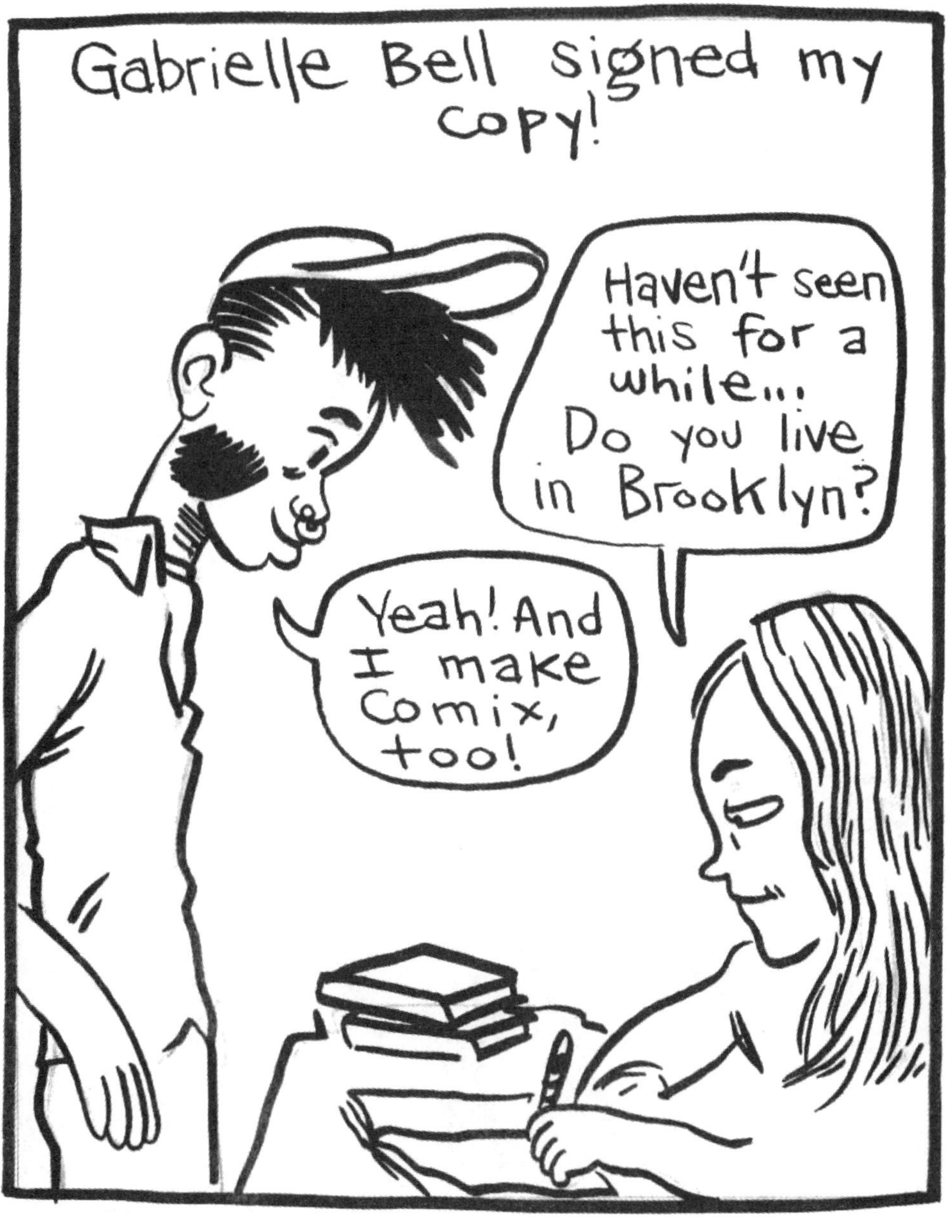
Gabrielle Bell signed my copy!
Haven't seen this for a while... Do you live in Brooklyn?
Yeah! And I make Comix, too!

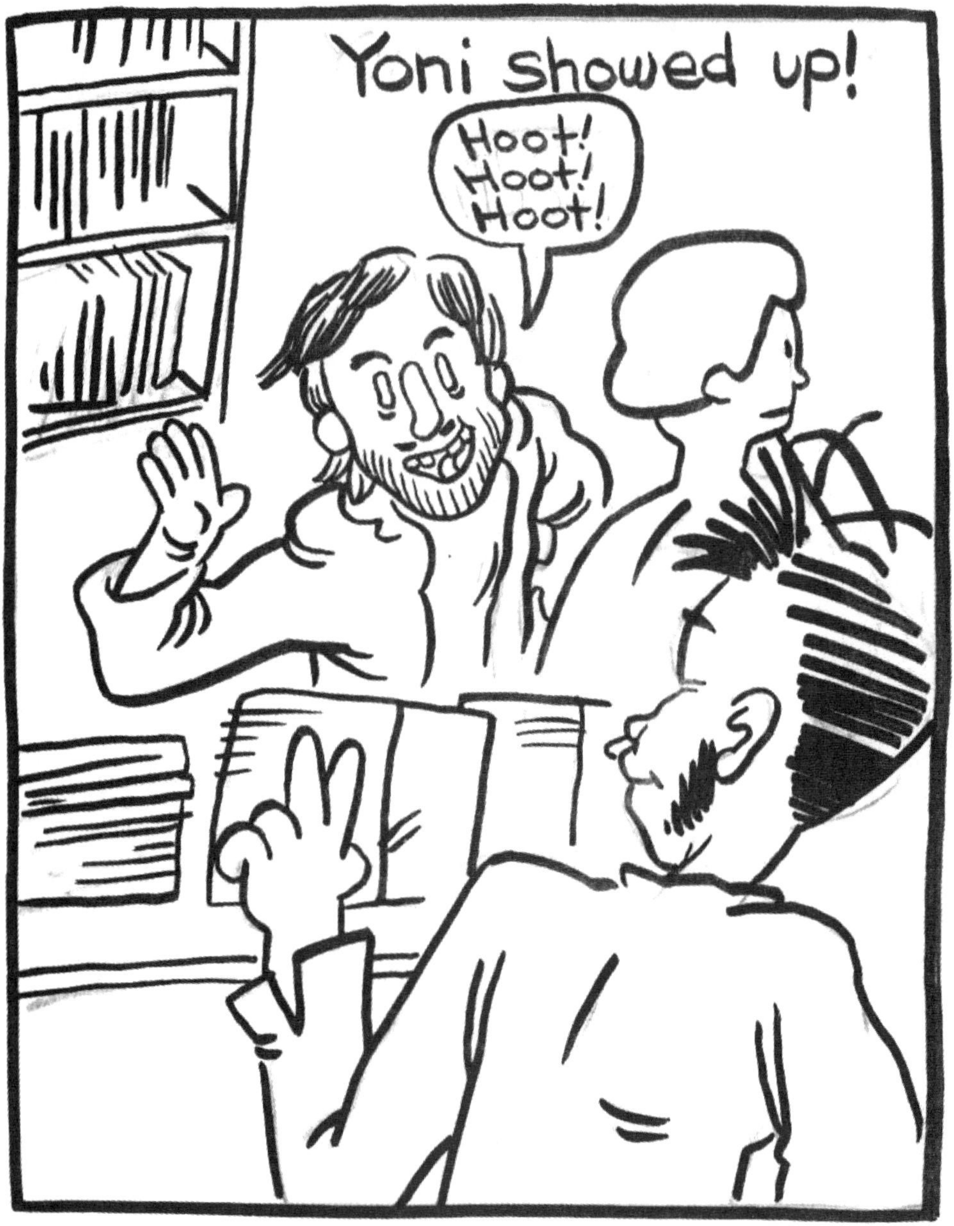
Yoni showed up!
Hoot! Hoot! Hoot!

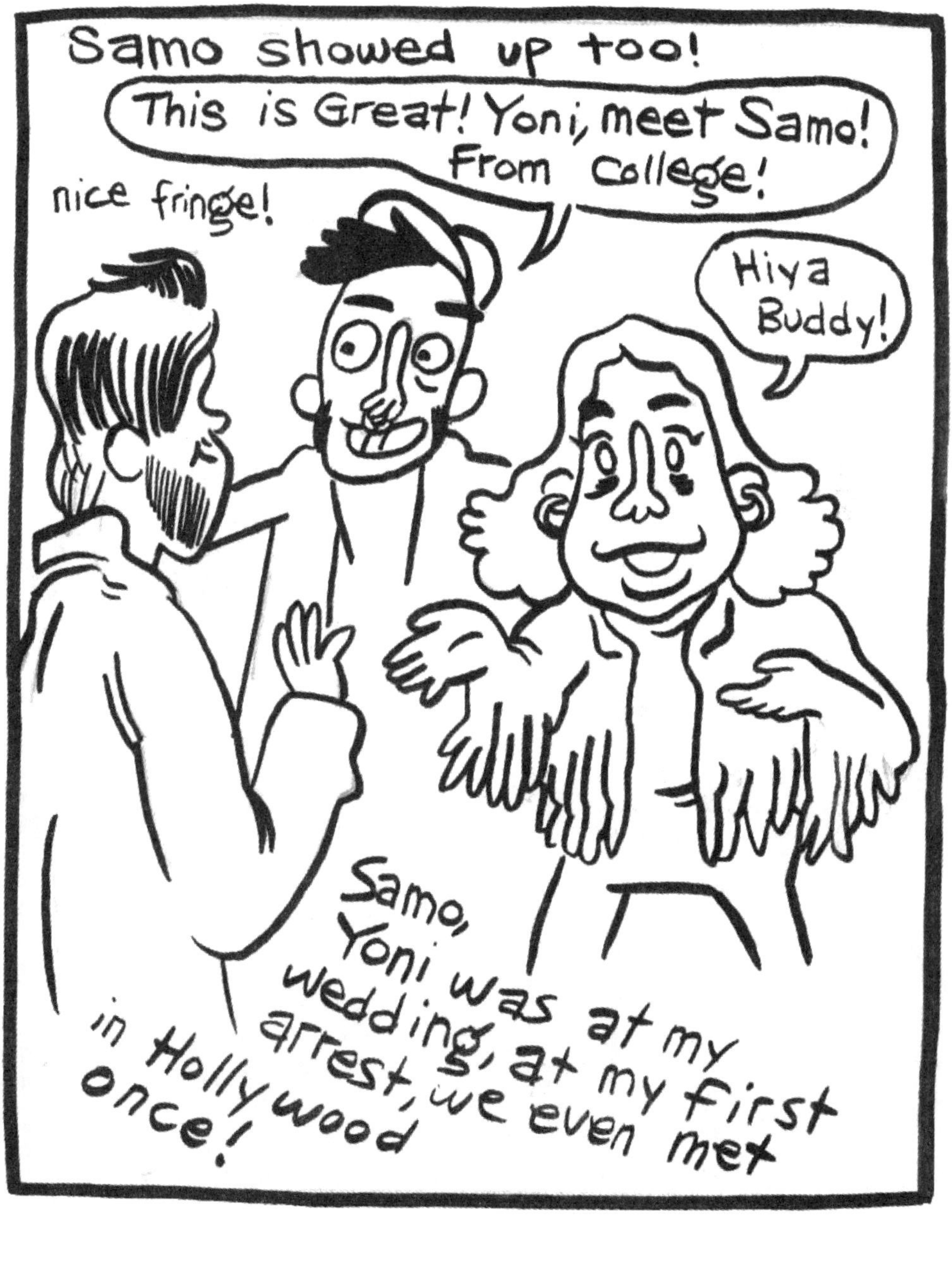
Samo showed up too!
This is Great! Yoni, meet Samo! From College!
nice fringe!
Hiya Buddy!
Samo, Yoni was at my wedding, at my first arrest, we even met in Hollywood once!

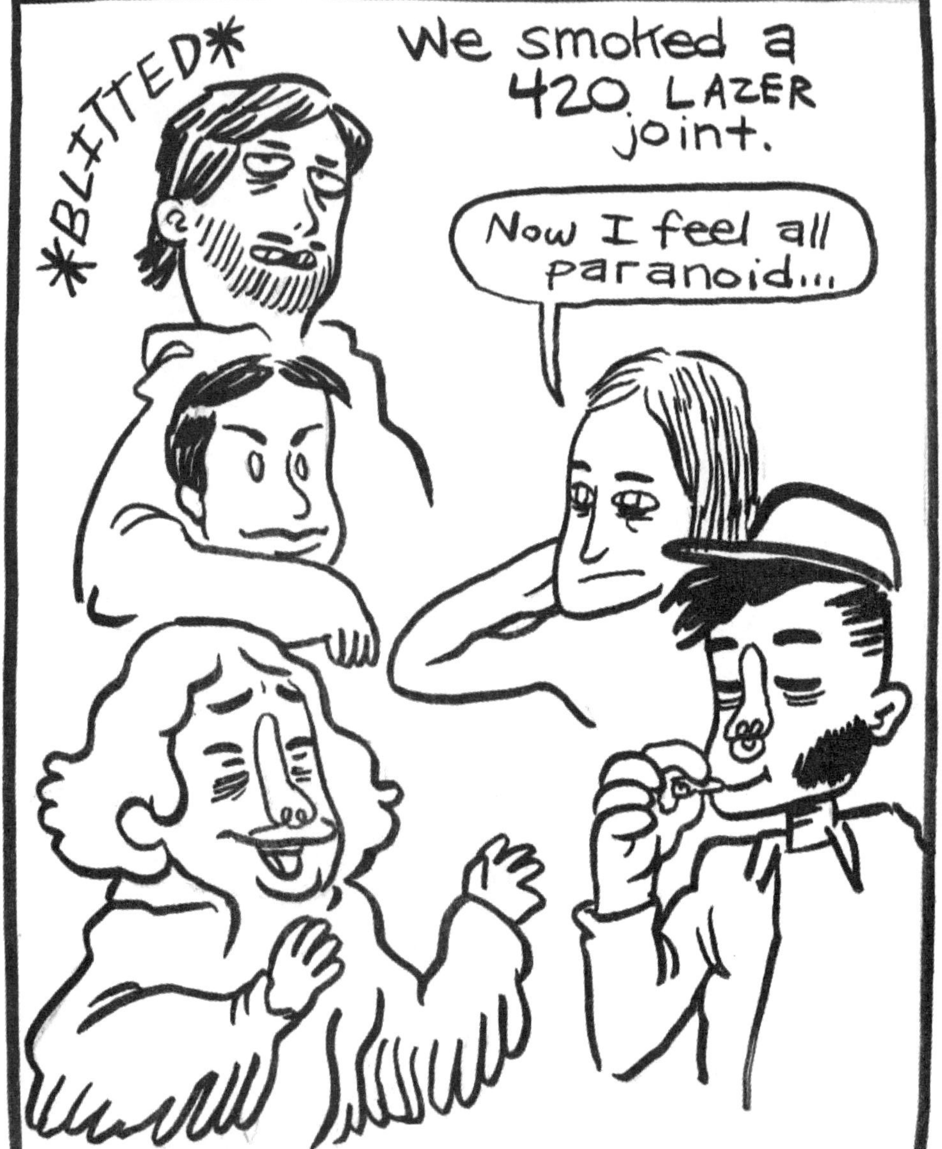
BLITTED
We smoked a 420 LAZER joint.
Now I feel all paranoid...

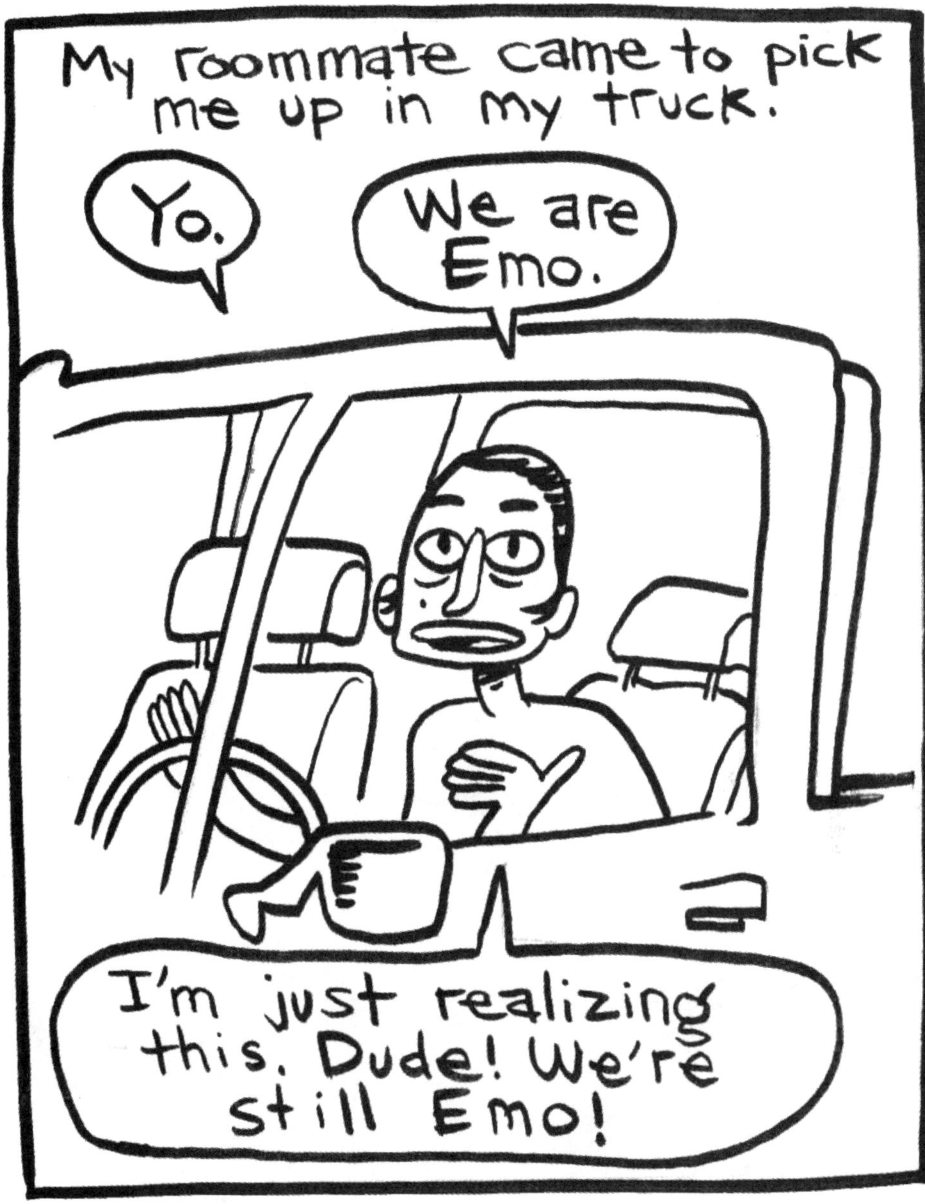
My roommate came to pick me up in my truck.
Yo.
We are Emo.
I'm just realizing this. Dude! We're still Emo!

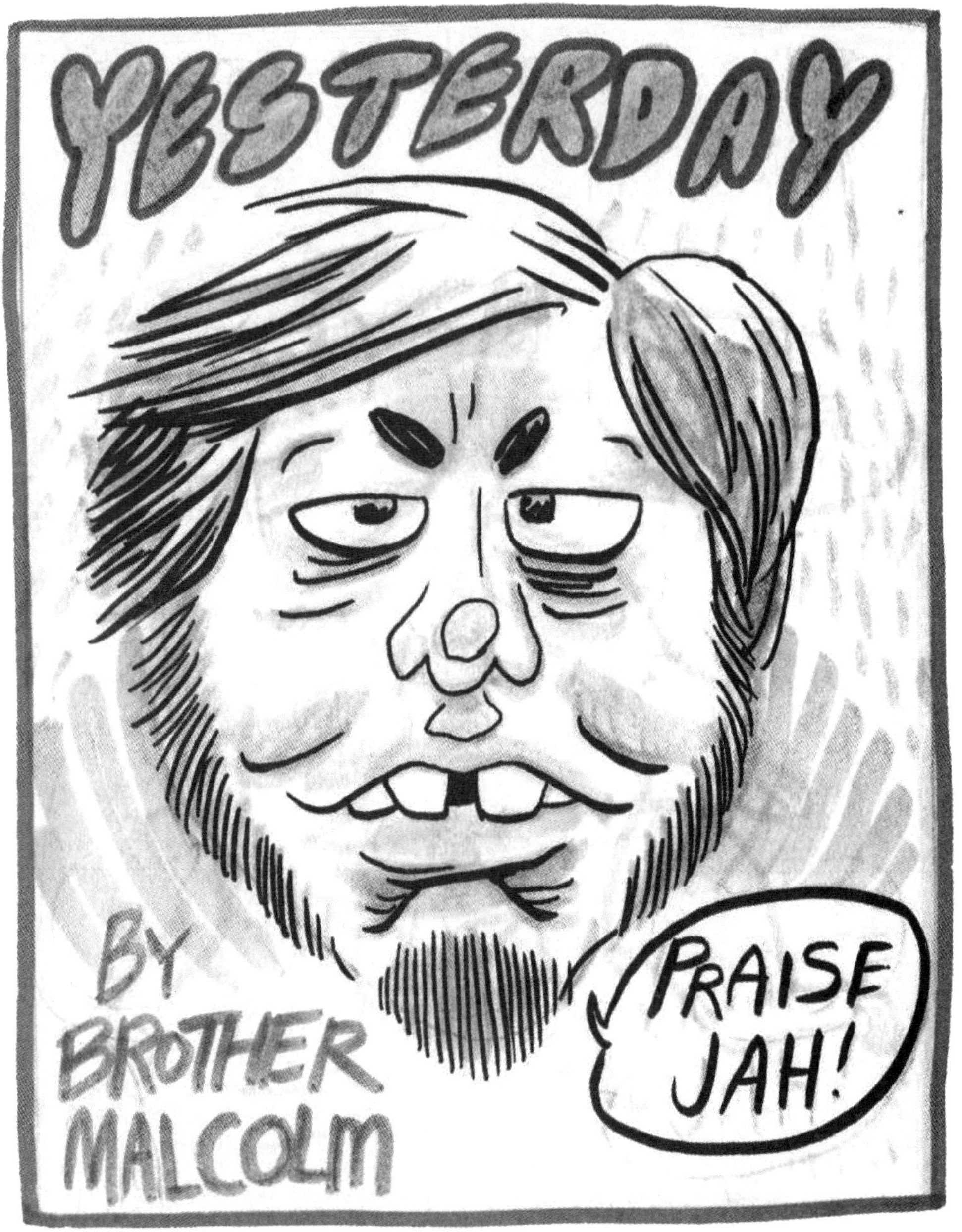
YESTERDAY
BY BROTHER MALCOLM
PRAISE JAH!

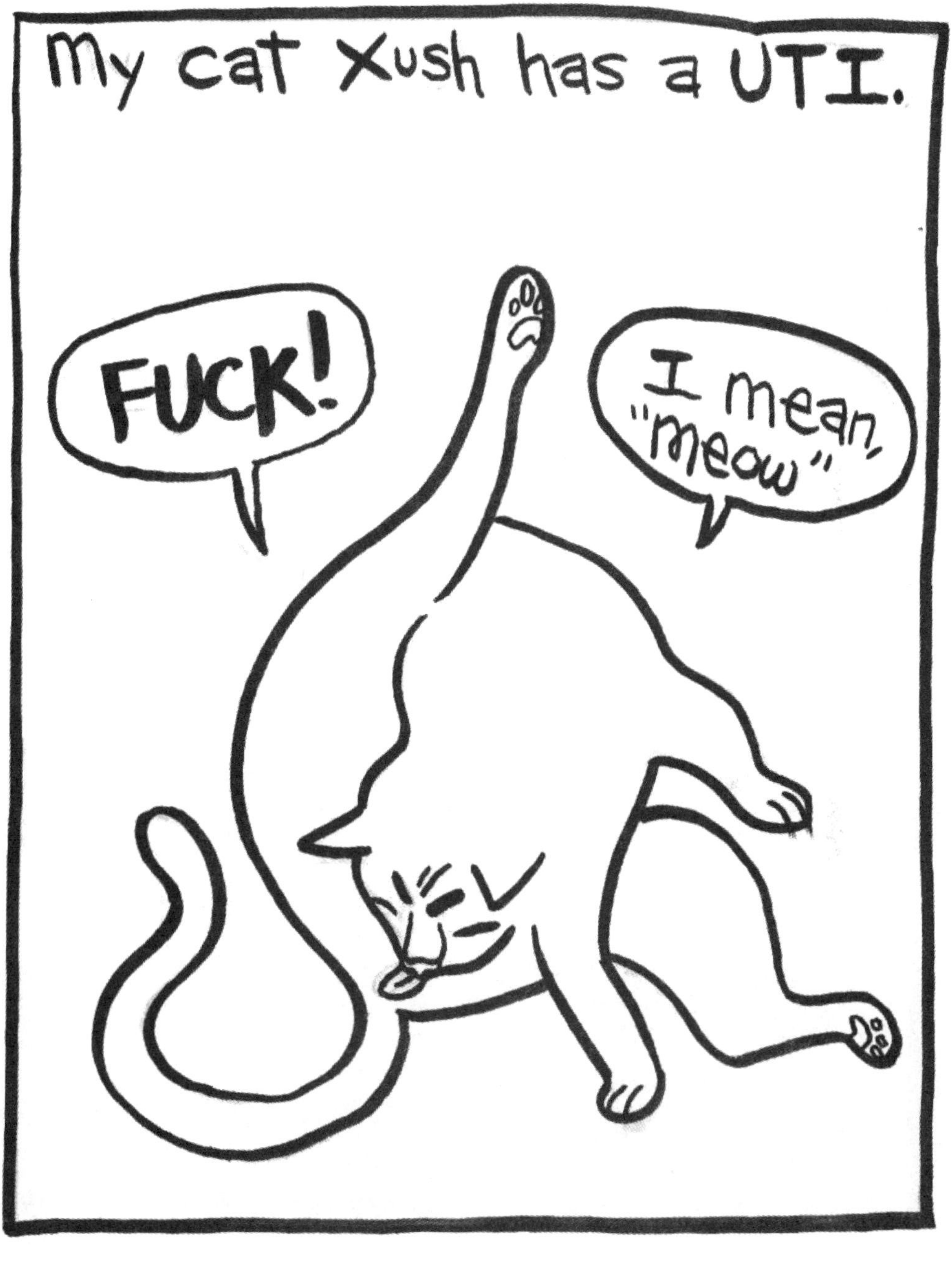
My cat Xush has a UTI.
FUCK!
I mean, "meow"

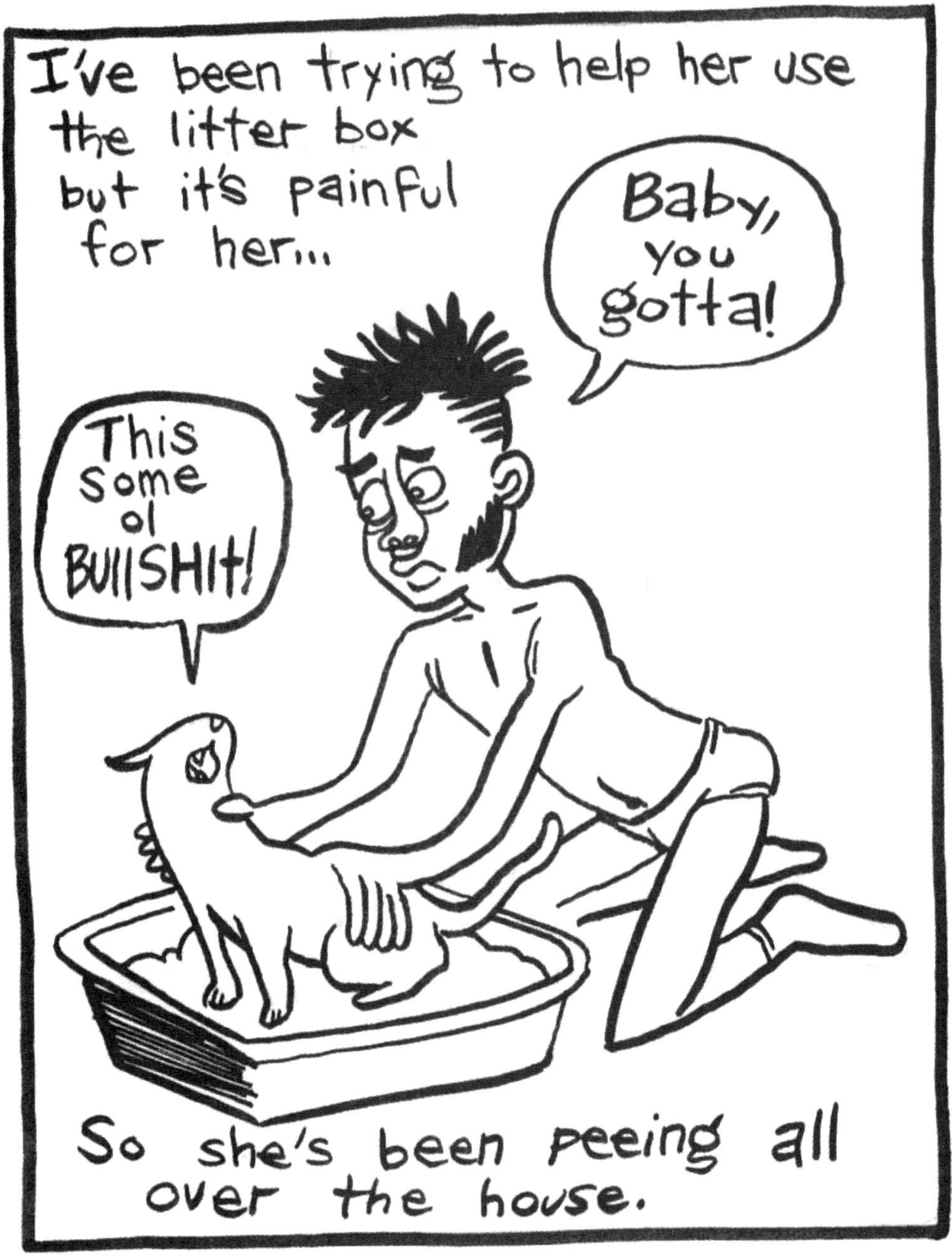
I've been trying to help her use the litter box but it's painful for her...
Baby, you gotta!
This some ol BULLSHIT!
So she's been peeing all over the house.

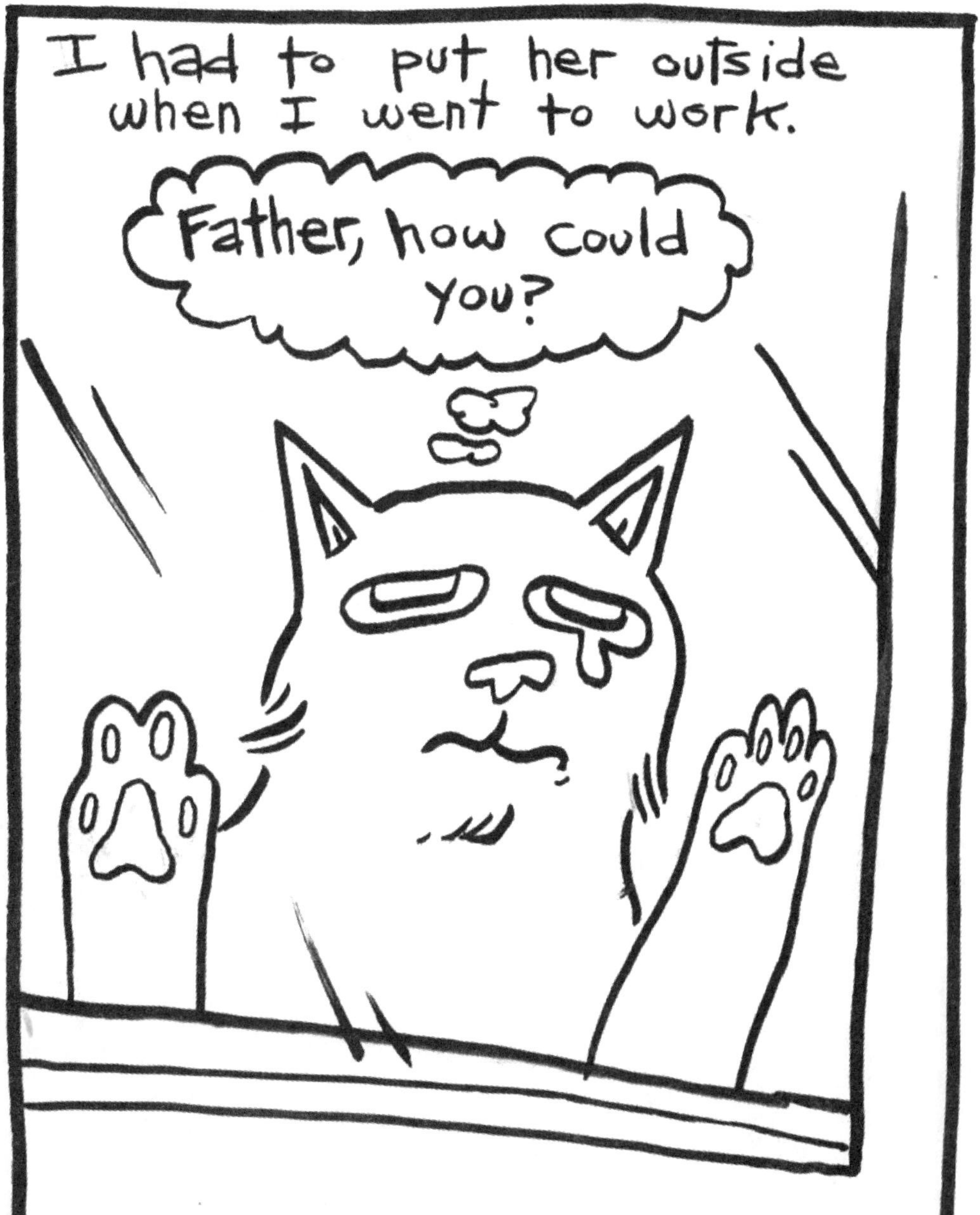

I had to put her outside when I went to work.
Father, how could you?

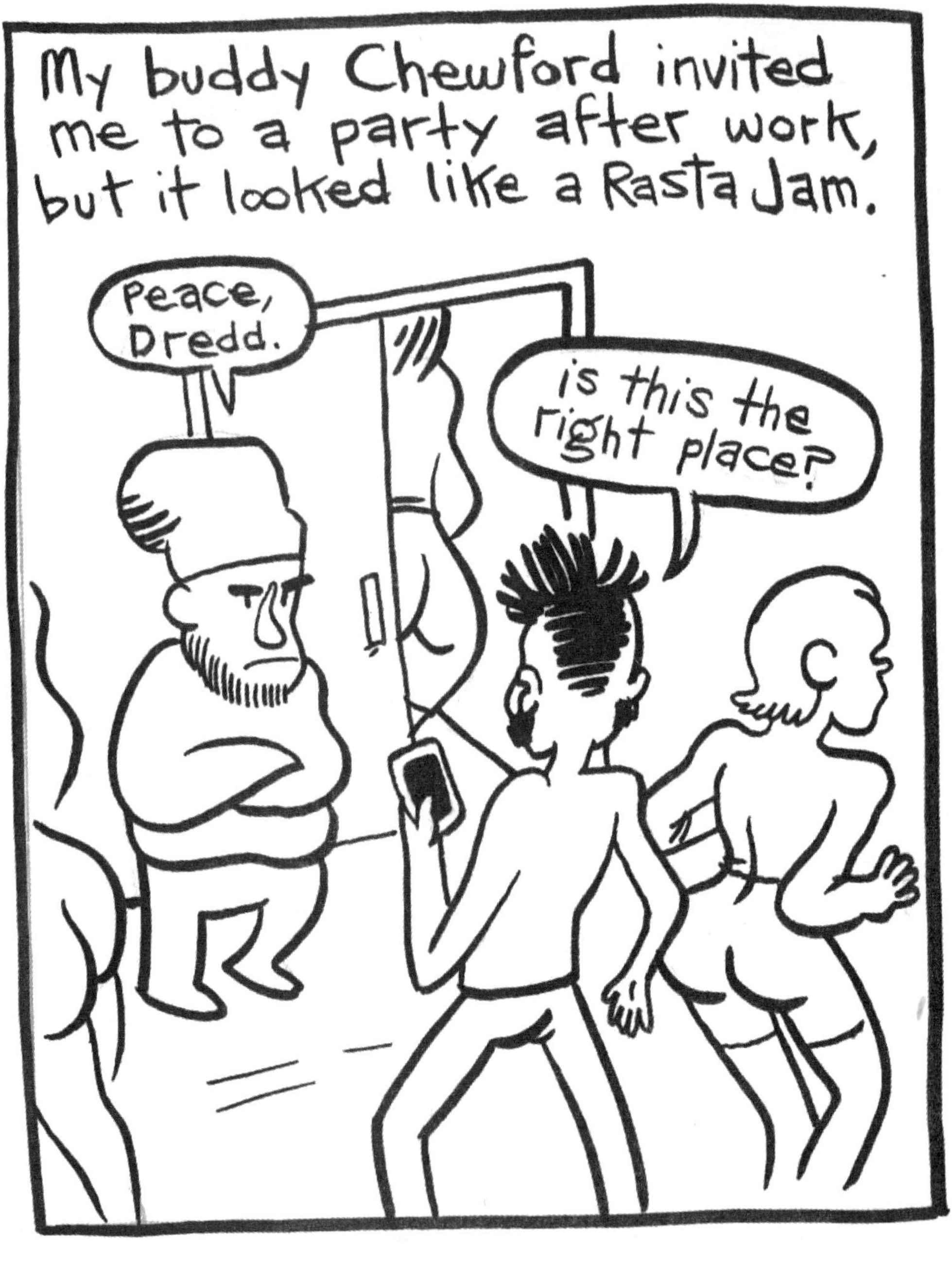
My buddy Chewford invited me to a party after work, but it looked like a Rasta Jam.
Peace, Dredd.
is this the right place?

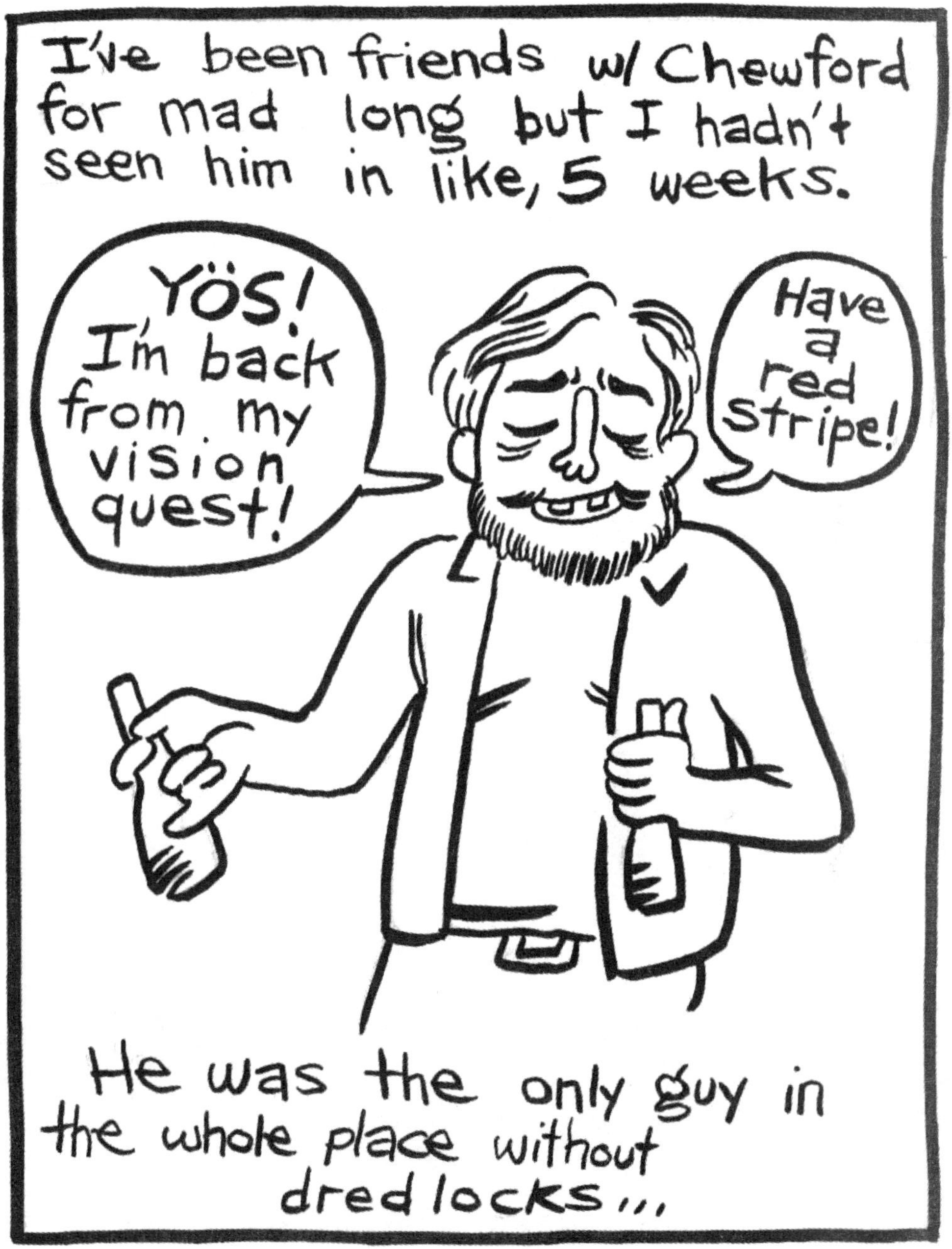
I've been friends w/ Chewford for mad long but I hadn't seen him in like, 5 weeks.
YÖS! I'm back from my vision quest!
Have a red stripe!
He was the only guy in the whole place without dredlocks...

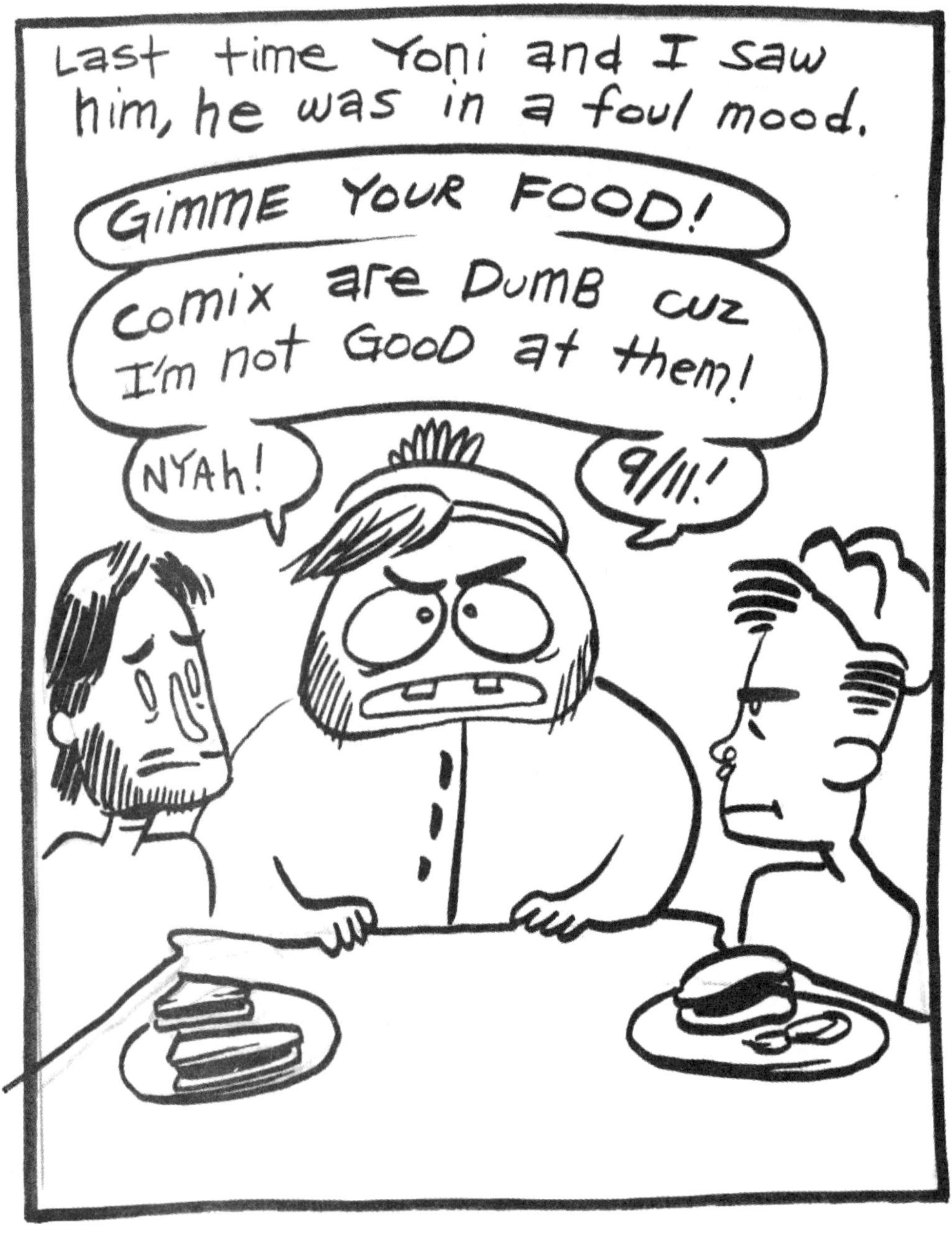
Last time Yoni and I saw him, he was in a foul mood.
GIMME YOUR FOOD!
Comix are DUMB cuz I'm not GOOD at them!
NYAh!
9/11!

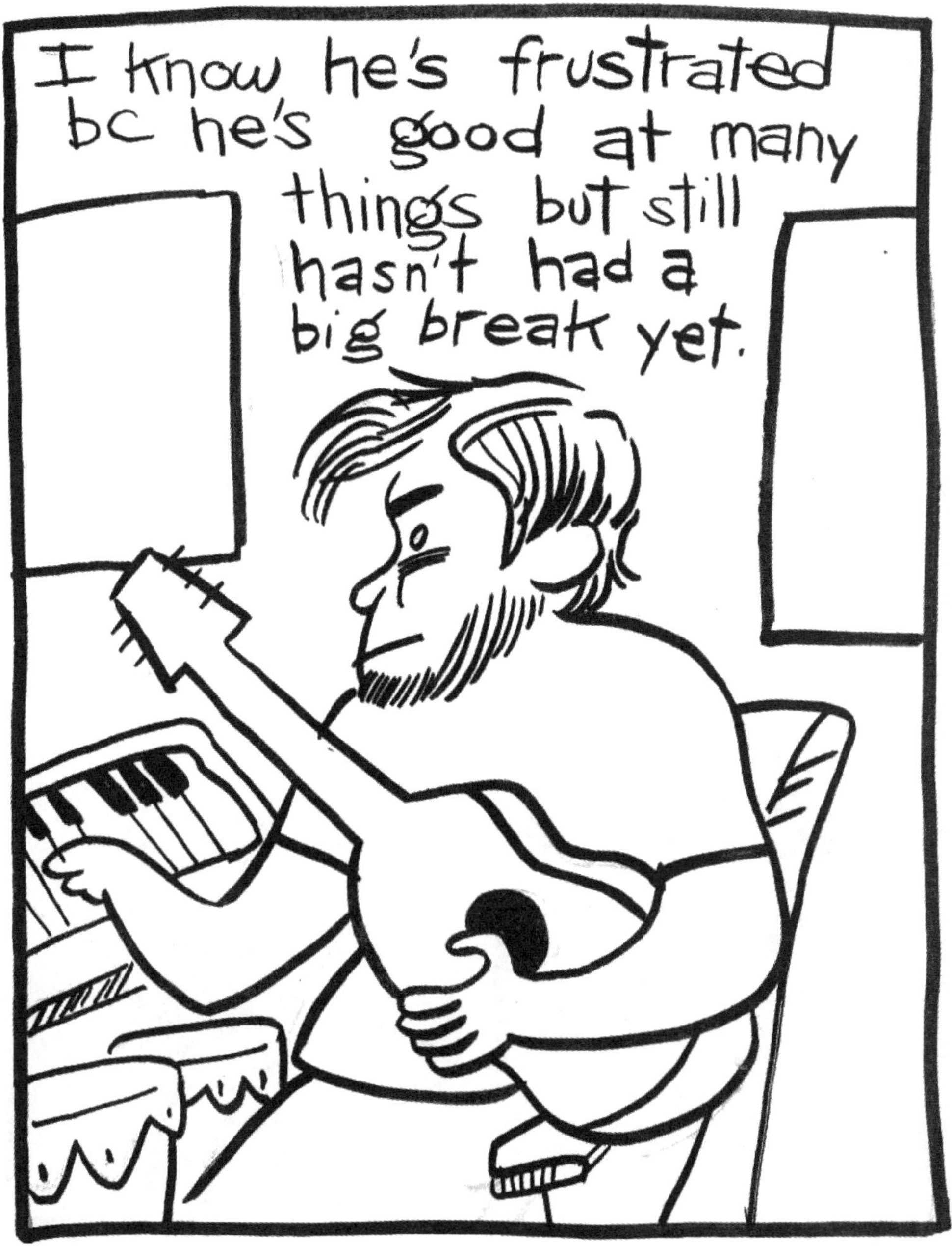
I know he's frustrated bc he's good at many things but still hasn't had a big break yet.

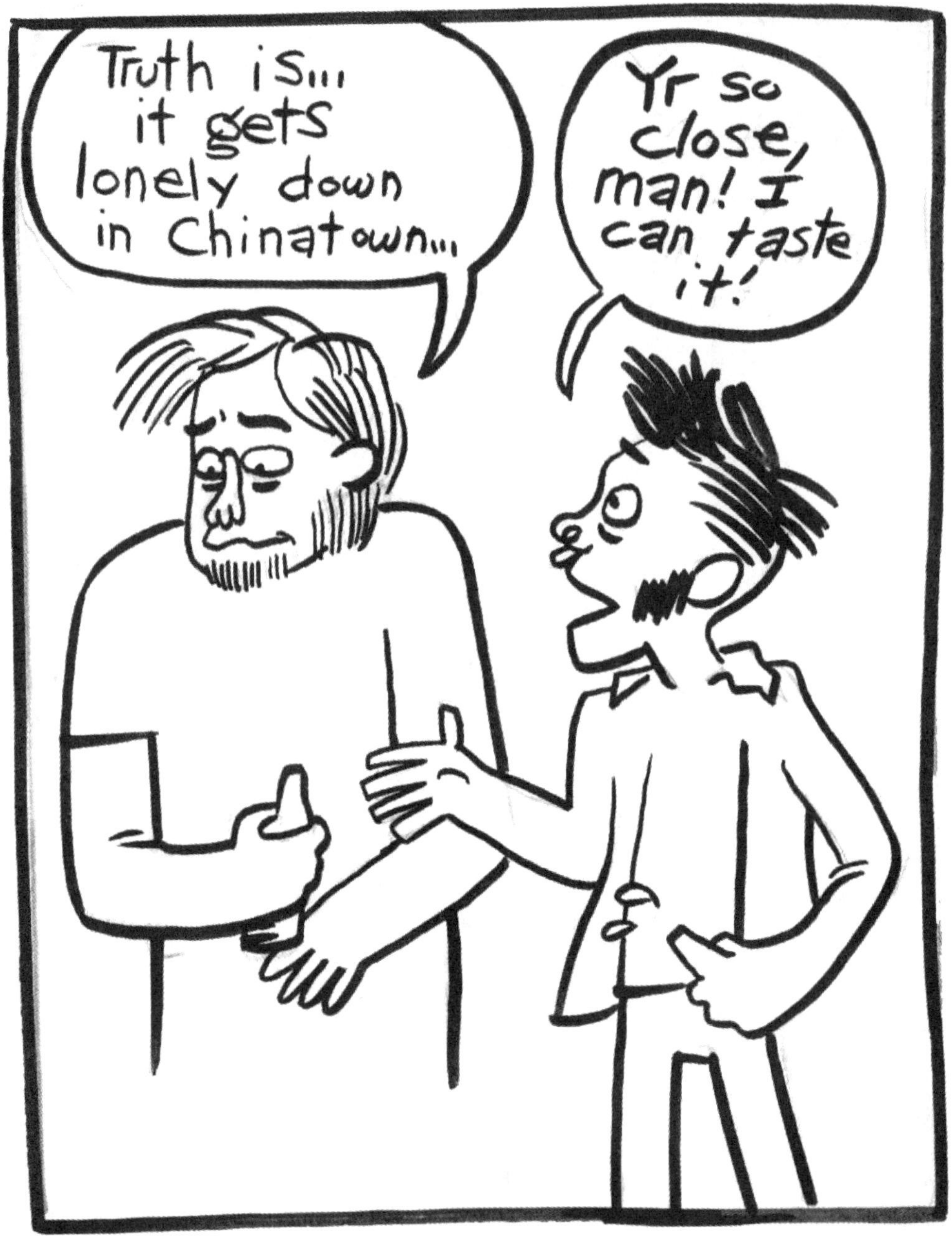
Truth is... it gets lonely down in Chinatown...
Yr so close, man! I can taste it!

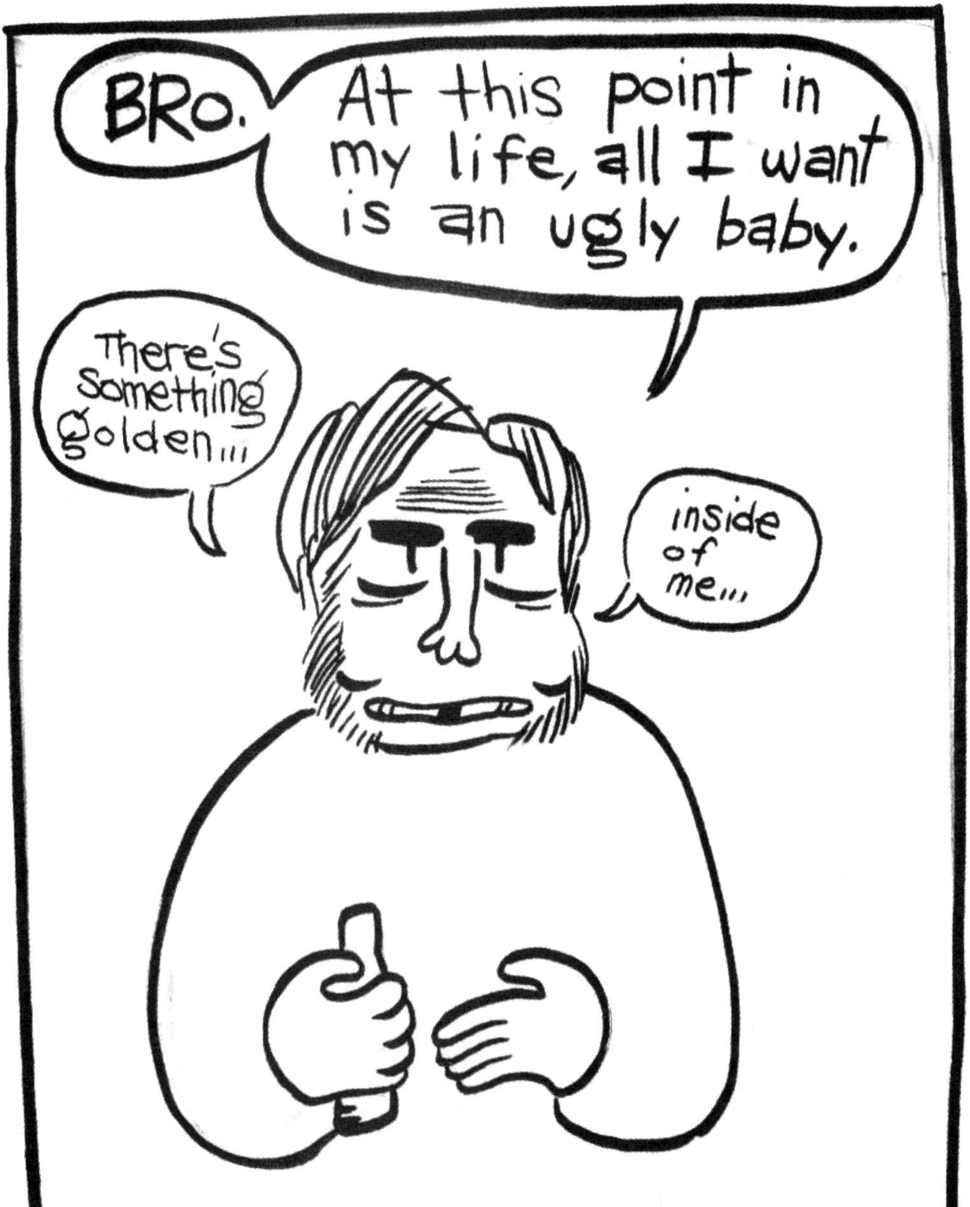
BRO.
At this point in my life, all I want is an ugly baby.
There's something golden...
inside of me...

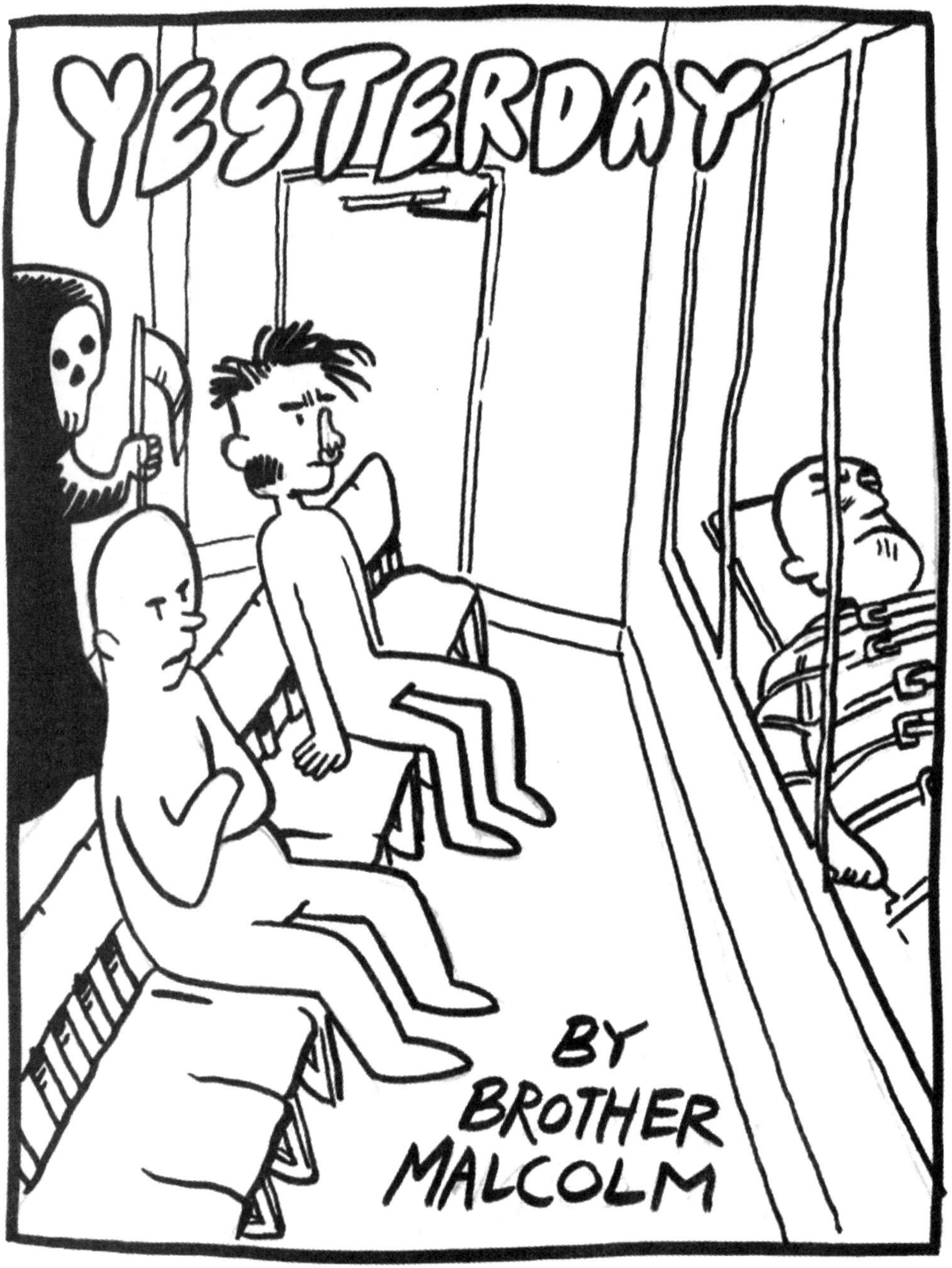
YESTERDAY
BY BROTHER MALCOLM

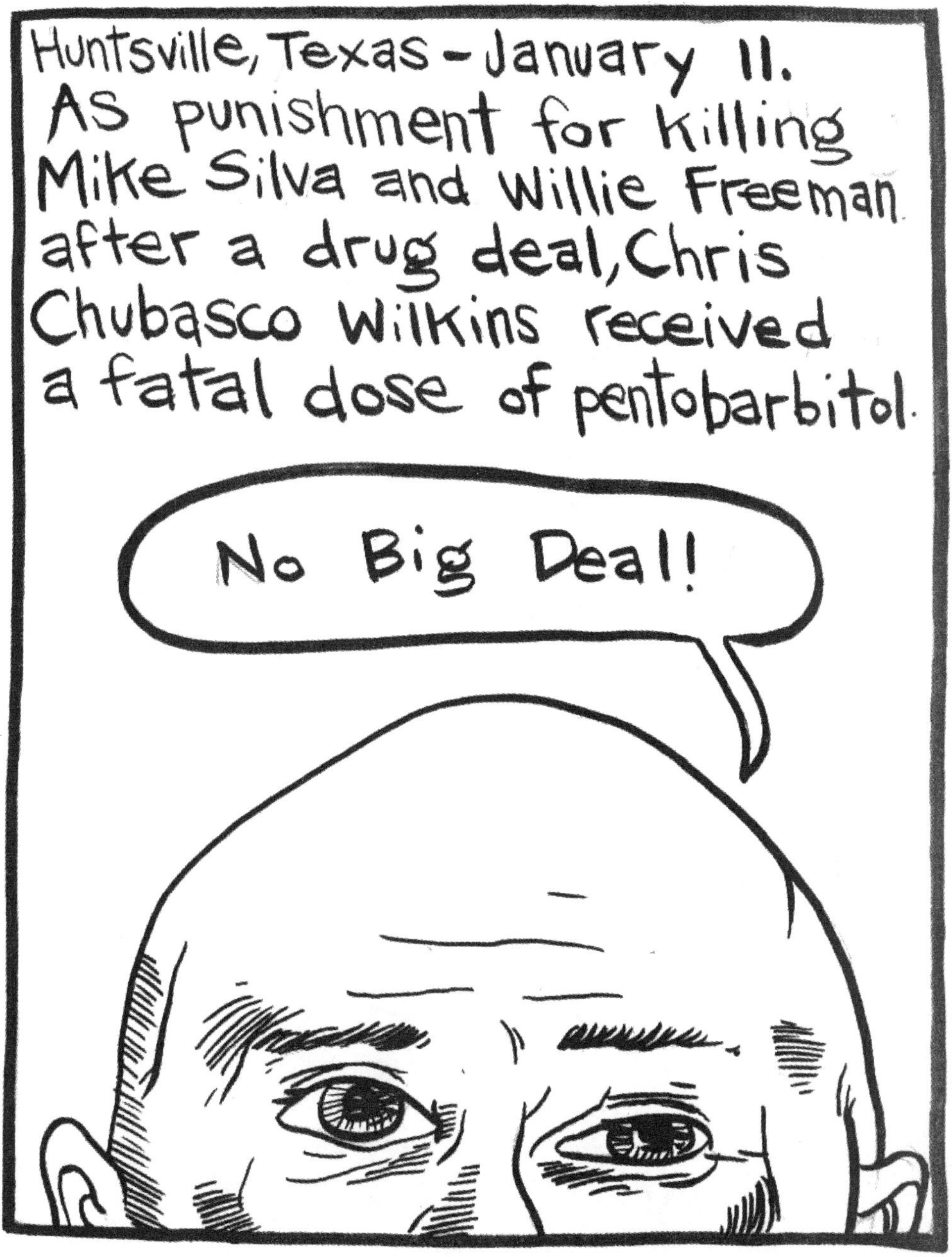
Huntsville, Texas - January 11.
As punishment for killing Mike Silva and Willie Freeman after a drug deal, Chris Chubasco Wilkins received a fatal dose of pentobarbitol.
No Big Deal!

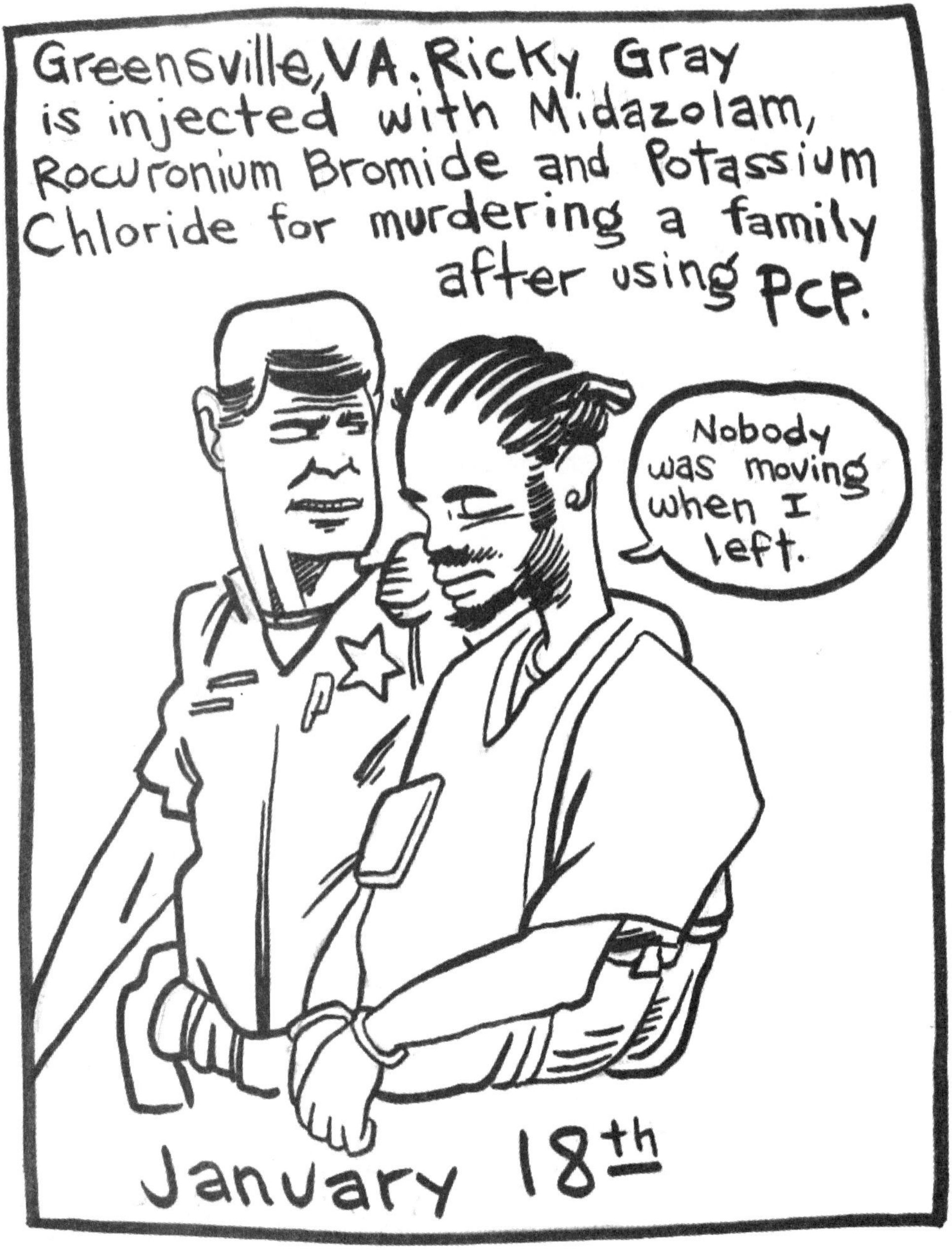
Greensville, VA. Ricky Gray is injected with Midazolam, Rocuronium Bromide and Potassium Chloride for murdering a family after using PCP.
Nobody was moving when I left.
January 18th

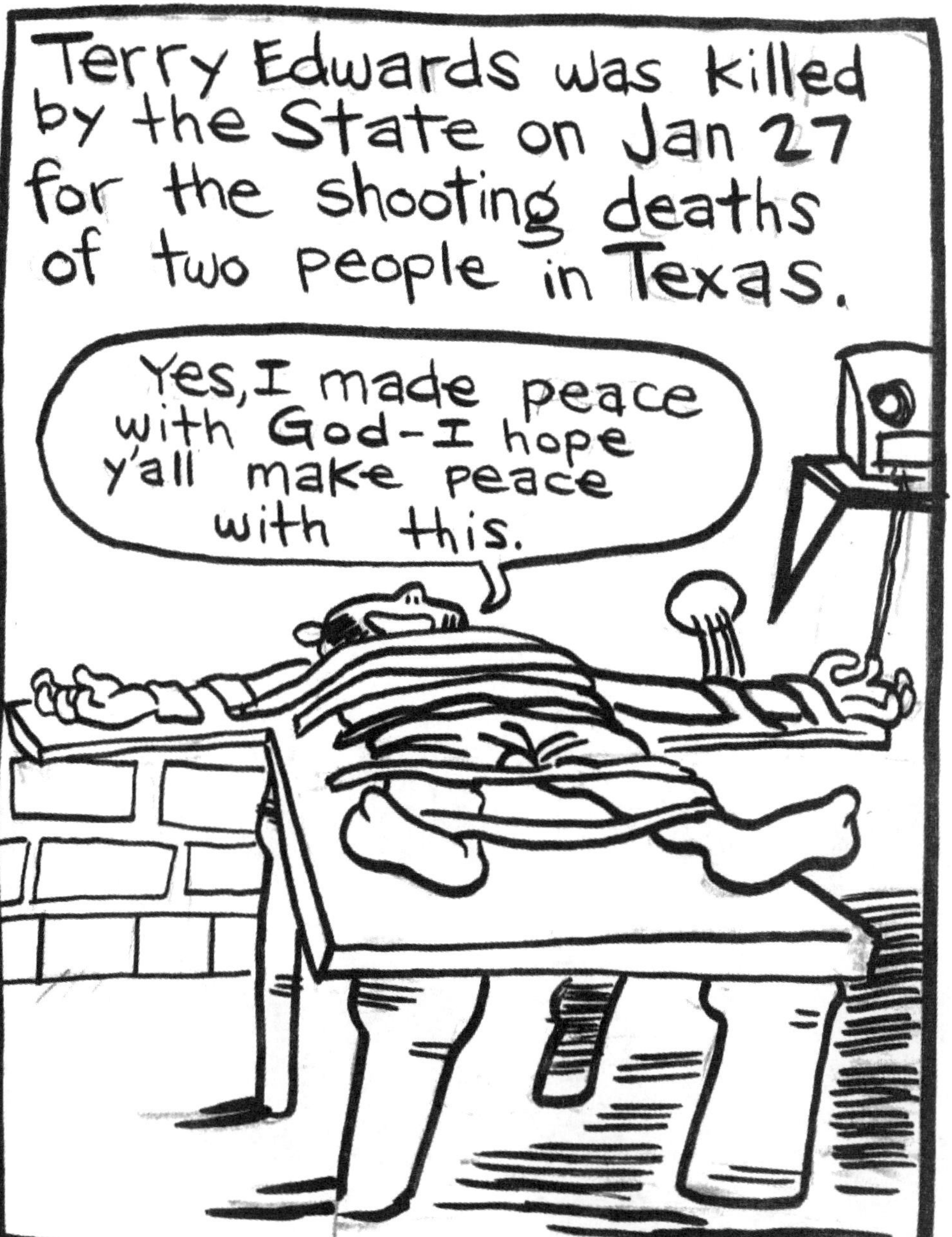
Terry Edwards was killed by the State on Jan 27 for the shooting deaths of two people in Texas.
Yes, I made peace with God-I hope y'all make peace with this.

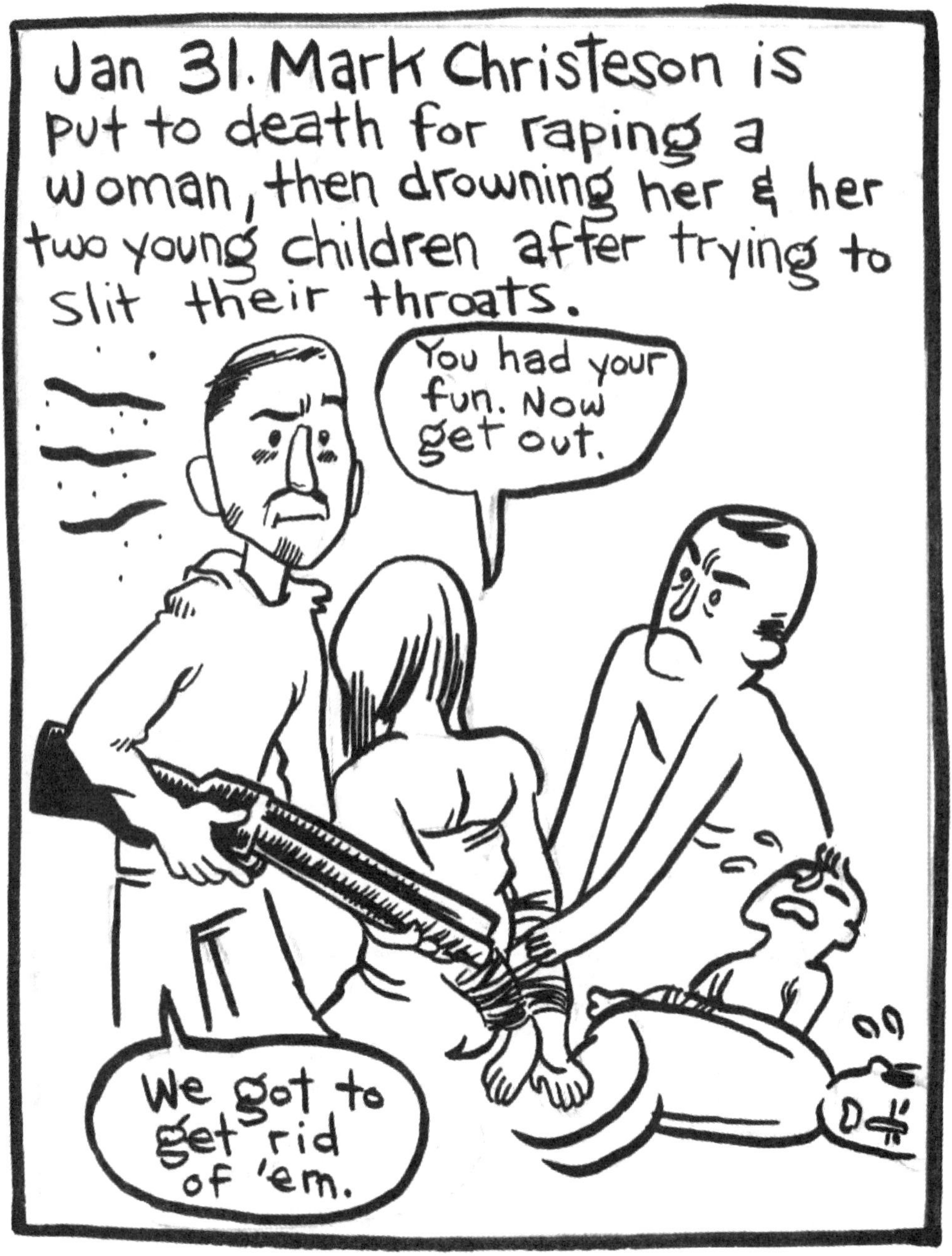
Jan 31. Mark Christeson is put to death for raping a woman, then drowning her & her two young children after trying to slit their throats.
You had your fun. Now get out.
We got to get rid of 'em.

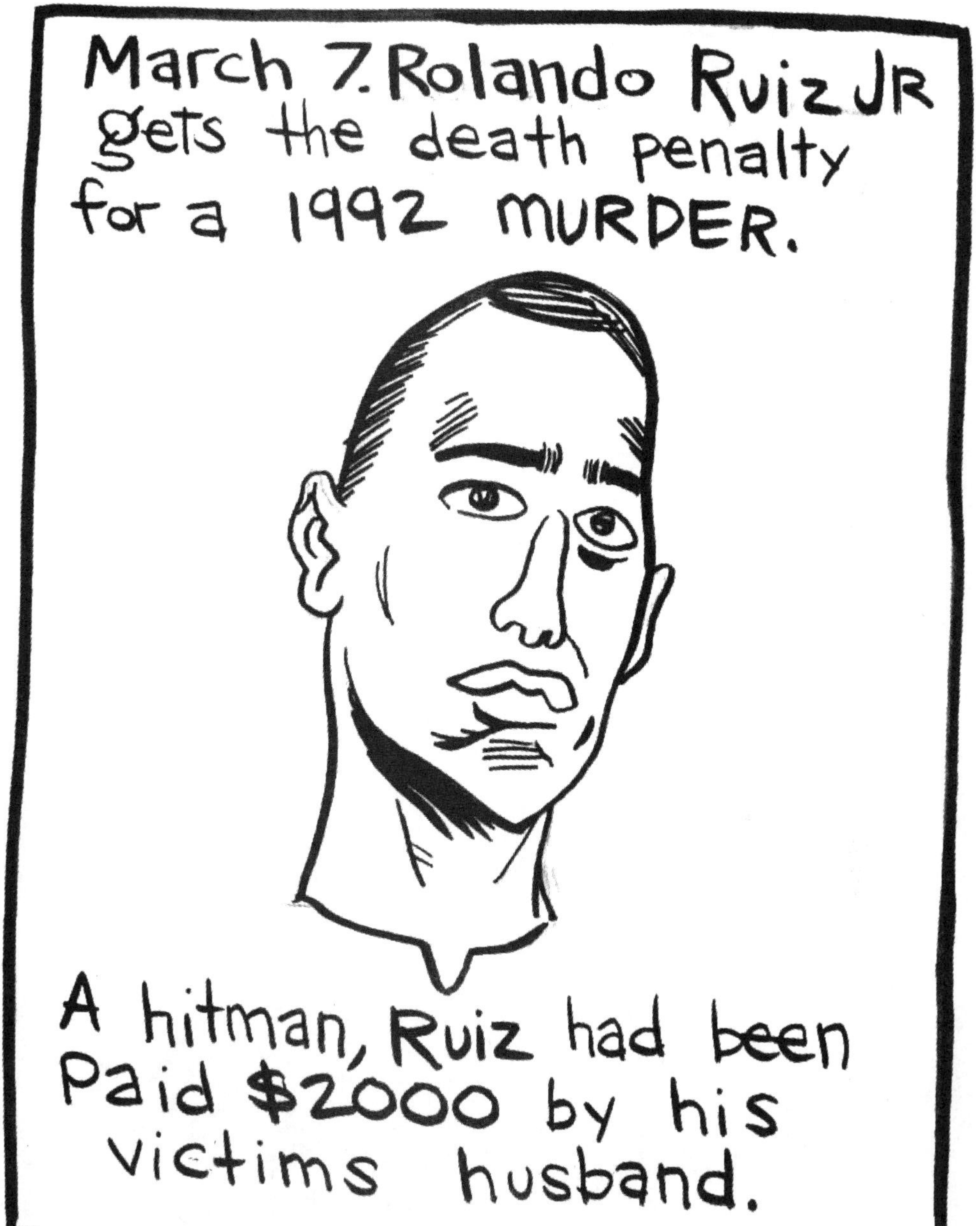
March 7. Rolando Ruiz JR gets the death penalty for a 1992 MURDER.
A hitman, Ruiz had been Paid $2000 by his victims husband.

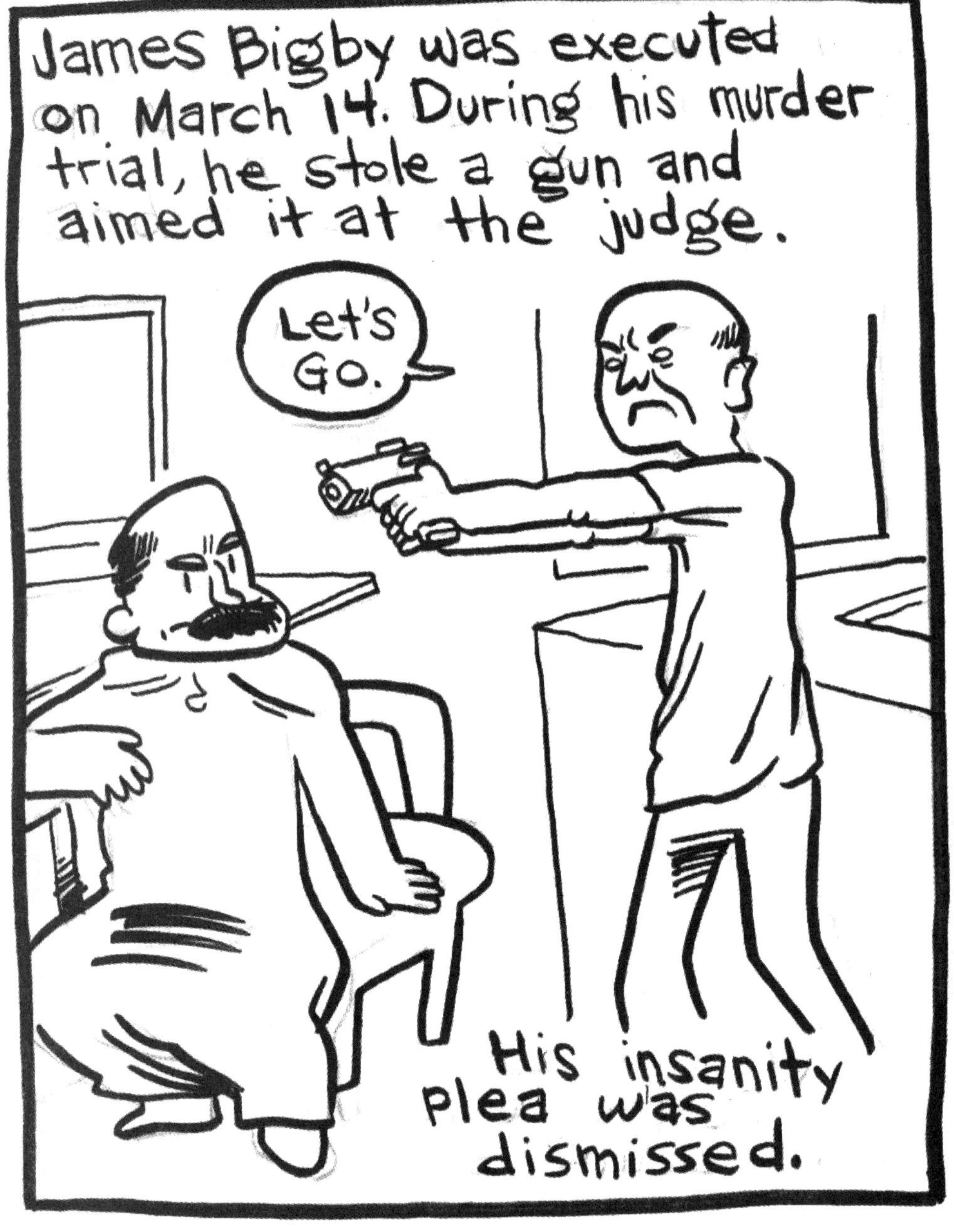
James Bigby was executed on March 14. During his murder trial, he stole a gun and aimed it at the judge.
Let's Go.
His insanity plea was dismissed.

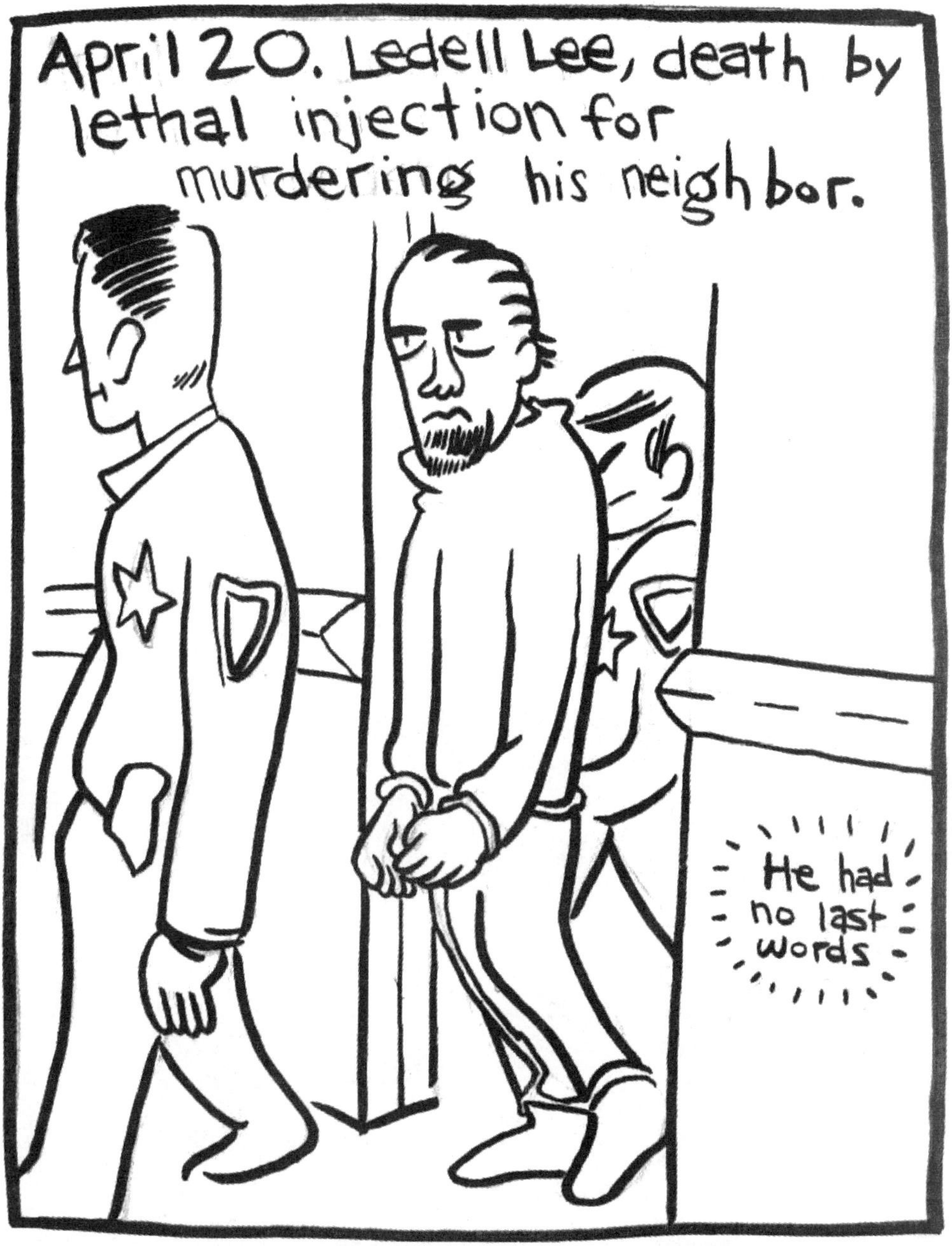
April 20. Ledell Lee, death by lethal injection for murdering his neighbor.
He had no last words

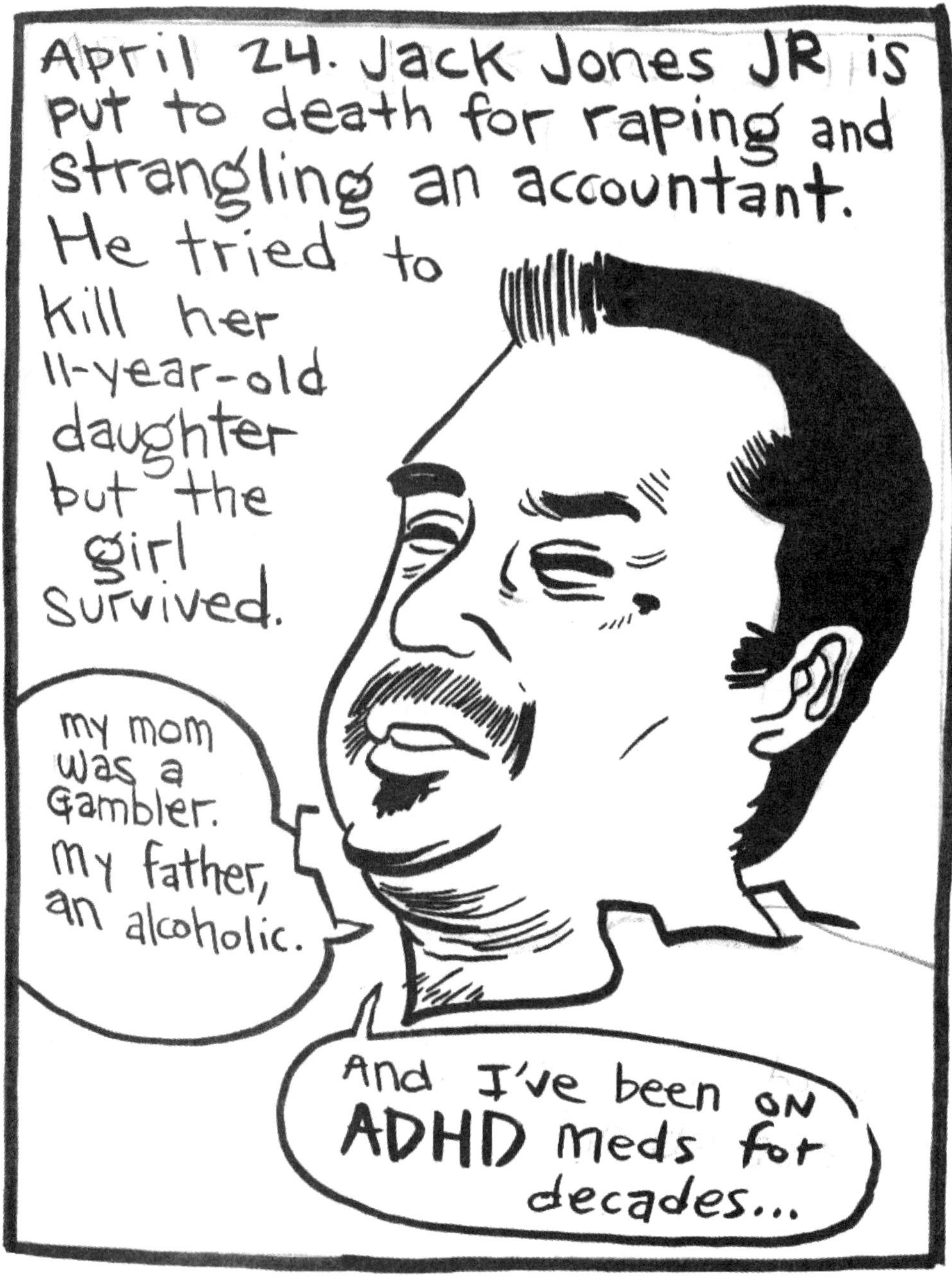
April 24. Jack Jones JR is put to death for raping and strangling an accountant. He tried to kill her 11-year-old daughter but the girl survived.
my mom was a gambler. my father, an alcoholic.
And I've been ON ADHD meds for decades...

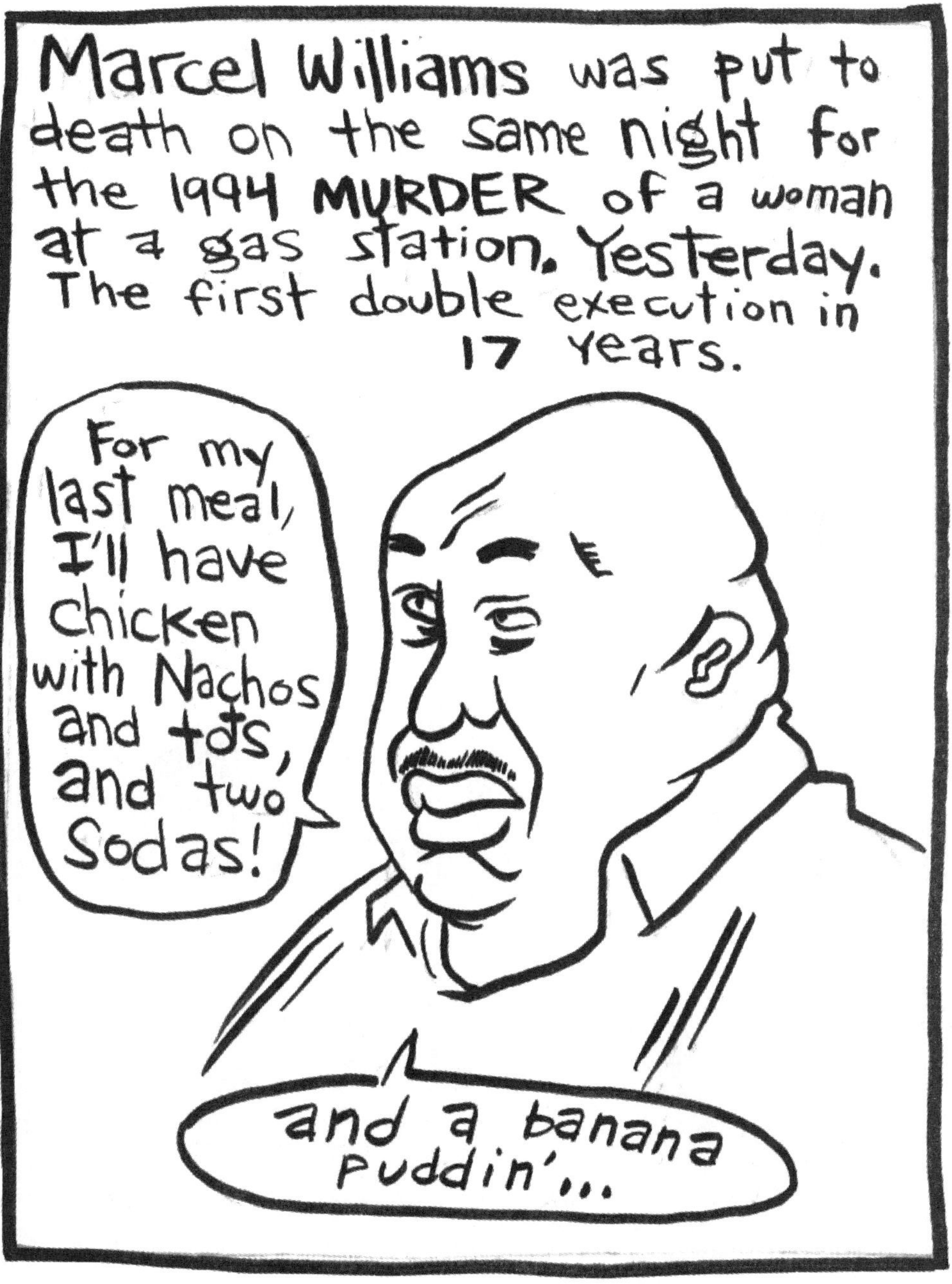
Marcel Williams was put to death on the same night for the 1994 MURDER of a woman at a gas station. Yesterday. The first double execution in 17 years.
For my last meal, I'll have chicken with Nachos and tots, and two Sodas!
and a banana puddin'...

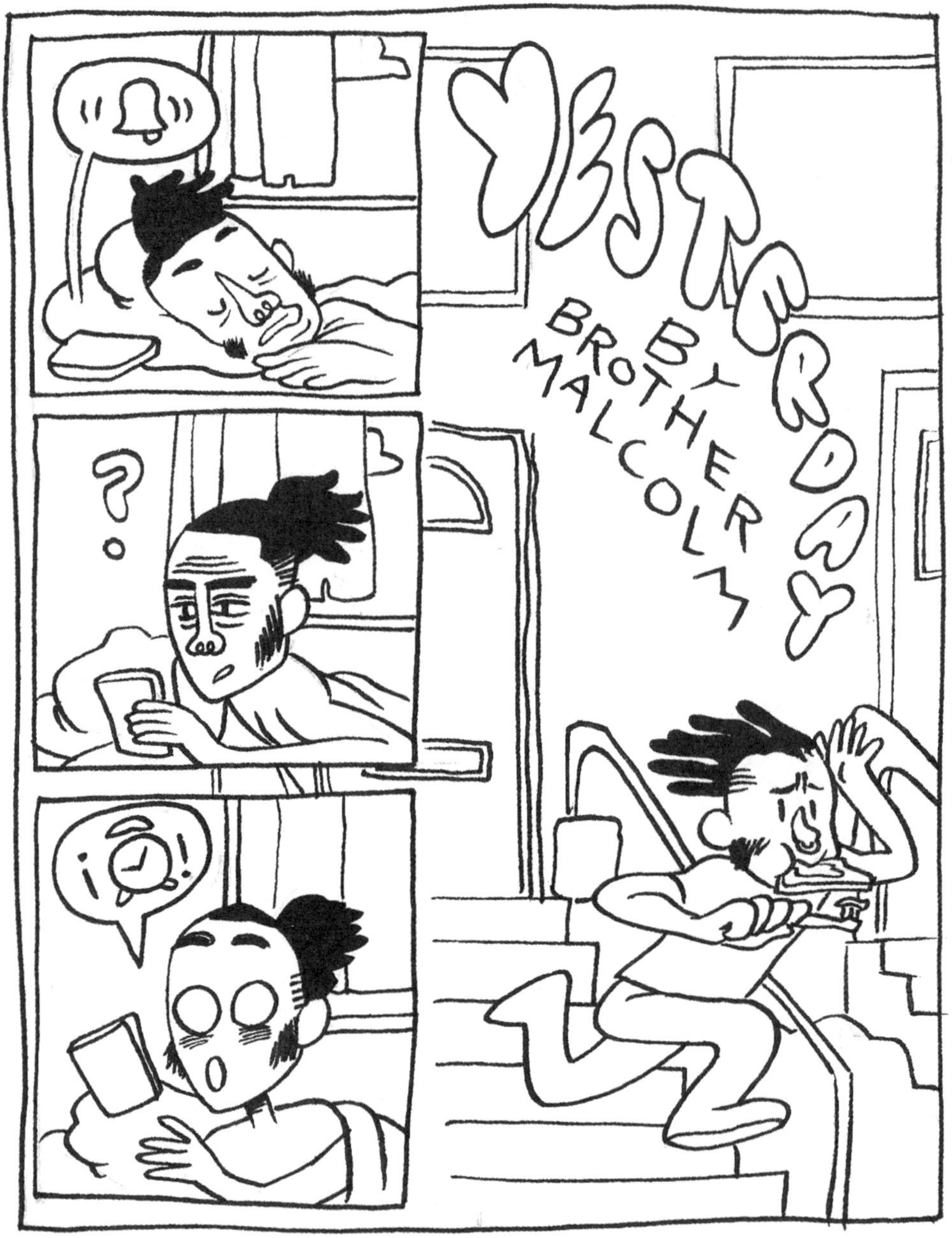
YESTERDAY
BY BROTHER MALCOLM
?
¡!

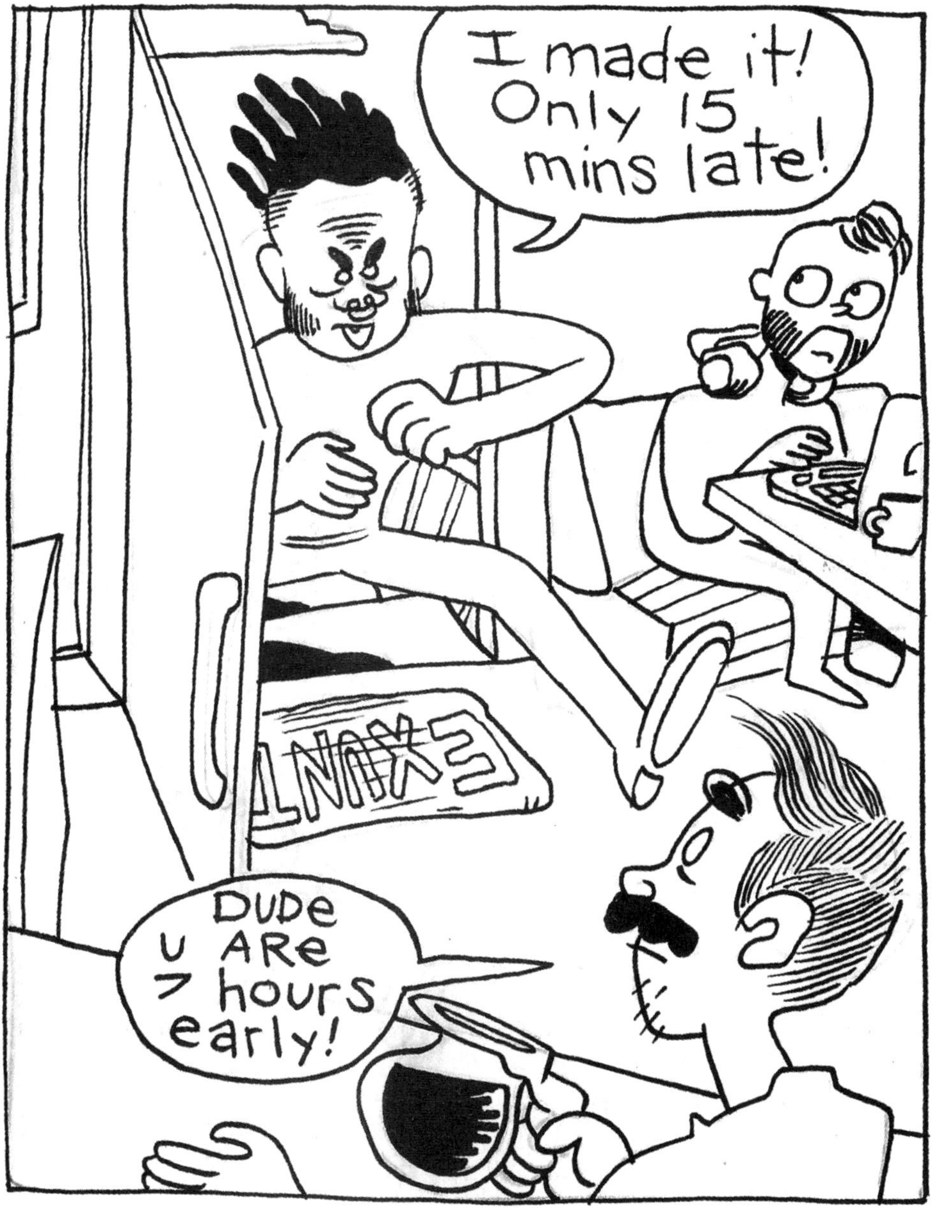
I made it! Only 15 mins late!
Dude U ARe 7 hours early!

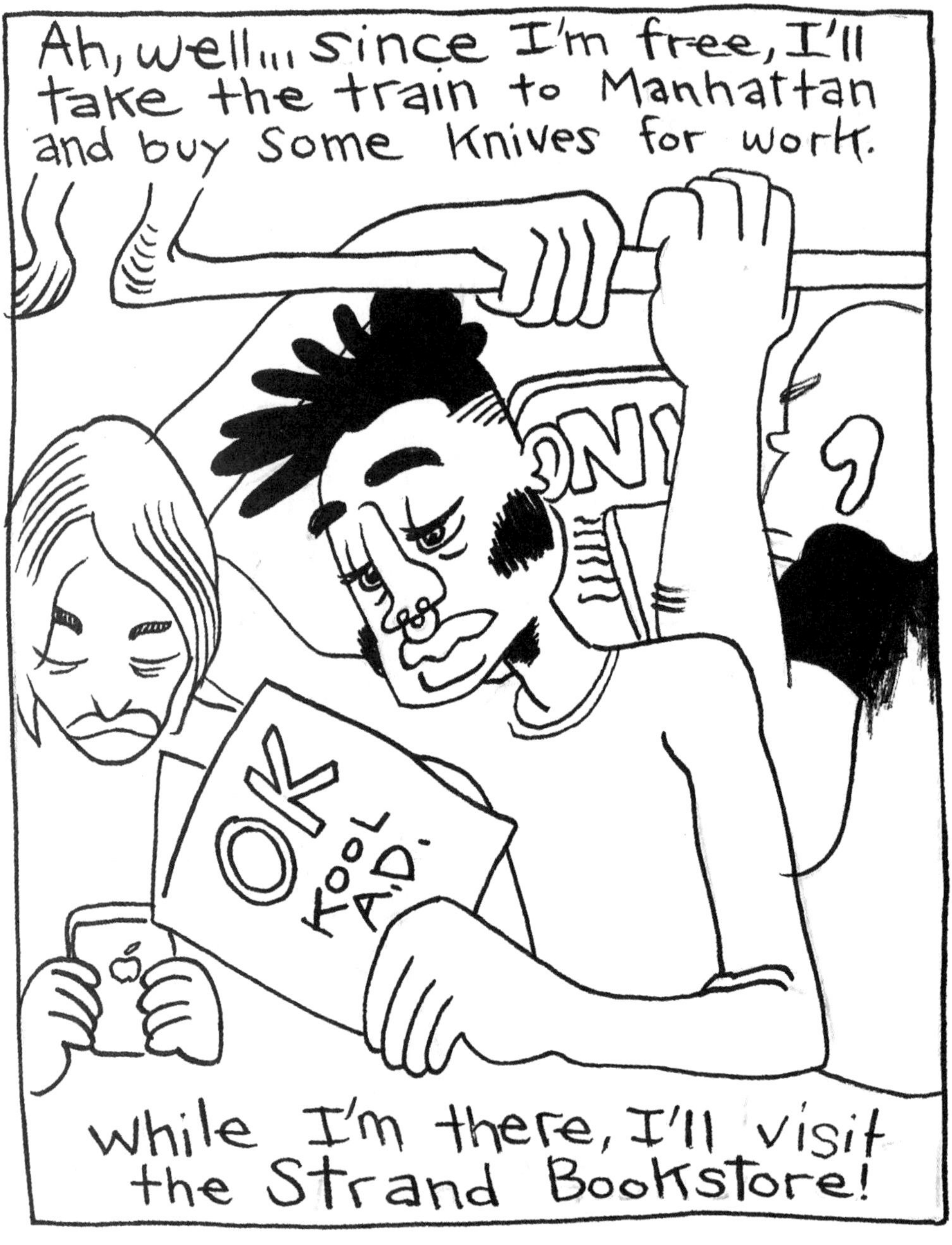
Ah, well... since I'm free, I'll take the train to Manhattan and buy some knives for work.
NY
OK
KOOL A.D.
While I'm there, I'll visit the Strand Bookstore!

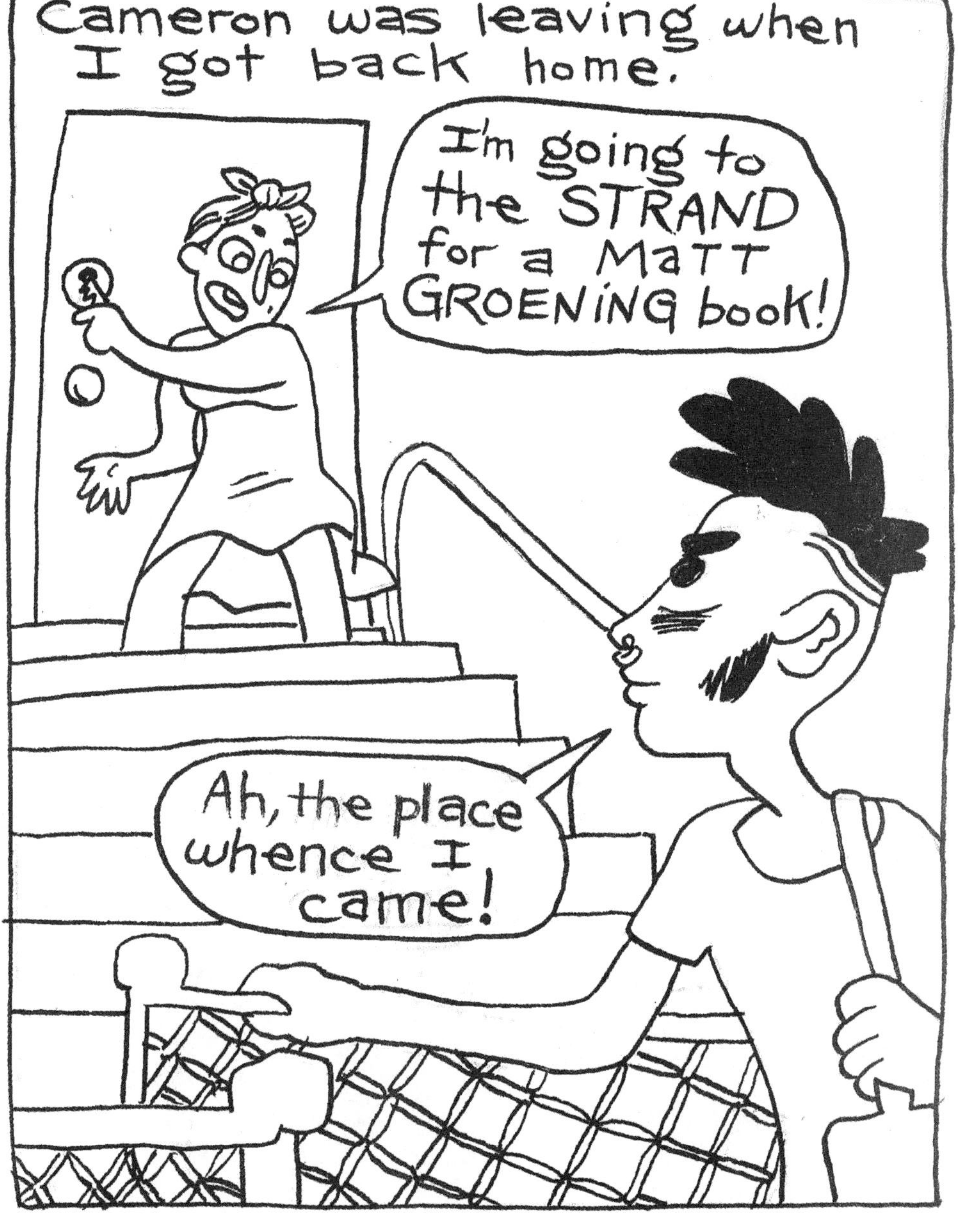
Cameron was leaving when I got back home.
I'm going to the STRAND for a MATT GROENING book!
Ah, the place whence I came!

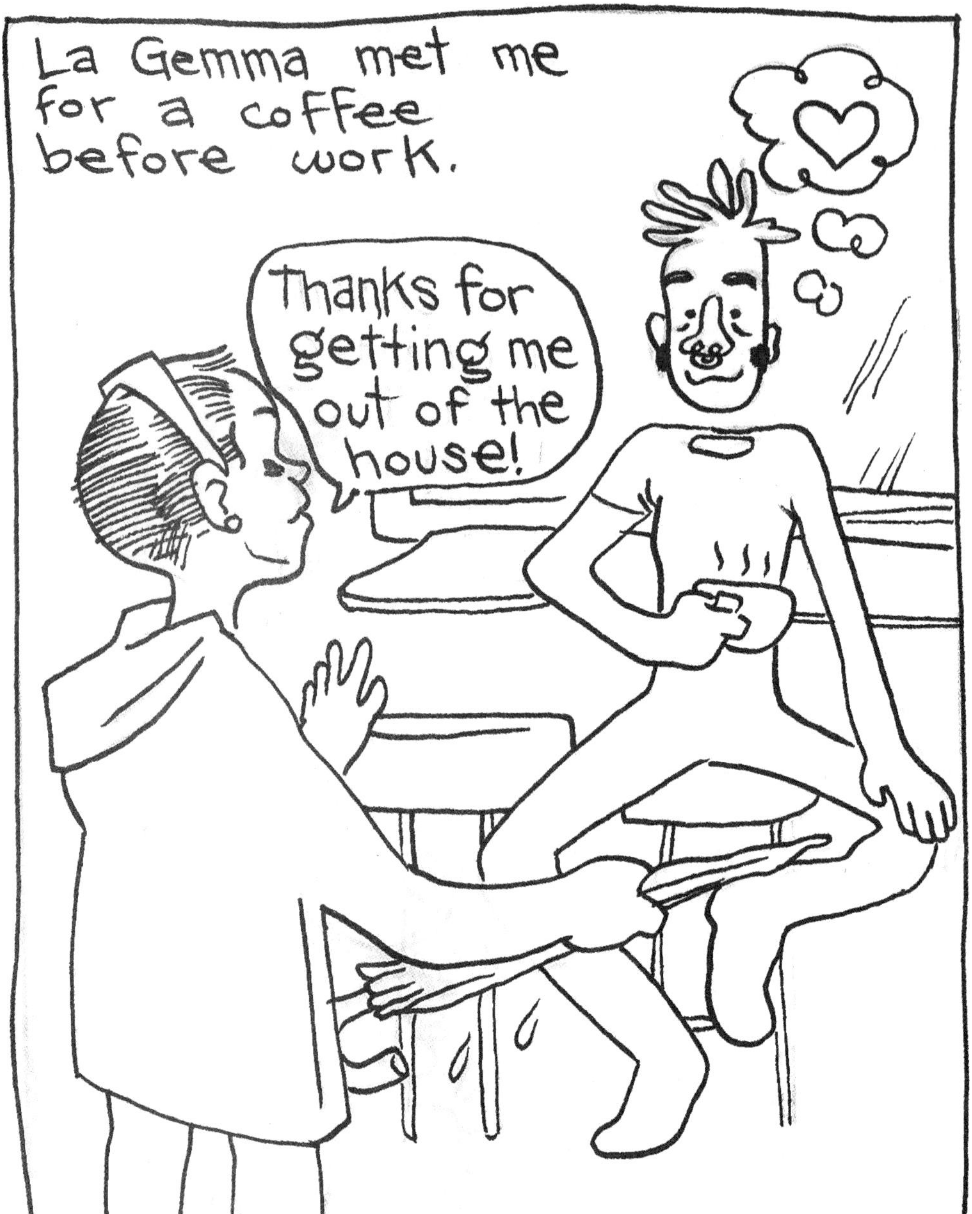
La Gemma met me for a coffee before work.
Thanks for getting me out of the house!

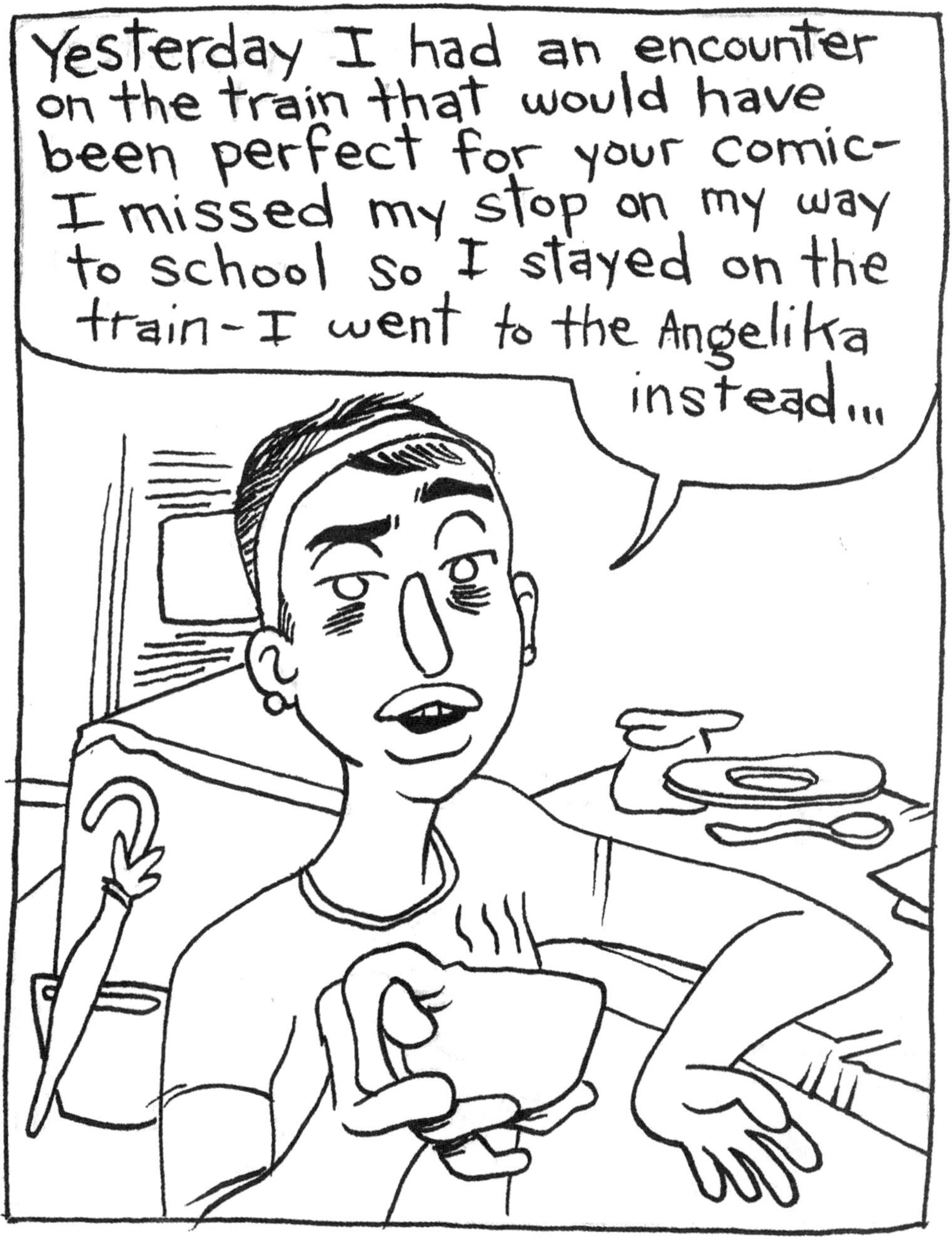
Yesterday I had an encounter on the train that would have been perfect for your comic- I missed my stop on my way to school so I stayed on the train- I went to the Angelika instead...

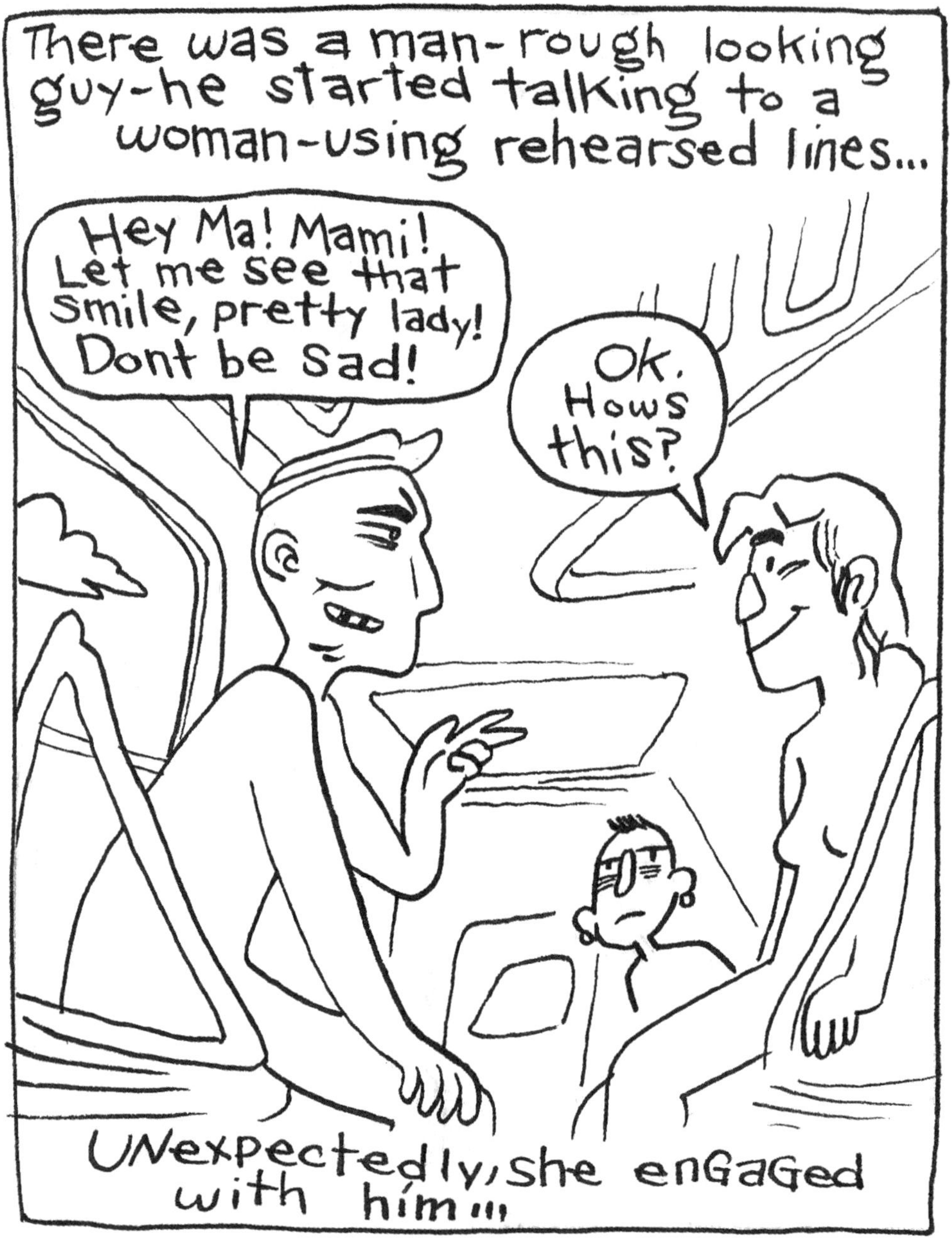
There was a man-rough looking guy-he started talking to a woman-using rehearsed lines...
Hey Ma! Mami! Let me see that smile, pretty lady! Dont be sad!
Ok. Hows this?
UNexpectedly, she enGaGed with him...

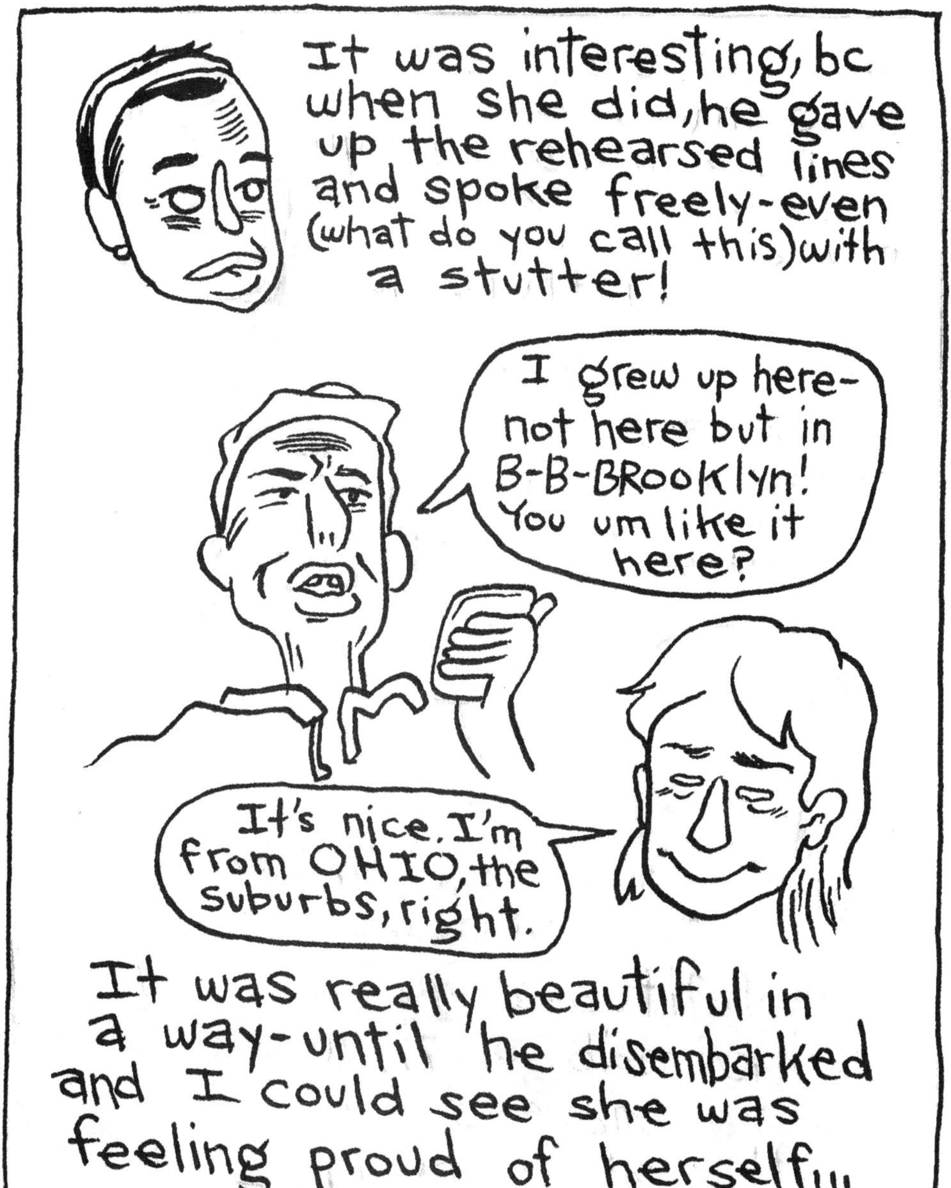

It was interesting, bc when she did, he gave up the rehearsed lines and spoke freely-even (what do you call this) with a stutter!
I grew up here-not here but in B-B-BROOKLYN! You um like it here?
It's nice. I'm from OHIO, the suburbs, right.
It was really beautiful in a way-until he disembarked and I could see she was feeling proud of herself...

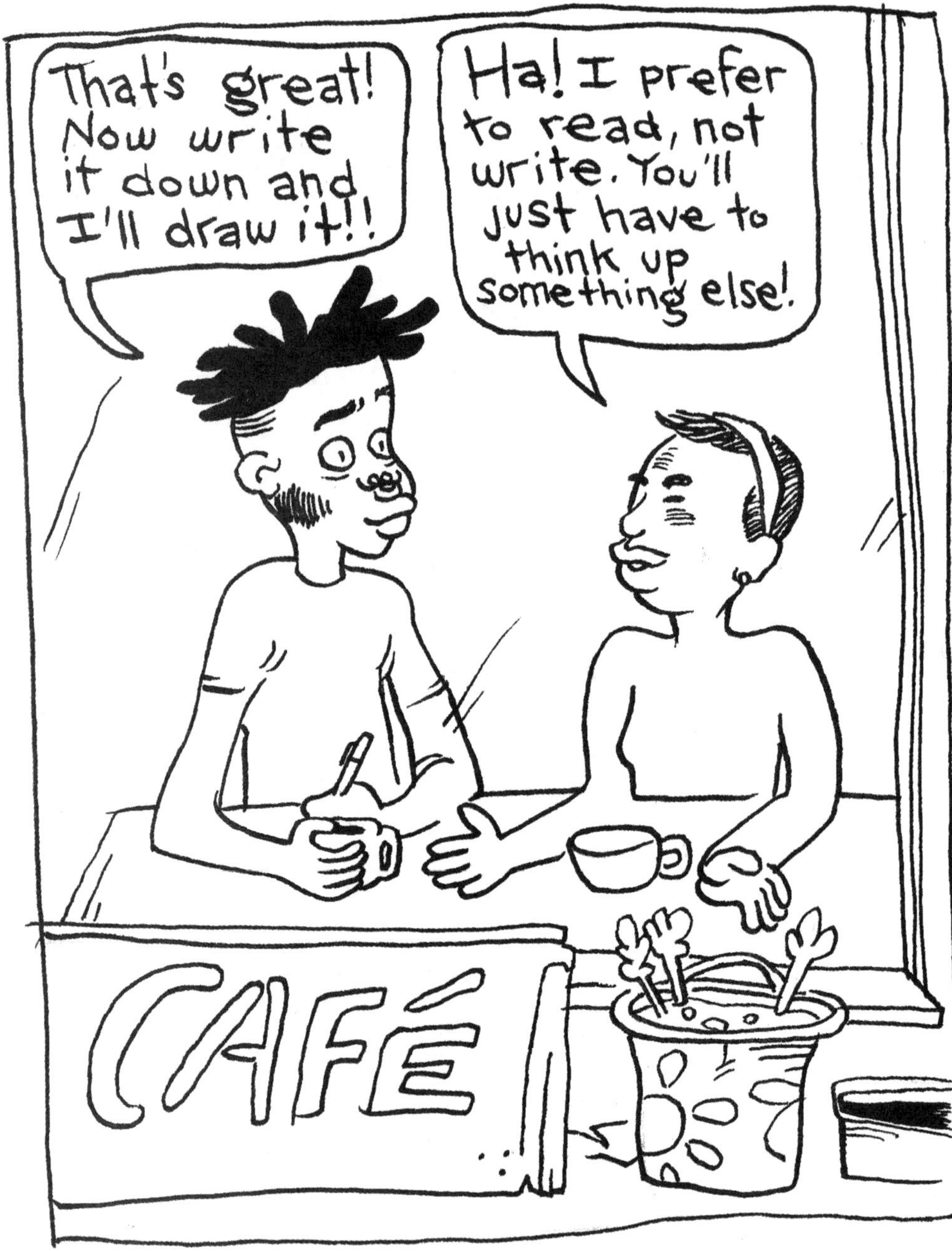
That's great! Now write it down and I'll draw it!!
Ha! I prefer to read, not write. You'll just have to think up something else!
CAFÉ

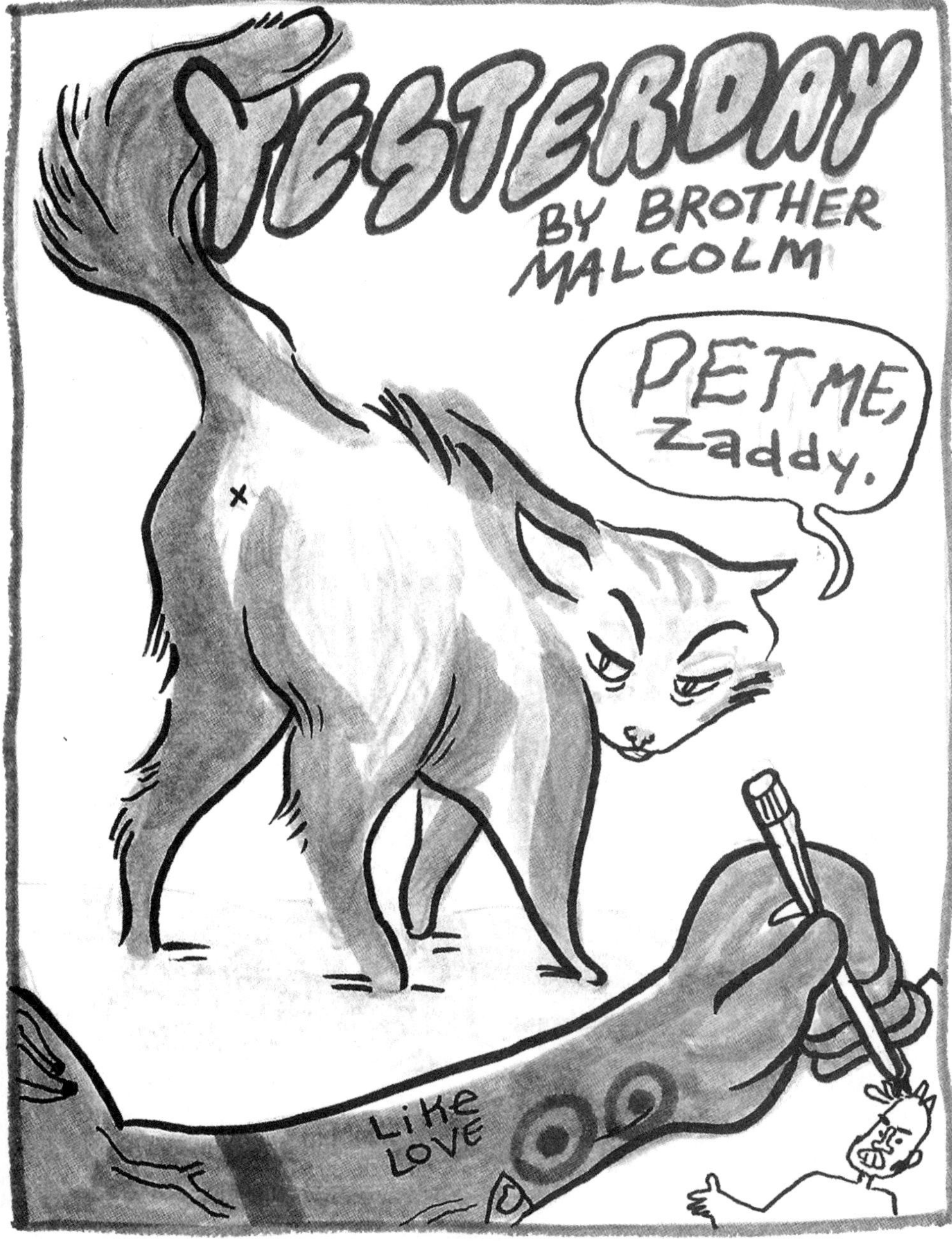
YESTERDAY
BY BROTHER MALCOLM
PET ME, Zaddy.
LIKE LOVE

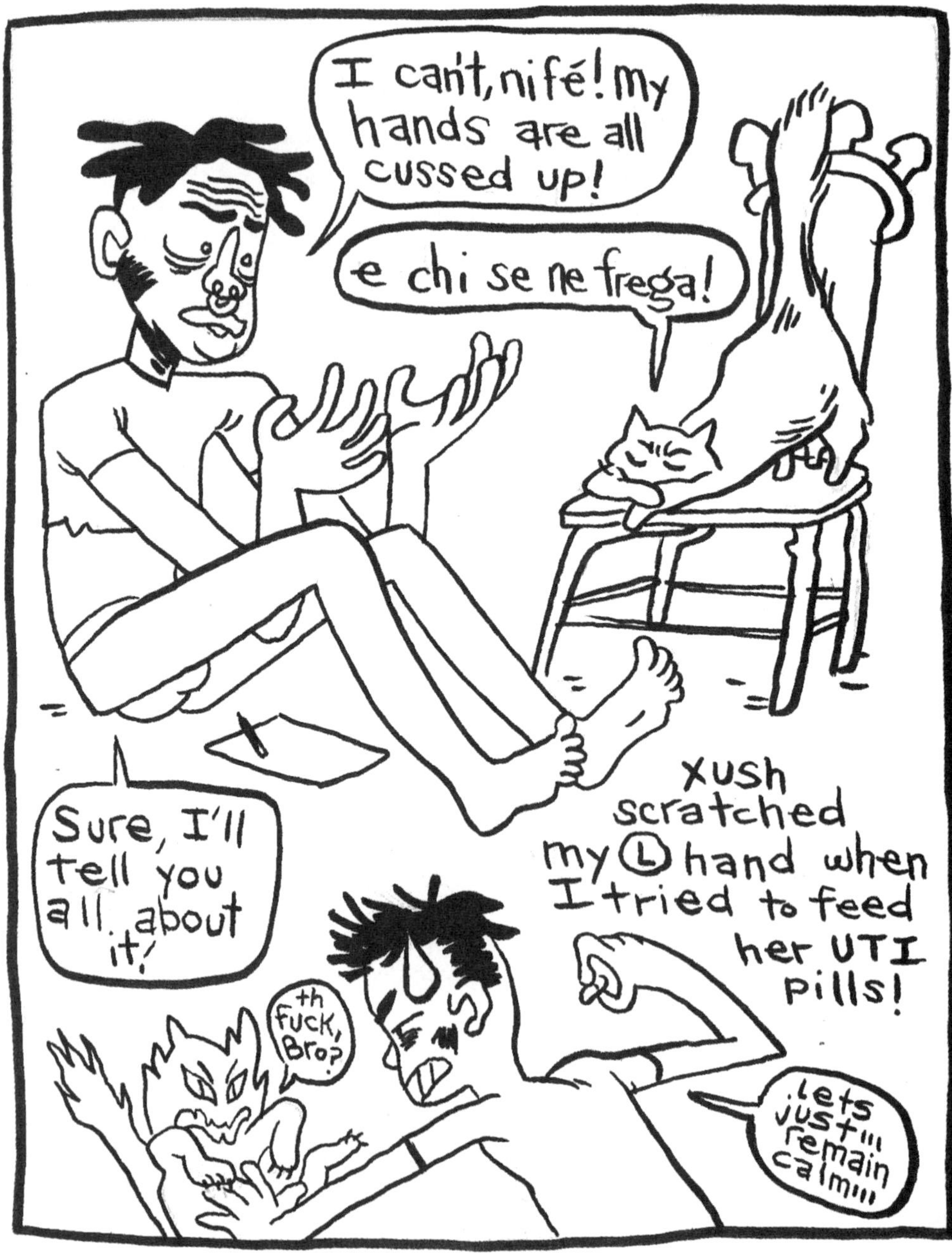
I can't, nifé! my hands are all cussed up!
e chi se ne frega!
Sure, I'll tell you all about it!
Xush scratched my Ⓛ hand when I tried to feed her UTI pills!
th fuck, Bro?
lets just... remain calm...

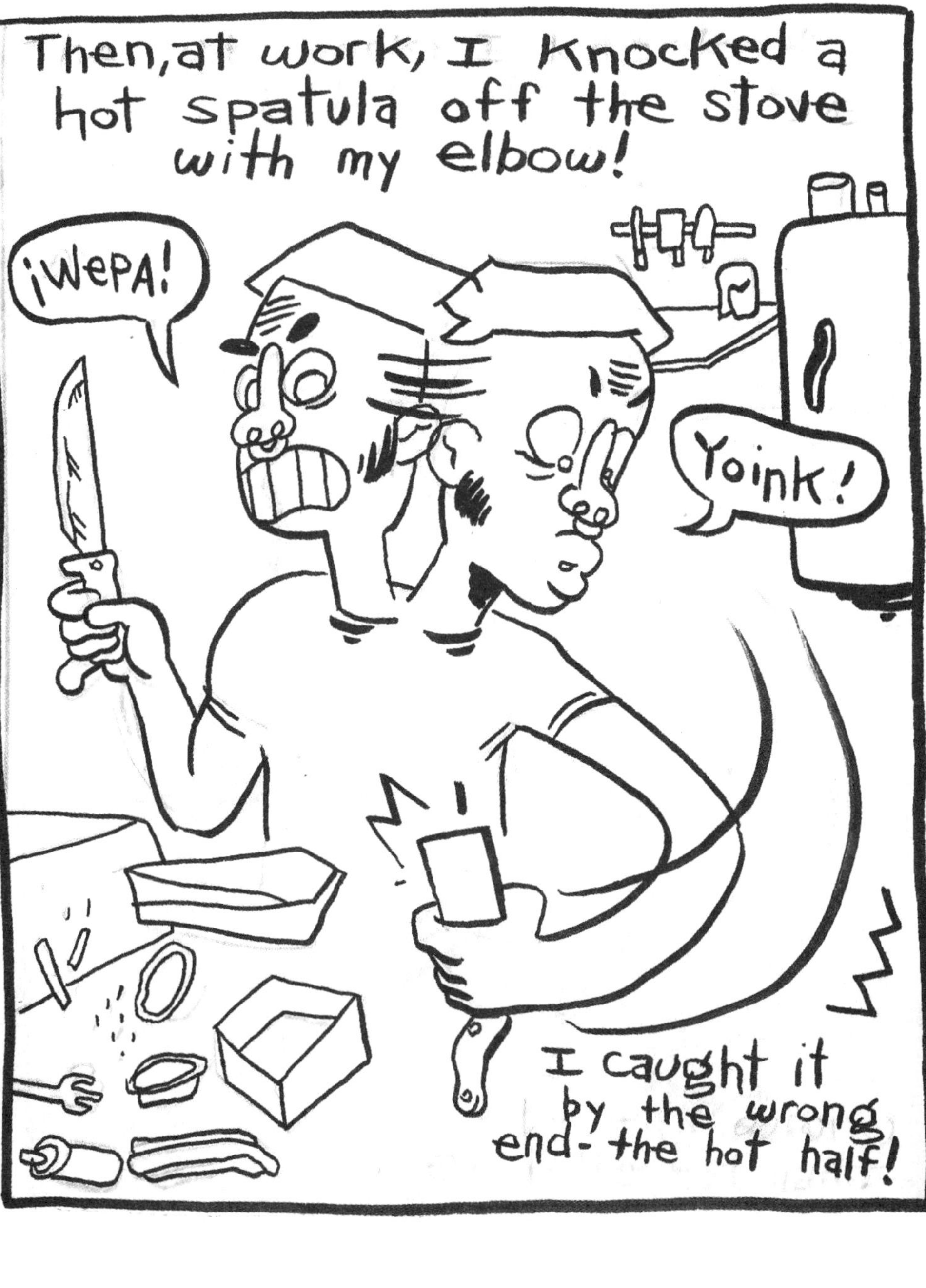

Then, at work, I knocked a hot spatula off the stove with my elbow!
¡WEPA!
Yoink!
I caught it by the wrong end- the hot half!

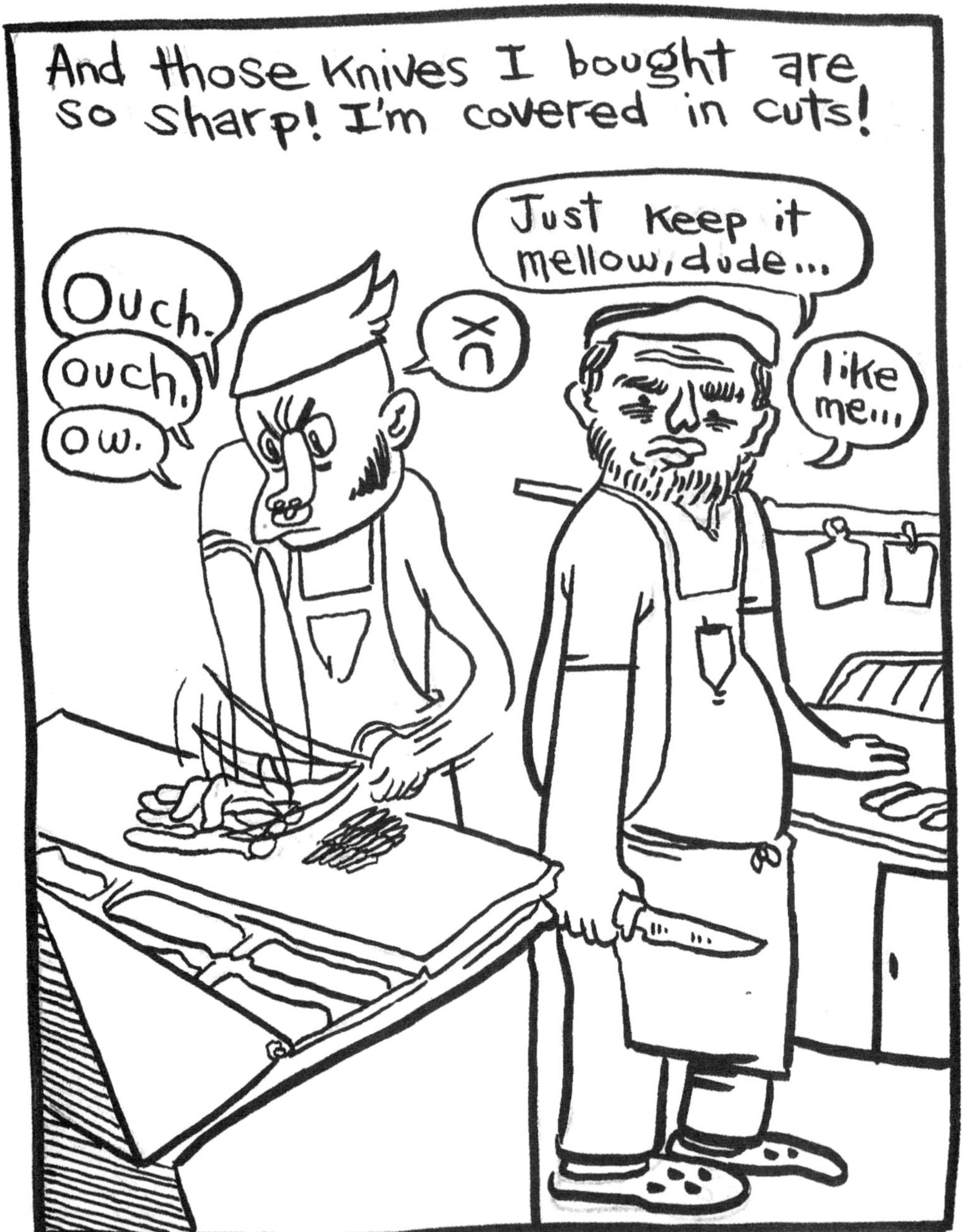

And those knives I bought are so sharp! I'm covered in cuts!
Ouch.
ouch.
ow.
Just keep it mellow, dude...
like me...

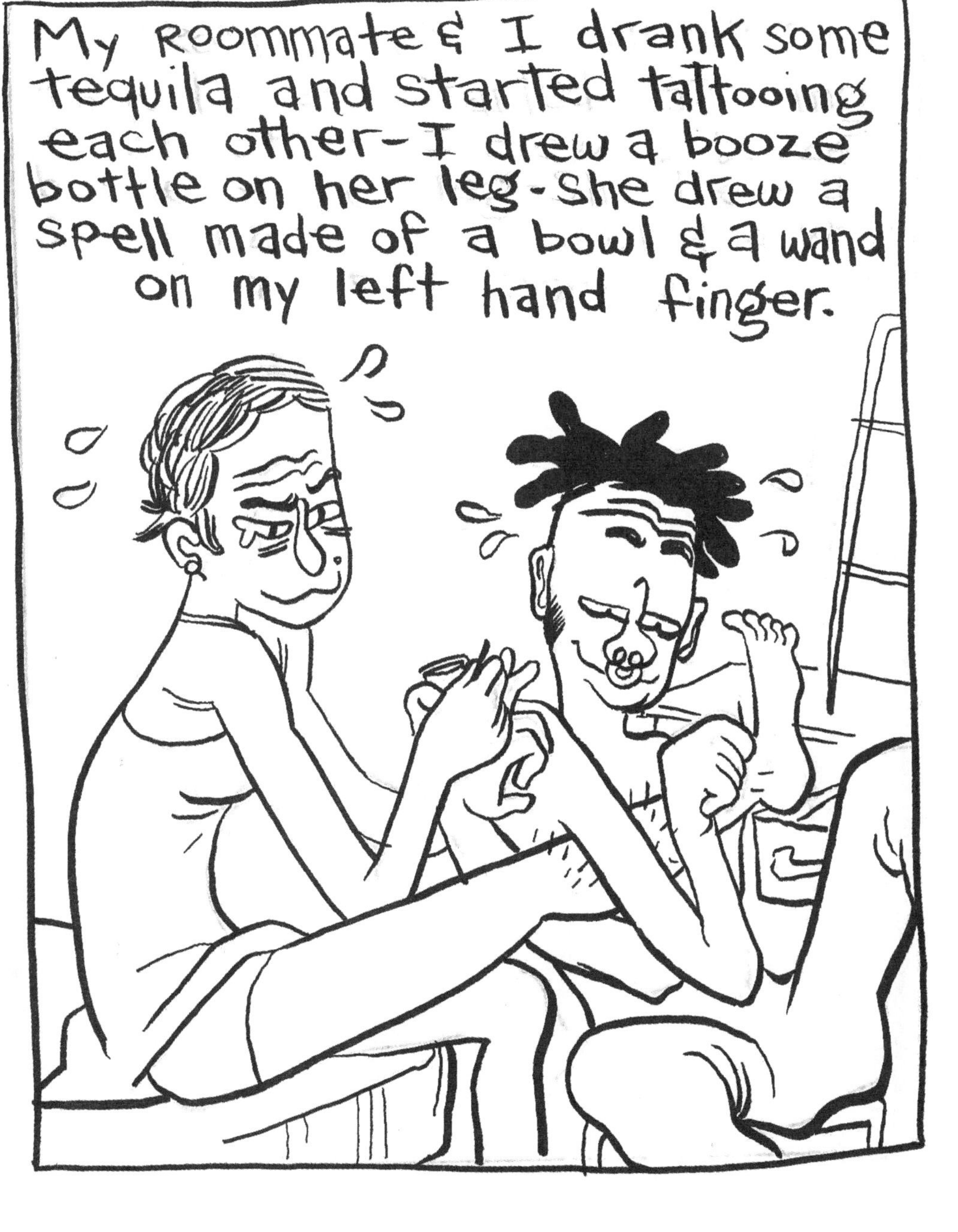
My roommate & I drank some tequila and started tattooing each other - I drew a booze bottle on her leg - she drew a spell made of a bowl & a wand on my left hand finger.

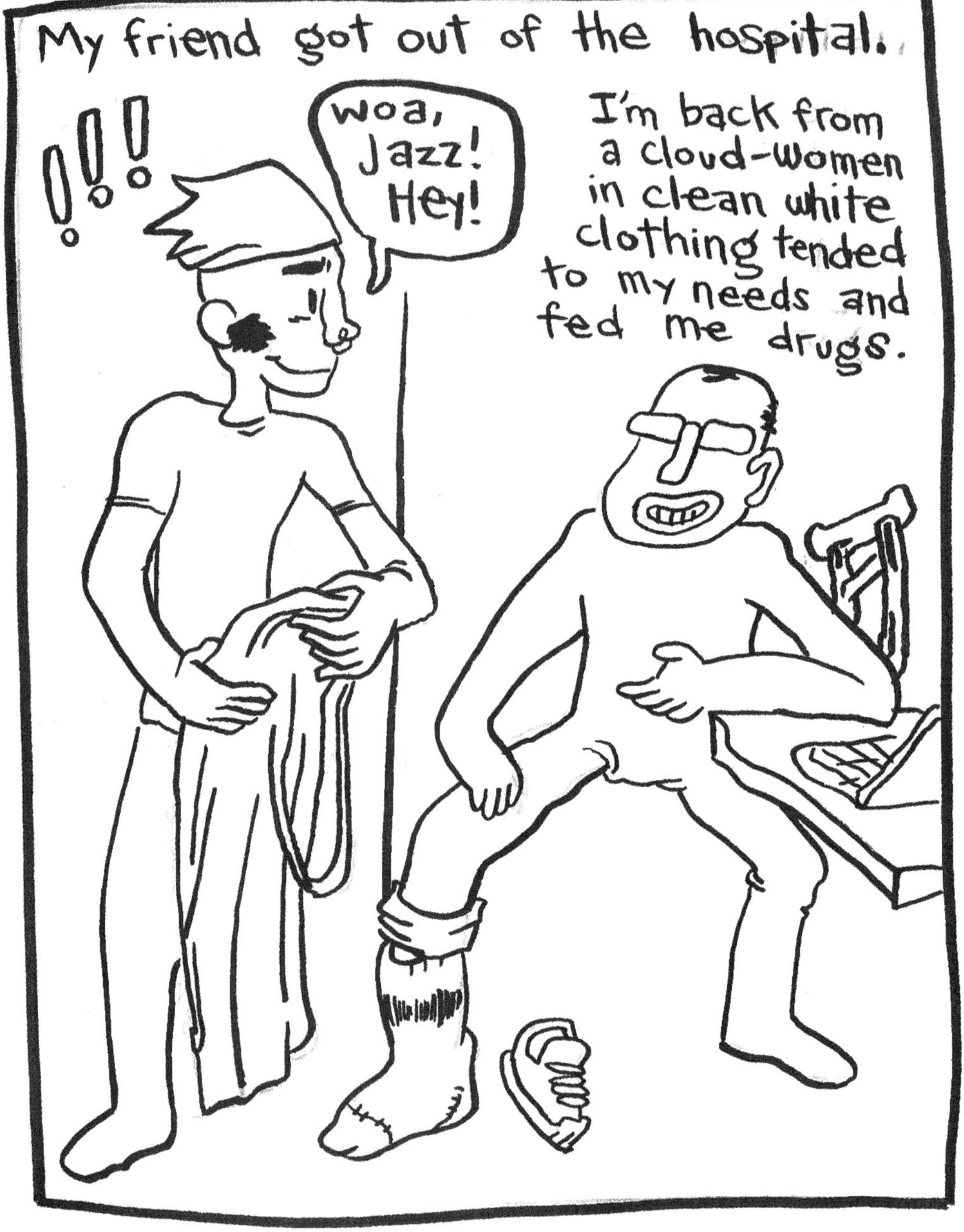
My friend got out of the hospital.
!!!
woa, Jazz! Hey!
I'm back from a cloud-women in clean white clothing tended to my needs and fed me drugs.

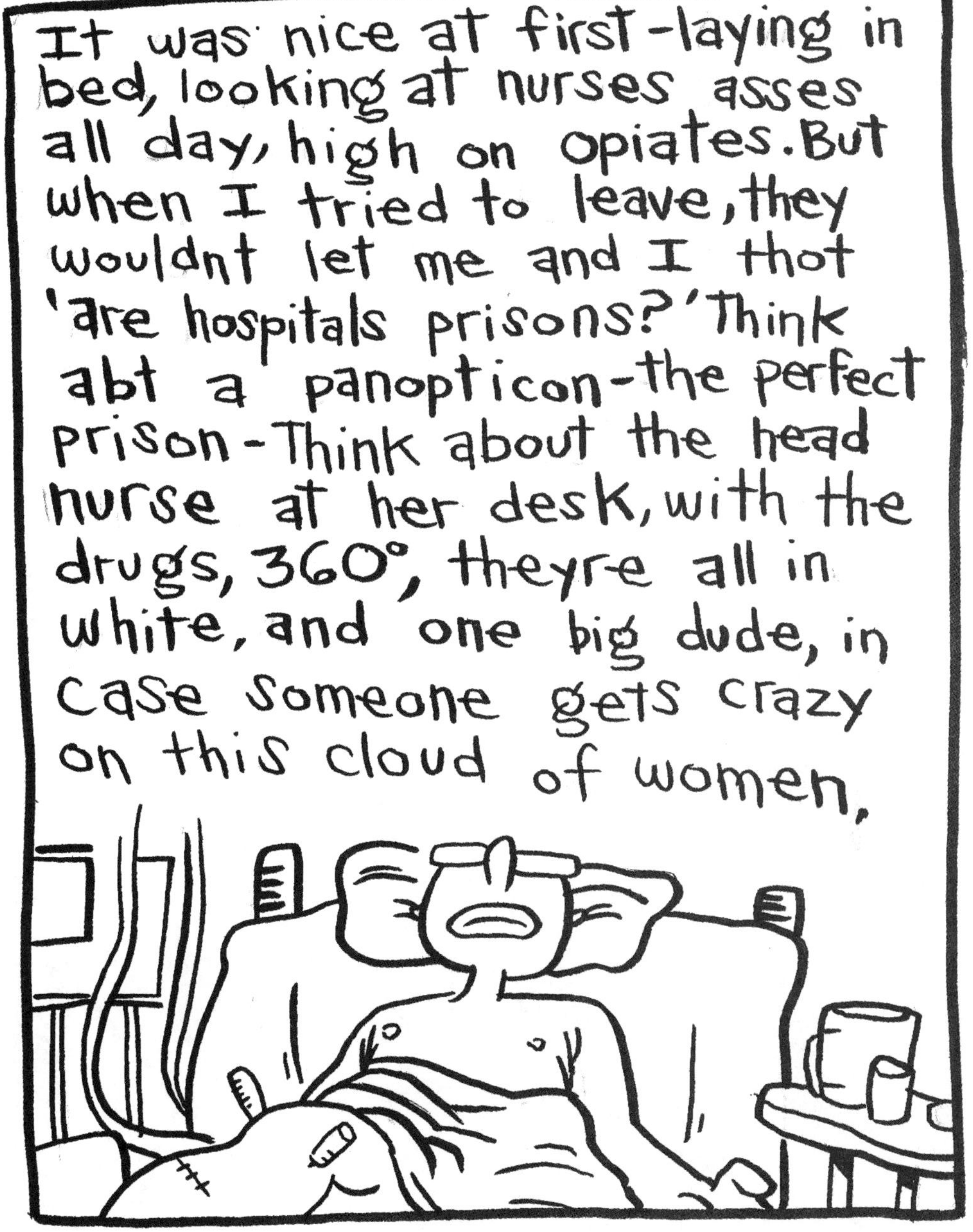
It was nice at first-laying in bed, looking at nurses asses all day, high on opiates. But when I tried to leave, they wouldnt let me and I thot 'are hospitals prisons?' Think abt a panopticon-the perfect prison-Think about the head nurse at her desk, with the drugs, 360°, theyre all in white, and one big dude, in case someone gets crazy on this cloud of women.

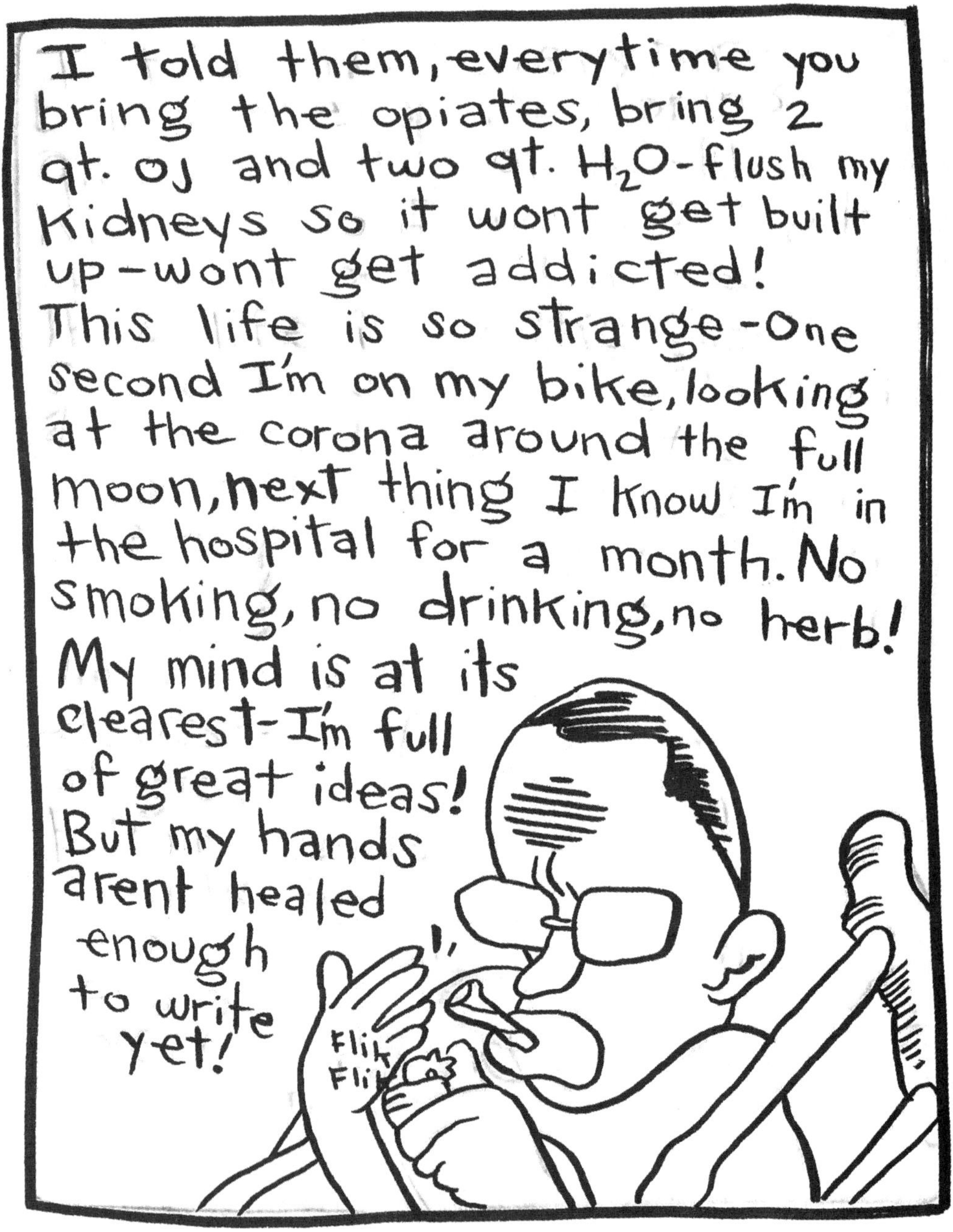
I told them, everytime you bring the opiates, bring 2 qt. OJ and two qt. H_2O-flush my Kidneys so it wont get built up-wont get addicted! This life is so strange-One second I'm on my bike, looking at the corona around the full moon, next thing I know I'm in the hospital for a month. No smoking, no drinking, no herb!
My mind is at its clearest-I'm full of great ideas! But my hands arent healed enough to write yet!
Flik
Flik

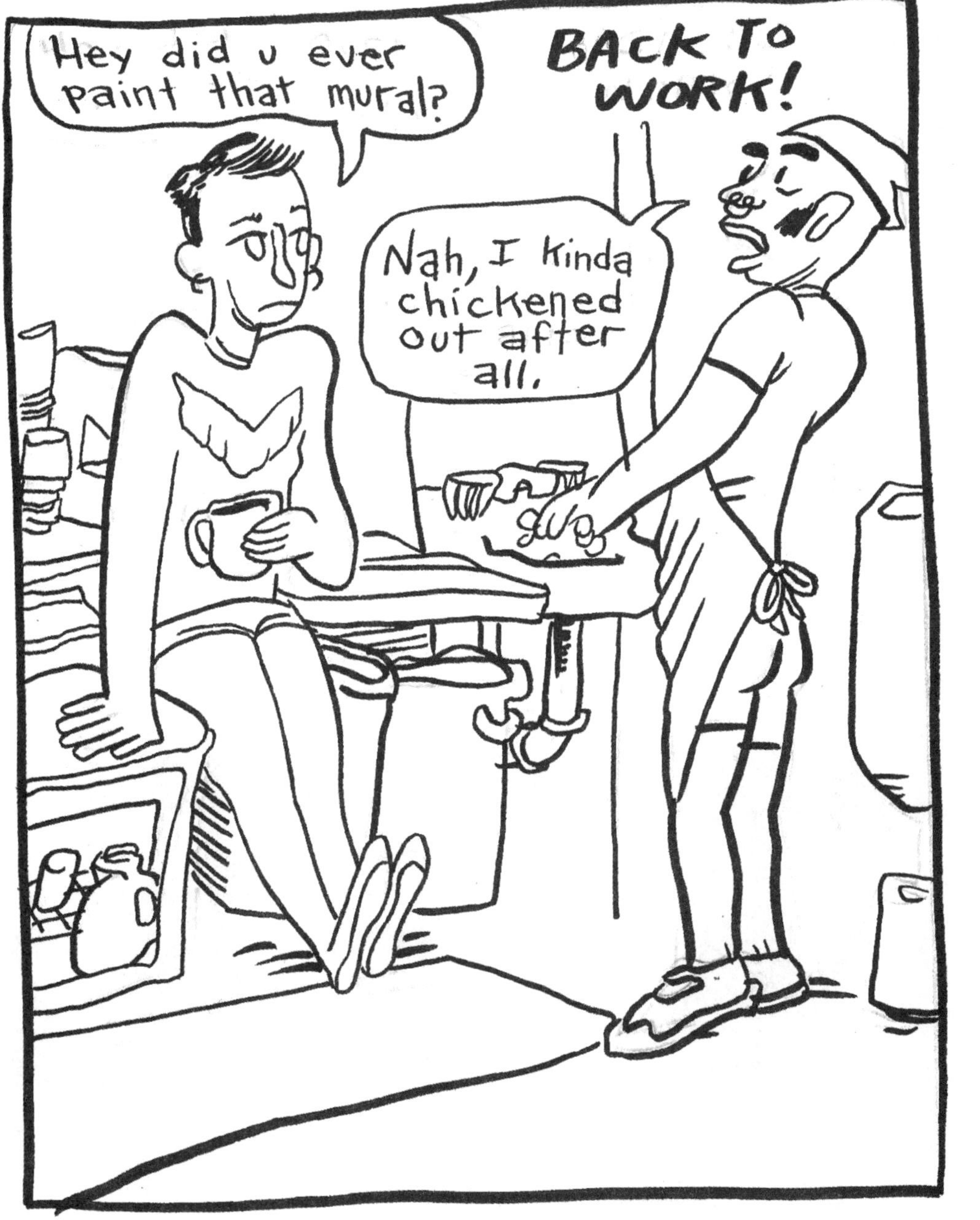
Hey did u ever paint that mural?
BACK TO WORK!
Nah, I kinda chickened out after all.

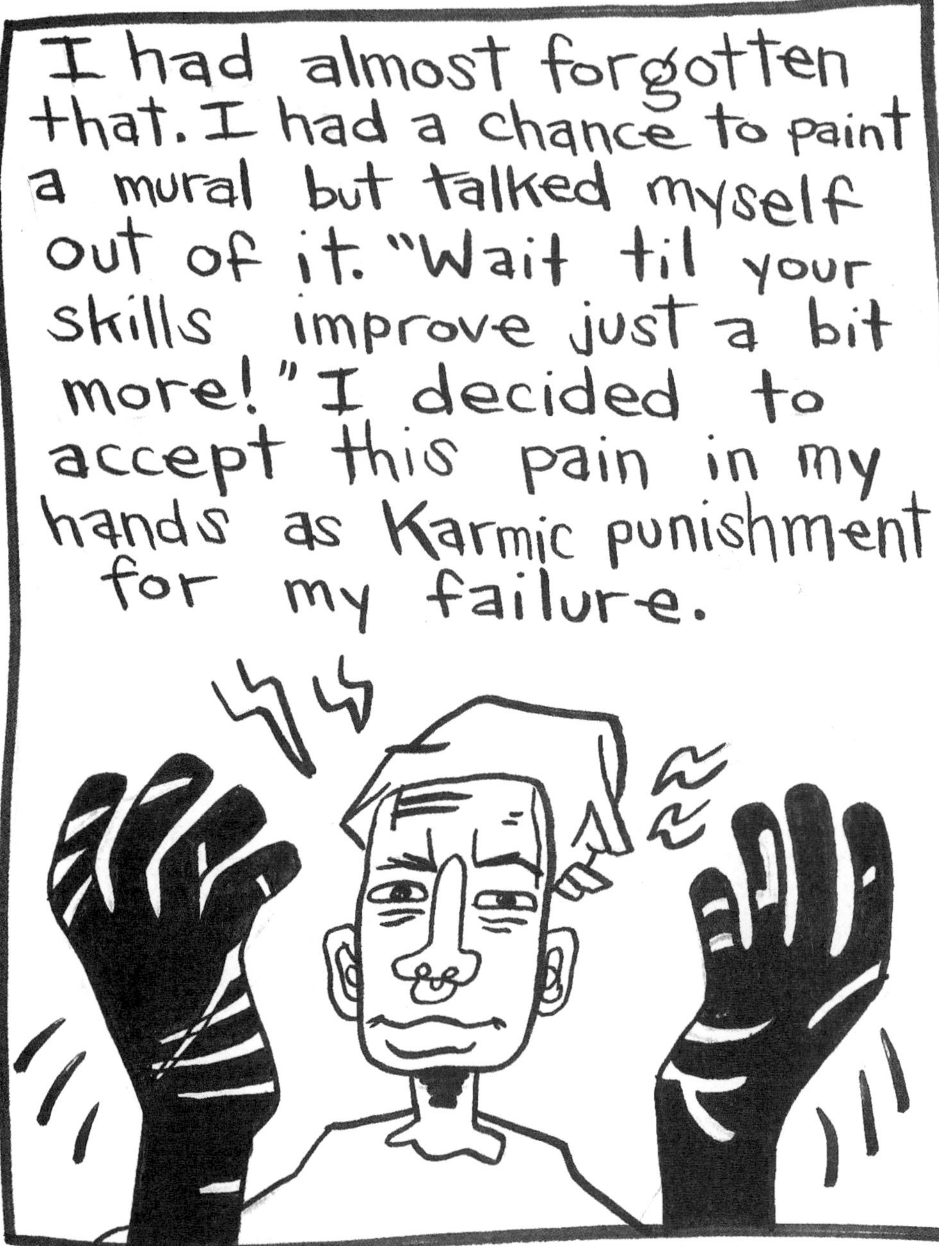
I had almost forgotten that. I had a chance to paint a mural but talked myself out of it. "Wait til your skills improve just a bit more!" I decided to accept this pain in my hands as Karmic punishment for my failure.

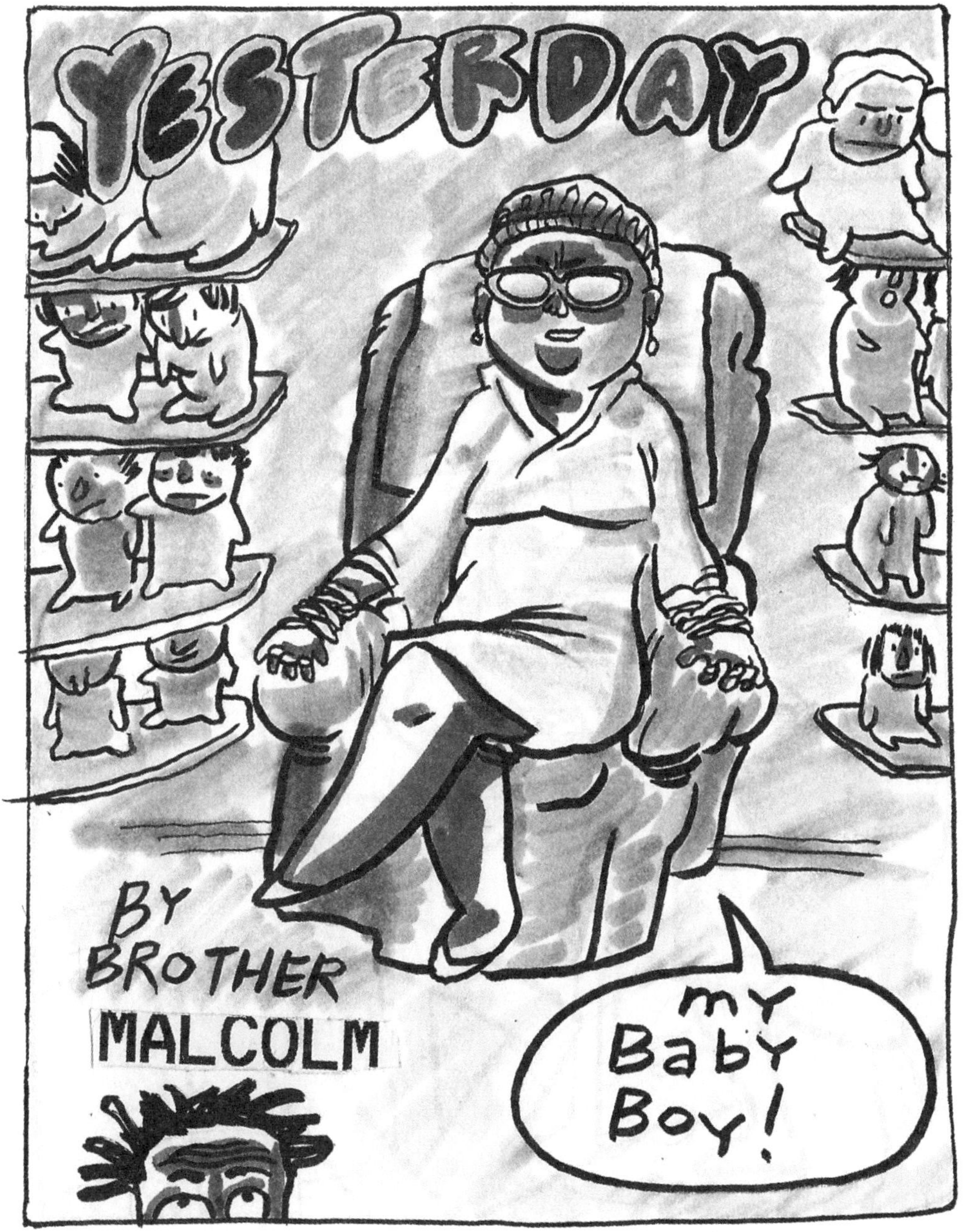
YESTERDAY
BY BROTHER MALCOLM
my Baby Boy!

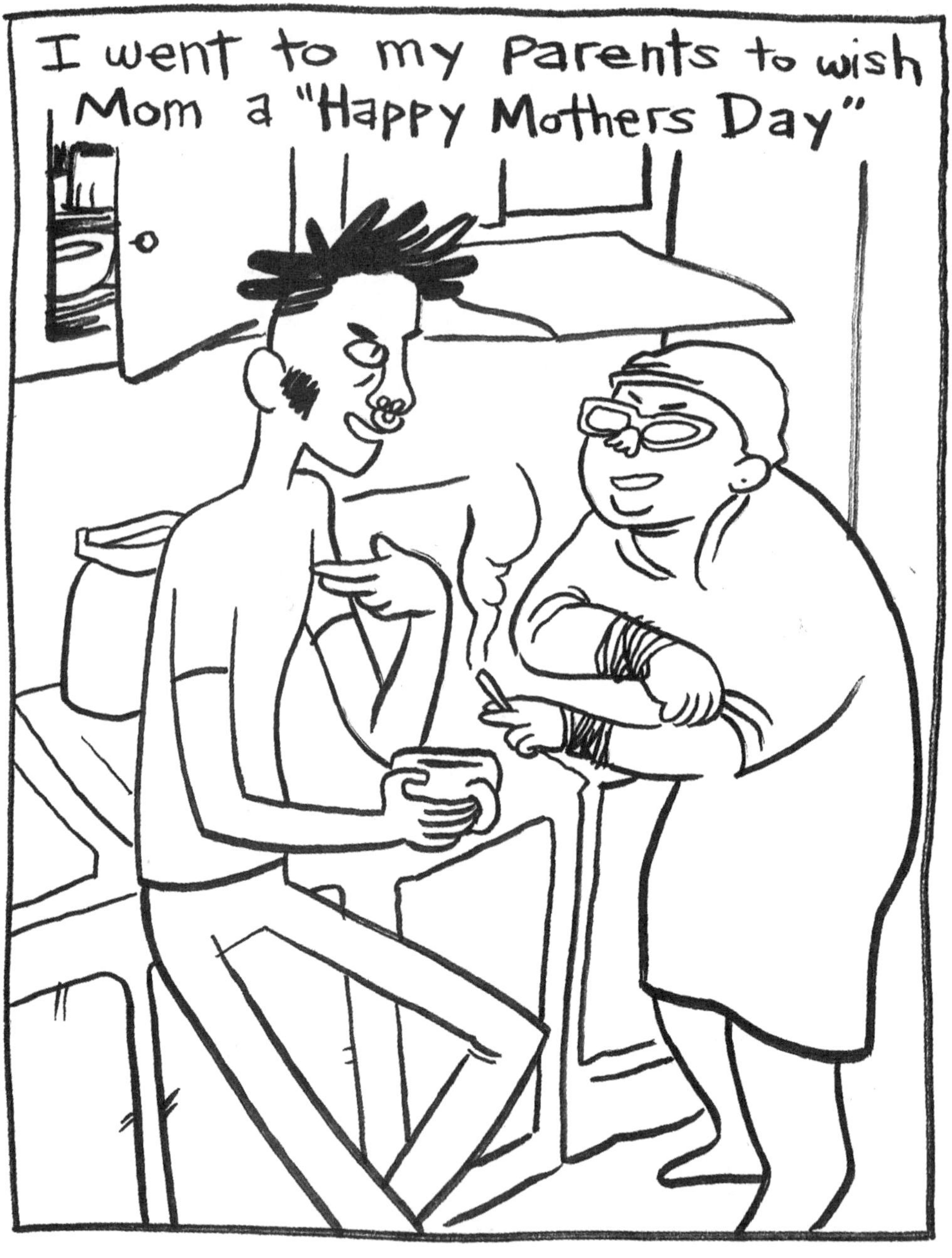
I went to my Parents to wish Mom a "Happy Mothers Day"

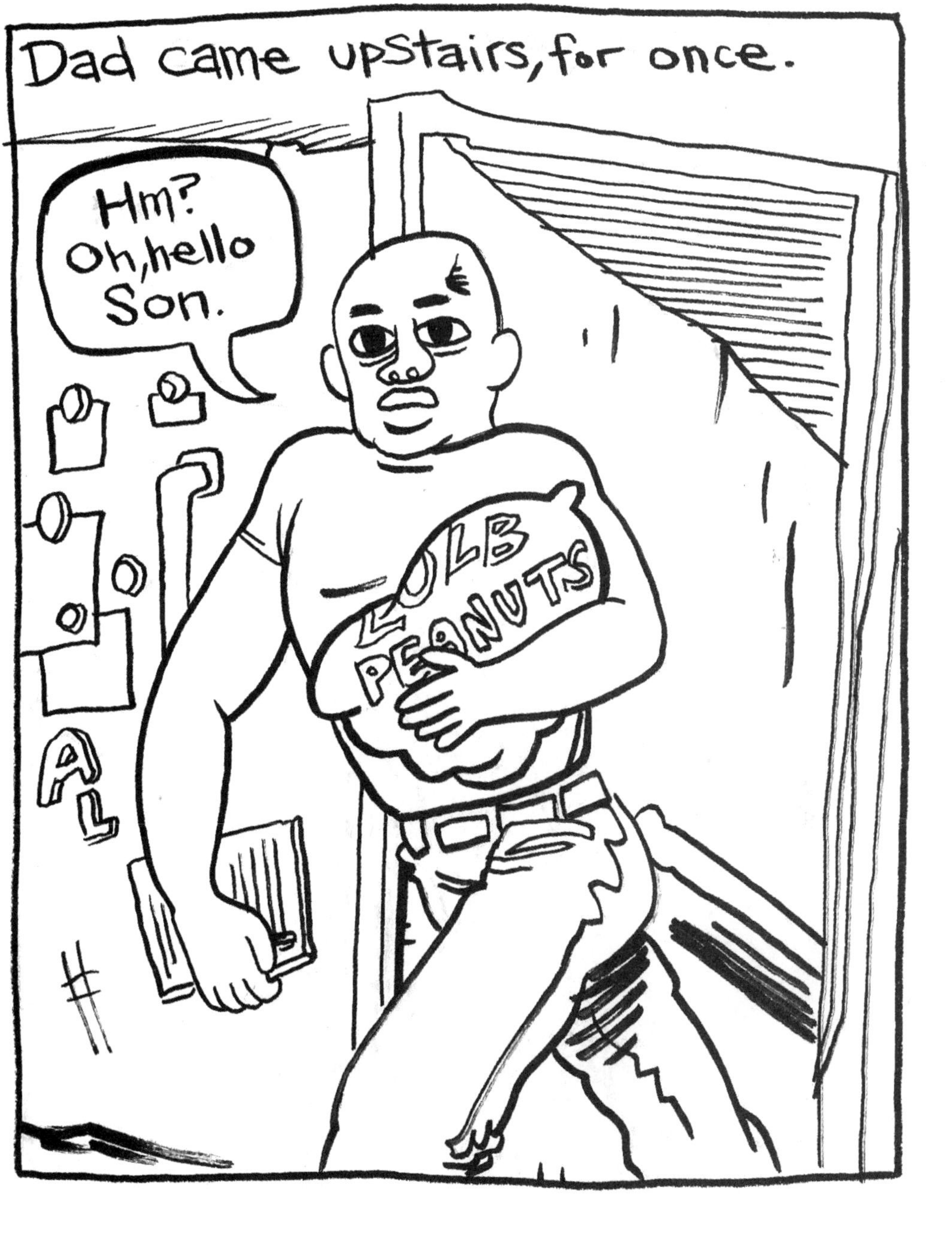
Dad came upstairs, for once.
Hm? Oh, hello Son.
20LB PEANUTS
AL

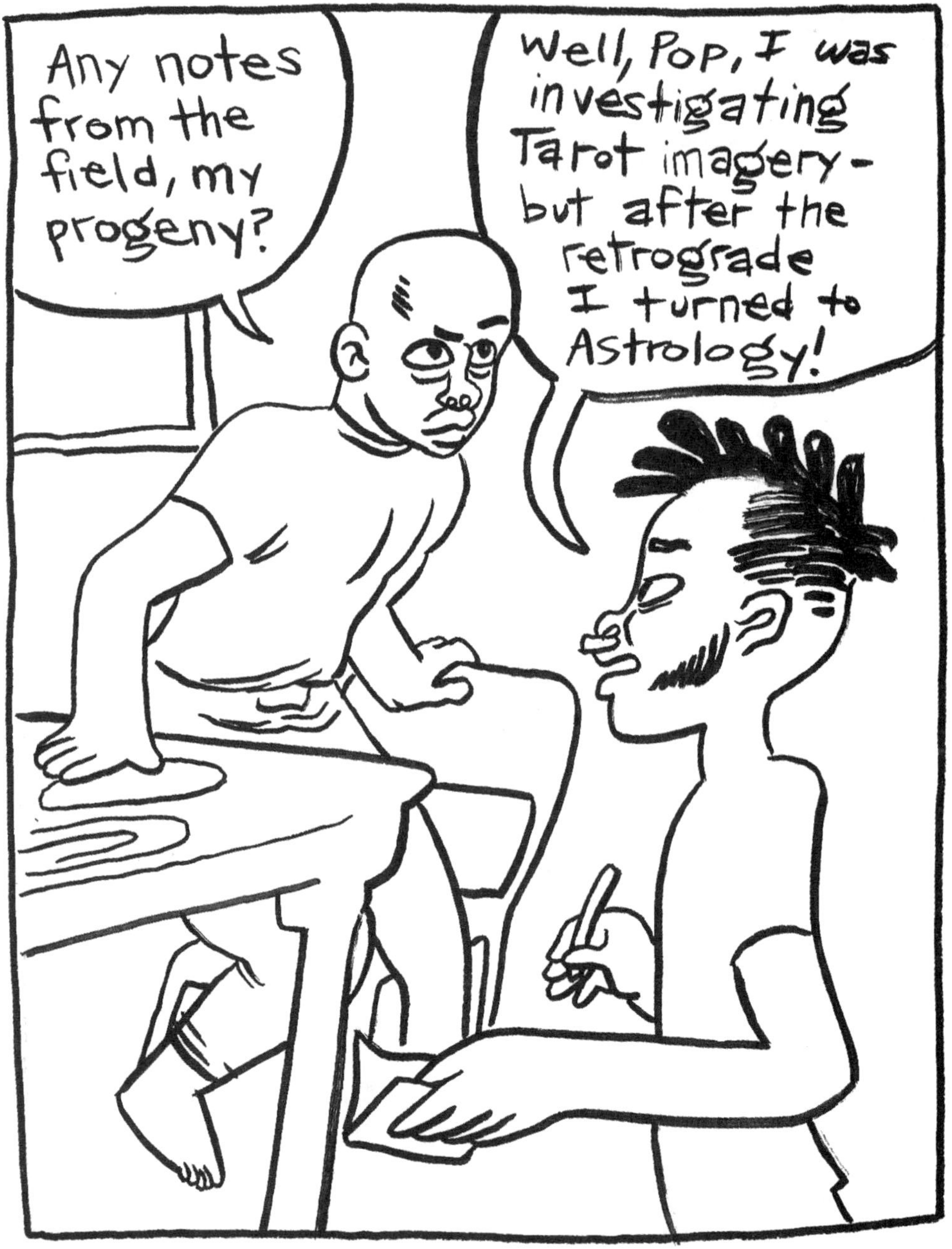
Any notes from the field, my progeny?
Well, Pop, I was investigating Tarot imagery - but after the retrograde I turned to Astrology!

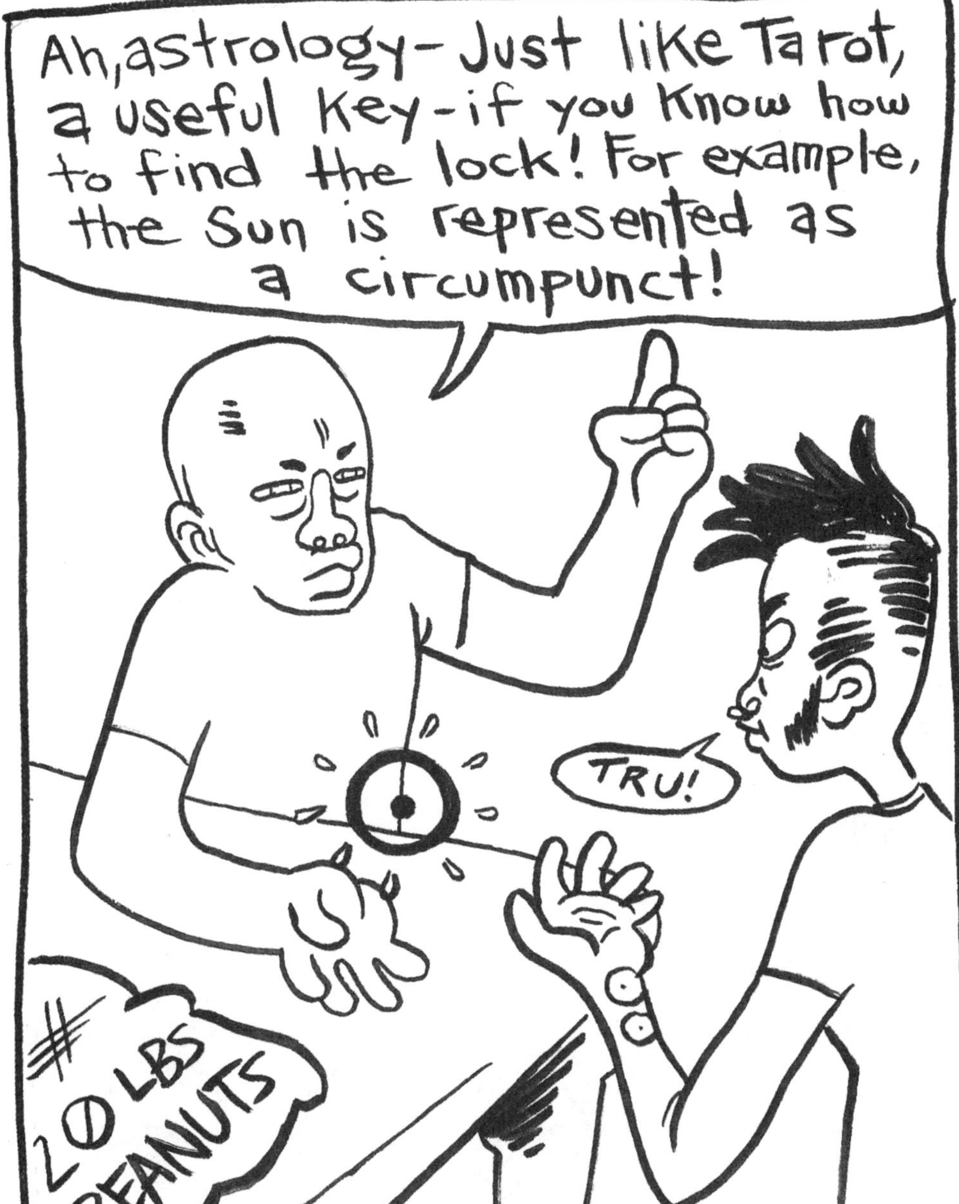
Ah, astrology - Just like Tarot, a useful Key - if you Know how to find the lock! For example, the Sun is represented as a circumpunct!
TRU!
20 LBS PEANUTS

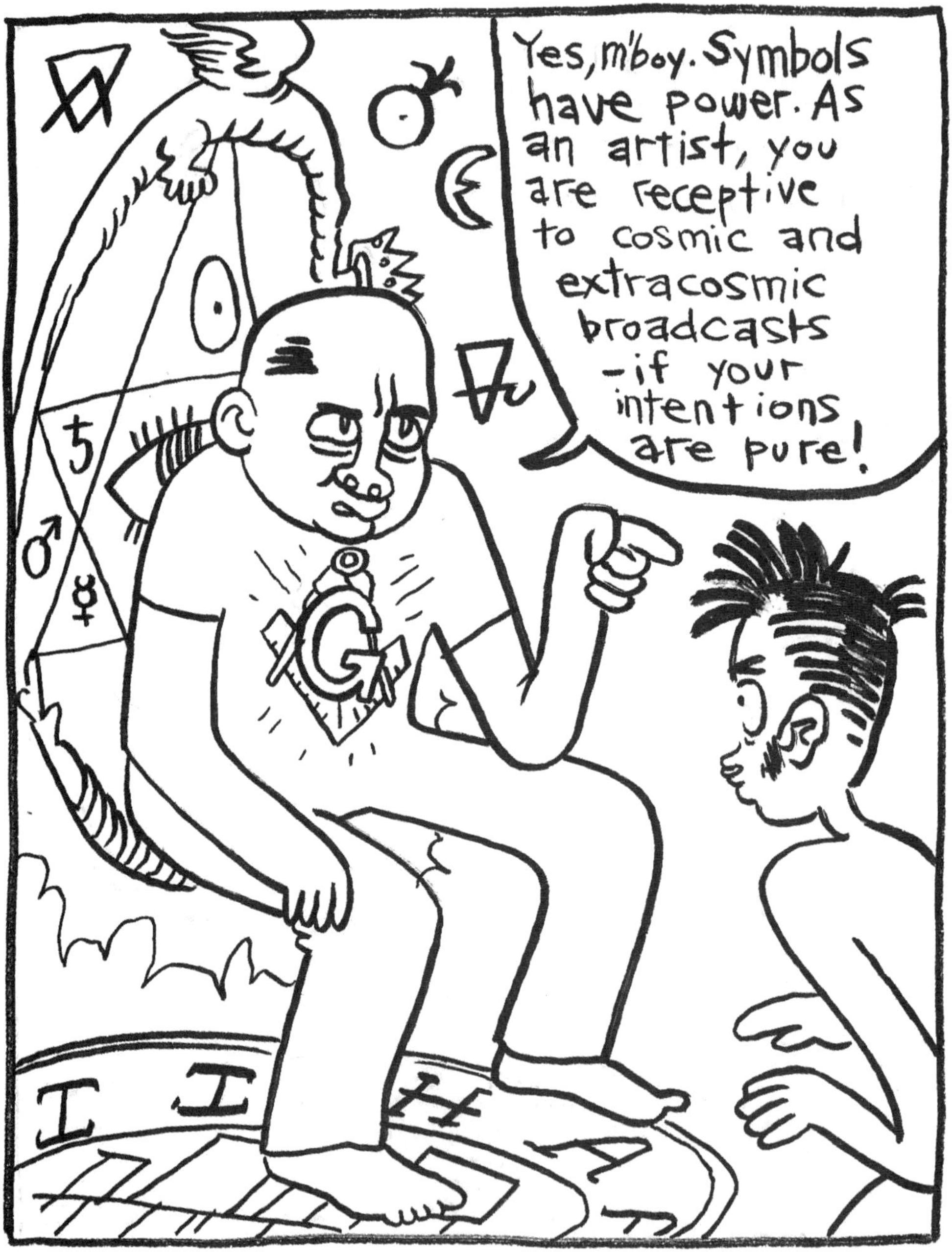
Yes, m'boy. Symbols have power. As an artist, you are receptive to cosmic and extracosmic broadcasts -if your intentions are pure!

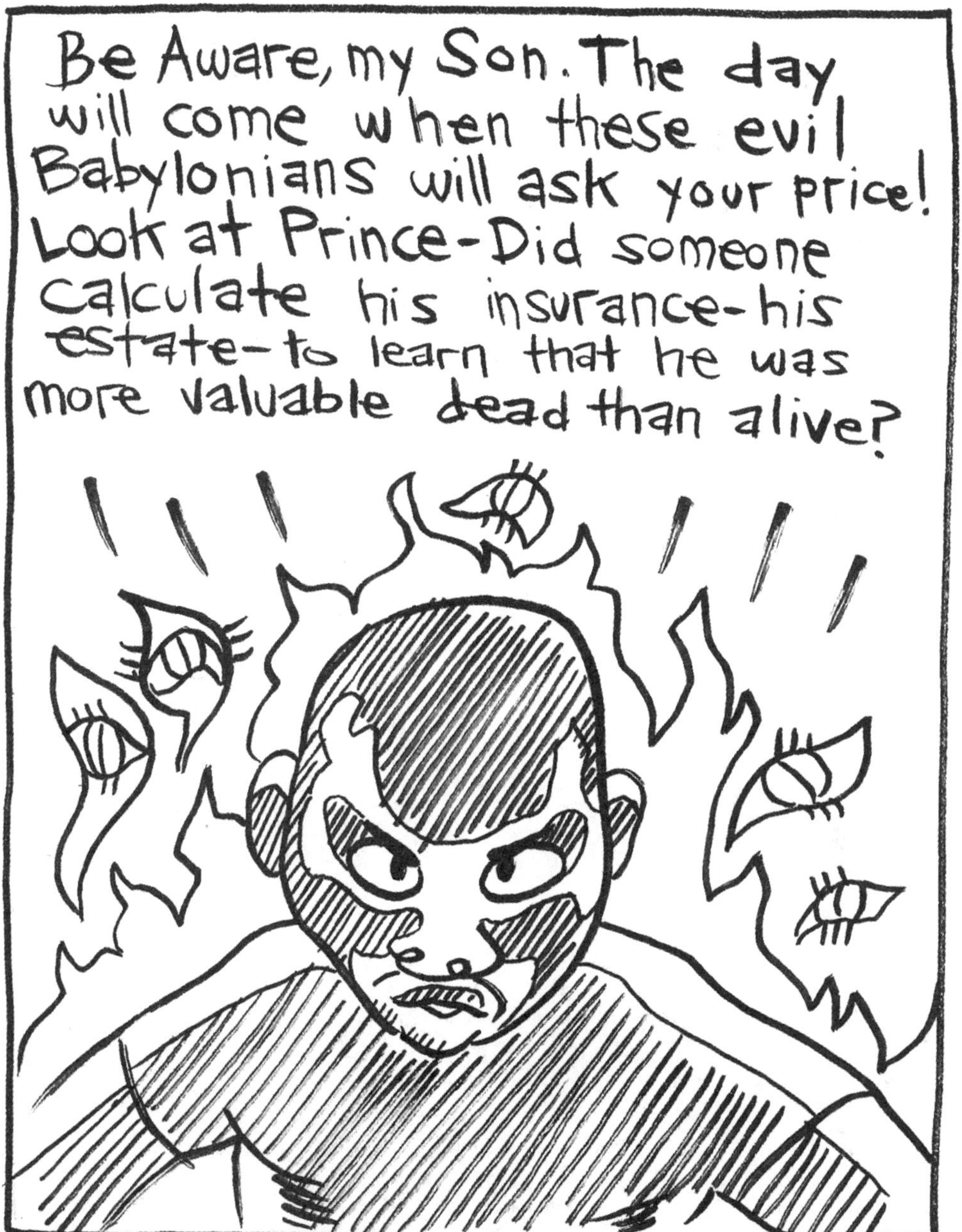
Be Aware, my Son. The day will come when these evil Babylonians will ask your price! Look at Prince - Did someone calculate his insurance - his estate - to learn that he was more valuable dead than alive?

Talking to Pop for two hours was equivalent to reading three books, or one semester studying esotericism. He left me with seven principles to research on my own:

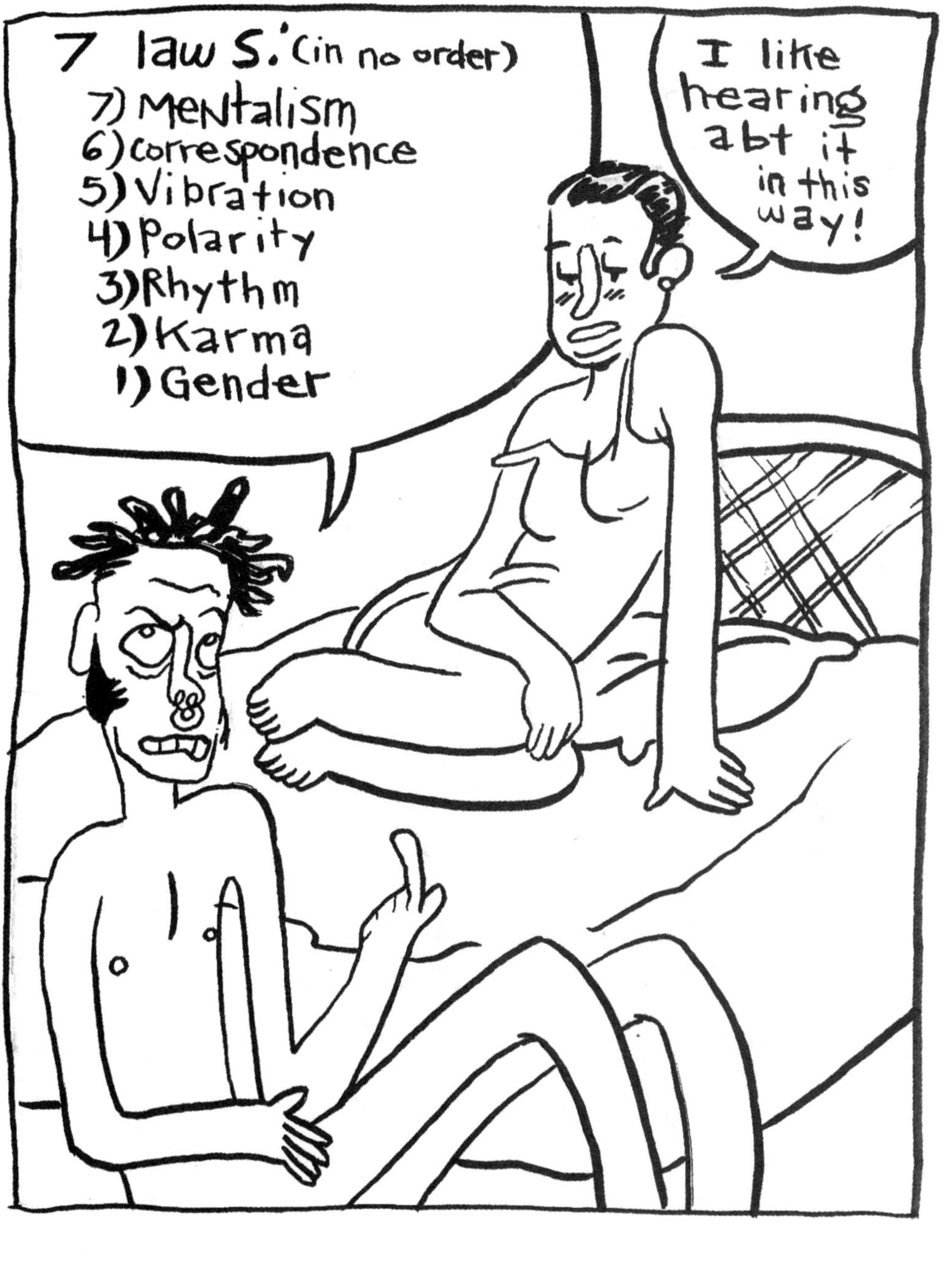
7 law S.: (in no order)
7) Mentalism
6) correspondence
5) Vibration
4) Polarity
3) Rhythm
2) Karma
1) Gender
I like hearing abt it in this way!

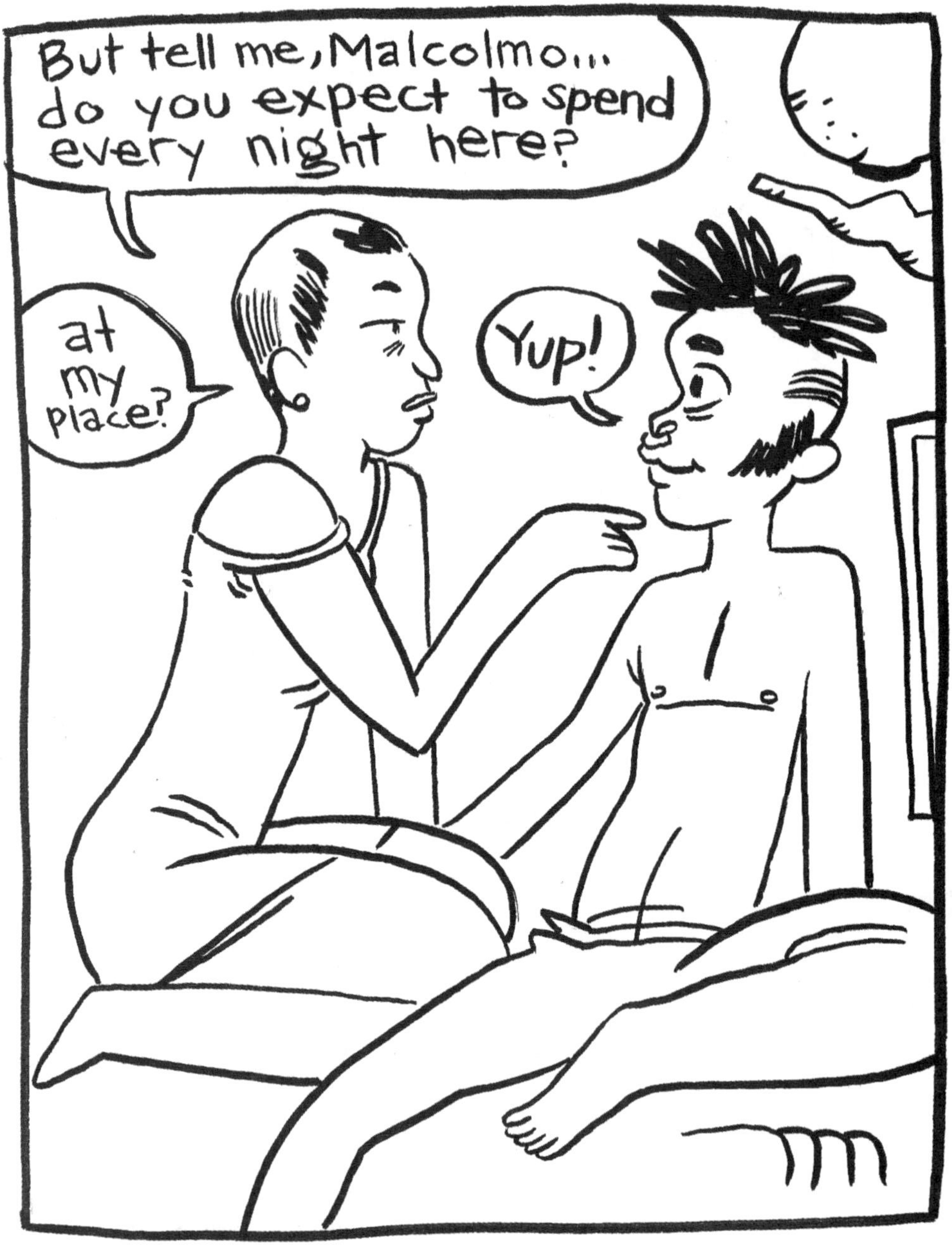
But tell me, Malcolmo... do you expect to spend every night here?
at my place?
Yup!

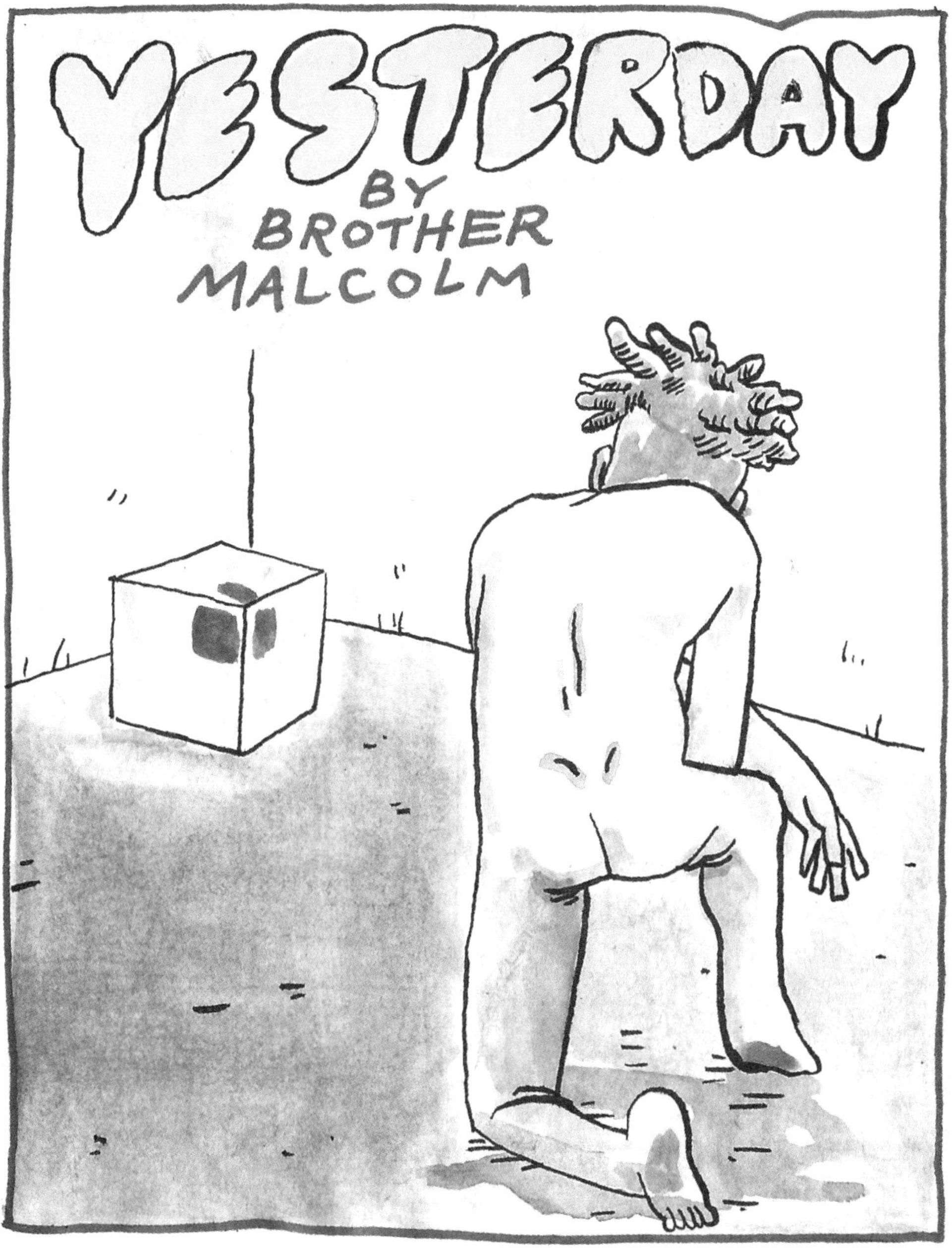
YESTERDAY
BY
BROTHER
MALCOLM

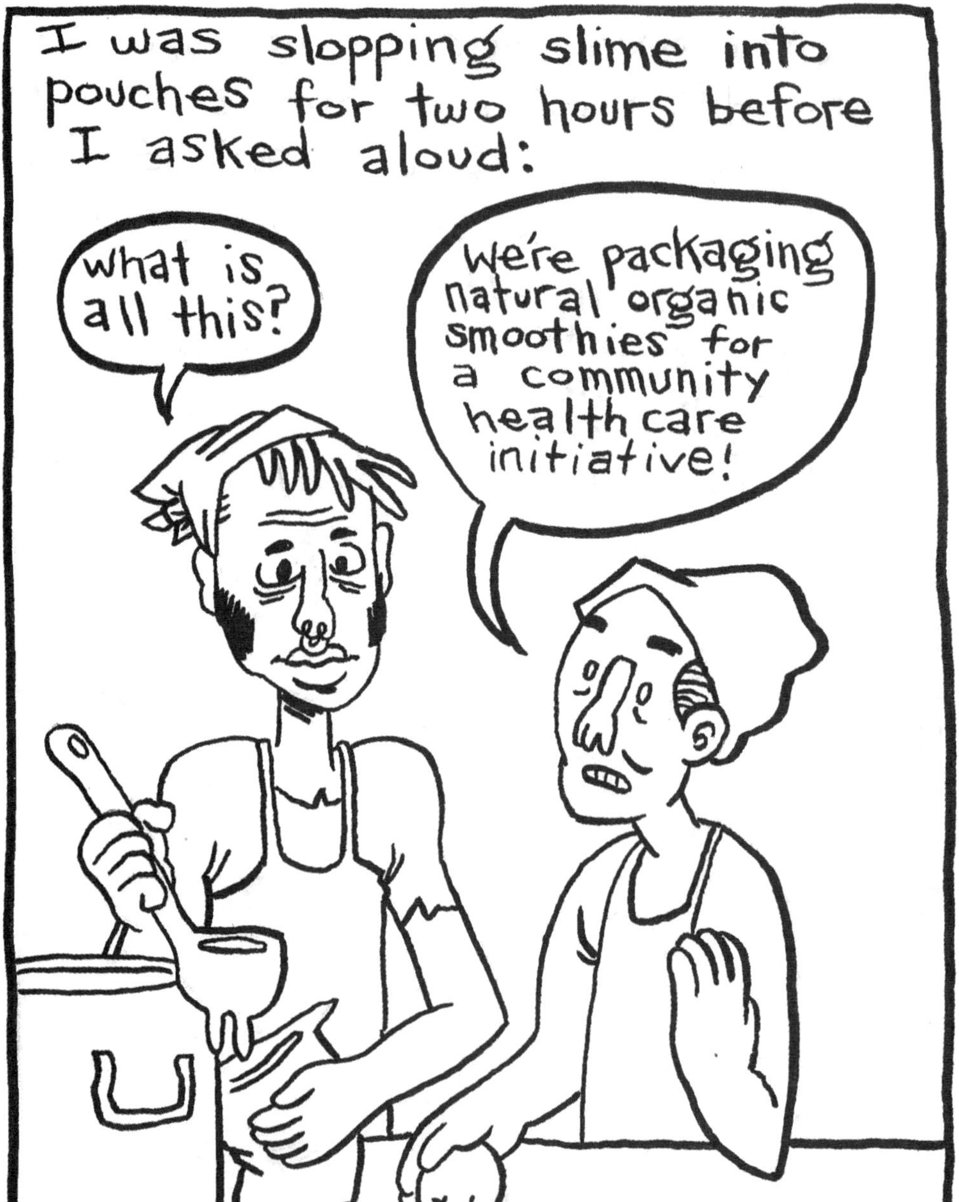
I was slopping slime into pouches for two hours before I asked aloud:
what is all this?
We're packaging natural organic smoothies for a community health care initiative!

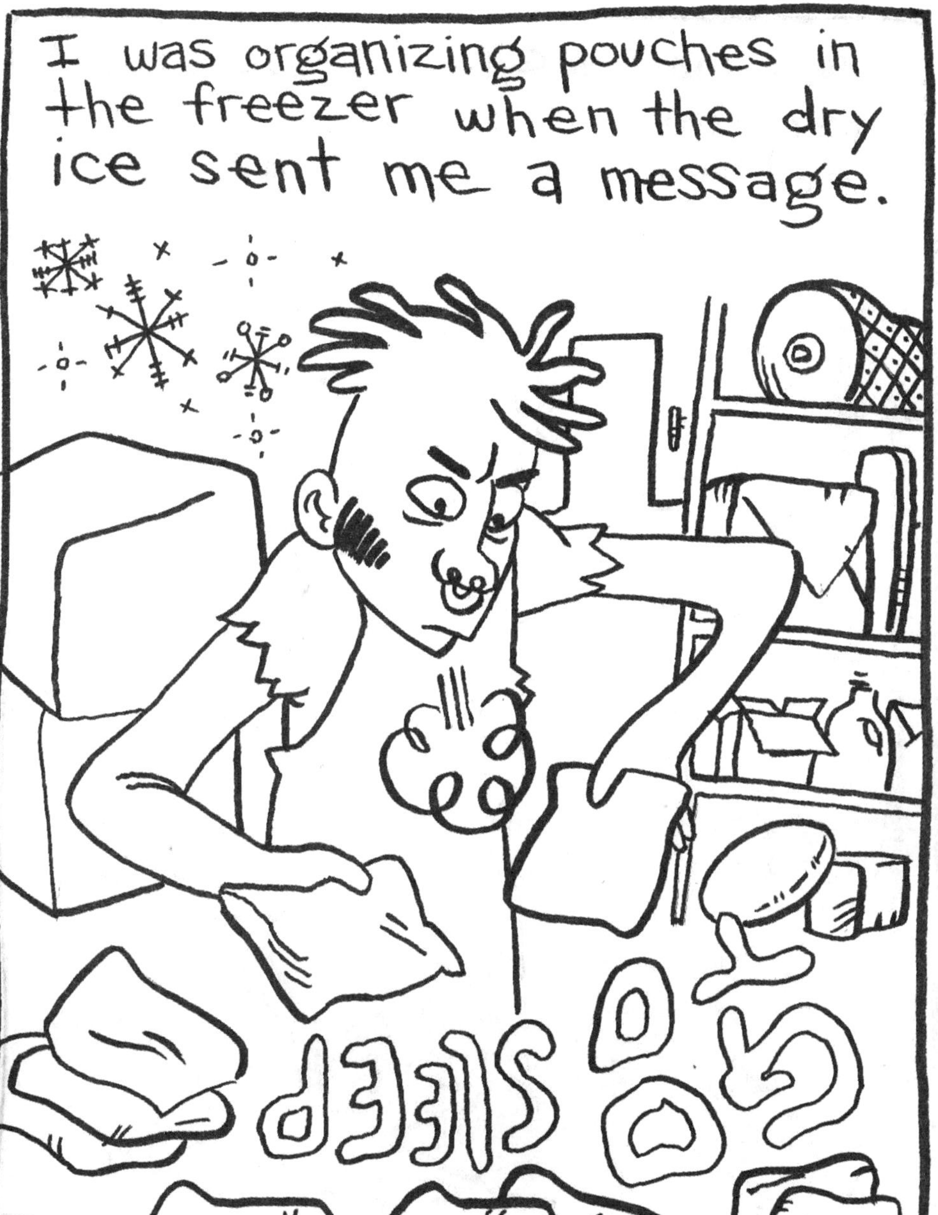
I was organizing pouches in the freezer when the dry ice sent me a message.

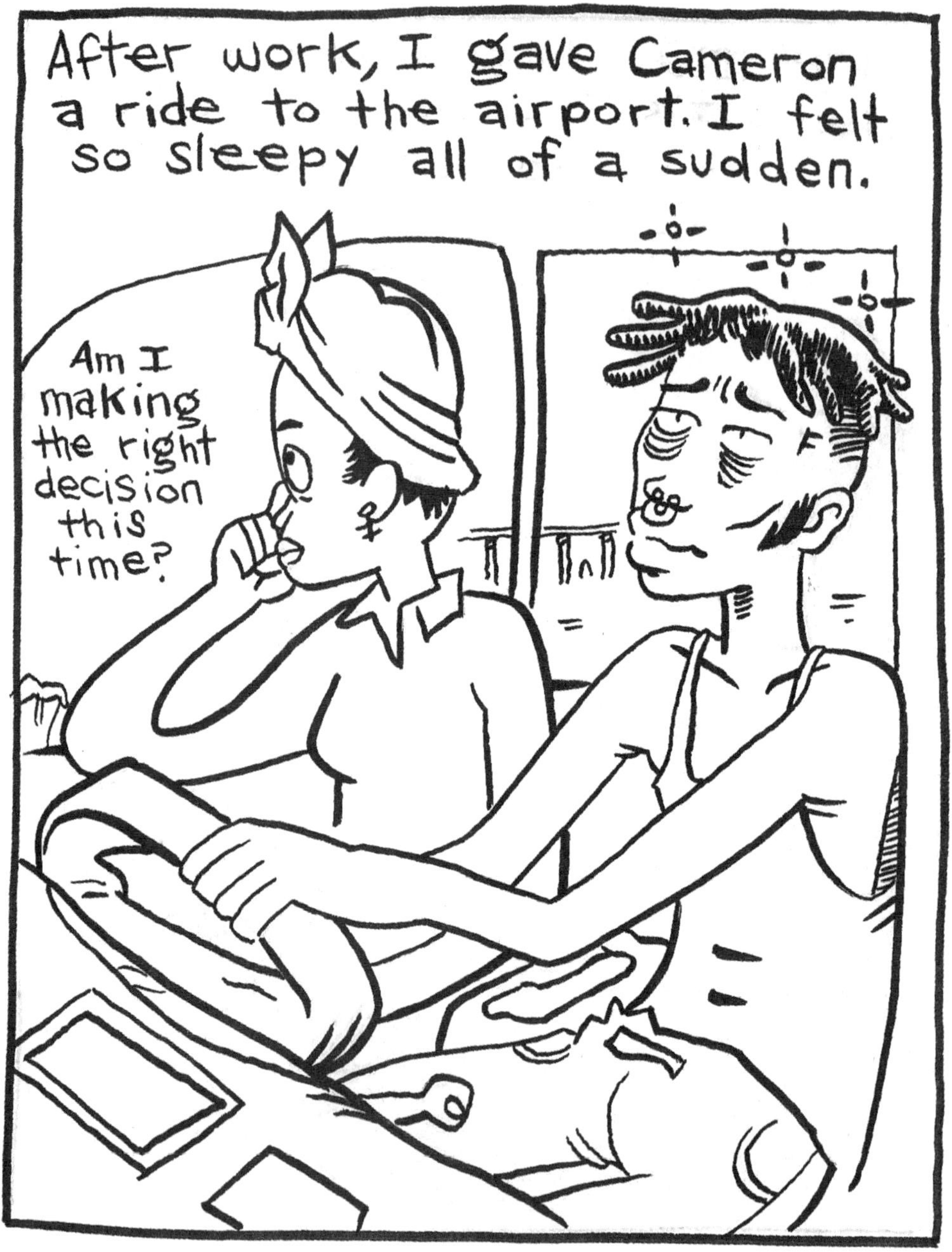
After work, I gave Cameron a ride to the airport. I felt so sleepy all of a sudden.
Am I making the right decision this time?

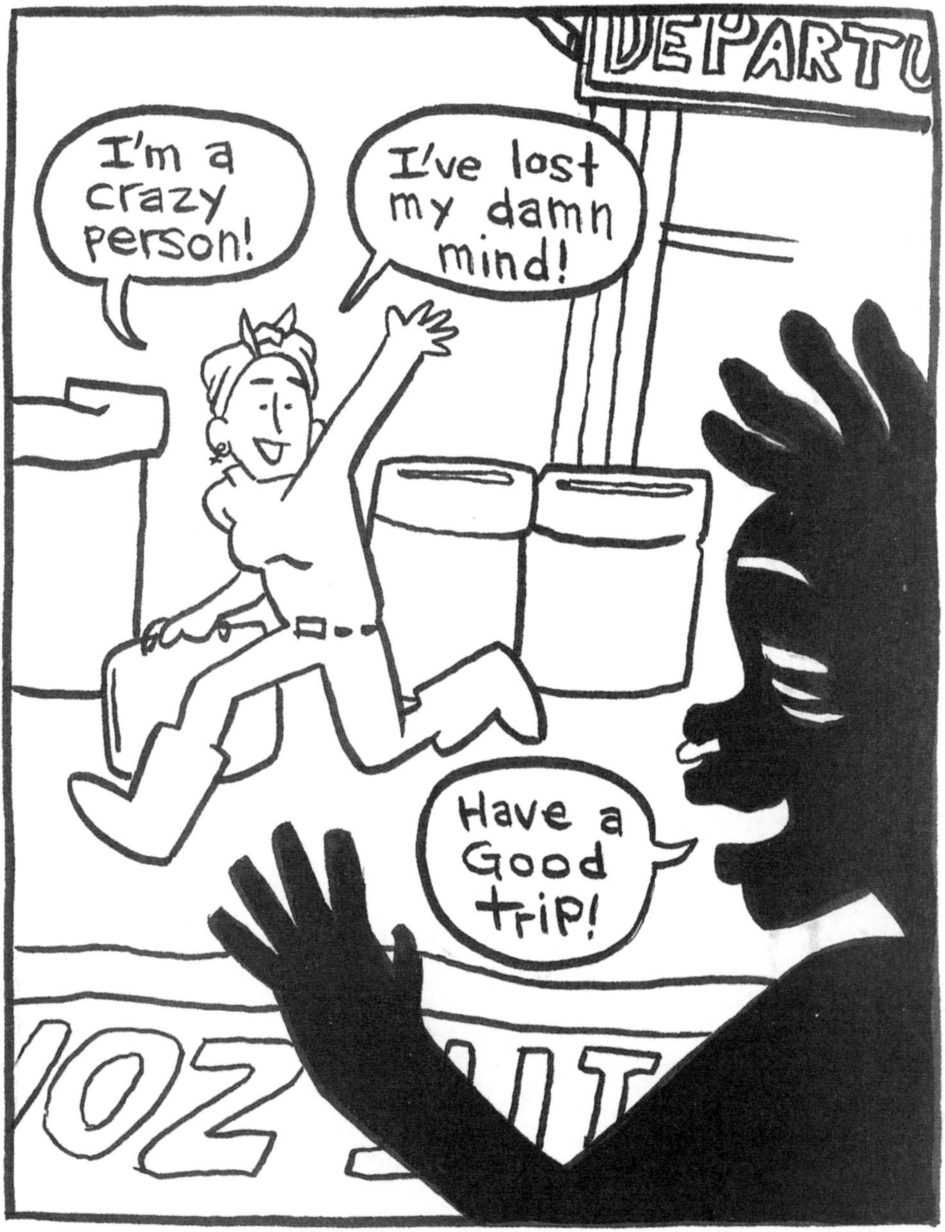
DEPARTU
I'm a crazy person!
I've lost my damn mind!
Have a Good trip!

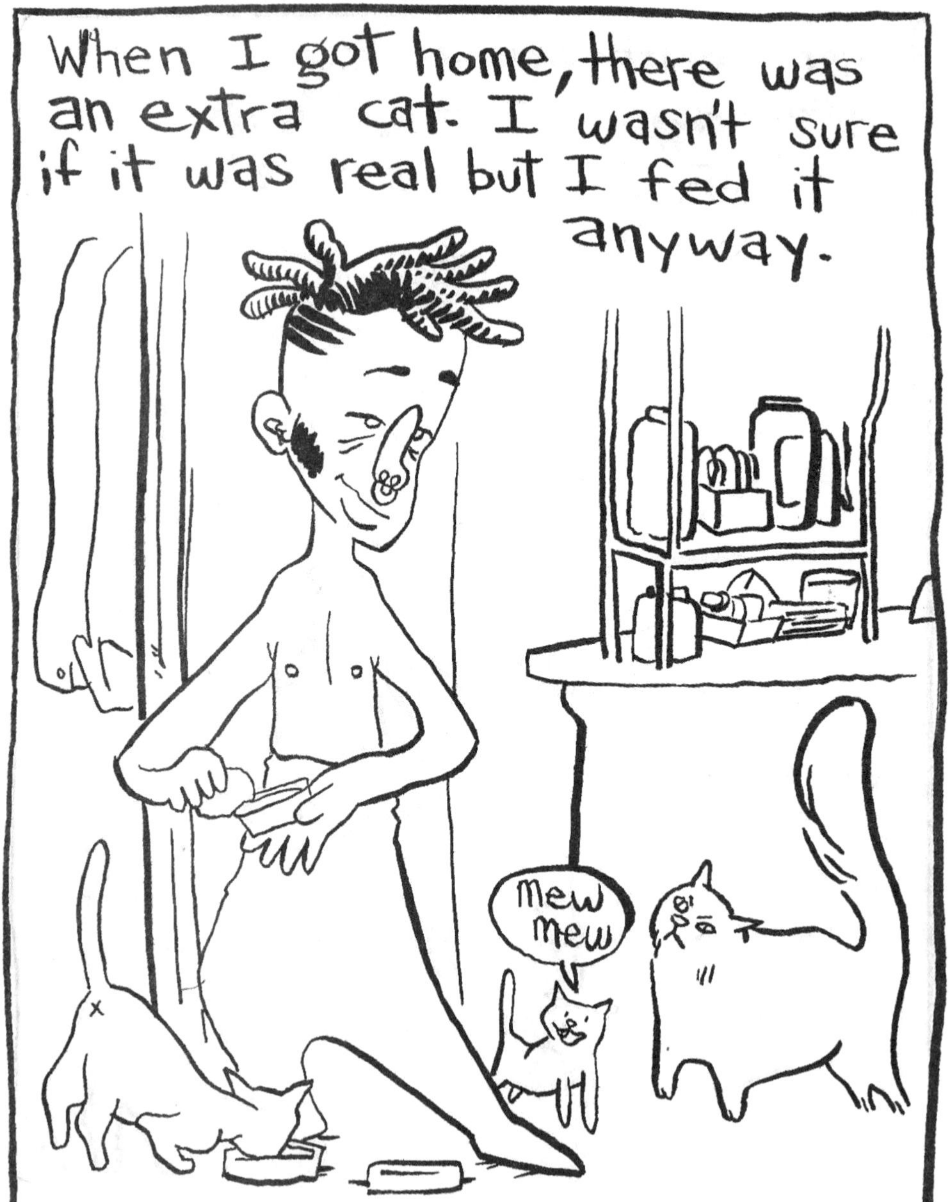
When I got home, there was an extra cat. I wasn't sure if it was real but I fed it anyway.
Mew Mew

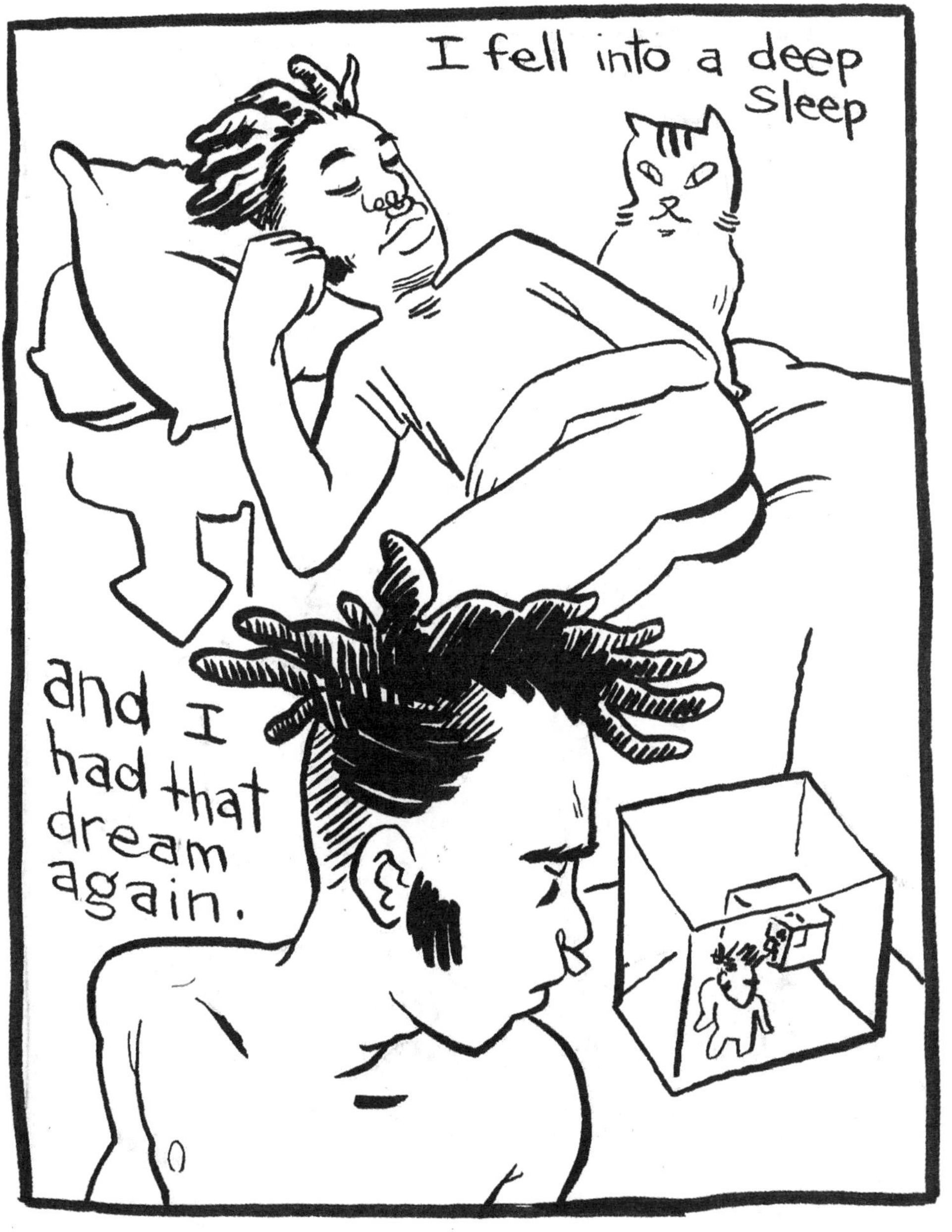

I fell into a deep sleep
and I had that dream again.

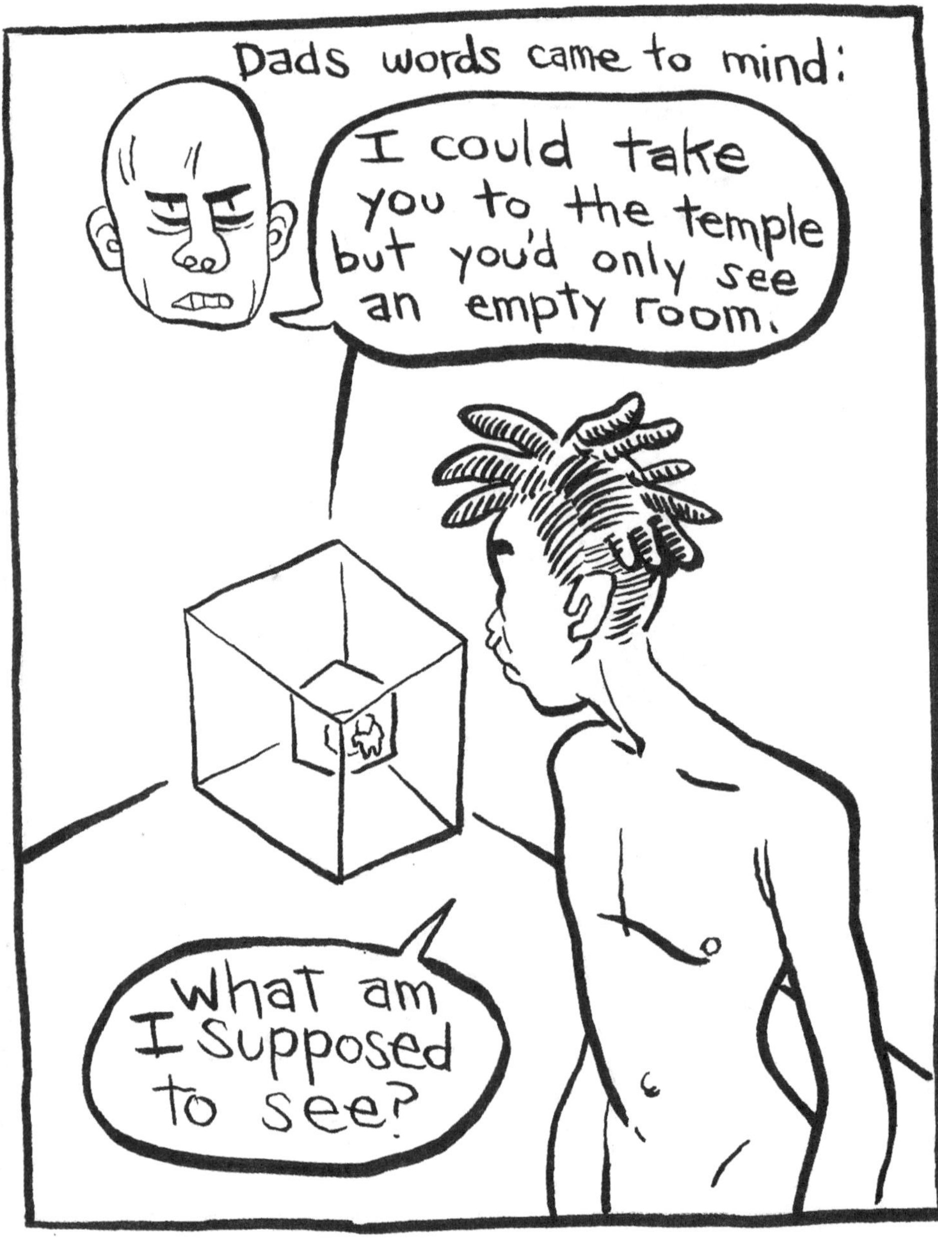
Dads words came to mind:
I could take you to the temple but you'd only see an empty room.
What am I supposed to see?

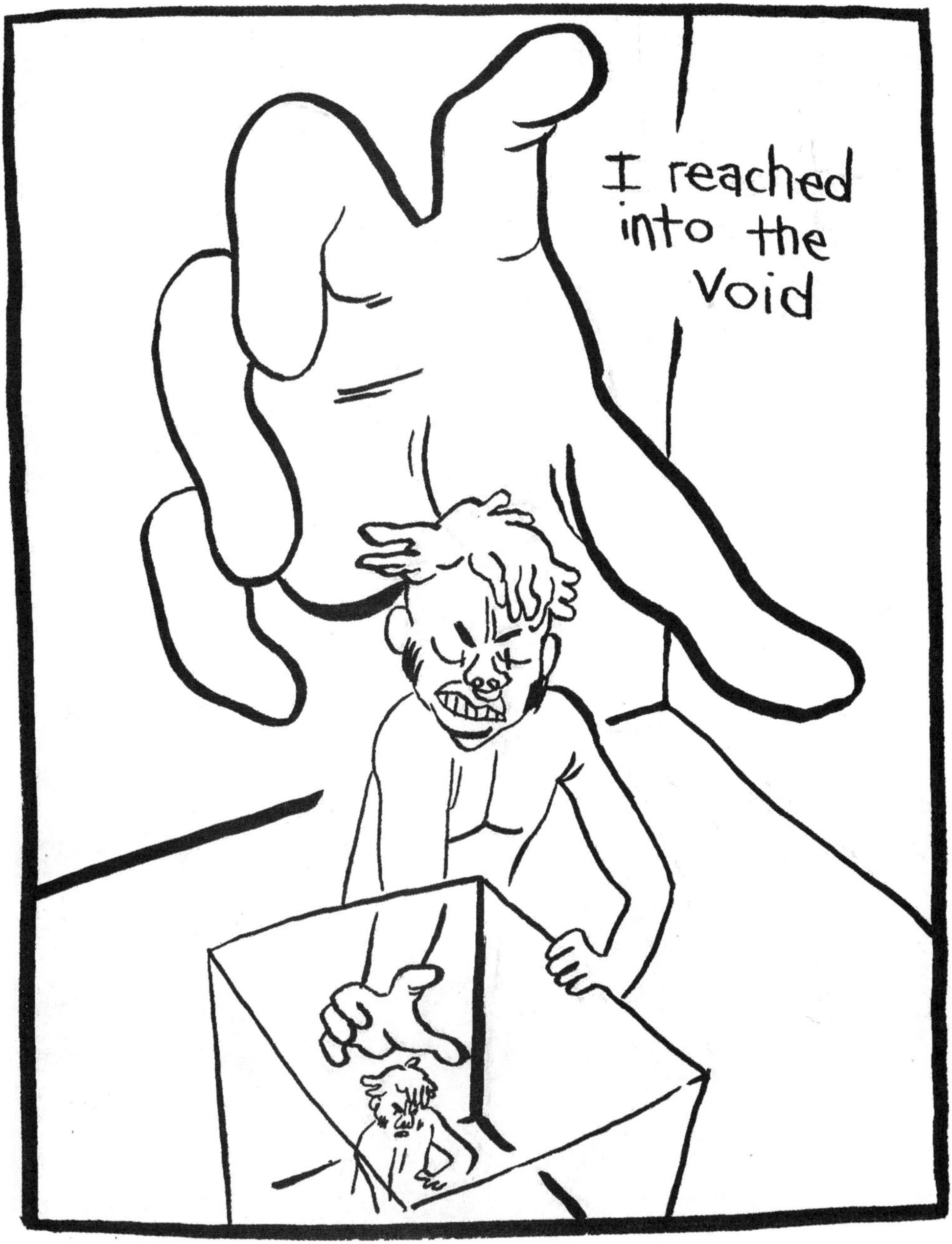
I reached into the void

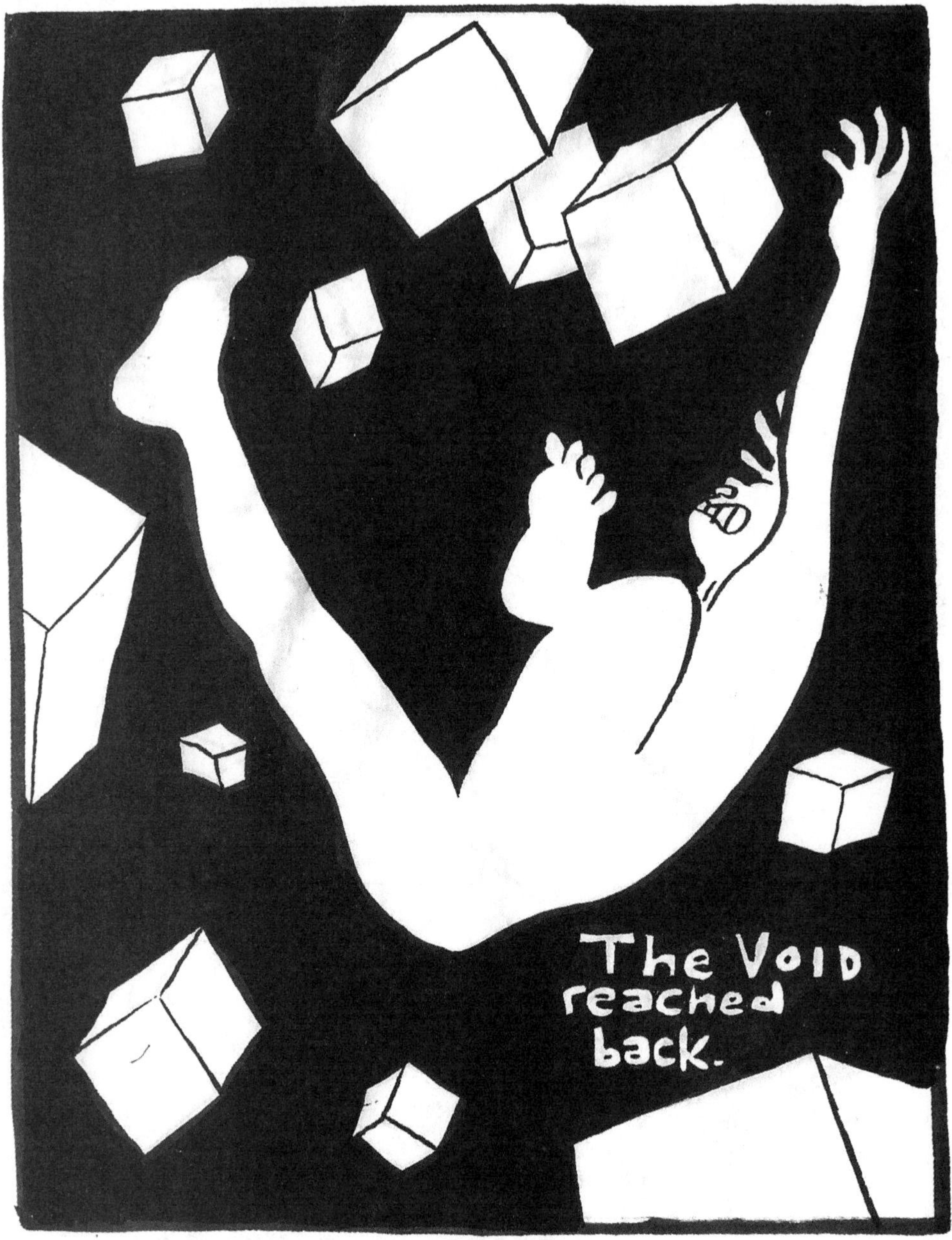
The VOID
reached
back.

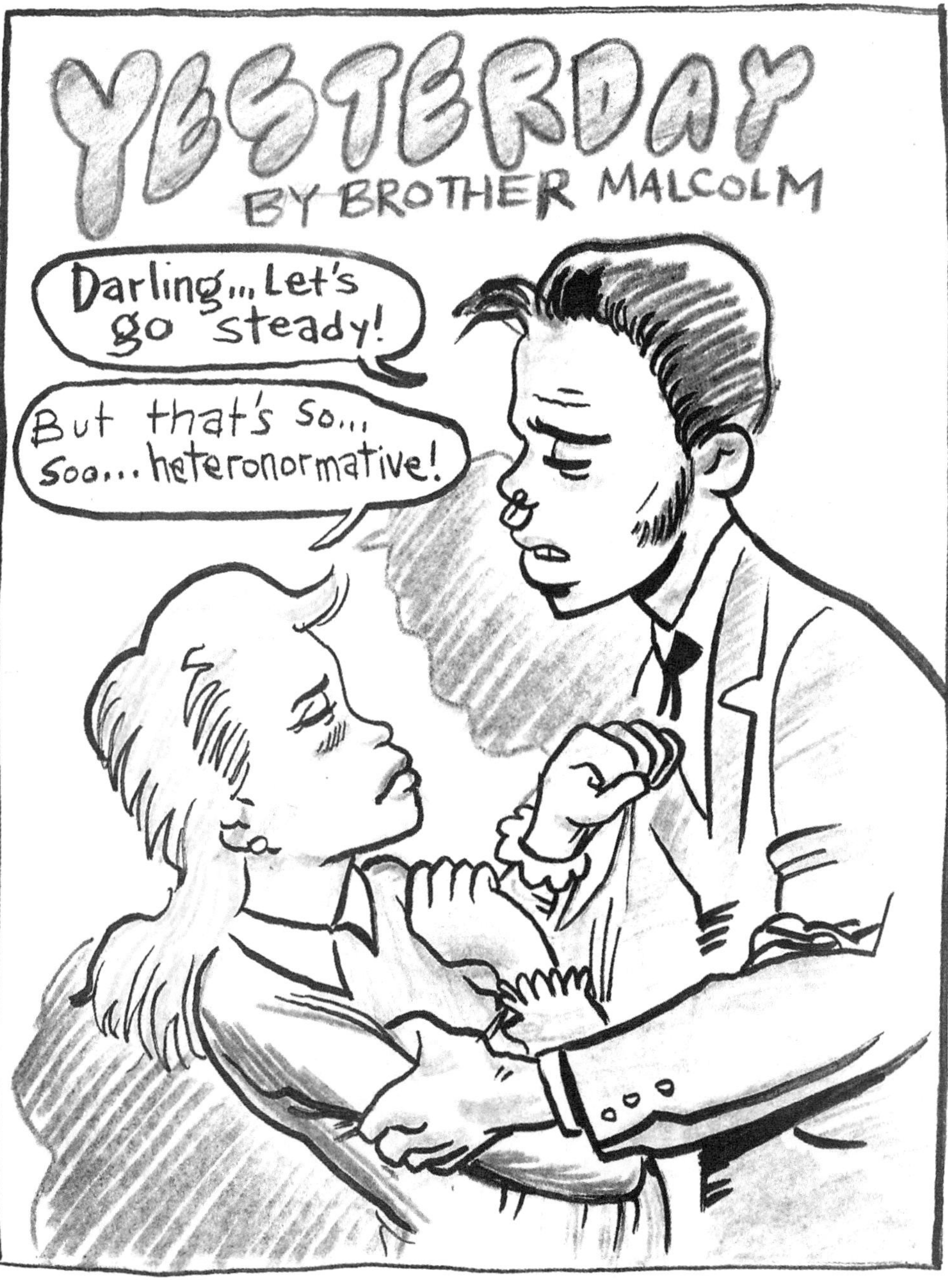
YESTERDAY
BY BROTHER MALCOLM
Darling... Let's go steady!
But that's so... soo... heteronormative!

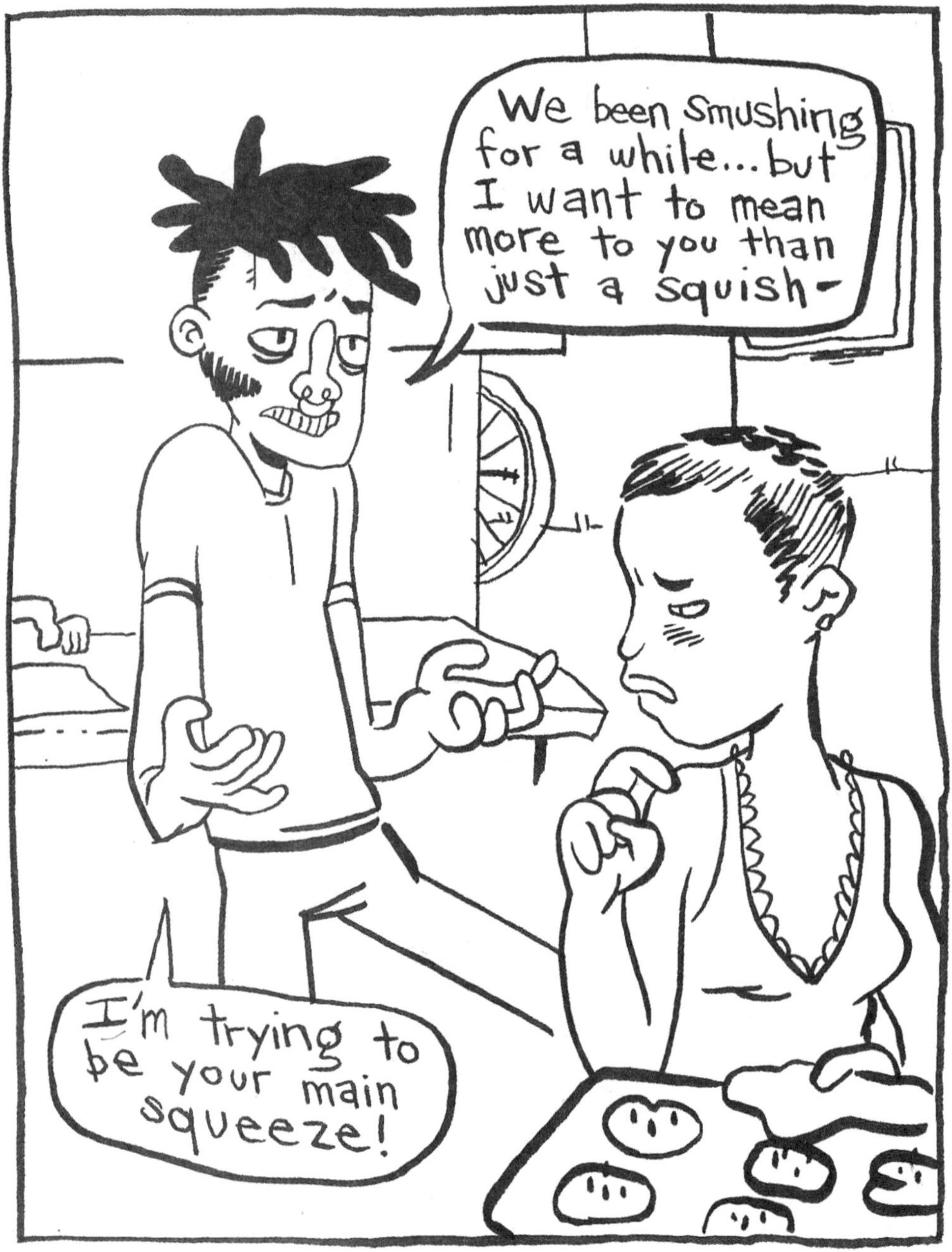
We been smushing for a while...but I want to mean more to you than just a squish-
I'm trying to be your main squeeze!

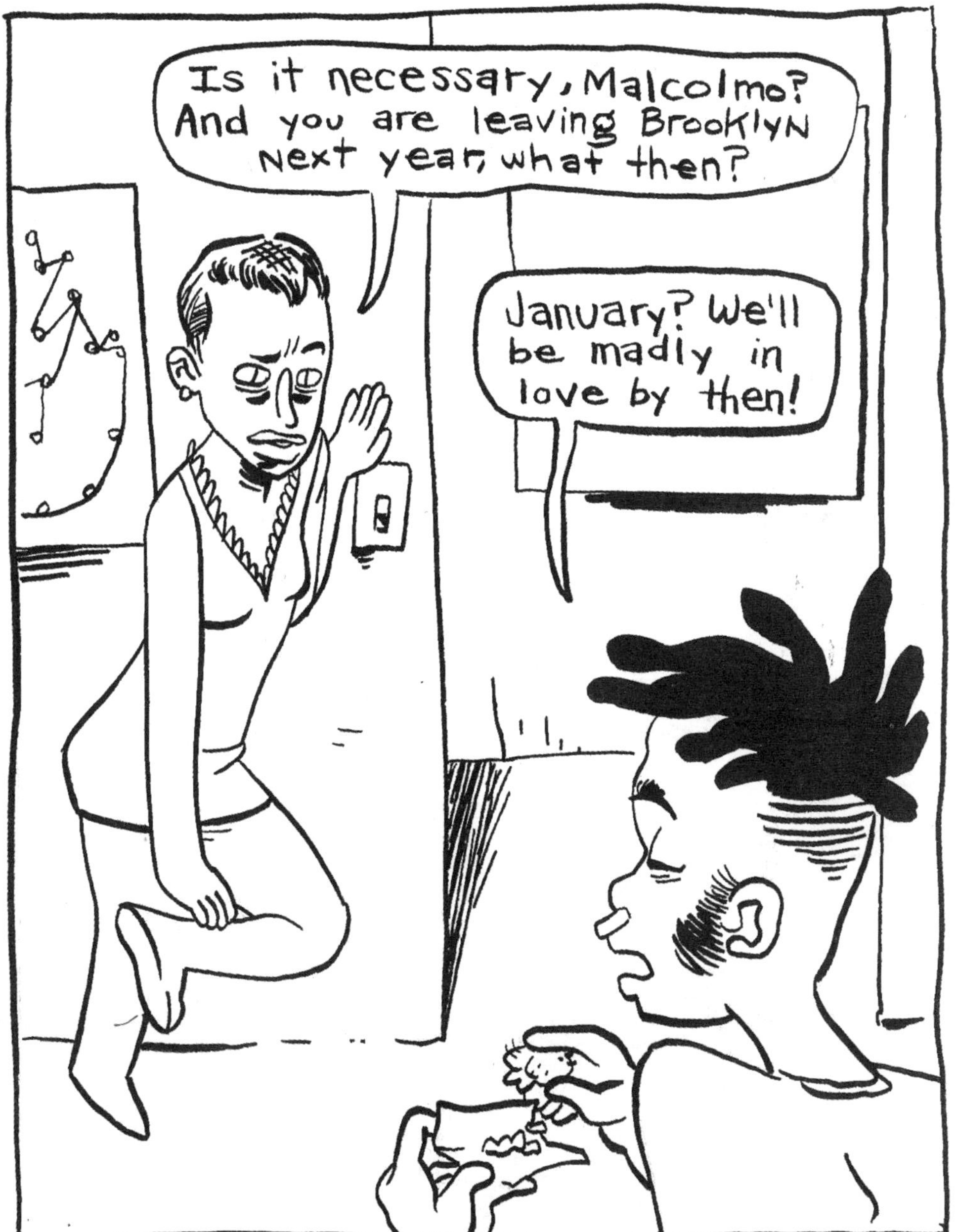
Is it necessary, Malcolmo? And you are leaving Brooklyn next year, what then?
January? We'll be madly in love by then!

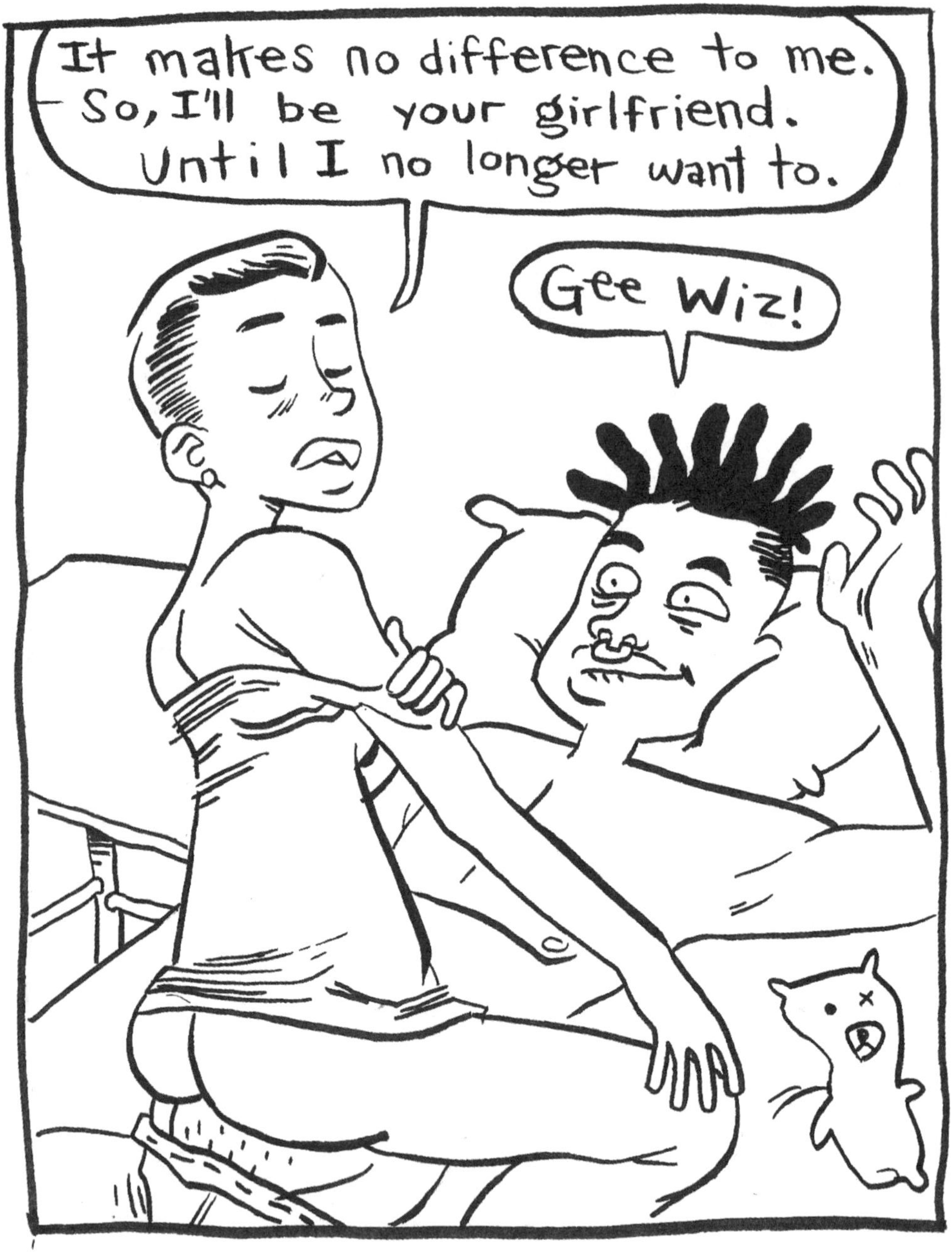
It makes no difference to me. So, I'll be your girlfriend. Until I no longer want to.
Gee Wiz!

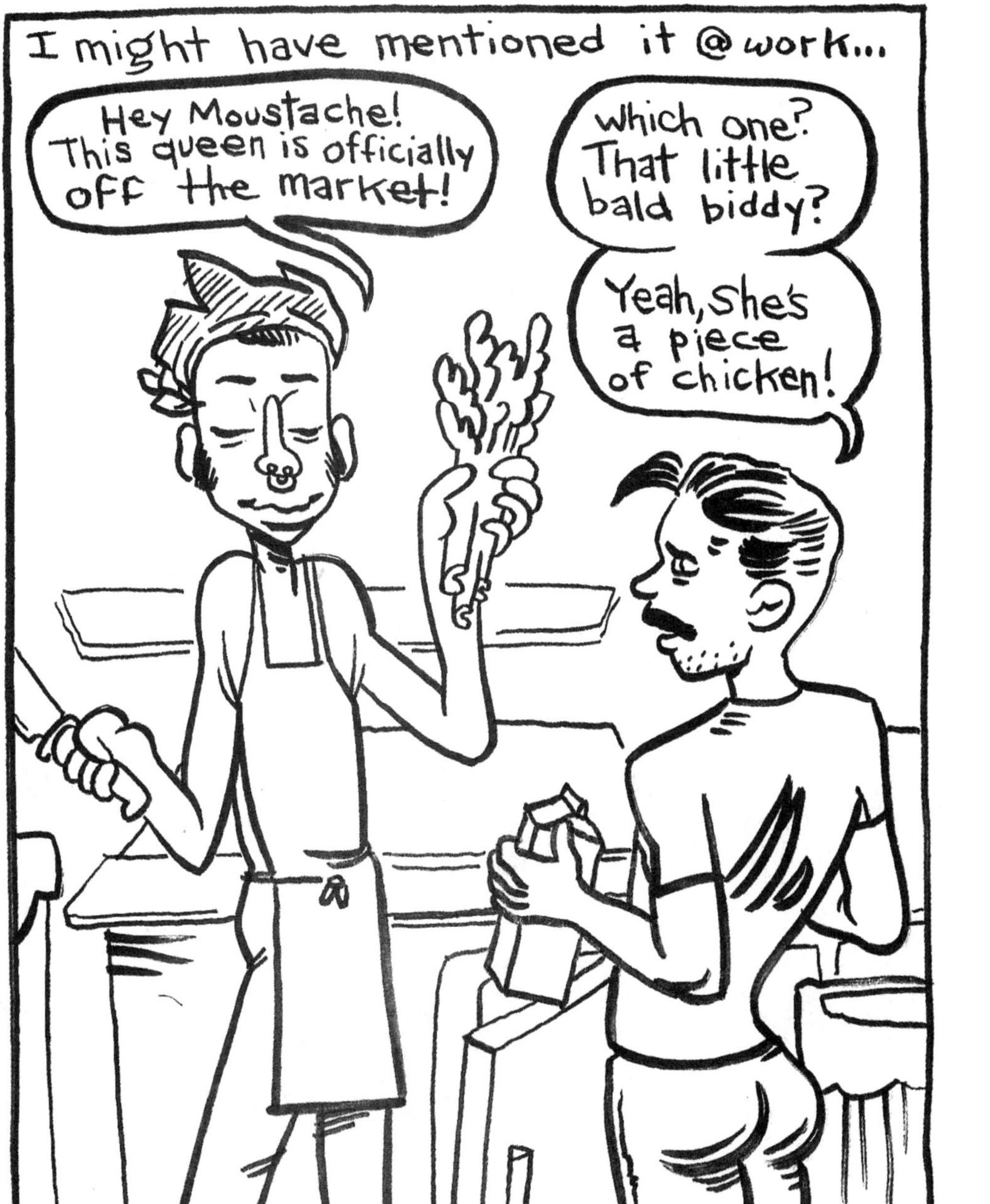
I might have mentioned it @ work...
Hey Moustache! This queen is officially off the market!
Which one? That little bald biddy?
Yeah, she's a piece of chicken!

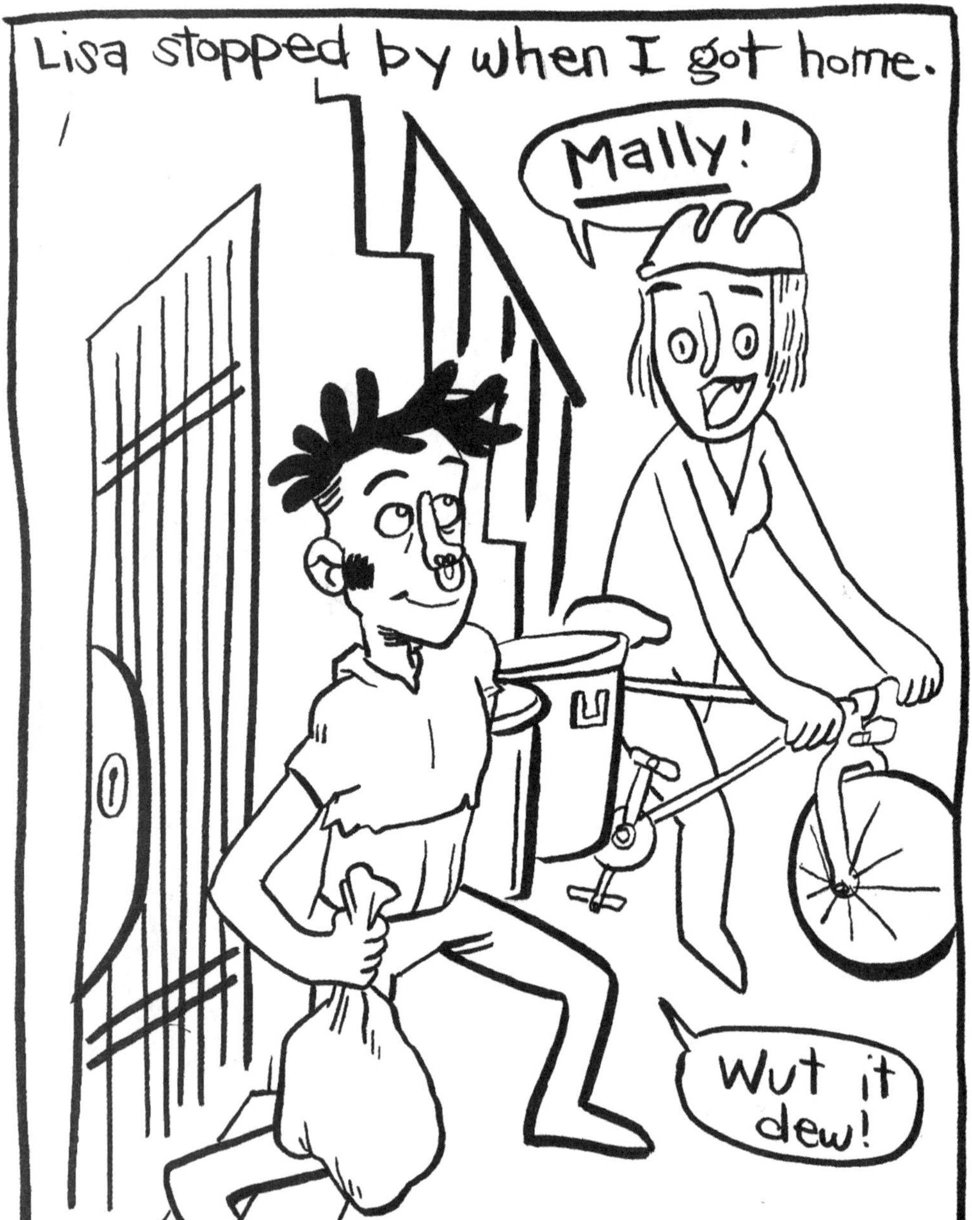
Lisa stopped by when I got home.
Mally!
Wut it dew!

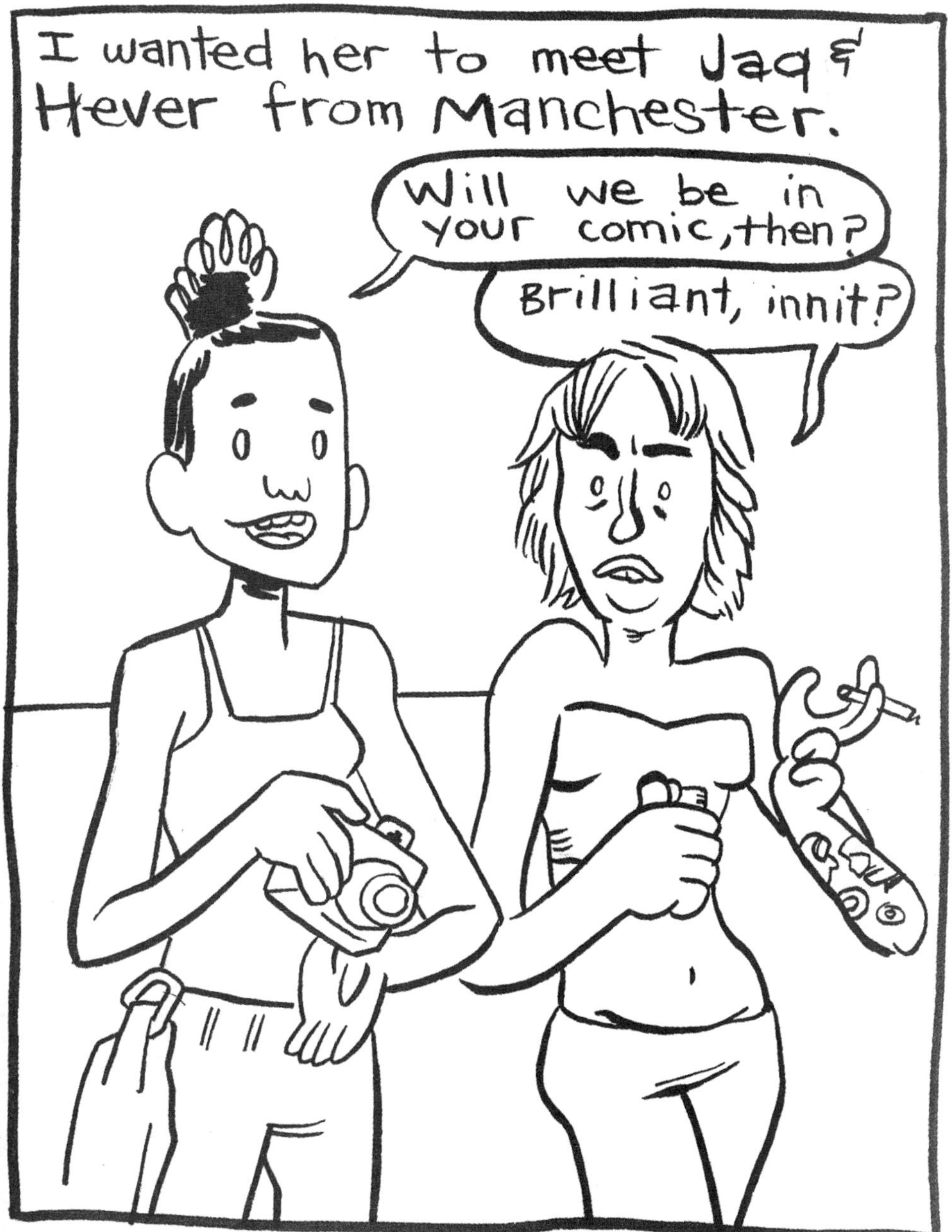
I wanted her to meet Jaq & Hever from Manchester.
Will we be in your comic, then?
Brilliant, innit?

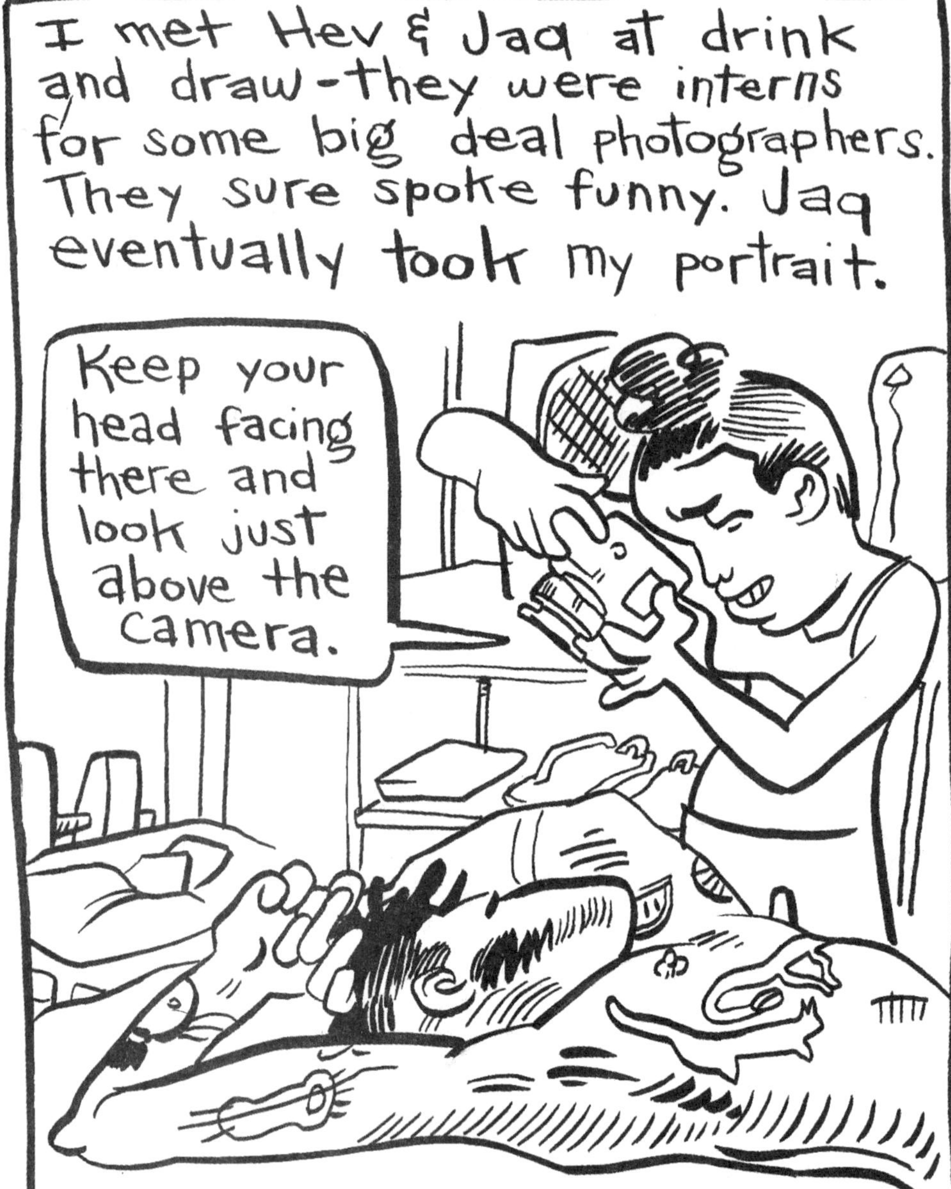
I met Hev & Jaq at drink and draw-they were interns for some big deal photographers. They sure spoke funny. Jaq eventually took my portrait.
Keep your head facing there and look just above the camera.

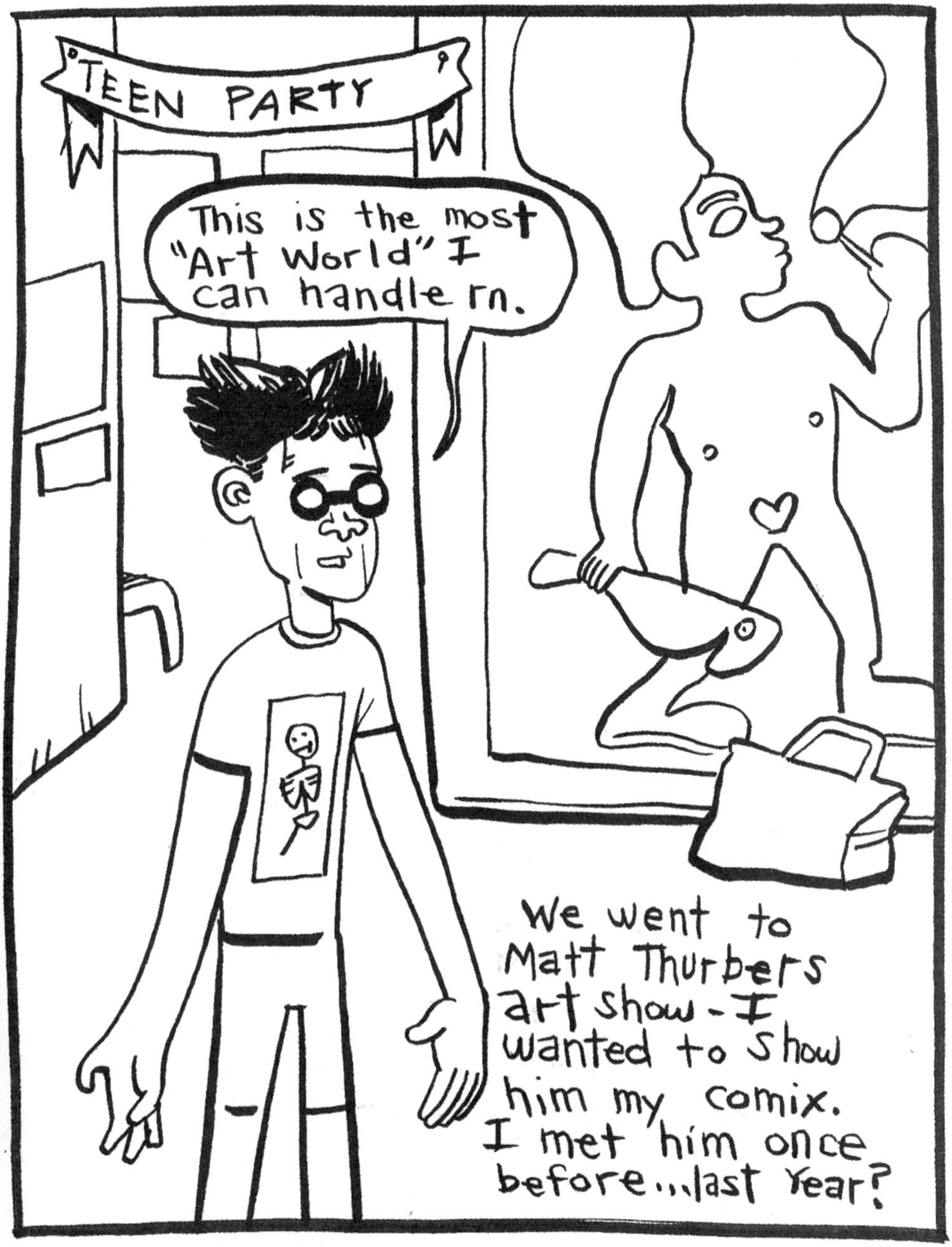
TEEN PARTY
This is the most "Art World" I can handle rn.
We went to Matt Thurbers art show - I wanted to show him my comix. I met him once before...last Year?

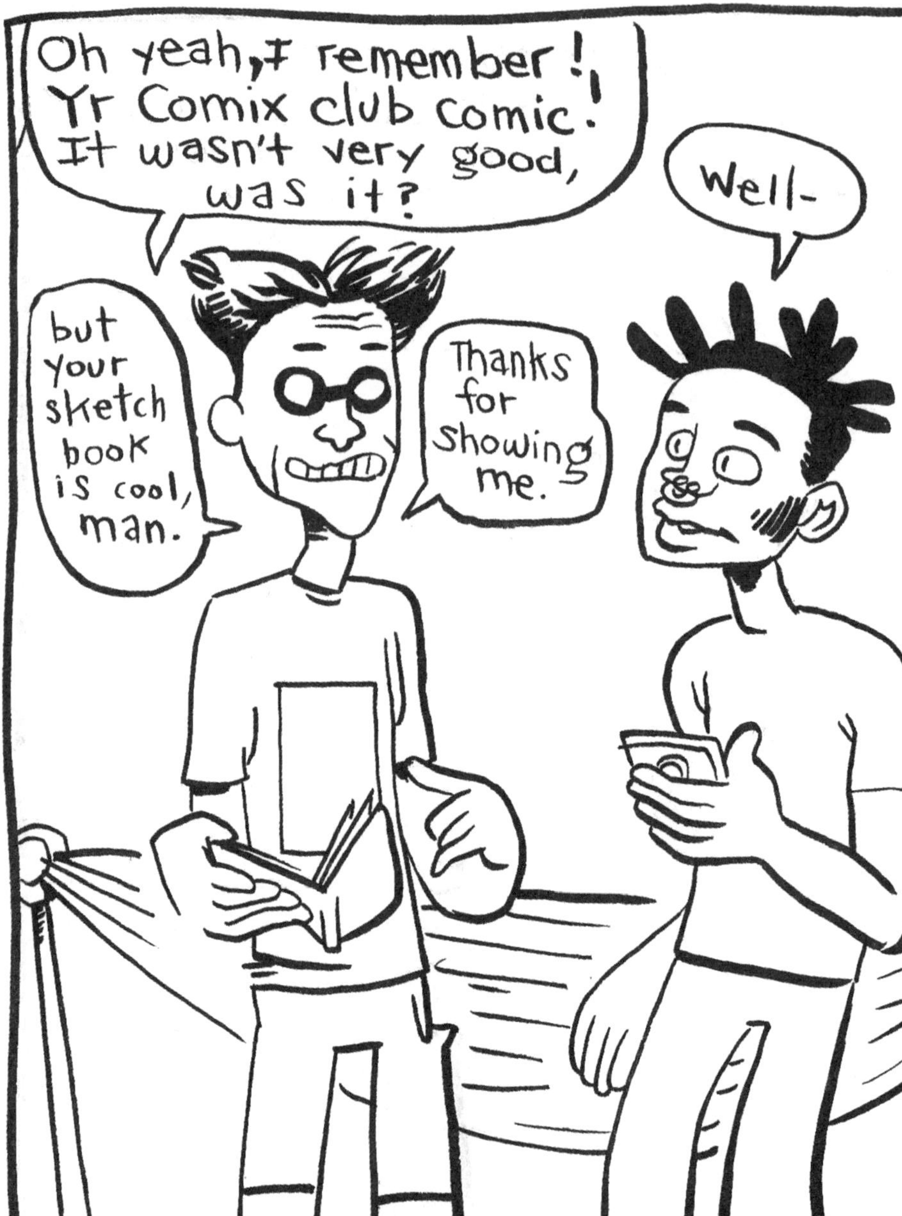
Oh yeah, I remember! Yr Comix club comic! It wasn't very good, was it?
Well-
but your sketch book is cool, man.
Thanks for showing me.

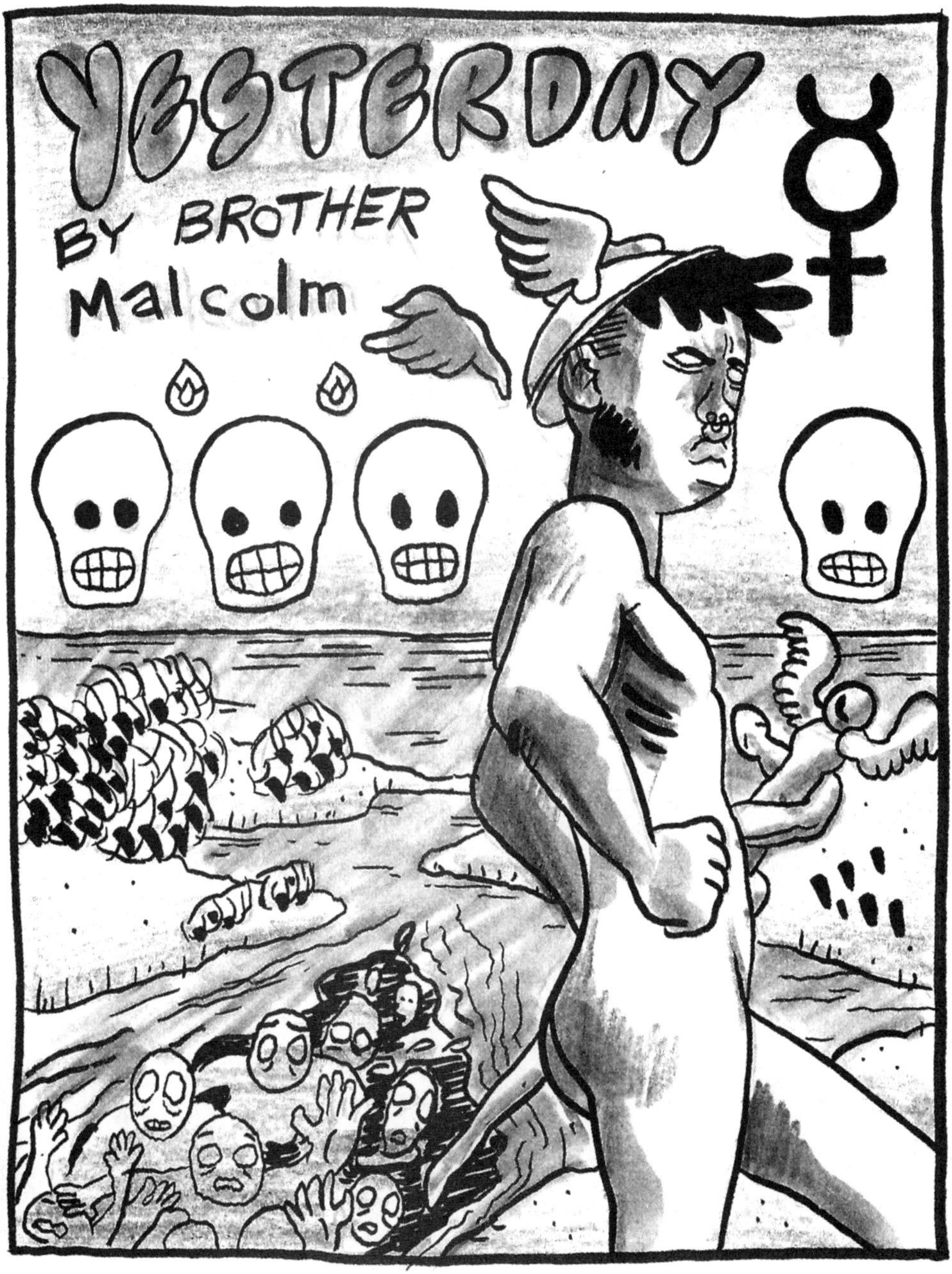
YESTERDAY
BY BROTHER
Malcolm

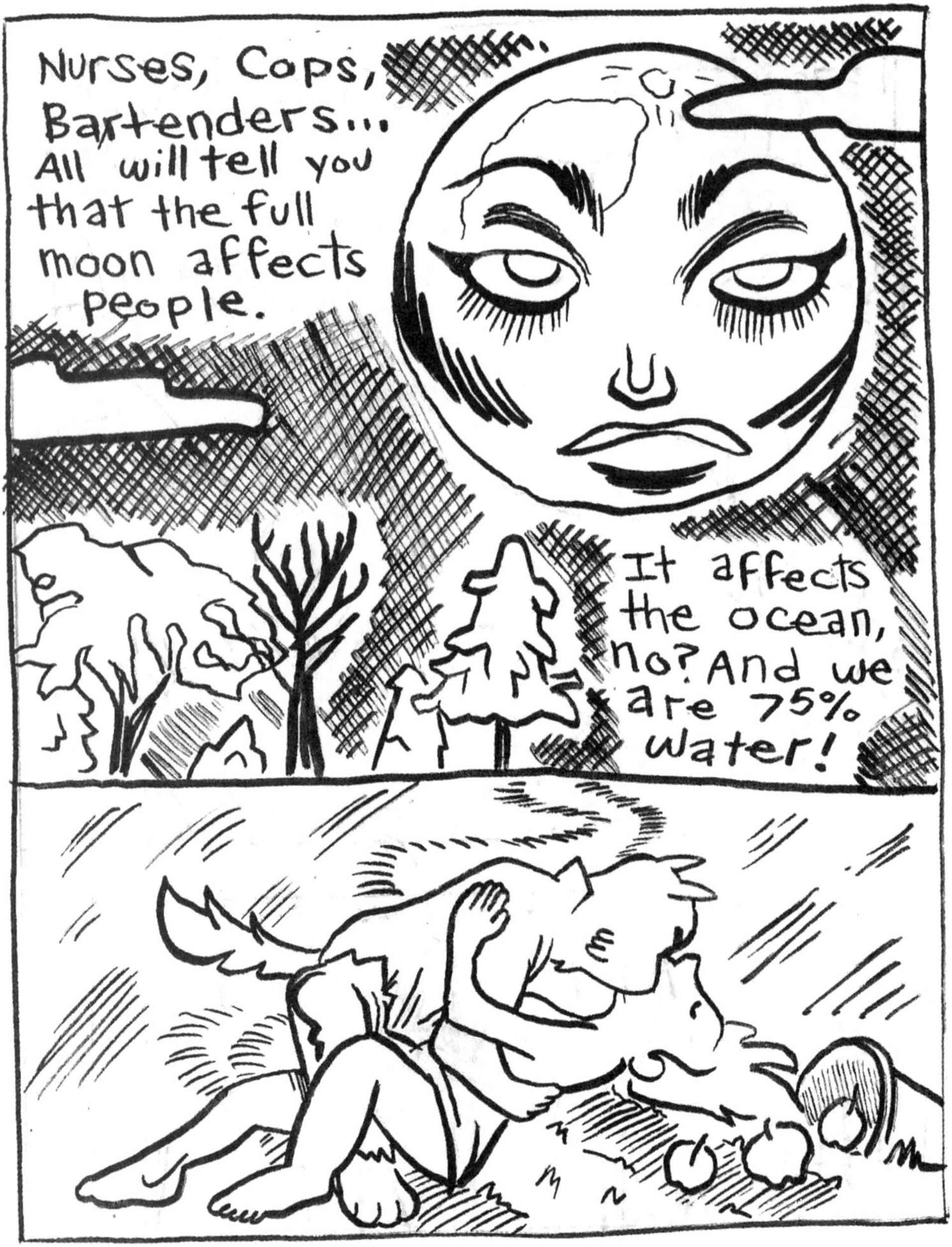
Nurses, Cops, Bartenders... All will tell you that the full moon affects people.
It affects the ocean, no? And we are 75% water!

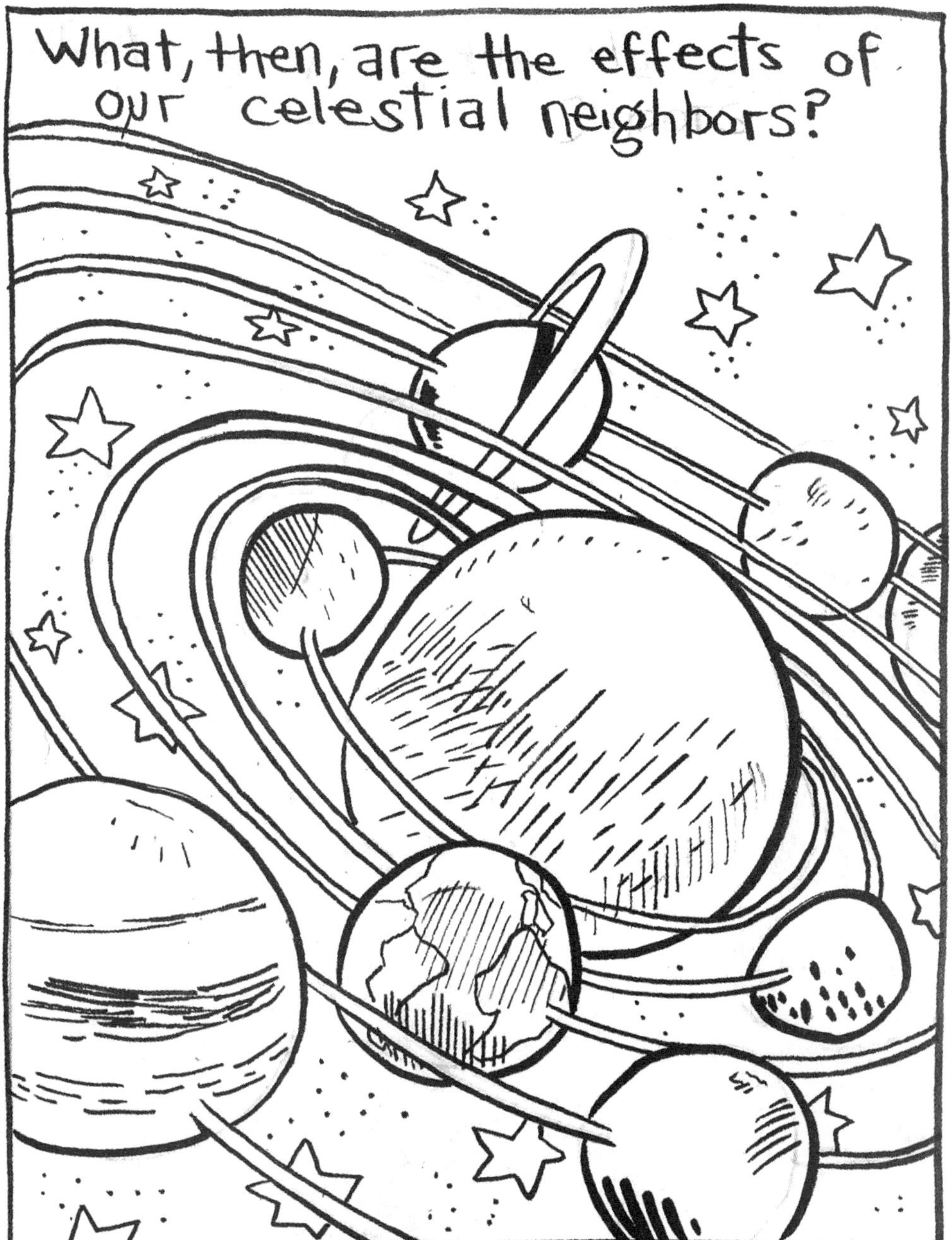
What, then, are the effects of our celestial neighbors?

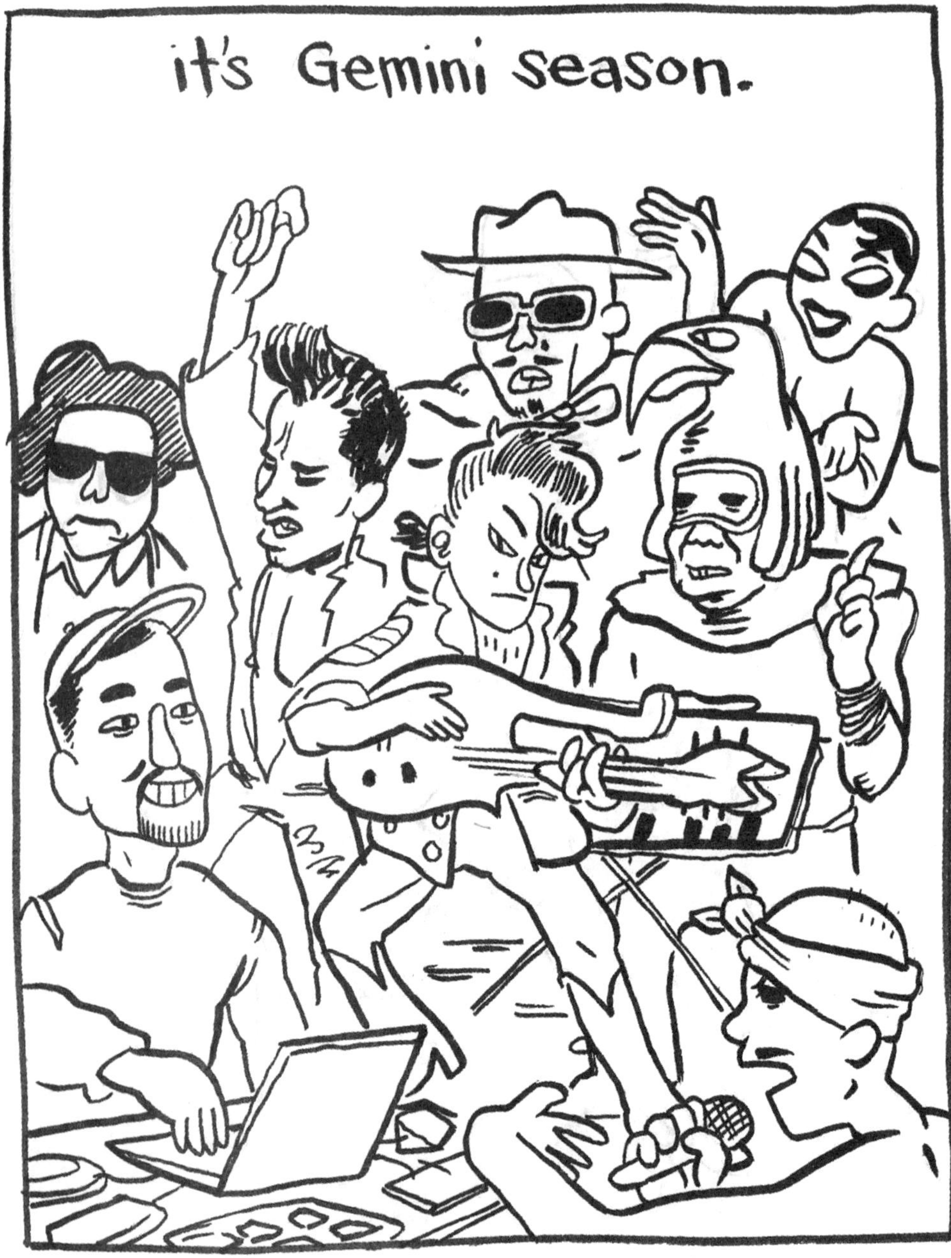
it's Gemini season.

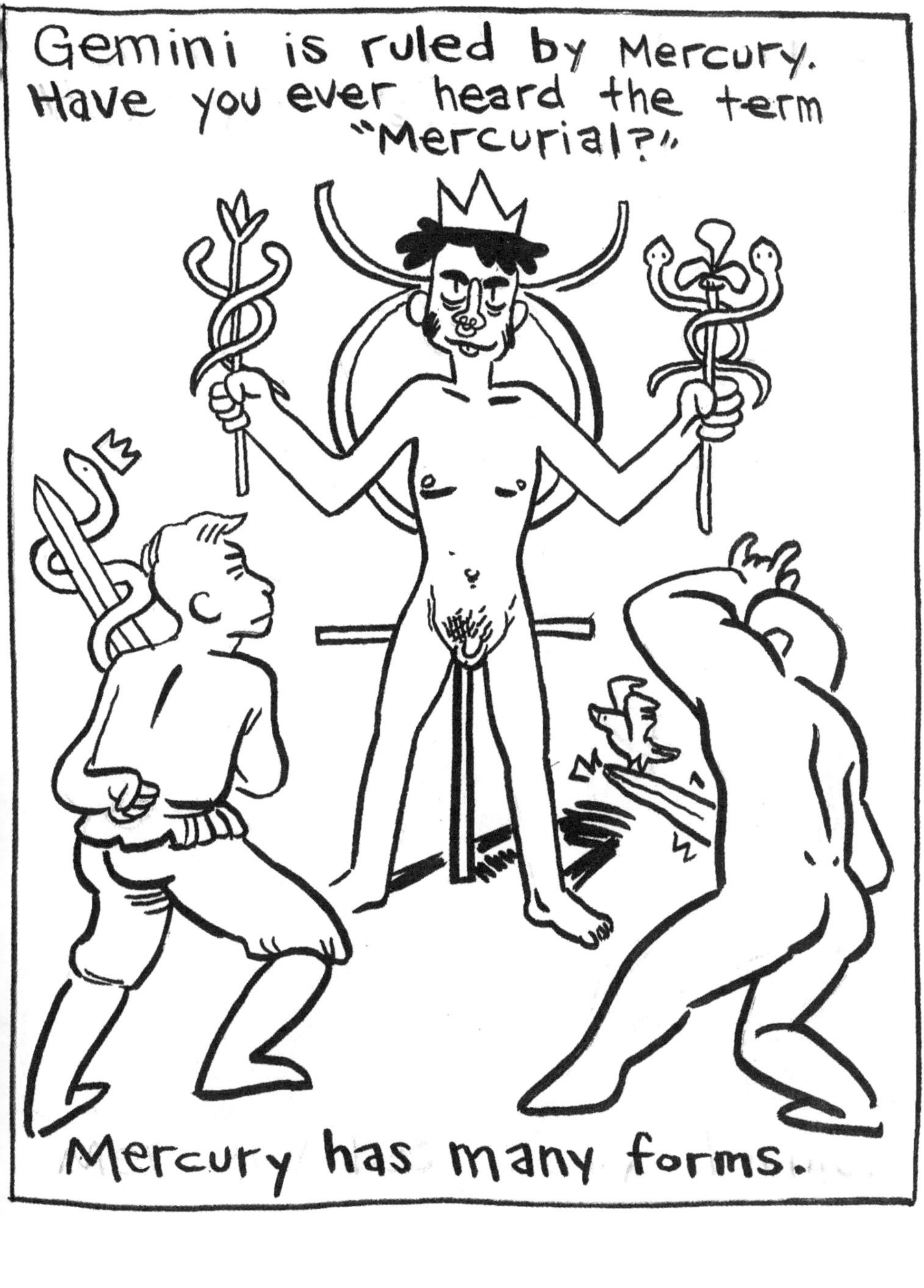
Gemini is ruled by Mercury. Have you ever heard the term "Mercurial?"
Mercury has many forms.

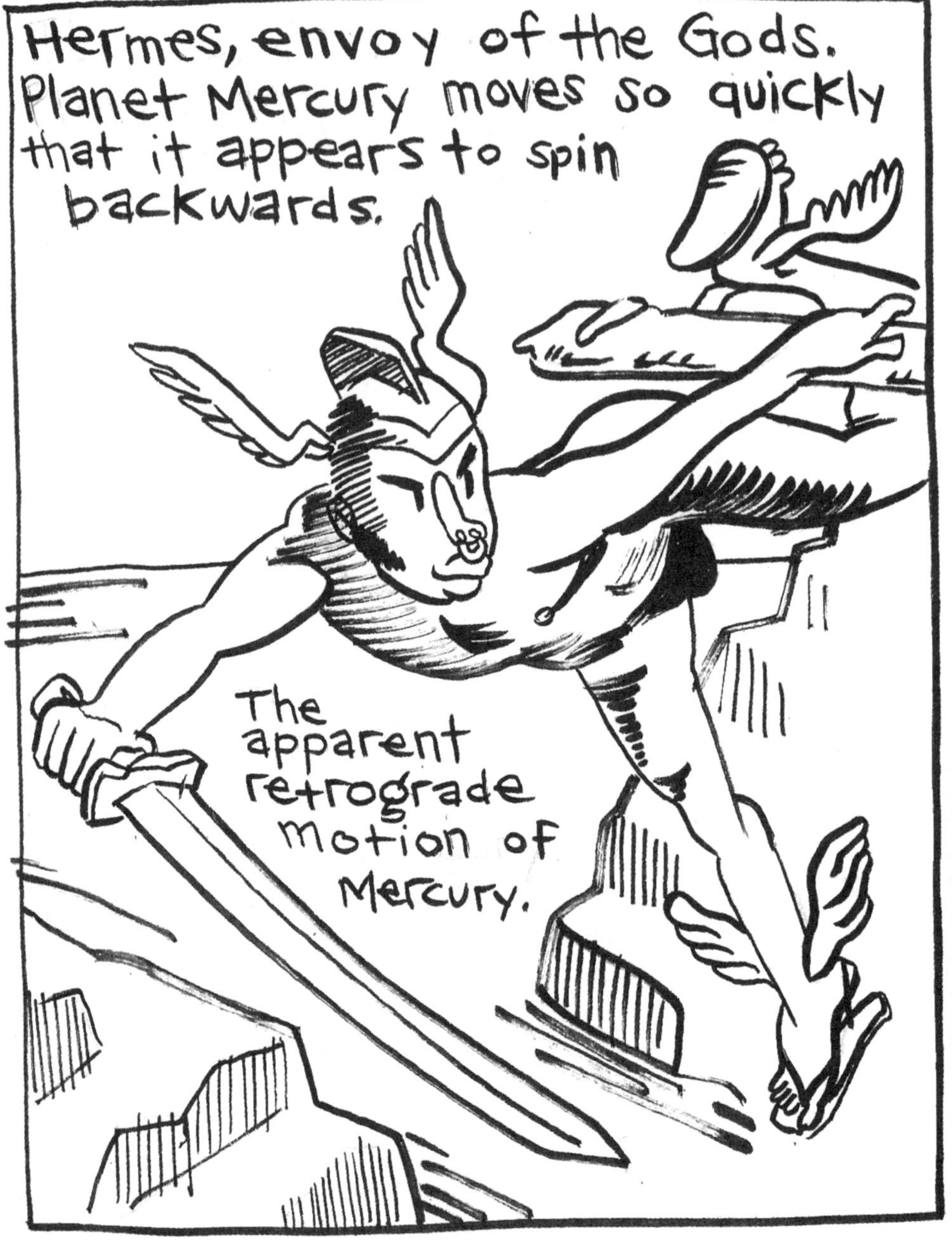
Hermes, envoy of the Gods. Planet Mercury moves so quickly that it appears to spin backwards.
The apparent retrograde motion of Mercury.

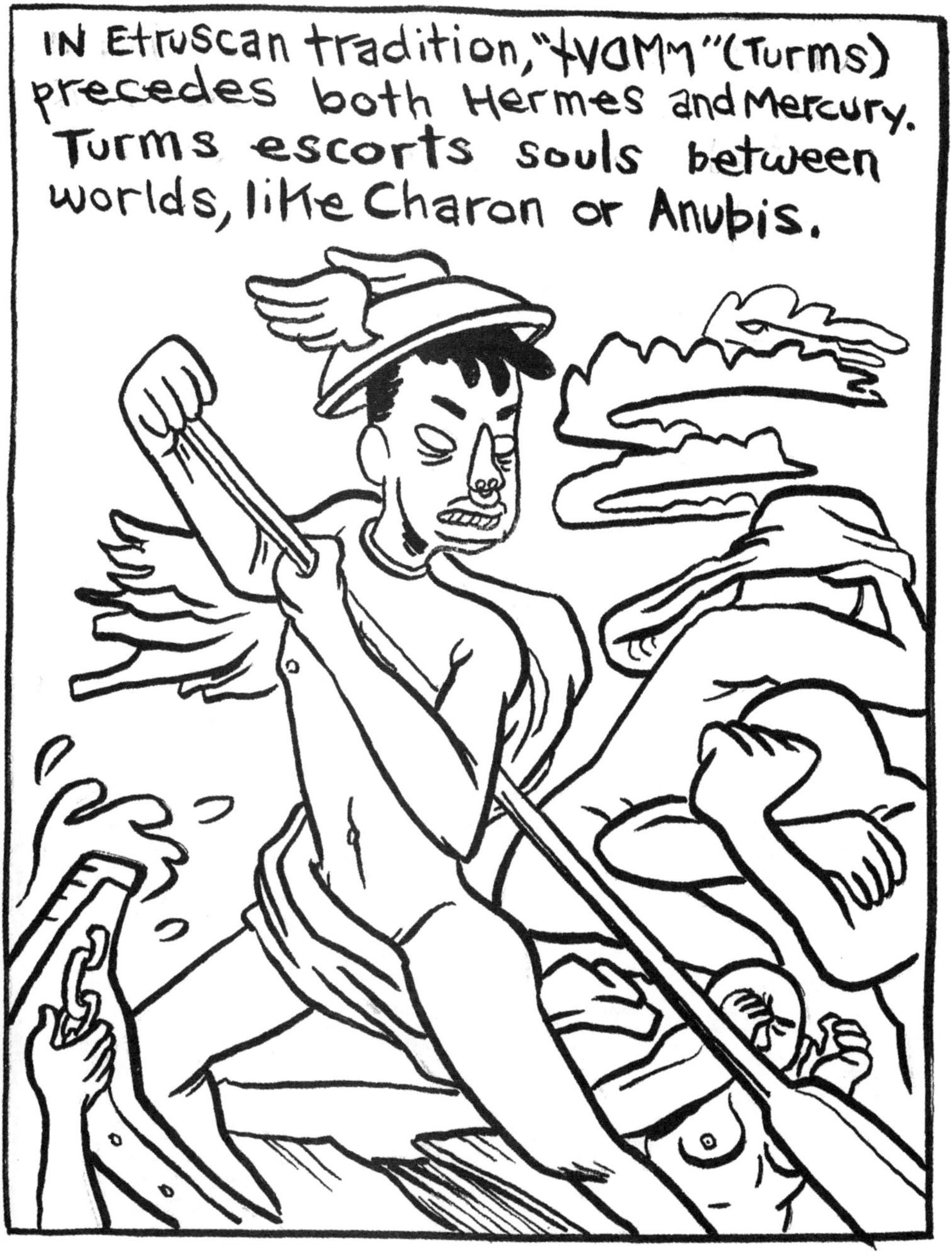
IN Etruscan tradition, "ϮVꓷMM" (Turms) precedes both Hermes and Mercury. Turms escorts souls between worlds, like Charon or Anubis.

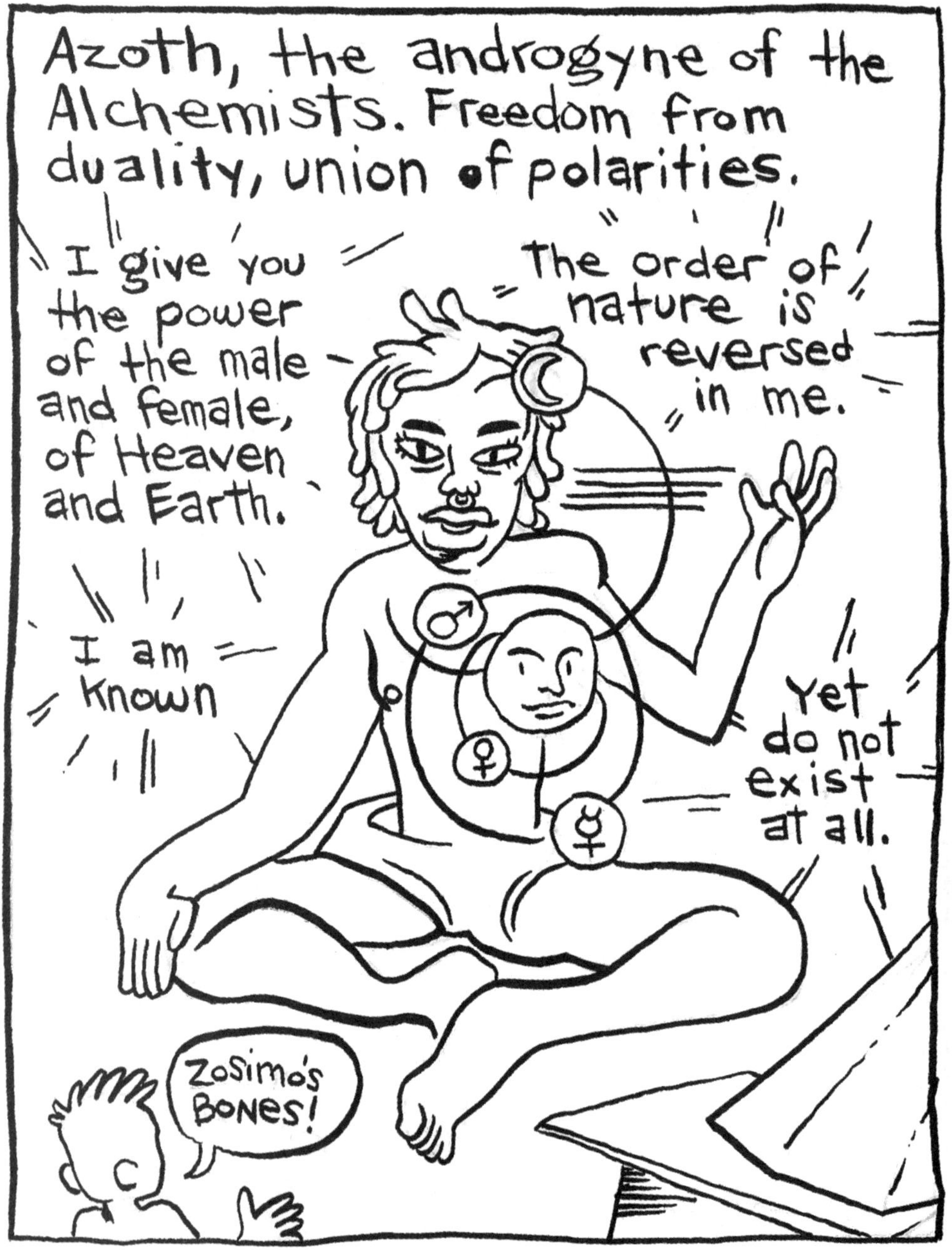
Azoth, the androgyne of the Alchemists. Freedom from duality, union of polarities.
I give you the power of the male and female, of Heaven and Earth.
The order of nature is reversed in me.
I am Known
Yet do not exist at all.
Zosimo's Bones!

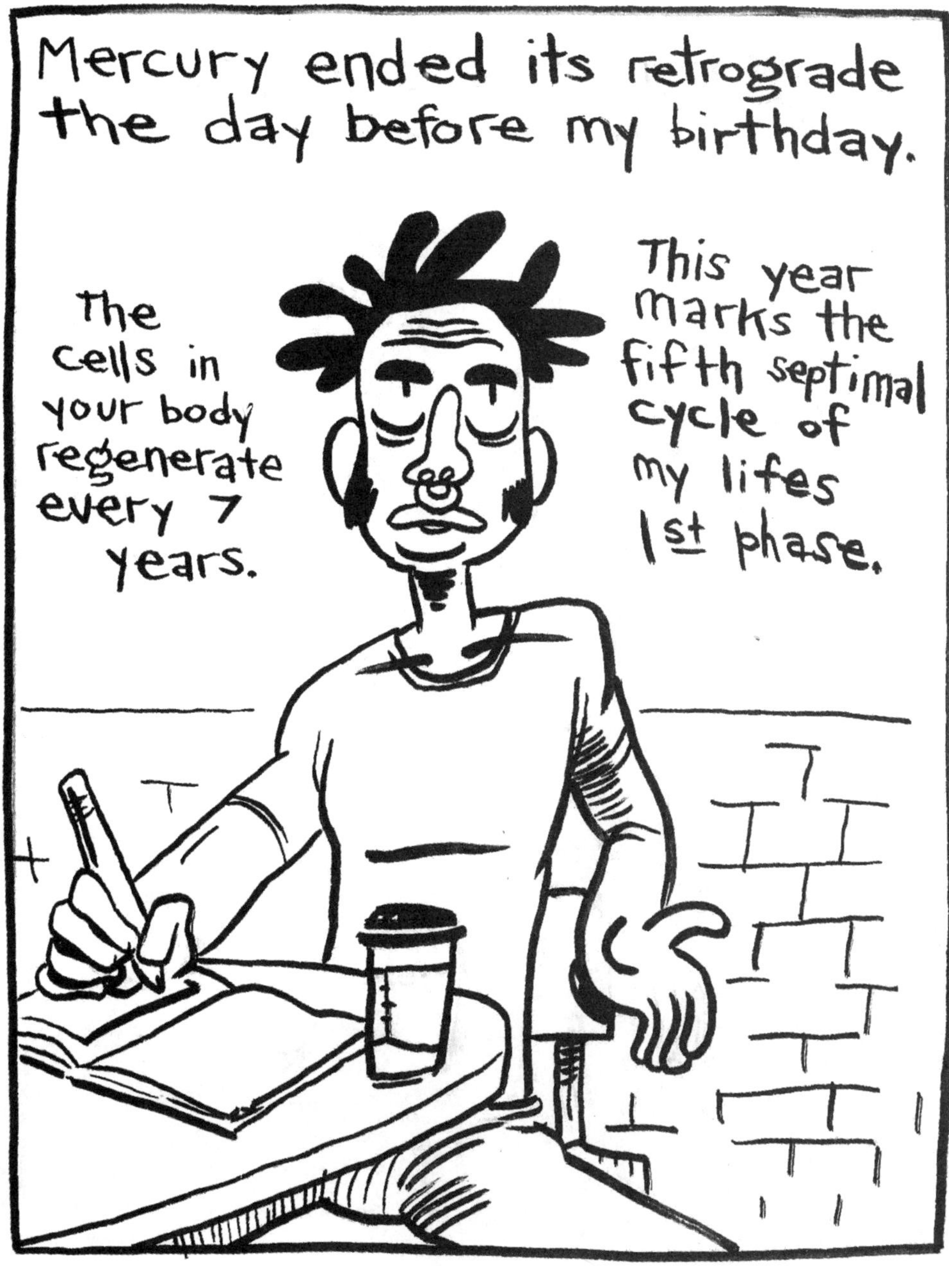
Mercury ended its retrograde the day before my birthday.
the cells in your body regenerate every 7 years.
This year marks the fifth septimal cycle of my lifes 1st phase.

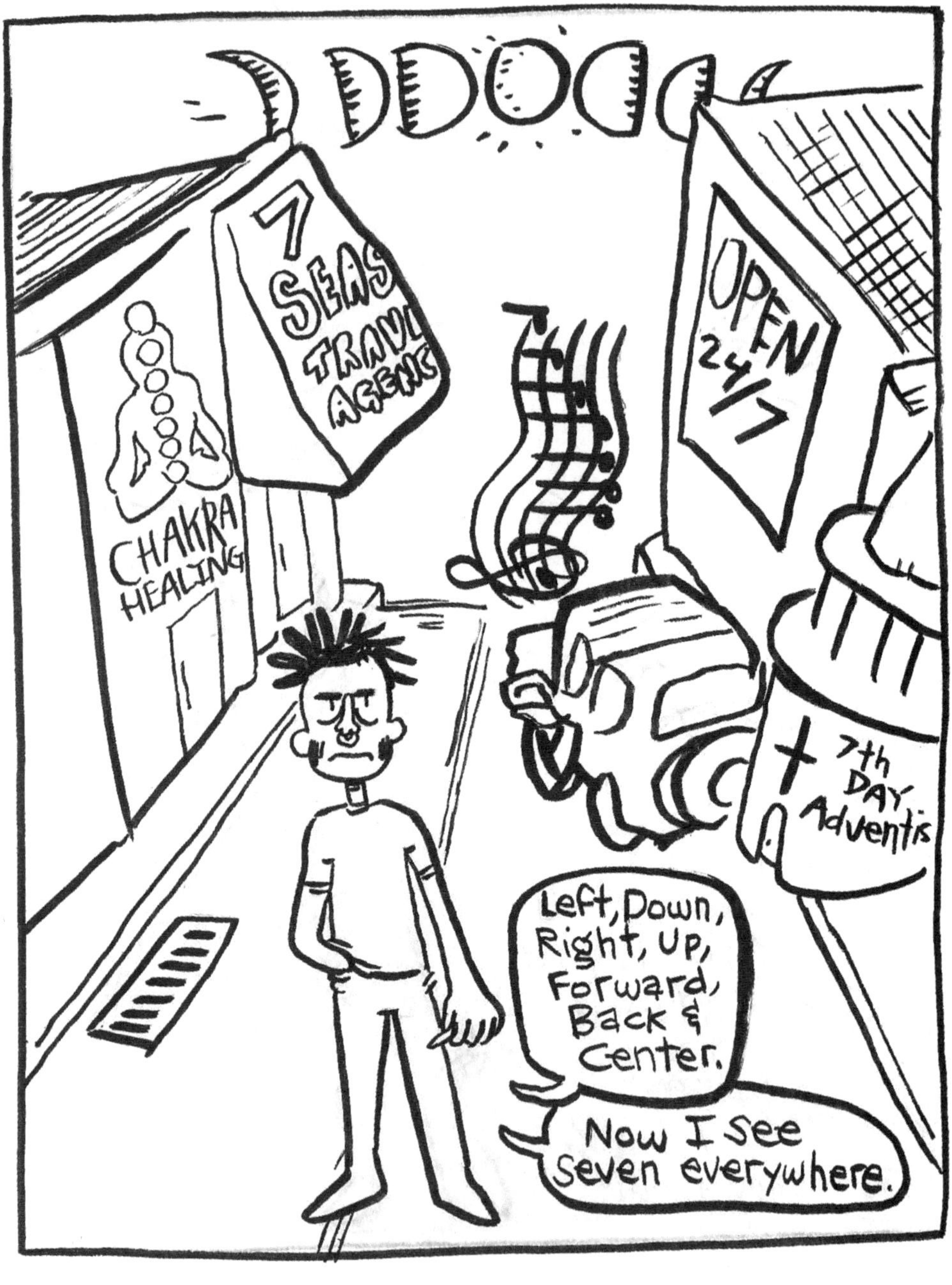
7 SEAS TRAV AGENC
OPEN 24/7
CHAKRA HEALING
7th DAY Adventis
Left, Down, Right, Up, Forward, Back & Center.
Now I see seven everywhere.

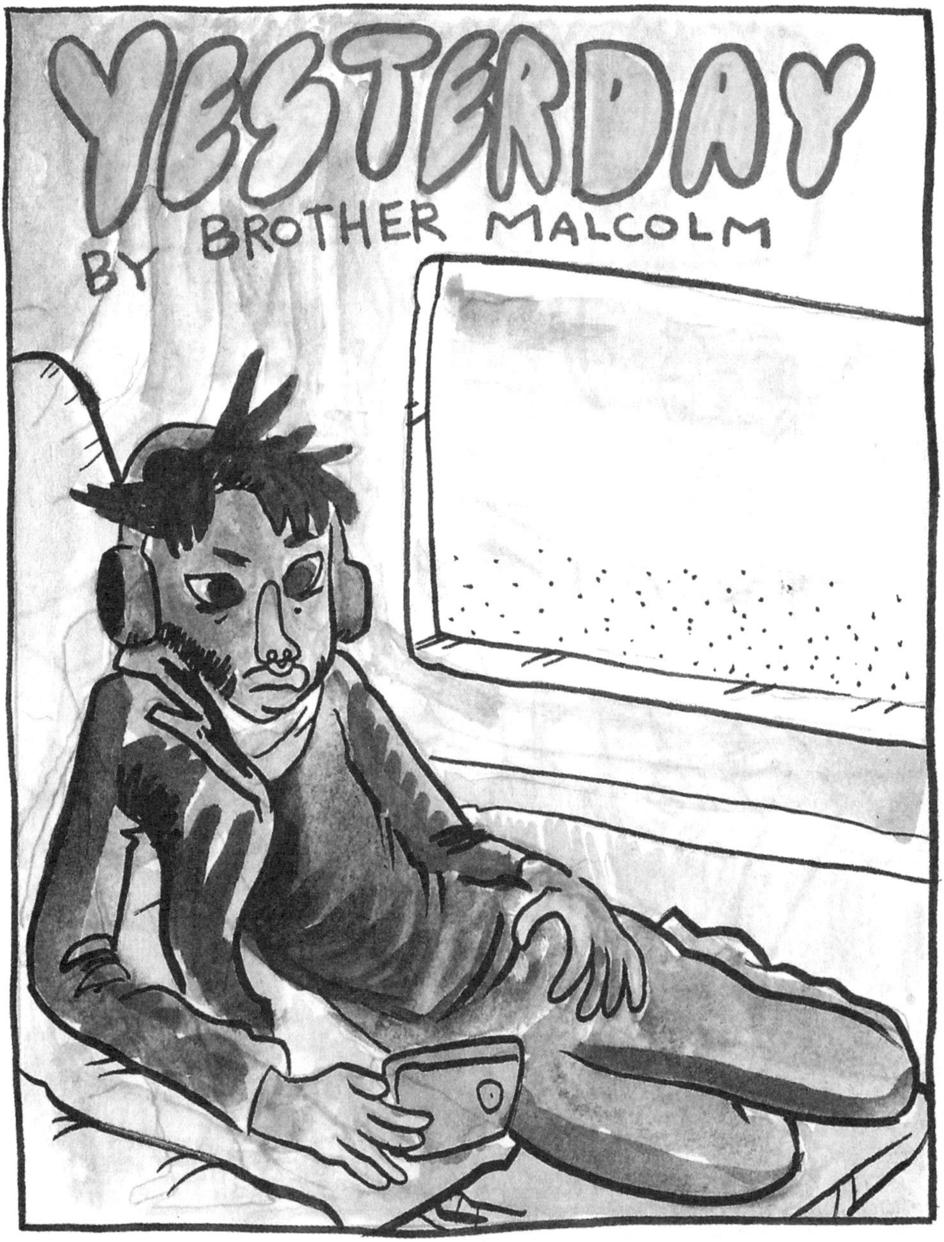
YESTERDAY
BY BROTHER MALCOLM

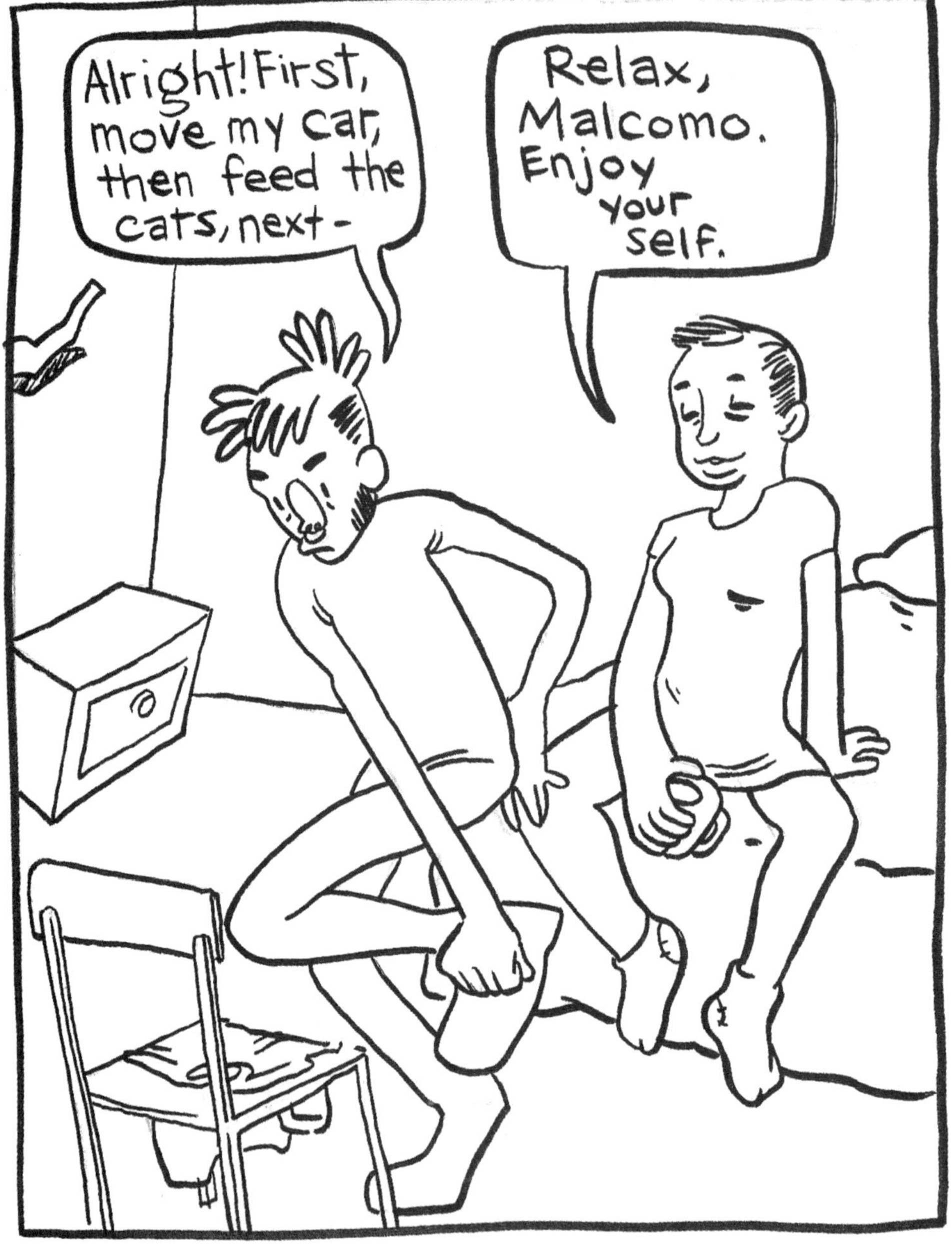
Alright! First, move my car, then feed the cats, next-
Relax, Malcomo. Enjoy your self.

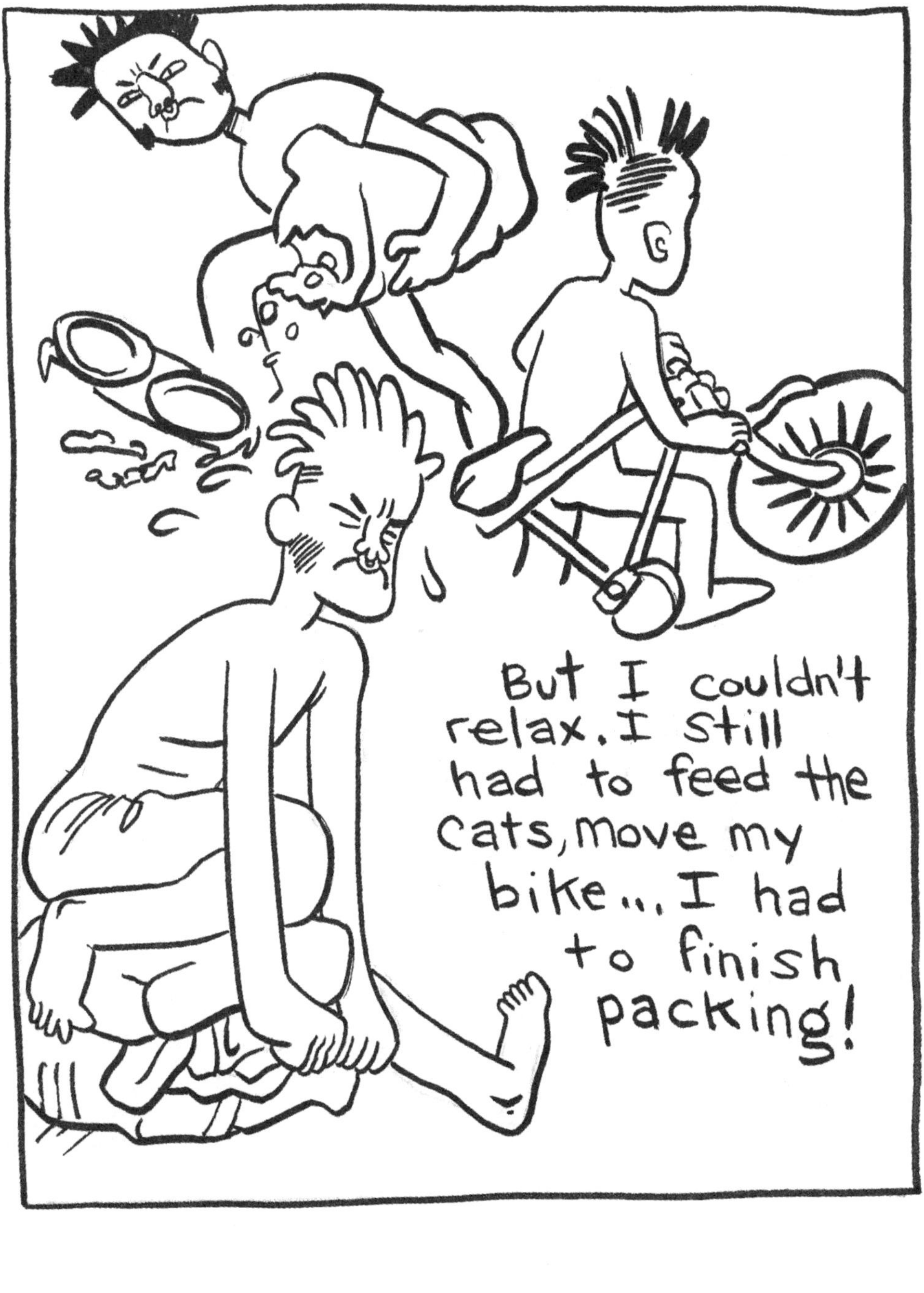
But I couldn't relax. I still had to feed the cats, move my bike... I had to finish packing!

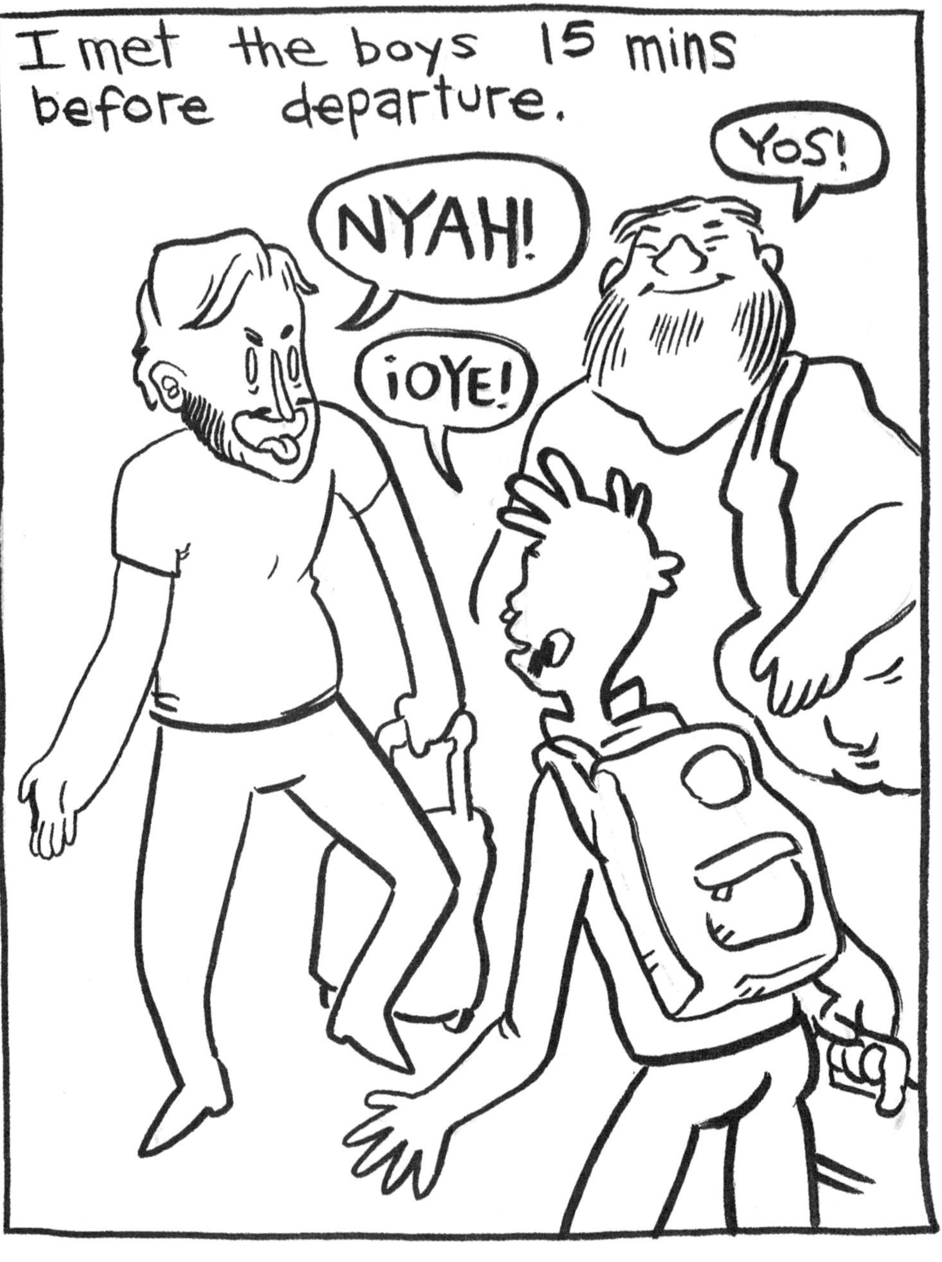
I met the boys 15 mins before departure.
NYAH!
¡OYE!
YOS!

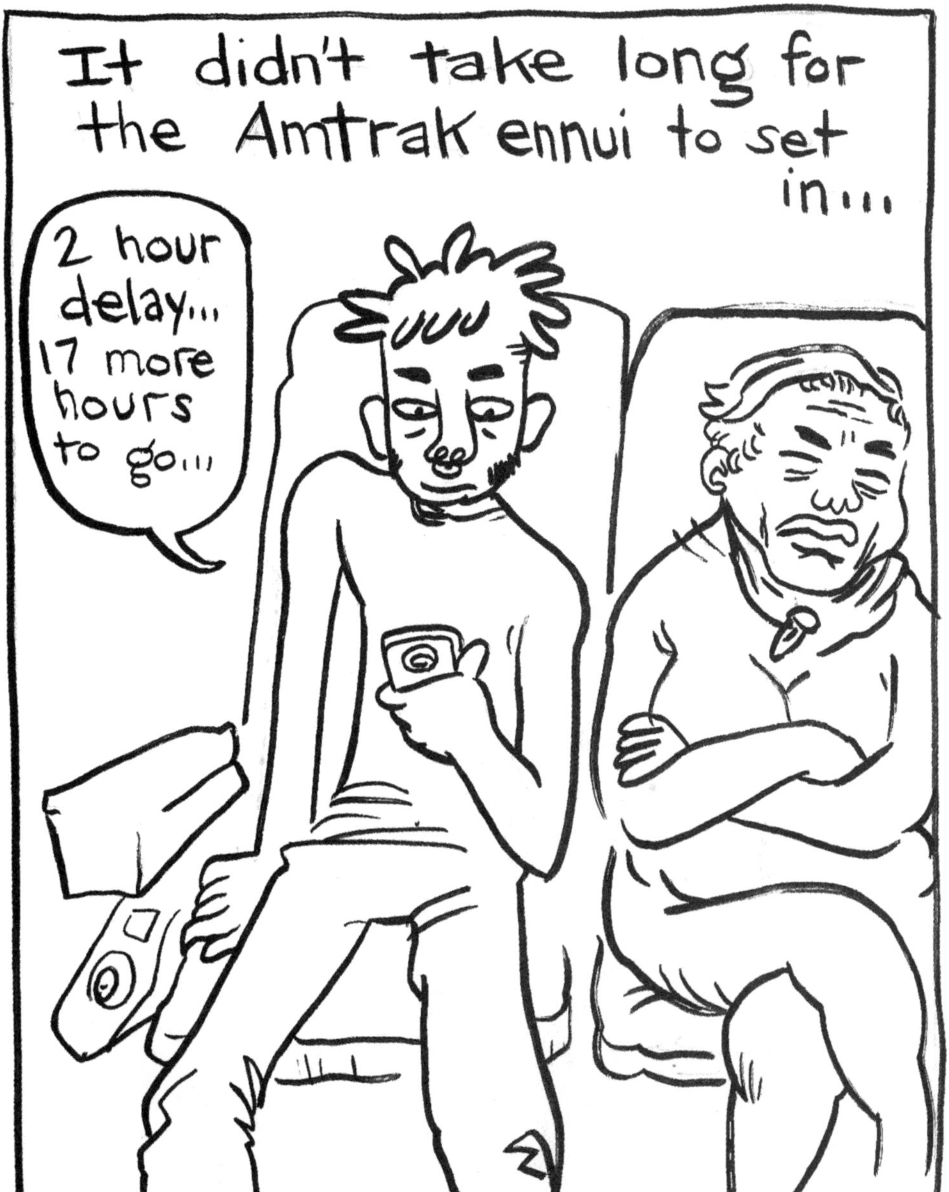
It didn't take long for the Amtrak ennui to set in...
2 hour delay... 17 more hours to go...

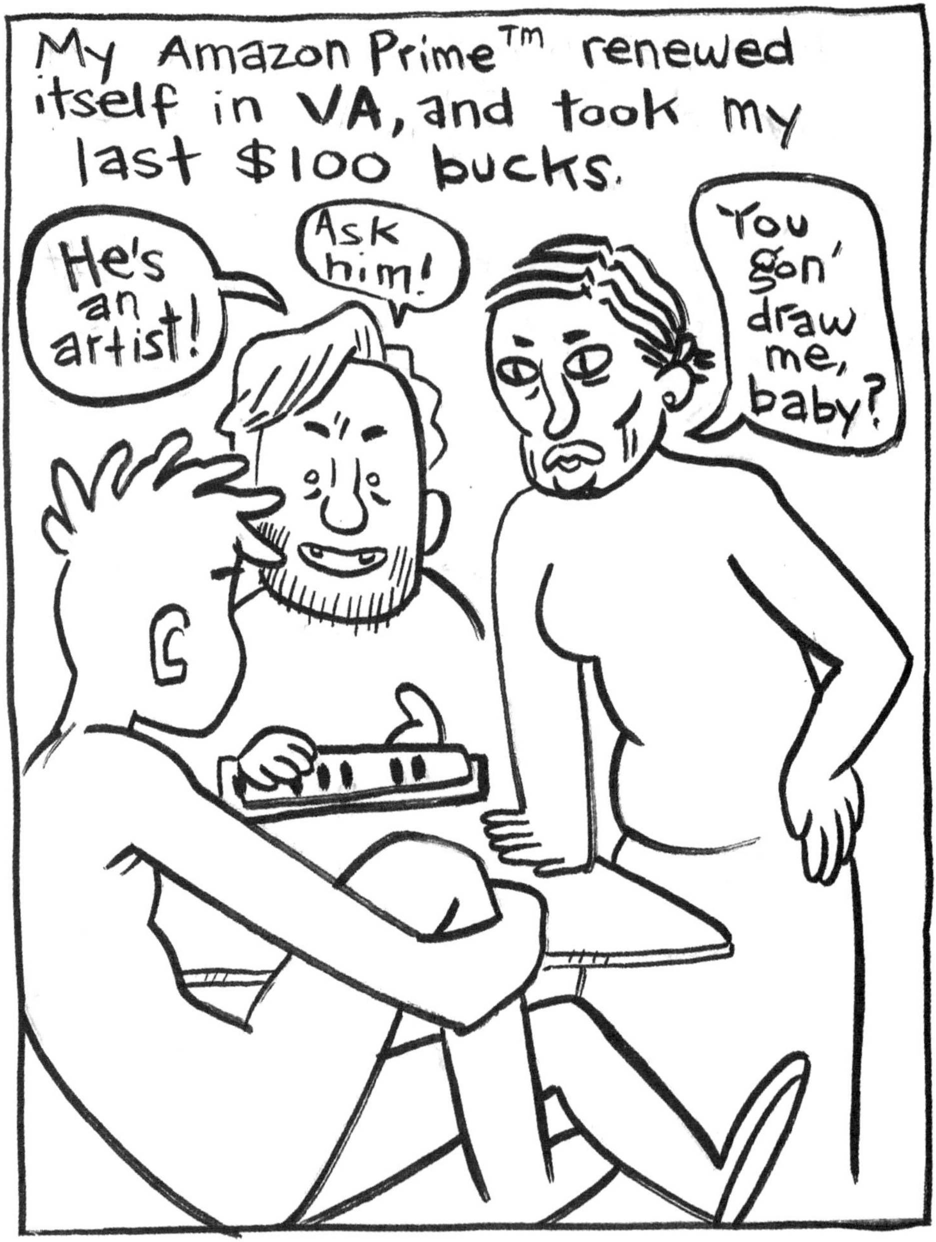
My Amazon Prime™ renewed itself in VA, and took my last $100 bucks.
He's an artist!
Ask him!
You gon' draw me, baby?

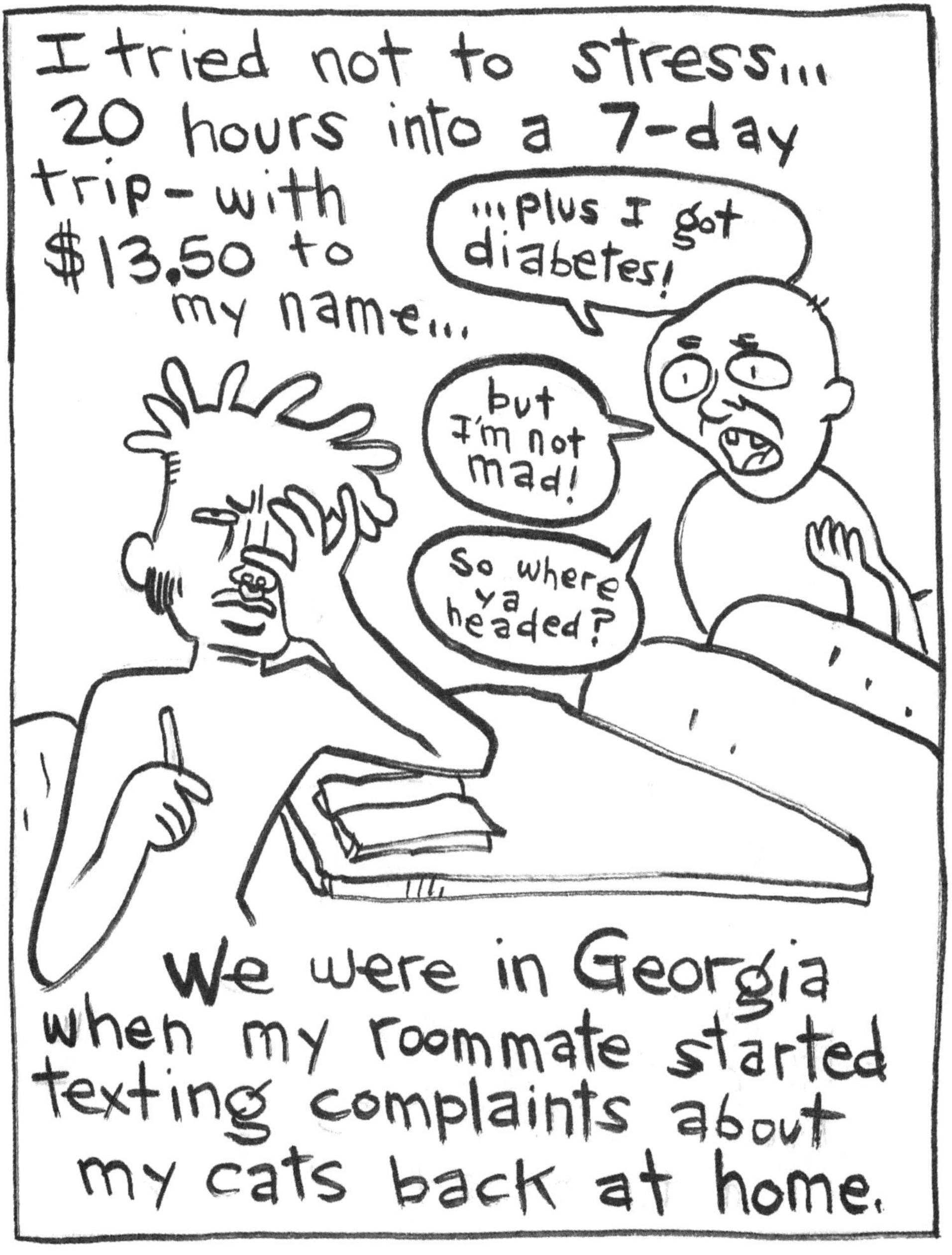
I tried not to stress... 20 hours into a 7-day trip- with $13.50 to my name...
...plus I got diabetes!
but I'm not mad!
So where ya headed?
We were in Georgia when my roommate started texting complaints about my cats back at home.

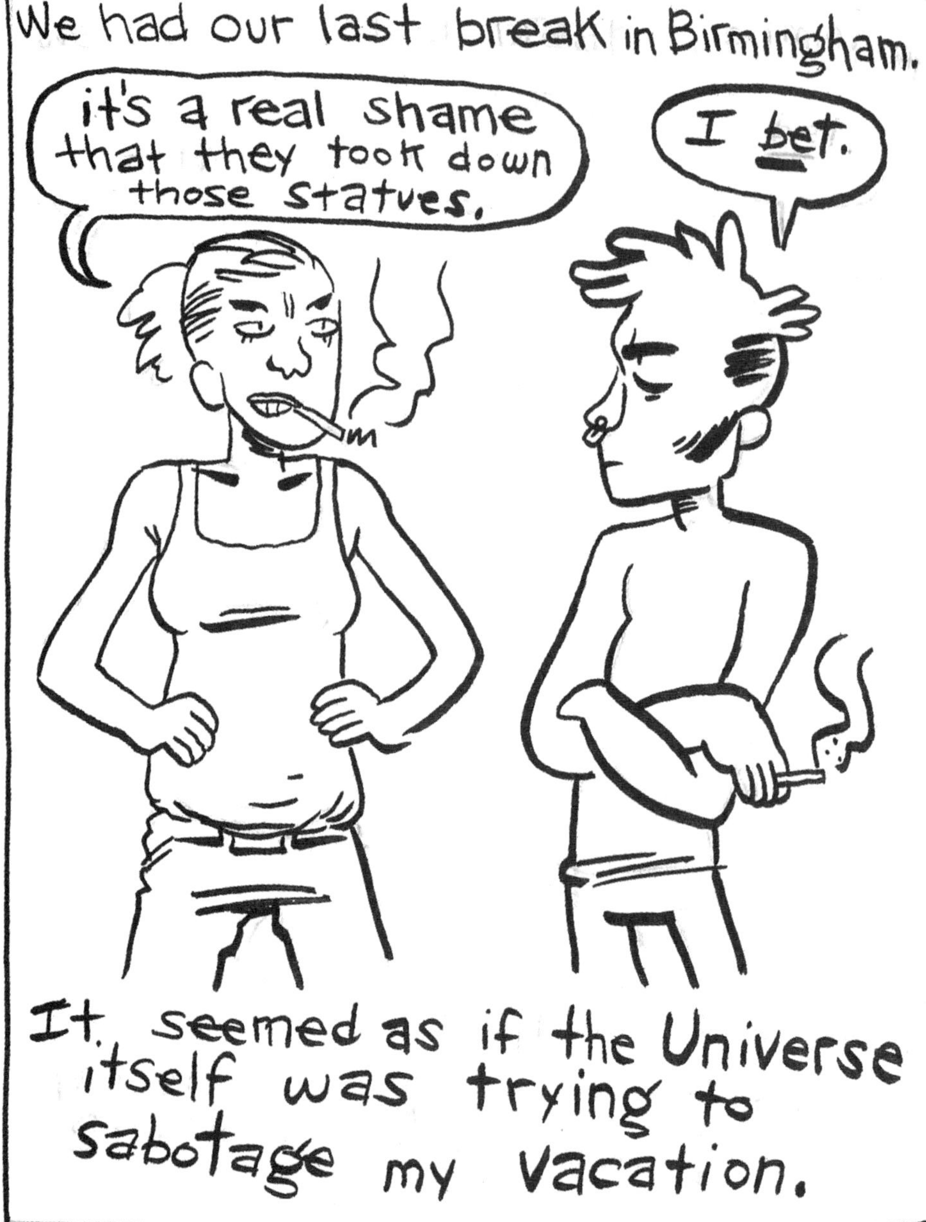
We had our last break in Birmingham.
it's a real shame that they took down those statues.
I bet.
It seemed as if the Universe itself was trying to sabotage my vacation.

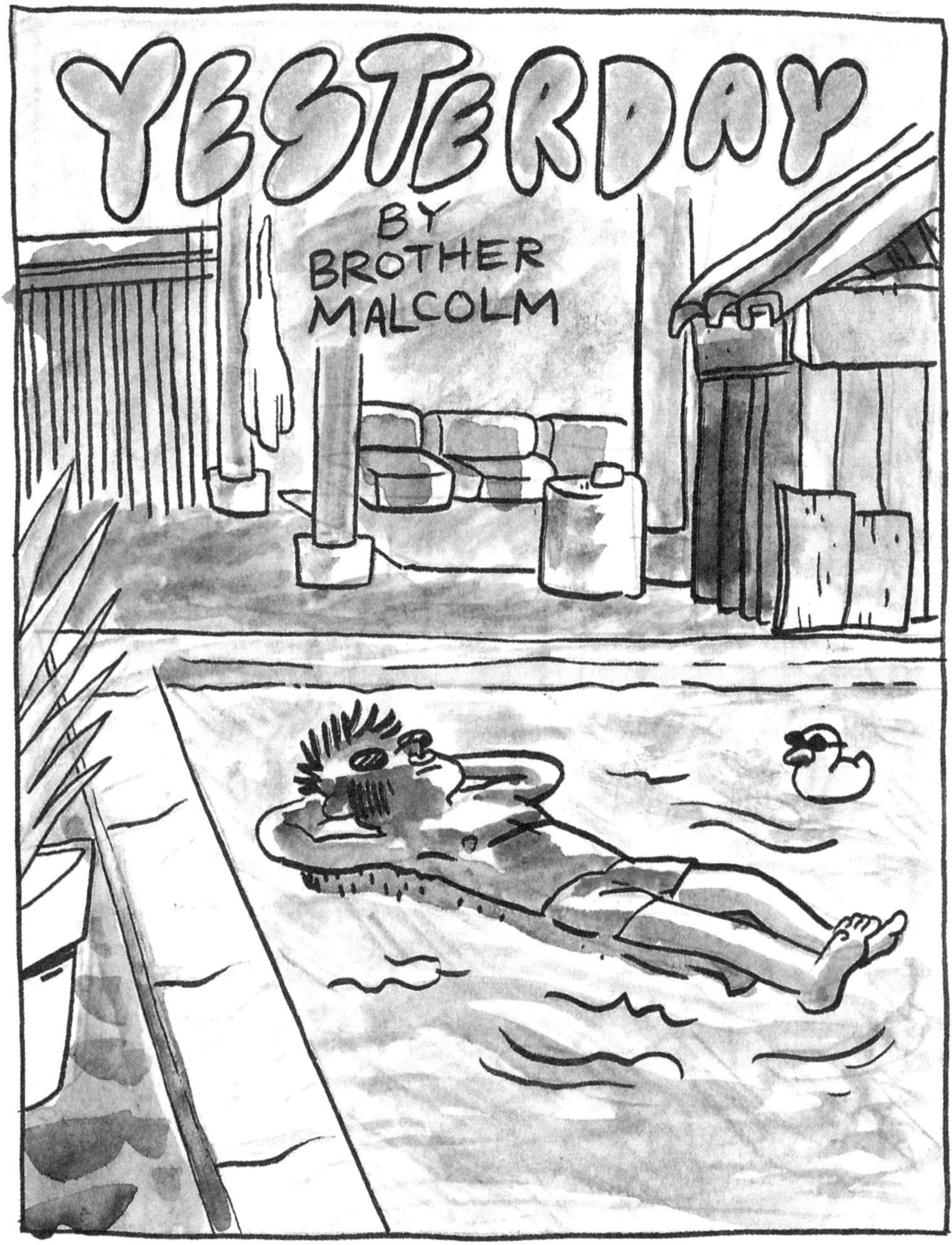
YESTERDAY
BY
BROTHER
MALCOLM

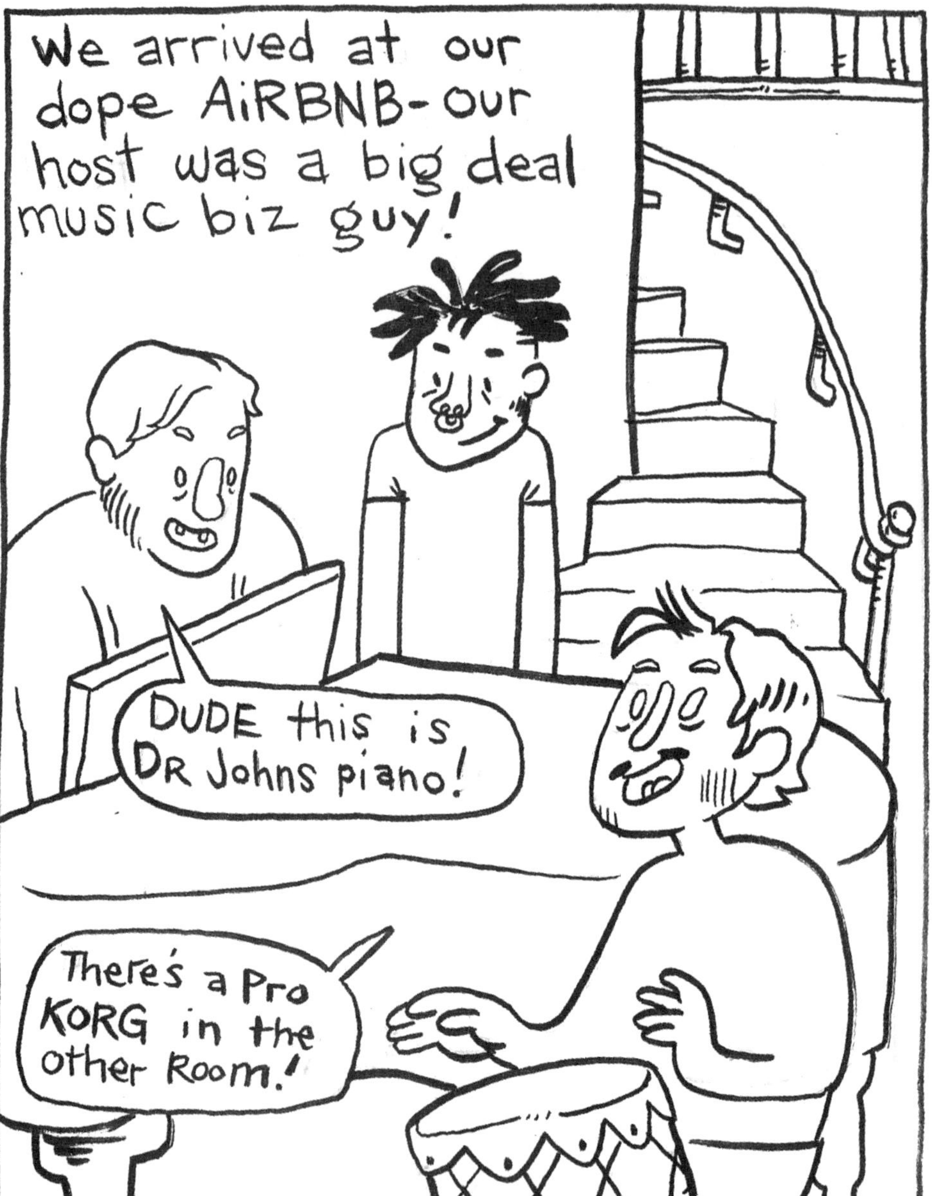
We arrived at our dope AiRBNB- our host was a big deal music biz guy!
DUDE this is DR Johns piano!
There's a Pro KORG in the other Room!

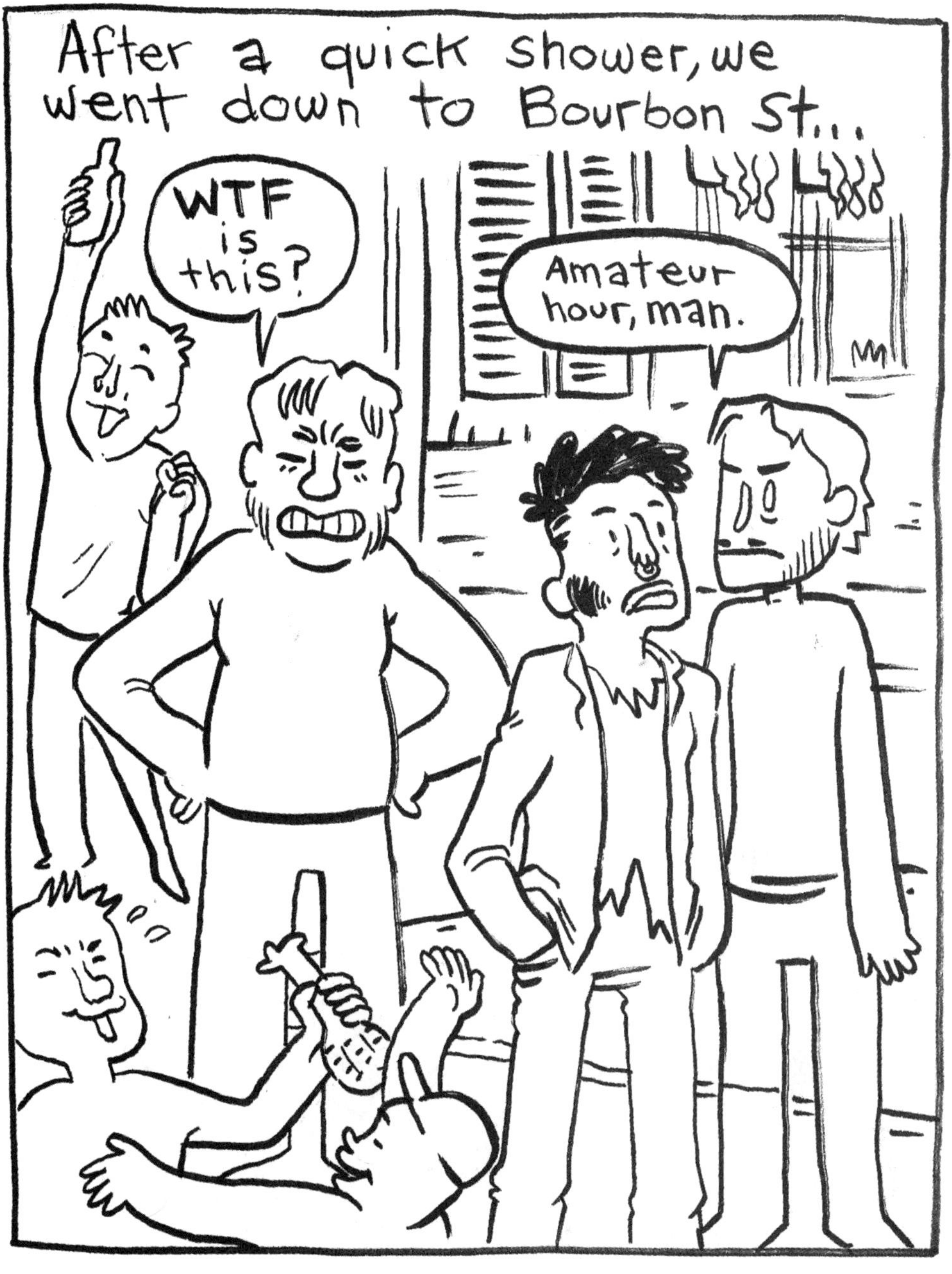
After a quick shower, we went down to Bourbon St...
WTF is this?
Amateur hour, man.

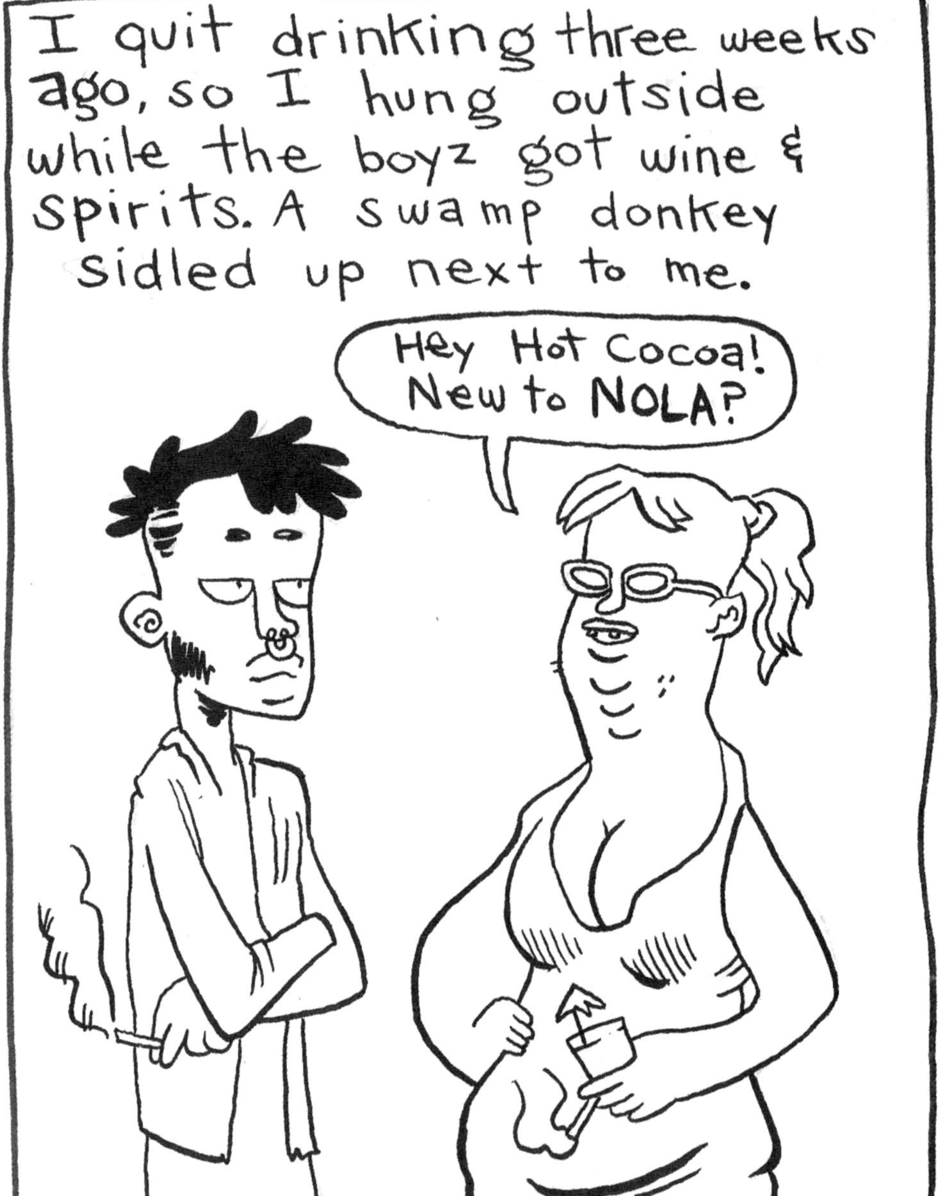
I quit drinking three weeks ago, so I hung outside while the boyz got wine & spirits. A swamp donkey sidled up next to me.
Hey Hot Cocoa! New to NOLA?

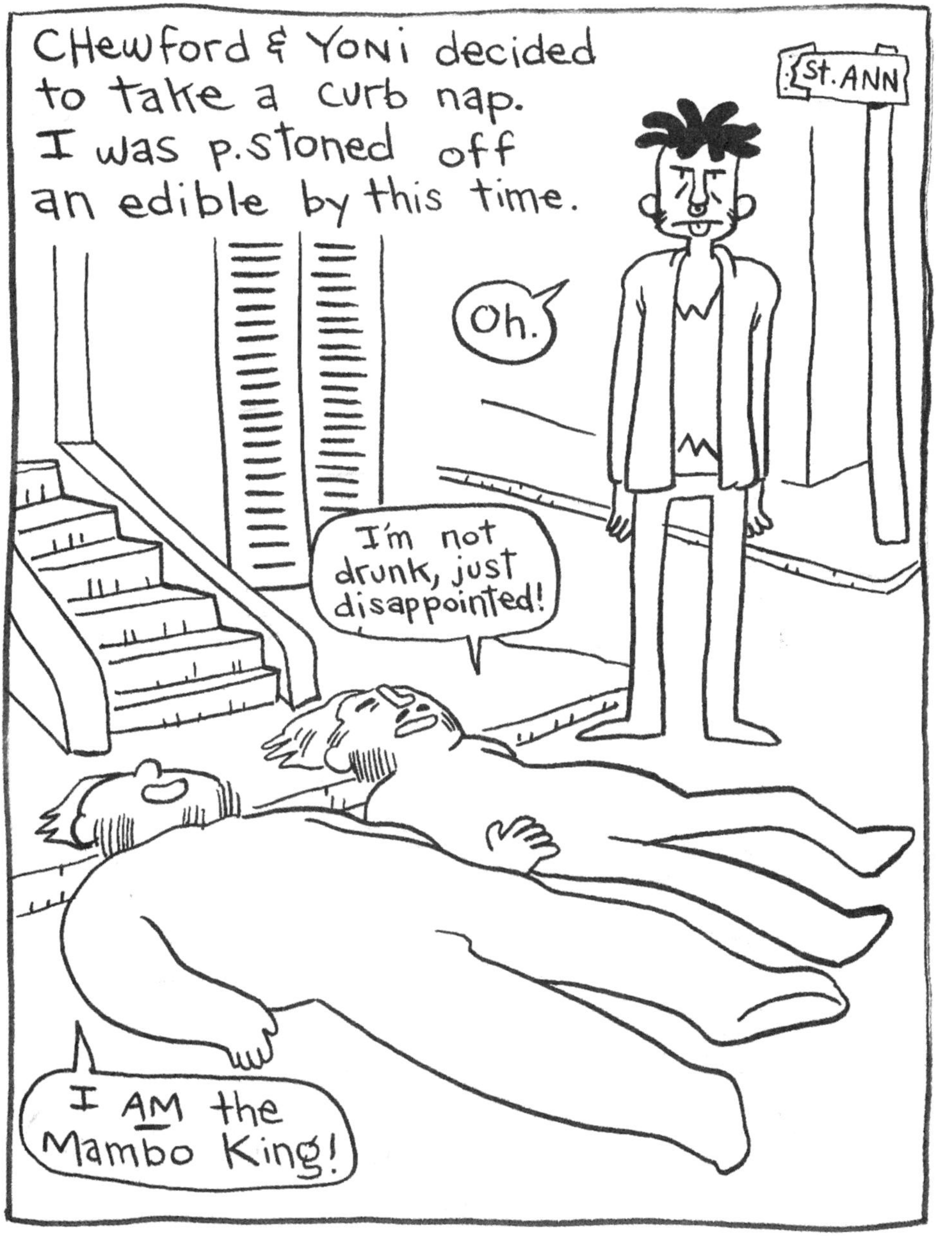
CHewford & YONi decided to take a curb nap. I was p.stoned off an edible by this time.
St. ANN
Oh.
I'm not drunk, just disappointed!
I AM the Mambo King!

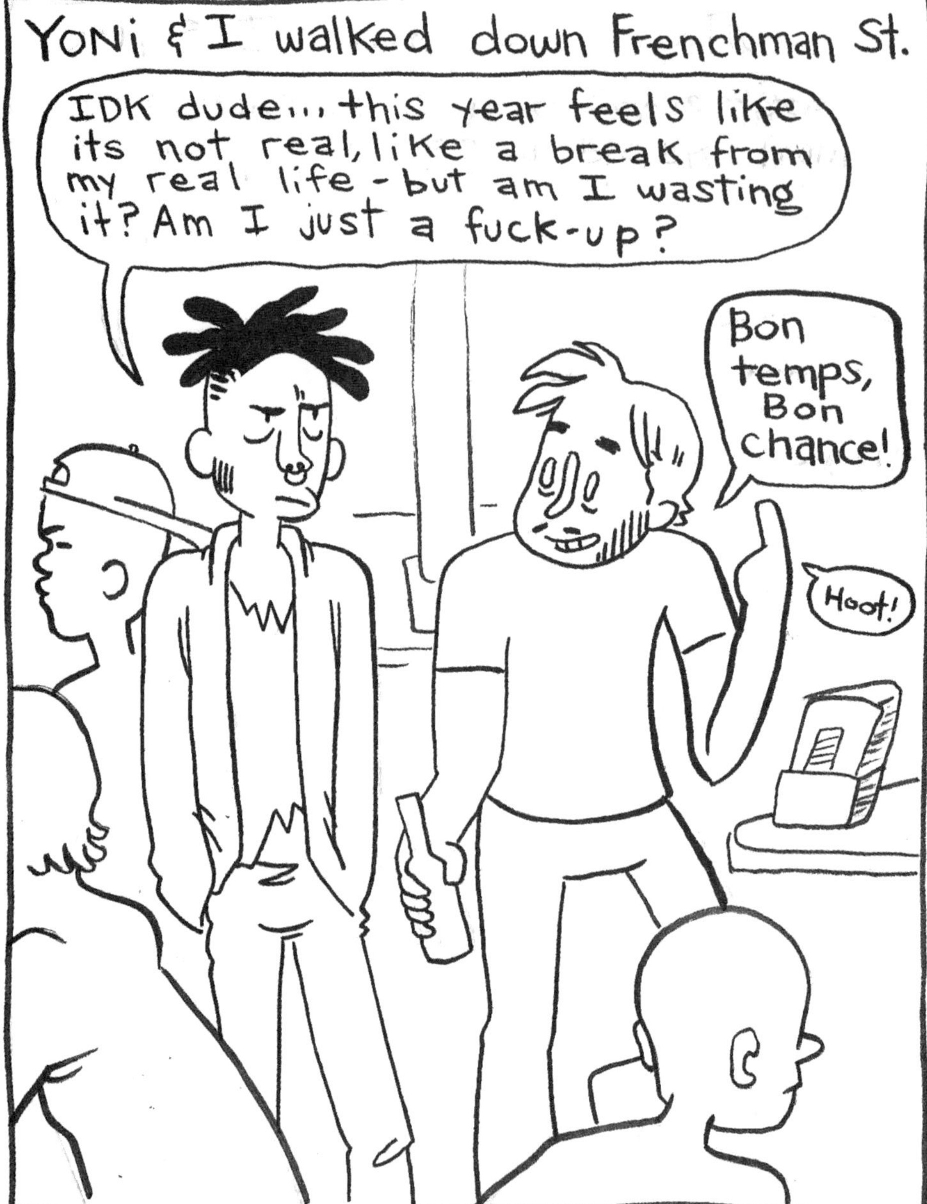
YONi & I walked down Frenchman St.
IDK dude... this year feels like its not real, like a break from my real life - but am I wasting it? Am I just a fuck-up?
Bon temps, Bon chance!
Hoot!

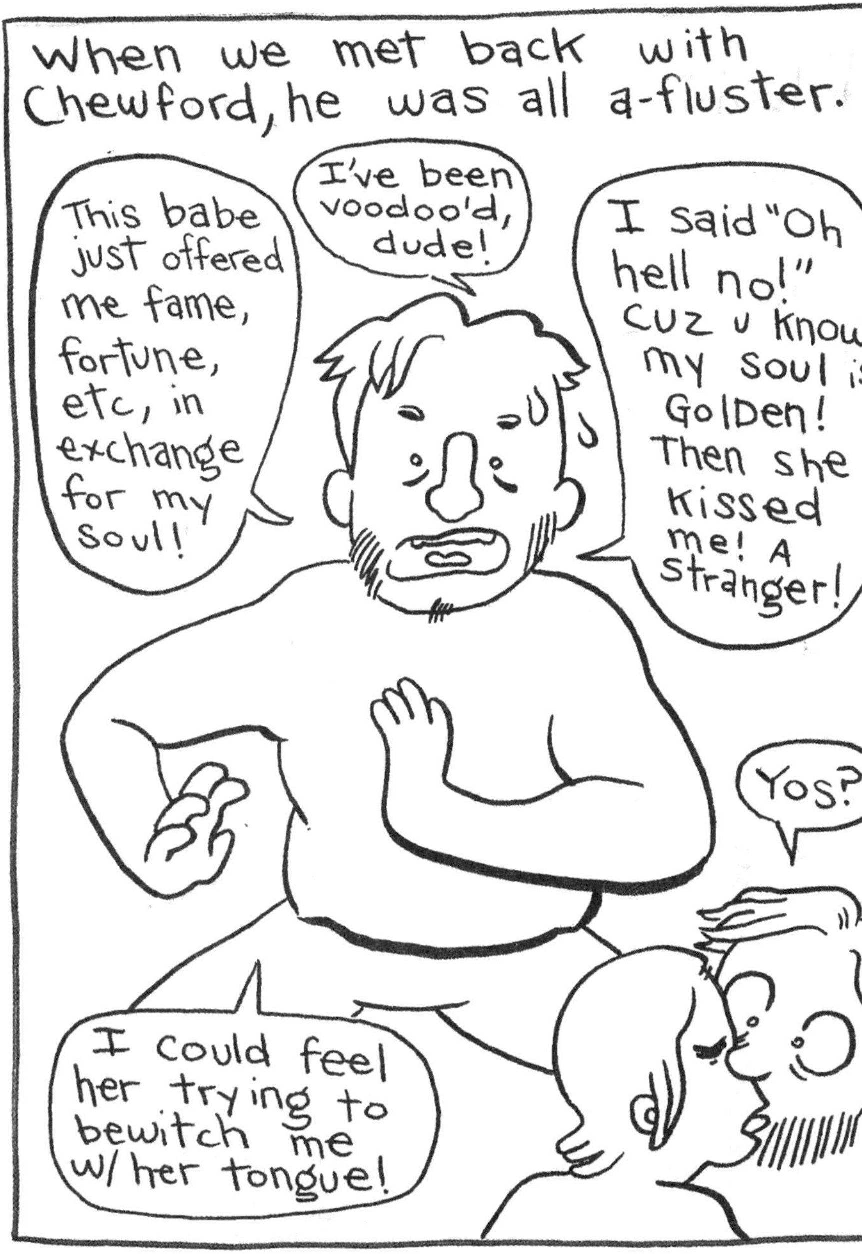
When we met back with Chewford, he was all a-fluster.
This babe just offered me fame, fortune, etc, in exchange for my soul!
I've been voodoo'd, dude!
I said "Oh hell no!" cuz u know my soul is Golden! Then she kissed me! A stranger!
Yos?
I could feel her trying to bewitch me w/ her tongue!

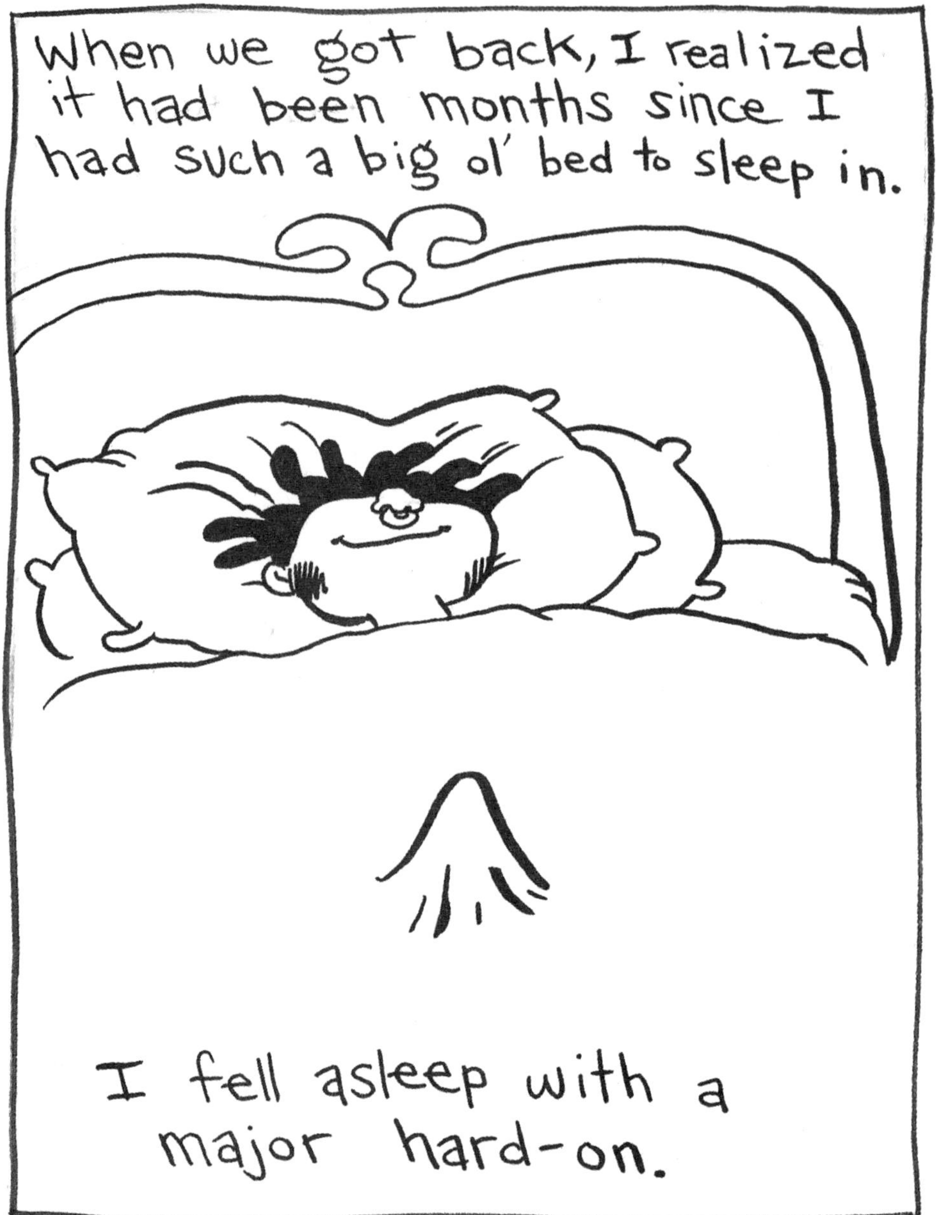
When we got back, I realized it had been months since I had such a big ol' bed to sleep in.
I fell asleep with a major hard-on.

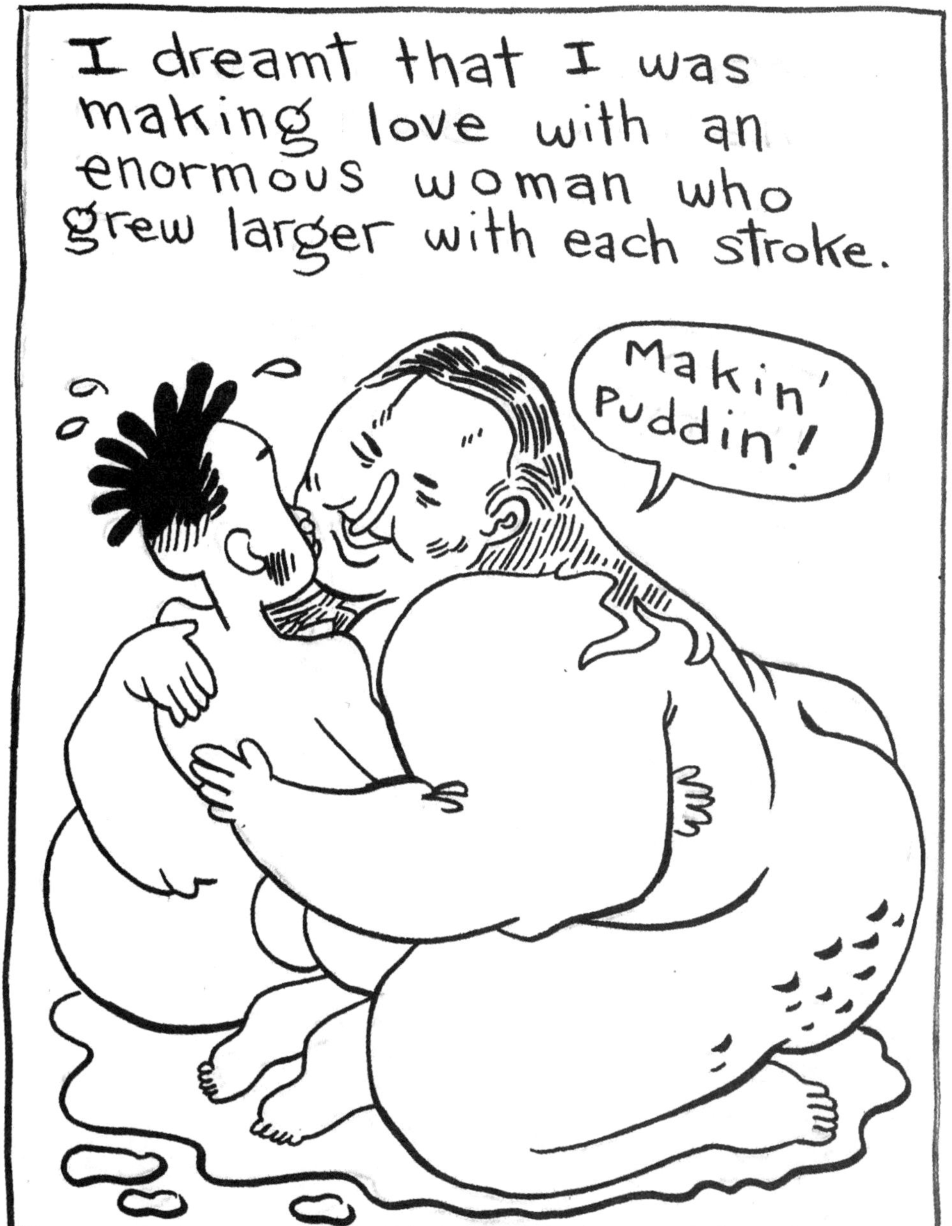
I dreamt that I was making love with an enormous woman who grew larger with each stroke.
Makin' Puddin!

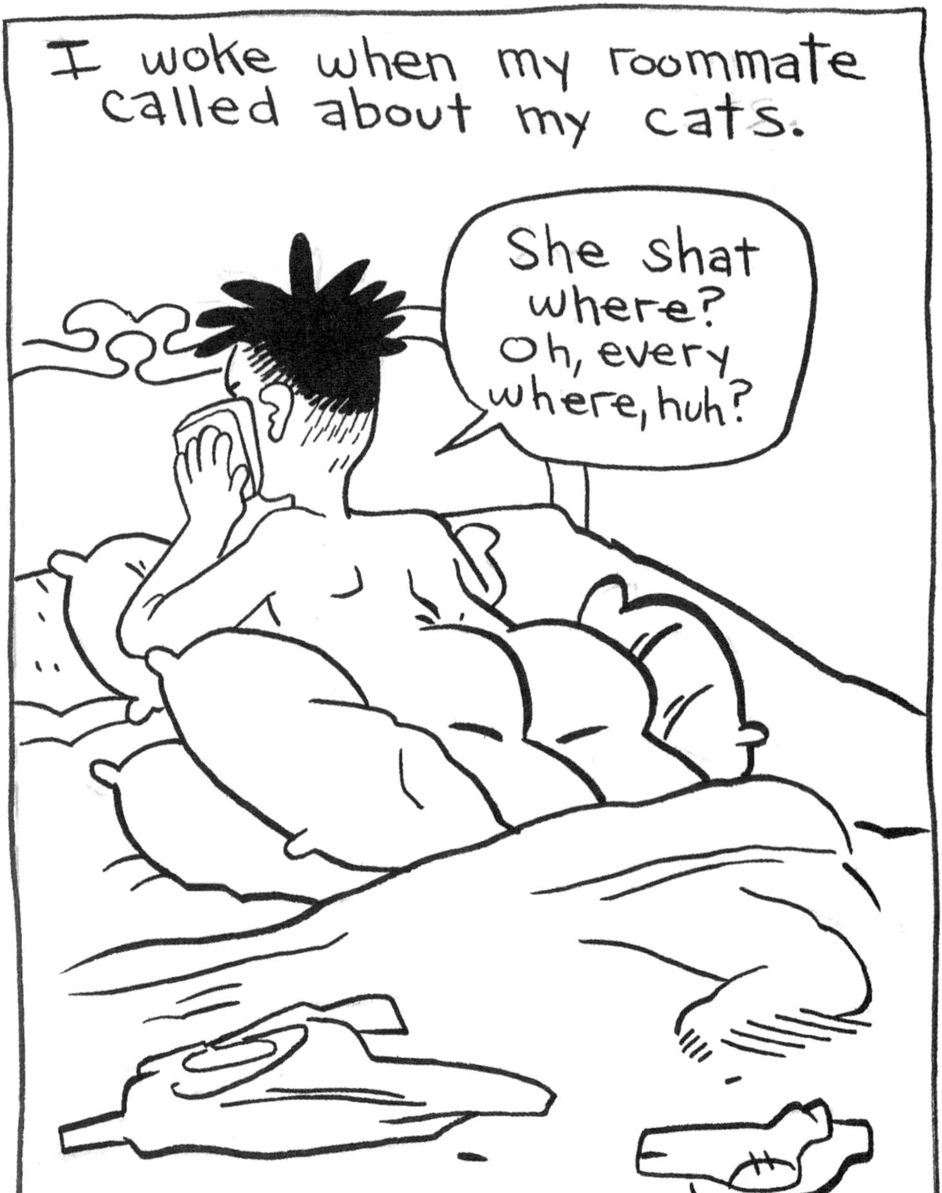
I woke when my roommate called about my cats.
She shat where? Oh, every where, huh?

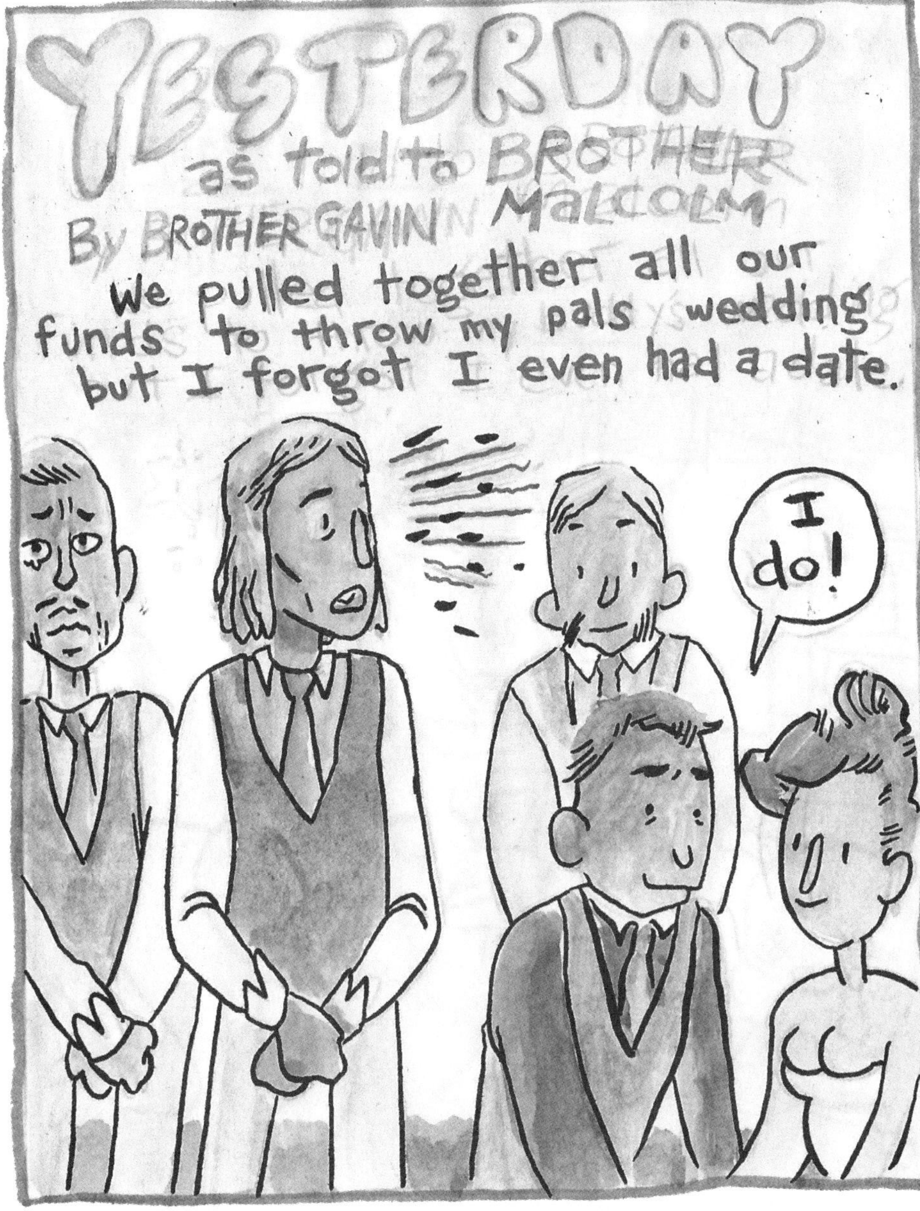
YESTERDAY
as told to BROTHER MALCOLM
By BROTHER GAVIN
We pulled together all our funds to throw my pals wedding but I forgot I even had a date.
I do!

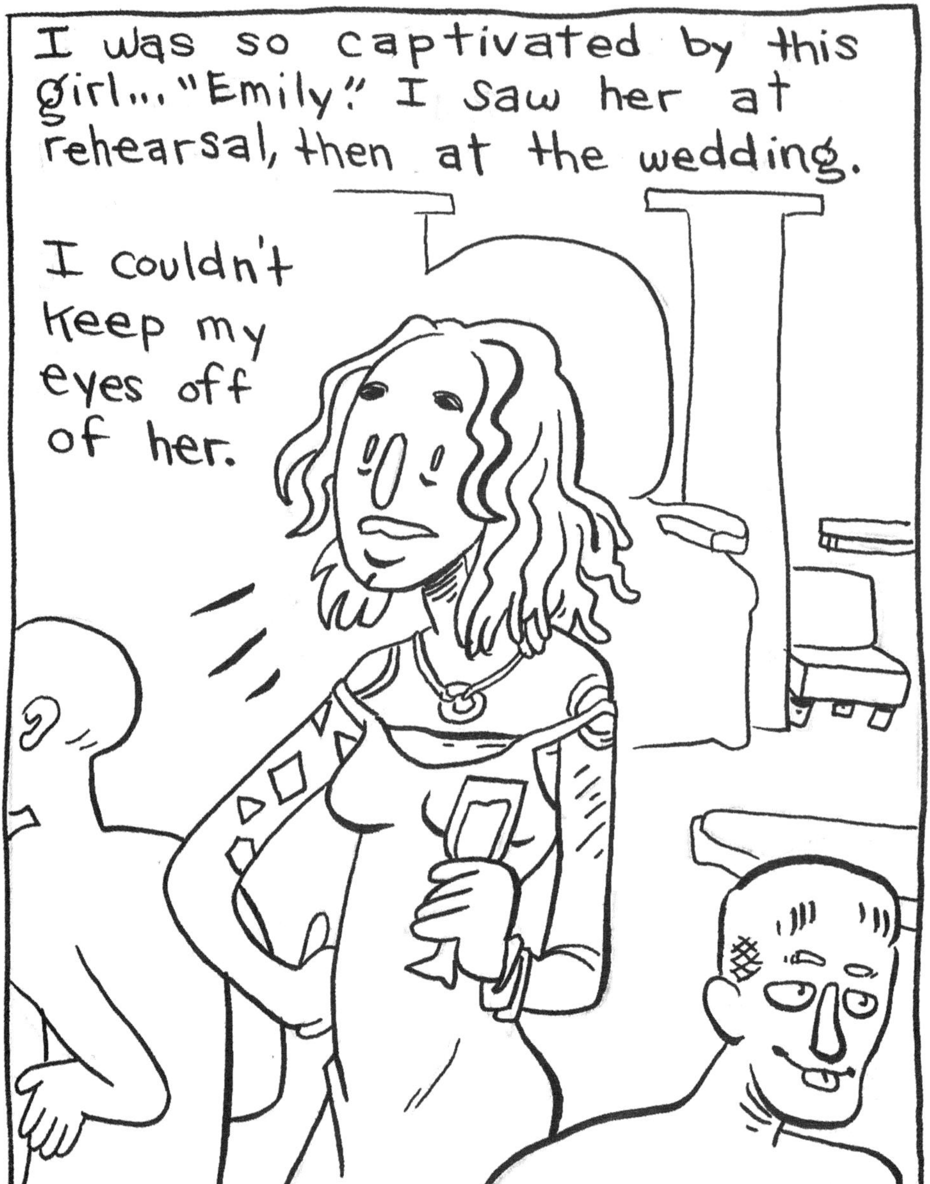
I was so captivated by this girl... "Emily." I saw her at rehearsal, then at the wedding.
I couldn't keep my eyes off of her.

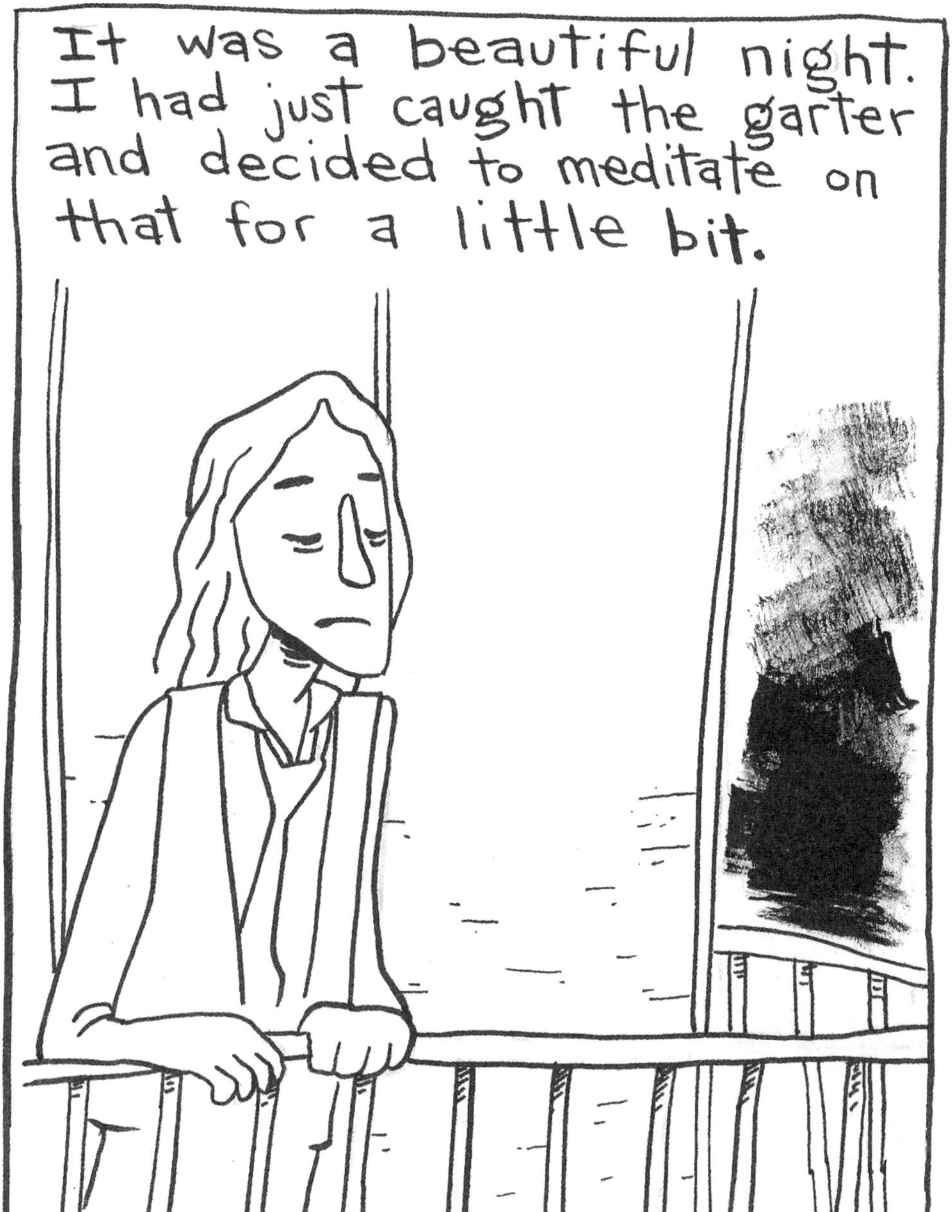
It was a beautiful night. I had just caught the garter and decided to meditate on that for a little bit.

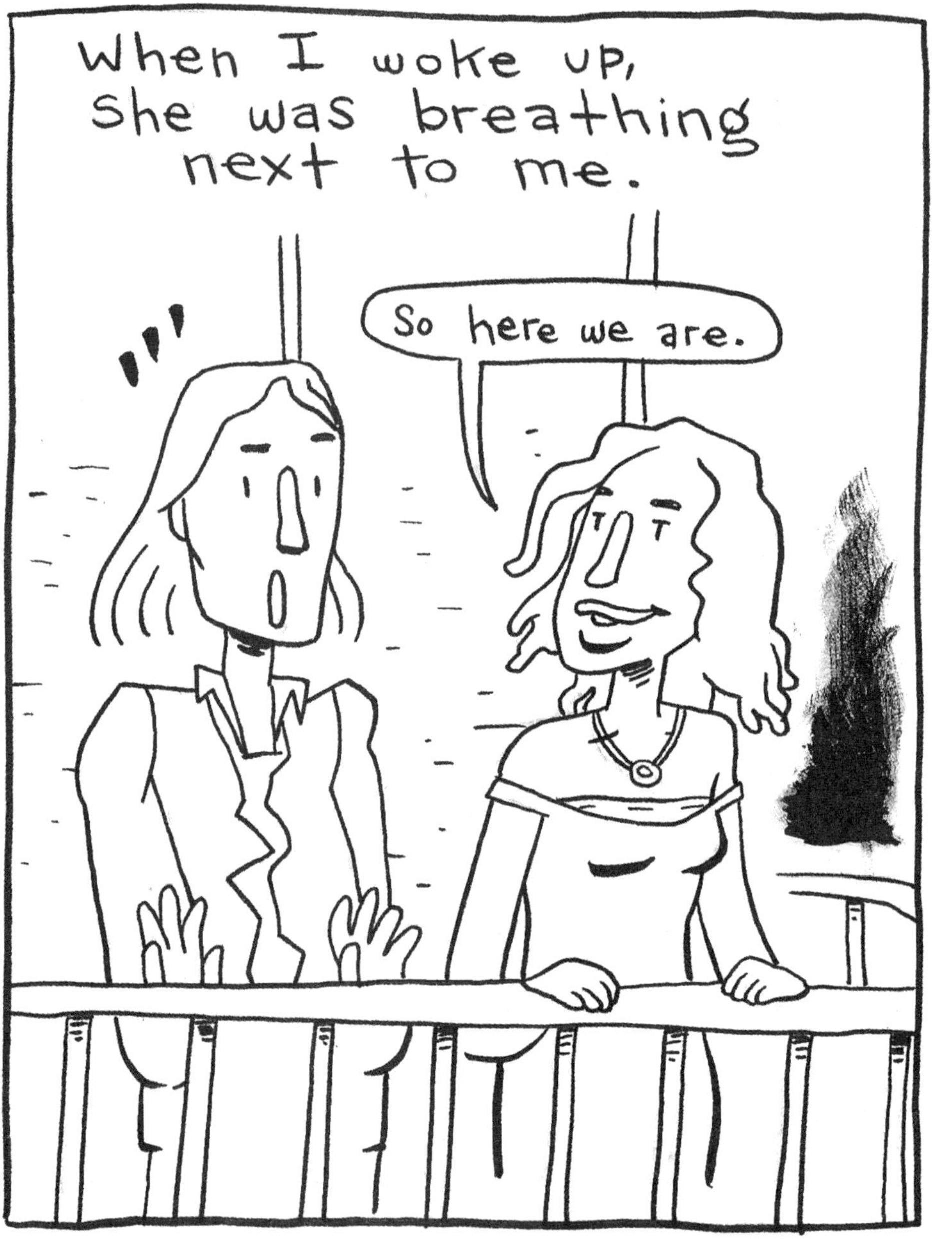
When I woke up, she was breathing next to me.
So here we are.

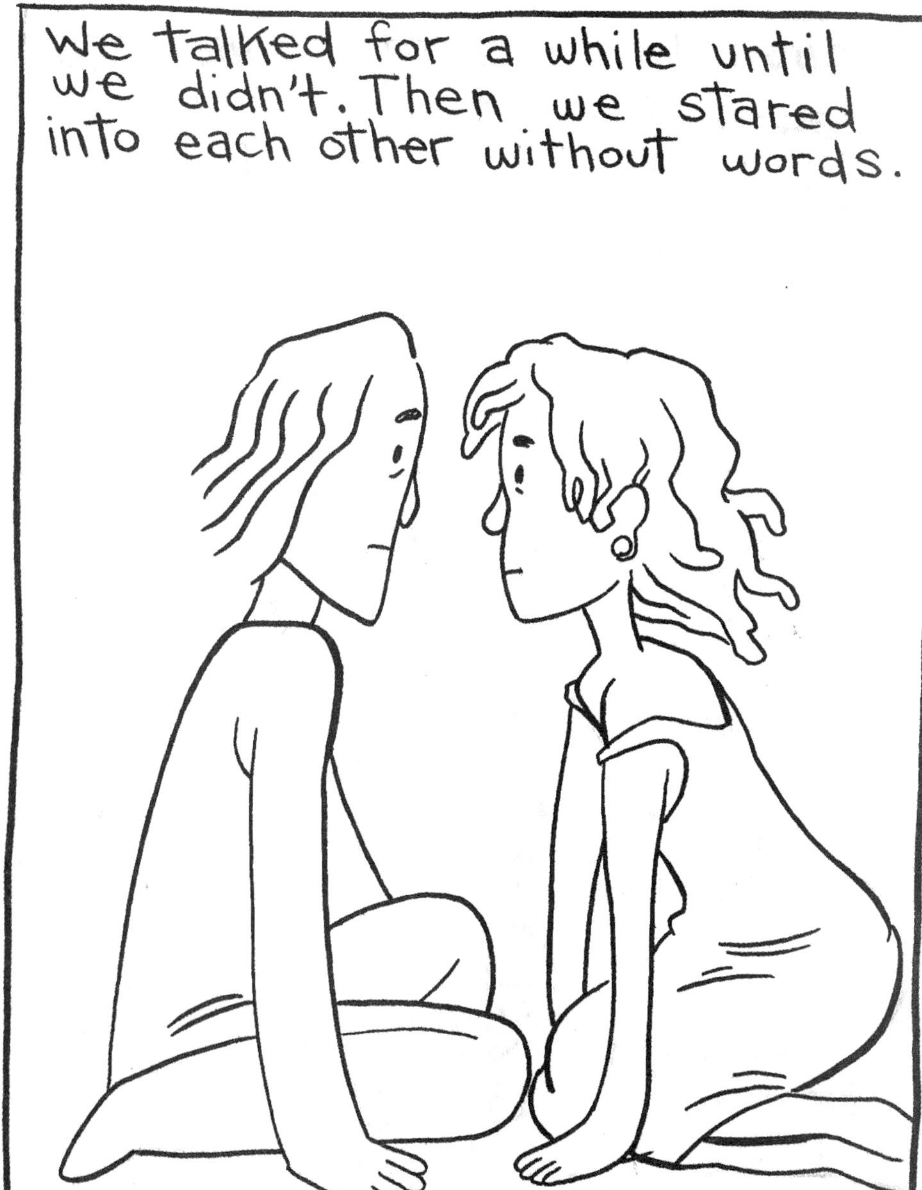
We talked for a while until we didn't. Then we stared into each other without words.

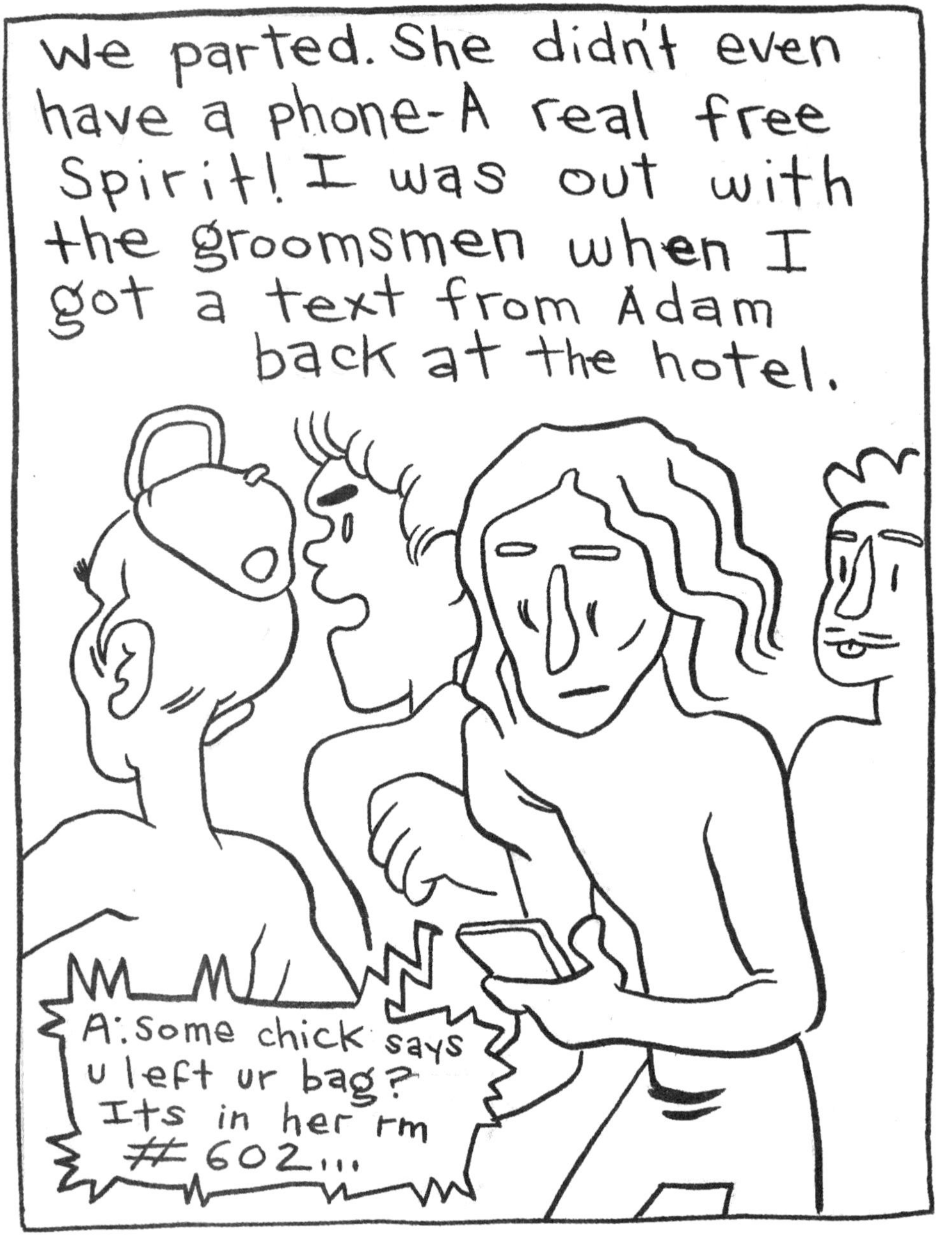
We parted. She didn't even have a phone-A real free Spirit! I was out with the groomsmen when I got a text from Adam back at the hotel.
A: Some chick says u left ur bag? Its in her rm #602...

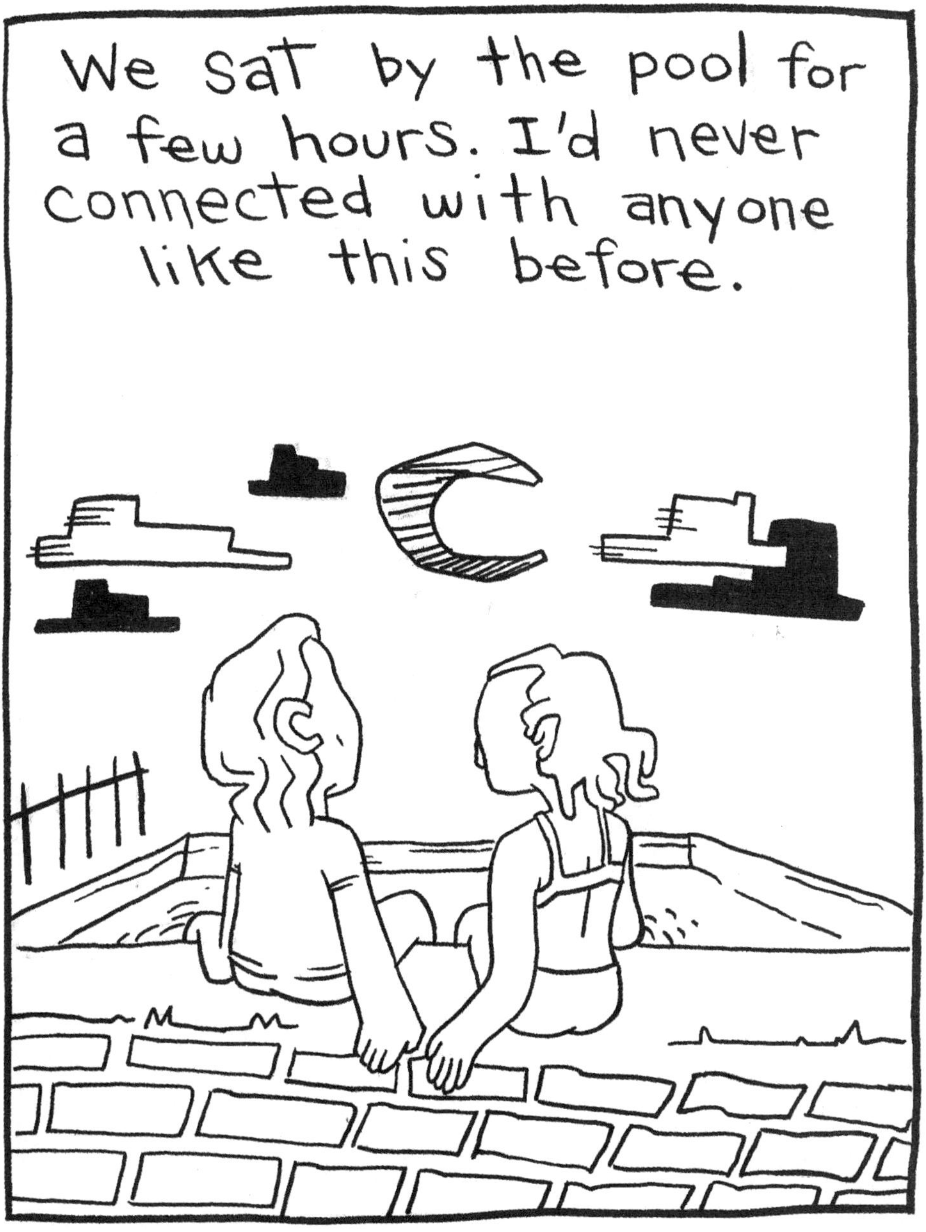
We sat by the pool for a few hours. I'd never connected with anyone like this before.

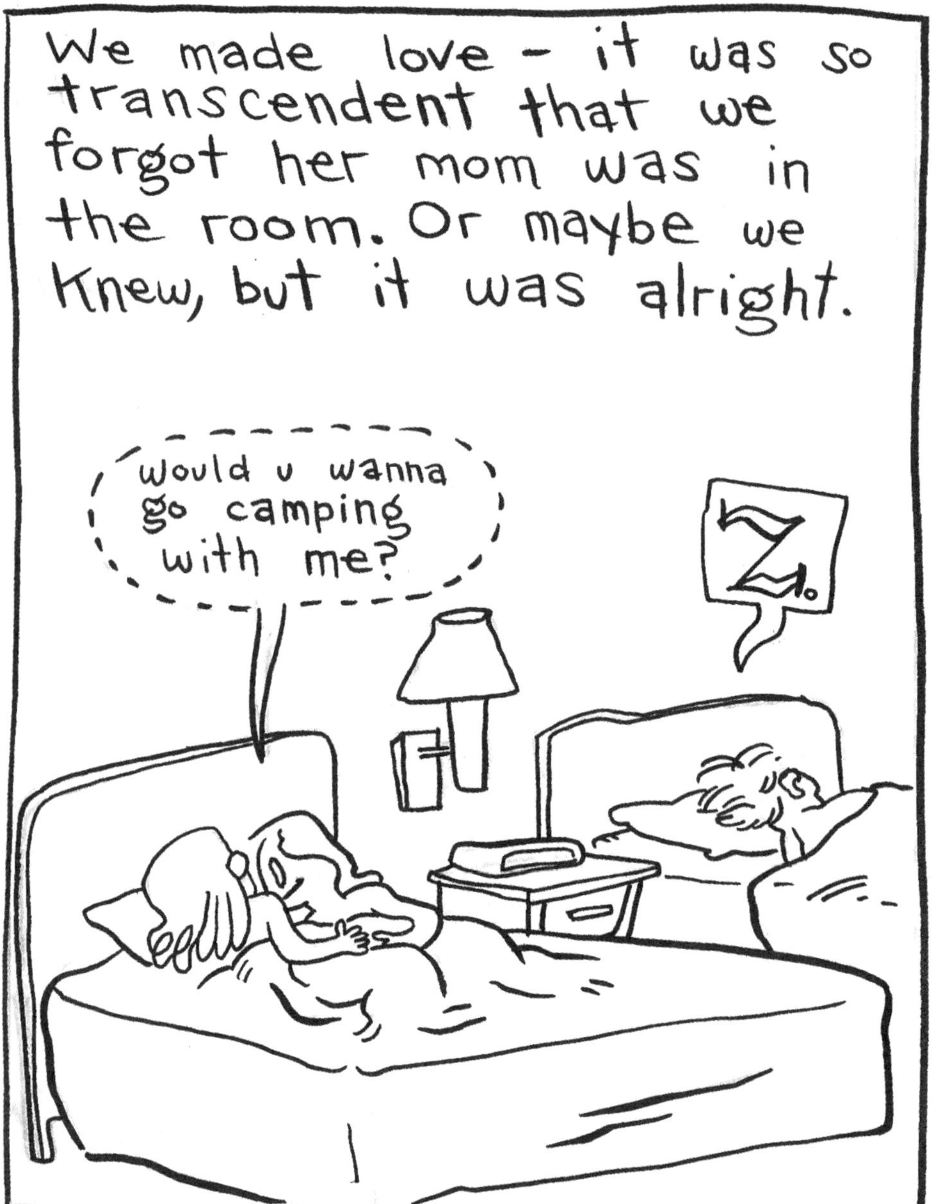
We made love - it was so transcendent that we forgot her mom was in the room. Or maybe we Knew, but it was alright.
would u wanna go camping with me?
Z

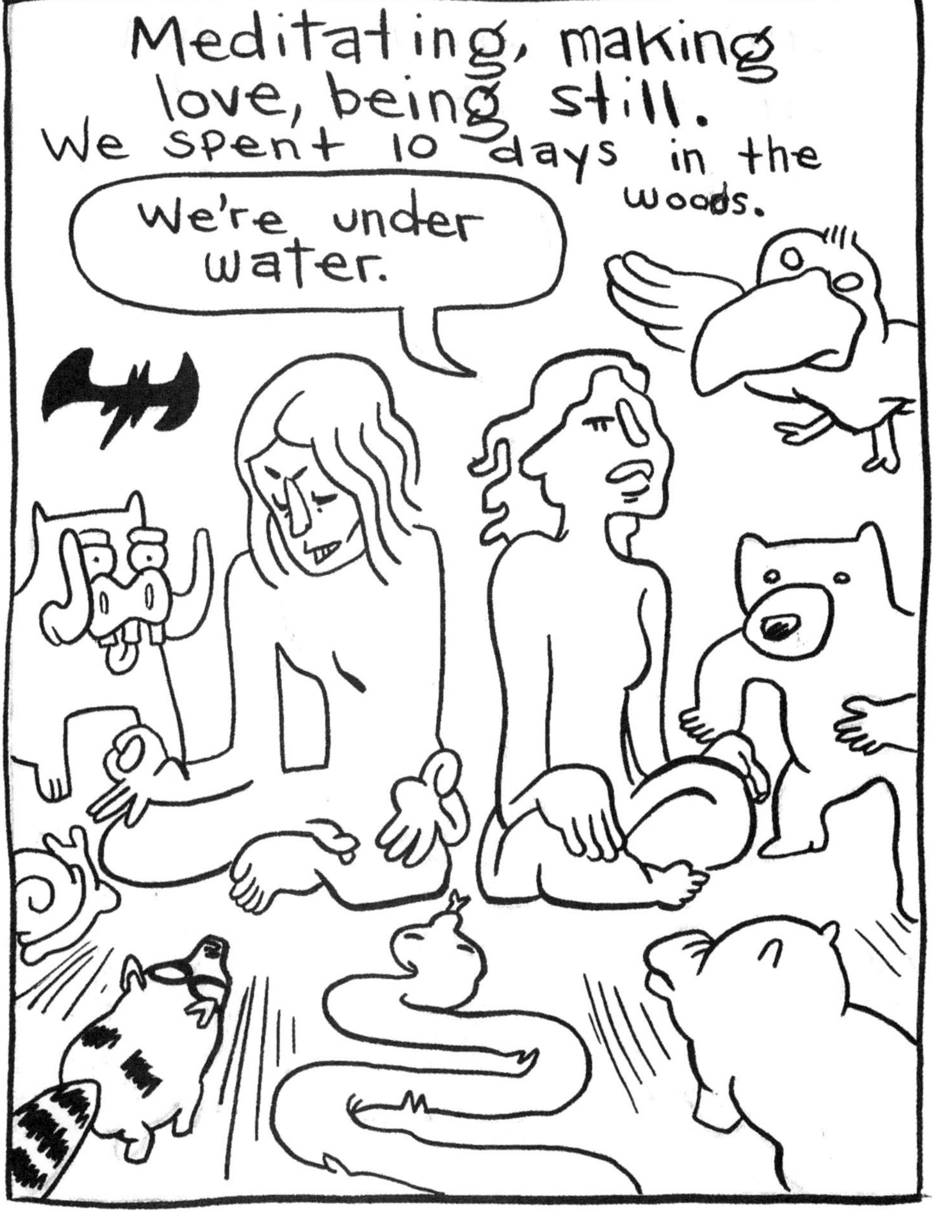
Meditating, making love, being still.
We spent 10 days in the woods.
We're under water.

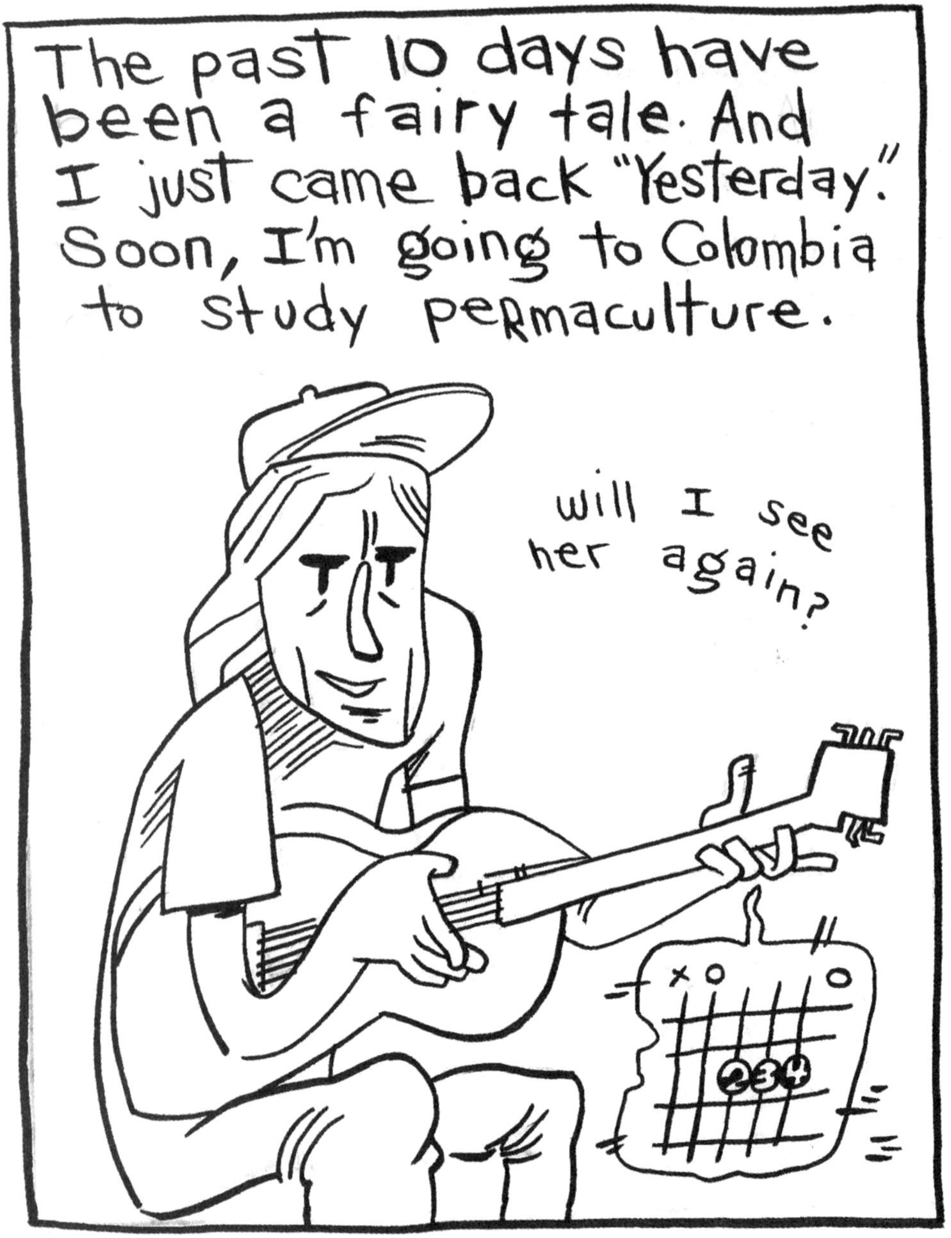
The past 10 days have been a fairy tale. And I just came back "Yesterday." Soon, I'm going to Colombia to study permaculture.
will I see her again?
x o o
234

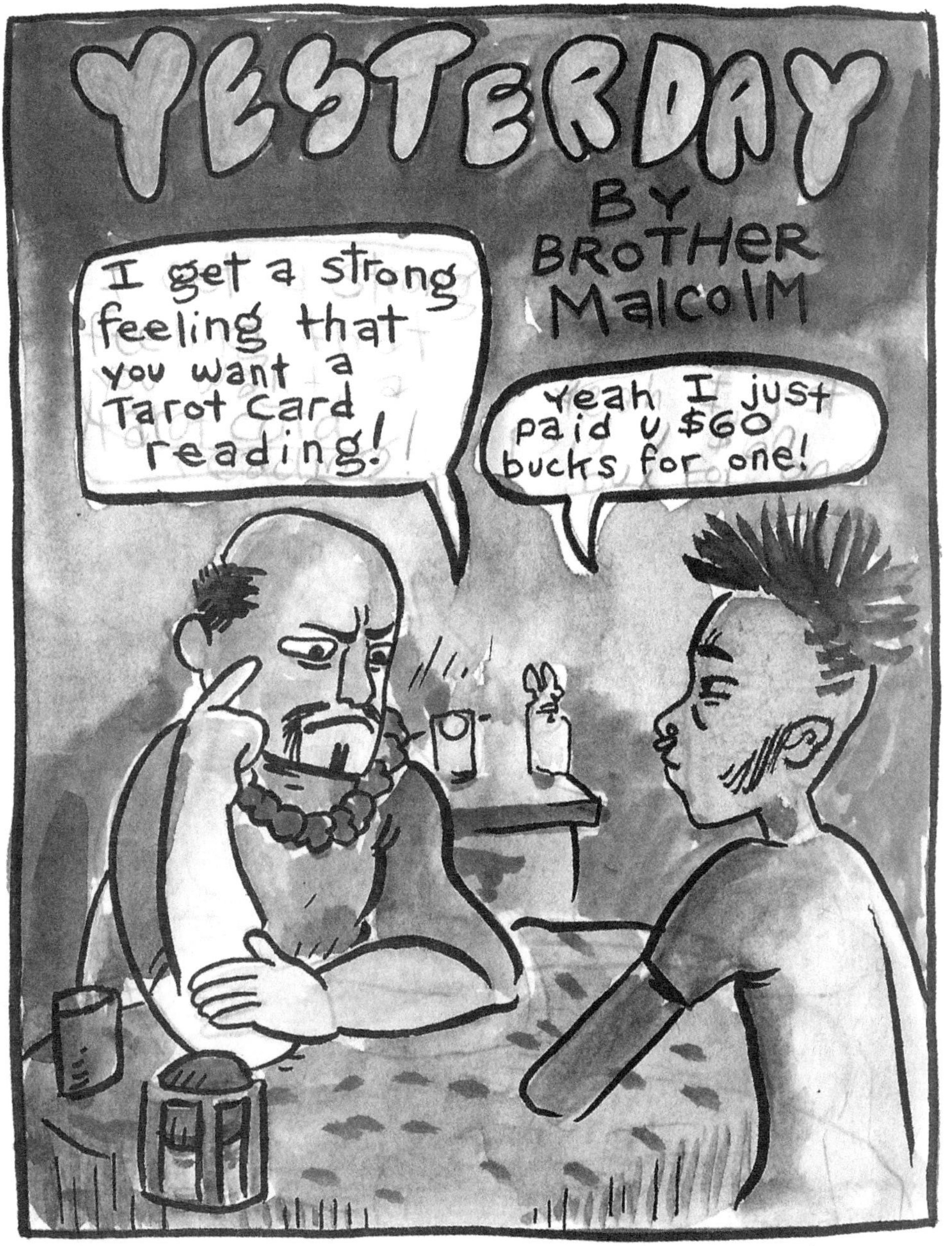
YESTERDAY
BY BROTHER MalcolM
I get a strong feeling that you want a Tarot Card reading!
Yeah I just paid U $60 bucks for one!

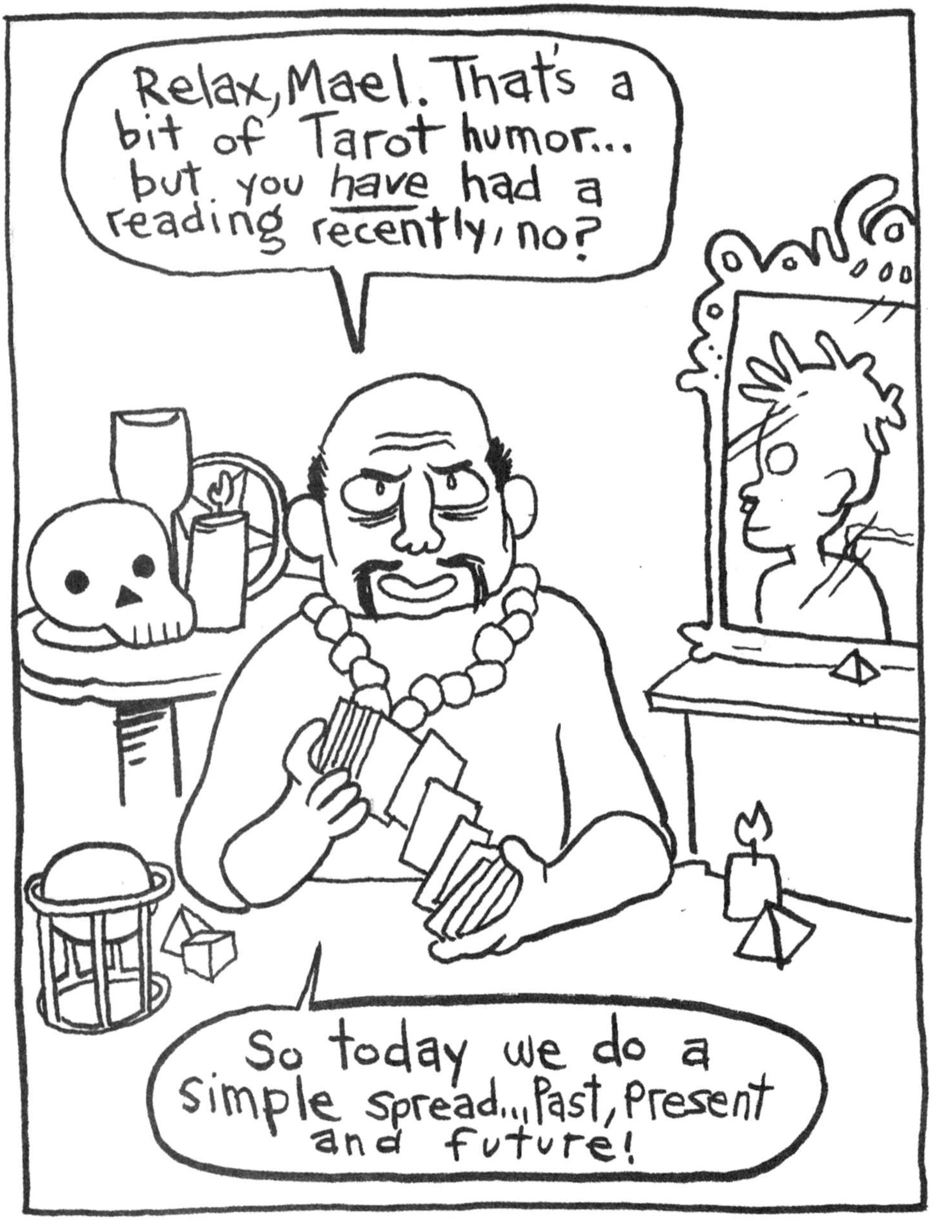
Relax, Mael. That's a bit of Tarot humor... but you have had a reading recently, no?
So today we do a simple spread... Past, Present and future!

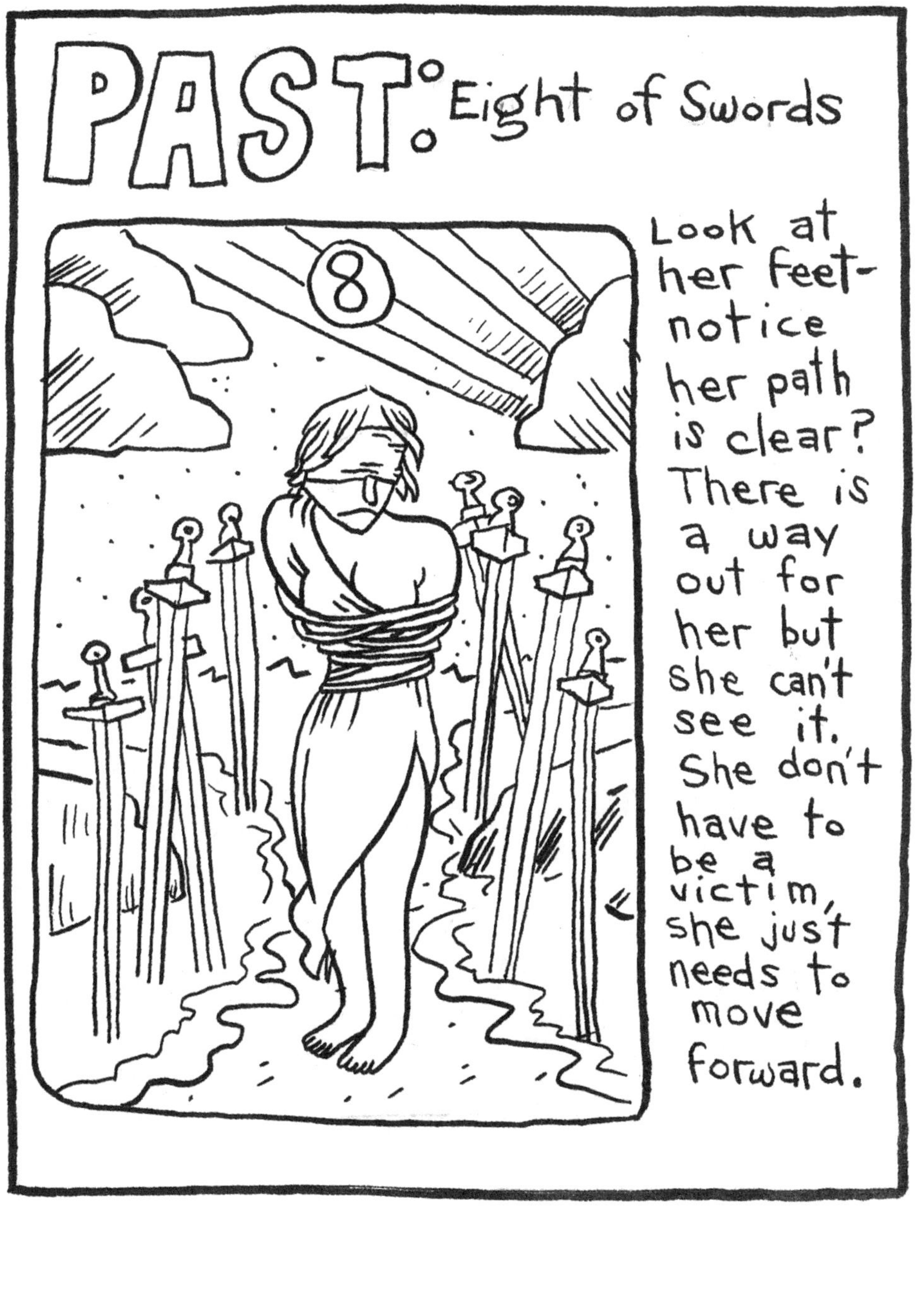
PAST: Eight of Swords
8
Look at her feet- notice her path is clear? There is a way out for her but she can't see it. She don't have to be a victim, she just needs to move forward.

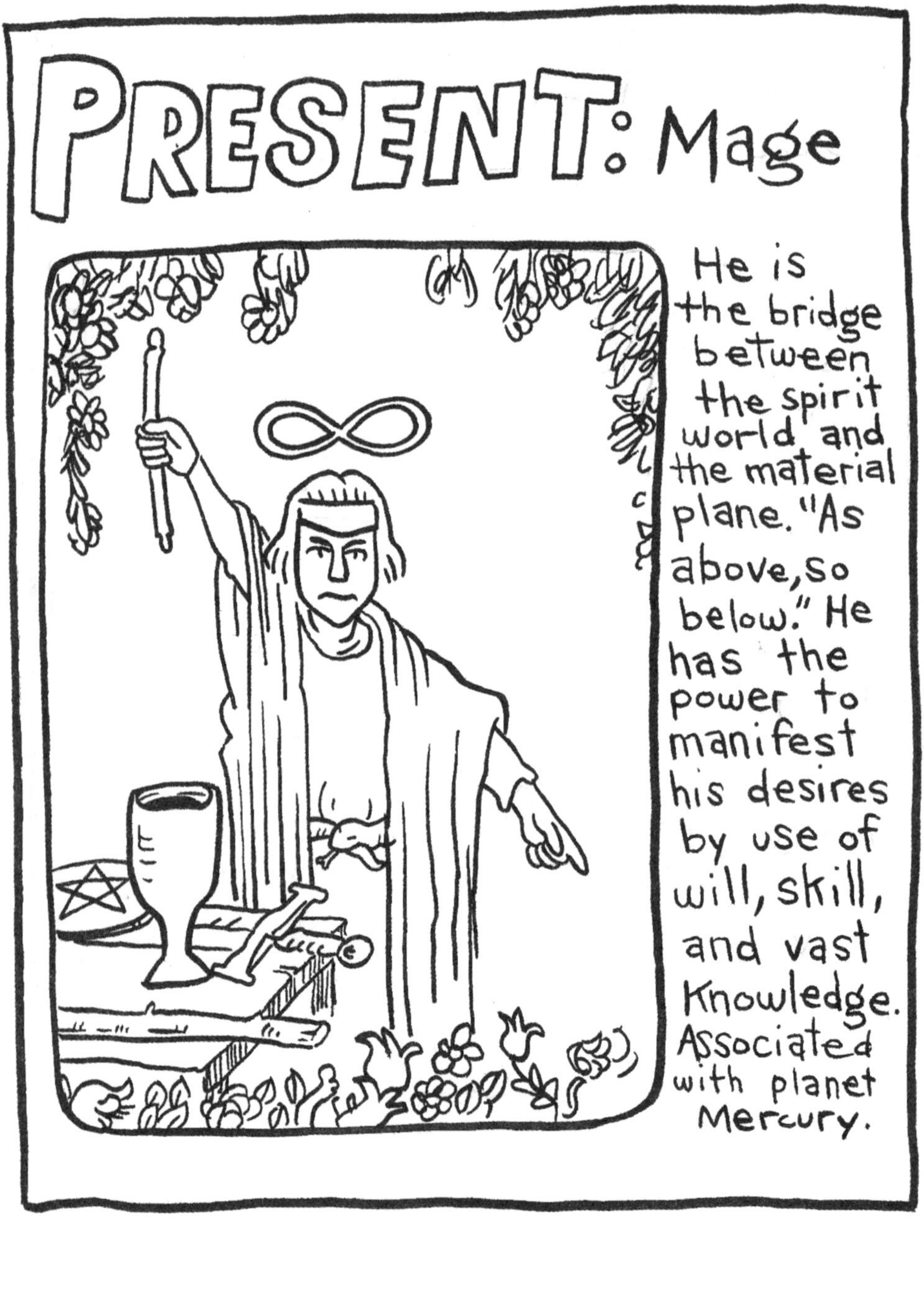
PRESENT: Mage
He is the bridge between the spirit world and the material plane. "As above, so below." He has the power to manifest his desires by use of will, skill, and vast Knowledge. Associated with planet Mercury.

FUTURE: Four of Swords

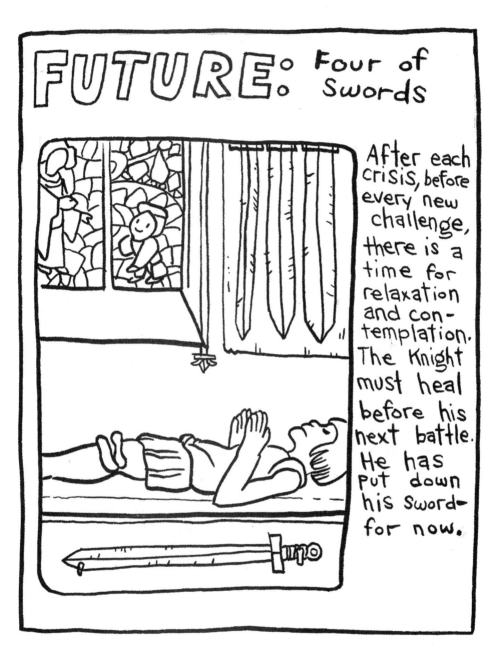

After each crisis, before every new challenge, there is a time for relaxation and contemplation. The Knight must heal before his next battle. He has put down his sword for now.

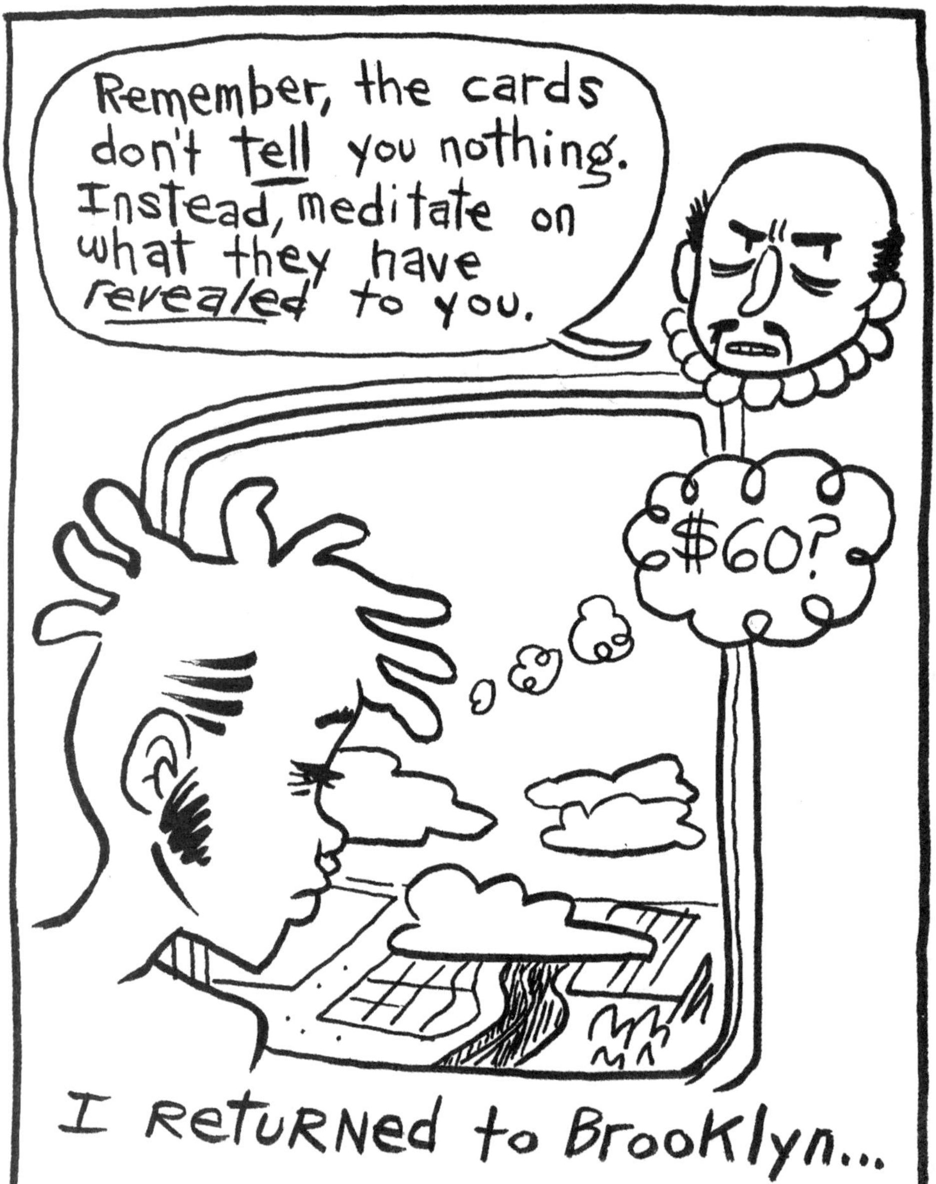
Remember, the cards don't tell you nothing. Instead, meditate on what they have revealed to you.
$60?
I returned to Brooklyn...

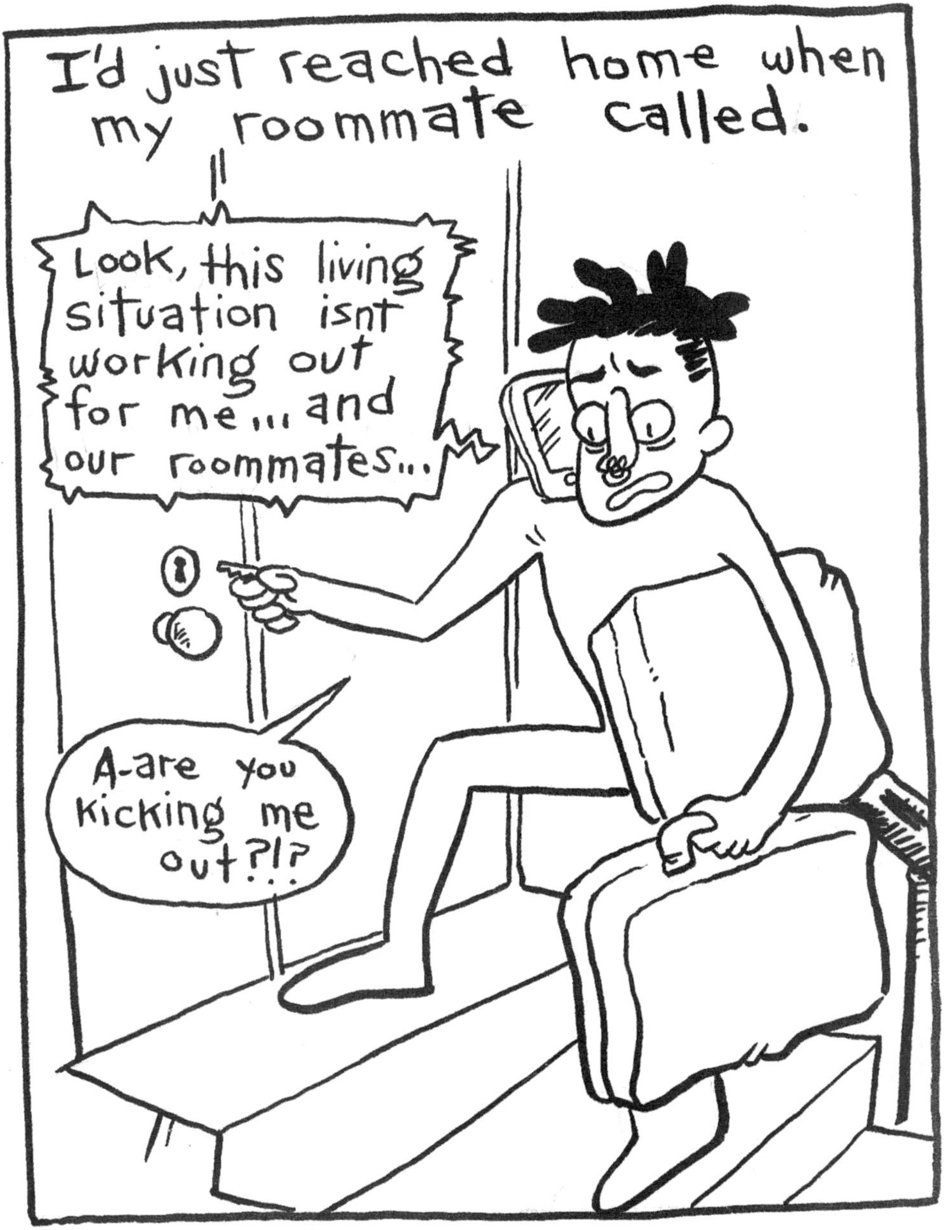
I'd just reached home when my roommate called.
Look, this living situation isnt working out for me... and our roommates...
A-are you kicking me out?!?

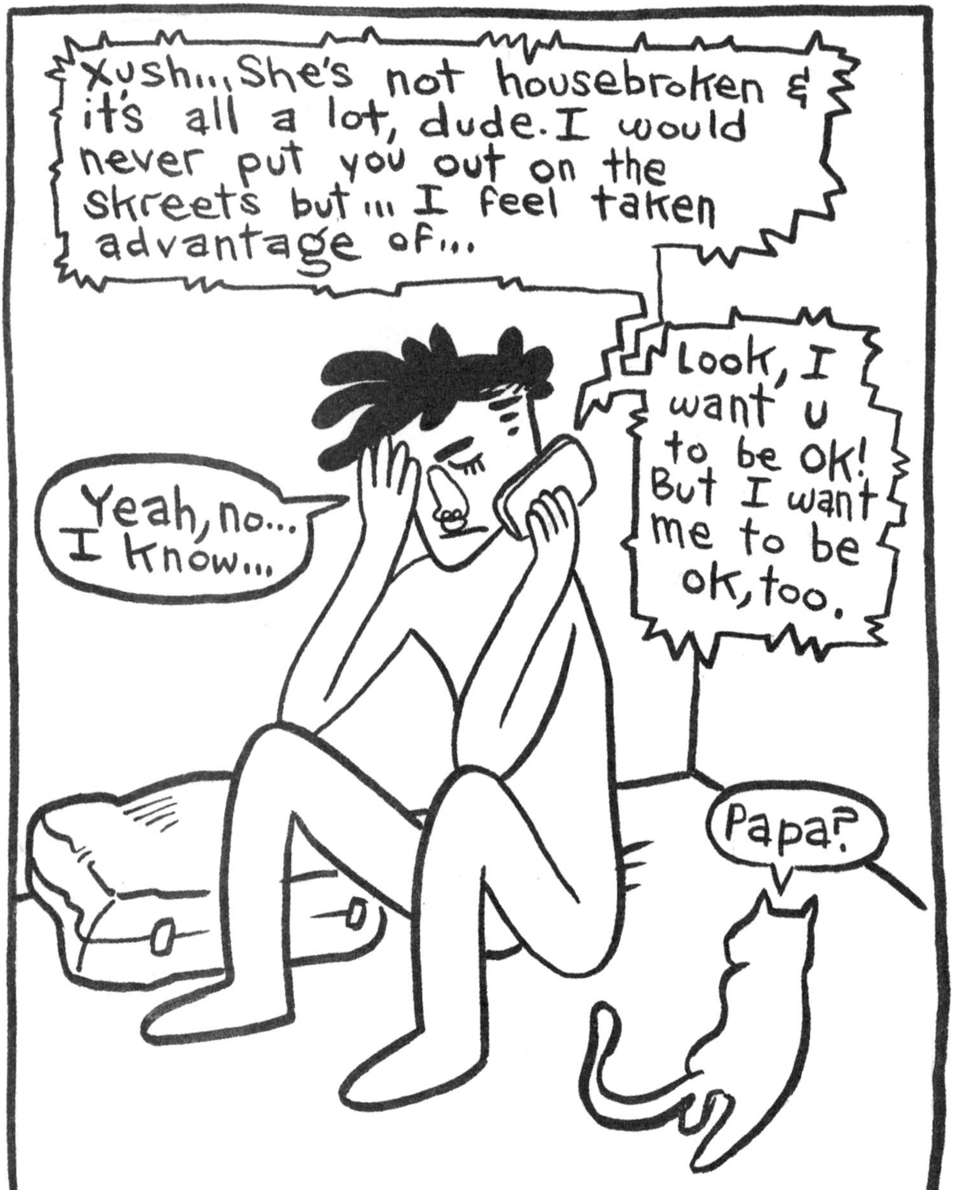
Xush... She's not housebroken & it's all a lot, dude. I would never put you out on the skreets but... I feel taken advantage of...
Yeah, no... I know...
Look, I want u to be OK! But I want me to be ok, too.
Papa?

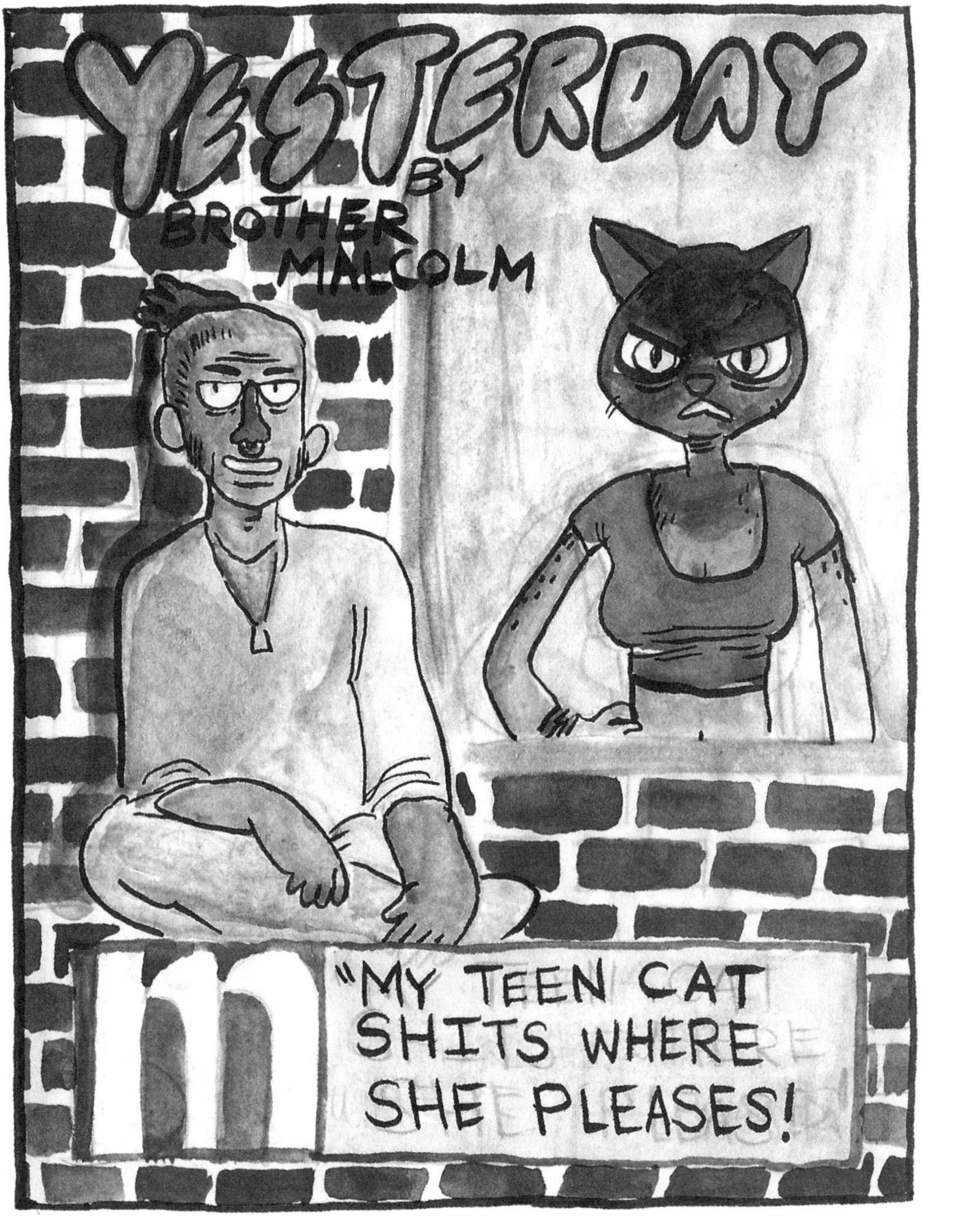
YESTERDAY
BY
BROTHER MALCOLM
m
"MY TEEN CAT SHITS WHERE SHE PLEASES!

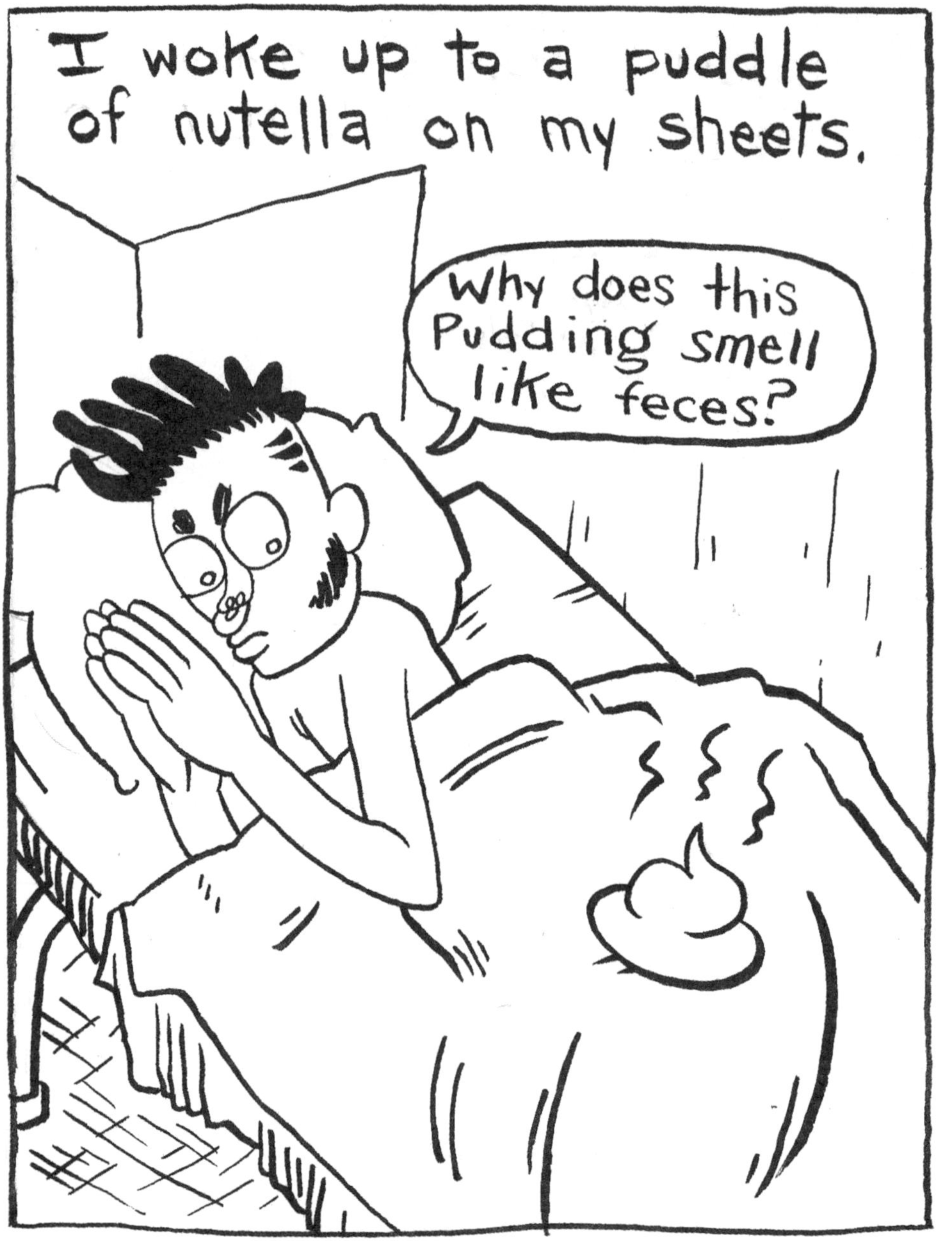
I woke up to a puddle of nutella on my sheets.
Why does this Pudding smell like feces?

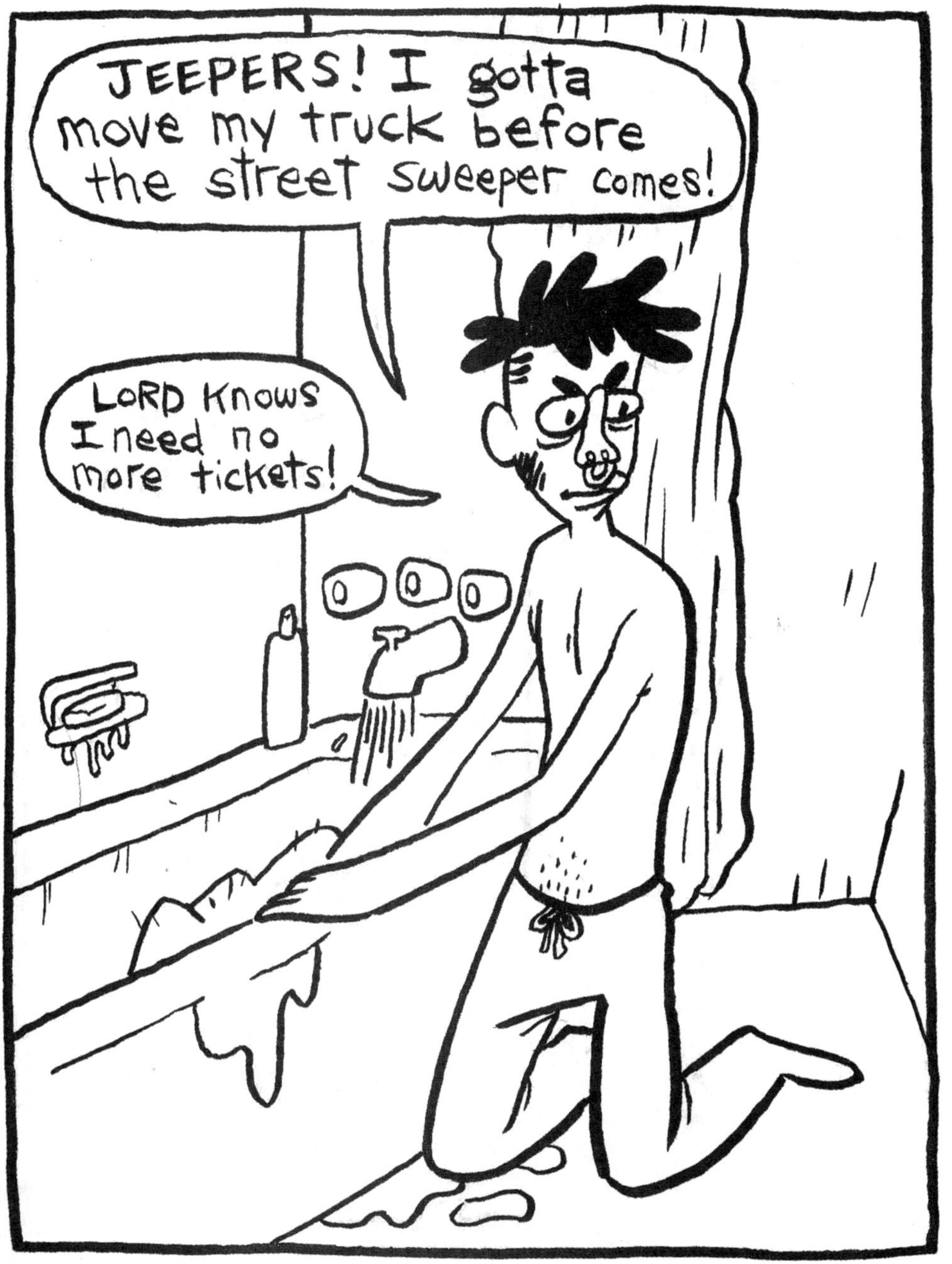
JEEPERS! I gotta move my truck before the street sweeper comes!
LORD Knows I need no more tickets!

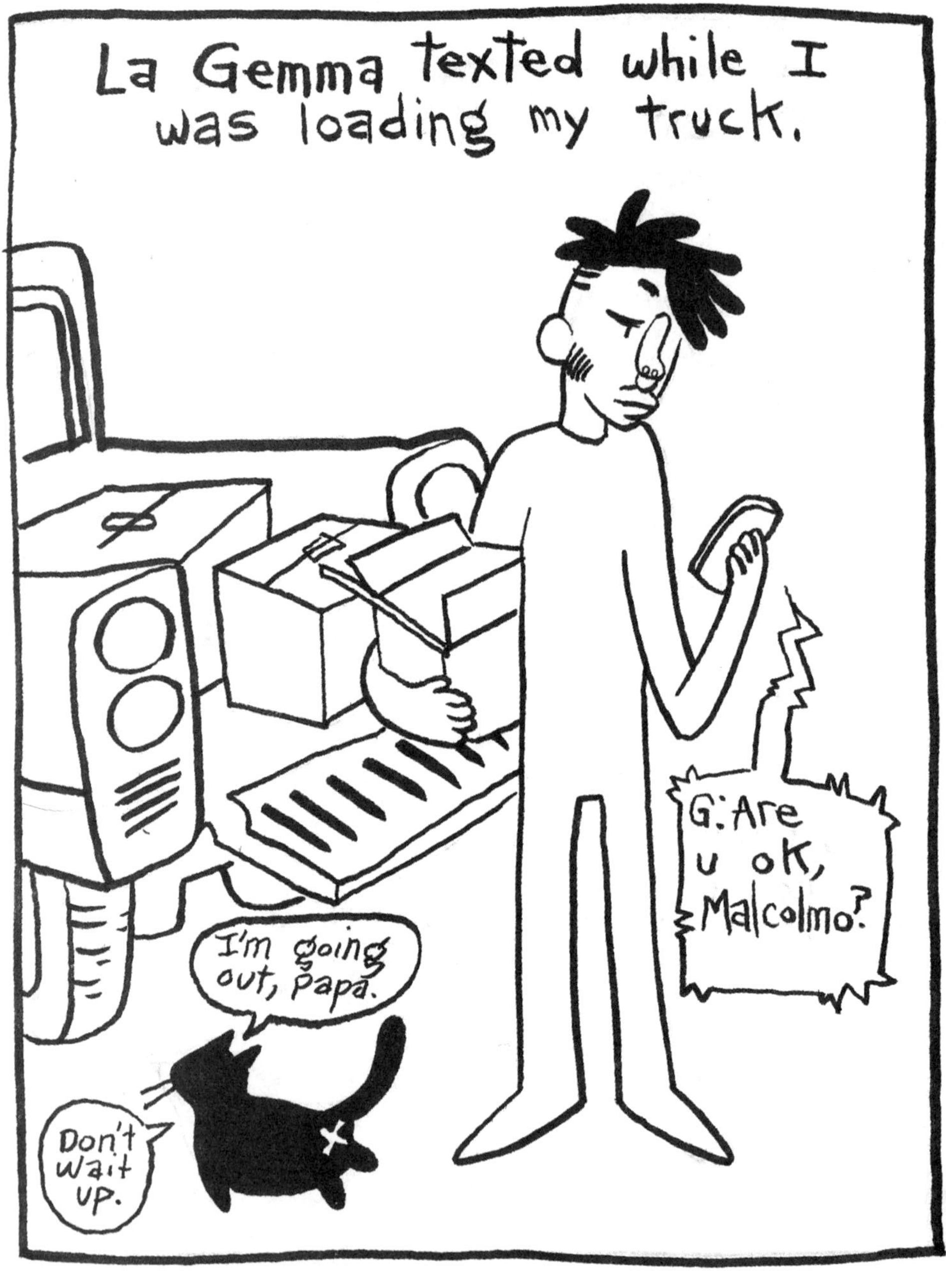
La Gemma texted while I was loading my truck.
G: Are u ok, Malcolmo?
I'm going out, papa.
Don't wait up.

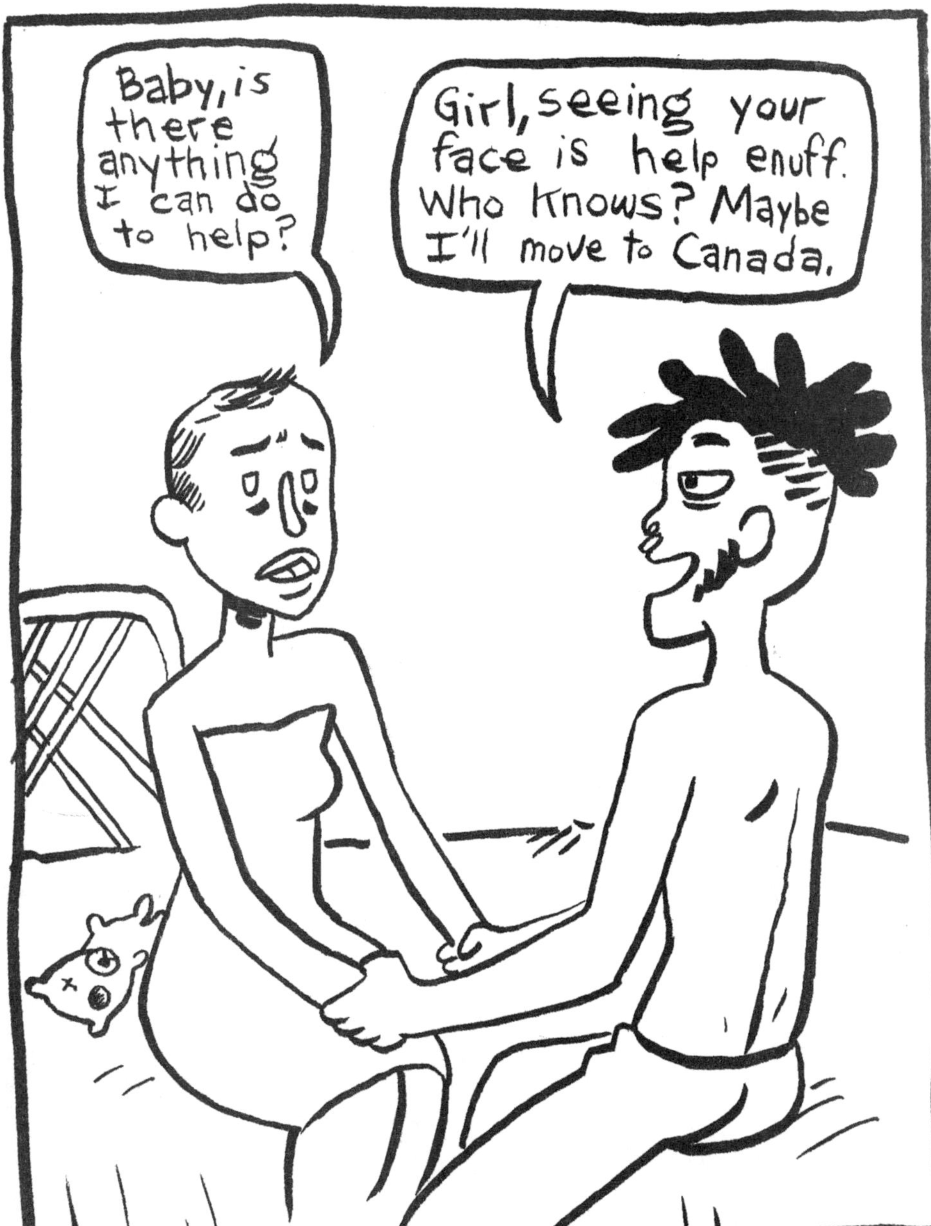
Baby, is there anything I can do to help?
Girl, seeing your face is help enuff. Who knows? Maybe I'll move to Canada.

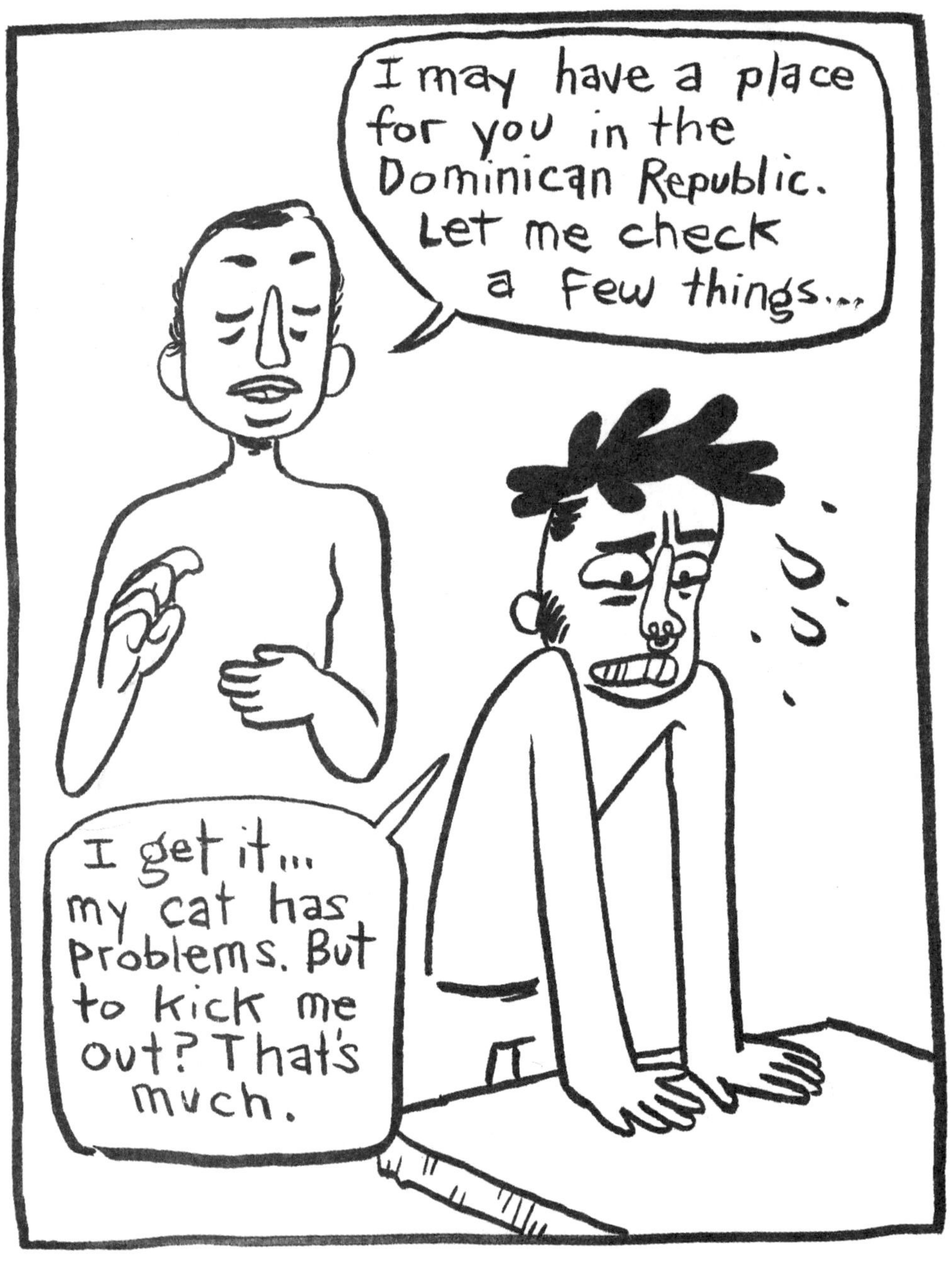
I may have a place for you in the Dominican Republic. Let me check a few things...
I get it... my cat has problems. But to kick me out? That's much.

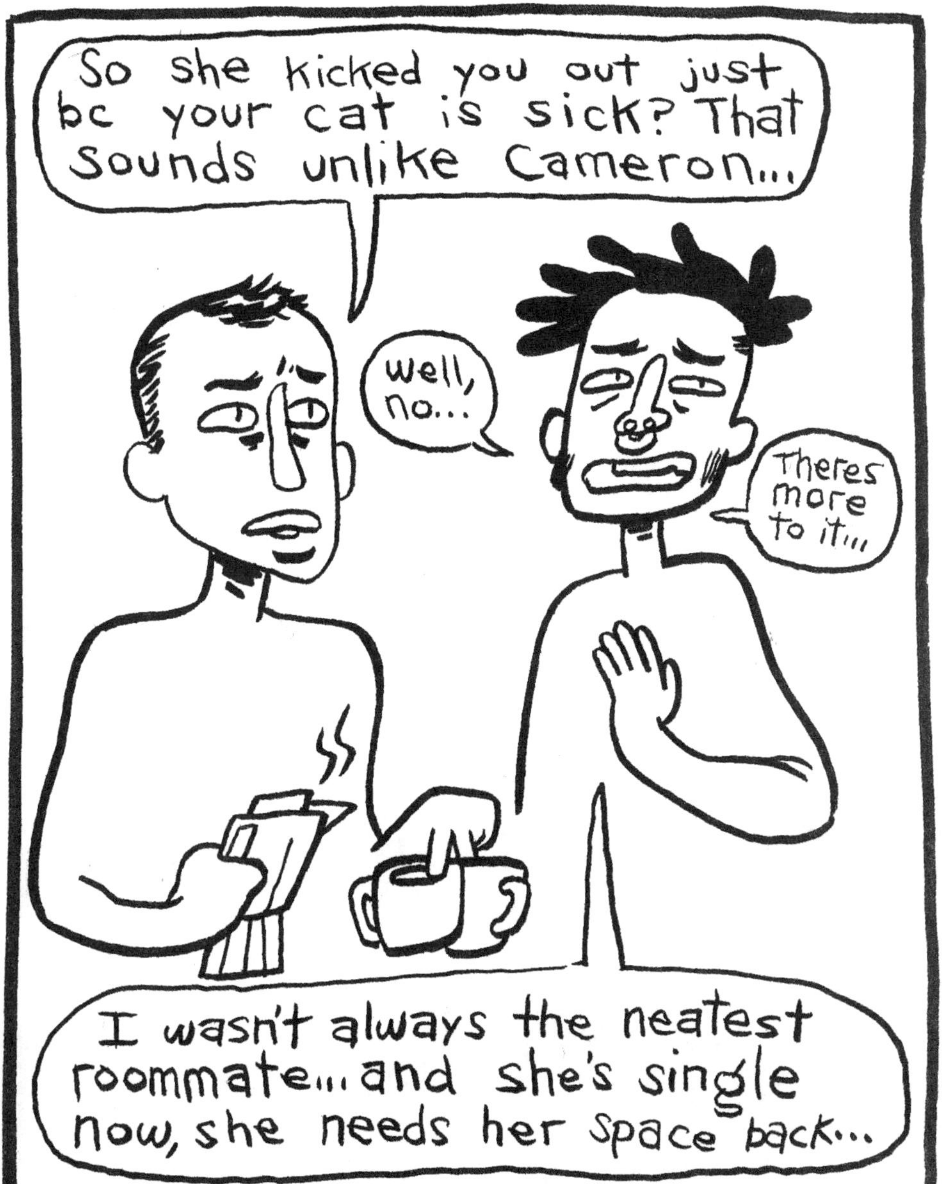
So she kicked you out just bc your cat is sick? That sounds unlike Cameron...
Well, no...
Theres more to it...
I wasn't always the neatest roommate... and she's single now, she needs her space back...

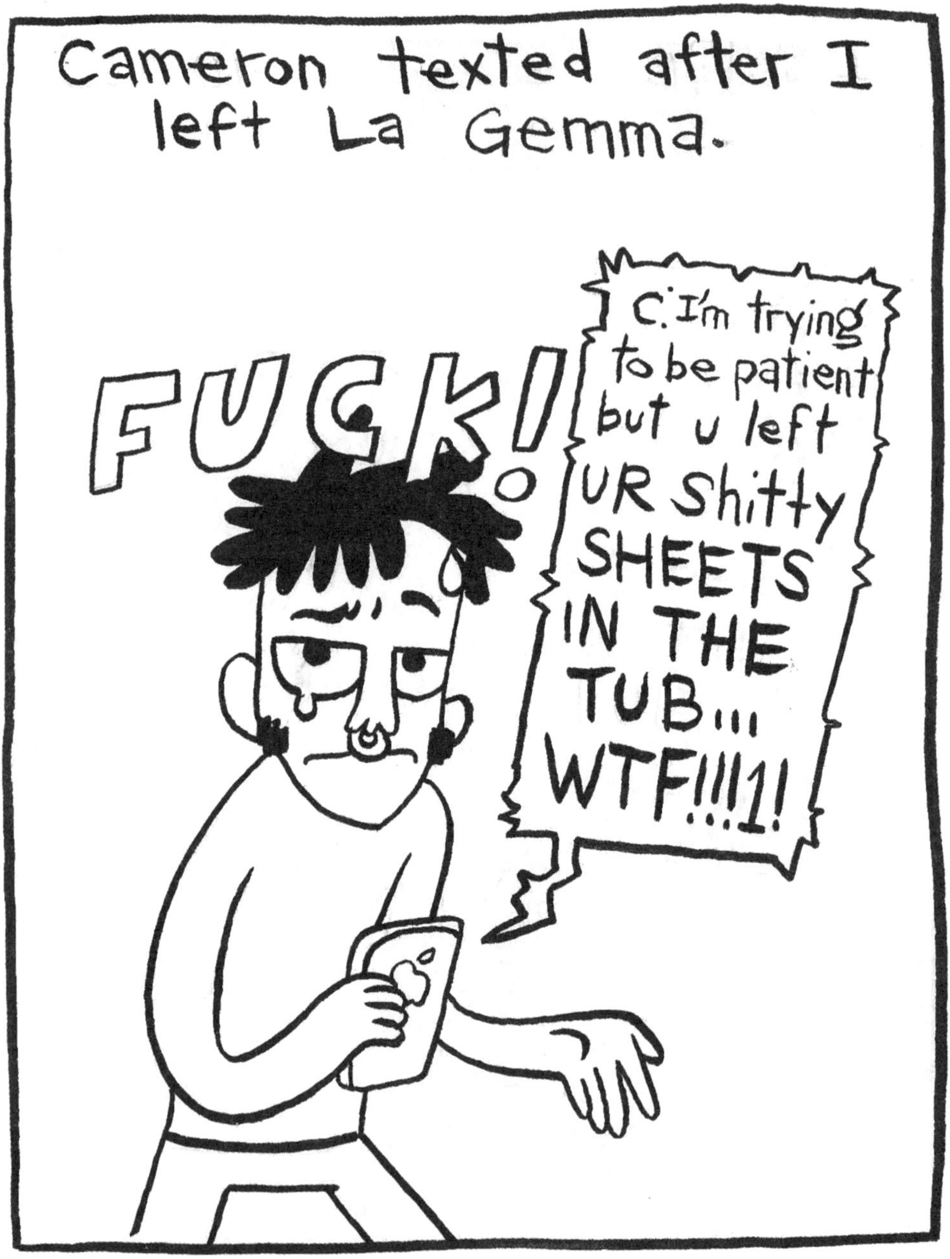
Cameron texted after I left La Gemma.
FUCK!
C: I'm trying to be patient but u left UR Shitty SHEETS IN THE TUB... WTF!!!1!

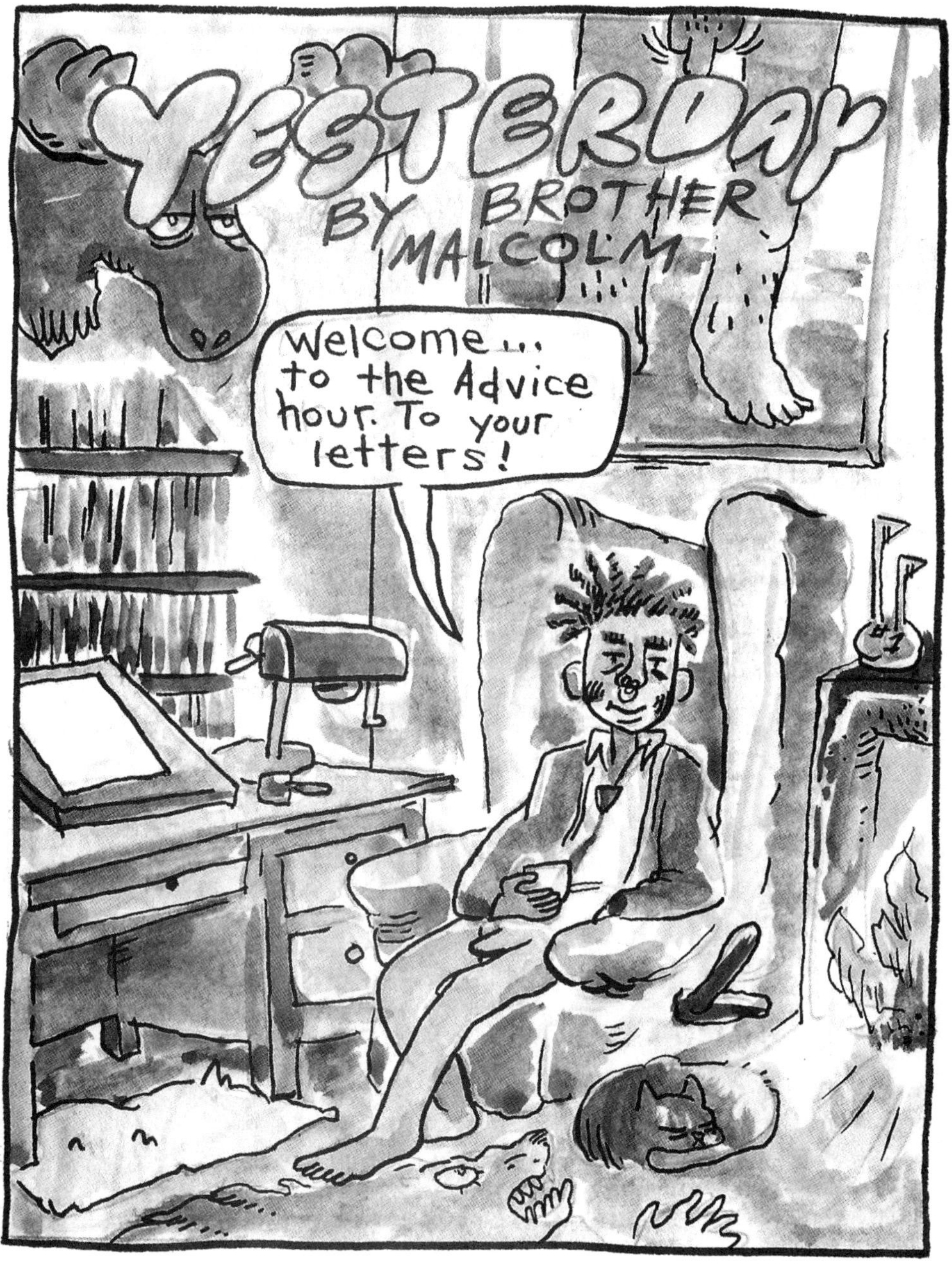
YESTERDAY
BY BROTHER MALCOLM
Welcome... to the Advice hour. To your letters!

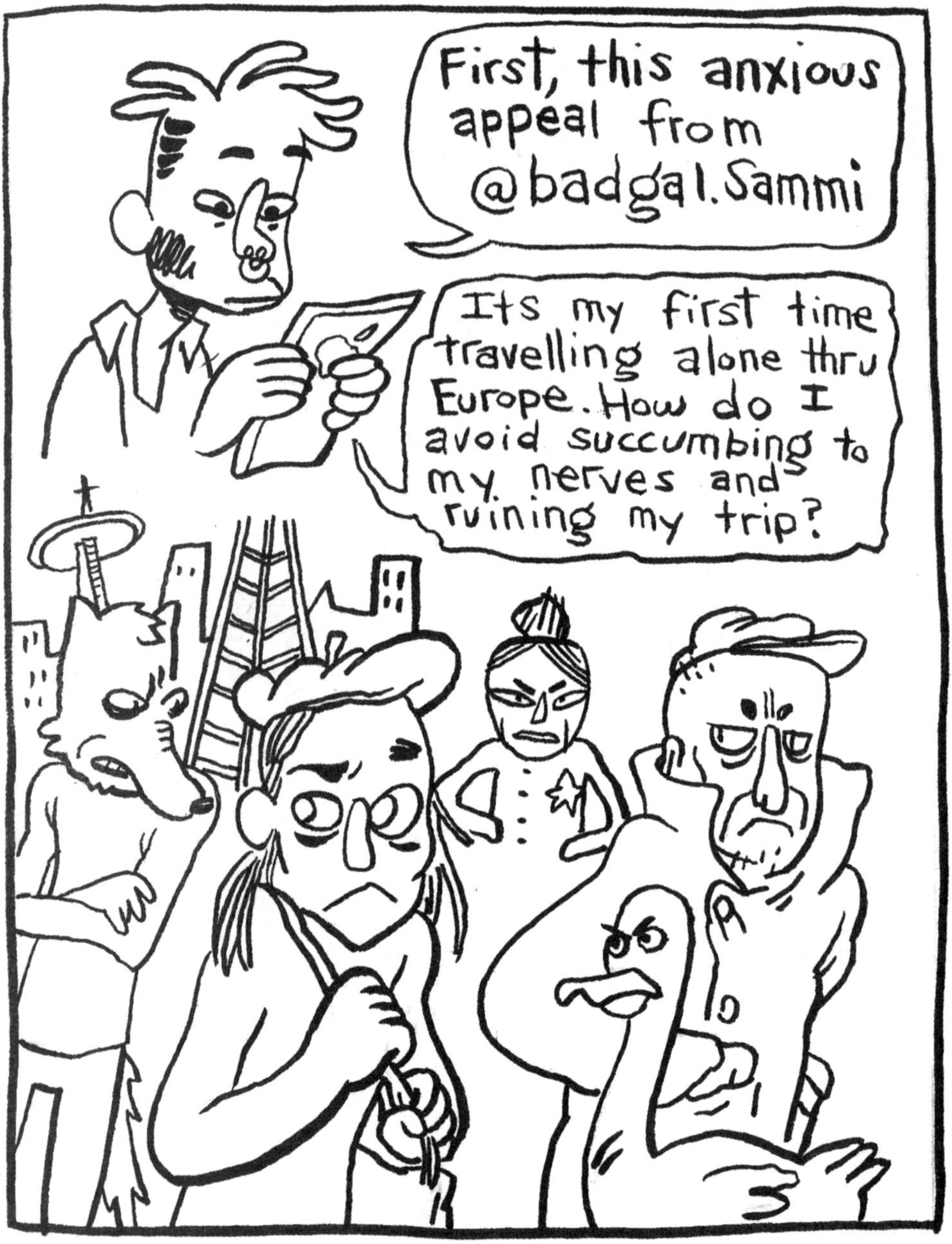
First, this anxious appeal from @badgal.Sammi
Its my first time travelling alone thru Europe. How do I avoid succumbing to my nerves and ruining my trip?

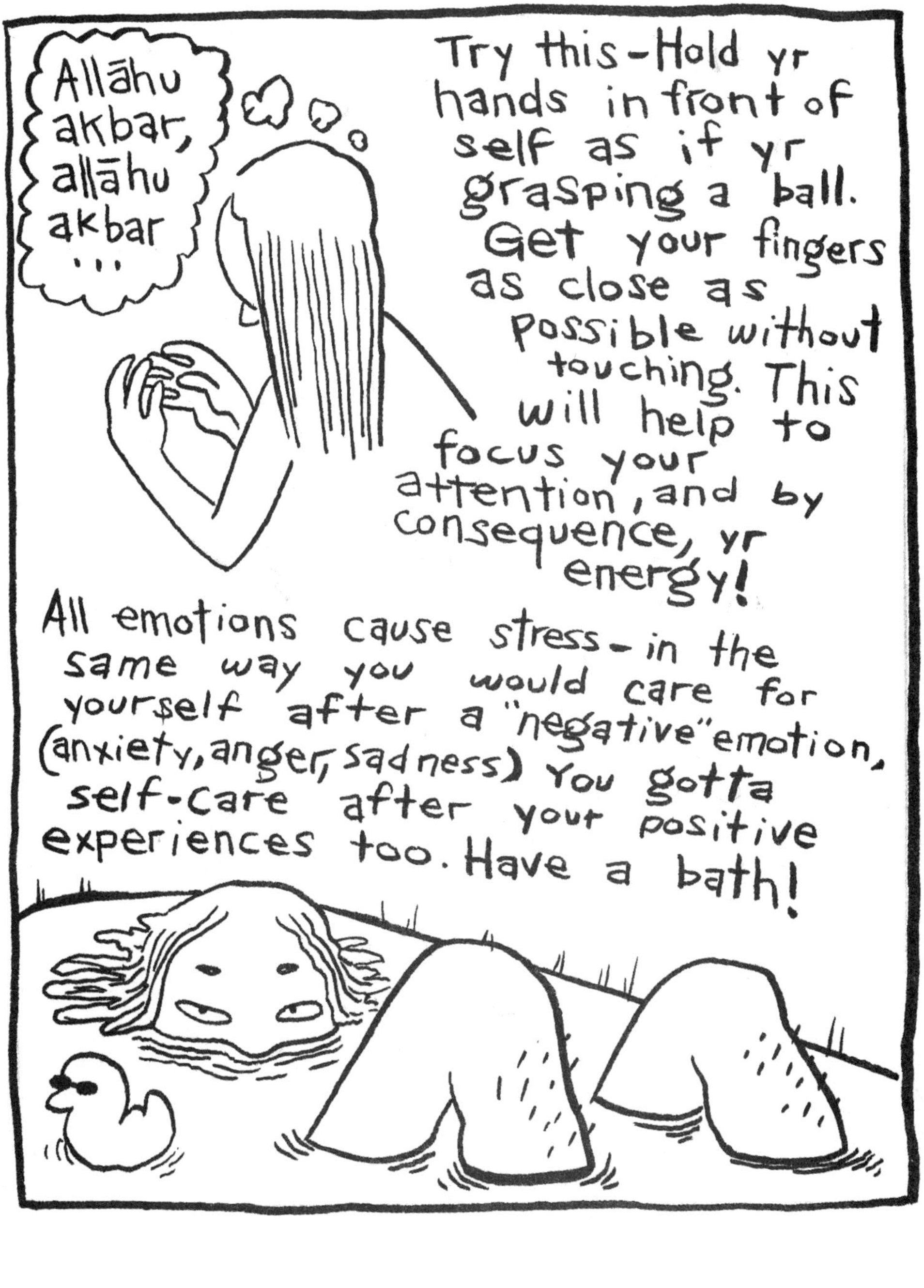
Allāhu akbar, allāhu akbar ...
Try this-Hold yr hands in front of self as if yr grasping a ball. Get your fingers as close as possible without touching. This will help to focus your attention, and by consequence, yr energy!
All emotions cause stress - in the same way you would care for yourself after a "negative" emotion, (anxiety, anger, sadness) You gotta self-care after your positive experiences too. Have a bath!

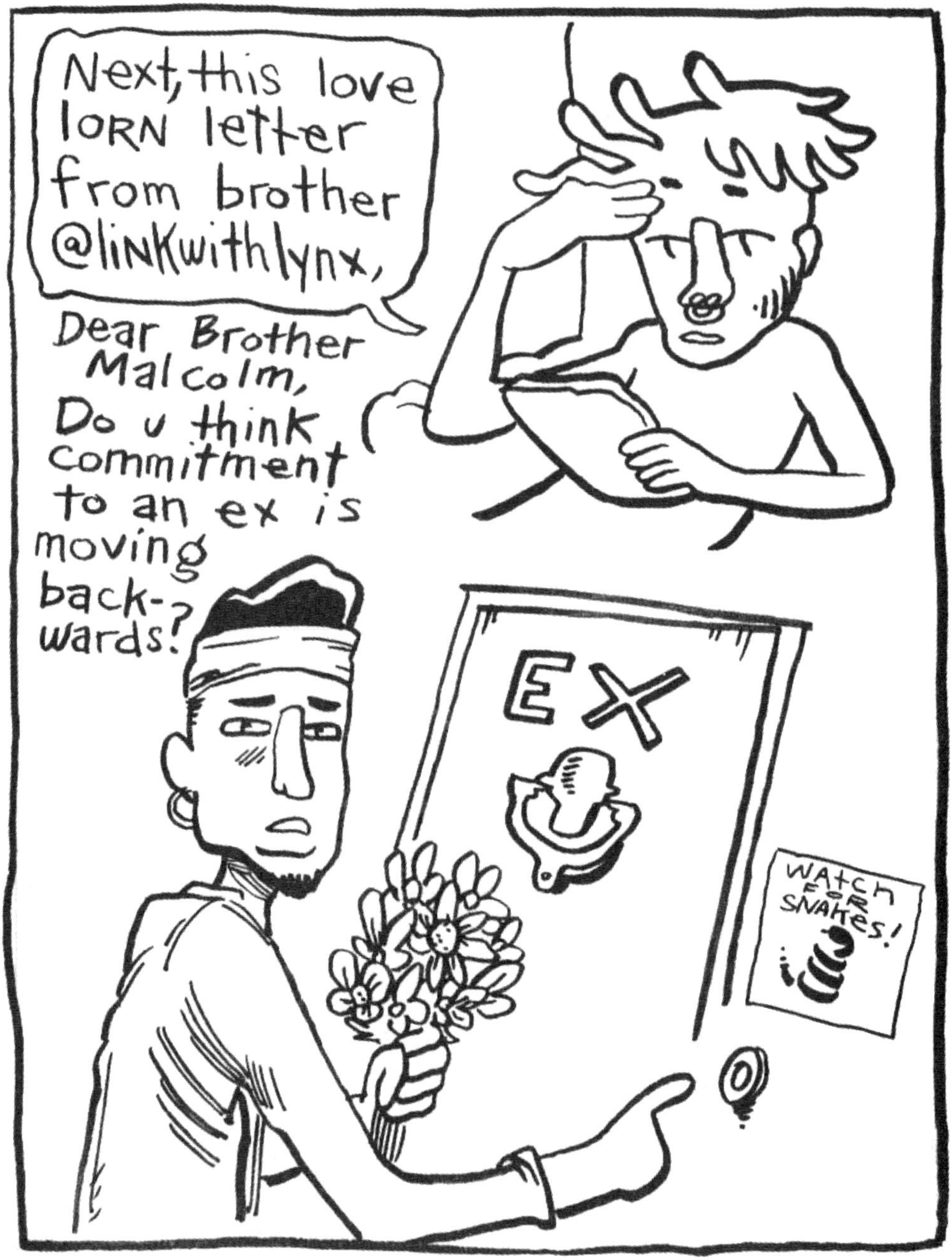
Next, this love lorn letter from brother @linkwithlynx,
Dear Brother Malcolm, Do u think commitment to an ex is moving back-wards?
EX
WATCH FOR SNAKES!

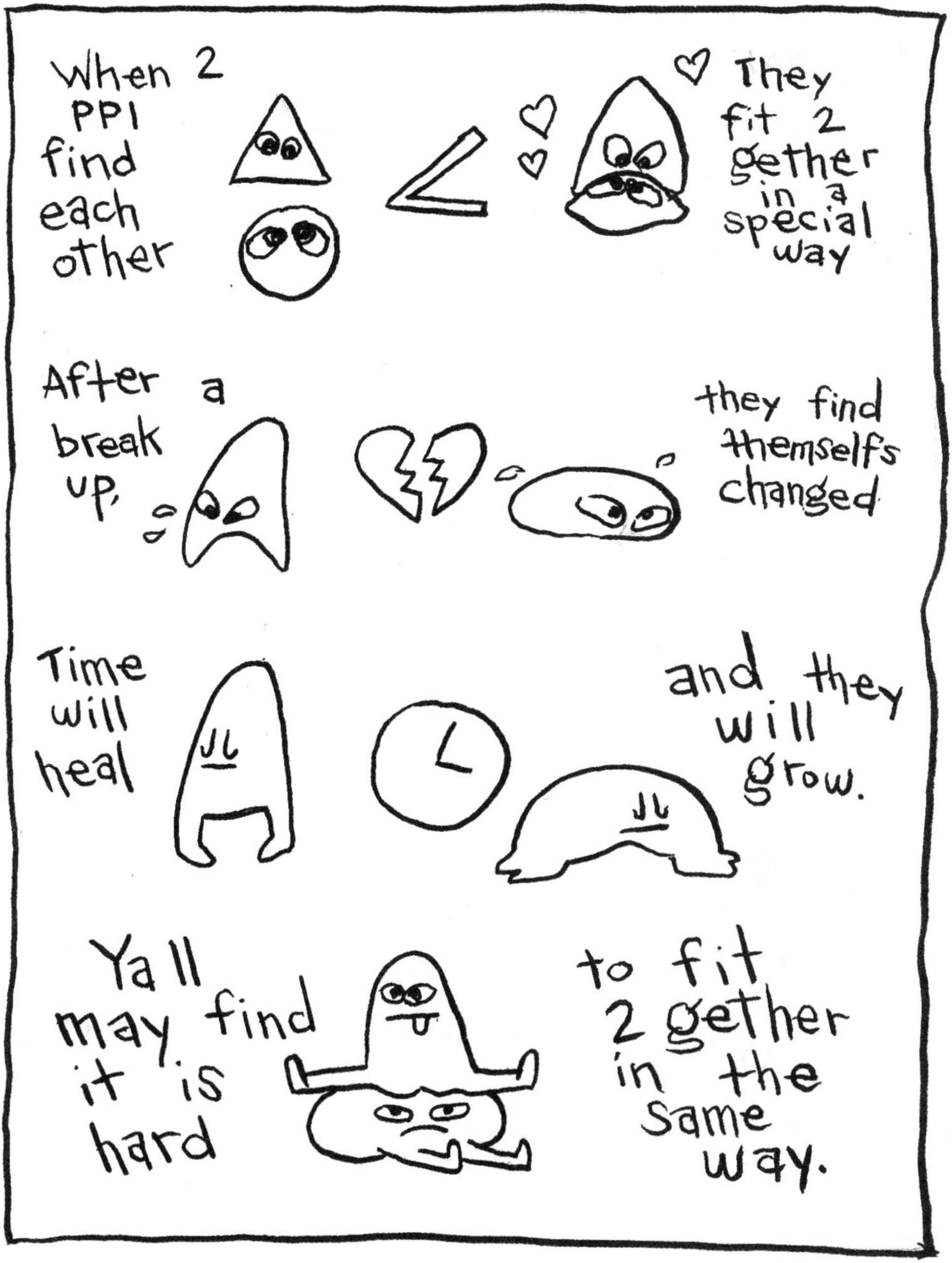
When 2 PPl find each other
They fit 2 gether in a special way
After a break up,
they find themselfs changed
Time will heal
and they will grow.
Yall may find it is hard
to fit 2 gether in the same way.

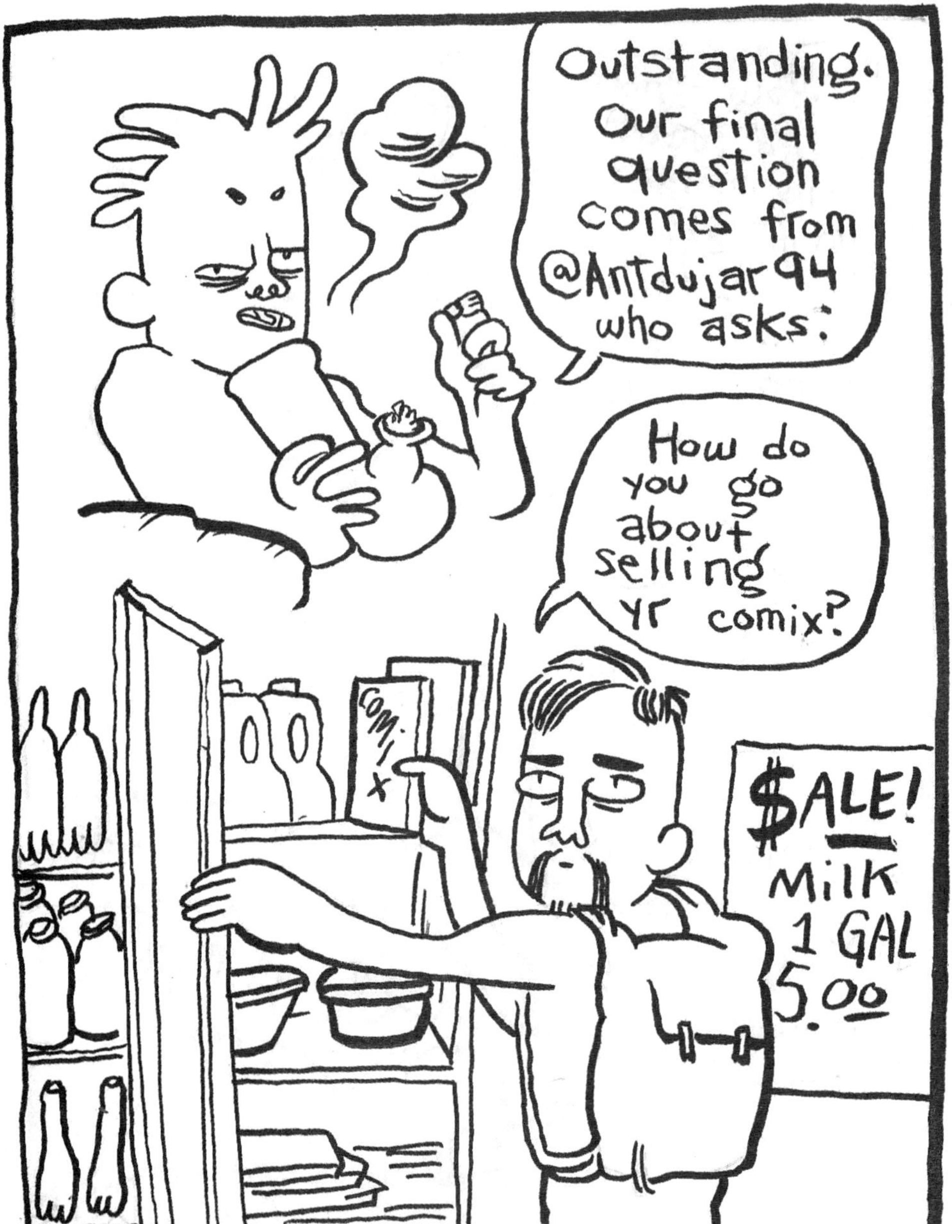
Outstanding. Our final question comes from @Antdujar94 who asks:
How do you go about selling yr comix?
COMIX
$ALE! MILK 1 GAL 5.00

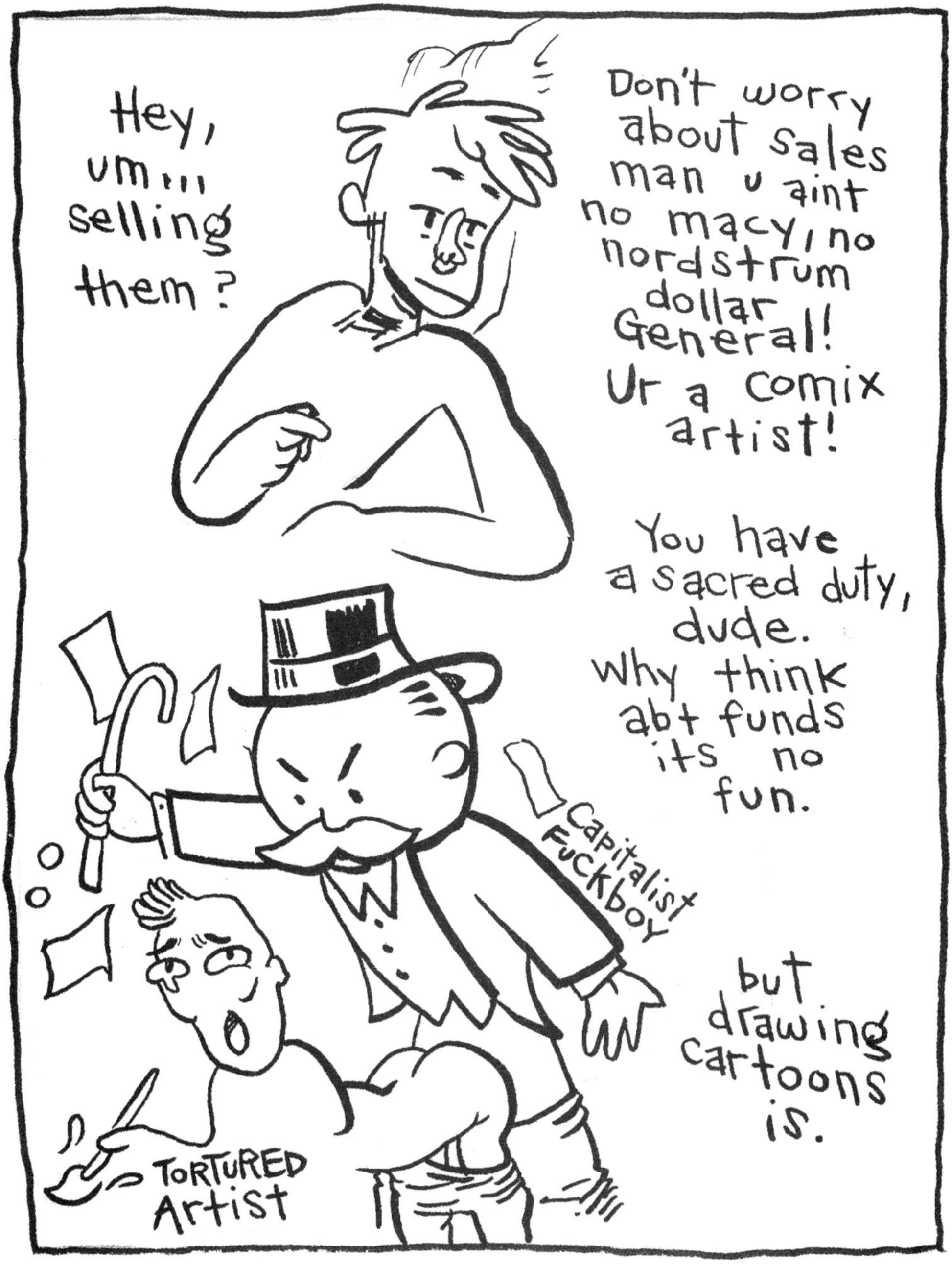
Hey, um... selling them?
Don't worry about sales man u aint no macy, no nordstrum dollar General! Ur a comix artist!
You have a sacred duty, dude. Why think abt funds its no fun.
Capitalist Fuckboy
but drawing cartoons is.
TORTURED Artist

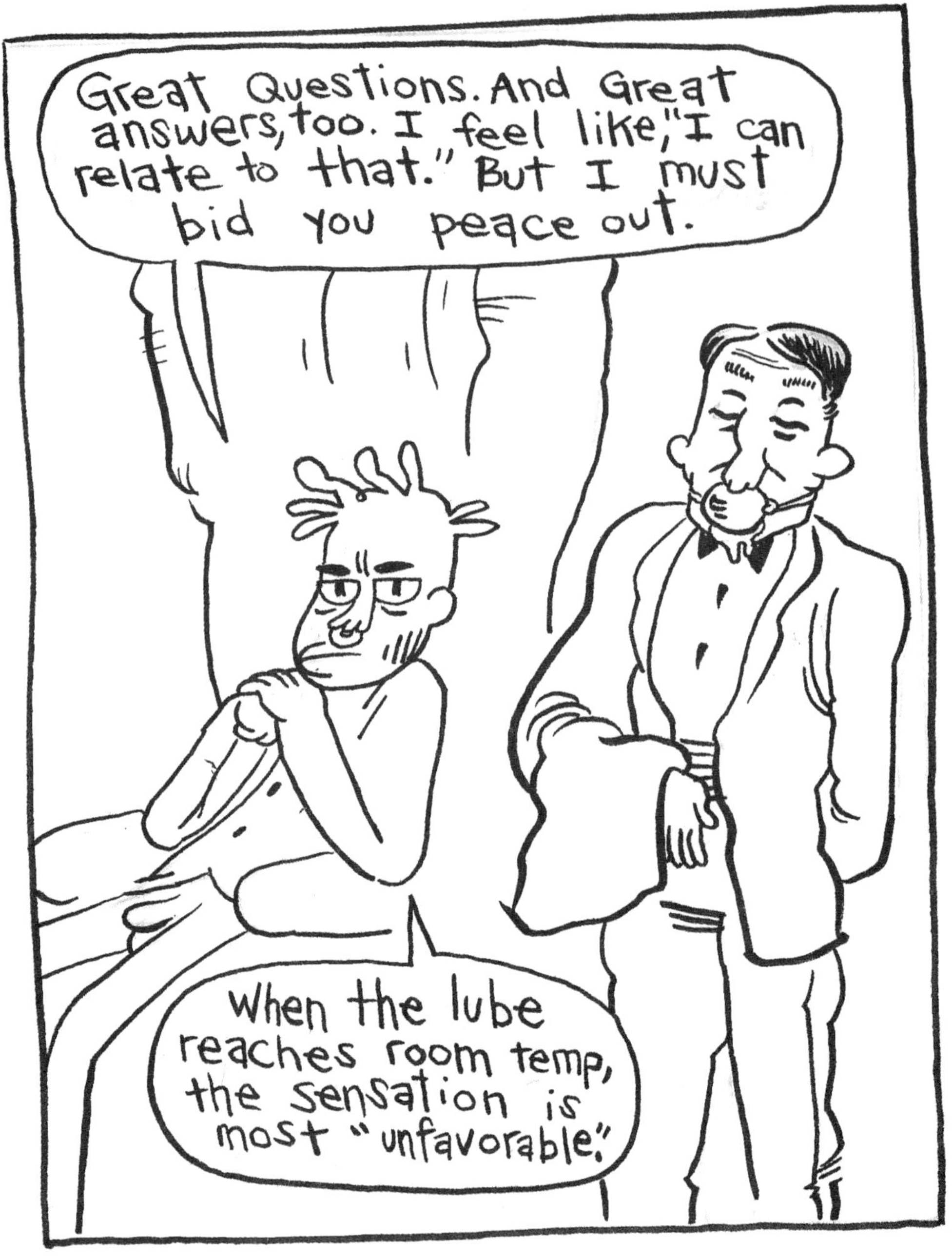
Great Questions. And Great answers, too. I feel like, "I can relate to that." But I must bid you peace out.
When the lube reaches room temp, the sensation is most "unfavorable."

"YESTERDAY"

by Brother Malcolm

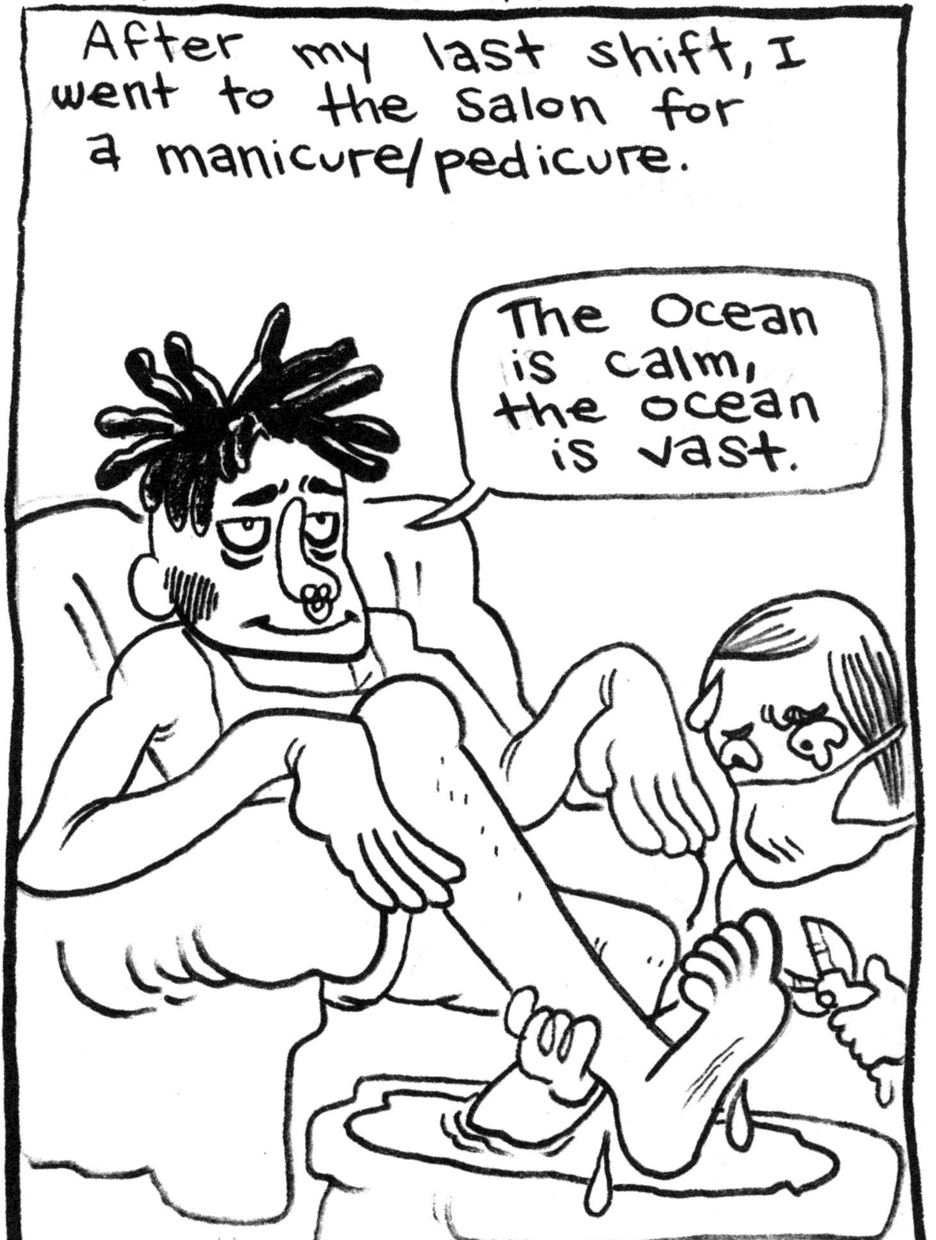
After my last shift, I went to the Salon for a manicure/pedicure.
The Ocean is calm, the ocean is vast.

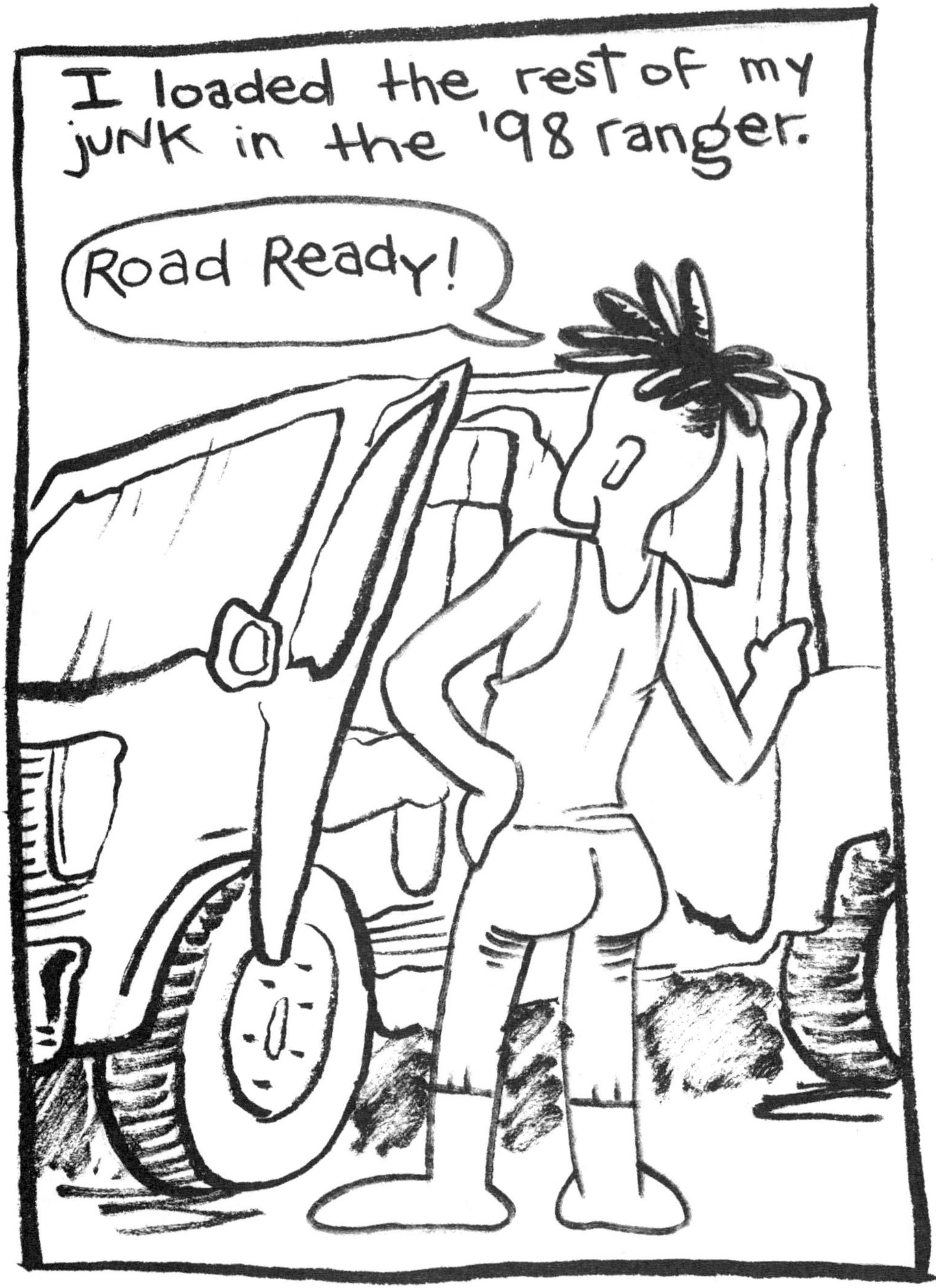
I loaded the rest of my junk in the '98 ranger.
Road Ready!

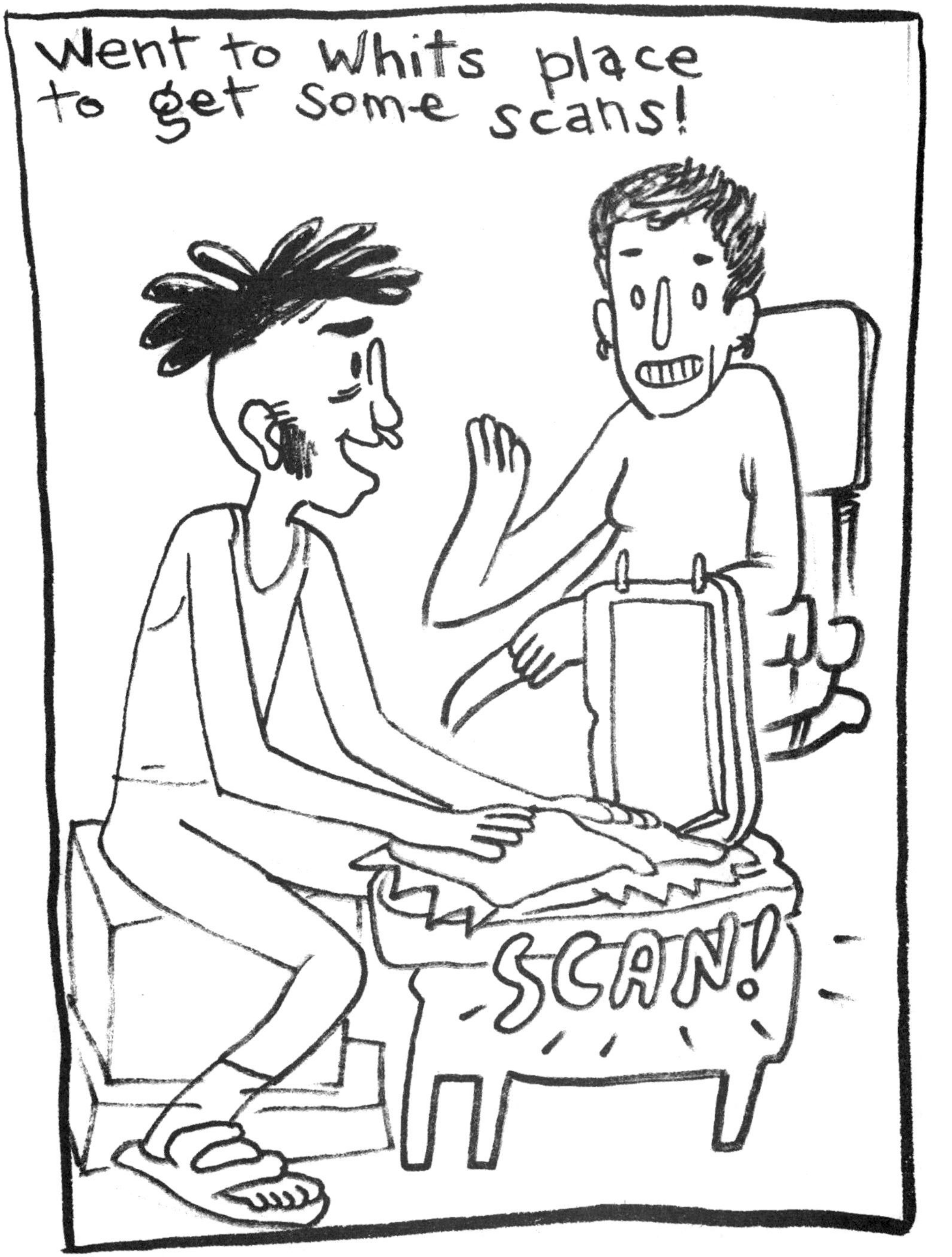
Went to Whits place to get some scans!
SCAN!

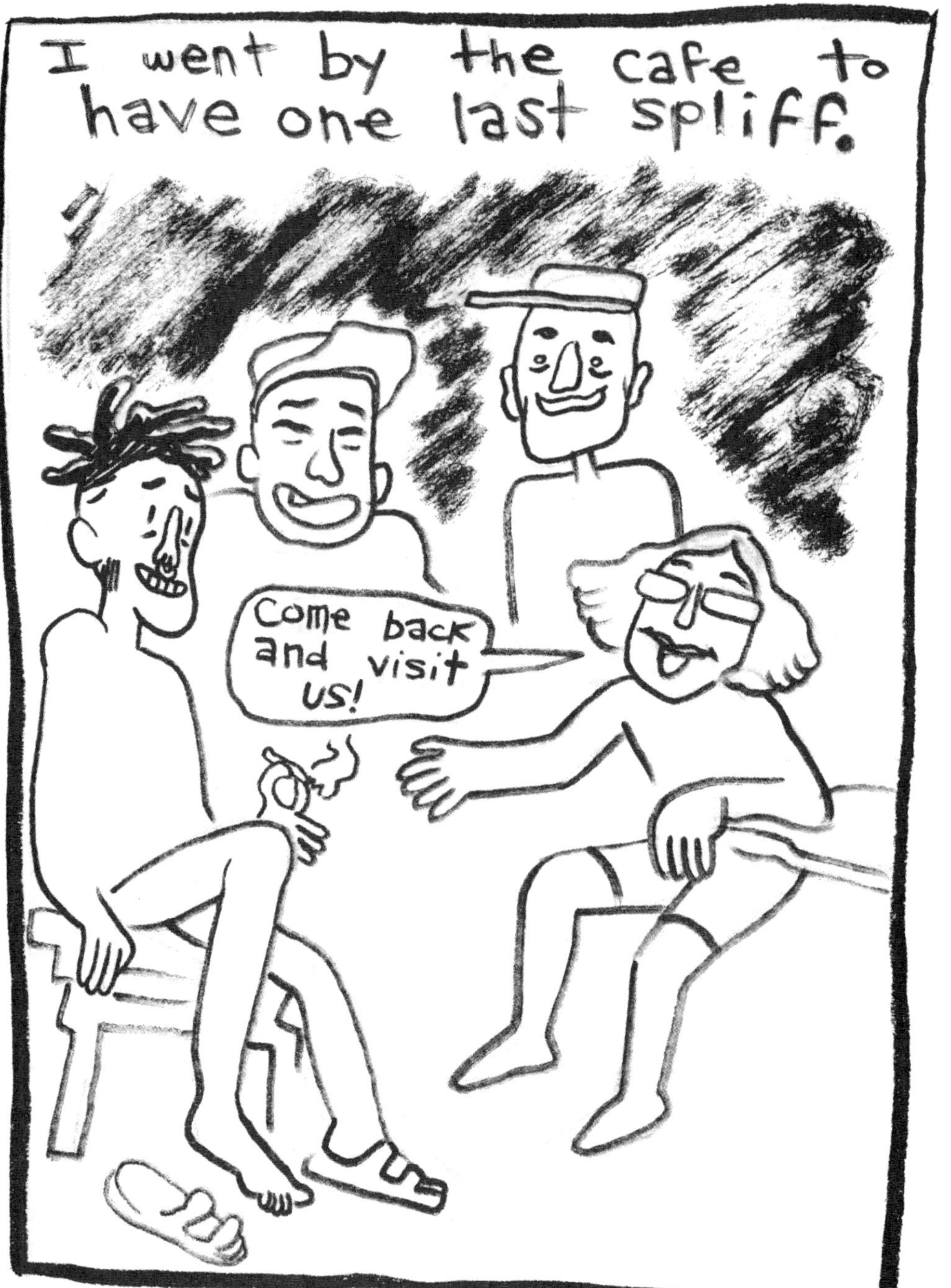
I went by the cafe to have one last spliff.
Come back and visit us!

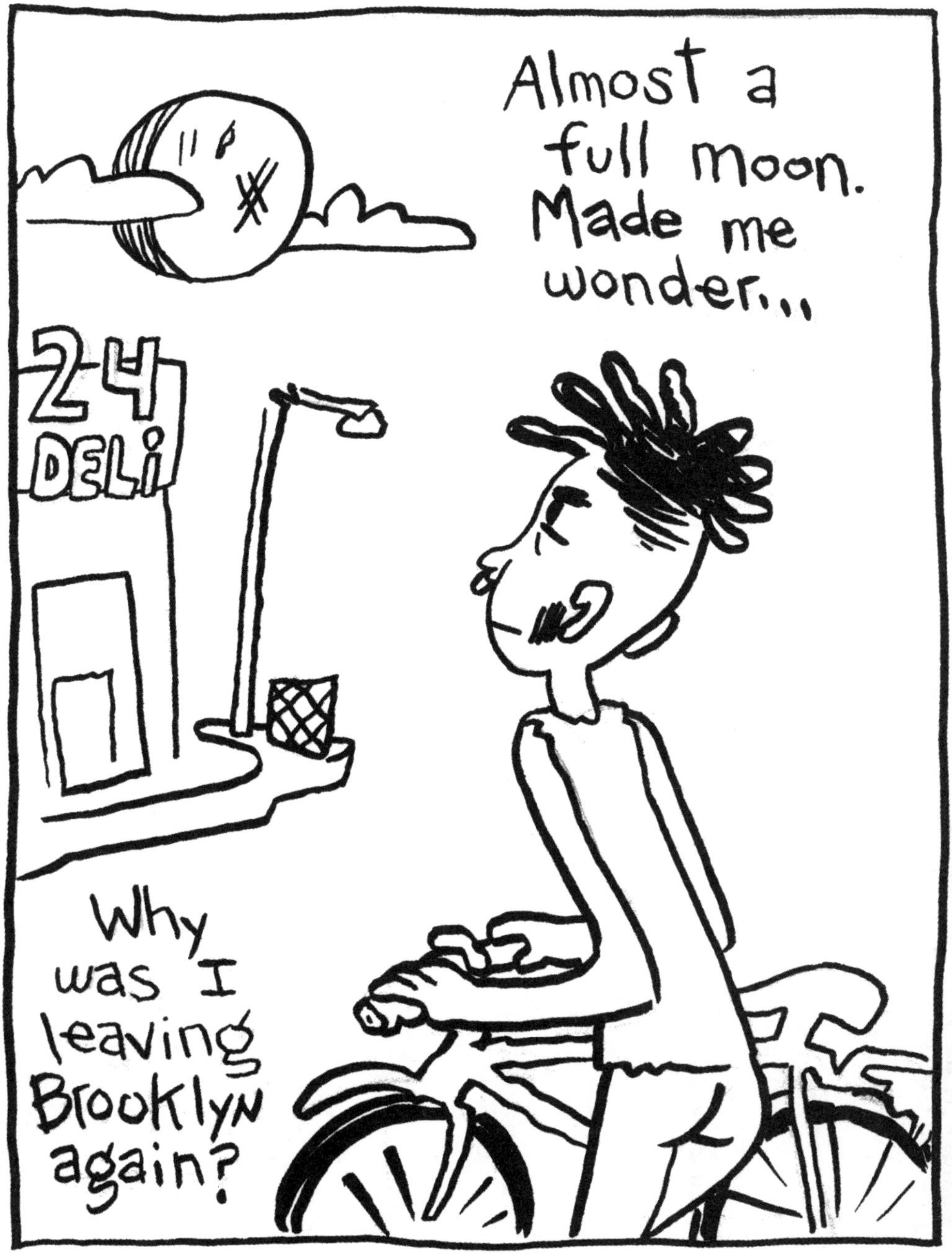
Almost a full moon. Made me wonder...
24 DELI
Why was I leaving Brooklyn again?

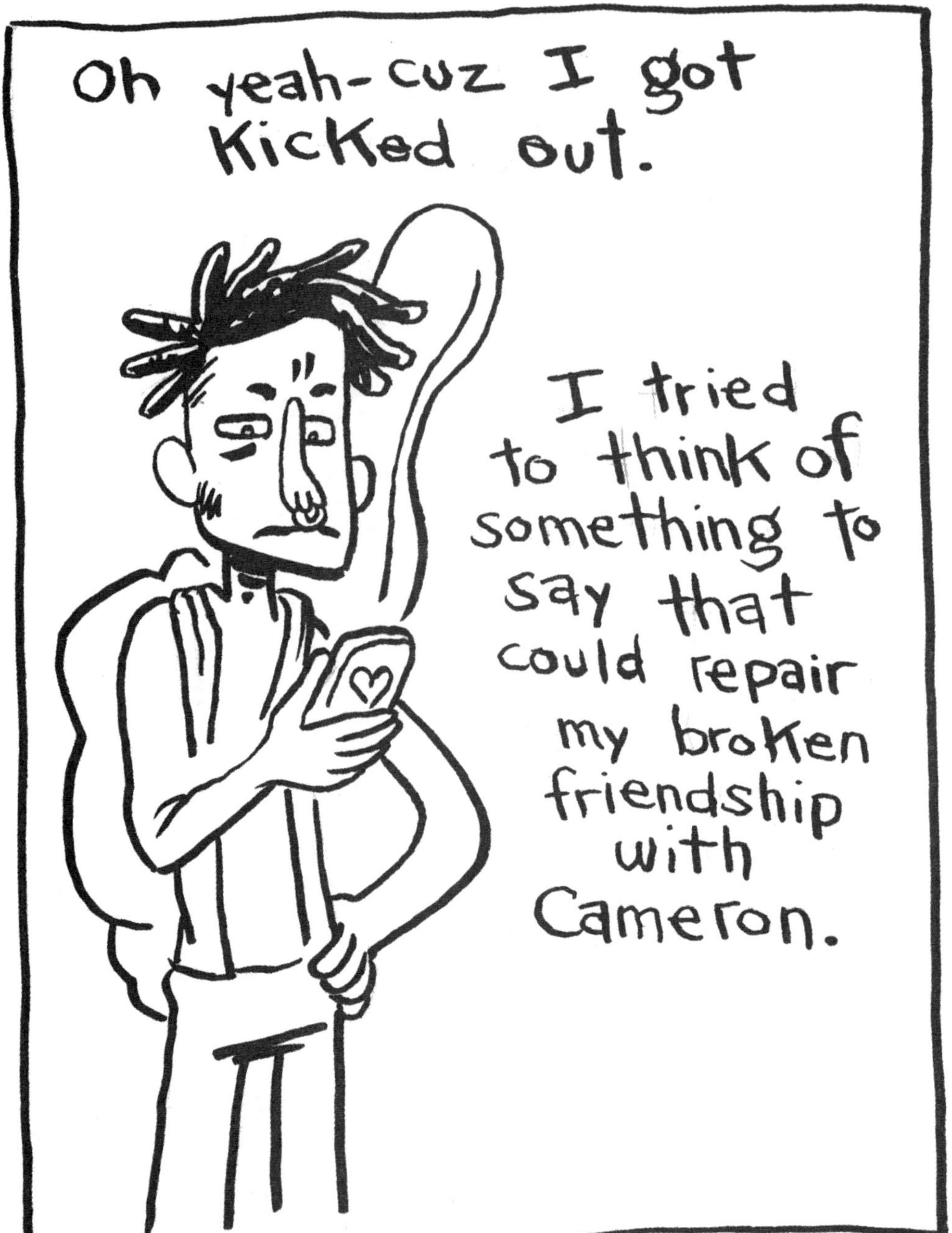
Oh yeah-cuz I got Kicked out.
I tried to think of something to say that could repair my broken friendship with Cameron.

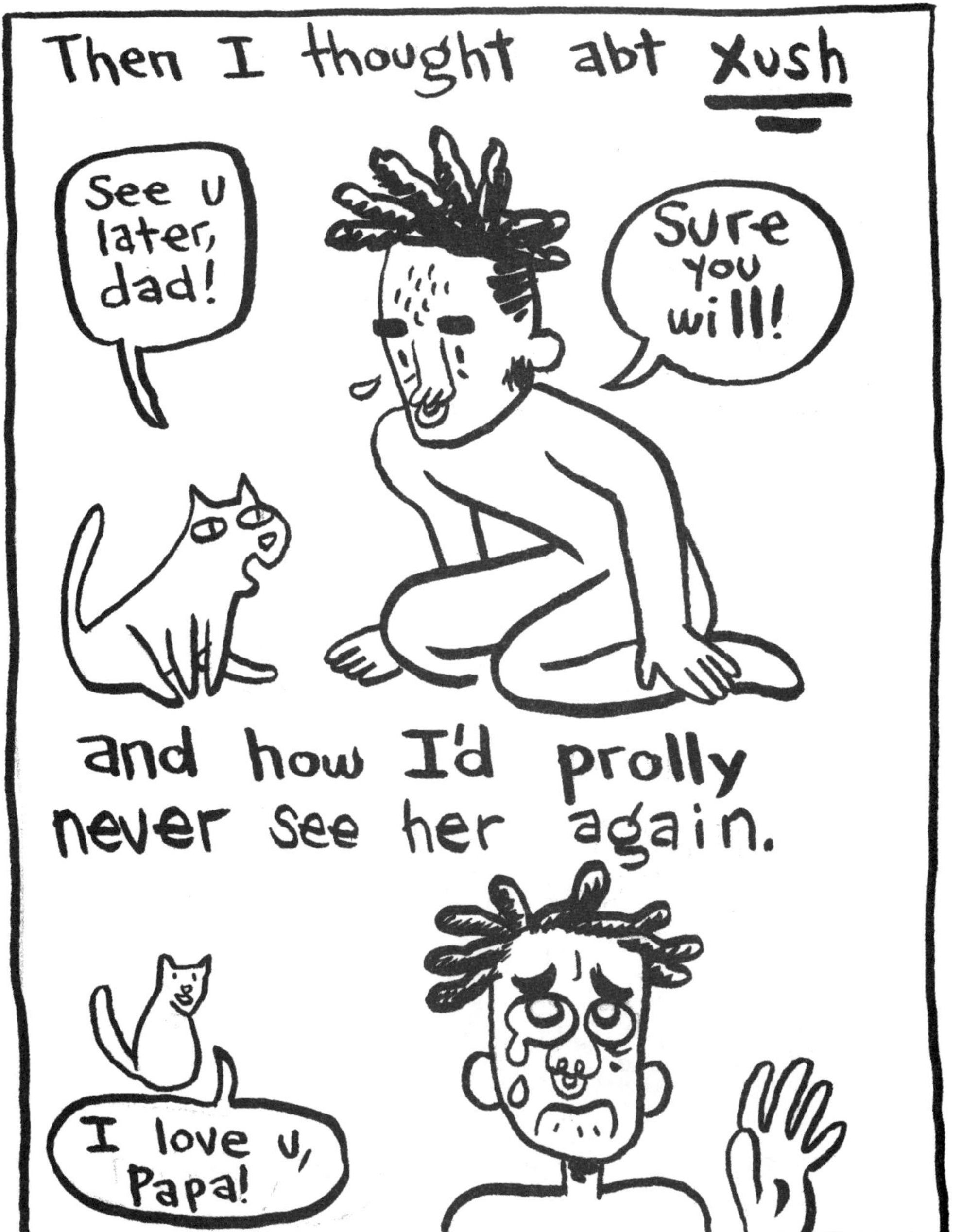
Then I thought abt Xush
See u later, dad!
Sure you will!
and how I'd prolly never see her again.
I love u, Papa!

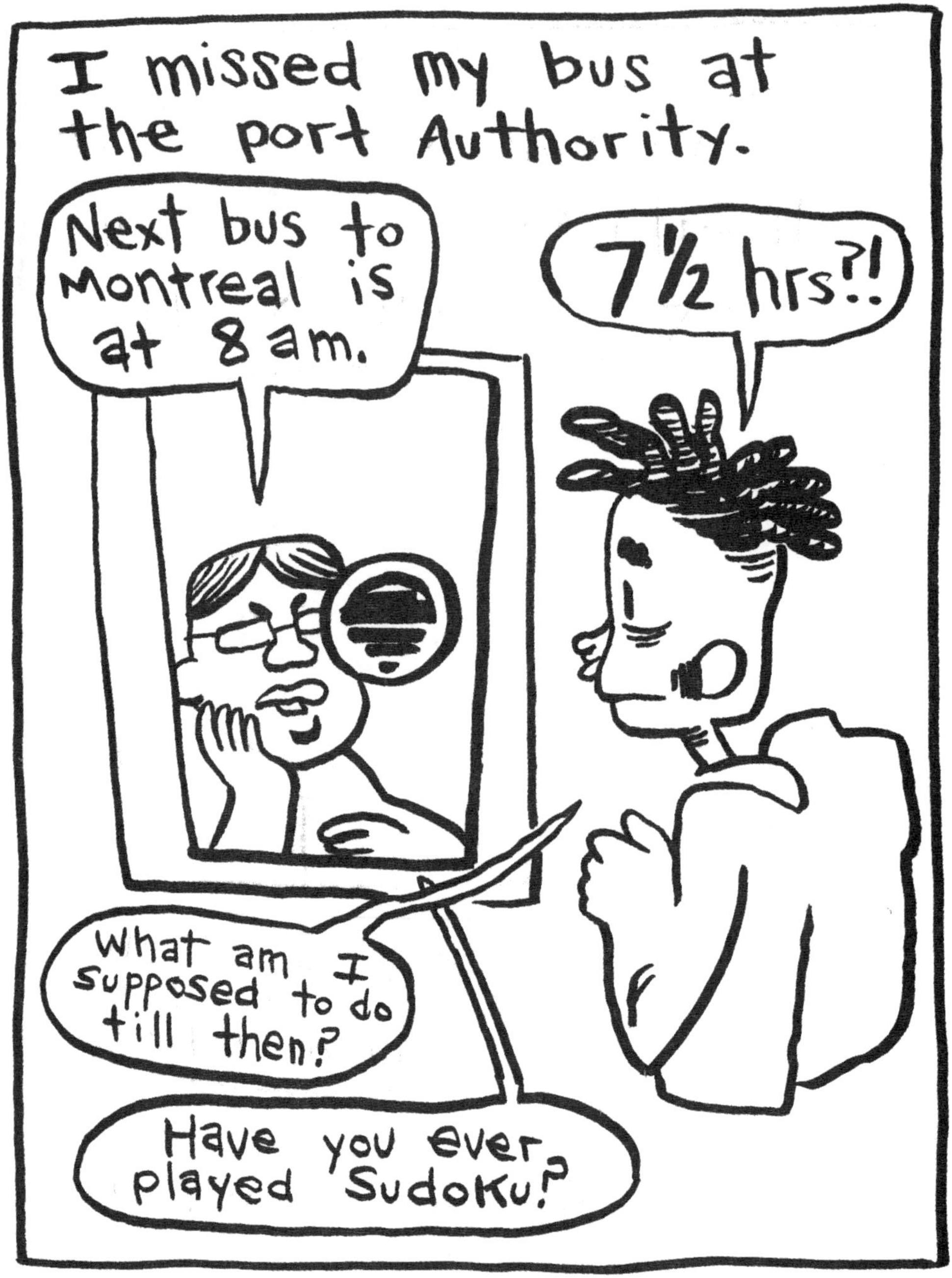
I missed my bus at the port Authority.
Next bus to Montreal is at 8 am.
7½ hrs?!
What am I supposed to do till then?
Have you ever played Sudoku?

YESTERDAY by Brother Malcolm

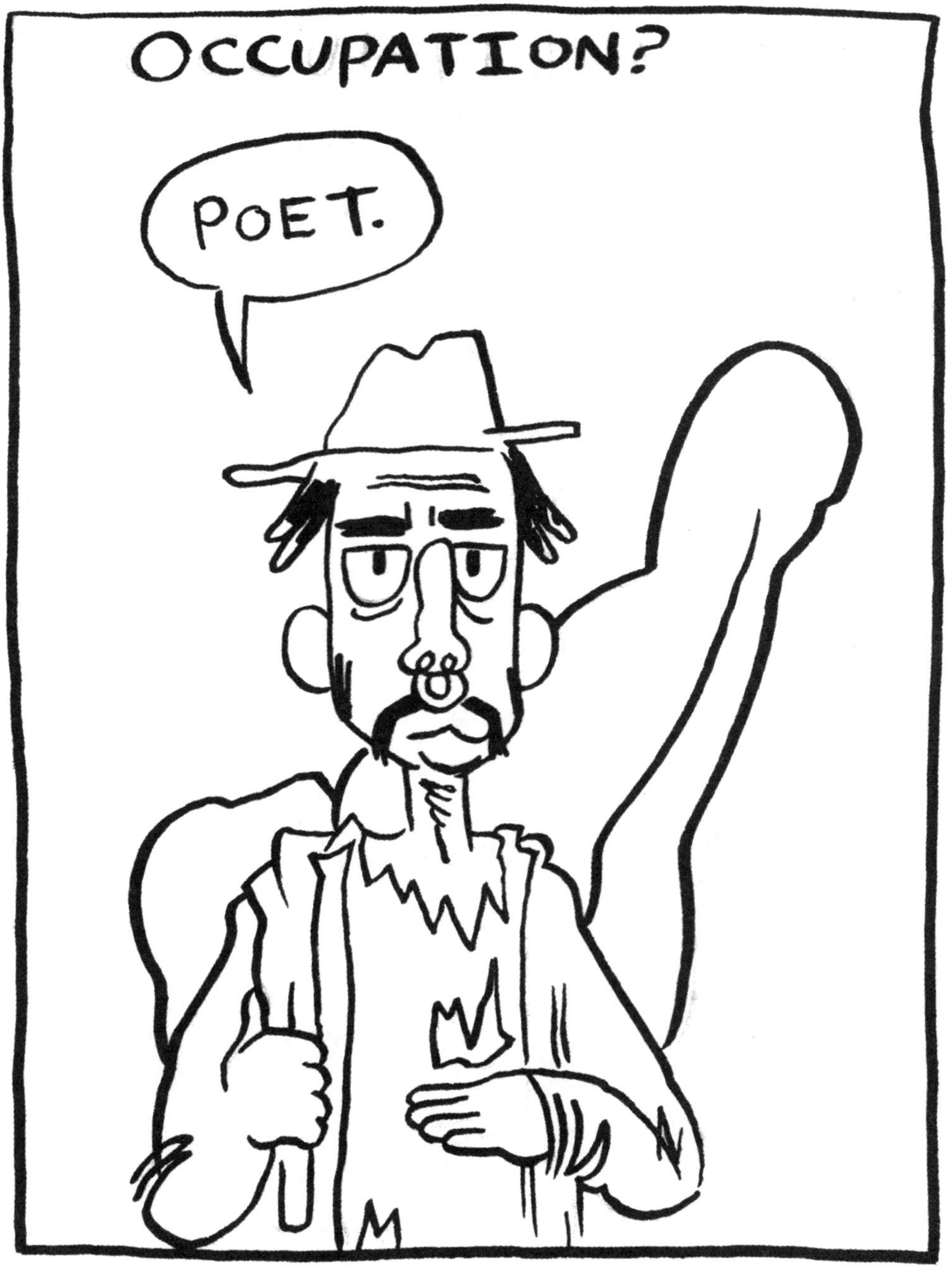
OCCUPATION?
POET.

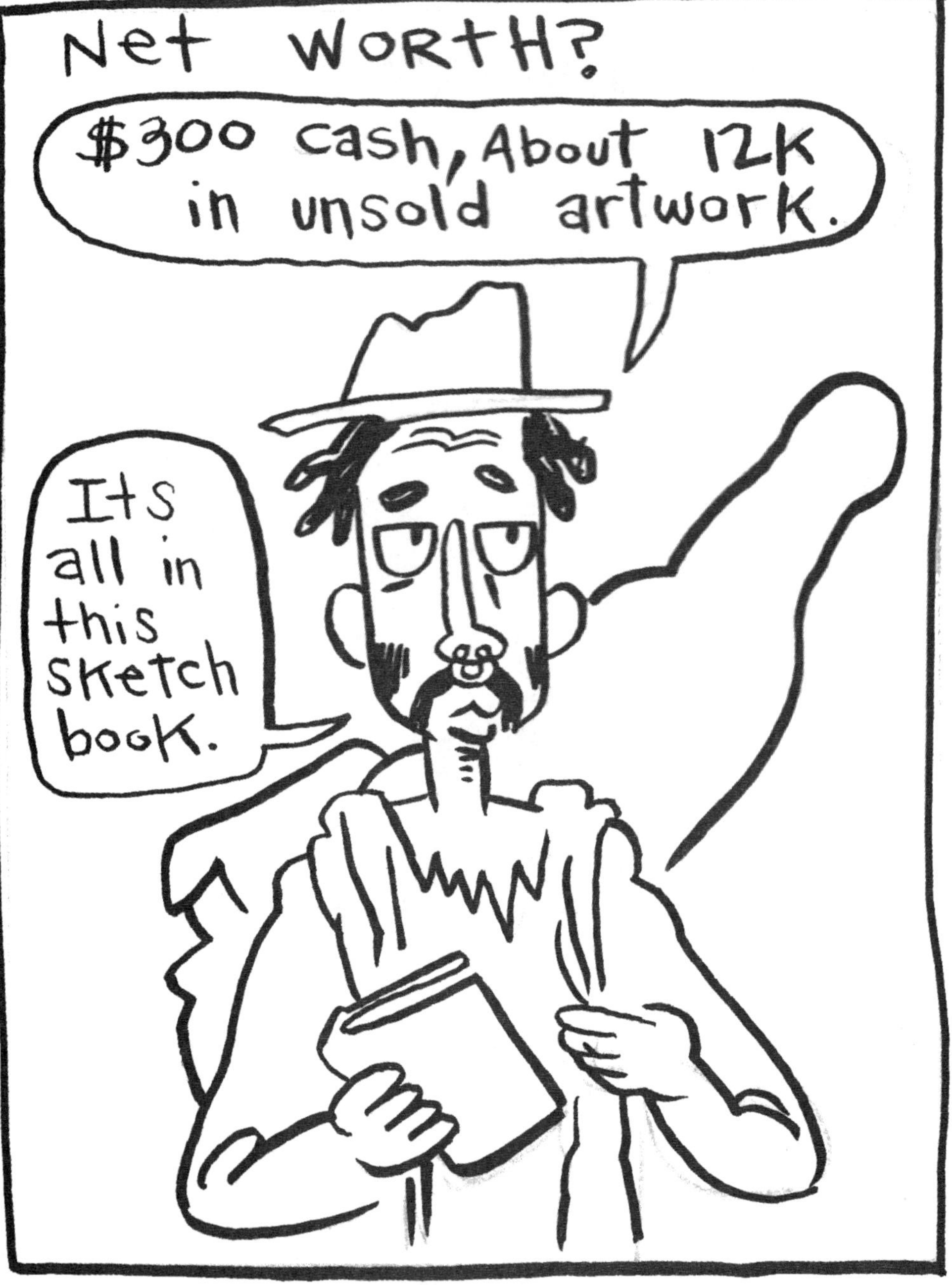
Net WORTH?
$300 cash, About 12K in unsold artwork.
Its all in this sketch book.

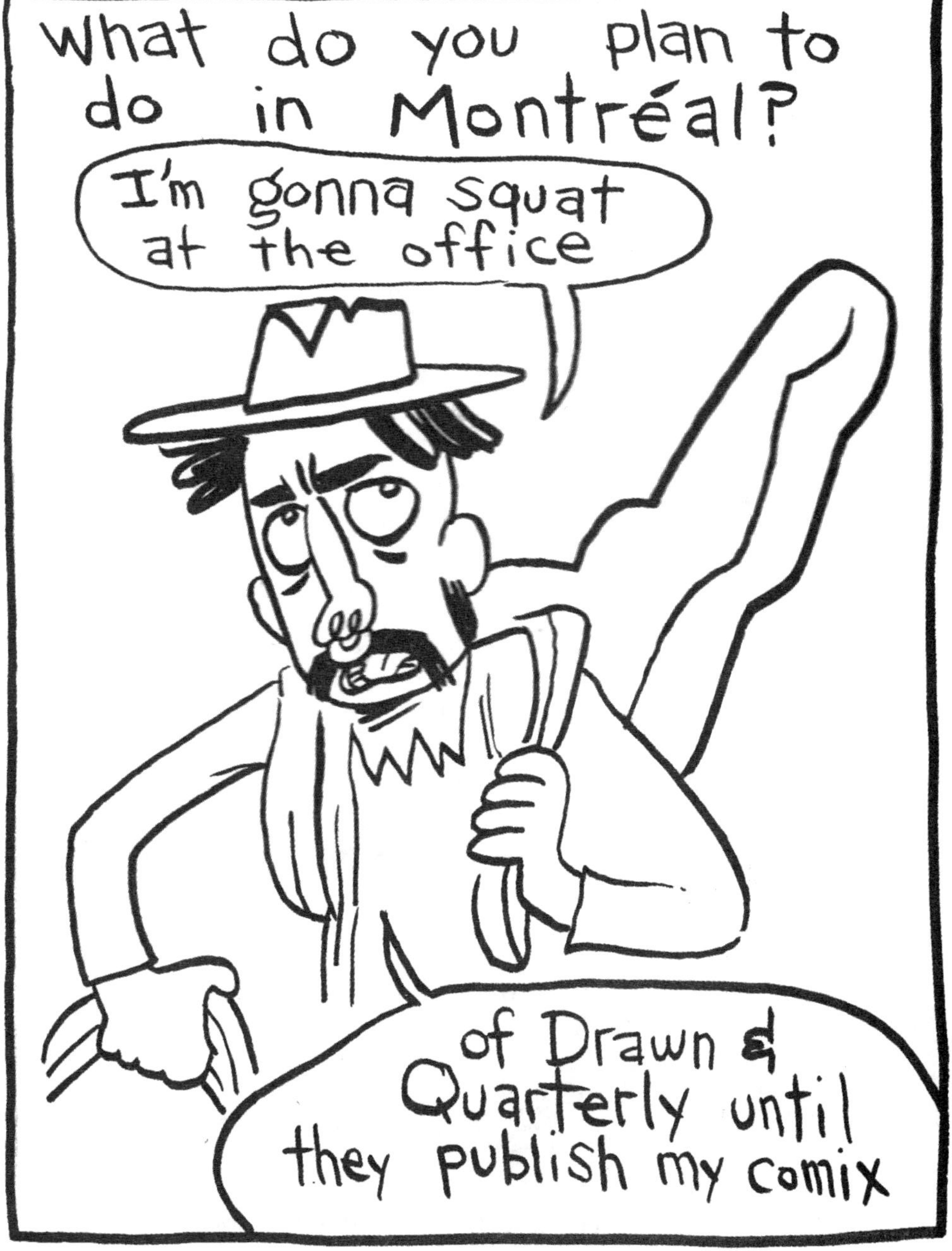
What do you plan to do in Montréal?
I'm gonna squat at the office
of Drawn & Quarterly until they publish my comix

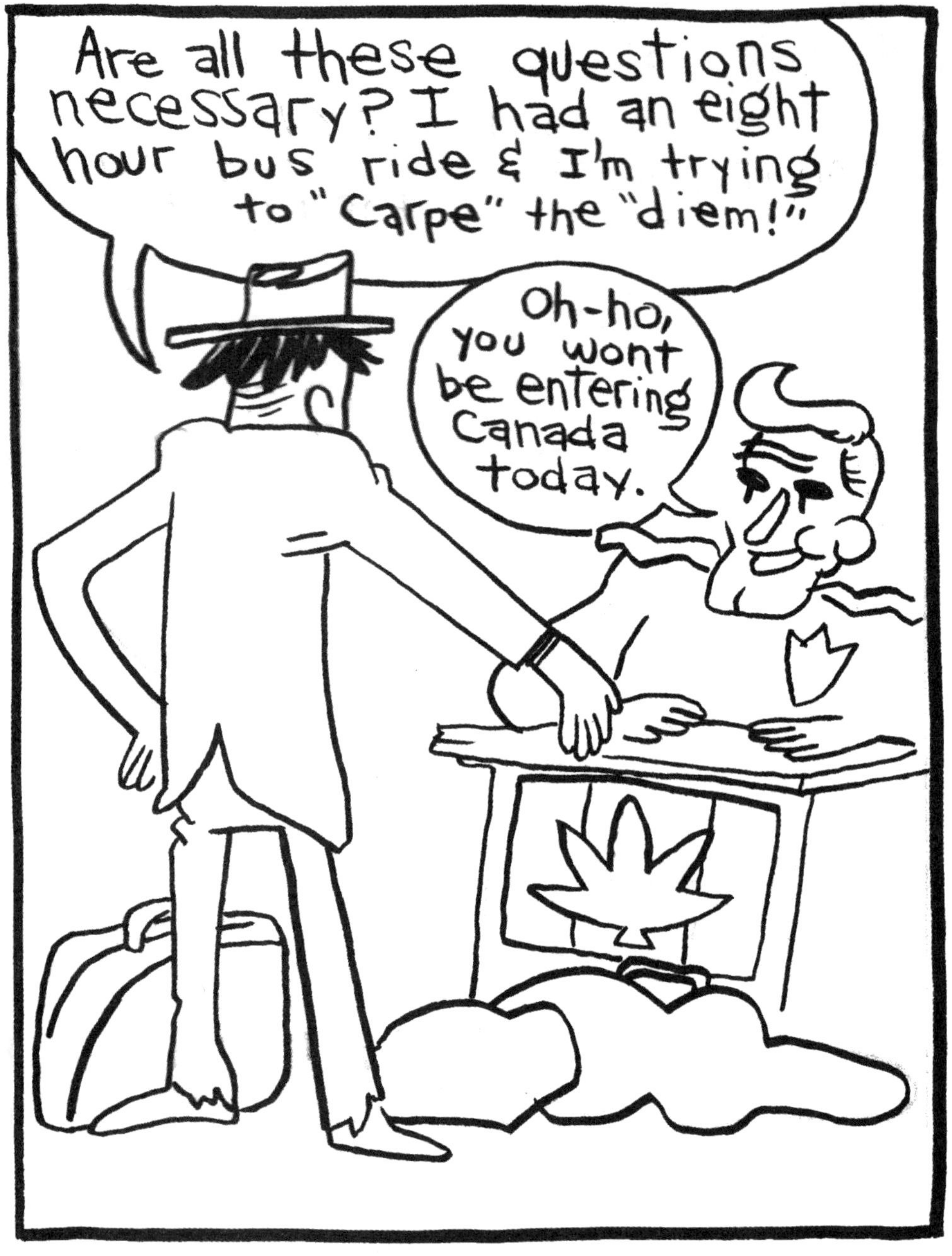
Are all these questions necessary? I had an eight hour bus ride & I'm trying to "Carpe" the "diem!"
Oh-ho, you wont be entering Canada today.

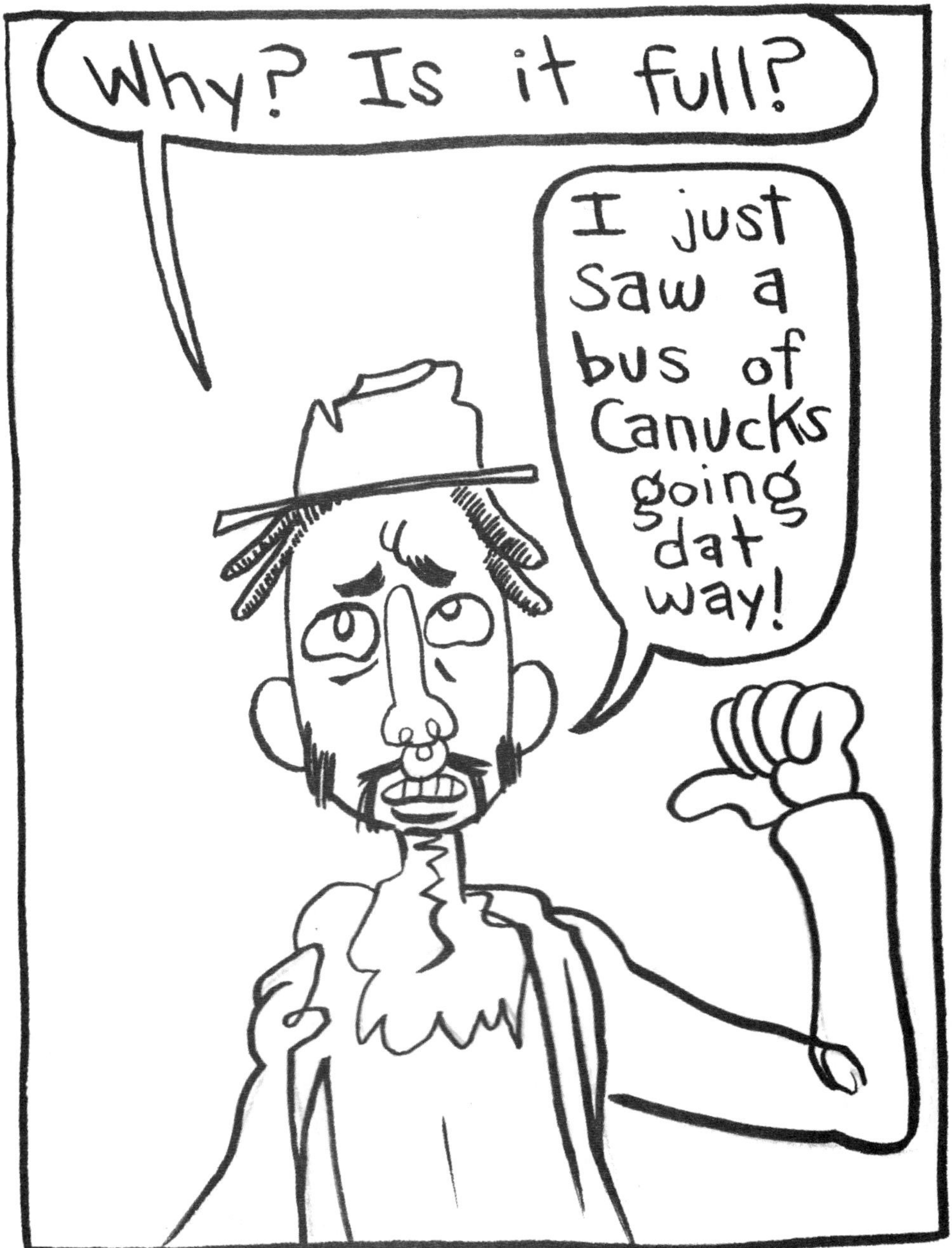
Why? Is it full?
I just saw a bus of Canucks going dat way!

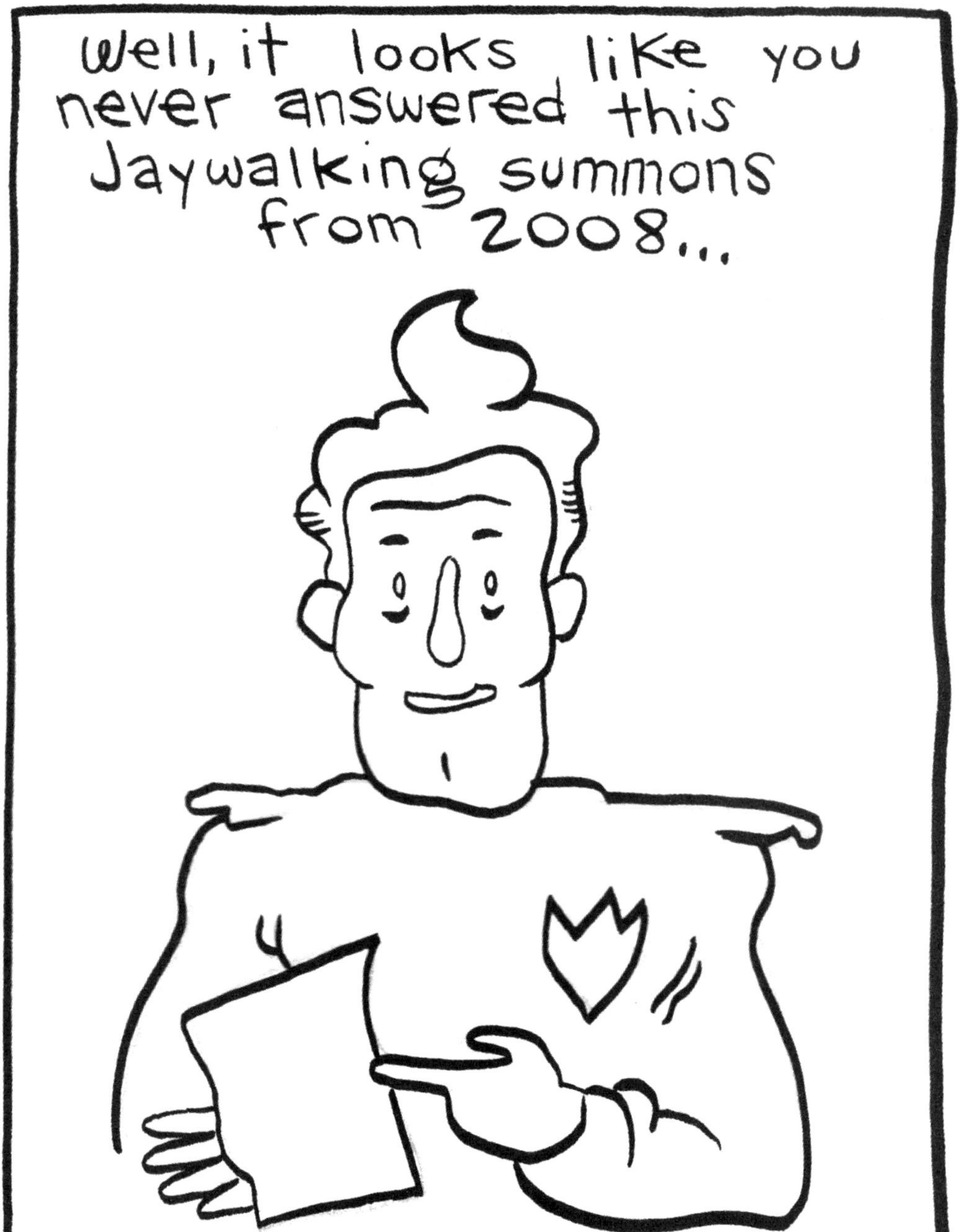
Well, it looks like you never answered this Jaywalking summons from 2008...

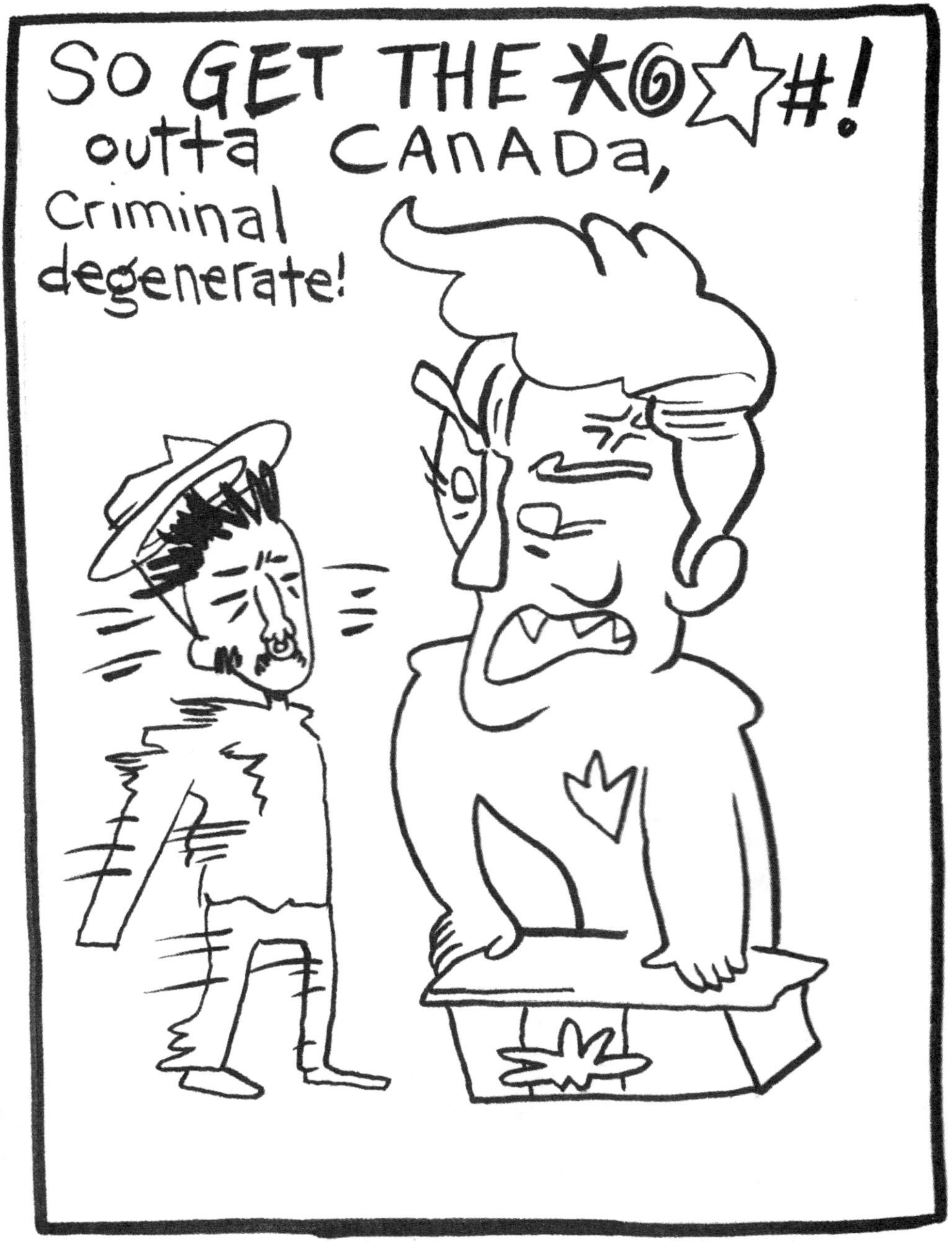
SO GET THE *@☆#!
outta CANADA,
Criminal degenerate!

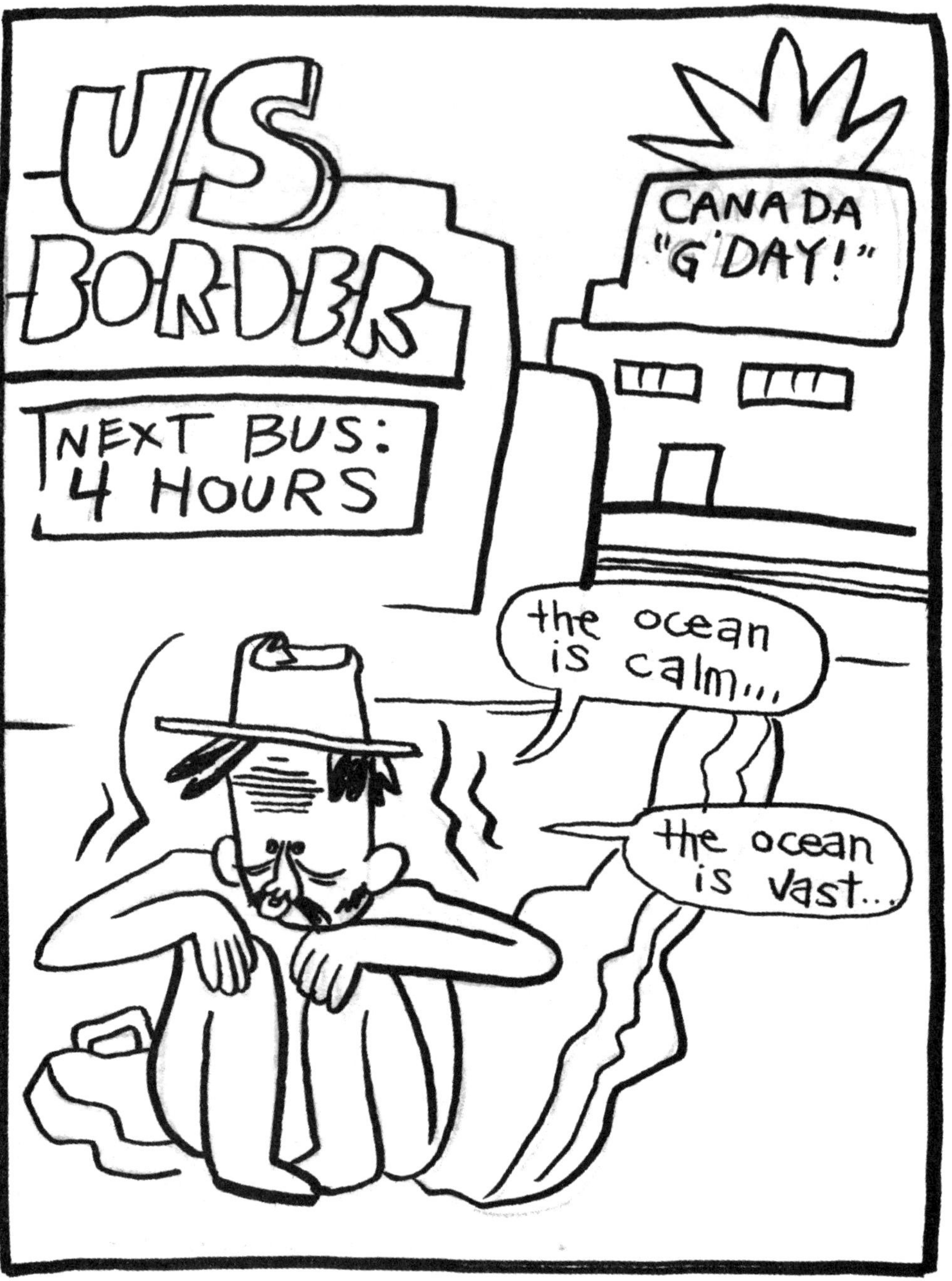
US BORDER
NEXT BUS: 4 HOURS
CANADA "G'DAY!"
the ocean is calm...
the ocean is vast...

YESTERDAY BY BROTHER Malcolm

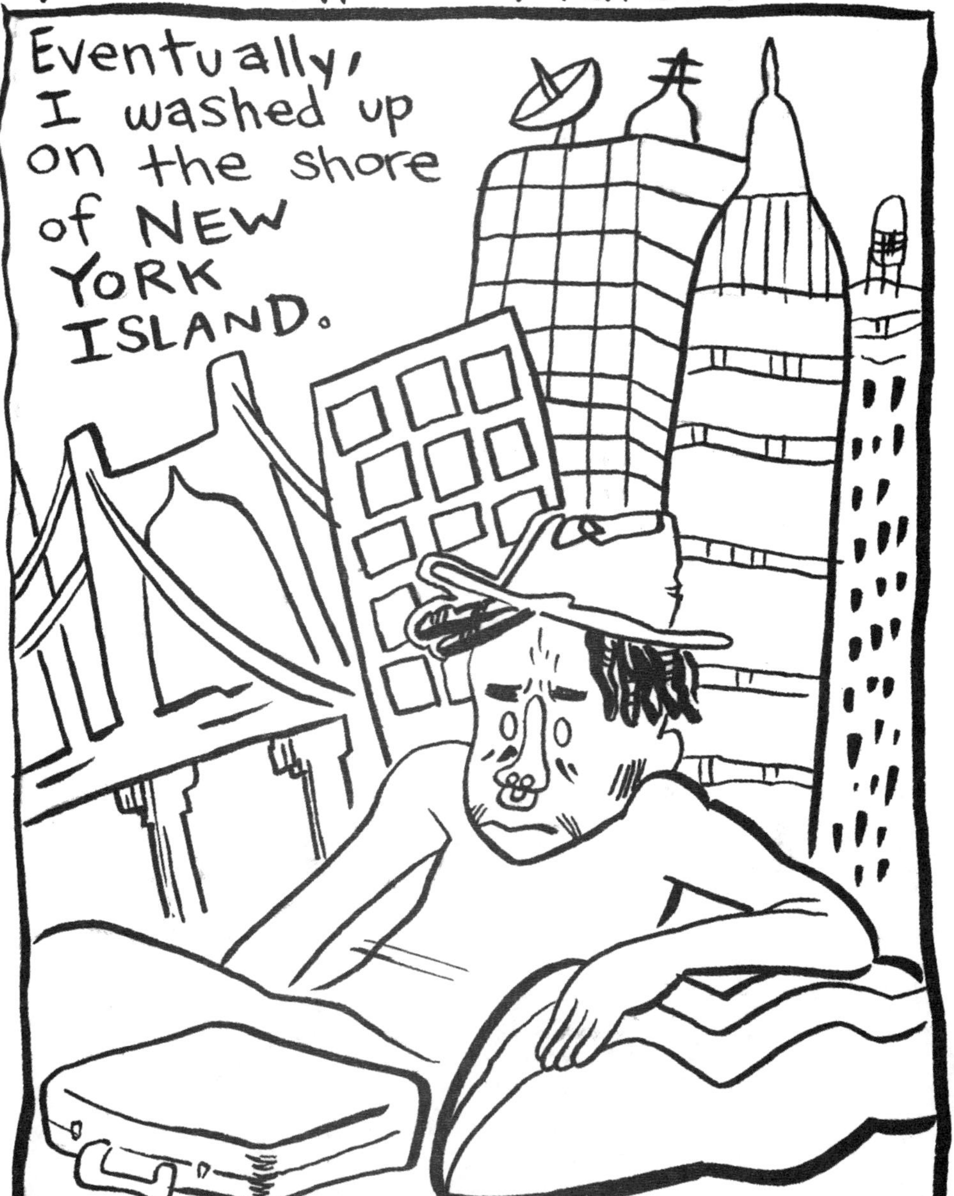

Eventually, I washed up on the shore of NEW YORK ISLAND.

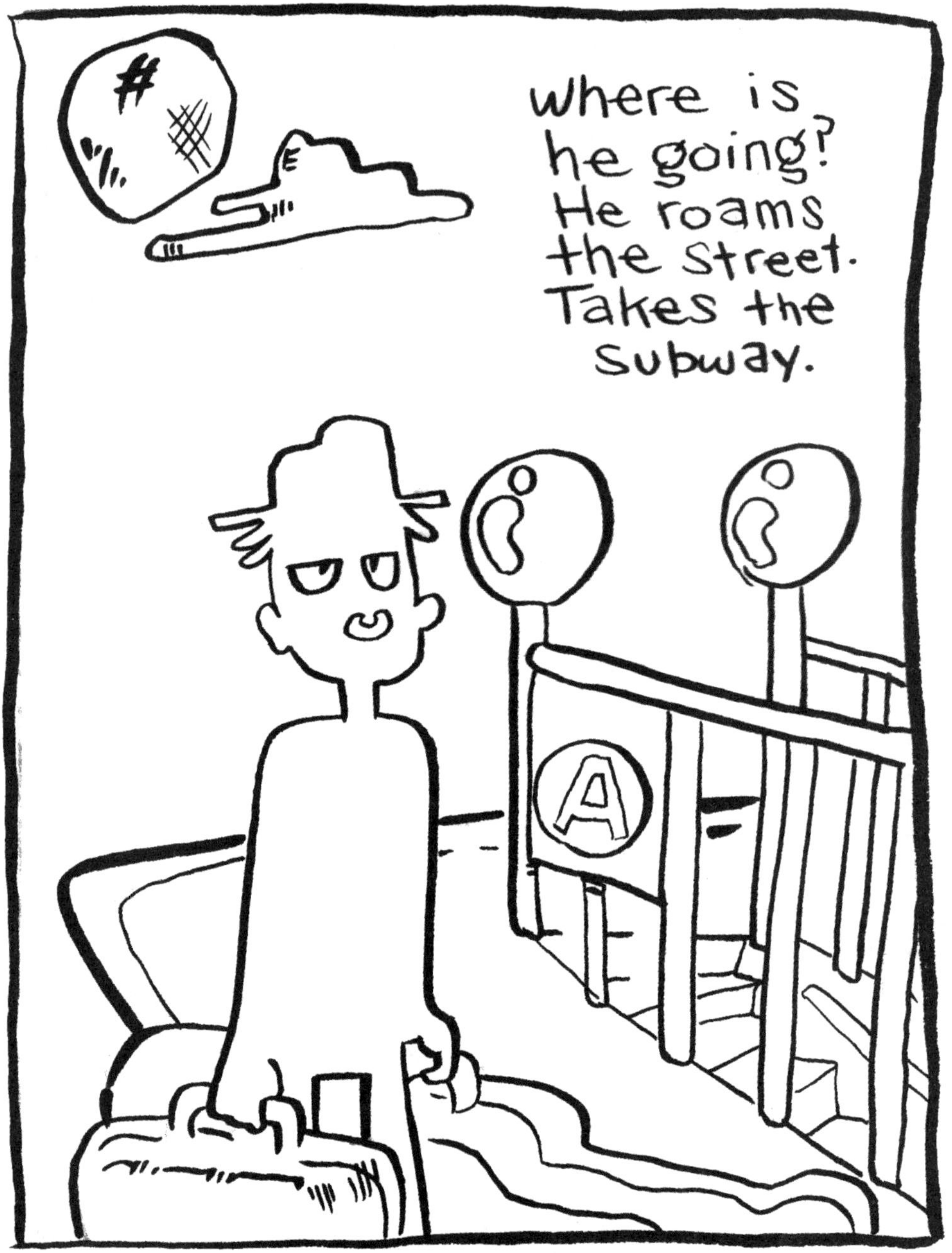
where is he going? He roams the Street. Takes the subway.
A

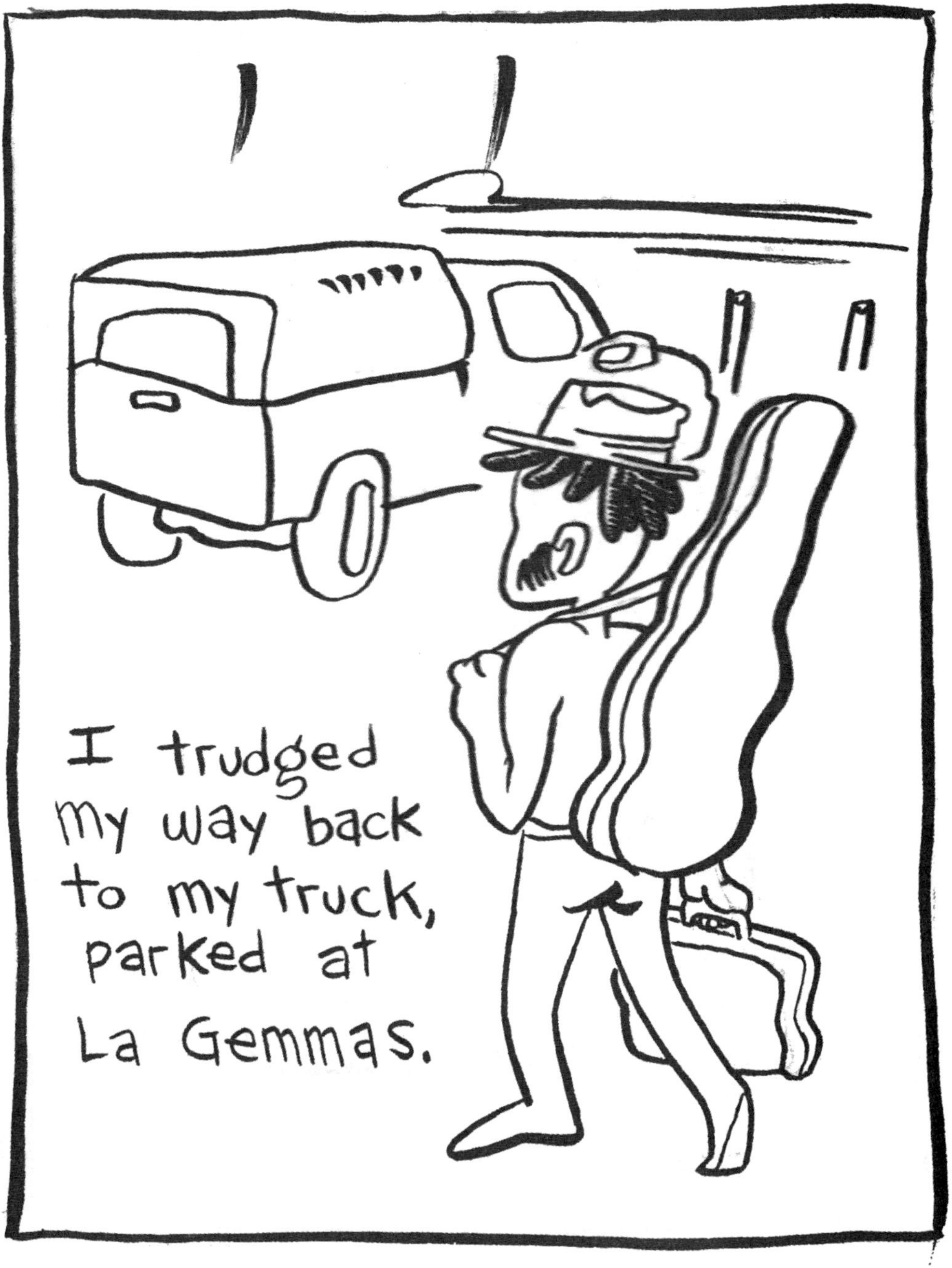
I trudged my way back to my truck, parked at La Gemmas.

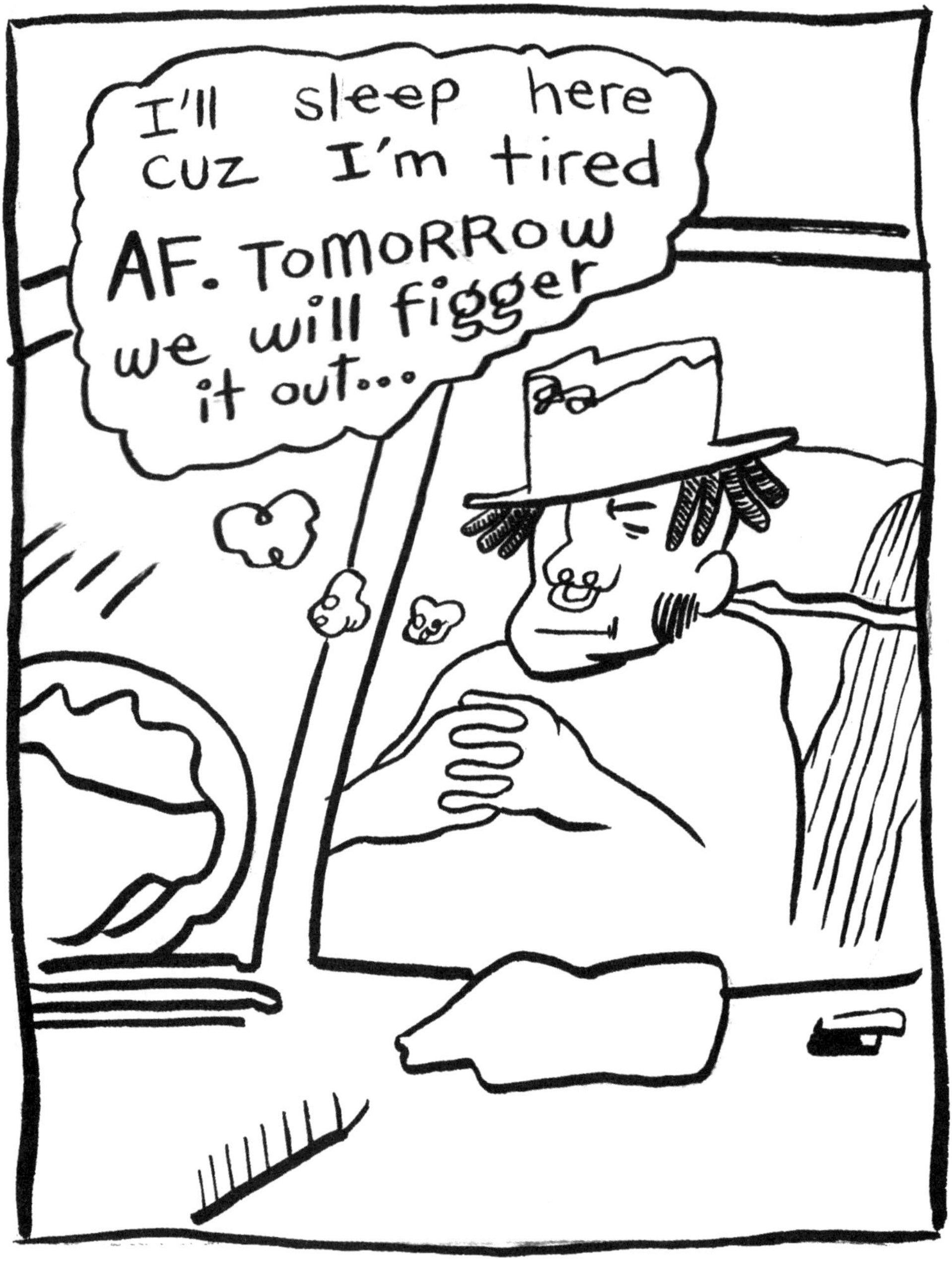
I'll sleep here cuz I'm tired AF. TOMORROW we will figger it out...

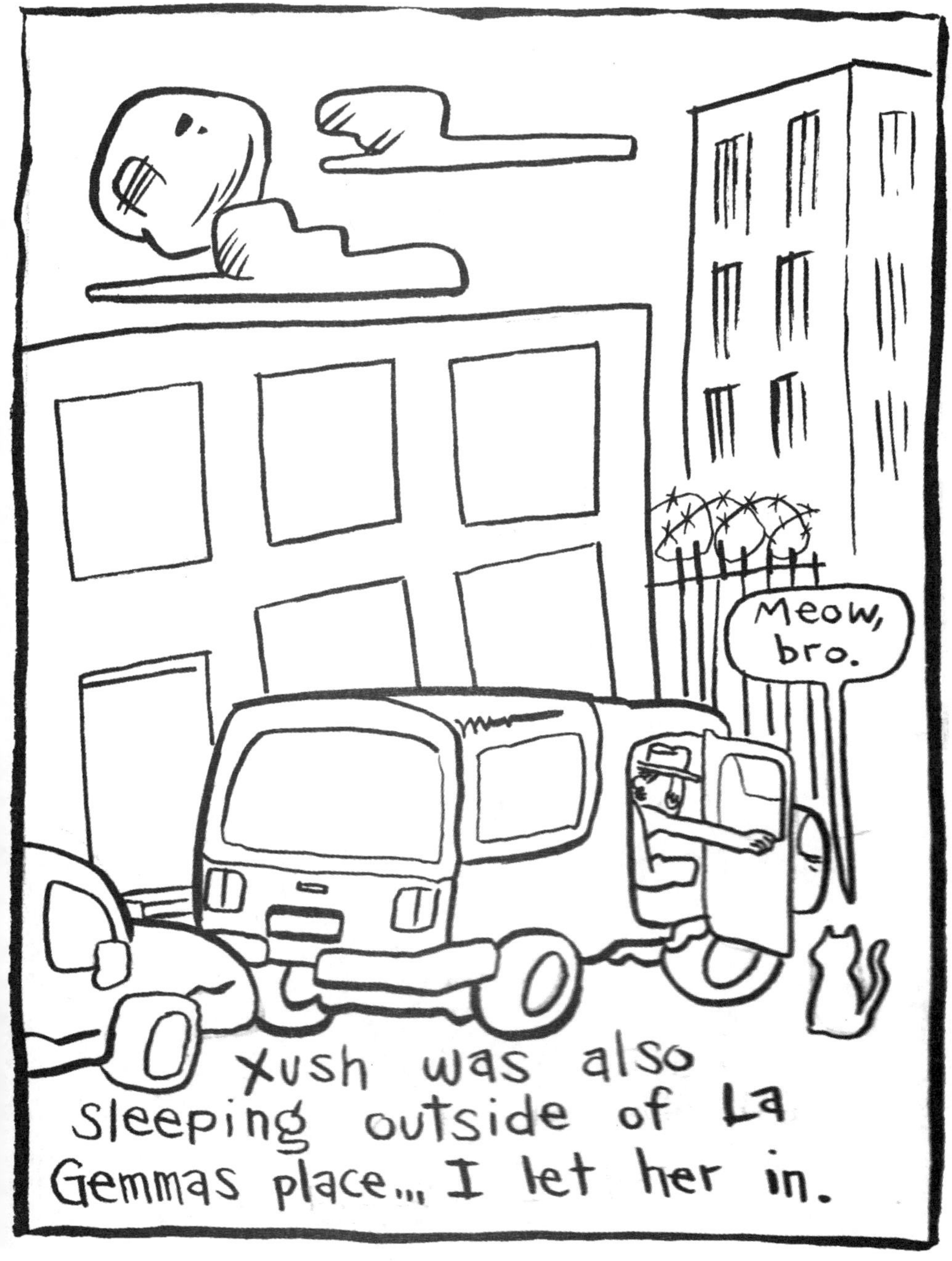
Meow, bro.
Xush was also sleeping outside of La Gemmas place... I let her in.

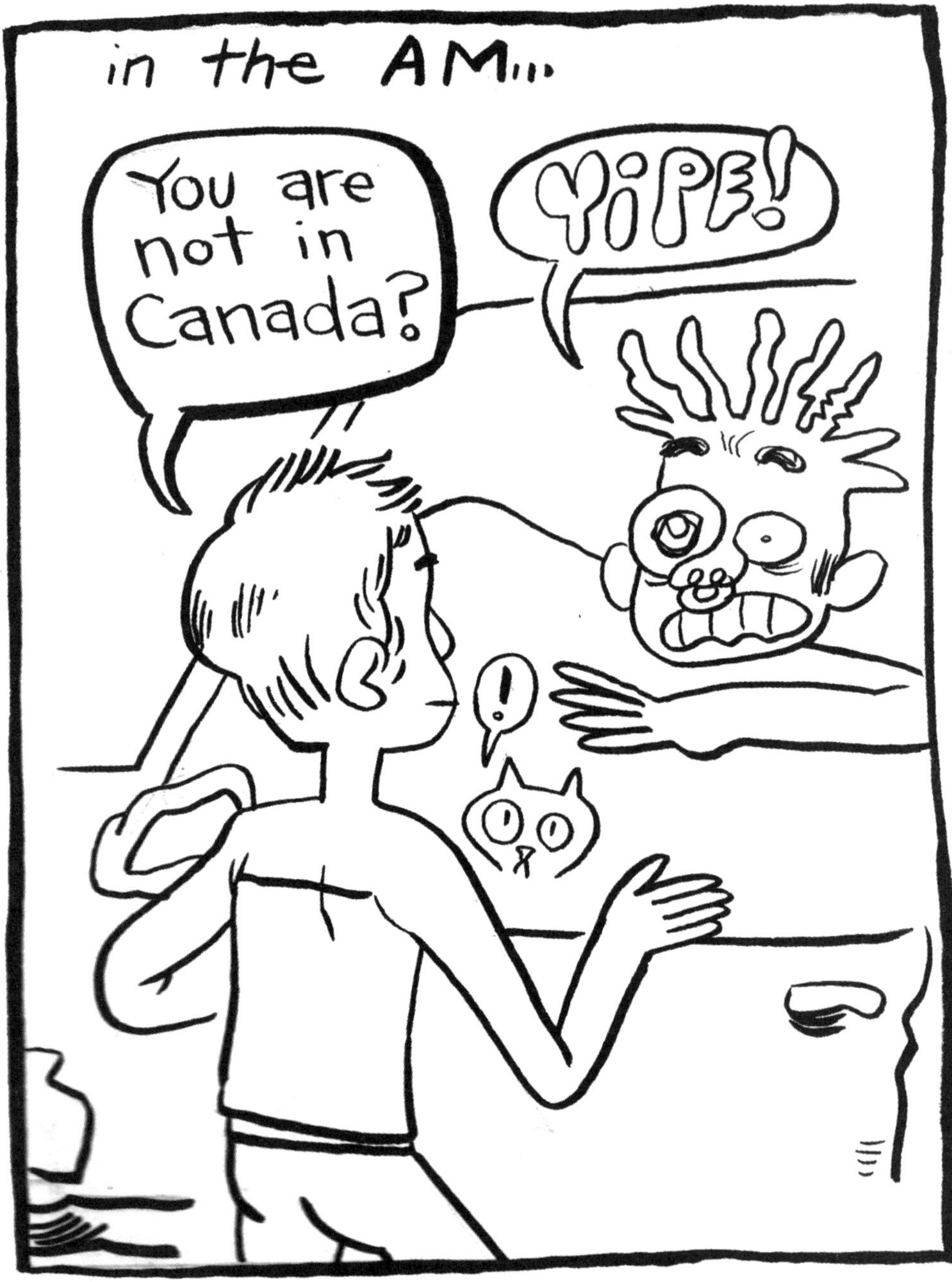
in the AM...
You are not in Canada?
YIPE!
!

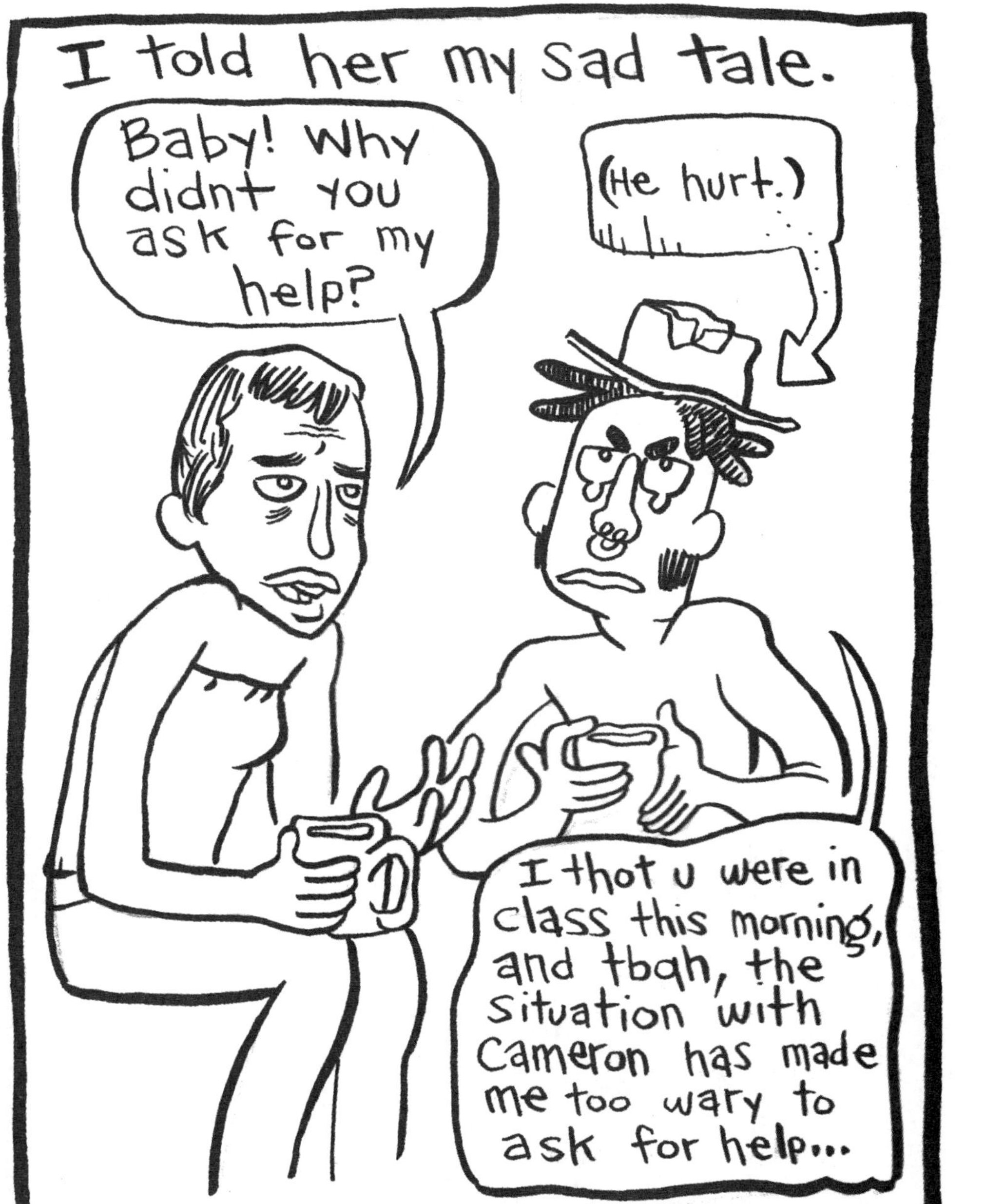
I told her my sad tale.
Baby! Why didnt you ask for my help?
(He hurt.)
I thot u were in class this morning, and tbqh, the situation with Cameron has made me too wary to ask for help...

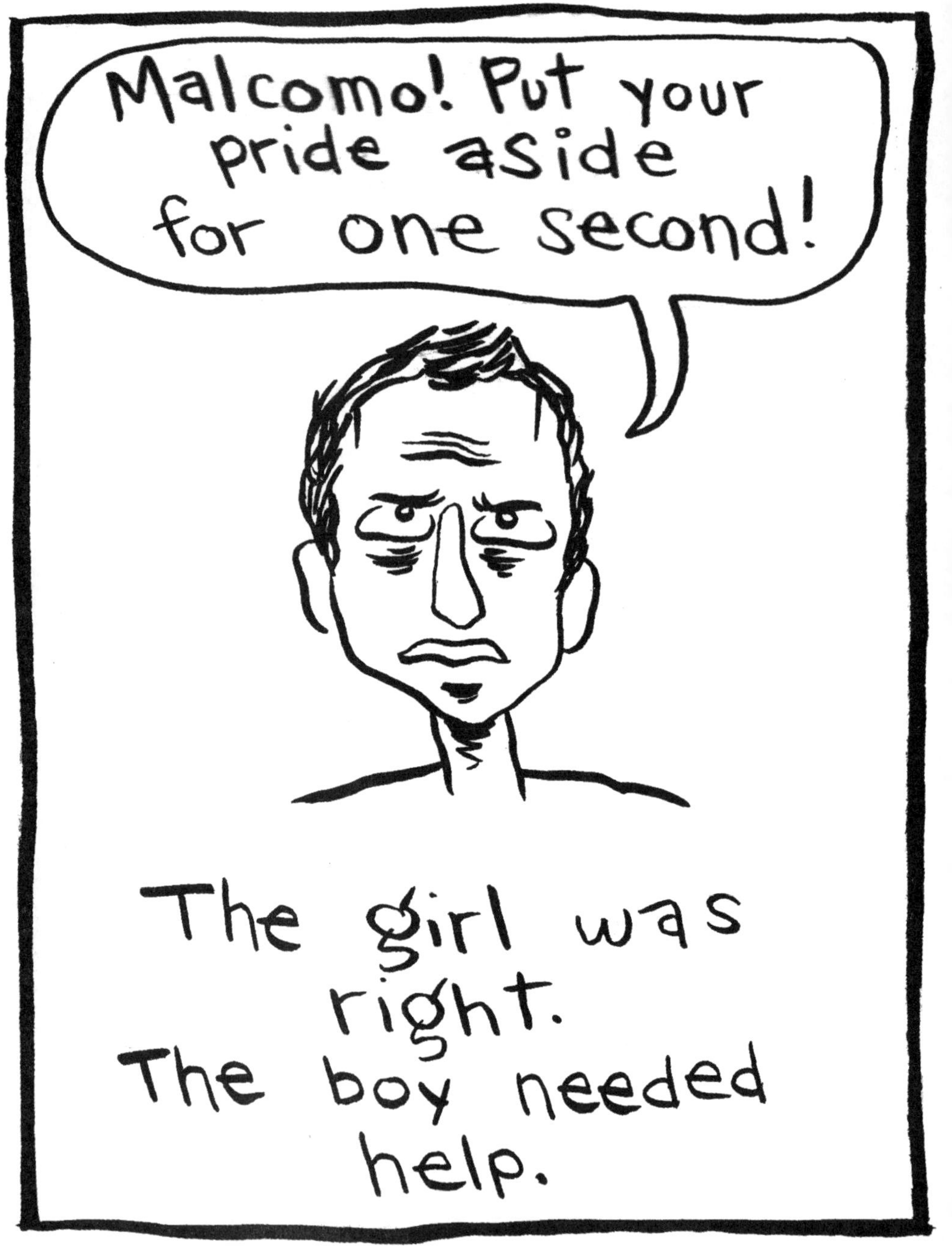
Malcomo! Put your pride aside for one second!
The girl was right. The boy needed help.

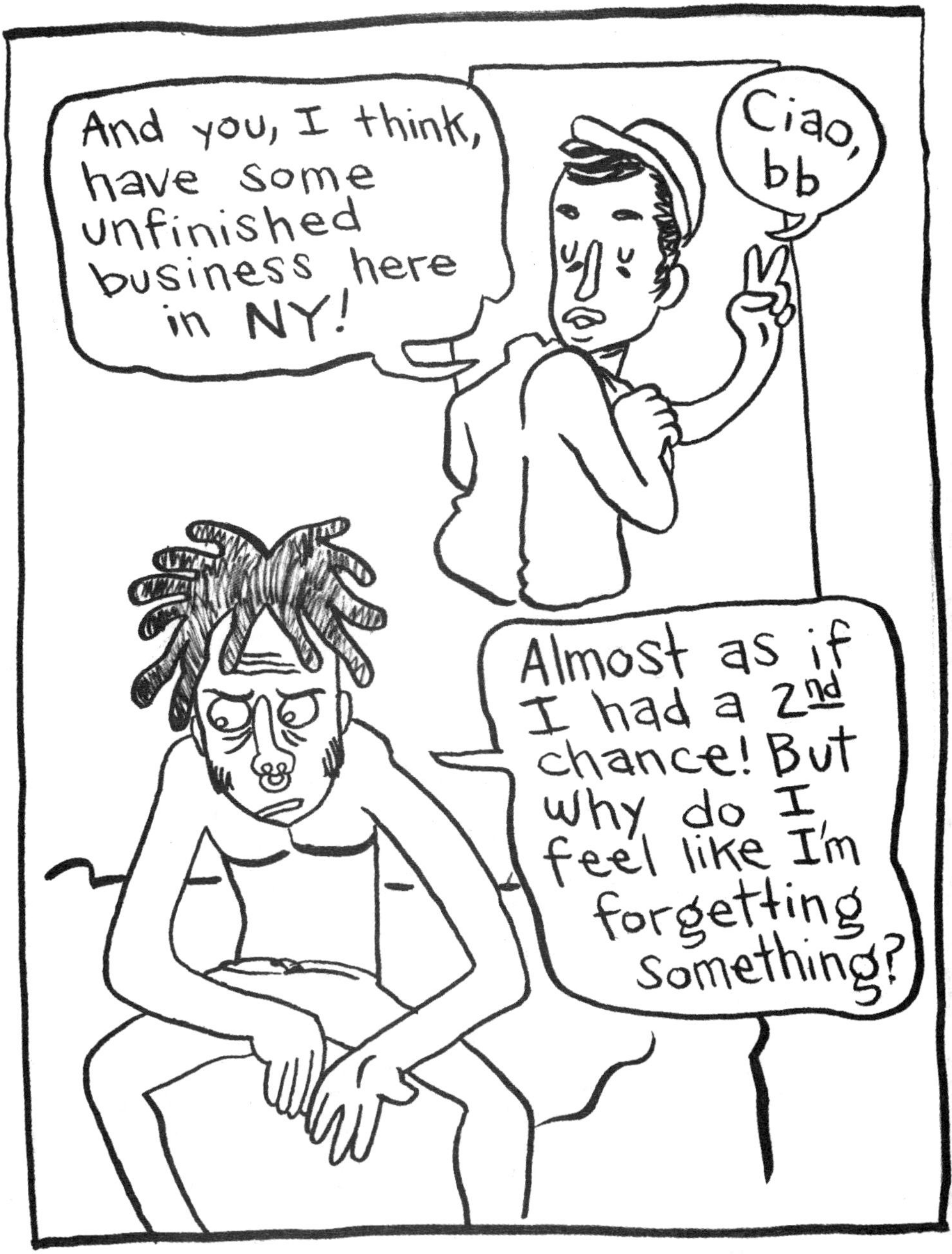
And you, I think, have some unfinished business here in NY!
Ciao, bb
Almost as if I had a 2nd chance! But why do I feel like I'm forgetting something?

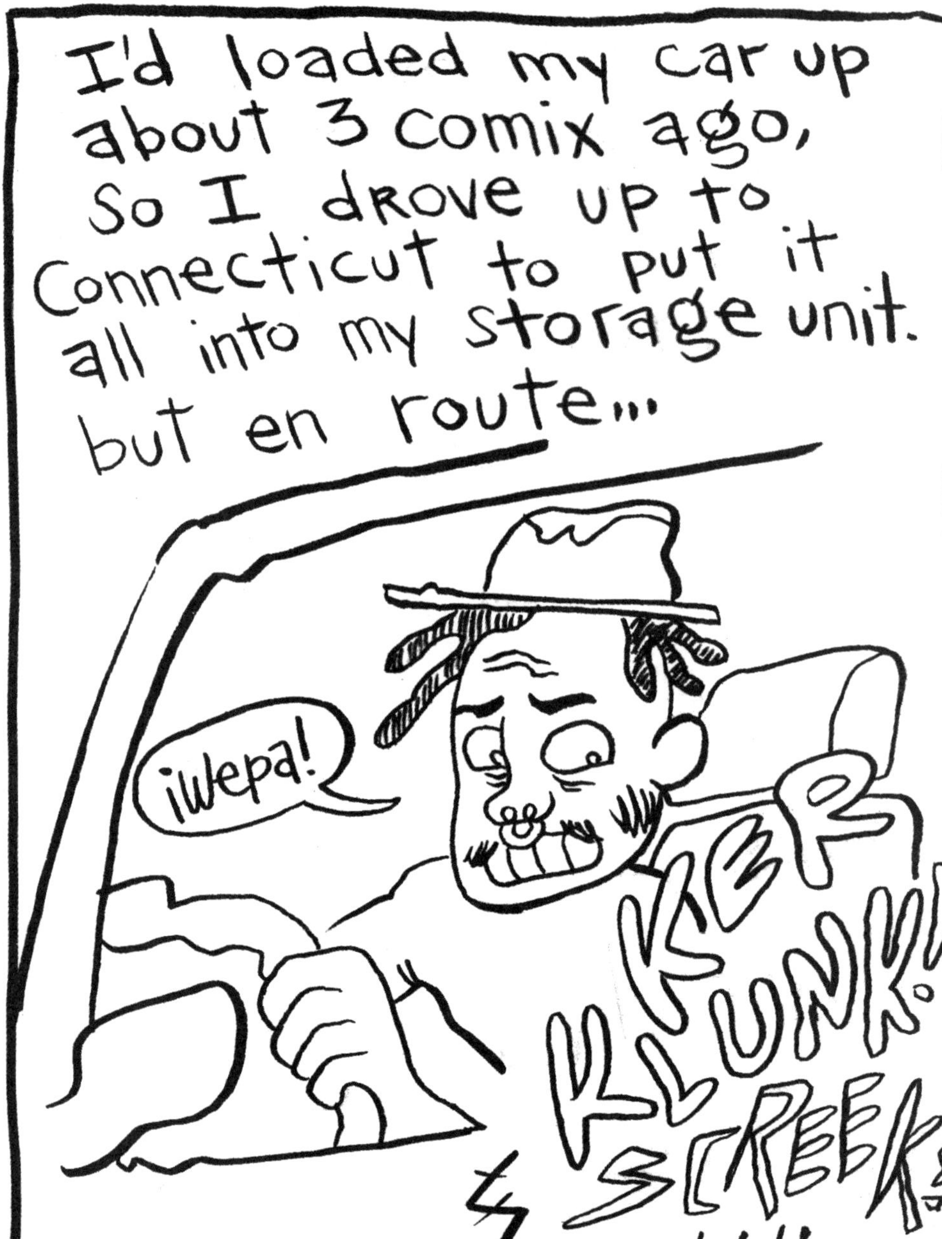
I'd loaded my car up about 3 comix ago, So I drove up to Connecticut to put it all into my storage unit. but en route...
¡Wepa!
KER KLUNK!
SCREEK!

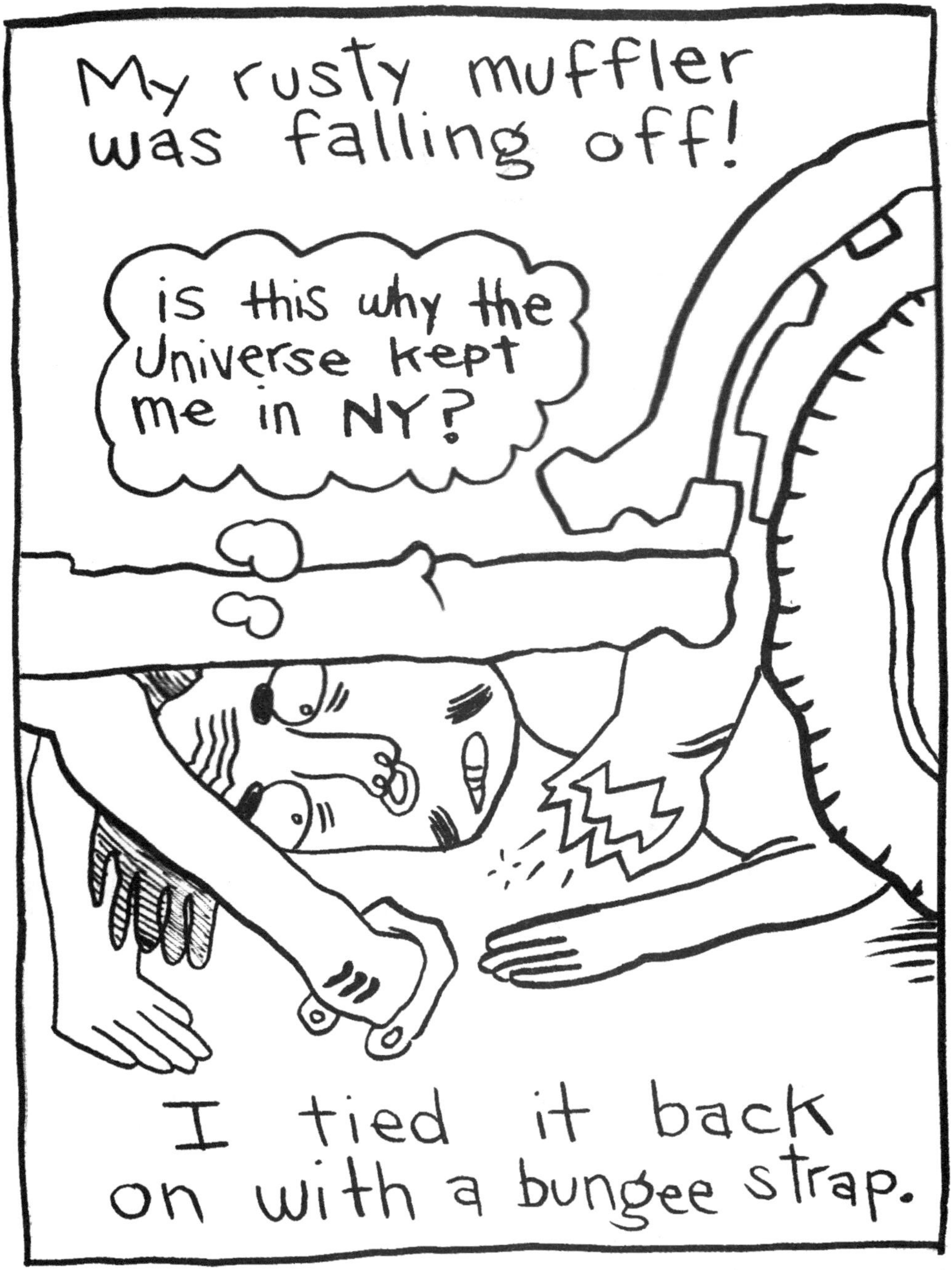
My rusty muffler was falling off!
is this why the Universe kept me in NY?
I tied it back on with a bungee strap.

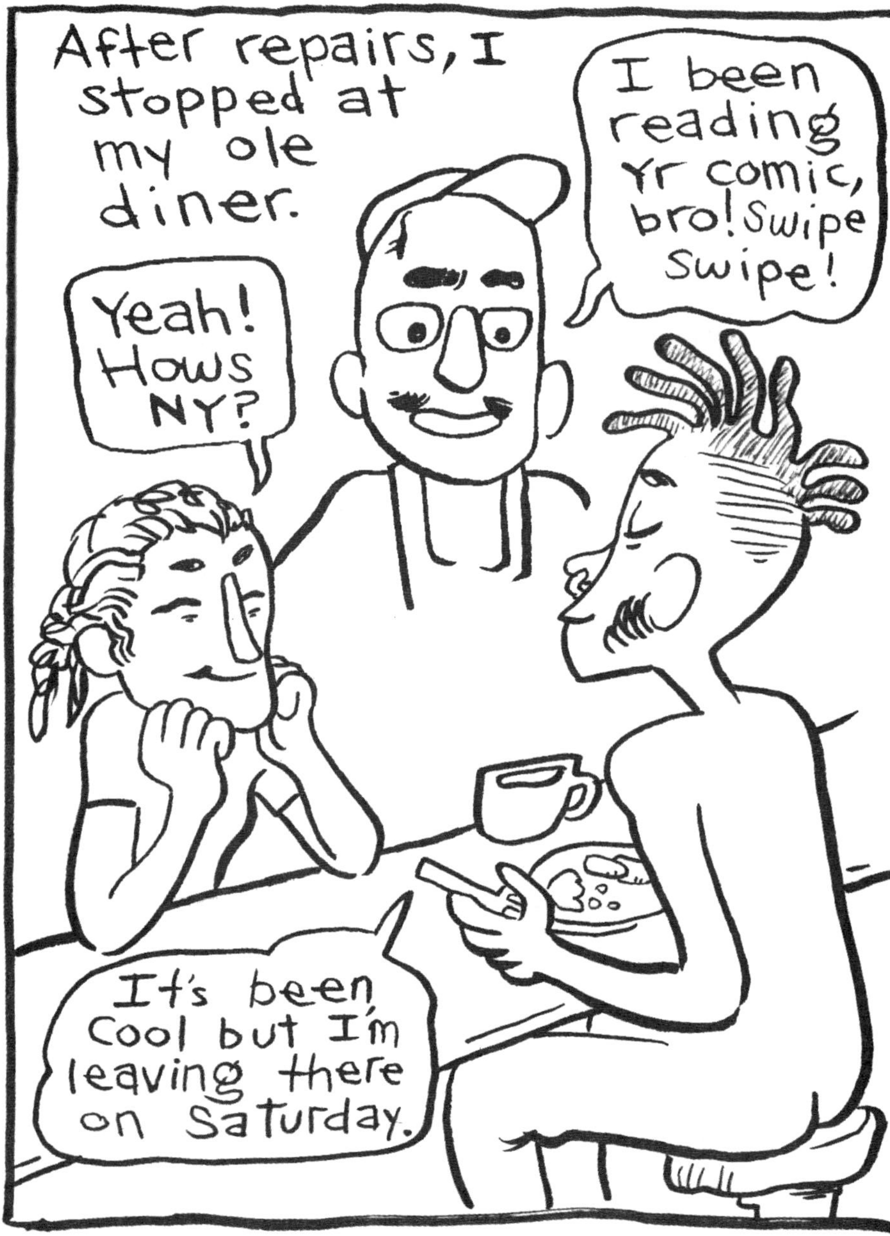
After repairs, I stopped at my ole diner.
I been reading yr comic, bro! Swipe Swipe!
Yeah! Hows NY?
It's been cool but I'm leaving there on Saturday.

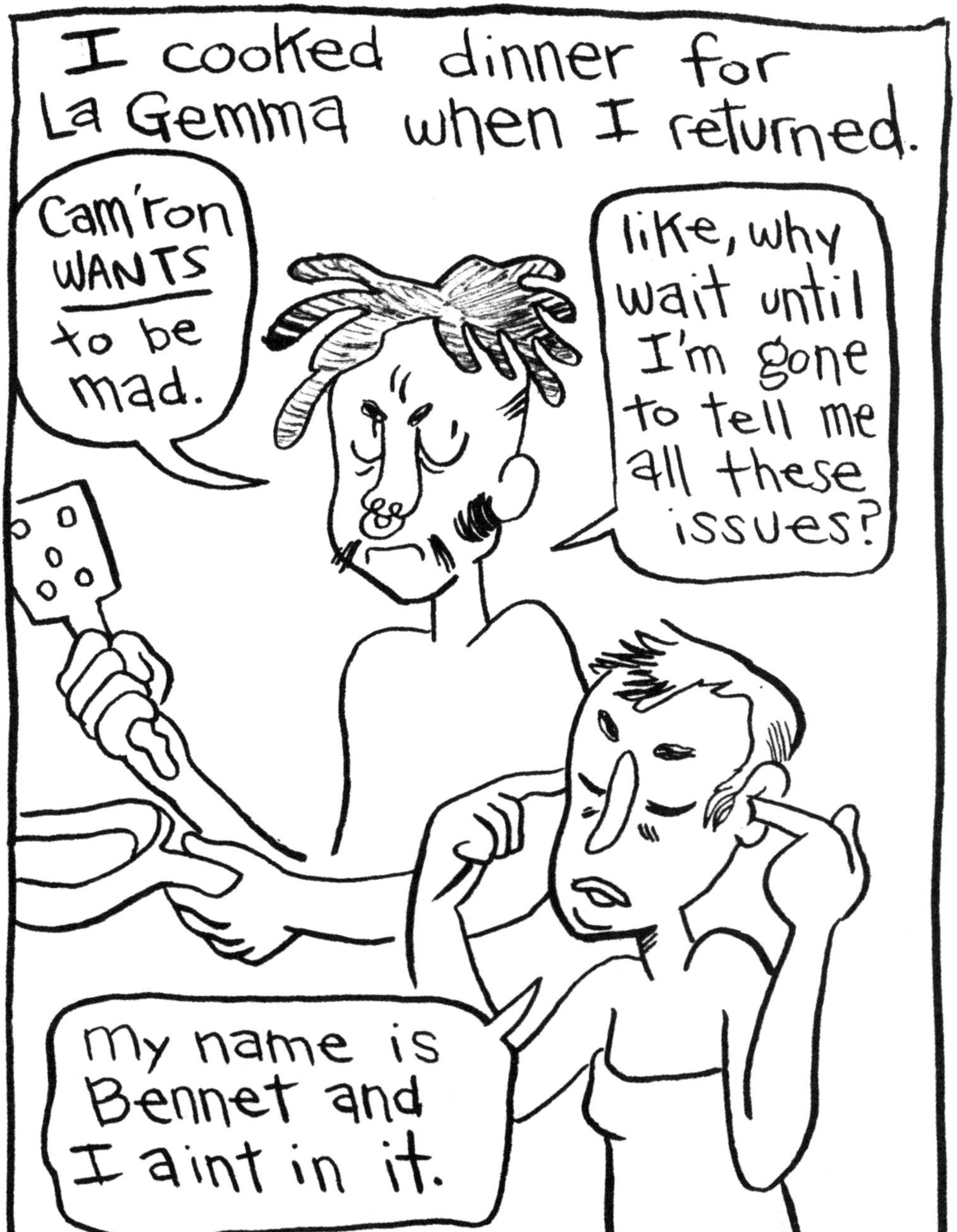
I cooked dinner for La Gemma when I returned.
Cam'ron WANTS to be mad.
like, why wait until I'm gone to tell me all these issues?
my name is Bennet and I aint in it.

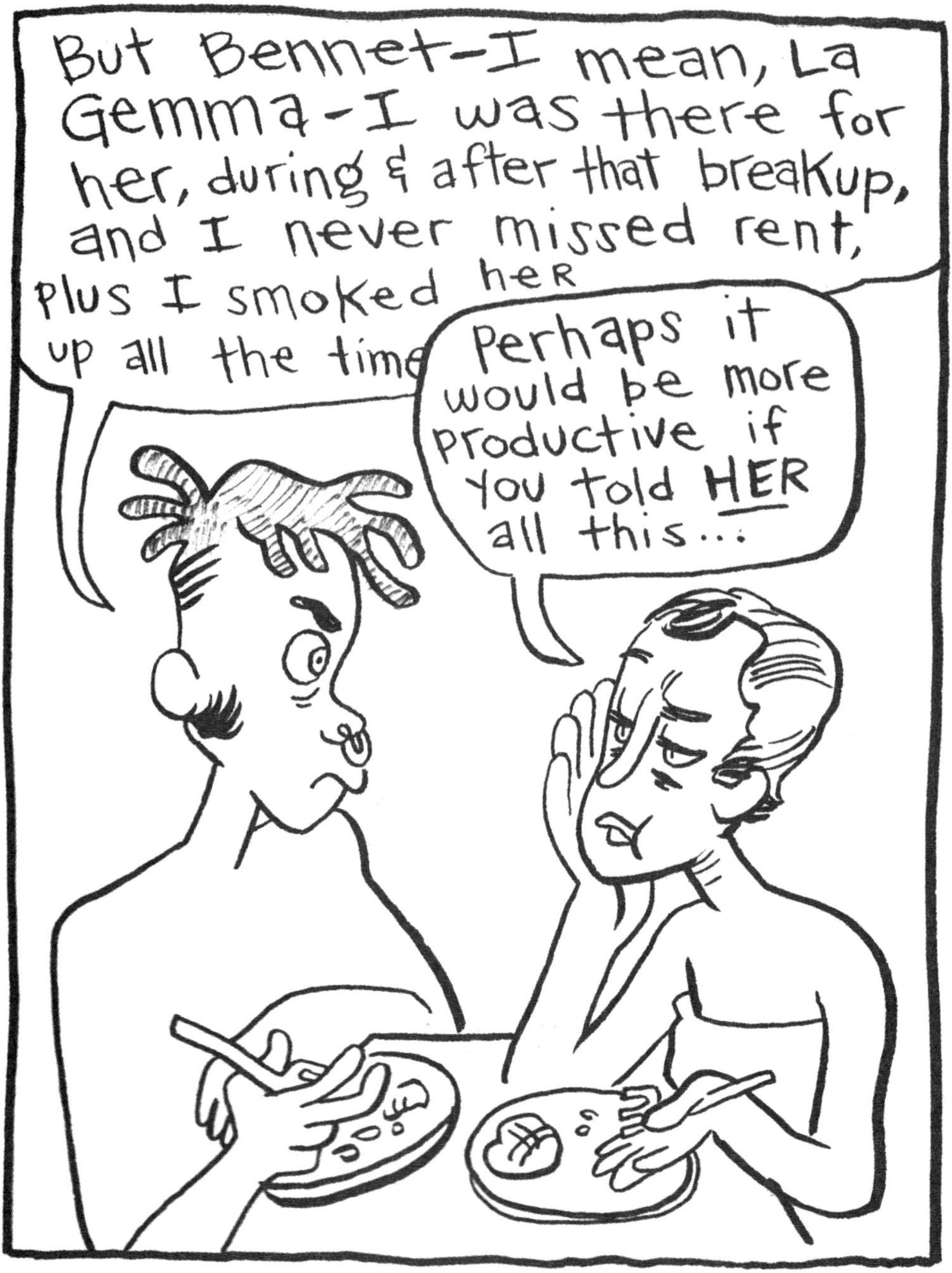
But Bennet—I mean, La Gemma—I was there for her, during & after that breakup, and I never missed rent, plus I smoked her up all the time
Perhaps it would be more productive if you told HER all this...

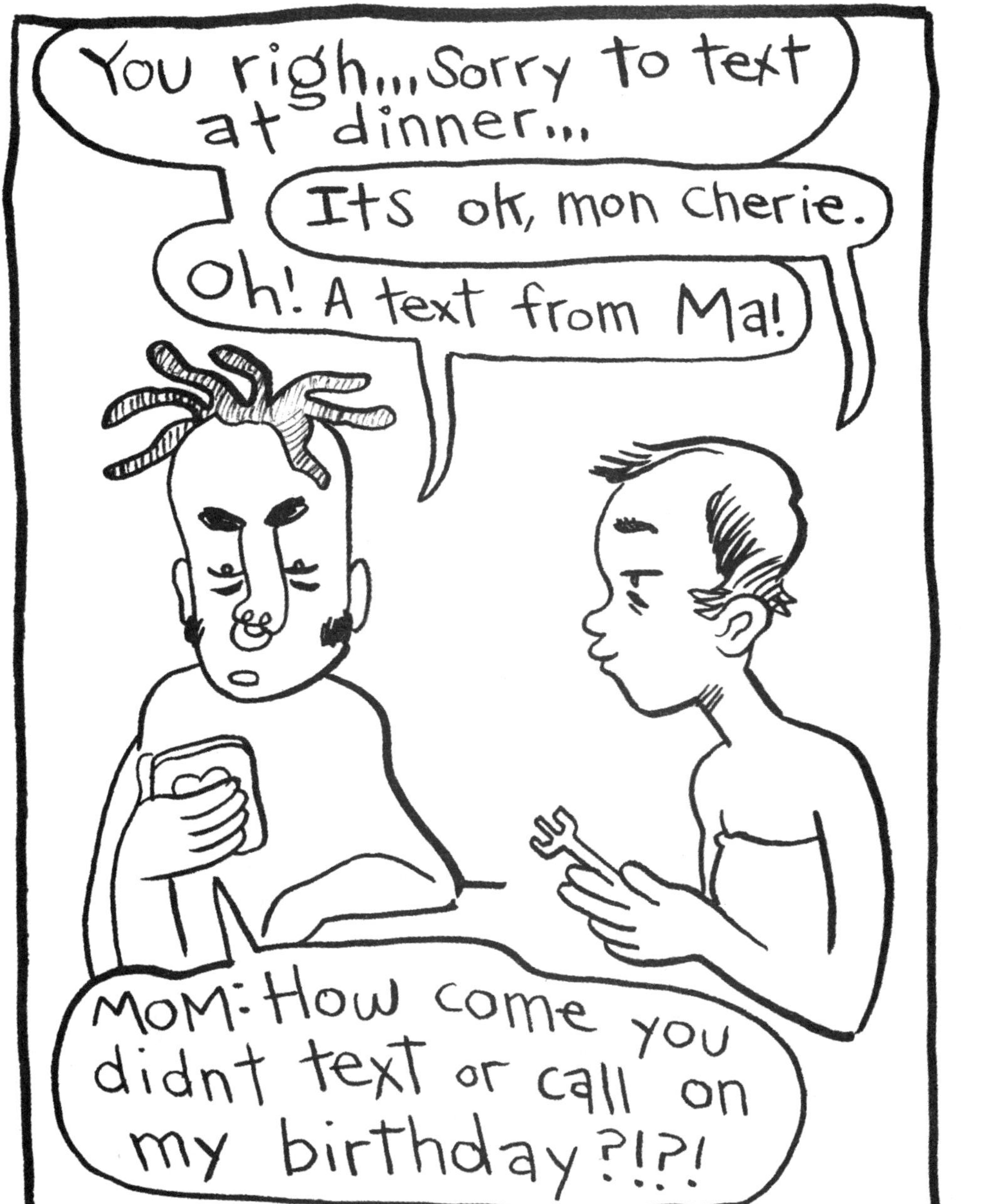
You righ,,, Sorry to text at dinner,,,
Its ok, mon Cherie.
Oh! A text from Ma!
MOM: How come you didnt text or call on my birthday?!?!

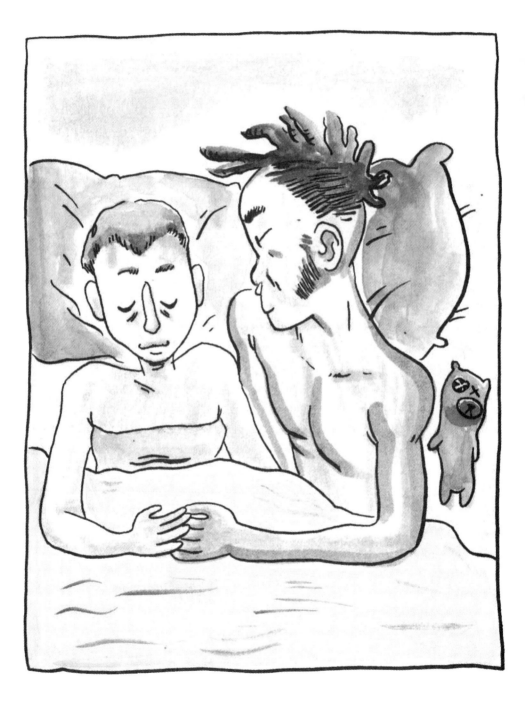

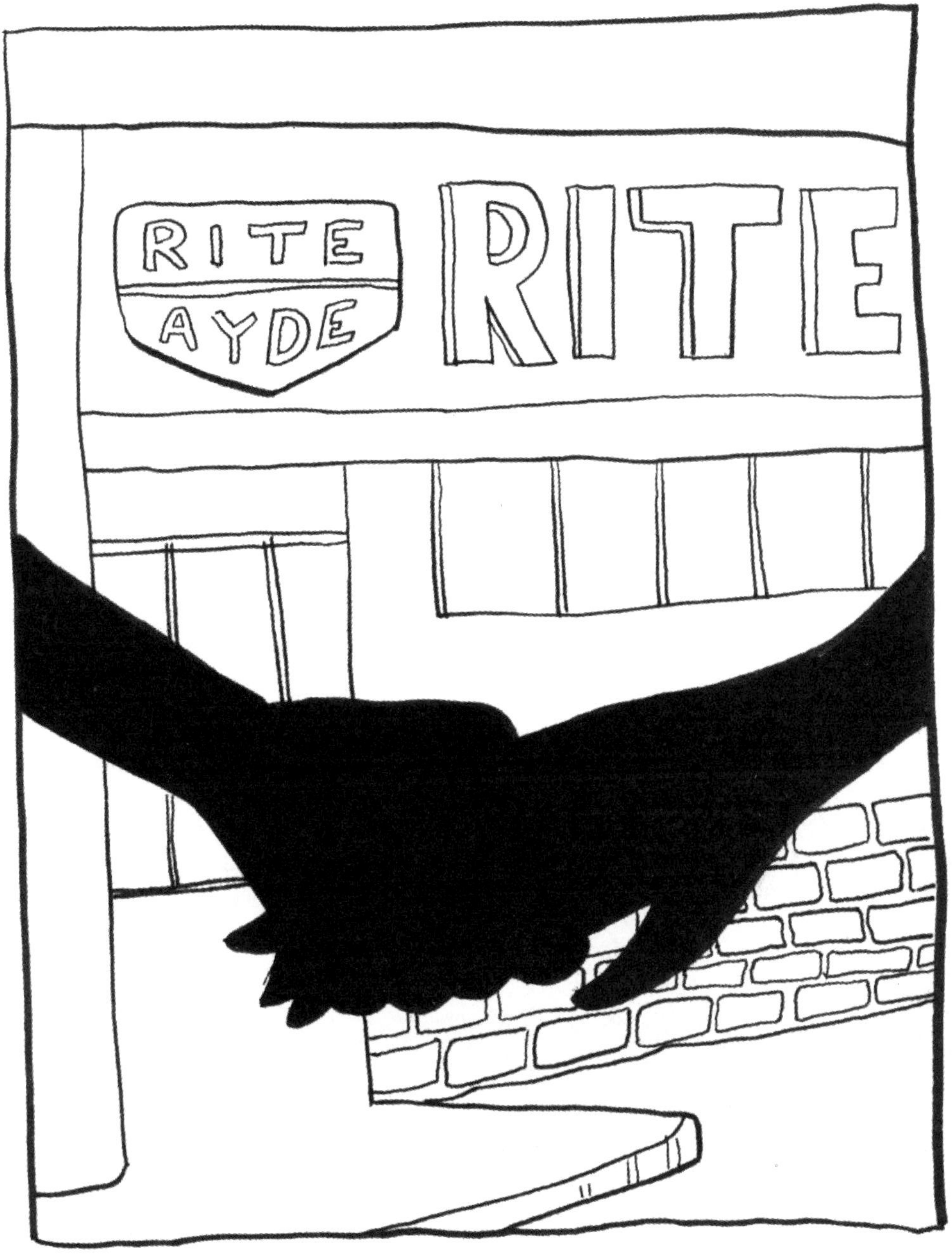
RITE AYDE
RITE

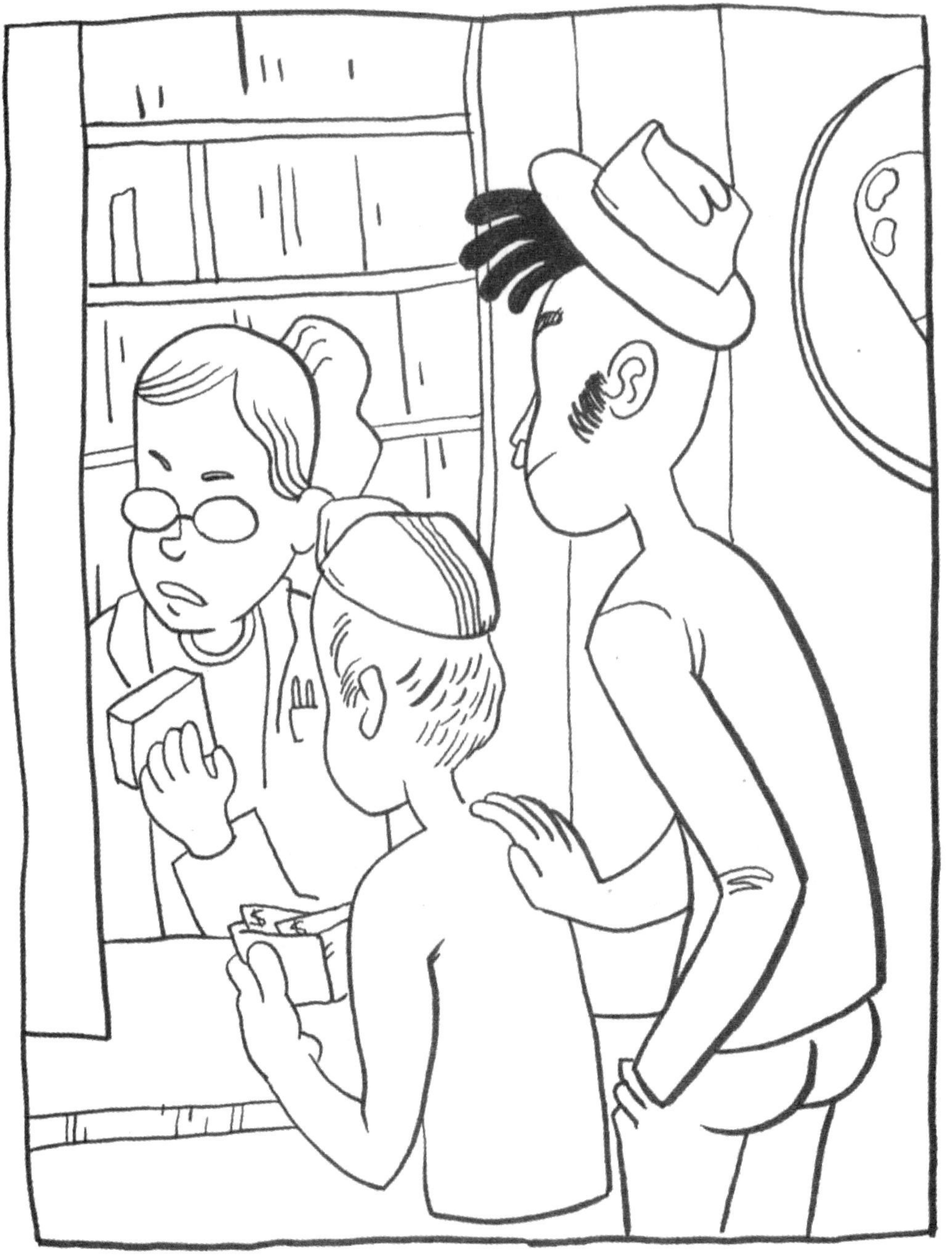

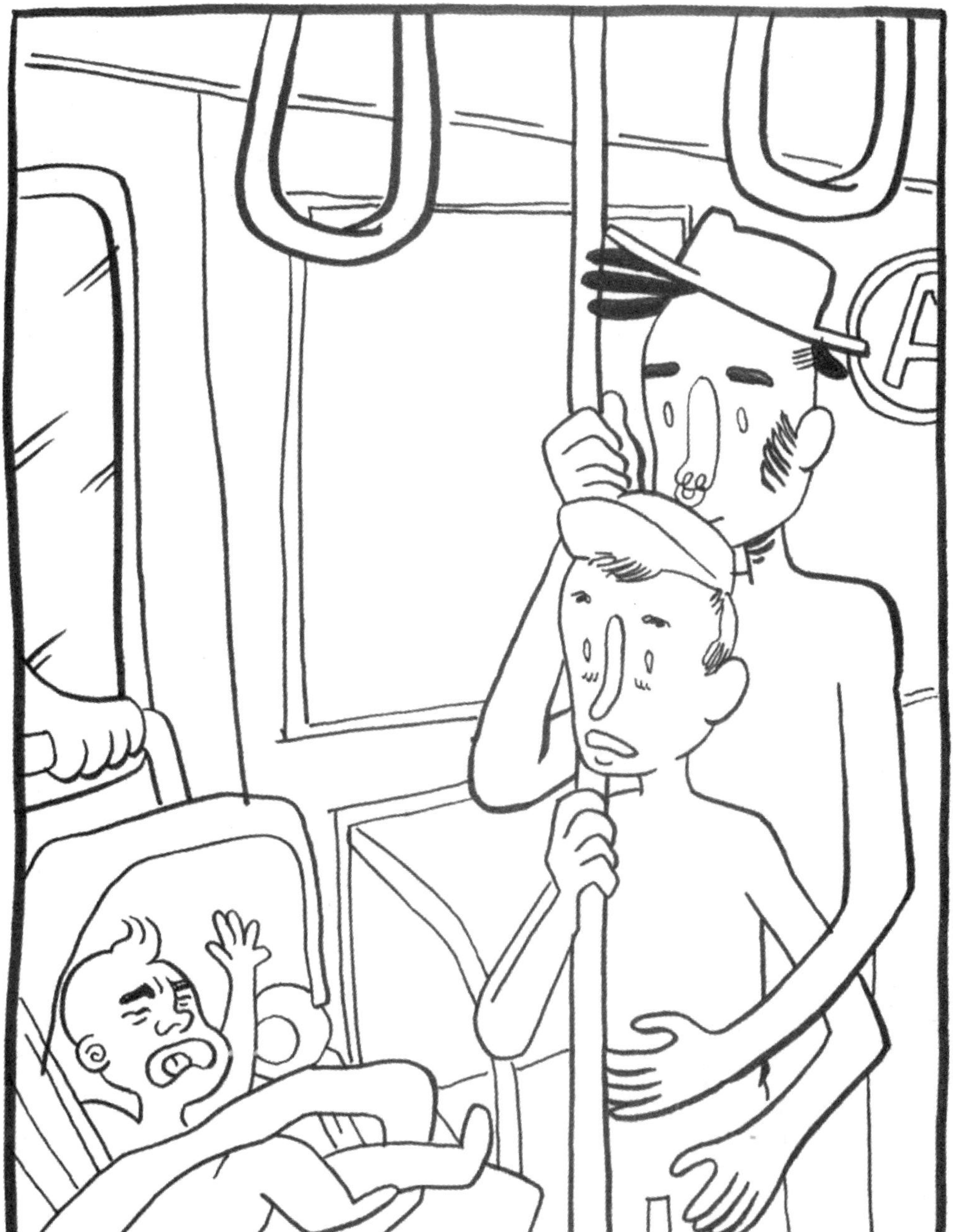
A

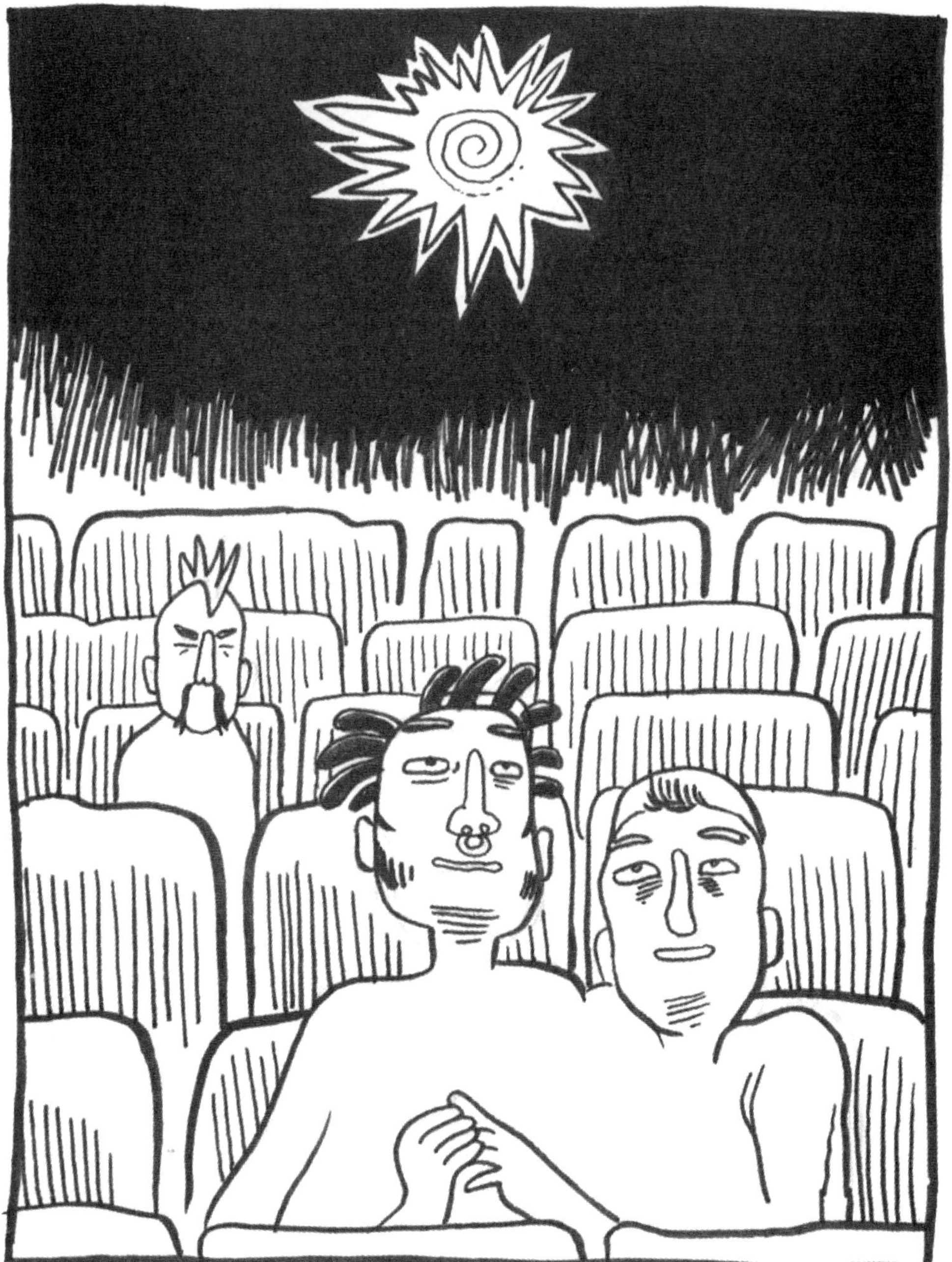

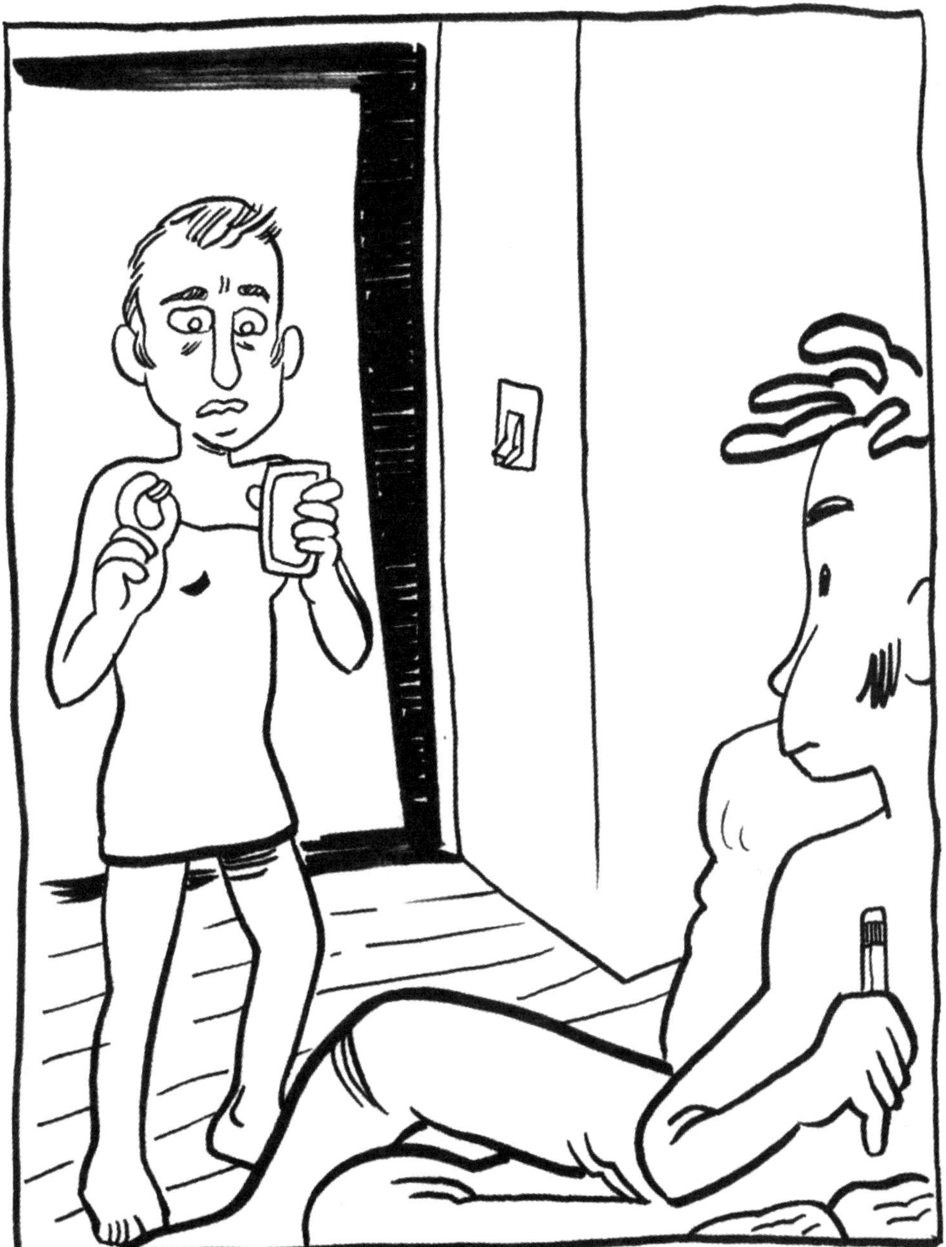

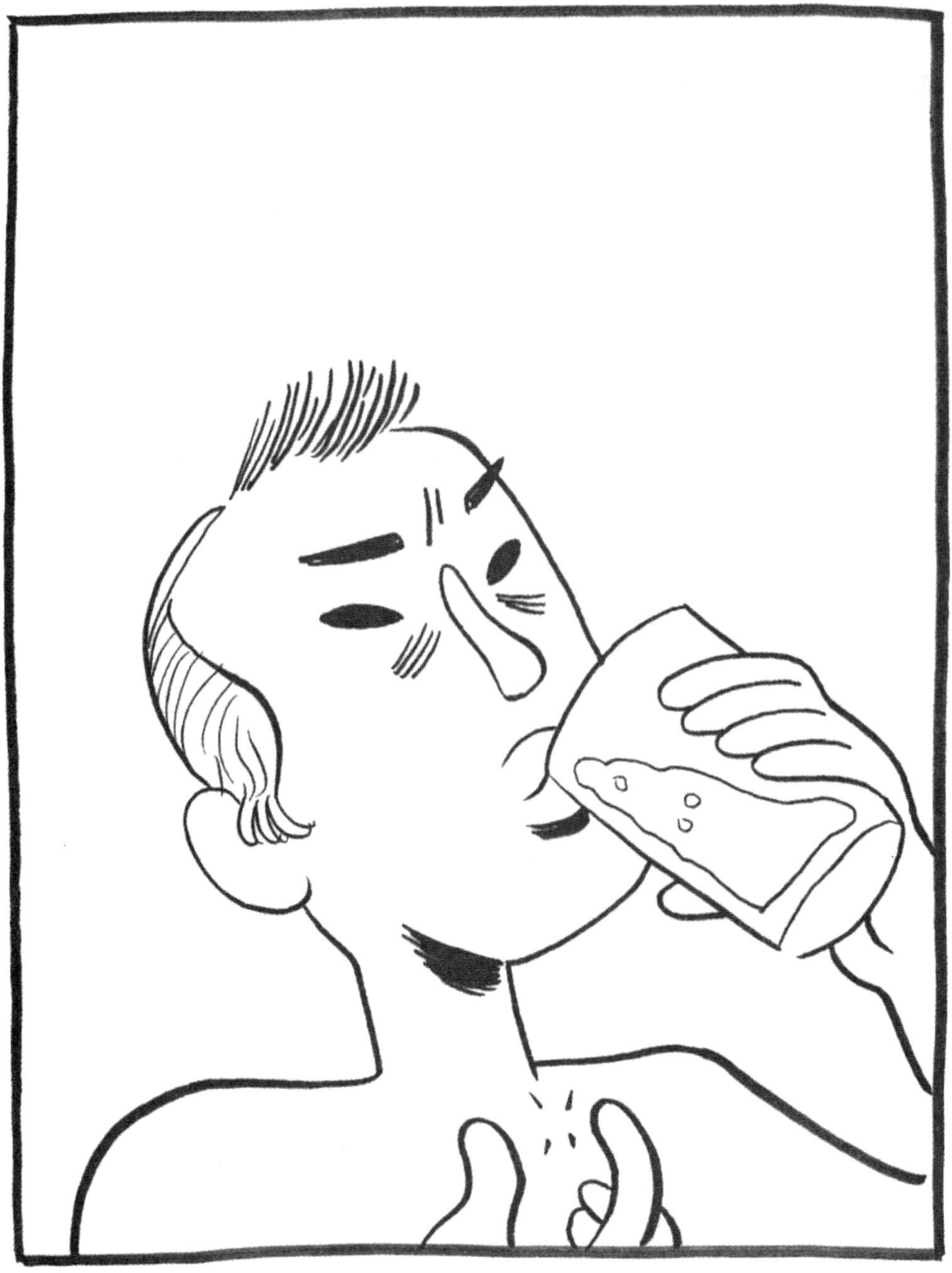

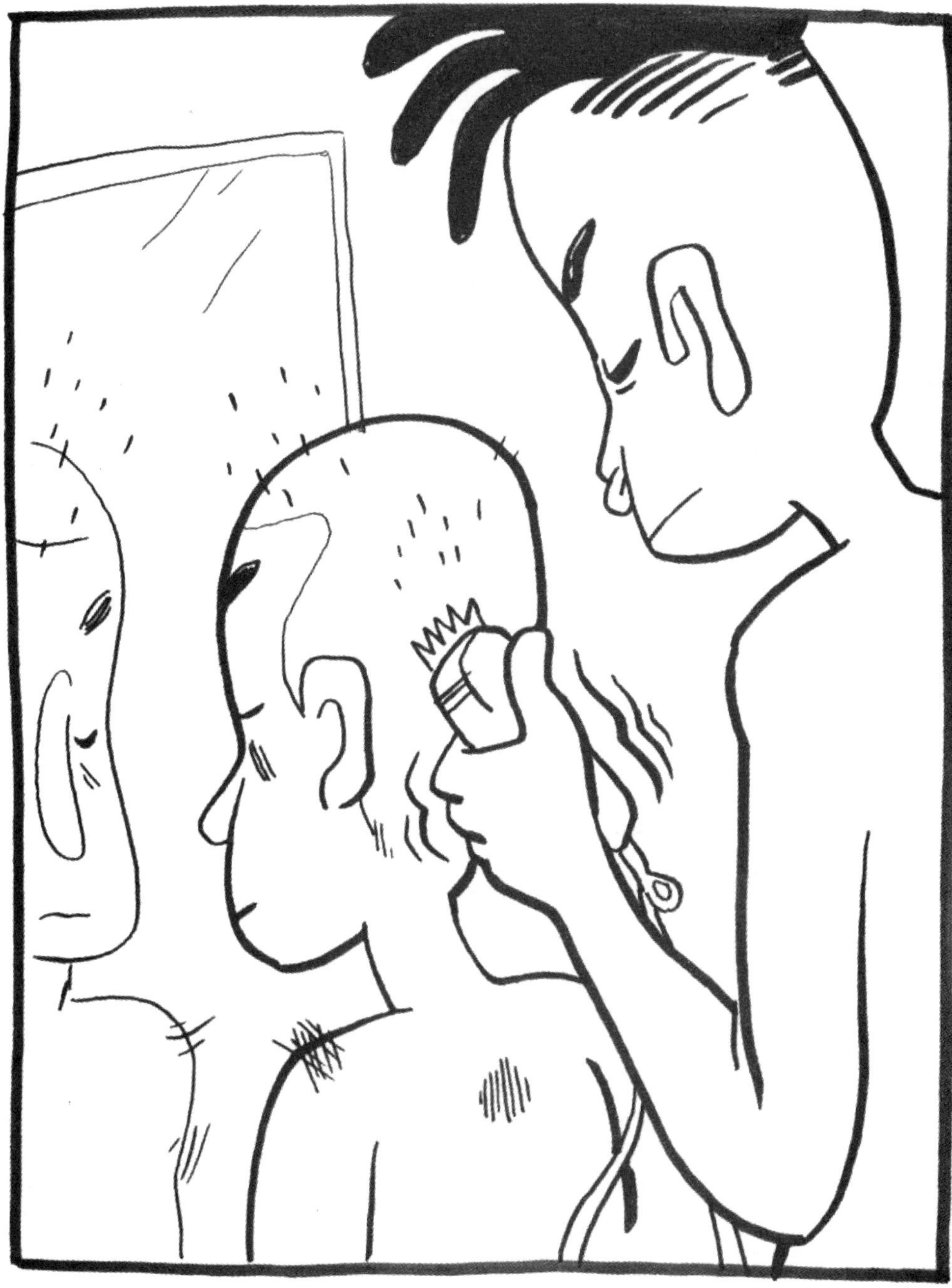

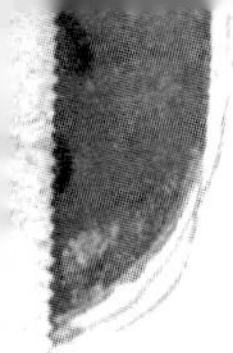

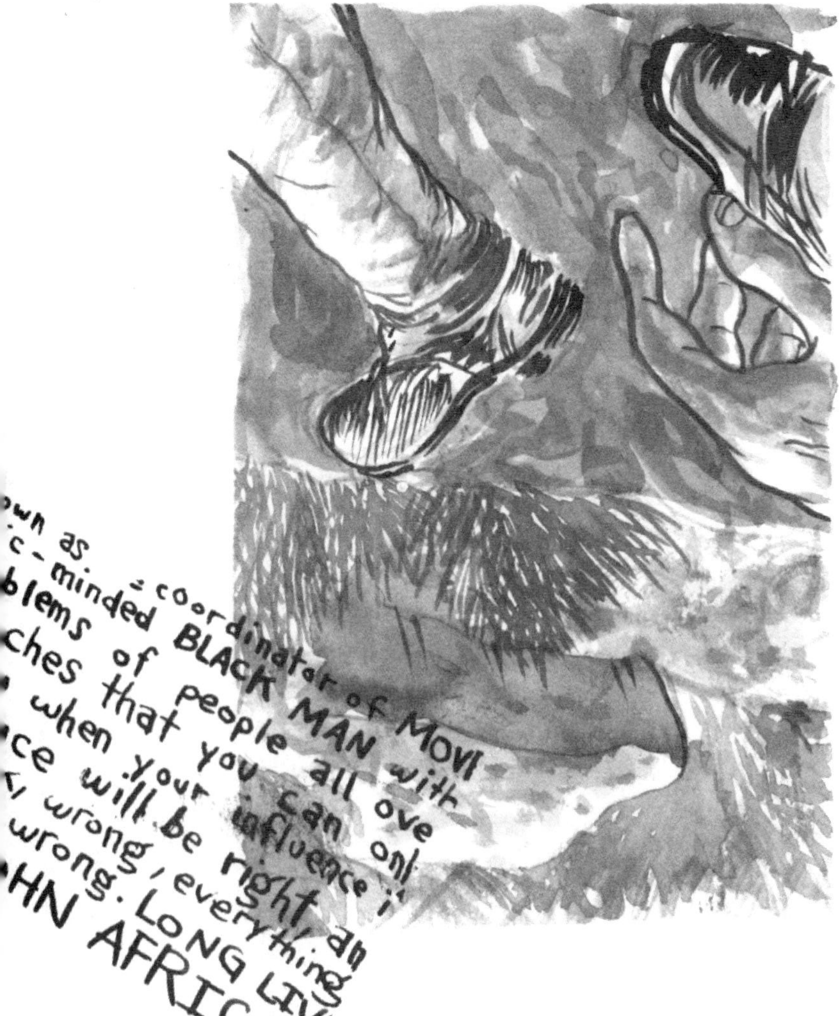
own as ...coordinator of MOVI
c-minded BLACK MAN with
blems of people all ove
ches that you can onl
when your influence i
ce will be right an
wrong, everything
wrong. LONG LIVI
HN AFRICA!

Public Market
480 MAIN ST
DLETOWN, CT 06457
860-346-3340
333302130

DEBIT CARD
DEBIT SALE

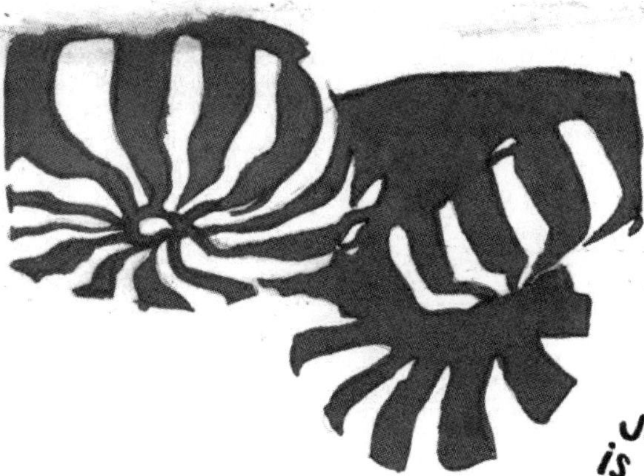

John AFRica, most widely
is a wise, PERCEPTIVE, strat
the solution to all the
the world. John Africa
influence your influence,
right, everything you influ
when your influence is we
you influence will be wea

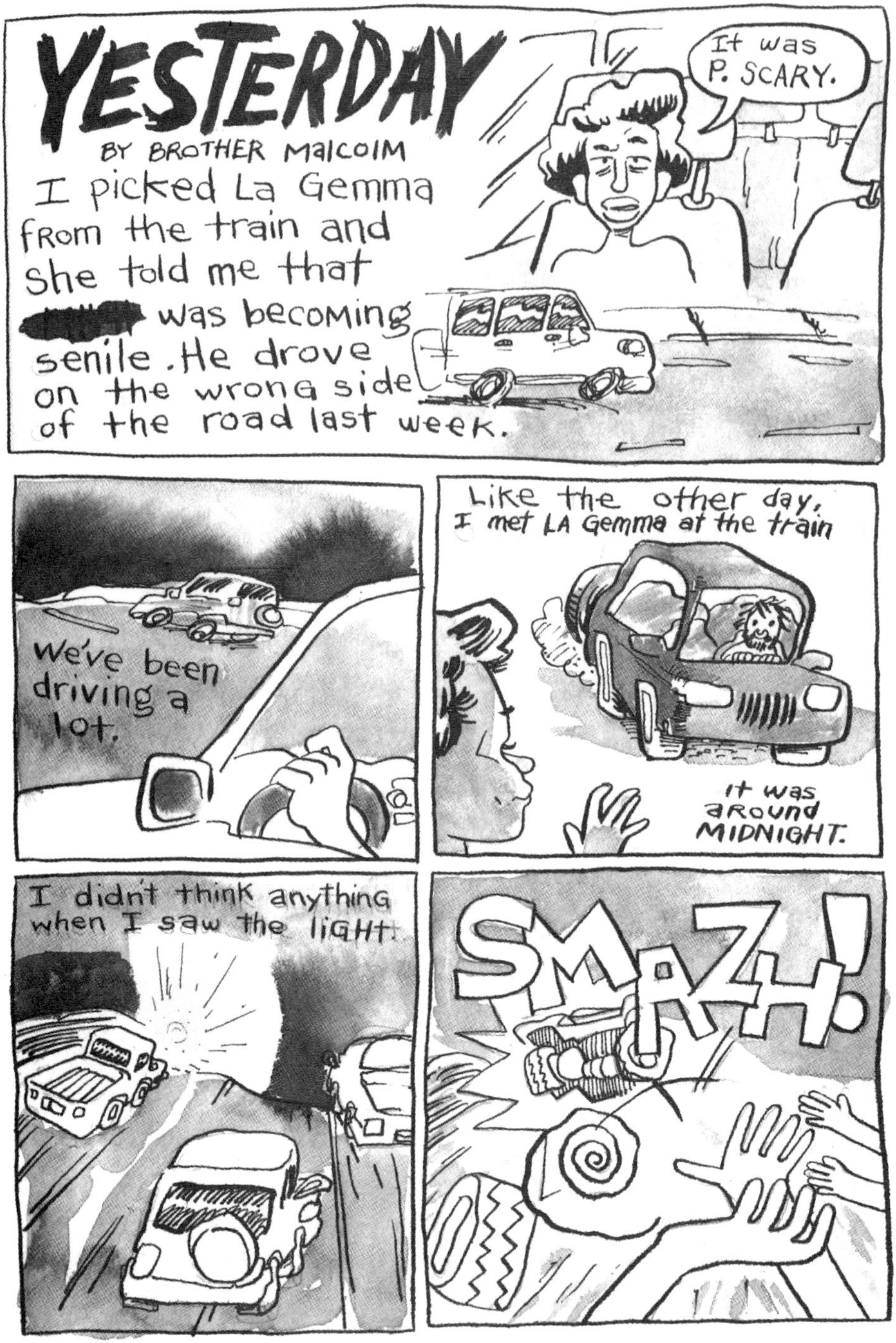
YESTERDAY
BY BROTHER MalcoIM
I picked La Gemma from the train and she told me that [redacted] was becoming senile. He drove on the wrong side of the road last week.
It was P. SCARY.
We've been driving a lot.
Like the other day, I met LA Gemma at the train
it was around MIDNIGHT.
I didn't think anything when I saw the light.
SMAZH!

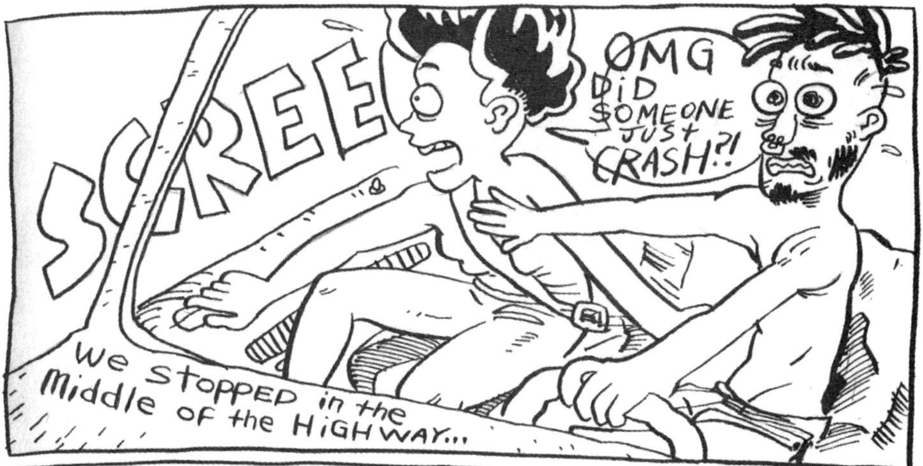
SCREE
OMG DID SOMEONE JUST CRASH?!
We STOPPED in the Middle of the HIGHWAY...

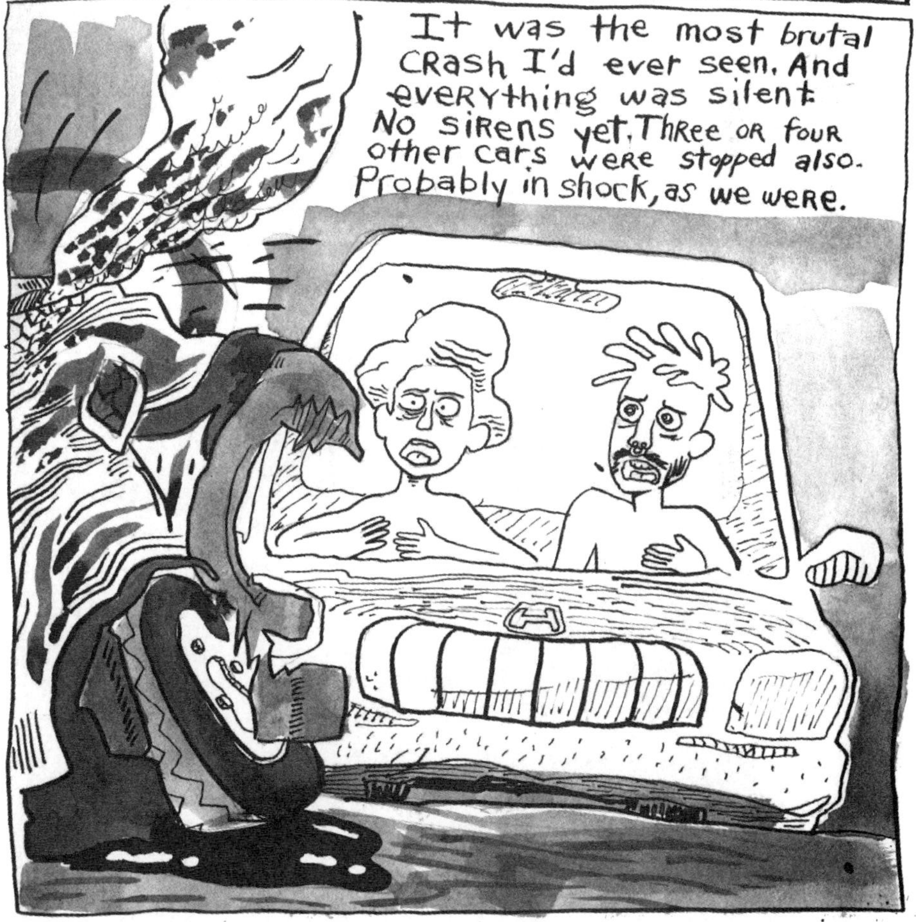
It was the most brutal CRASH I'd ever seen. And everything was silent. No sirens yet. Three or four other cars were stopped also. Probably in shock, as we were.

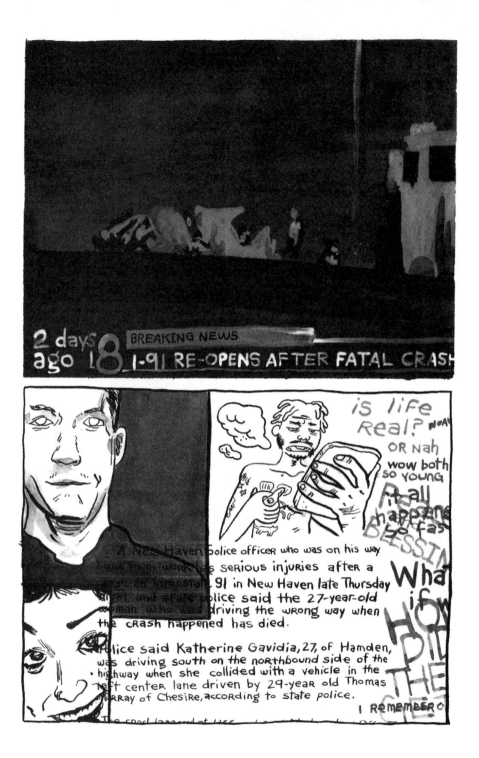

2 days ago 18 BREAKING NEWS I-91 RE-OPENS AFTER FATAL CRASH

is life Real? NOAH

OR NAH

wow both SO YOUNG

It all happene TRACCAS BLESSIN

Wha if w

HOW DII THE

I REMEMBER O

A New Haven police officer who was on his way home from work has serious injuries after a crash on Interstate 91 in New Haven late Thursday night and state police said the 27-year-old woman who was driving the wrong way when the crash happened has died.

Police said Katherine Gavidia, 27, of Hamden, was driving south on the northbound side of the highway when she collided with a vehicle in the left center lane driven by 29-year old Thomas Murray of Cheshire, according to state police.

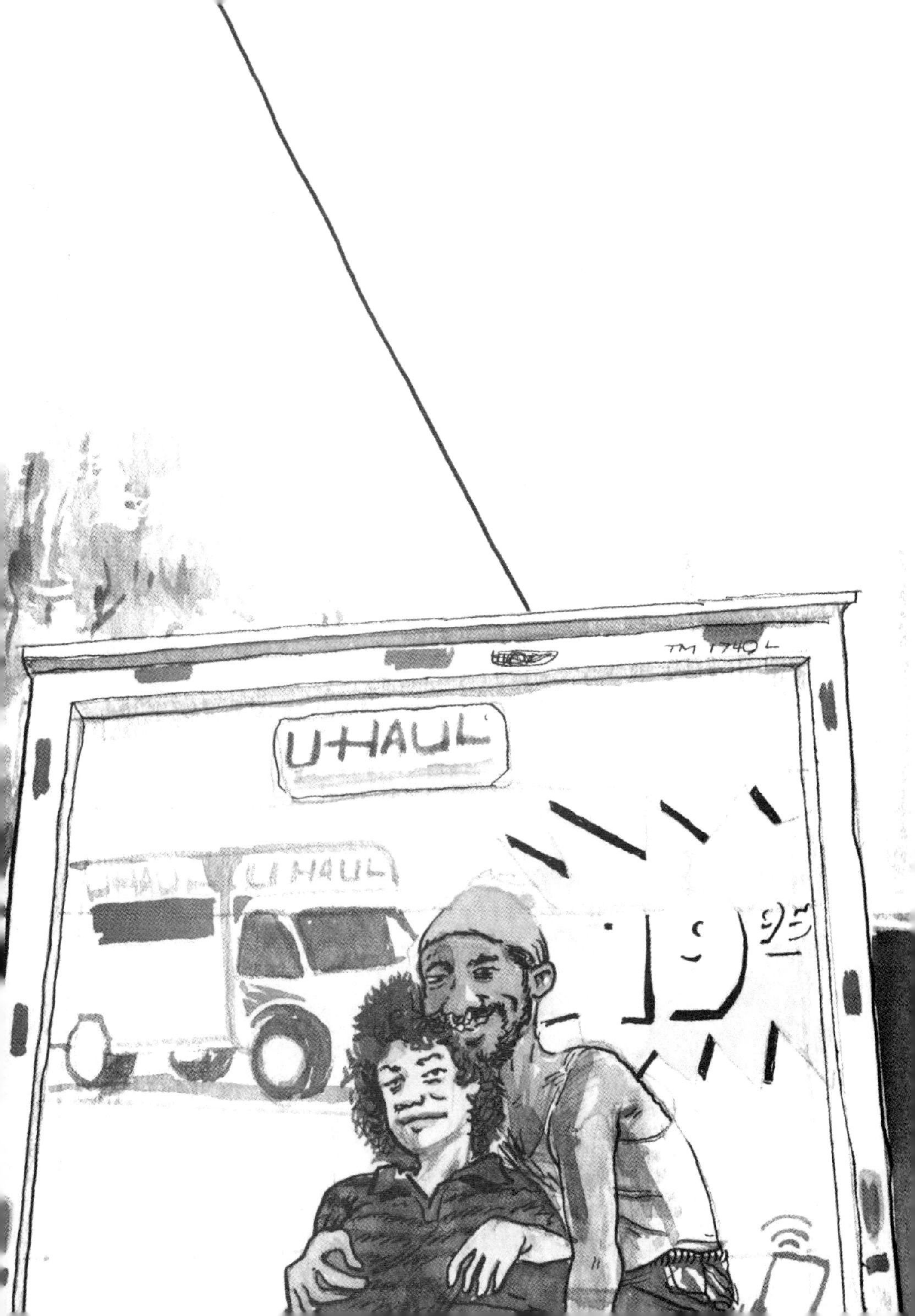
TM 1740 L
U-HAUL
U HAUL

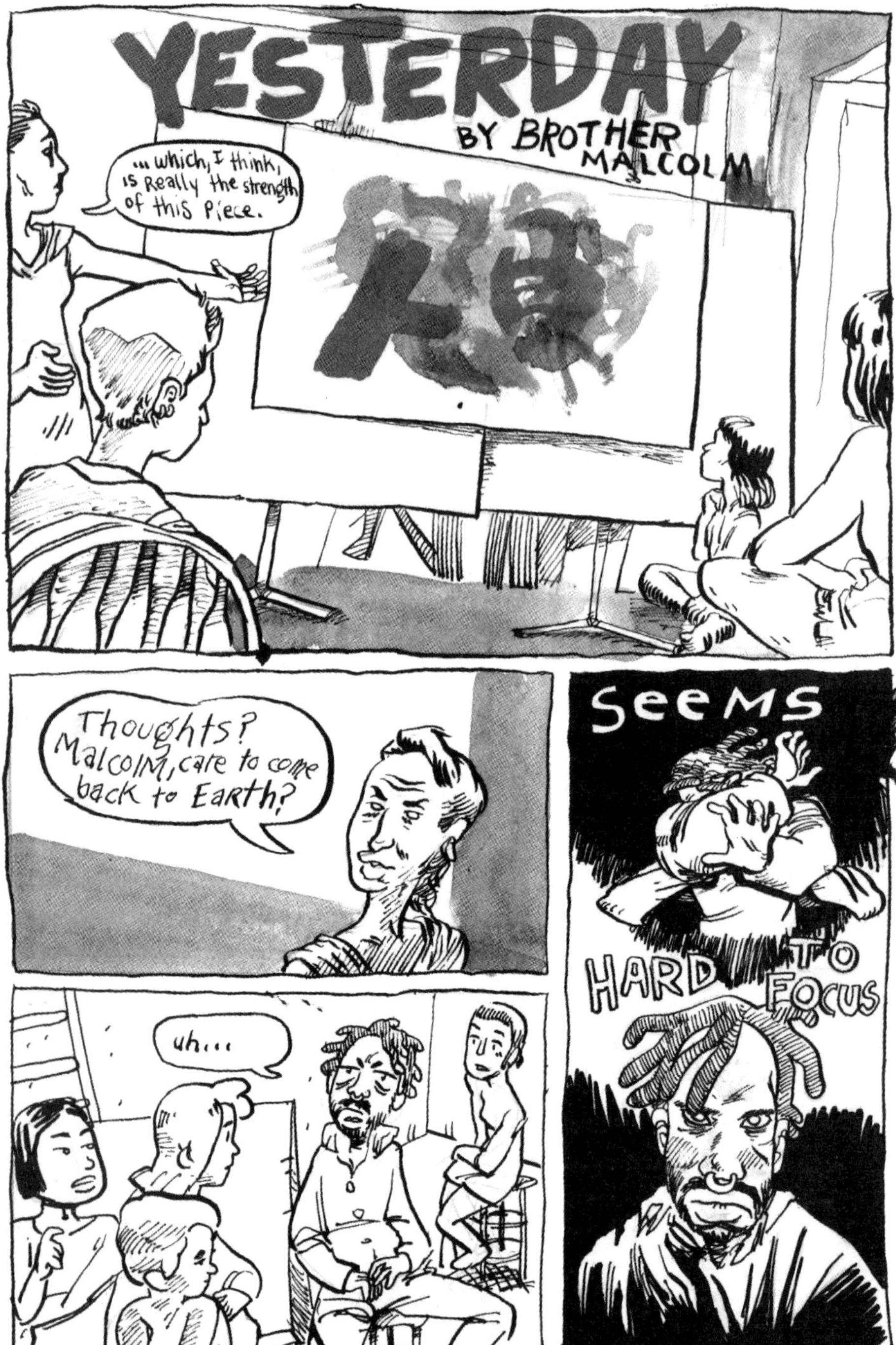
YESTERDAY
BY BROTHER MALCOLM
... which, I think, is Really the strength of this piece.
Thoughts? Malcolm, care to come back to Earth?
uh...
SeeMS
HARD TO FOCUS

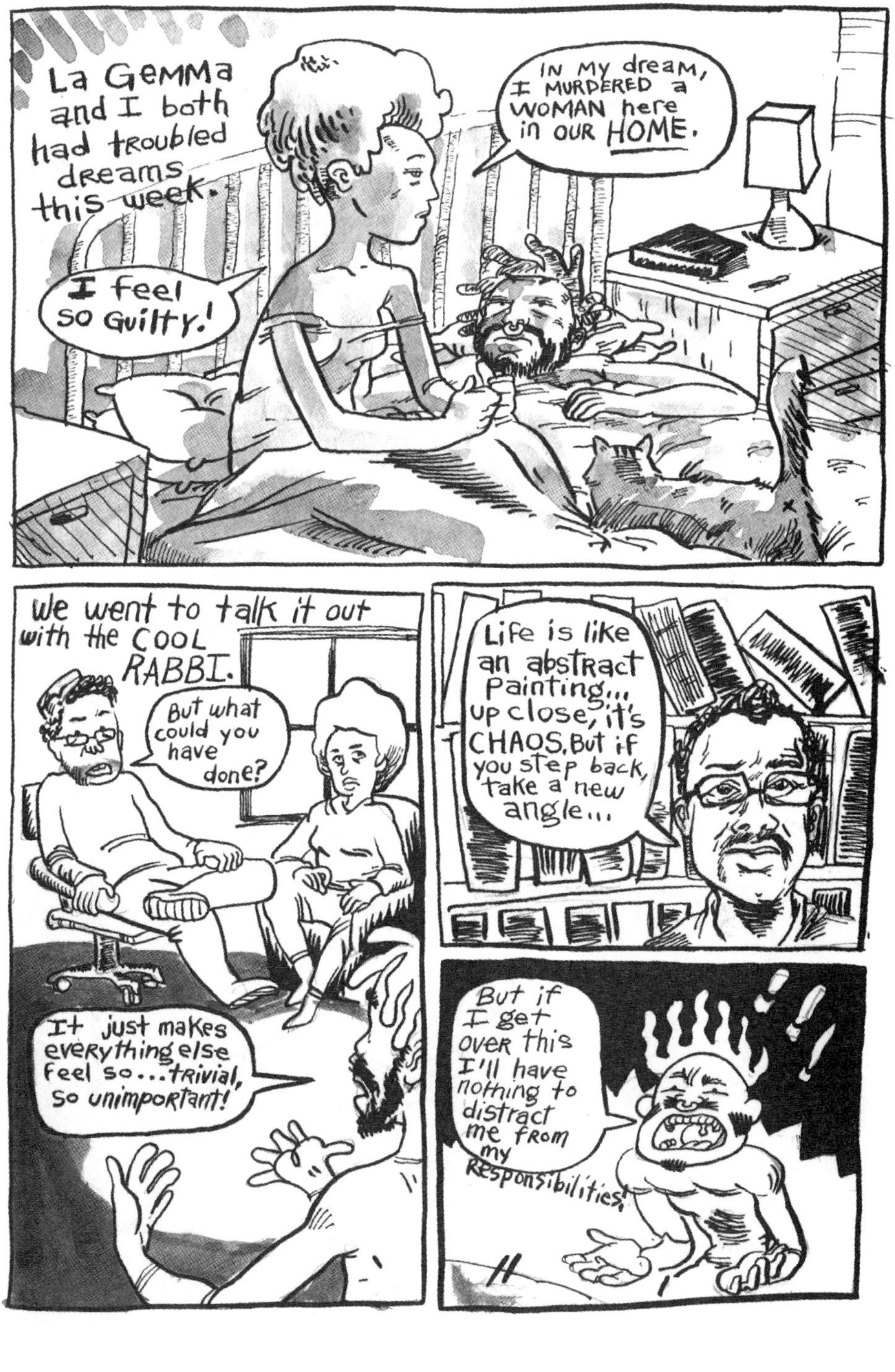
La Gemma and I both had troubled dreams this week.
IN MY dream, I MURDERED a WOMAN here in OUR HOME.
I feel so GUILTY!
We went to talk it out with the COOL RABBI.
But what could you have done?
Life is like an abstract painting... up close, it's CHAOS. But if you step back, take a new angle...
It just makes everything else feel so... trivial, so unimportant!
But if I get over this I'll have nothing to distract me from my Responsibilities!

YESTERDAY

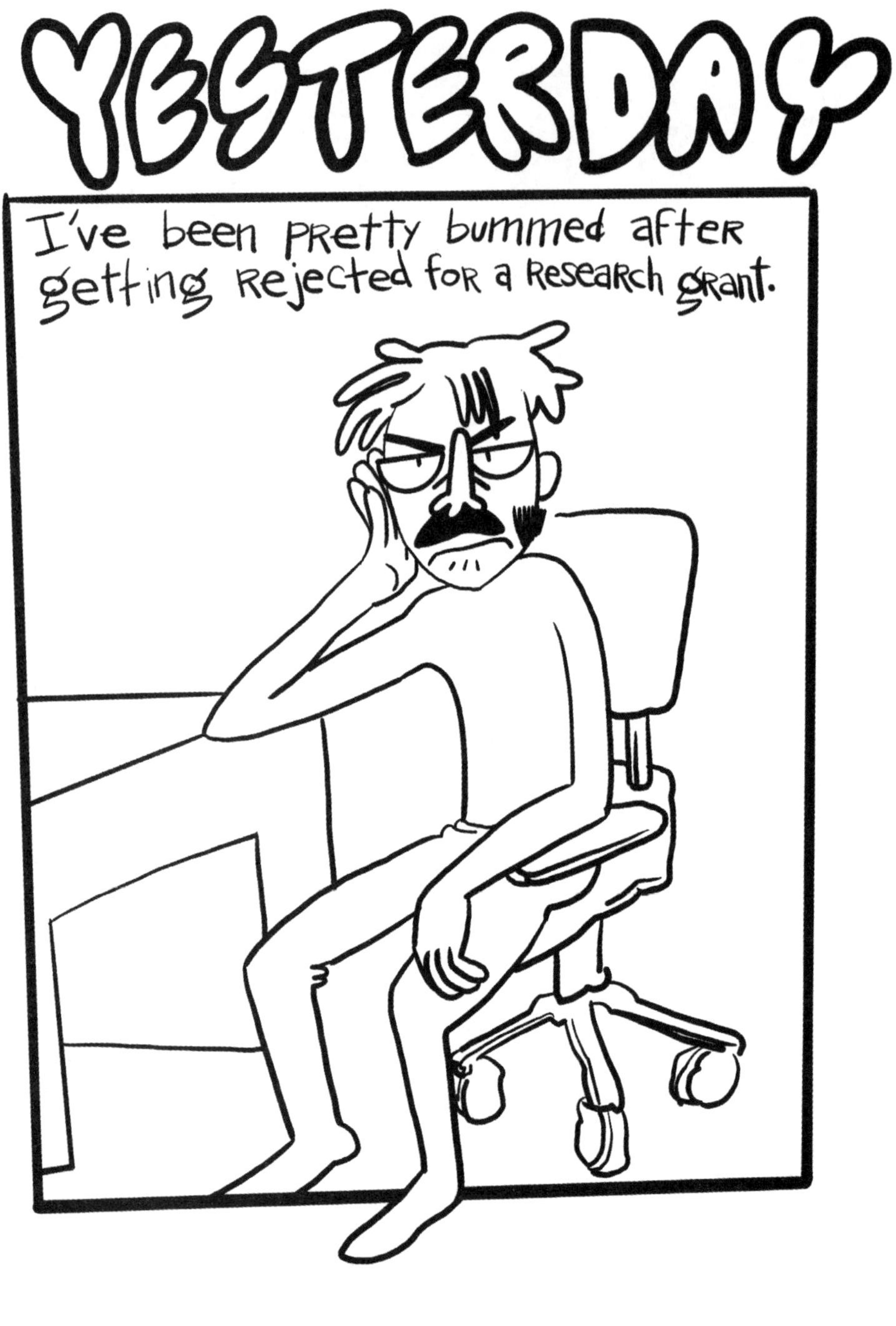
I've been pretty bummed after getting rejected for a research grant.

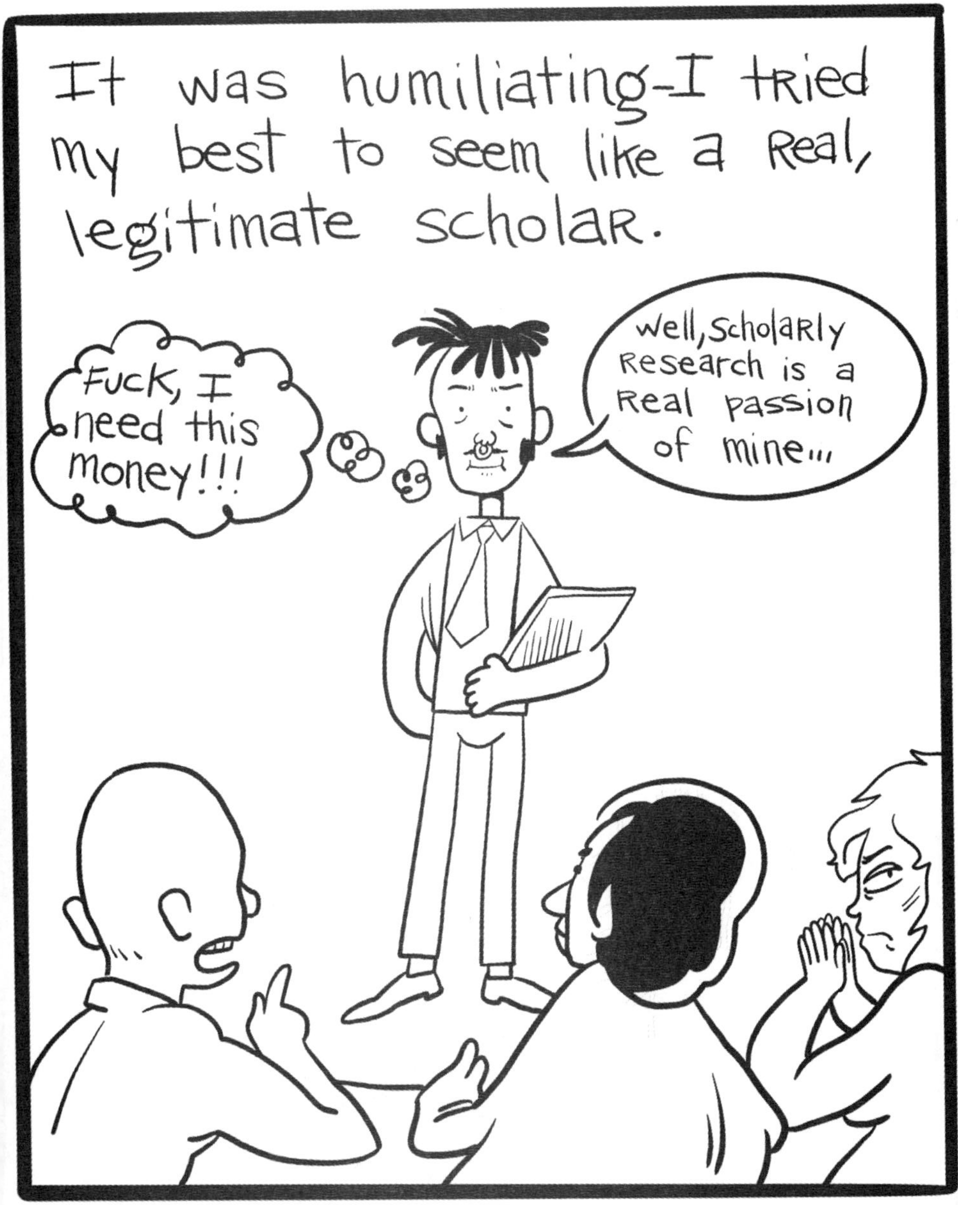
It was humiliating–I tried my best to seem like a real, legitimate scholar.
Fuck, I need this money!!!
Well, scholarly research is a real passion of mine...

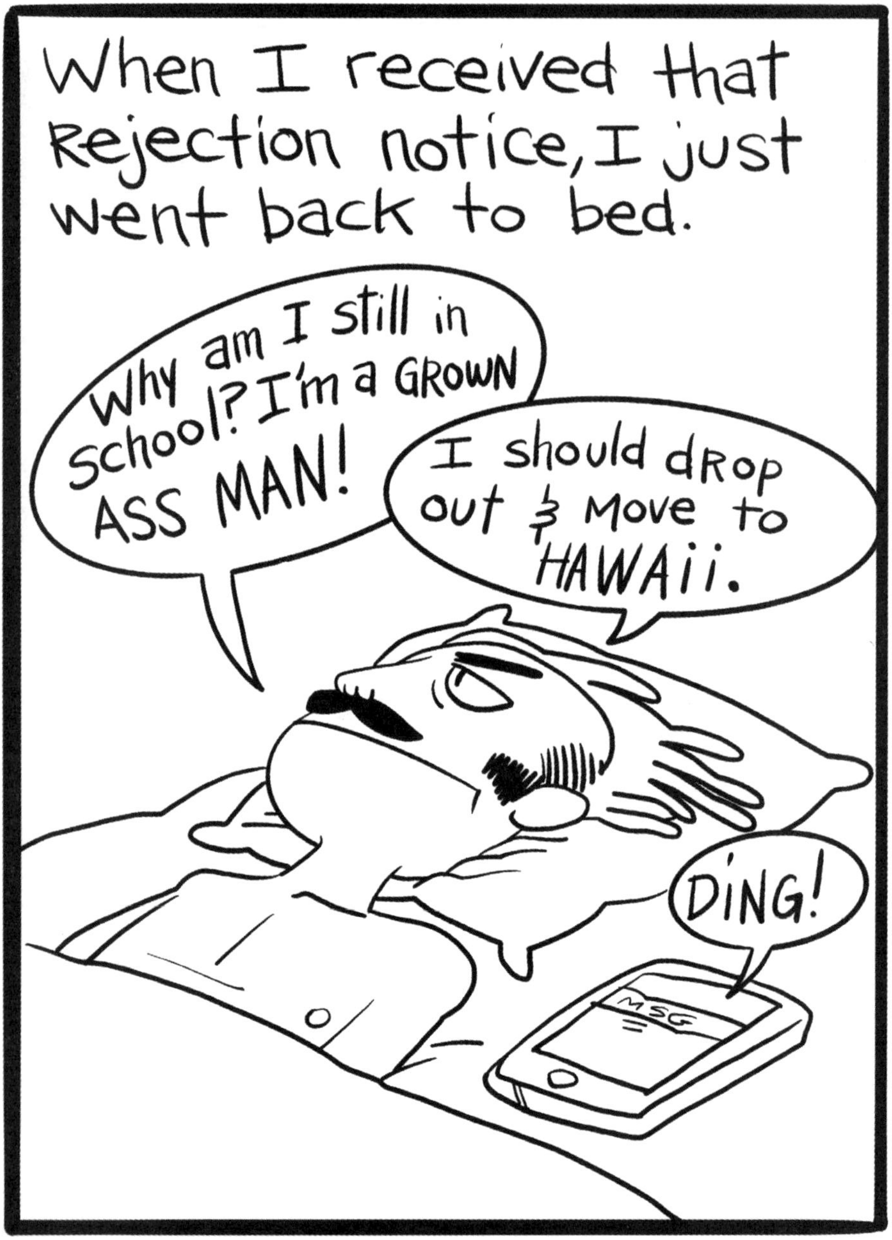
When I received that Rejection notice, I just went back to bed.
Why am I still in School? I'm a GROWN ASS MAN!
I should drop out & Move to HAWAii.
DING!
MSG

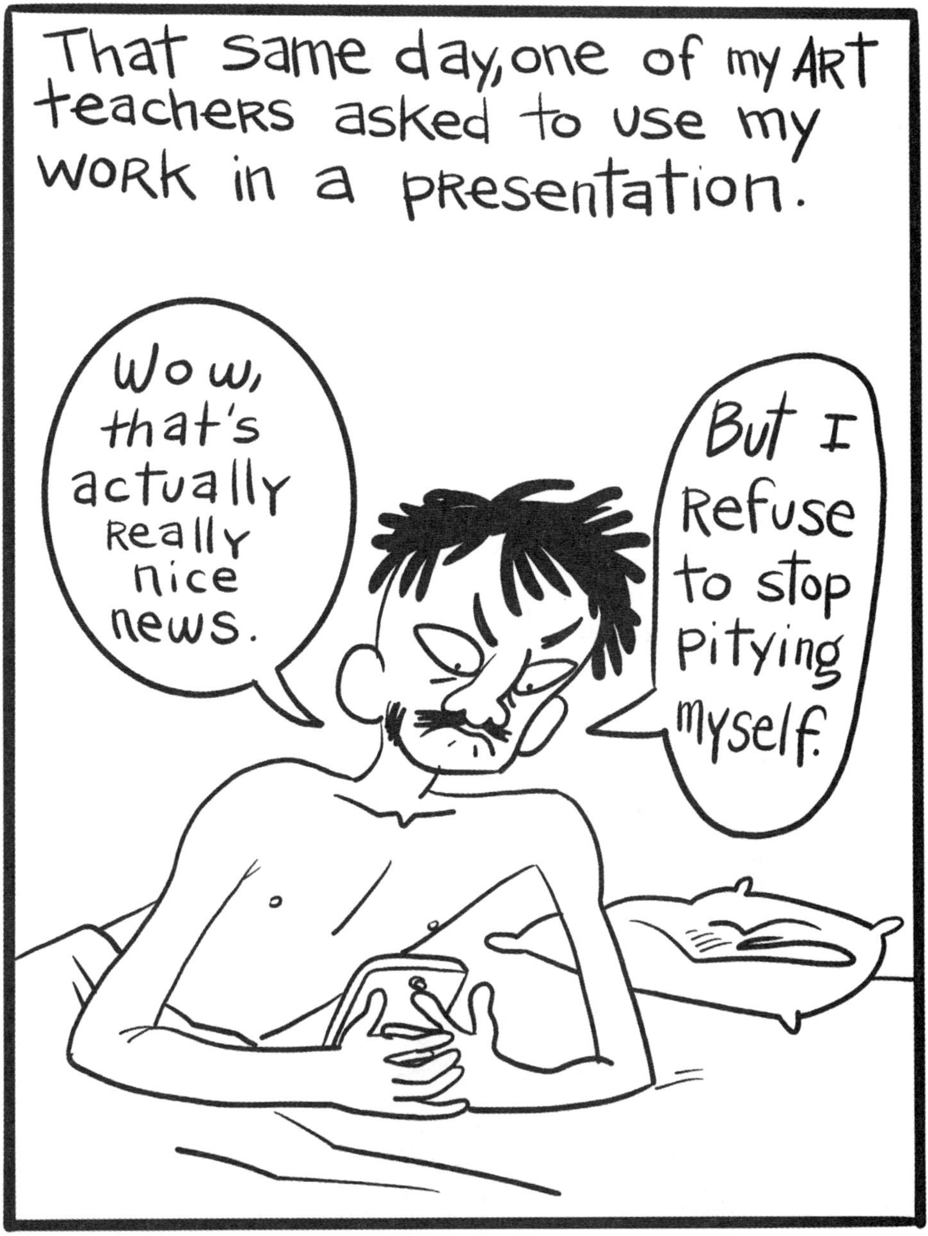
That same day, one of my ART teachers asked to use my work in a presentation.
Wow, that's actually really nice news.
But I refuse to stop pitying myself.

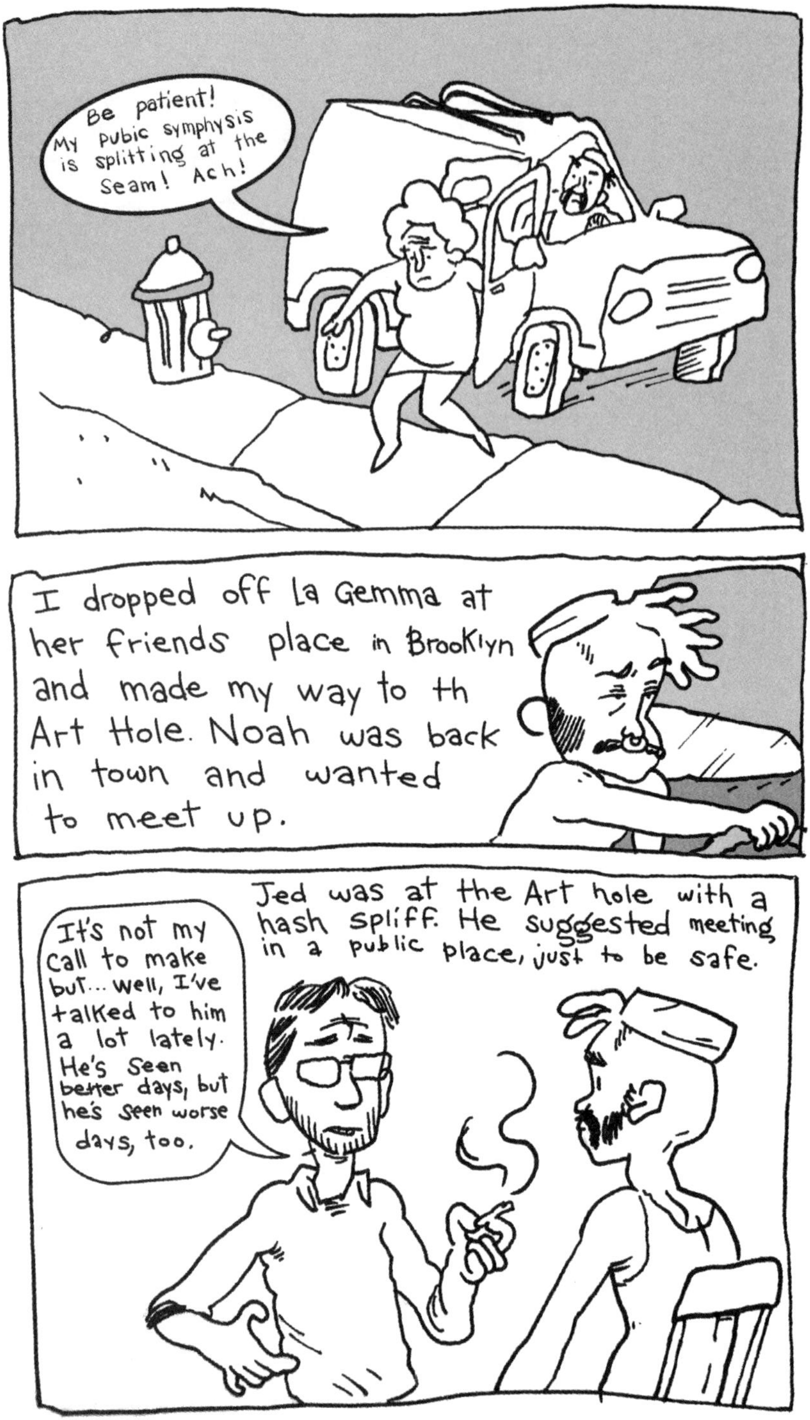
Be patient! My pubic symphysis is splitting at the seam! Ach!
I dropped off La Gemma at her friends place in Brooklyn and made my way to th Art Hole. Noah was back in town and wanted to meet up.
Jed was at the Art hole with a hash spliff. He suggested meeting in a public place, just to be safe.
It's not my call to make but... well, I've talked to him a lot lately. He's seen better days, but he's seen worse days, too.

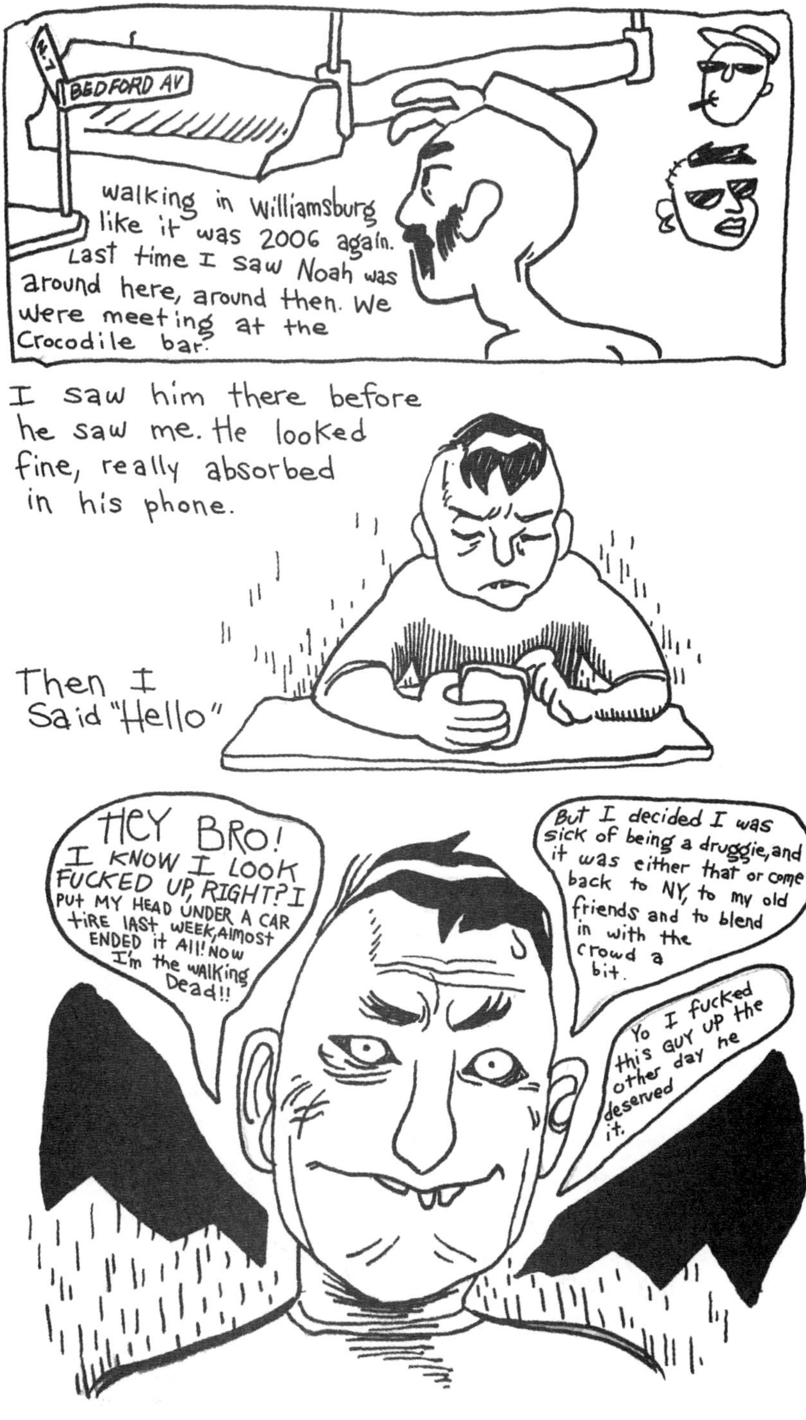

L M
BEDFORD AV
walking in Williamsburg like it was 2006 again. Last time I saw Noah was around here, around then. We were meeting at the Crocodile bar.
I saw him there before he saw me. He looked fine, really absorbed in his phone.
Then I Said "Hello"
HEY BRO! I KNOW I LOOK FUCKED UP, RIGHT? I PUT MY HEAD UNDER A CAR TIRE LAST WEEK, ALMOST ENDED it All! NOW I'm the WALKing Dead!!
But I decided I was sick of being a druggie, and it was either that or come back to NY, to my old friends and to blend in with the crowd a bit.
Yo I fucked this GUY UP the other day he deserved it.

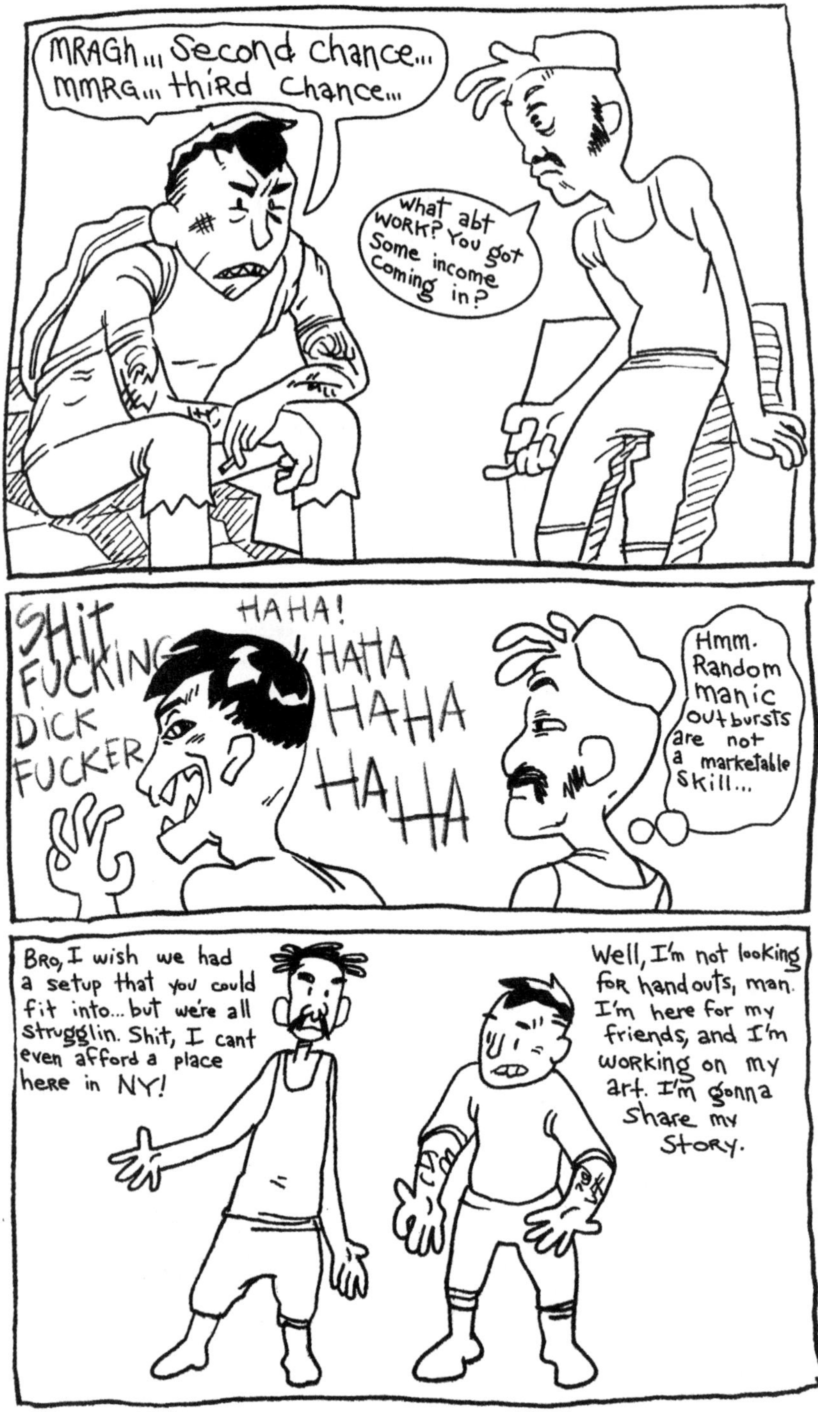
MRAGh... Second chance... MMRG... third chance...
What abt WORK? You got Some income Coming in?
SHit FUCKING DICK FUCKER
HAHA! HAHA HAHA HAHA
Hmm. Random manic outbursts are not a marketable skill...
Bro, I wish we had a setup that you could fit into... but we're all strugglin. Shit, I cant even afford a place here in NY!
Well, I'm not looking for handouts, man. I'm here for my friends, and I'm working on my art. I'm gonna share my STORY.

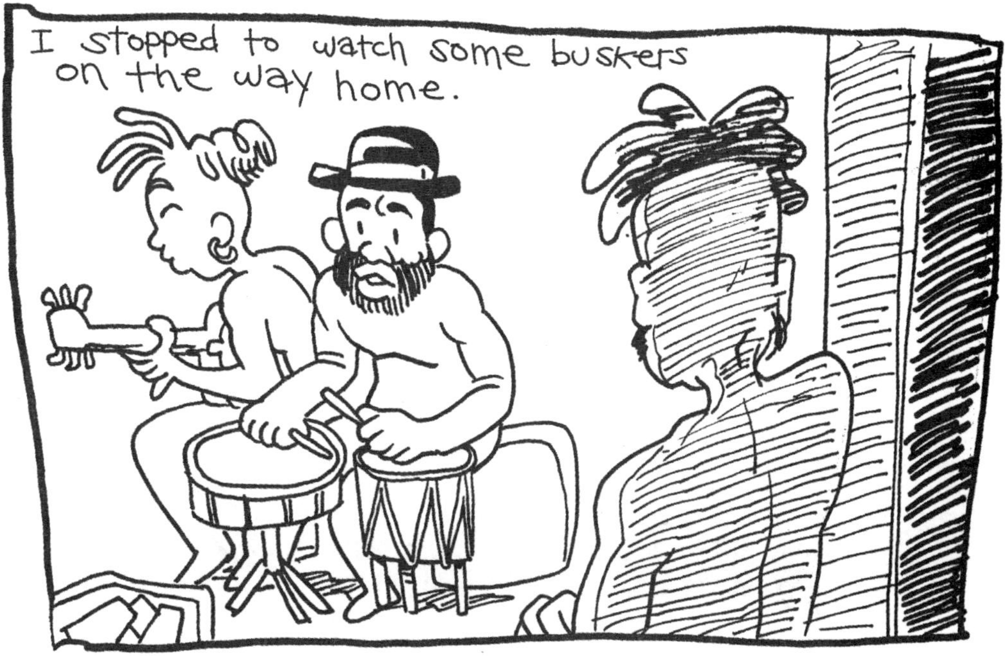
I stopped to watch some buskers on the way home.

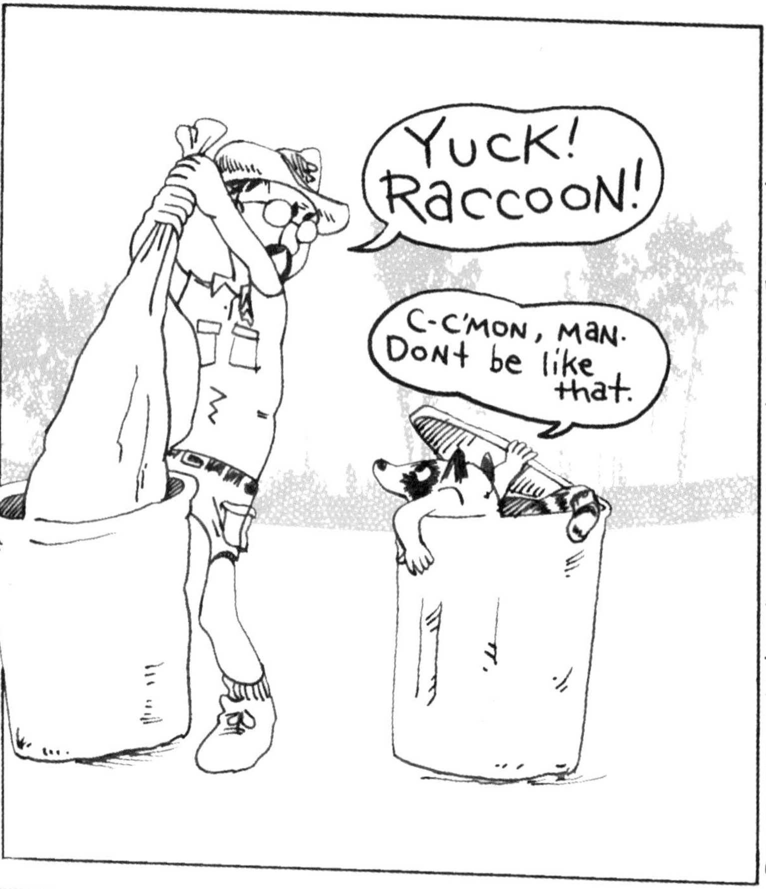
YUCK! RaccooN!
C-C'MON, MAN. DONt be like that.

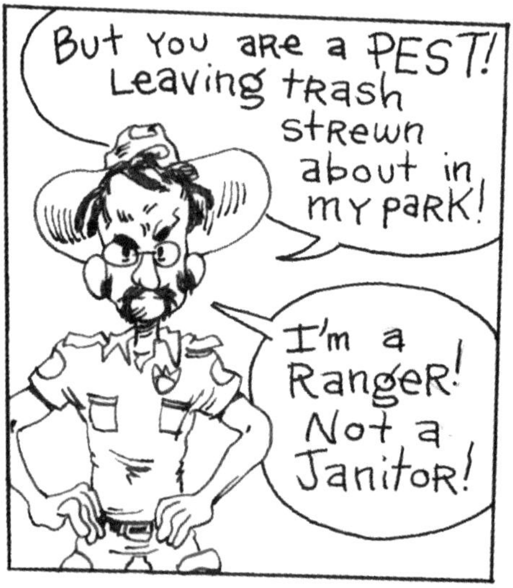
But YOU are a PEST! Leaving trash strewn about in my park!
I'm a Ranger! Not a Janitor!

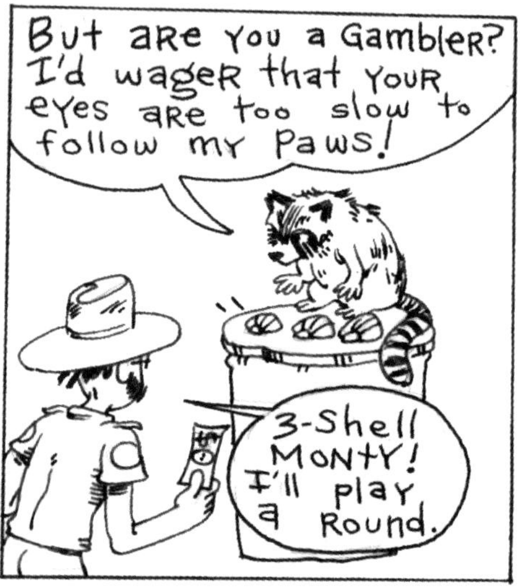
But are you a Gambler? I'd wager that your eyes are too slow to follow my Paws!
3-Shell MONTY! I'll play a Round.

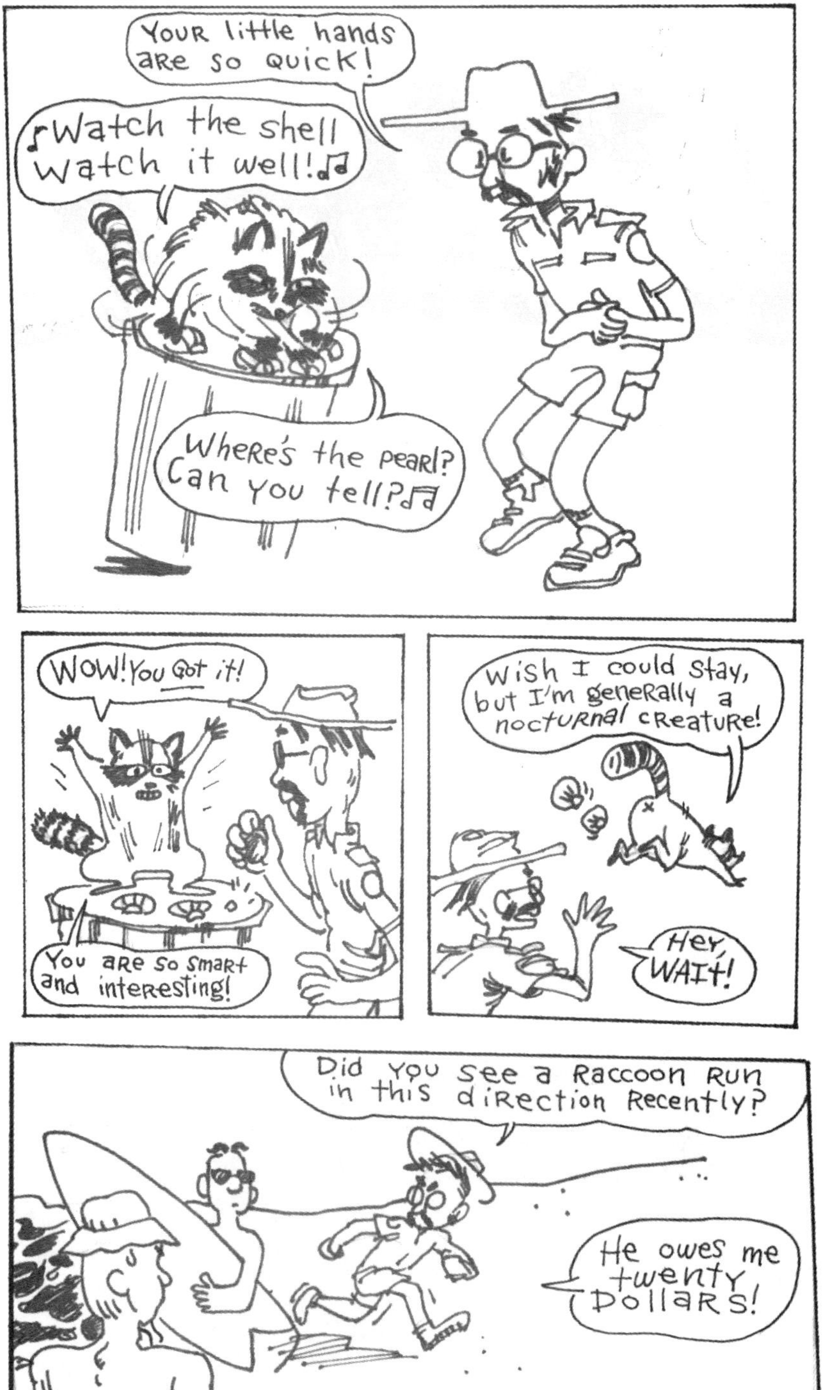
Your little hands are so quick!
Watch the shell watch it well!
Where's the pearl? Can you tell?
WOW! You got it!
You are so smart and interesting!
Wish I could stay, but I'm generally a nocturnal creature!
Hey, WAIT!
Did you see a Raccoon Run in this direction Recently?
He owes me twenty Dollars!

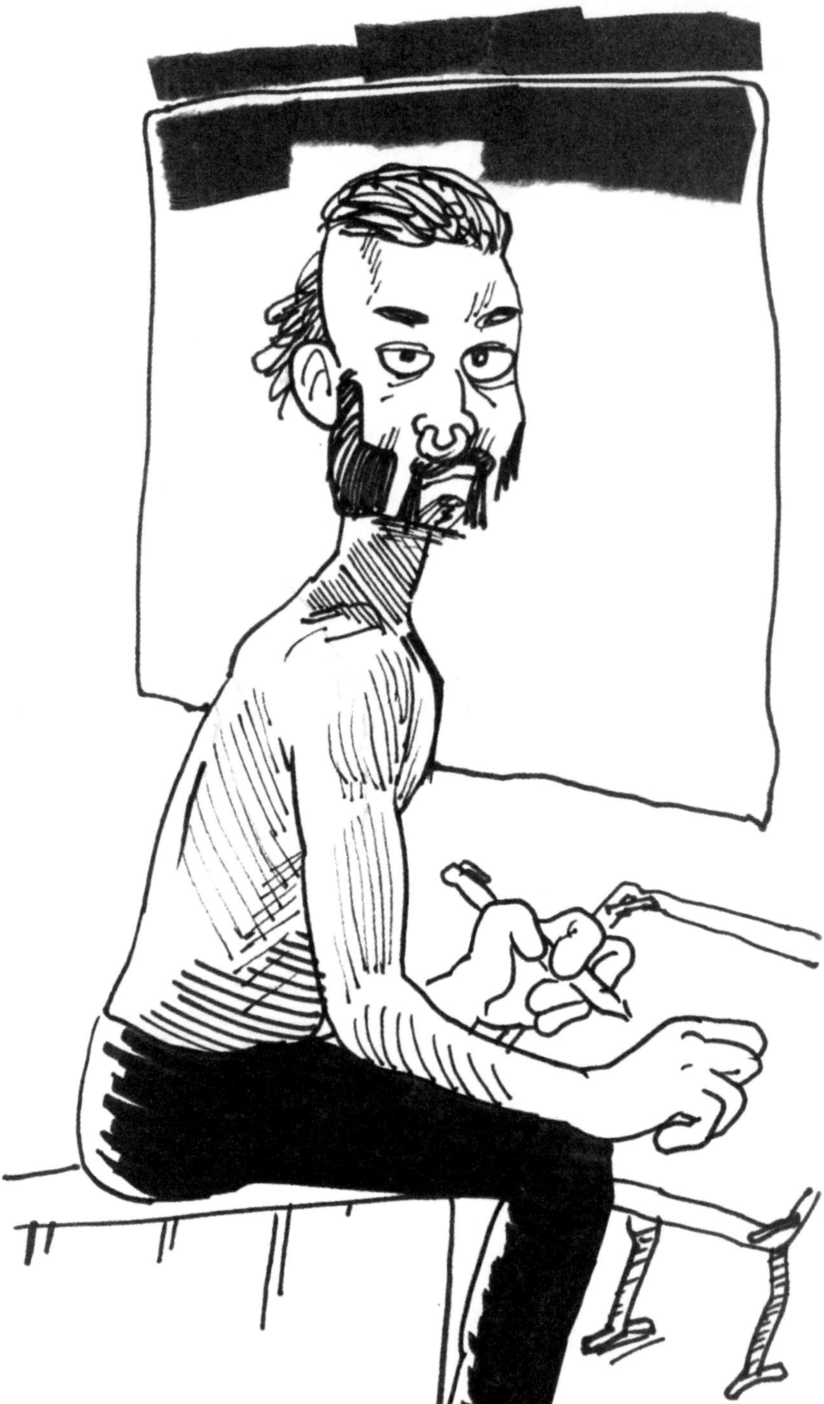